THE RELIGION OF THE VEDA

HERMANN OLDENBERG

The Religion of The Veda

Die Religion des Veda

Translated into English
by
SHRIDHAR B. SHROTRI

MOTILAL BANARSIDASS PUBLISHERS
PRIVATE LIMITED • DELHI

First Edition: Delhi, 1988
Reprint: Delhi, 1993, 2004

ISBN: 81-208-0392-2

MOTILAL BANARSIDASS
41 U.A. Bungalow Road, Jawahar Nagar, Delhi 110 007
8 Mahalaxmi Chamber, 22 Bhulabhai Desai Road, Mumbai 400 026
120 Royapettah High Road, Mylapore, Chennai 600 004
236, 9th Main III Block, Jayanagar, Bangalore 560 011
Sanas Plaza, 1302 Baji Rao Road, Pune 411 002
8 Camac Street, Kolkata 700 017
Ashok Rajpath, Patna 800 004
Chowk, Varanasi 221 001

Printed in India

BY JAINENDRA PRAKASH JAIN AT SHRI JAINENDRA PRESS,
A-45 NARAINA, PHASE-I, NEW DELHI 110 028
AND PUBLISHED BY NARENDRA PRAKASH JAIN FOR
MOTILAL BANARSIDASS PUBLISHERS PRIVATE LIMITED,
BUNGALOW ROAD, DELHI 110 007

Preface to the First Edition

An attempt to expound the Vedic Religion necessarily presupposes extensive excursions in the domain of the Vedic mythology. To draw a precise dividing line between them and to exclude at the very outset facts and questions of the purely mythological order would amount to attempting the impossible, and as such, it has not been contemplated at all. However, a selection has been made from amongst the Vedic myths, and only the most striking ones have found a place in the present study. The very nature of this work forbids the inclusion of those myths which are available to us only as meagre narrative fragments, or also those whose interpretation appears to be ever and again despairingly unsatisfactory.

Kiel, August, 1894 *Hermann Oldenberg*

Preface to the Second Edition

I did not find any reason in principle to modify this book which was published in 1894. But here and there, my further research and the work of other scholars have understandably unearthed new material in this vast field of research; old views have been either corrected or refuted. Accordingly, I have taken pains to improve upon my first edition and to enlarge it.

December, 1916 *Hermann Oldenberg*

Translator's Foreword

Hermann Oldenberg (1854–1920) is no strange name to Indologists. His outstanding contributions to the field of Buddhist and Vedic studies are universally acknowledged and cited even today with approval by scholars. His *Die Religion des Veda*, first published in 1894, became a classic, and a second revised edition was brought out in 1916. In this conspectus of the Vedic religious belief and its cult practices and customs, Oldenberg has brought to bear on the subject not merely the weighty apparatus of critical scholarship, but also his intimate knowledge of ethnology, folklore and philology. With pioneering spirit, he seeks to unravel the various links between the Vedic *Zeitgeist* and prehistoric times, links which extend beyond the common existence of the Indo-European peoples but have become blurred with the march of time.

Strangely enough, Oldenberg's classic has remained inaccessible till now to scholars not familiar with German. This endeavour to fill that lacuna was prompted largely by the encouragement given to me by the noted Vedic scholar Shri Shaṃ Bā Joshi, winner of the Sahitya Academy award 1970, and by late Shri Sundarlal Jain, grandfather of the present publisher, Shri N. P. Jain.

In translating this work, I was hampered a great deal by my lack of familiarity with Indological studies, and not to an inconsiderable extent by the ponderous, laboured syntax, so typical of nineteenth century German dons. Ironically enough, Oldenberg who accuses the Vedic poets of delighting in secret-mongering and obfuscatory phraseology, almost invites the same charge himself. In my attempt to decode his deep structures, I have refrained from excising many a reduntant turn of phrase, mainly with a view to fidelity to the text.

My thanks are due to Dr. V. N. Deshpande, Dr. S. H. Ritti, Dr. C. Venugopal and Mr. Arya Acharya for helpful suggestions and to the editors of the Bibliographisches Institut, Mannheim, for clarifications.

And last but not the least, I wish to acknowledge the unstinting help received from Dr. B. Subramanian who read and revised my manuscript thoroughly in the light of the original.

'Rajanigandha',
2/1 Belgaum Road, Dharwad-580 008.

Shridhar B. Shrotri

CONTENTS

Introduction

THE SOURCES

Chapter I

THE VEDIC GODS AND DEMONS IN GENERAL

Chapter II

THE INDIVIDUAL GODS AND DEMONS

Chapter III

THE CULT

Chapter IV

ANIMISM AND THE CULT OF THE DEAD

INTRODUCTION

The Sources

ANCIENT INDIA AND THE ṚGVEDA

Characteristics of the People in Ancient India

The Vedic Indians, whose beliefs and cults are to be examined here, settled on the banks of the river Indus and in the Punjab during the period in which the oldest texts were composed. According to very rough estimates—and we can go by only rough estimates—this period is around 1500 to 1000 BC. The Vedic Indians were divided into numerous small tribes, ruled mostly by petty *rājās* and nobles of the warrior class; besides these, there was the priestly nobility which formed a closed caste-like group even at that time. They lived in villages; there is no trace of cities and city-life in the oldest texts. Animal-breeding, especially cattle-breeding, was much more predominantly significant than agṛiculture: a condition whose effect is to be noted even in the religious sphere. The art of writing was as yet not developed, but was compensated by the achievements of the astonishing power of memory cultivated by the priestly schools.

The immigration of these tribes to India from the north-west and their separation from the Indo-European sister tribes of the Iranians, with whom they had remained one for a very long time, are remote events even for the Vedic Indians, if one were to go by the extant literary documents of this period. However, the remoteness of this period has to be judged on a much humbler scale than, say, the tremendous intervals of Egyptian or Babylonian history.[1] The separation of the Indians from the Iranians meant for the tribes migrating south-east a complete dissociation, if not the last step towards dissociation, from participating in that great rivalry amongst the nations out of which the healthy manliness of the Western nations emerged. In the abundant peace of their new home, the Aryans, brothers of the eminent nations of Europe, mixed with the dark-skinned primitives of India and acquired more and more the characteristics of the Hindus. The immigrant Aryans, who grew up in the moderate climatic zones of the earth, became slack through the tropical climate—a climate not congenial to their likes, and which could not but cause grave damages to them. They became slack through the passive enjoyment of what the rich country offered them, after easy victories over their unequal opponents, i.e. the primitives incapable of any resistance. They were further rendered passive by the absence of great challenges; the harsh sufferings and the grim necessities of life that steal the spirit were missing. The intellectual work done by these people lacks traces of that difficult struggle that alone can plumb the farthest depths of reality and help mould their own inner worlds amidst joyful vigour. With playful light-heartedness, they surrounded the upper surface of things with images that emanated mostly from their fantasy, sometimes graceful, sometimes strangely adorned, rich in colours, but wanting in firm, energetically drawn-out lines, now blending together, now distinguishing themselves and interlacing themselves again and again into new shapes.

The first signs of this passivity are manifest in the oldest document of Indian literature and religion, the hymns of the *Ṛgveda,* in the sacrificial songs and litanies with which the priests of the Vedic Aryans invoked their gods to the templeless sacrificial places of sacrificial fire surrounded by grass. Barbaric priests invoked barbaric gods who came through the celestial realms astride steeds and in chariots to feast upon the sacrificial cake, butter and meat, and to invigorate themselves with courage and divine strength with the intoxicating *Soma*-juice.

Before setting out to survey the sources of our knowledge regarding the ancient Indian religion, we must, first of all, examine the special nature of the poetry of the *Ṛgveda.*

Characteristics of Ṛgvedic Poetry

The bards of the *Ṛgveda,* who hail from certain families that are at the point of forming a caste-like independent unit, compose poems in traditional style for celebrations of sacrifice. Above all for that sacrifice where poets get the richest reward, namely, for the great and the gorgeous *Soma*-sacrifice. Therefore, they do not want to talk about the god they celebrate, but to praise him. They are not interested in human listeners, their listener is the god himself whom they call upon to accept the offerings mercifully. So they vie with one another with untiring and pedantic zeal in heaping upon the god, in prayer and in song, all superlative epithets at the command of a blandishing plump eloquence endowed with a fantasy which is fond of the loud and the garish. Of course, there is no god at whose wink, no immortal head, at whose nod, the heights of Olympus tremble. Yet there is a long series of gods, amongst whom every one like the other is called 'very great' or 'the greatest', whenever the singer addresses him, 'very shining', 'very mighty', 'beautiful to look at' and 'very generous to the pious'. The god exterminates all enemies, shatters the citadels of the enemies; he has secured the ends of the earth with his might and stretched the heaven above. Everywhere, superlatives abound, no restraint and no form. The contours emerge rather unobtrusively—in the common glow of light that envelops the gods—outlining one figure from the other. However, in this glorification of the gods, one chief effect is the play with the mysterious. It would be, however, an exaggeration to say that there is preference for this sort of a play throughout the whole of the *Ṛgveda.* Many a song, rather a series of songs, speaks of Uṣas, the ruddy light of dawn, sparkling with lovely charm; of Indra, the omnipotent destroyer of foes, of demons and monsters; of Agni, the kindly shining guest of the human dwellings—all in a language from which the breath of fresh simple nature has not yet vanished. But besides these, there is a vast number of hymns imbued with another spirit. If the song is to be beautiful, it is said, in order to please the god, it should be artistic. But that poem, above all, is artistic, which is devised by the learned and is intelligible only to the learned, which through veiled hints half-reveals the thought and half-canceals it. Poetry of this type could be created only in a closed circle of priest-technicians of the sacrifice. Posing and solving spiritual riddles was a favourite pastime amongst these priests, and even the gods, influenced by priestly nature, seemed to favour it. The gods love, so goes a repeated saying in the later Vedic texts, the hidden, and hate what is manifest. Pleased at the mysterious depths and subtlety of his own being and also with the mortal adept in them, the gratified god shows his mercy when flattered. The poets, therefore, repeat again and again the old intelligible or unintelligible allusions, paradoxes and riddles and chase new ideas to surpass what is already existing. Catchwords abounding in mystical ambiguities play a confusing game with profound and, at times, not so profound ideas. Thus, one speaks of the navel of immortality, of the mysterious names of cows, of the first-born of righteousness and of the highest heaven of speech. One reveals in pursuing the being, the god to be hailed, through his manifold manifestations and living places usually hinted at with great fondness as the 'highest secret abode' of god. Milk libations are called 'cows' and a wooden vessel 'forest'; the substance present in the product of which it is made, is referred to in artificial allusions. One discovers in the world of the gods fathers who are the sons of their sons or, sons who are the fathers of their fathers, and daughters or sisters who are at the same time consorts or beloveds. The age-old tendency of the myth towards the motif of incest receives, as it were, added substance from this fancy for the mysterious intricacies of blood relationship. Monstrosities, intended absurdities and riddles of this sort, fill many songs completely, and are juxtaposed without break.

The priestly master-song, which speaks of gods and divine things, can also be said not to possess the rhythm and the music in what it has to say about human souls and human fate; it also lacks the eloquence of suffering; we rarely hear the tunes from which speak the warmth and the depth, the soft trembling of a pious heart. This poetry knows little of the abysses of misery and guilt. Here speak only the fortunate and the wealthy who, by performing sacrifices, appeal to the gods for acquisition of cattle and horses, for longevity and progeny. More often, it is not the sacrificers who speak, but the professional bards in their employ. These bards who have succeeded in securing lucrative assignments against competition from their intriguing rivals, now practise their professional art with sober virtuosity for the sacrifice whose overwhelming intricateness must, of its own accord, retard all vigour and momentum. From where then should emerge the real, deep, strains of the within, and the subtle insight into the orderliness of happenings? From where can arise, amidst these narrow and shallow circumstances concerning their petty dynasties at rivalry with one another, the sobriety, gravity and pride, of the great national consciousness illumining their culture?

The outward form given by the singers of the *Ṛgveda* to their poems had the character of simplicity, which was not in contradiction to the basically naive artificiality of the contents. The language relied on nothing more than the elementary basic form of a sentence-structure which did not have the finesse to express complicated movements of thoughts with their side-currents and counter-currents. Also, the narrow scale of the verses almost uniformly ending in a sentence, namely, the verse measure of *Gāyatrī* with its 3x8 syllables, made the formation of a great thought-structure difficult. They did not possess the art of forming and mastering the organization of such thought-structures. The one was put in sequence with the other with continuous repetitions, as chance allowed it. The individual structure, mostly in eulogistic vein, was not developed fully. Where the poetic language once left its simplicity of expression, it would lose itself rather in a confused and unclear sinuosity than elevate itself to versatility. The frequent comparisons touching all the fields of human experience form a welcome interruption from the monotonously alternating eulogies and obscure mysteries: the shining sun and the canopy of the sky decorated with stars, the never-tiring wind, the river with the surging waves of its waters hurrying into the depths, the shepherd driving his cows, the virgin going to a rendezvous or sprucing herself up for a marriage, the blameless wife loved by her husband, the father's caring love and the son, who touches the seam of his father's shirt; it is of this that these brief similes speak. Their simplicity is not quite different from the rich poetic development manifest in those similes which adorn later the spiritual sayings and hymns of the Buddhists.

Later Parts of the Ṛgveda

The poetry of the sacrificial songs described here reached its culmination mainly around the end of the *Ṛgvedic* times. Even in the later parts of the large collection of hymns, it is no longer quite vivid as in the earlier style; the liturgic technique asserting itself more and more firmly—one could say, technique becoming more and more rigid—prescribed for all the sacrificial rituals certain hymns from amongst those inherited from the old. This left no further scope for poetic production. There begins in its place now the poetry of philosophical, particularly of cosmogonic, speculation. A number of narrative stories, blended of prosaic and poetic elements, begins to emerge in the older style.[2] A number of minor cult-activities, lacking literary merit, was now adorned with songs in the manner of old hymns dating to the *Soma*-sacrifice, or with a series of *mantras* in poetic form. Thus, for instance, the marriage and—what is especially important for our research—the funeral rites. Further, all sorts of magical actions: charms to drive away the demons, to cure diseases, charms to promote married life and the like. Not this magic itself, which is of course very old, but the literature—as far as it is preserved—of songs and verses belonging to this magic, goes back in its origins to the latest parts of the *Ṛgveda*, only to continue in greatly increasing dimensions through the later Vedic texts. The practice of magic of the earlier period satisfied itself mainly with the short prosaic form of incantation. And even when the poetic production of the magic hymns was in its fullest bloom, the prosaic magic incantation stood its ground. It can be clearly seen at many a place how a prosaic incantation was subsequently rhymed, for the original form is still clearly discernible. Particularly, however, the old prosaic form of the magic hymns in incantations of this sort has remained almost untouched in the *mantras* of this type where they refer to the big sacrifices belonging to the magical actions;[3] the conservative peculiarity of the sacrificial practice guaranteed here prolonged protection against the introduction of the poetic form. We shall have to consider this literature on magic incantation, briefly discussed now, later on when we shall discuss the *Yajurveda* and the *Atharvaveda.*

The Ṛgveda as a Religio-historical Source

Let us now see what consequences result from the peculiarities of Ṛgvedic poetry with respect to its evaluation and its application as the oldest direct source for the beliefs and cults of the Vedic period.

It is in the nature of this hymnal poetry that it touches upon the different aspects of religious life and the existence of the myth in an extremely uneven way. All light is focused almost exclusively on the great gods, who are in the foreground in the *Soma*-sacrifice and in the eminent cult of the princes and the rich. It is clearly discernible how the singers of the Veda have understood the character of these gods and their relation to human beings. Where vague outlines remain, the vagueness is not for want of our sources, but in the object itself. The individual deeds of just the same gods are featured indistinctly, in part too much indistinctly, except, of course, those that stand in the foreground, just like Indra's victory over Vṛtra. Even the lesser deeds in epic texts would have claimed somewhere full attention, but in the narrow framework of the sacrificial hymns, the stereotyped praise and those heroic deeds claim so much space each time that only short allusions—often in the course of long enumerations—can be made to the less significant deeds: in which case, they refer mostly to one and the same aspect at numerous corresponding places of the collection of hymns, obfuscating everything else necessary for the understanding of the whole. As these myths have disappeared to a great extent,[4] their origin and their full import remains inaccessible to posterity.

The rites of the sacrifice dedicated to gods receive as much uneven treatment as their conceptions and deeds. As the hymns of the *Ṛgveda* are mainly litanies meant for the *Soma*-sacrifice, it is not all too difficult to ascertain the classification of these litanies and with that the classification of the offerings brought to different gods while taking the later texts representing the ritual of the same sacrifice into consideration. We ascertain with that the facts about only one side of this specific sacrifice. The *Ṛgveda* fails completely to describe a great part of the relevant concrete preliminaries. It also fails to describe the magical actions connected with the sacrifice like, e.g. the preparatory *dīkṣā* which is surrounded by multiple magic to which the sacrificer has to subject himself. It also fails to describe other similar rites and observances partly of superior cultural and historical significance. The *Ṛgveda* further fails completely, apart from negligible accounts, with respect to the other sacrifices. Of the Animal-sacrifice, e.g. only its most splendid form, the Horse-sacrifice, appears in some detail in two homogeneous hymns. Besides this, we know nothing more from the *Ṛgveda* than the naked, basically obvious, fact that the Animal-sacrifice was known. It is important to note that such deficiences in our information derived from the *Ṛgveda* are explained completely, as already pointed out, by the peculiar nature of these works of poetry that mainly concern only one definite aspect of the *Soma*-sacrifice: reason enough to be extremely careful when one has to conclude about the later origin of the rites not mentioned in the *Ṛgveda*.

The fragmentary nature of the Ṛgvedic traditions will be strongly felt, if one turns from the major gods and their cult to the sphere of minor demons, goblins, spirits of diseases, ghostly animals, etc. to the primitive magic cult, further to the incantations and exorcisms and, particularly, if one turns to the souls, to the ghosts and to the cult of the dead. The poetry of the *Soma*-sacrifice had no reason to deal with all this. It is even probable that it would have been considered polluting and dangerous, if the souls of the dead were to be invoked or even mentioned in the hymns on the sacrifice to gods.[5] The silence of the *Ṛgveda*—apart from its later parts—is so deep here that one is even tempted to dispute in the older Ṛgvedic age altogether the place of Yama, the god of the dead, and the whole sphere of ideas connected with him with reference to life after death. This is an assumption not proved by the *Ṛgveda*—one may take here into account the one-sidedness of the source in question—but decisively contradicted by other factors.[6]

We have already pointed out earlier that the later parts of the *Ṛgveda* fill up, though partly, the gaps mentioned by us. Given the poor amount of material available to us, the picture of the belief in souls and demons and in the magic powers obtained from them lacks that completeness and vividness that would enable one to dispense with the wealth of additional material to be gained from the later Vedas. And in many respects, one believes, one can observe an after-effect of the excellent, yet narrowly limited exclusiveness in that little portion contained in the *Ṛgveda*. This exclusiveness is confined chiefly to the older layers of that poetry. Thus, the belief in immortality is evident in the dirges of the last book of the *Ṛgveda*, notably in their bias towards the aristocracy whose members are sure that they will be received into the bright celestial abode by their divine friends with all honours. But the concepts of souls dwelling in the bowels of the earth, of the souls hovering and whizzing over graves and human dwellings, of souls entering into animals and of ghosts: all this is as good as absent in these funeral hymns.

While concluding these remarks on the *Ṛgveda*, it must be emphasized that, in the vast maze of ideas contained in these hymns, what is part and parcel of people's faith has often been indiscernibly mixed up with the impulsive inspirations of individual poets. The nature of these literary productions as we have described them—i.e. the competition between countless poets and poet-families, and the straining for effect through obfuscation, often overdone—explains sufficiently the grand usurpation of individual ideas and also the attempts, now and then, to impart a refreshingly new look or an aura of mystery to old well-known ideas by arranging them afresh. Proper evaluation of such fleeting ideas—we do not really always possess the means to recognize them—is part of the basic conditions without which we cannot hope to understand correctly the religious thought of the *Ṛgveda*. It is not enough, for research purpose, to arrange side by side the ideas that are found in the old hymns with those that appear at regular intervals as if in a register.[7] They have to be there in their proper perspective. The casual play of thoughts to which a poet has succumbed sometimes should not be linked with those thoughts that appear continuously and at regular intervals to form an apparent organic system. Our research will have ample opportunities to illustrate the principles laid down here.

THE YAJURVEDA

Sacrificial Magic Mantras

While the priests entrusted with the recitations and hymns—the *Hotar* and the *Utgātar*—recited the hymns of the *Ṛgveda*, to praise the gods and to invite them to be present at the sacrifice, the other priests, the executors of the real act—the *Adhvaryu* and his companions—accompanied their manipulations with prose-hymns (*yajus*)[8] which brought blessings or averted misfortunes. As a rule, they did not address the gods, at least not directly, but the sacrificial utensil that was being used, the chores, the proceedings that were at the moment in progress. They endowed things with mystical names that refer to their innate secret powers or to the nature of divine assistance; they believed that mystical links existed between the mundane and the divine. Therefore, they regarded the conditions of the sacrifice as representatives of analogous conditions of the universe; they turned—what used to happen at the place of sacrifice—to the lord of the sacrifice for blessing and for 'the destruction of the one who hates us and whom we hate'. Whenever the priest took hold of some object, he did it at 'the impulse of the god Savitar, with the arms of the Aśvins and hands of Pūṣan'. He said to the corn-swingle braided from reed, 'you have grown through rain'; whenever he put the corn in the sacrificial meal, he would say to the corn, 'may it embrace you who have grown in the rain', and cleaned it from the hull with the words, 'the demon is done away with, the fiends are removed'. At the fitting up of the chariot filled with the sacrificial meal, he touched the pins of the chariot-yoke with the words: 'You are the yoke-pin (*dhur*); evil to the evil-doer (*dhūrva dhūrvantam*); harm the one who harms us; harm the one whom we harm.' Whenever he poured water over flour while preparing the sacrificial meal, he would say: 'The waters have become one with the plants.,[9] the plants with the juice, and the rich should unite with the mobile,[10] the sweet with the sweet.' It can be seen how the periphrases try to reproduce the mysterious nature of the objects from all sides and to make magic effective through them.

It is probable that such *mantras* were already spoken during the sacrifice of the Indo-Iranians; the Avesta has preserved several of them, and they are exactly similar to the Vedic.[11] Explicit proofs confirm the existence of *Yajus*-hymns during the period of the *Ṛgveda*.[12] The comparison of the collection of such hymns[13] at our hand with the *Ṛgveda* makes us recognize in them their later appearance at every turn; many words missing in the *Ṛgveda* or beginning to appear isolatedly in its later parts are already common here.[14] Thus the form of these *mantras* compared with the admirable rigidity of the *Ṛgveda*-text, has to be more flexible.[15] These *mantras* must have been more open to progressing modernization in a different proportion than those of the *Ṛgveda*.

The contribution of the *Yajus*-formulas to the understanding of the Vedic gods is, of course, negligible compared to that of the *Ṛgveda*. The gods are here subordinate. One has the impression that they are placed just here and there as accessories, not quite in place. And, therefore, what they have to do accidentally in the context of the sacrificial act has a very loose connection with their real nature. For the compilers of the *Yajus* this aspect of the gods has faded altogether. On the whole, compared with the prime of the Vedic theistic belief, there is obviously a fresher approach to these *mantras* which has asserted itself over the old form of sacrifice: a philosophy for which, heaven and earth, inhaling and exhaling, human senses and powers and verse-measures are as important as or, perhaps, more important than, Indra and Varuṇa. In addition, the *Yajus* are extremely important for the understanding of the sacrificial ritual. They accompany it step by step, often down to the minutest of procedures. In the process, evidence of these procedures, which would have ordinarily rested upon the *Brāhmaṇa*- and *Sūtra*-texts, is dated back to a more ancient age. Therefore, they are a major source for our understanding of the mysterious occurrences, of the magic forces at work at the sacrifice and, further, for our understanding of the cultic means used to influence those occurrences and forces.

THE ATHARVAVEDA

The Contents

The third Veda, the *Atharvaveda*,[16] which is important for our research, continues, according to its contents, with the poetry of the magic hymns beginning in the later parts of that Veda and also with the songs and verses concerning customs of family life.[17] Compared with the *Ṛgveda*, the *Atharvaveda* is, in its poetic expression, more skilful, albeit more lax at the same time. The comparatively small collection of verses about marriage and funeral rites, contained in the last book of the *Ṛgveda*, recur here in a greater detail; also an extensive new literature on conjurations of all sorts—*mantras* meant for blessing of man and cattle, for banishment of demons of diseases and other demons, for warding off of evil magic and similar things—is added to the magic hymns of the *Ṛgveda* that are also repeated to a very great extent here. In addition, there are, in part, extensive texts, which have little to do with the so-called popular magic, but more with the new inventions of shrewd priests, say, in developing or reconstructing the great sacrifices as magic acts of different types; then there are, with dubious repetitions, texts extolling the virtue of pious alms-giving to the priests. This theme is alluded to only modestly here and there in the *Ṛgveda*. It can be said that, for the *Atharvaveda*, the centre of gravity of meritorious deed has shifted straight from the cult of gods to rewarding, feeding and honouring the Brahmanas.

I think one may unconditionally maintain that the *Atharvaveda* as a whole or its various constituent elements is of a later origin than the *Ṛgveda*. Nowhere, I feel, do the language, metre and contents confirm the view expressed by a few research scholars that some sections of this Veda—of course, apart from those borrowed from the *Ṛgveda*—reach back into the Ṛgvedic age.[18] Yet, how far the world of ideas of this magical poetry matches or even supersedes in the maturity of its contents the world of ideas of the sacrificial hymns will be examined further in the discussion on the cult of magic.

Priestly Character

One believes one can find in the *Atharvaveda* traces of composer-circles, different, not only chronologically, from those of the *Ṛgveda*, for, apart from the priests, people belonging to the lower strata appear to have also had a say in the matter. There is some truth in it, for it is evident that the realm of concepts, in which charms against diseases, love-charms or marriage customs find a place, cannot have that exclusive priestly character found, for instance, in the liturgy of the *Soma*-sacrifice. Yet, the reader of the *Atharvaveda* will have the impression that what was originally popular has gone through the priests' hands. For example, how the great marriage-hymn and the large number of marriage-*mantras* are infused with the Vedic learnedness and the theological pursuit of symbols, how similes and epithets betray the priestly background of the authors time and again. The poet, who wants to master reason (*medhā*) with the aid of a charm, calls reason 'the one rich in holiness, moved by holiness, which the wise singers have praised and from which the pious pupils have drunk' (VI, 108, 2). The author of the charms against field-vermins drives them away, so that they may leave the corn untouched, like the Brahmana an unfinished oblation (VI, 50, 2). When one goes well beyond the magic spell, one finds at every stage such examples of the priests' scholastic wisdom, for example, the hymn extolling the remnant of the offering (*ucchiṣṭa* XI, 7). It probably deals with the remnant the priest had received or wished to receive: the strength of all the sacrifices lives in the remnant of the offering; and now follows a long list of all possible sacrifices with their main and subordinate forms, of different sections of the liturgic diction of the hymn, etc. all that has gone into the remnant with its mysterious power. One may, further, think of that endless paean of heavenly reward and of the mysterious splendour that are coupled with the honouring and feeding of the priests; all this and more must lead one to think that the circles of composers of the *Atharvaveda* are akin to those of the *Ṛgveda* in their social position.

The Atharvaveda as a Source of Magic

The *Atharvaveda* with its appropriate ritual laid down in the *Kauśikasūtra* is, obviously, as a collection of magic hymns, an inexhaustible main source for the understanding of the whole; it deals with the primitive demon-folk, with the artifice through which man wins over this demon-folk, reconciles himself with it, scares it or outwits it. It is in the nature of things that the inter-connections of most of the Atharvan hymns along with their appropriate manipulations are considerably closer than in case of the hymns of the *Ṛgveda* which soar so often to abstract heights. The picture of the ritual of the magical actions handed down by tradition is, on the whole, quite reliable, and, often enough, vivid; the fact that, here and there, additions have been made freely to the text or created subsequently from some features of the text hardly prejudices the reliability of the entire picture.

Gods and Myths in the Atharvaveda

Remarks made earlier with reference to the *mantras* of the *Yajurveda* hold good also for the role played by the superior gods in the Atharvan poetry: how so often the gods may be called, their nature stands only in superficial or perhaps no relationship with the contents of the invocation. We have to do overwhelmingly here with the aims of day-to-day life and with the age-old magic rites intended for achieving these aims. These magic rites have basically nothing to do with the conceptions, say, of Indra or the celestial gods of light. But they are, in part, certainly older than these. Of course, one tried to humour as many divine helpers as possible in order to achieve a particular aim; thus the simultaneous invocation of numerous deities is common here, whereas the extensive flattery in the Ṛgvedic hymns is usually directed only to one deity at a time. 'Heaven and Earth have anointed me; Mitra has anointed me here; may Brahmaṇaspati anoint me; may Savitar anoint me'. Or, 'May Maruts anoint me, Pūṣan and Bṛhaspati. May this Agni bless me with offspring and wealth.' The *Atharvaveda* is full of rich prayers to a whole series of deities, and often the requirements of prosody must have simply decided whether a god be addressed more often or less often.[19]

On the contrary, hymns in the style of the Ṛgvedic hymns praising extensively a single god are comparatively rare; the excellent occasion offered by the *Soma*-sacrifice for composing hymns was, as already mentioned above, essentially exhausted. In those we can find—like the splendid hymn to the Earth (XII, 1) or a series of homogeneous hymns to Agni, Indra, Vāyu and other deities (IV, 23ff)—we feel, in comparison to the hymns of the *Ṛgveda*, a difference in description of the colours attributed to the appearance of the gods. There is predominantly a more rational tone, easier intelligibility, immediate correlation with the real and the visible. The hymn to the Earth details, in a manner hardly imaginable in the *Ṛgveda,* all that is found on earth: hills and dales and plains, shrubs of varying potency, trees, resolute monsters of the forest; corn, rice and barley that grow on the rain-soaked soil; also song and dance, battle-cries and beating of drums; prowling beasts of prey, lions, man-eating tigers and wicked demons; birds flapping their wings; Mātariśvan, the wind, causing mists and shaking the trees.

The hymns composed in this new style allude often enough to the deeds of the gods which are mentioned in the old myths. The stereotyped phrases, used frequently earlier to describe these deeds, are repeated here also. But one feature of the myth almost missing is hardly ever supplemented by the *Atharvaveda.* The old world of gods and myths had lived itself out; and the next generation was interested more in comprehending the vivid, intelligible reality of natural life hidden behind the gods.

THE LATER VEDIC LITERATURE AND THE LITERATURE OTHER THAN THE VEDAS

Brāhmaṇas and Sūtras

The sacrificial ritual forms the main content of the later Vedic texts composed in prose (*Brāhmaṇas* and *Sūtras.*) The ritual of the great sacrifices, especially of the *Soma*-sacrifice, that was in a state of flux in most ancient times, acquired a comparatively stable form in an epoch that must be later than the concluding age of Ṛgvedic poetry.[20] In this form, with all its numerous variations depending upon the different schools, yet concurring in the main, it has been handed down to us in the extensive literature of the Brāhmaṇa texts and in the later *Sūtras* which were based on them and which took great pains to depict the text briefly and all too briefly. As pointed out earlier, the analysis proceeding from this ritual has the possible object of arriving at the older, at the same time, simpler and more fluid form of the ritual for which the *Ṛgveda* was composed. If the historical research shuttles constantly back and forth between the older and the later data in such a manner that, with the progress of time within the literature, our knowledge of the entire concept of the sacrifice increases, then the important question will be: how much of this increasing wealth of information rests upon the addition of fresh constructions? How much rests upon the altered shape of the sources? In the treatment of these alternatives, one may say, lies the secret of success in the examination of the Vedic cult. Of course, an answer cannot always be found. Yet, in many cases, one can arrive at a certain or near-certain solution. Much will then turn out to be new constructions merging with the sphere of ideas which we are to encounter in their later vivid and developed form. Many cultural concepts and customs are such that, even if they are ancient, their origins cannot be altogether absent in the older sources, notwithstanding their fragmentary character. On the other hand, cases, where the sources maintain silence, will confirm the observation that the constructions in question cannot be explained away by referring to the well-known sphere of ideas of the later Vedic theologians. A trained eye can discern, in such cases, the characteristic stamp of remnants of ancient ideas that are incommensurate with the views of the Vedic age. The parallels—they may be within the sphere of related nations or they may overlap boundaries—we shall come back to the importance of such parallels later—will contribute to strengthening the evidence of the extreme antiquity of the phenomenon in question, in spite of its later appearance.[21]

As it is known, the *Brāhmaṇa* texts—not likewise the *Sūtras*—contain, besides the description of the sacrificial customs, an attempt at their interpretation. It is quite obvious that the interpretation had to fail; firstly, the original meaning of the countless rites lay far beyond the field of view of these theologians; and, secondly, they did not have to be necessarily Indians in order not to introduce all the time their own favourite speculations about the potentials of the course of nature and about the functions of human life, while interpreting ancient customs. The other side is easily overlooked on account of these conspicuous defects. Not quite seldom do the *Brāhmaṇa* texts offer useful explanations; the real old logic of sacrificial art had not died away altogether with the priests who spent their lives at the sacrificial place that we moderns had nothing to learn from them in order to understand procedures that are so strange to us.

The ceremonies of the family cult, the marriage, the initiations for the child and for the entry into the age of puberty, the ceremonies of the house, fields, herds, etc. were depicted only later in literature than the great sacrifices solemnized with the three fires.[22] We possess from them only the description, no interpretation in the style of *Brāhmaṇa* texts.[23] To the ritual books of this class, the *Gṛhyasūtras* (books dealing with domestic ritual), are to be added the *Dharmasūtras* (Books of Law) which, while refraining, however, from specific references to the sacrificial ritual, deal with the entire field of law and custom in private and public life, but quite obviously from the point of view of theorizing Brahmanism. Obviously, these texts also allude frequently to the problems with which we are concerned.

Historical Background and the Stories

As it is well-known, the historical tradition of the pre-Buddhistic period does not link up with the various branches of the Vedic religious tradition; there is a gap here, save for a few negligible fragments, which, however, do not concern us. No words are needed to express how severely our research has to suffer on account of this lacuna which, though characteristic of the Indian spirit, has lamentable consequences for the research on India. The absence of fixed chronology also hits us hard. But, above all, it is this that is denied to us, namely, to see the forces of culture at work in the historical context. At first, a certain compensation is made by the old Buddhistic literature with its poetry and truth about the period of life of the Buddha and his disciples, at any rate by the otherwise abundant stories and fables, some set on the plane of human reality, some in fairyland, so also by the literature of the Jainas, which has become recently a subject of more and more zealous study; and further compensated by the poetry of the great epics and generally by the later narrative and dramatic literature. The importance of these texts for the visualization of the world of religious ideas need not be emphasized now; we shall confirm it for us in many ways, even if it surpasses the powers of an individual to master more than a small portion of this gigantic bulk of material. What would the Veda teach us, only to take an example, about the belief in ghosts which is important for the entire concept of life after death? Here, sources like the Buddhistic collection of ghost-stories (*Petavatthu*) or something similar must come forth to supplement the information. Here, then, the research has an urgent duty to be constantly aware of the doubts resulting from the application of such later sources and to be armed with all available precautions.

THE VEDA AND THE AVESTA

The Discoveries of Bogaz-köi

A survey of the sources for our understanding of the nature of the Vedic religion must also consider the closely related literature of the Avesta.

It may be said at the outset that gods with Vedic names have appeared not only in the literature of Iran but also further westwards in a monument discovered most recently. Deeds of contract in Babylonia were discovered in Boghaz-köi (Asia Minor), dating to the period around 1400 BC. In these deeds the following gods are invoked amongst those of the Mitani (in northern Mesopotamia): Mi-it-ra, U-ru-w-na, In-dar, Na-š̆a-at-ti-ia: the last name in plural which also includes the area of Dual in the Babylonian language.[24] It is clear that they are Mitra-Varuṇa, further Indra and the Nāsatyas (Aśvins). On considering the distance, I think, it is quite improbable that these gods were brought there from India during military adventures. There may perhaps be more of the old Iranian deities in them, well beyond the reach of available Iranian tradition and representing the existence of the old Indo-Iranian community;[25] or the gods belong to the third branch of the Indo-Iranian race besides the Indian and the Iranian. One way or the other, the pre-Vedic, pre-historic existence of these Vedic gods is confirmed. Simultaneously, light is thrown on the question as to which of the gods preserved in the Veda were respected even in very ancient times as the most noble and powerful.

From this highly significant discovery, which awakens a hope for further similar discoveries, we shall now turn to the literature of the Avesta and its importance for the history of the Vedic religion.[26]

From the point of view of Vedic as well as Avestic research, there is a clear tendency, considered valid for a long time, to separate strictly one field from the other. Basically, it should only be with regard to language, which, being the most conservative factor in life of the people, binds together both the literatures.[27] Thus, the Veda is to be considered and understood as purely Indian, and the Avesta purely Iranian. This tendency may be understandable as a reaction against that superfluous and rash enthusiasm of comparing, which tends to overlook the uniqueness of a nation. But I feel that it has overshot the mark. Such a tendency appears, at times, to be scarcely avoidable in the newly established fields of science, given current research trends.

The Veda and Avesta from the Viewpoint of Language

To keep at first to the language, one can, in fact, state that the language of the older Vedic hymns is closer to the language of certain parts of the Avesta in many respects than, say, to the language of the *Mahābhārata* and Kālidāsa. If the sound-shift establishes a gap between the Veda and the Avesta, which is, however, rarely greater than the one between two Greek dialects spoken at places quite far away from one another or between Old High German and Old Low German, then the correspondence of the syntactical basic relationships connects both the languages, and so also the simplicity of the same type in the sentence-structure and, further, the essentially identical vocabulary. The Vedic diction has a great number of favourite expressions which are common with the Avestic, though not with the later Indian diction. In addition, there is a close resemblance between them in metrical form, in fact, in their overall poetic character. If it is noticed that whole Avesta verses can be easily translated into the Vedic alone by virtue of comparative phonetics,[28] then this may often give, not alone correct Vedic words and phrases, but also the verses, out of which the soul of the Vedic poetry appears to speak.[29]

From the Viewpoint of Contents, Gods and Rituals

The contacts between the religious and mythological contents does not lie far behind the formal in its importance. How could it also be different? Because even if it were true—what is indeed only a one-sided expression for the relationship, which cannot be so easily disposed of—that in the Veda as also in the Avesta we meet completely separated people living secluded in their unique world,[30] even then this can never mean creating afresh a whole range of spiritual ideas out of nothingness, in fact even there where historical destinies give a new shape to the people's individualities. The old will project itself, however, into the new in countless remnants and traces, sometimes fused with the new. Therefore, howsoever far-reaching the transformations of the religious world of ideas might have been, which are associated with the name of Zoroaster, one should not overlook the whole foundation of the indelible mythical views and cultural customs which have crossed over intact from the past to Zoroaster's religion and connect them with the Vedic. It is true that, for example, such an important figure of the old mythology like Indra, the Vṛtra-killer, has at least partly disappeared from the Avesta: and yet the victorious god Verethraghna maintains clearly his place in the Avesta, where the ancient God of Storm had once stood. The sublime royal figure of that great Asura, addressed both in the Veda and in the inscriptions of Boghaz-köi as Varuṇa, called in the Avesta Ahura Mazda, the highest god of all goodness, has been preserved in both nations, complete agreement prevailing even in details. Like Varuṇa, the Avestic Ahura is also the highest lord of law or order (Vedic *ṛta*, same word as Avestic *aša*); like Varuṇa, Ahura of the Avesta forms a closely connected pair with Mitra; like Varuṇa, Ahura is the first in the circle of seven gods; just as Varuṇa holds the sun so that it may not fall down from the sky as it moves across the vault of heaven, Ahura too holds the earth so that it does not fall, and he guides the course of the sun and the stars.[31] One may add further: the whole range of such gods[32] who course through the ethereal realm on chariot driven by swift horses with ease and poise are unaffected or hardly affected by the traits of malice, horror and lust; they do not also possess the secret of the Olympian divine beauty. It is this type of the princely Aryans elevated to celestial heights that is predominant in the Avestic as well as in the Vedic world of gods. It is similar with concepts held by both the nations about the first man, the first dead, the ruler of the dead, Yama, Vivasvant's son (Avestic Yima, son of Vivahvant). These concepts are closely related and they explain one another mutually. This is true of the sacrifice as well. Both the peoples considered the intoxicating juice of the *Soma* (*Haoma*) as the most distinguished offering one could make.[33] Priests of both peoples celebrated *Soma* as the lord of the plants, the one growing on the mountains, watered by heavenly rain and brought down by eagle or eagles. In Iran as well as in India, the juice was pressed from the *Soma*-plant, it was purified with a sieve made of hairs and mixed with milk and water. God Indra, the true *Soma*-drinker, is really absent from the Avestic sacrifice: he had to make way for the Zoroastrian spiritualization of religious life, and, therefore, the feast of the drunken god had faded into a confused maze of consecrations and symbolic remnants of rites of all sorts. But the original relationship of the rituals on both sides is visible everywhere. There was, for instance, at the Avestic and at the Vedic sacrificial place a cushion and a bundle of plants, originally meant as a seat for the deity, called by both peoples with closely related names (*Barhis, Baresman*)[34] described by the Iranians, though the external form of application had changed in their case, and also by the Indians as 'spread out' (*stereta, stīrṇa*). Accordingly, the pious sacrificer was called in both the countries as the man with 'spread out' *Barhis* or *Baresman*. Amongst both the peoples a priest—both had the same name (*Hotar, Zaotar*) for him—recited those prayers while seated. We have already referred to their poetic character: many forms from among the prayers, composed by Zoroastrian priests for spiritual goods, are common to the Avesta and the Veda, and introduce us to the language of prayer of the Indo-Iranian period—the prayer to go safely past enemies, to remain protected from the thief and the wolf, the prayer for the protection of men and cattle, the prayer that the horse be swift in battle, that robust male descendants should continue the race; also the prayer where the devotee delivers himself to the god leaving everything to the wish of the deity.

While reading the Veda, one may form an impression quite different from that which one gets from the reading of the Avesta, for Avesta's sphere of ideas has been influenced by greater change. But while reading the Veda, there is an impression that what is said here in broad sections could have been already said in the Indo-Iranian period or that something similar must have been said. There is really no doubt that the world of thoughts and expressions has become more complicated, but at the same time more stereotyped during the transition from the pre-historic period to the period of the oldest Vedic hymns; there is no doubt that particularly the overgrowth of spiritual poetry with allusions, mysteries and intricate obscurities was essentially a special Indian process. But nothing points to the fact that the changes which affected the mind of the people and the religious thinking during this period of time could have been even remotely so profound as those of the period between the oldest Veda and Buddhism.[35] The change of the geographical scene from the pre-Indian to the Indian period of life for those Aryan races contained the seed of incalculable effects for the future, but these effects did not occur in a day. The tempo of change which the culture of a people has to sustain accelerates with its progress, with its enhanced self-awareness and freedom of thought and with the birth of individuality: the Upaniṣadic thinkers, perhaps also the circle around Zoroaster, have experienced and brought about a profound transformation of the entire inner world. Those ancient times appear to have progressed quite slowly along peaceful lines. So, we cannot consider it proper to hinder forcefully the explanation of the Veda against the light thrown upon it by the remnants and the traces of ancient religious traits present in the Avesta. Just as the grammar of the Vedic language has been decisively influenced by Avestic grammar, so, too, one believes—and there are sufficient grounds for this belief—can the comparison with Avestic religion and mythology provide the cautious, yet bold researcher the yardstick with which he can differentiate, at more than one point in the Vedic texts, inherited structures from new constructions; it can also help him to supplement what had survived fragmentarily and to explain what had become incomprehensible.

INDO-EUROPEAN AND GENERAL COMPARISON OF RELIGION

Indo-European Gods and Myths

When we progress from the Indo-Iranian to the comparison of Indo-European myths and cults, we are not on sure ground and the outcome of research is meagre.[36] The distances of space, time and race which helped the comparison between India and Iran were comparatively negligible. But the distances from India to Europe—to the Greek and the Germanic worlds—are great. What sort of contacts are there between the eastern descendents of the same race with the people of an altogether different stock with a mixture of races from different surroundings, economic and social conditions! The disturbing and obscuring nature of those factors will be felt in our research. More so, because the changes themselves which have been effected in the religious and mythological concepts, particularly in their higher spheres, are more difficult to ascertain than, say, those in the field of language. Word-changes in the course of history are to a great extent the product of relatively simple factors which can be expressed frequently with mathematical exactness. On the other hand, in the history of gods and of myths, there are ever-recurring cross-currents of various influences which can never be surveyed even approximately. Spiritual processes relating to the sphere of the unknown intermingle with known preoccupations like primitive composition and speculation. External interests play their part, so do rivalries, the battle for possession or influence, vanity and many other similar motives. If all this is taken into consideration, it is then evident that the path that leads from the Vedic deities to Zeus or to Wodan can never be the same as the path, say, that leads from the Indian sibilants and optative forms to those of the Greek or the German language. And yet the scepticism is hardly correct which altogether denies superior forms of deities to the Indo-European people and lets them have only the belief in souls and inferior demons like forest-ghosts, wind-spirits, water-nymphs and spirits of diseases: in this case, a comparison of an Indian deity with the Greek or the Germanic would have to be rejected in principle. It is, therefore, understandable that such scepticism can result from the disillusionment over the failure of attempts at comparisons like Kuhn's comparison of *Sarameya* and *Heremeias,* and at the same time from the deeply impressive concurrences in the realm of lower mythology—concurrences extending likewise only in the main to Non-Indo-European fields—especially discovered by Mannhardt. Yet Mannhardt himself warns against throwing out the baby with the bath-water. Calm reflection will find no cause to reduce the Indo-Europeans to the status of the savages during the period of their separation. And care should be taken not to reject many important conclusions founded on the basis of their mythological contents along with those hasty comparisons that rest essentially upon etymologies and, no doubt, upon the products of the Storm and Stress period of etymological research. It is certain that the Indo-Europeans had a general notion of 'gods', that they used the term *deivos* to express the nature common to all the individual divine powers. The etymology of this term shows clearly that even during that period the most prominent gods were regarded as celestial beings.[37]. One of these celestial beings was 'Father Sky' himself who probably had a place of honour amongst the gods, but was preceded in power and importance by the Storm-God, who with his armour of lightning triumphed over the dragon and liberated the waters held in confinement by him. Other deities like the two divine youths, the Aśvins or the Dioscuri, perhaps also the god of paths and wayfarers, Pūṣan-Hermes (or Pūṣan-Pan?),[38] in addition to the smaller ones like the elves, water-maids, amongst others, can be traced back similarly to the Indo-European past with some measure of probability.[39] The same holds good for the myths and fairy-tales, which speak of the deeds and the experiences of these gods: of the conquering of the dragon by the Storm-God, of the liberation of cows by Indra-Herakles-Hercules, from the prison of Paṇis, of Geryones or Cacus, of the companionship of the Dioscuri with the sun-maiden.[40]

Of course, one cannot, rather, one should not, attempt here to give a complete survey of the existence of gods and myths that are of Indo-European origin; I wanted to refer only to the main points. I see the essential difference between the Indo-European and the Vedic world of gods in addition of Varuṇa and the gods of light connected with him: the acceptance of gods, I suppose, coming from outside, appears to me to be the most radical innovation of the Indo-Iranian period. The main progress—of course, connected to older beginnings—of the development of the *Soma*-cult and perhaps also the stronger accent on the significance of Agni, is to be ascribed to the same period. From the beginning to the end, and during the transition from the Indo-Iranian to the Indian conditions, one will never come across a real breach between the old and the new, howsoever immense in number the new developments may be, and however much the old forms have disappeared or have been affected.[41] After all this it should be clear that in describing the Vedic gods and myths one cannot ignore offhand the outcome—though very small—of comparisons covering the Indo-European field.

Transgressing the Indo-European Field

Finally, follow comparisons which, going beyond this field, reach across the whole world and are not bound by any frontiers.[42] They deal with figures of the primitive culture or the state of no culture and which have survived as remnants. These remnants are in themselves older than the creations of the Indo-European period, but exist in the midst of more recent religions like the Vedic.

Ethnology teaches us that certain crude types of religious concepts and customs recur with the widest possible distribution among the people of correspondingly low cultural niveau, in apparently strange but doubtless parallelism. What the observer of today sees there is, of course, ancient in its nature. And, therefore, those same forms as also the superior forms of religion prove to be rooted in the distant past. We have indeed noticed earlier that the vastness and certainty of our knowledge grows smaller as we pass from the Indo-Iranian to the Indo-European period. This appears paradoxical at first sight—now that we have descended into the still earlier past—but this decrease in knowledge does not continue and the opposite is the case. Here we arrive at that prehistoric period where the freedom of the people's individuality is not yet at play, but where necessities, that are to be expected, predominate and bring forth similar figures everywhere. The research work on religion takes on here almost the character of science. What it reports does not sound much different from a chapter on life of animals. There is very little talk of gods or heroes or of myths rich in poetry. It deals with something that is primitive, robust, crude: with goblins and monsters, with the cult of magic, with the devil-possessed, with the cult of primitive observances (like fasting, chastity, etc.), with the cult of the soul and with the funeral customs. In the field of our research, the elements of this primitive world of ideas are visible at numerous places beneath the progressive forms characteristic for the Vedic people and their times. Soon they extend coherently over a comparatively greater space; soon they appear elsewhere as isolated rudiments interspersed among another mass of concepts. They may be explained here and there by the immigration of the aboriginal tribes of India; on the whole, however, they point out without doubt to those distant preliminary stages of development. To ignore them, in order to let the religion of the Indo-European gods spring directly from the lap of nature, would appear similar to the intention of a language research scholar who wants to deny the whole rich prehistory of the Indo-European basic language rich in countless evolutions, and to stamp it as an aboriginal language.

The standards laid down by the study of primitive types of religion are definite enough to judge what is old and what is new in the world of Vedic ideas—a question which, as we have seen, cannot often be decided only on the basis of its appearance in the older or later texts; also, the parallels found here are invaluably important for explanations of those concepts and customs, which are present in the Veda in rudimentary form. Their (the concepts and customs) obstinate bizarreness becomes intelligible to us, the more we learn to look at them from the point of view of primitive thinking. Those parallels are endlessly important to us. They show us, also through myriad connections with the non-Indian forms, the world of Indian cult which is, for our superficial observation, a cult complete in itself and following its own laws. They teach us to understand what is Indian at many points as the specimen of a type, besides which there is a great number of other equally valuable specimens.

I would not be mistaken if I say that the one, who ventures to enter into these unforeseen fields of research that have been recently found, would often make many mistakes, particularly when one approaches them only as a stranger. But to forgo this hazard would be to forgo the first steps on a path that alone can lead the researcher of Vedic religion to the solution of many important riddles.

REFERENCES

1. The use of the (war) chariot was already known, when the Indians and the Iranians formed one people; this speaks for their earlier common culture.
2. Of those, only the metrical elements are preserved in the *Ṛgveda.* The prose matter for which no fixed wording was prescribed, has to be supplemented.
3. These are, namely, the so-called *Yaju*-incantations. See p. 7.
4. How urgently the brief allusions of the *Ṛgveda* need to be supplemented is especially illustrated by exceptions like the myth of Namuci (Bloomfield, *JAOS*, xv, 143ff; compare my remarks in *NGGW*, 1893, 342 ff.), which is interwoven peculiarly in certain cult-practices of the later Vedic period, and that is why it is treated comparatively favourably in the *Yajurvedas.*
5. Yet, there are few exceptions like *Ṛv.* VI, 52, 4; VII, 35, 12. Also compare VIII, 48, 12.
6. Hillebrandt (*Ved. Myth.*, small edition, 20 f.) explains the fact discussed in these pages as under: the Vedic year is divided into the rising half of the gods (*Devayāna*) and the falling half of the manes (*Pitṛyāna*); the *Ṛgveda*, however, owing to a definite bias in its compilation, serves mainly the earlier half. One should look for the material on the second half in the *Atharvaveda* and elsewhere. I think, however, that the calendar-point-of-view has been given too much importance by that. For my own view, see p. 4 above.

7. I believe to have shown with this the defects in the important work of Bergaigne, *La religion védique*.

8. Compare *ZDMG*, XLII, 245 note 2 for the meaning of this word. The *mantras* of this type are often connected with the work of the reciting and the singing priests; yet these *mantras* did not attain the literary fixation so early like the *mantras* of *Adhvaryu*, as they were obviously less numerous and considered less important than the actual recitations of those priests.

9. i.e. with the flour originating from the plant-kingdom.

10. The rich are the waters. 'Mobile' appears to be referring, somehow or other, to the flour (?), or to the cattle for whose prosperity this was meant.

11. Compare note 29.

12. *ZDMG*, XLII, 244 f.

13. I have tried to show in my *Hymnen des Ṛgveda*, I, 294 f., where these collections are retained in the whole text of the *Yajurvedas*.

14. See *ZDMG*, *op. cit.* 245.

15. Compare my *Hymnen des Ṛgveda*, I. 352.

16. Also Atharvāngirasaḥ, i.e. the Atharvan and the Angiras texts: the first referring to the useful, curative magic, the latter referring to the harmful magic. Bloomfield's *The Atharvaveda* (*Grundriß der indo-ar.* Phil., iii, 1B) is an excellent introduction to these Vedas. The *Sāmaveda*, the collection of melodies used in the cult, is different here from the four Vedas. The text of these melodies belong almost exclusively to the *Ṛgveda*.

17. The verses given in the different *Gṛhyasūtras* (Book of the Domestic Sacrificial Ritual) are similar and homogeneous with the material of the *Atharvaveda*; majority of them are found there.

18. I refer to my explanations in *ZDMG*, LIV, 186 ff.

19. There is a warning in what is said against the method popular here and there. It likes to base its conclusions about the oldest popular form, said to be peculiar to the image of any deity, basing them on the expressions of the *Atharvaveda* in contrast to those of the *Ṛgveda*. This is done on account of, in some sense, the older character (see in discussion of the cult) ascribed to the popular contents of the *Atharvaveda* than those of the *Ṛgveda*. The exorcisms, among other things, of the *Atharvaveda*, are certainly in their nature older than the *Soma*-sacrifice of the *Ṛgveda*, but at the same time it is quite certain that the manner in which the *Atharvaveda* involves the gods in these magical actions is quite secondary.

20. Compare my remarks, *ZDMG*, XLII, 246.

21. The initiation to the *Soma*-sacrifice (*dikṣā*) furnishes an illustration of both the contradictory series of arguments with reference to the same ritual. Ḥere, the series of concepts characterized by the pair of gods, Agni-Viṣṇu, betrays a new form; but the centre of the whole rite, in brief the *Tapas* (ascetic magic) practices, is obviously very ancient. Compare the discussion of the *dikṣā* in the section on the cult.

22. So also the poetic embellishment of the rites is considered later than the *Soma*-sacrifice. Compare above p. 9 and my explanations in *Sacred Books of the East*, XXX, pp. IX ff. Knauer (*Festgruß an Roth*, 64) says that the *Gṛhya*- ritual (i.e. the ritual of the domestic cult) is 'older than the Śrauta-ritual'—the ritual of the major sacrifices with the three fires—'from the point of view of the literary style and its contents, and judged from the basic features of the two rituals'. I think that his view is misplaced, in so far as it is the question of the literary treatment of both the domains of ritual.

23. With few exceptions: *SBE*, *op. cit.*, XVIII f.

24. Winkler, 'Vorläufige Nachrichten über die Ausgrabungen in Boghaz-köi im Sommer 1907' (*Mitteilungen der Deutschen Orientgesellschaft*, No. 35). Compare also Meyer (ed.), *Das erste Auftreten der Arier in der Geschichte* (Sitz. -Ber. Berl. Akad. 1908), 14 ff., and the discussion between Jacobi (*JRAS*, 1909, 721 ff.; 1910, 456 ff.) and me (*op. cit.*, 1909, 1095 ff; 1910, 846 ff.). I also refer here to Hommel's findings in *Proc. of the Society of Bibl. Arch.*, XXI, 138 f., which have escaped my verification: it concerns here the appearance of not only As-sa-ra Ma-za-aš in an Assyrian list of gods, but also of Mi-it-ra and Marun (to be pronounced as Varun) named in the inscriptions.

25. It should be—in fact, it could be—based on this antiquity that one writes here still Našatia and not, as one would expect in the historical Iranian language, say Nahatia.

26. In rewriting the Avestic words I shall keep, for practical reasons, to the practice followed so far. It does not mean that I doubt the justification of Andreas and Wackernagel in introducing innovations.

27. Pischel-Geldner, *Vedische Studien*, I, XXIX.

28. Bartholomae, *Handb. der altiran. Dialekte*, p. V. Compare Mills in *Festgruß an Roth*, 193 ff.; see also my *Vedaforschung*, 35, 40.

29. I think that also the prosaic formulas of solemnization and exorcism appearing in both the works at the time of the sacrifice go back to the same basic type. The Avestic priest, e.g. says to consecrated water (*zaothra*) which he draws and pours into the vessels: 'I draw you for the satisfaction of the sacred and the just.' He says to the tree from which he takes the Baresman branches: 'Hail to you, you good, sacred tree that has produced Mazda.' When he strikes the pestle on the four sides of the mortar at the *Haoma*-preparation, he says: 'A blow against the cursed Angra Mainyu', 'A blow against Aešma with the murderous weapon', 'A blow against the demons of Mazana', 'A blow against all demons and foes of Varena'. One who knows the language of the Vedic *Yajus* (compare above, p. 7f.) will notice the complete similarity between the two.

Incidentally, I would like to point out at least to the possibility that a common form appears to be preserved in the instructive enumerations as under: on the Iranian side, Yasna 10, 16: 'I belong to five things; I do not belong to five things; I belong to good thought; I do not belong to evil thought; I belong to good word; I do not belong to bad word, etc.' It is likewise in the Buddhistic texts, e.g.: 'A monk armed with five qualities should not perform the consecration..His morality is not perfect. His contemplation is not perfect, etc. A monk armed with five qualities should perform the consecration—His morality is perfect, etc.' *Vinaya Piṭaka*, Mahâvagga I, 36). Or: 'There is an illegitimate renunciation of penitence, a legitimate one. There are two...three (and so on upto ten) illegitimate renunciations of penitence, ten legitimate' (enumerations follow always with the juxtaposition of the opposites; Cullavagga IX, 3). Likewise, very often. One may even compare Vendīdād 13, 44: 'One dog can be compared with eight people: it has the character of a priest, the character of a warrior, etc.' (closer details are given) with the Buddhistic parallels as under (see my *Buddha* p. 213): 'A man can have seven wives. Which seven are these? One who resembles a murdereress, one who resembles a roberess, one who resembles a lady of the house, etc.'

30. Pischel-Geldner, *op. cit.*

31. We have to come back to this relationship between Varuṇa and Ahura in the section on Varuṇa and the Ādityas.

32. It may be noted, incidentally, that the Veda, as also the Iranian tradition, has preserved the formal number of thirty-three gods. (Darmesteter, *Orm. et. Ahr.* 39 note 5).

33. I refer here to Henry, *Soma et Haoma* (Paris 1907) and again to him in Caland-Henry, *L'Agniṣṭoma*, 469 ff.

34. I shall come back to the original identity of Barhis and Baresman in my discussion of the Cult of Sacrifice.

35. Thus, it is not saying much when it is said that the Vedic Varuṇa is closer to the Avestic Ahura than to the Varuṇa of later India, although one has to consider not only the distance between the Indo-Iranian and the Vedic age, but also between the Indo-Iranian and the Avestic for the difference between Varuṇa and Ahura. This means one has to consider the whole Zoroastrian cataclysm.

36. Of the enormous literature, I mention here only the lengthy and excellent article of O. Schrader, 'Aryan Religion' in the *Encycl. of Religion and Ethics*.

37. Incidentally, one should take care in selecting from this expression all too prominent concepts of divine superiority over the earthly maze. Celestial guiding gods are also present in the strata of primitive cultures.

38. See under the section 'Other Deities'.

39. See the section 'The Gods and Demons in Their Relationship to Nature, etc.' for the types of 'special Gods' and 'Lords' (Skt. *pati*) of this or that area.

40. The present position of research is unfourable for comparison of cult-forms which try to reconstruct the Indo-European state of affairs, at least with the intention of ascertaining here a characteristic special possession of the Indo-European people. There is no doubt that the Vedic and the Greek sacrifices show numerous and far-reaching contacts. But the semitic sacrifice is essentially silent over the concurrences obtaining among the remote peoples. Perhaps, the comparison of the Indo-European sources in the field of domestic rites are still the most productive.

41. Pischel and Geldner say (*Vedische Studien*, I, p. XXXVII):

> If we think on the one hand that the old Indo-Germanic gods in the Veda have almost no legends, that they have partially fallen into the background, like Dyaus, partially gradually displaced, and on the other hand, a large number of legends group around new, purely Indian, gods, then we are forced to conclude that a great shift has taken place in mythology, that the legend of the Vedic gods represents a more recent layer, which may contain reminiscences of the old Indo-Germanic myth, but in its character, it is purely Indian and it is rooted in the Indian folklores.

My view, as seen from what I have already said, is decisively opposed to this view. Indra, for example, or the Aśvins are, I think, figures of gods to whom many legends have been added anew during the Indian period, but they have brought with themselves a distinctive stamp of the Indo-European past in their basic features; just as Varuṇa and Ādityas have brought them from the Indo-Iranian period.

42. We may refer here to the excellent speech of Caland; '*De studie van het Sanskrit in verband met ethnologie en klassieke philologie*' (1906).

CHAPTER ONE

The Vedic Gods and Demons in General

THE VEDIC GODS AND DEMONS IN THEIR RELATIONSHIP TO NATURE AND TO THE REMAINING SUBSTRATA OF MYTHICAL CONCEPTION

Nature-Deities and Anthropomorphism

THE religious or semi-religious activity of the Vedic Indians refers to the forces which are of various types. There are impersonal forces or forces represented as substances and fluids and having at best a shadow-personality, like the solidity present in the stone, forces like diseases and dangerous things of all kinds, the sanctity and efficacy of the holy word, magic formula, the secret power of numbers, etc. It is the duty of the priest or of the magician to lead all this to or away from friend and foe. Further, the souls of the dead—of relatives and enemies—now as protectors, now as originators of harm, must be appeased or warded off. Animate beings, friendly or inimical to man, fill the whole world, heaven and earth, mountains, forests, trees and animals, the terrestrial waters and the celestial waters borne by the cloud. Life is also present in the object prepared by human hand. The warrior respects the god in the ploughshare; the gambler, in the dice; the sacrificer—about whom we have the most exact information—in the pressing-stone which presses the *Soma,* in the bed of straw on which the gods sit, in the pole to which the sacrificial animal is bound. In the same way, human life is influenced by the demons who bring cure or spread diseases. These demons, through contact with such natural beings or objects or by virtue of being in origin the souls of the dead that have entered wholly or almost completely into human, animal or monstrous forms, are able to move freely. The world of superior gods exhalts itself over inferior forms of all different kinds. They have the character of anthropomorphism, of course not spelt out in every case everywhere, but certainly predominant. They are men elevated to power, greatness and glory. Men with human passions, but not subject to death like human beings though born as humans. In this way, the gods of the Indo-European people were also given form, at least in the period preceding the separation: these gods were the 'Father Sky', the heroic Storm-God and the youthfully handsome Dioscuri.

One could think of attempting a survey of these various types of superhuman beings, at least the beings beyond human characteristics, together with the forms of human activity ascribed to them in an order corresponding to the course of historical development moving from the lower to the upper order. Perhaps, it may be possible to envisage an approach to this ideal of presentation. I do not think the time is now ripe enough for that. Even if the main trends of such development begin to emerge from the science of religion with satisfactorily increasing reliability, the features which can be recognized here are still not so distinct as to enable one to undertake classification of the whole matter according to them. The requirements at the moment—one may consider this as a pioneering work for that very urgent task—will be to draw the picture as its outlines emerge within the purview of the Vedic period: more exactly, corresponding to the nature of our sources, within the purview, above all, of the priestly classes of that period. Yet, it is obvious that even a presentation arranged wholly in this sense cannot, without doing violence at places, disregard the fact that the old and the new lie side by side within the Vedic development and after that within the development reaching far beyond the Vedic.

The typically marked condition of religion was attained long ago in Vedic India through many preliminary stages. For this condition, characteristic is the predominance of the beings named at the end of the survey above, i.e. of the supreme gods worshipped through prayer and sacrifice. These gods are quite predominant, or they were at least in the pre-Vedic period, divine nature beings, the active personalities influencing the great natural events. So, we have to concern ourselves here with the relationship in which they stand to their natural substrata. This relationship varies with different gods, the process of individualization and humanization of the god with respect to that strata being either regressive or progressive. For example, the Fire-god Agni stands in this context essentially apart from the Storm-god Indra, and the Sun-god Mitra apart from the Sun-god Sūrya. I think, for this difference, the form of the concerned substratum in nature itself is of considerable significance, apart from many other factors. These factors are the influence of the name which expresses or does not express the identity of the god with the natural object, the influence of the period of the idea in question, the effect of the contradiction between the independently developed gods and the gods accepted from outside, and finally—we shall come back to that later—the effect of the interference, say, of ethical interests remote from natural existence. One may compare the form of Agni or Uṣas (Dawn) with that of Indra. The fire, the dawn presents a clear phenomenon complete in itself. One sees Agni or Uṣas. But in the storm,[1] the figure of Indra is not visible. One sees the dark mountains of clouds from which Indra releases the waters; one sees the waters; one sees the flashing weapon of the god: but where is he himself? There is a gap here, and this is filled by a spirit fond of creating myths with the figure of a hero;[2] and the less is restraint placed on the imagination by the outline determined by nature, the more human[3] characteristics does he acquire. Also a chronological factor plays its part here. The constant presence of Agni, the regular coming and going of Uṣas restrains the mythical perception which, in Indra's case, takes place unhindered: there is not always a storm, not at regular intervals at least—surely Indra has gone here or there on account of his unpredictable whims; he performs deeds which have nothing to do with the storm, yet they show the same character of heroic sublimity. Therefore, it is possible that the connection with the natural phenomenon, standing originally in the centre, is forgotten through the strong accentuation of this near-human quality that lures mythical ideas into treading separate new paths. But the understanding of an object like Agni could not possibly become extinct in view of the constantly present natural objects.

Agni and Fire

We shall dwell further on Agni to know more in detail about the type of the deity closely connected with the natural phenomenon.

Should the Vedic concept of relationship of Agni to the fire be understood to the extent that this is the privileged abode and domain of god who has at his disposal also other abodes and domains or, are the two entities, Agni and fire, inseparable? Is, can one say, this element the house of the god or the body of the god?

The name Agni itself supports the second view; the god is called 'fire'. He is present where there is fire; I scarcely find the *Ṛgveda* considering this god as present where there is no fire. If there is talk of Agni hidden in the waters or plants, then the god is not separated from fire; it only means that the fire is present latently in water or in wood.[4] One who produces the sacrificial fire with fire sticks does not create the ungodly element and then ask god to enter it, but he creates god or gives him birth. 'Men have produced Agni, the worshipped one, from fire sticks with devotion through the movement of hands.' 'Rub, you men, the wise one without falsehood, the expert, the immortal, the beautiful-faced; produce you men, the banner of the sacrifice, the first one, the Agni, the merciful.'[5] The expressions which attach human form to Agni become more scarce and less marked than, say, in the case of Indra: one sees Agni's body before one's eyes, and sees that he does not resemble the human body.

The identification of the god with the natural object is indeed fraught with difficulty in the case of Agni, and, to that extent, this example is perhaps not the most favourable for an illustration. The natural fire appears unlimitedly in many simultaneously occurring phenomena. In a way, the god Agni participates in this multiplicity: he is 'the one Agni, the multiply kindled' (*Ṛv.* VIII, 58, 2), and doubtless, there was a time when he was worshipped here only in isolation or in plurality as a demoniac form of this or that fire. Obviously, the example of such gods as the Sky-god or the Sun-god induced a change. Corresponding to their inherent natural subtrata, these gods were considered as incomparable, world-dominating superior beings. Agni became similar to them and equal in birth; 'the multiply kindled' became at the same time the 'one Agni'.[6] A treatment or solution of this contradiction between the unity and the multiplicity was not attempted by the Ṛgvedic poets; they let it remain along with countless enigmas and paradoxes. It is, however, clear that the understanding of Agni as one of the few gods did not fit in with his identity on earth. Therefore, we find also, besides the concept of the god emerging time and again from the fire sticks mentioned above, the idea of his entry and descent into the fire which man produces or kindles. This idea is really isolated, and if I am not mistaken, foreign to the earlier contents of the text. One cannot refer to this with certainty, when one addresses the fire while producing the sacrificial fire by friction: 'Climb down Jātavedas, make the gods once more aware of our sacrificial meal.'[7] Here it does not mean the god's descent from celestial heights, but simply refers to his stepping out of concealment from the fire sticks.[8] It signifies more when one prays at the time the fire-altar is being built and the fire is being kindled: 'Come out from afar, O god with the red horses.'[9] The custom to be discussed further below, i.e. of keeping a white horse looking in the direction of the fire being kindled, can also suggest the idea that the god Agni represented by the horse is to unite with the freshly kindled fire although one cannot always definitely conclude from such magical practice that this bears exact resemblance to some idea. The presence of a fiery-looking animal only means that one wished to encourage the fire to step out of the fire sticks, whereby nothing would show for the relationship between god and element. It may be mentioned here that when a later Vedic poet (X, 12, 1) calls Agni, lit for sacrifice, as the god who sits down to help the mortals in the capacity of a priest 'going to his spiritual existence', there is an expression here which is used preferably to indicate the soul entering the world of spirits.[10] In the sacrifice made by humans, the god reaches his goal and his home like the soul reaching the other world. Obviously, this separates the god from the visible element.

It is not necessary to collect further details: what is here the original idea and what is secondary appears to be clear. Basically, Agni is the element endowed with the divine soul and only then an ideal being who could be thought of as apart from the element. If, as we noticed, the contradiction between the multiplicity of the concrete fire and the unity of god favoured this separation, then, in other cases the identity of the god with natural phenomena appears to be undisturbed as in the case of the identity of Sūrya with the sun, Uṣas with the dawn. In their cases, a unique natural being corresponds to the unique deity[11] or, as in the case of Āpas, it corresponds to the waters whose natural multiplicity is retained in the pluralistic nature of the deity.[12] Wherever the dawn shines, the Vedic Indian sees in it the shining goddess who reveals her bosom; when the sun shines he sees in it Sūrya visible from afar, and where the waters flow there go past the indefatigable goddesses; the poet who speaks of a drink of wholesome water attributes its beneficial effects to the presence in it of the Āpas, the goddesses.[13]

Obscurities and New Forms

But not in the case of all gods who represent natural objects in this way is the connection with them (the natural objects) still so clearly evident in the Veda. Like Sūrya Mitra is also a Sun-god; I think it is hardly less certain that Mitra's divine companion Varuṇa was originally a Moon-god.[14] But in the hymns addressed to Mitra and Varuṇa the relationship between the god and the natural objects appears to be different from the one, that is, between Agni and

Uṣas. This relationship is not at all directly present in the consciousness of the Vedic poets; they know only a series of features associated with the image of those gods which are to us, the traces of those original objects, but to them they are simply given facts. Mitra and Varuṇa are kings of light who sit on the celestial throne and supervise right and wrong among the human beings. They have opened the path for the sun; the sun is their eye. Here is a trace of Mitra's original nature, but for the Veda, the sun is also the eye of Varuṇa. The belief crops up that Mitra has a special mastery over the day, and Varuṇa over the night; the latter points our attention to the moon. In place of the faded natural significance, the being here which is similar to man is rather markedly developed than in the case of Agni or Sūrya. One feature is sufficient to characterize the difference: Mitra and Varuṇa have the sun as their eye; Sūrya himself is the eye. The Avesta shows an intermediate stage between the oldest stage in which Mitra must have been a divinely animated sun and the stage in the Veda of complete dissociation of the god from the natural body. This is done by the Avesta when it lets Mithra, as the first of the holy gods, reach across the Hara-mountain, seize the beautiful peak and survey the dwellings of the Aryans 'before the immortal Sun with the swift horses'.[15] The Sun-god is so much detached here from the sun that he appears ahead of the sun, in fact in close conjunction with his rising. It is a mistaken principle to search for a natural phenomenon on the basis of such expressions and adapt these to suit the occasion—like the identification with Mithra of the light that accompanies the sun and precedes it: the natural object is the sun himself but the condition in which the concept of Mithra agrees exactly with this substratum is no longer stable in the Avesta.

What motives have given this particular Sun-god in the Avesta and throughout in the Veda an altogether different form from the Sun-god Sūrya, and have also allowed the Moon-god appearing in the Veda as Varuṇa to free himself completely from the moon? Here, perhaps, we should consider the strange origin of these gods[16] which, as I believe, is to some extent probable. Their nature was not firmly imbedded in the consciousness of the Aryans. At the same time, the consistency of the name linking the god with the natural object is missing. Finally and above all, a sphere of moral concepts was peculiar to Mitra and Varuṇa alone. These concepts were enlarged by the process of progressive ethical absorption and these, in turn, contributed considerably in restraining the natural significance of those gods. It can be said that the religious factor drained especially energetically the mythological complex of ideas of its force. The sun and the moon, and whatever might happen in their case, did not stand any more in the foreground. What mattered was the concept of all-seeing, all-righteous kings with whom one wanted to be on good terms. In place of the old feeling of helpless dependence upon the natural forces, it was more and more the human, the social and the political conditions of life which furnished the prototype for the concept of higher powers: the dependence upon the king, the strong warrior, the wise priest, the rich. Therefore, there came, in place of the idolized nature-being the figure of a divine hero or donor increasingly detached from nature. In place of Mitra and Varuṇa, there came divine kings and judges.

We may refer here in passing to a further example of separation of the Vedic gods from their natural substratum: the two Aśvins, the Indian Dioscuri. They are probably, according to their original meaning, the morning star and the evening star.[17] In the Veda, however, they are two radiant youths who course together along their heavenly path and bring help to human beings in distress. They have become, quite like Mitra and Varuṇa, near-human ideal figures with the remnants of attributes accorded to them by the original natural significance, yet so much free of them, that their attributes as present in the Veda directly contradict that meaning in part: like Mitra and Varuṇa, the Sun-and the Moon-god who have the sun for their eye, so too the two Aśvins, the morning- and the evening-star, move across the morning sky.

We contrasted earlier Indra, the Storm-god with the type represented by Agni, Sūrya and Uṣas, for a more dominant anthropomorphism appears to have been peculiar to him from the beginning. We must add here that even with respect to the secondary obscuration of the original meaning, Indra of the *Ṛgveda* is different from those gods and is comparable, at least approximately, with Mitra or the Aśvins. We shall show that Indra's first great deed, the liberation of the celestial waters in the storm from the bondage of the mountains of clouds, had changed for the Ṛgvedic poets into the liberation of the earthly rivers from the bondage of the rock, whence they originate. Therefore, the obscuration here of the original complex of ideas takes place at first in the proportion in which an equally concrete new complex of ideas that displace it can be expressed through the former by the same words (water = rain or river; mountain = cloud or mountain): whereby, as can be seen, the metaphorical use of the word has partly overlept its real meaning.[18] As the earlier natural meaning of Varuṇa recedes behind the ethical and is obscured by it, there surface features to which the religious interest is tied up especially firmly, and which allow the original natural character of Indra to become blurred: it is the powerful hero bestowing victory and riches to whom the prayers are addressed, and not the Thunderer.

Thus we find that the features of the Vedic gods as they emerge from the perception of the natural objects and natural events survive clearly only in part. Another portion is present in a form which is already far removed from the original type as a result of the obscuration of the old and the addition of new ideas. Such things happen in the sphere of mythology and are not quite different from what happens in the sphere of language which sometimes faithfully preserves very old constructions or sometimes modifies them into modern forms or replaces them by new constructions. Like both the transforming forces at work in language, viz. the sound shift which is mainly the result of phonetical corruption and the analogy which builds new forms, so also there are two similar processes, opposed to each other, in the history of divine figures and myths—it may be mentioned, also in the history of the cult. These processes are the fading away, the emptying of the mythical idea, and the filling of this emptying vessel with the new contents. It is natural, as already pointed out above—and it may be remembered once more—that, even at the outset, it is impossible to attempt to trace back the disintegration of the myth along so a clear pattern as science has shown in the process of linguistic disintegration. And the analogy, whose influence is no doubt felt both in language and in mythology, does not find in this as in the former comparable framework like paradigms. Such framework could enable research to trace back its effect, if only approximately, to such distinctive types that have remained unchanged as in grammar. Above all, unaccountable factors intervene here like national and personal fates, priest's speculation and poet's creative urge: they give their products the character of fortuitousness or also of freedom, and their effect can at best be confirmed, given favourable circumstances, but can never be calculated in advance.

Nature-Myths: Other Elements of the Myths

From what has been said one expects the nature-myths to be the basis of the Vedic myths: the description given in the language of the myths of the natural events which the gods or demoniac beings bring about or sustain.[19] Throughout all the obscurations and new forms, a number of such nature-myths have remained perceptible with near-certain or at least with some probability: thus Indra's victory over Vṛtra, i.e. the storm; the liberation of the imprisoned cows, i.e. perhaps the appearance of the dawn; the coming down of Agni, i.e. the kindling of fire on earth through lightning; the companionship or the marriage of Aśvins and Sūryā, i.e. perhaps the combined appearance of the morning star and the sun. Such myths must have hardly ever been numerous. Originally, they were very brief, not certainly because the practice of visualization and the narrative skill were inadequate for the description of complicated events but because the matter made available by nature contained just very little. In lieu of it they seem to have a certain obstinate rigidity about them which is missing in the chequered existence of other stories. Though numerous deeds of Indra have been reported, the Vṛtra-victory has always remained the best.

If now, such myths, which one would like to denote as mythical molecules or monads in contrast to the complicated newer forms, fuse together, then one does not have to see in the resultant fusion something like the mythical image of a longer, more complicated natural event. The elements reach out directly to nature; their union does not any more reflect a concatenation of natural occurrences but the free work of poetry and speculation. Mostly, however, those monads do not develop through mutual union, but through gradual appearance of elements of other origin. The fantasy utilizes the old motives as a starting-point for independent creation.[20] It mixes with the myths the features from the treasures of fairy-tales, present surely in large numbers in the older period. The need for poetic embellishment and refining made its influence felt; the demands of indigenous poetics also begin to show its influence. When the celestial drink is brought to the god by a bird,[21] the fantasy, suggested by the usual course of things in human life, adds that the guard who has to protect the drink follows the bird closely. He shoots but does he hit the mark? A feather falls; the bird, however, luckily escapes with its precious booty. Does the shot mean a natural occurrence, the feather a natural object? I do not think so. The episode rests only on the efforts to lend life to the whole event, to create suspense which resolved itself happily: an episode certainly common among hunters and stories of hunting of those times must have suggested the motive.

The gods also take over quite willingly a rôle that can by no means be derived from their natural character, in numerous stories which are intended to explain the origin of some peculiarity in the evolution of nature, in animals or plants, in human custom and order, that can evoke curiosity. And, further, the belief in god's intervention in human life had to give rise to stories which illustrated this intervention, and depicted the gods as bestowers of gifts and blessings and as saviours of the hopeful. Indra is the strongest of the strong gods: so he usually makes his presence felt whenever it counts to overpower a strong opponent for the best of the beloved of gods. The Aśvins bring the kind, rescuing light after the horrors of the night. Thus, they always turn up to lead those oppressed by dark dangers to salvation.[22] The Apsaras, the charmingly adorned nymph, takes over the role of the beloved or the wife of the human hero. This hero himself was, at least in the stories that were circulated in the higher social circles, as a rule, an eminent personality like a king or a famous warrior of earlier times, or—one should take into consideration the role of the priestly class in the building up of the Vedic traditions—the founder, the ancestor, the name-giver of a priests's family. The motives of these stories originate from various walks of human life, or, at least, from the spheres with which the more important persons come in contact, from war and sport, and then from various situations of family life. The question how human beings learnt to perform the sacrifice and further how the gods rewarded this or that sacrifice of an earlier period with special blessings drew the priest-poet's immediate attention: here, then, the sphere of mythological stories merge unwittingly with the reminiscences of something that actually happened.[23]

Minor Demons, Souls

We shall have to return to the major gods in this survey in order to refer to the types not dealt with so far. But first it is better to think of the minor ones amongst the supernatural and non-earthly beings like spirits of the forest and the field, goblins, monsters and devils. In a large number of most ancient texts which are full of excessive praise for the high as well as the highest celestial gods, there is hardly any talk of these lower classes of beings. It was already mentioned that they surface more clearly only in the later strata of the *Ṛgveda*; they are in the foreground in the *Atharvaveda* and even more so in the texts which portray domestic cult practices. They assume a significant place in the narrative literature of the great epics and also in the collection of the stories of the Buddhists.

One should not, of course, deduce from this relatively later appearance of the mass of concepts in the literature in question that the concepts are of later origin than the myths and cults of the major gods. Nowhere else is the divergence between the chronology of literary and religious history so pronounced as in this case. Ethnology and folk-psychology have already explained this sufficiently. We know now that the belief in hosts of benevolent or malefic minor nature-demons and souls inhabiting the earth and also the magic art of rendering these beings harmless or beneficial to man, and identical in their basic features, have spread across the whole earth, down to the most primitive peoples. In the process of development, a higher divine world is then built upon the common foundation of that belief, and on the common foundation of that magic, a higher cult—both acquiring different forms, depending upon the character and the fates of the individual peoples. But those lower forms of religious life that were pushed gladly into the background, though not wholly, by representatives of advanced faith, who formed something like a guild, do assert themselves in many remnants in the midst of higher cultures and survive almost unaltered, in their old and crude form among the inferior strata of people. The data of the Vedic traditions are in convincing agreement with the concept of the course of events briefly referred to here and have been confirmed by research. References to the beliefs in a widely spread world of demons find mention also in the older strata of Ṛgvedic poetry, and if these references are sparse and poor in content, it can be explained sufficiently by the character of these hymns which have a different purpose; it would be against all possibility, if one were to accept, therefore, that the colourful and crude concretion, later to become characteristic of these concepts, was not there in them earlier. Like in the case of hymnic poetry, we get to know the sacrificial ritual in its oldest phase, full of customs reflecting the mental attitude of primitive practitioners of magic.[24] We have no doubt reached here the stratum of very ancient forms of perceptions and magic cult which, like the structures of the religio-historical Stone Age, form the background behind all higher religious systems.

Amongst the spirits and the demons with whom the Vedic magic is concerned, the malefic spirits predominate, probably because the superior gods who are thought of exclusively as good and benevolent have ousted the benevolent demons from their sphere of activity. It is also probable that those monsters evolved, at least partially, from the souls of the dead. We shall see how old Indian belief, which in this respect is an extension of most ancient beliefs, allows the existence of the living to be surrounded by the souls of dead friends and enemies. These souls hover far and wide, now invisible, now revealing themselves in ghosts, animals and in many other forms, whole as well as misshapen. That they bring to the living danger in various forms is proved by the various precautionary measures provided for in the cult of the dead. The same process of the fading away of the old and the coming up of new ideas, which changed the Storm-god Indra into the performer of heroic deeds and the Moon-god Varuṇa into the discerner and chastener of sins, could let the souls turn into the demons of diseases, etc. These demons, then, obviously develop separately their peculiarities with reference to this or that type of malefic influence. I think many things point to concrete traces of such developments in India, as also in many other countries, for example, in closely related Iran.[25] The later literature of India is rich in stories like the one in the '*Thirty-two Stories of the Throne*' about the man who, deceived by his wife, dies of sorrow and returns every night in the shape of an evil spirit to torment her.[26] For the contemporary world, Monier Williams[27] confirms it as a general belief of the Hindus that the majority of evil spirits are from dead human beings: here haunts the ghost of a milkman killed by a tiger, there the ghost of a potter, the terror of the whole neighbourhood. The connection with the memory of this or that deceased is naturally lost, in the course of time, in the case of these ghosts, and only the idea of an evil monster torturing the people remains. The right of such folk-belief to provide hints for research on the Vedic period can hardly be disputed, even if this belief were to be bracketed with the theory of metempsychosis with the intention of severing it from its connection with the older Vedic belief. Probably, it will become clearer that the theory of metempsychosis is nothing more than the process of making use of elements—a process that systematizes, stereotypes and raises the particular to the level of the unforeseeable. These elements become less important for us in the tradition, but they are as old, nay, older than Indian belief and folklore: and that the concepts just mentioned here belong to such elements is quite likely on account of their wide propagation among the lowest cultural regions. Direct evidence for the association of different types of demons with the souls of the dead is not—it may be noted—altogether missing in the older literature. In a magic hymn of the *Atharvaveda* (II, 14, 5), the goblins present in the cow-stall, in the cart-shed and in the foundation of the house are driven away thus: 'If you are of the endemic ones, if sent by men, or if you are born of the Dasyus.' Here the reference to the evil spirits of the dark-skinned aboriginals approximates almost to the concept of hostile souls. So also, in the cult of the dead, 'the Dasyus who have entered into the fathers assuming the physiognomy of the relatives' are warded off from the sacrifice.[28] It appears that the hostile souls want to partake of the sacrificial meal along with the friendly ones. Elsewhere, there is a direct reference to 'the Asuras, Rakṣas who sojourn among the fathers';[29] the reference to the sojourn of evil spirits, recurring often in the cult and the liturgic hymns,[30] can be explained as pointing to the nature of souls of these spirits or at least of many amongst them. Thus, even in the older Buddhist literature, there are weird spirits of all kinds dwelling in graveyards and in tombstones.[31] A 'ghost that grants wishes' living in a tree says of himself in a Buddhist story: 'I am not god, no Gandharva, no Indra who destroys fortresses: know that I am one no more living who has come here from Bheruva.[32] At another place in the same collection of stories the pious are advised to give gifts 'in the names of those who have died earlier or in the names of the deities (*vatthudevatā*)'[33] residing there. The later deities are thus placed alongside the souls, whose fate in the other world can be made easy through pious gifts.

One cannot deny the possibility that souls increased in strength where their activity assumed greater dimensions,—the strength that would let them appear to be equal in birth to the celestial gods. It would be, therefore, natural to understand Yama, the ruler of the dead, in this sense.[34] And perhaps, also, the only really evil one amongst the greater Vedic gods, viz. Rudra. We shall come back again to this problem while studying him more closely later. Somehow, a definite solution is made difficult besides by the hazy state of affairs and the apparent great estrangement of the concerned concepts from their origin.

Abstract Deities

Here we have to speak of different groups of minor and major deities, whose characters are more abstract than those discussed so far. First, the gods who are characterized by their names as rulers and masters of certain spheres or mechanism of influence: they are active themselves in the appropriate sense or are patrons of those who are thus active. At the harvest the 'collector', the 'accumulator', the 'piler' helps. The 'restorer' (*Nivarta, Nivartana*) looks after the return of the cows. The god 'scare' (*Uttuda*) scares the girl in love away from her bed: all proper 'special gods' in the sense Usener has taught us to understand them. It may be said they have a certain linguistic uniformity: they often prefer names formed with the suffix *-tar*, a very common suffix for the nouns which denote the doer of some action. One finds in every epoch of the history of language, apart from word-structures which, having lost their effectivity, have merely survived in the constructions inherited from the past, also word-structures that possess vitality and can be used by every speaker for the formation of more and more new words. Therefore, the religio-historical method of deriving names of gods ending with *-tar* in the Vedic age and in the age immediately preceding it must be credited with the greatest vitality and productivity. There are gods like Trâtar (guardian-protector), Dhâtar (maker), Netar (leader) with their corresponding feminine forms like the goddesses Vārutrīḥ (protectresses), etc. It is seen that the scale of these divinely hypostatized ideas reaches up to very broad generalities. Basically, it is quite similar to this kind of hypostatization, when one does not worship indeed any divine 'angry one' and 'lover', any 'speakress', 'plenty givnig one','destroyeress', but the god 'anger' (*manyu*) and the god 'love' (*kāma*), the goddesses 'speech' (vāc), 'plenty' (*puraṃdhi*), 'destruction' (*nirṛti*).[35] One may further refer here to the clearly dominant group of 'masters' (*pati*) of this or that sphere, and of this or that substance, another highly vivacious type of the Vedic period. There is the 'lord of lineage' (*prajāpati*), the 'lord of the field' (*kṣetrasya pati*), the 'lord of the place' (*vāstoṣpati*), the 'lord of thinking' (*manasas pati*), 'the lords of truth' (*satyasya patayaḥ*), etc. and in which case it is not always correct to call the gods abstract. Where the one that is ruled by them is a natural object, they are on the side of the nature-gods or nature-demons; only that within this type, the relationship to nature represents only one case amongst other possible cases and, so to say, the machinery which keeps the god in contact with the substance ruled by him, works here with abstract, schematic universality. Compared to gods like Indra or Varuṇa, these beings are that much poorer in plasticity and personal vitality.[36] At every moment, the momentary situation or a sudden inspiration can increase these mythological cheap merchandise according to desire. One would scarcely doubt that most of the gods belonging to the species introduced here are fairly young, just as Fides and Pax are younger than Jupiter and Mars. All the same, the goddess 'plenty' (*puraṃdhi*, compare Avestic *pārendi*) originates, for example, from the Indo-Iranian period. And the types as such date back obviously still further: the numerous Roman 'special gods' like Vervactor, Reparator, etc. and the Lithuanian[37] *pati*-gods leave hardly any doubt about their Indo-European origin.

The individual specimens of these types of gods could, under especially favourable circumstances, understandably cast off their hereditarily acquired paleness and gain new life—a process that brought them closer to the nature-gods by merging them with some sort of concrete complexes of ideas.

Both these remarkable cases shall be discussed here in brief.

Savitar

Myriad movements criss-cross the world life: who causes them? To answer this question the god 'Stimulator' or 'Impeller' Savitar[38] was created. He had finished features already in the Ṛgvedic times. He underwent later a bit of development. The name of this god expresses his character: he stretches out his golden arms to impel all movements that take place on heaven and earth. As one likes to use for the god 'Maker' (*Dhātar*) the verb 'make' (*dhā*), for the god 'Protector' the verb 'protect' (*trā*), so also for this god 'Impeller' the verb 'impel' (*sū*), without prefix and with prefixes, in verb-forms and in noun-derivatives. Repeatedly, the essence of the verses addressed to him is that he impels, he impelled, he should impel. The objects to which this 'impelling' refers are quite different: men, gods, animals, the living and the dead, water and light.[39] Just as he impels men to do their work at morn, he allows man and beast to rest at nightfall. He allows the sun to begin his daily course and heralds the coming of the night. As sun himself completes the mightiest movement in the universe and governs thereby all other movements, Savitar stands, naturally, in close relationship with him. Thus, the inclination to transfer to him the attributes of the Sun-god. But it would be misunderstanding the structure of the whole complex of ideas, if one were to consider, therefore, both the original and the Ṛgvedic Savitar as the Sun-god. The essential feature of the concept of Savitar is not the idea of the sun or the idea of the sun moving in a particular direction, namely, towards life and movement; rather it is the abstraction of this 'impelling' itself that also provides a framework which includes concepts relevant to Savitar.

But the scale on which these ideas are entrenched, the force with which they arrest attention indicates that, in contrast to the profusion of abstract gods sandwiched between Savitar and other deities, an attraction for Savitar became pronounced, endowing him with concrete, colourful features. The Ṛbhus come to the house of Savitar on their wanderings. He 'infuses' them with immortality. Savitar sets the marriage procession of the goddess Sūryā in motion. That proximity in which the god 'Impeller' stands to the sun lets him finally—after Ṛgvedic times—merge with the sun and then become in reality the Sun-god. When we compare the Sun-god with Sūrya or Mitra, it is more so educative for the historical observer to know as to how from different stuff this Sun-god was originally made of.

Bṛhaspati

The 'Lord of prayer' Bṛhaspati or Brahmaṇaspati[40] takes a similarly privileged position amongst the gods named as *pati*, like Savitar amongst the gods with the names ending in *-tar*. The nature of this god is expressed by his name: he is 'the oldest king of prayers', 'Creator of all prayers'. He himself sings the sacrificial songs and utters the magic-charged prayer formulas that awaken the mercy of gods, 'the *mantra* that finds favour with Indra, Varuṇa, Mitra and Aryaman', or he gives such a prayer to priests who invoke him for that—'I shall give you a brilliant word', says Bṛhaspati to the priest who sought his help for a rain-bringing sacrifice (*Ṛv.* X, 98, 2). Thus, besides Agni, the sacrificial fire, Bṛhaspati is the divine incarnation of priesthood in so far as this had power and duty to guide the course of things through prayer or conjuration; Bṛhaspati is himself a priest, the house-priest (Purohita) of the gods.

Now, it is important to pursue how concrete shape is assumed by this god, in whom one could have been inclined to expect a certain abstractness. Prayer and conjuration, besides the power of weapons, dominate battles; the priest accompanies the king's general to the battle. Thus, Bṛhaspati appears as a priest-god of war beside Indra, the heroic war-god. 'Bṛhaspati, fly with your chariot! You, who destroys evil spirits and keeps enemies at bay! The wrecker of armies, the subduer of enemies and the victor in battle! May your blessings accompany us' (*Ṛv.* X, 103, 4). He does not miss the mark with his fleet bow and arrow; the string of his bow is *Ṛta* ('Law', 'Order', *Ṛv.* II, 24, 8): therefore, the magic power of the holy word rooted in the order of things is effective like an arrow in the hands of Bṛhaspati.[41] Like Indra, together with whom he is invoked, he wrecks hostile fortresses, the forts of Śambara; he shakes all that is firm; he dispels darkness and wins light. Above all, it is the myth of the forcing of rock-cave and the liberating of the cows in which Bṛhaspati, the gods' priest, has found a firm place together with the ancestors of the human generations of priests. We shall show[42] that this Indo-European myth—whatever may be its original meaning—has become in the Veda the story of how the cows were taken away from the niggards who had withheld them from the Brahmanas. No other god fits in the train of thoughts of this story so exactly like Bṛhaspati, the divine *Purohita,* the representative of Brahmanism amongst the gods, the possessor of the magic power of the holy word, which brings to fall the miserly despisers of the Brahmanas. So, it had to be Bṛhaspati who split the rock asunder with his sacred hymns and got the cows; the legend which classical antiquity attributed to Herakles-Hercules, the conqueror of Geryone-Cacus is extended to him. It would be difficult to find a more positive example to show how a late, abstract conception receives tangible concreteness through the mingling of the old mythical substance.

Gods and Animals[43]

The relationship of the Vedic gods and demons to the animals deserves special treatment.

Strongly predominant animal traits amongst gods and demons can be taken for granted for the remote antiquity, according to the results obtained by ethnology. The god is frequently an animal or becomes an animal; he oscillates between human and animal nature. Blurring of the boundary between the two is just a part of the features characterizing the philosophy of the primitive races.

If now—as we have seen—the anthropomorphic view carried the day during the Indo-European period itself in the case of the great gods ruling the world, the animal kingdom stretches out into the gods' world in numerous remnants and traces for the Vedic belief. It must be first emphasized here that the real animal the Vedic Indian meets—apart from where it is the messenger or the representative of god—appears to him frequently, so to say, in its own right, as a bearer of demoniac nature: thus, particularly, the frightful or evil beasts like serpents difficult to be warded off. Then useful animals like the cow, the very essence of the blessing of nourishment.

Animal Worship

Even a sort of a personal deification can be applied to each of the individual animals endowed with specially radiant qualities. There take place, especially with regard to Serpent worship,[44] celebrations with offerings and invocations to the serpent kings and serpents at the beginning and the end of the rainy season when the danger from the serpents is especially great. The serpents are given water for bathing, a comb, paint, flowers, eye-soothener, cord of thread for clothing and ornamenting. One surrounds oneself with relatives around the merciful. 'Hail to the celestial group of serpents', so it is said; also the serpents of the air, of the world-regions and the serpents on earth—all are hailed one after the other. In a way, the serpents are elevated here to the demoniac supernatural, their existence extending by fantasy beyond the whole universe. But the real serpents and protection against them are the main thing.[45] Similarly, for example, the ants are transposed to the sphere of demoniac existence, when sacrifice to counter their spread is made to the 'king of white ants in the east and the king of black ants in the south'[46] etc. The tortoise which one immures as a water-related, rain-bearing being in the brick altar and which remains there in the dark, unaffected by the glow of the sun and the fire and which 'ought to go whither the earlier ones have gone', is elevated to divine and demoniac heights as the 'lord of waters'.[47] Also, the well-known song of the frogs in the *Ṛgveda* (VII, 103) is an invocation of the frogs awakened by the rainy season, following the course of the year like the sacrificing priests armed with magic power over the waters. We shall refer only briefly to the mystic qualities of the cow. The fact that one receives in it the essence of all the abundance of nourishment and the embodiment of the goddesses Iḍā and Aditi[48] must have influenced, even during olden times, the attribution of some sanctity to it. The sources do not permit us to define for this period the exact nature of this sanctity; but in any case it was far away from the extravagances of later Indian cow-worship. It may be further mentioned here that the Vedic poets pay divine respect to the horse, Dadhikrāvan. This is real horse:[49] the gods Mitra and Varuṇa have lent it to Trasadasyu, the king of Pūru; every Pūru is glad when it comes storming from afar like a falcon, overtaking all the chariots like the wind. This Dadhikrāvan is invoked together with the morning deities in a number of hymns; it is said of him that he 'produced strength and vigour and the sun'. 'May Aditi make one free of sin who praises the horse Dadhikrāvan, when the flame is kindled at the break of dawn, he[50] of one mind with Mitra and Varuṇa.'

Animal-shaped Demons and Gods

Thus, we find animals in the Vedic period who give some occasion or the other to be respected divinely or demoniacally as species or as individuals. Further, however, the great gods standing in the foreground, more or less similar to human beings, are surrounded by a kind of divine animal world: numerous primitive gods, particularly, creatures hostile to the gods, demons causing diseases, etc. have animal form.[51] Two creatures, which scarcely have the capacity to appear independently and which appear to have survived only as relics, are encountered often as a rule in longer lists of gods who are invoked: the '*serpent of the ground*' and the '*one-legged goat*' (*ahi budhnya* and *aja ekapād*). We know very little definite about both these. The serpent has its abode at the bottom of the waters. Serpents living in waters appear in the mythologies of several peoples; one comes across even in later Indian literature the idea of water as the home of serpent-demons. The goat is described as the supporter of all living beings, as a pillar of heaven and earth; it appears with its one foot, considered as an animal-demoniac pillar, upon which the universe rests.[52] *Cow formed* goddesses or those oscillating between the cow and the human form figure many times. The abundance of food given by the cow—for the pastoral tribes the essence of all prosperous blessing—is personified in the goddess Iḍā: when, for instance, *Ṛgveda* once attributes to her 'handful of butter', i.e. the human form, or when a legend of the Brāhmaṇa period describes her as the wife and daughter of Manu with her footprints sprinkled profusely with butter; yet she appears, on the other hand, also as a cow in the *Ṛgveda,* as a mother of herds, and in the sacrificial ritual the cow is hailed with the words: 'Come Iḍā, come Aditi!'[53]. The second part of this form teaches us to understand one more cow-formed goddess Aditi,[54] herself the mother of seven gods of light, as the name suggests, embodying freedom and closely connected with the idea of liberation from the guilt of sin in many Vedic prayers, is at the same time cow; the gods descending from her are 'cow-born': it appears that, in the midst of highly developed, ethically steeped sphere of ideas, it is the trace of a primitive myth which lets the celestial light be born of a divine cow. Another cow, the 'colourful one' (Pṛśni), is the mother of the Maruts. The goddess Saraṇyū becomes mare[55] and gives birth to the Aśvins, the 'Horsemen'. Should we not—as it has been presumed long since—interpret these gods as tinged with an anthropomorphism from which their mother standing further in the background has escaped, so that the 'Horsemen', the children of the mare, were once themselves divine horses?[56]

Just as we find here on several occasions the human-shaped gods themselves to be children of the animal-shaped god-mothers, so we find that the animals surround further the anthropomorphic divine world in so far as the beings inimical to gods are animal-formed like the monsters fought by Indra, the serpent Vṛtra, the 'wild animal' (*mṛga*), the 'spider child' (*aurṇavābha*).[57] We shall discuss below those minor, often animal-shaped demons who afflict man with misery and disease, further also magicians or spirits ruled by them assuming temporarily animal forms.[58]

Animals as the Possession of Gods

Further, a number of animals appear as the possession of gods or as those serving them: thus the eagle which brings *Soma* to Indra; the divine bitch Saramā which tracks the cows to their hide-out; the cows themselves which the god takes from the enemy; the horses which Indra and other gods drive; and the goats driven by Pūṣan, etc. As a matter of fact, such animals are in perfect agreement with the prevalent anthropomorphism; as man owns animals, the man-like god must own the same animals, or he would be waited upon here or there by the other animals depending on the queer character of divine existence. Yet, in both cases, it can be asked whether the animal which belongs to the god is not given the progressive anthropomorphic trend, the remnant of an animal which was a god or whose form he used to take. That the 'Horsemen' (*aśvins*), the children of the mare, must have had once a horse-form was already expressed as a guess. The Irānian parallels should be considered first in connection with the eagle which brings *Soma* to Indra. The bird Vārənjina or Vāraghna, which a coin shows on the helmet of the Vṛtra-killer is similar to the eagle described in the Avesta as the incarnation of a god; Verethraghna[59] appears in the shape of the bird Vāraghna, the fastest of the birds which soars up[60] into the sky around the dawn. Further, a Germanic myth is to be compared which corresponds to the story of the theft of the *Soma*: here the god transforms himself into an eagle and flies to the god's realm with the mead of Suttung.* Thus, we may ask whether Indra's eagle is not the vestige of Indra's incarnation in the form of the eagle.[61] Similarly, Pūṣan's goats could point out to the original goat-shape of this god. Pūṣan is the knower of all the difficult paths that protects one from going astray; the goat, on the other hand, is the animal which finds its way through the most impossible terrain. At the Horse-sacrifice, in addition to the horse, a he-goat is given in sacrifice as 'Pūṣan's share to announce the sacrifice to the gods' (*Ṛv.* I, 162, 2–4). The goat thus, acts as a guide on the way to the divine world. A similar association is in play when a goat is burnt along with the corpse at the cremation.[62] Thus, Pūṣan's assumption of goat's form would give a distinct meaning to these rites. Of course, we cannot but hazard a guess here.

The association of the animals with the gods, whose emissaries they are, stands out particularly in the case of animals considered as ominous. The bird of prey perching with meat in its beak is 'a horrible bolt of lightning sent by the god'; the bird, mentioned already in the *Ṛgveda*, which cries 'in the celestial realm of the forefathers (in the south)', is understood to have been sent by the forefathers; the hyena howls 'when forced to do so or through its own will'; the owl is the 'bird going to the house of the gods' and 'messenger of evil spirits'; the 'blood-stained beast of prey with bloody mouth' and 'vulture that plunders corpses' are 'messengers of Yama' or 'messengers of Yama and Bhava'. If we consider the belief in the appearance of eerie, ghost-like characters in the shape of animals, the suggestions are obvious that these god-sent animals had in themselves once the demoniac nature and have become since the servants of the divine employer.[63]

Animal Fetishism

The researcher on the relationship of the Vedic gods to the animals must also observe a few cases where the animals represent god in the ritual—an instance of animal-fetishism or its less distinct remnant coming into practice, if we may be permitted to say so.

The *bull*[64] is the animal with which Indra is mostly compared in the language of the hymns, and whose name is used preferentially to refer explicitly to Indra. Now a bull is 'invoked' to take up the offerings brought for Indra in the *Sākamedha*-sacrifice; the sacrifice takes place only when it bellows.[65] A Brāhmaṇa remarks: 'With that, one invokes Indra in his form to kill Vṛtra. For the bull is Indra's form.... When it bellows one should know: Indra has come for my sacrifice; my sacrifice enjoys the presence of Indra'.[66] It appears clear that here the action of the cult operates with a concept, closely connected with animal-fetishism.[67]

Just as the strong Indra is described as a bull, the hymns speak in similar vein of the fleet-footed Agni as a horse. In that context, one should observe

*Suttung is the name of a giant of the North-Germanic mythology. He was in possession of mead which gave wisdom and capacity to write. Odin succeeds in stealing it.

the following directions for the setting up of the holy fire. The *Adhvaryu* orders: 'Lead a horse this way.' This horse stands near the place where the fire is kindled, so that the horse should look at the process. As far as possible, the horse is white or red with black knees; corresponding to the age of Agni, which is being created at the moment, the horse should be young or just being harnessed.[68] When then freshly struck fire is carried to the east, the horse leads it; the fire is put down on its footmarks.[69] No doubt, the horse embodies Agni. It is also seen in the relevant hymns. As a matter of fact, these hymns do not appear to be old. When fire is produced by friction in the presence of the horse, it is said: 'O Agni, be born together with Agni, together with treasures', etc.[70] And later, the sacrificer says into the ear of the horse: 'O sturdy horse, please bring forth whatever element is present in cattle which purifies Agni', etc.[71] The horse, therefore, bears the characteristics of Agni. Besides the horse, the text also mentions yet another animal, obviously of equal importance, a goat with black spots—'goat is like Agni', it is remarked; the fire is set up by some on the footprints of this goat.[72]

Our understanding of the horse and the goat is strengthened by similar customs connected with characteristic hymns at the time of building of the Agni-altar. This may be quite modern as a ritual, but many of its individual practices have come down from hoary antiquity. I am reminded here of the construction-sacrifice[73] connected with the shaping of the clay from which the most sacred fire-pan (*ukhā*) is prepared. Three animals: horse, ass and goat[74] stand nearby. Hymns are addressed to them, of which the one addressed to the horse clearly identifies with Agni: 'Swift horse, come running along upon the broad track. Your highest birth is in heaven, your navel is in the air and your home on the earth.'[75] Then the animals are led to the clay-pit, and the horse, while setting its foot upon it, indicates the place from where the clay is to be dug out. We may point out that Agni himself selects the material for the pan which would serve him. The clay is dug out, and the priest holds it high. Here follows again the invocation of the three animals standing nearby and the horse is again identified most clearly with Agni; 'he praises the horse', as a commentator aptly says, 'while the horse is made into Agni'; it is an Agni-verse of the *Ṛgveda* which he applies to it: 'You are born the corporal fruit of both the worlds, Agni, spreading yourself well among the plants'.[76] And 'the goat in the shape of Agni' is similarly treated, quite in agreement with what has been said above about the setting up of fire, just to speak with that commentator. The priest says to it: 'Be friendly to the human creatures, O Aṅgiras.[77] Do not attack heaven and earth with your glow, neither air nor trees.[78] The animals then escort the clay towards the sacrificial fire; it is put down near it, upon which the animals are driven away. Some of the hair cut from the goat is mixed with the clay to a verse that says: 'I mix you Jātavedas[79] of noble birth so that the diseases stay away from the creatures.'[80] It is clear that the meaning of all these rites is only this: Agni himself is to participate in the action in these incarnations and something of its substance is to be mixed with the earthly material. That was also visualized by the theologians of the Brāhmaṇas. In their explanations of this ceremony, the utterances like this are found: 'That is Agni, that is horse.' 'Agni-like is the goat. He brings it with himself, with his divinity.'[81] The only doubt is about the significance of the ass. It simply appears as the beast of burden in the hymns. Perhaps, a magical meaning was originally connected with it. Does it deal, so to say, with the magic of propagation otherwise associated with this animal?

A horse appears once more later in the ritual connected with the setting up of fire.[82] I think it also represents there Agni. When a place chosen for building up of the Agni-altar is marked out, and the bricks are to be removed, a white horse is made to stand beside these.[83] The order goes: 'Recite the hymn for the forward-movement of the fires'; the 'fires' are, however, the bricks burnt in fire and permeated by Agni. With the proceeding of the horse, the bricks are got into place, quite similar to the process of the setting up of fire described above. The horse is led around in prescribed directions on the place chosen for the building up of the altar, and finally the horse smells the bricks and is chased away. The meaning of the whole seems to be that the Agni-nature of the altar is distinguished and strengthened in as much as the Agni-animal is allowed to accompany the building material and take possession of the building-place at the same time.

The role of the goat mentioned above as the second Agni-animal comes out in the remarkable sentence that one can sacrifice in the right ear of the goat instead of at the sacrificial fire, when the fire does not appear even after rubbing; in that case one should not eat the meat of the goat. Or one sacrifices on the *Kuśa*-grass: then one should not sit on such grass. 'The goat is indeed like Agni: with that the fire-sacrifice is offered for it in the goat-Agni', explains a Brāhmaṇa.[84]

I think horse has another meaning in a certain form of *Soma*-sacrifice,[85] where the recitation of the hymns characteristic for this form takes place during sunset: here stands near the singers a white or a reddish-brown horse and beyond that a black horse. The singers keep gold in their hands during the recitation, doubtless a symbol of the sun. The horse also represents the sun,[86] the black obviously has a special connection with the setting of the sun.

The incarnation of the god appears to be particularly intensive in an animal during the 'horned cattle-sacrifice'[87], which is offered to Rudra. Two huts are erected near the sacrificial-fire, and in one of them is led an ox, in the other the 'donoress of grace', in the midst of both, 'the conqueror'—according to the traditional explanation, the 'wife' and the 'son' of the first ox. Water is given to these three animals, they are allowed to touch the sacrificial meal, which then is offered to Rudra, his spouse and the 'conqueror'.

These are the most important examples of animal-fetishism or something analogous to it in the higher cult; characteristically, they have to do only with the domestic animals. The role of this sort of incarnation of god in the Vedic period is obviously not significant. We may even say, not any more significant. The entire direction, into which at least the higher trends of religious life moved did not favour those forms of concepts. The abode of the most important gods in celestial heights, the form in which they were considered as heroic or as equal to royal men, the association one had with them during the sacrifice invisibly visited by the gods, winning over their goodwill not through magic, but by offerings and entreaties: all this was not done to associate oneself with the concept of incarnation of the god in an animal form. It may appear strange that, in spite of it, the remnants of animal fetishism and probably also new constructs based on old models are not wholly absent. The view that associated the Vedic age with this cultic use of animals did not invest the full majesty of the god in a bull or a horse: in that case these animals would have been paid other honours. But between a god and an animal, there exists a certain intercourse of the substance, an association that would constantly engage our interest further while considering the cult of magic. A magician makes an image of a person or a thing or something that is similar to that (person or thing), or which comes from that or which stands in touch with that in order to produce, as desired, good or bad effects in a person or a thing; effects which cannot be otherwise achieved directly. So, corresponding completely to this very common technique of magic, we meet manipulations with fire or gold or a wheel which are meant for influencing the sun.[88] In just the same way, the animal appears to stand with the god in a certain communion or commonality of character, and to that extent used to be considered as a handle for magic directed towards the god. It is not a constantly revered object of the cult but only its tool fulfilling a momentary role. Indistinct traces of a way of thinking are evident here. This thinking, if it had once brought about a close identity between the god and the visible object, would have left behind more valuable traces. At the same time, it would have promoted, like in Egypt, the development of the plastic arts, the existence of temple-like cult centres, the creation of animal idols and the care of sacred temple animals.[89]

Man and Animal

We cannot conclude our consideration of the world of mythical animals without casting a glace at relationships maintained between animals and humans. The idea of substantive unity between animal and man, which projects deep into India's past and naturally survives in the form of a relic is expressed at first in beings similar to a werwolf. Probably to them belong the human-tigers[90] and the Nāgas[91]; the latter apparently human beings, in reality, however, serpents, and as an old Buddhistic text says[92], their serpent-natures appear on two occasions, namely in copulation and in sleep.[93]

Totemism

It would be, above all important for research if one could find out whether traces of the belief, once held in the descent of human races and families from animal—(resp. plant—) ancestry (Totemism), existed also in India.[94] It is well known that this belief formed a dominating element of the religious and social life and customs connected with it amongst many primitive folks and later, as the progressive knowledge of reality displaced the belief itself, it often left its traces over long time as relics. Are such traces to be detected in the repeated naming of Vedic people or generations after animals? Thus appear the fish (Matsya), the goats (Aja), the horseradish-folk (Śigru): all as names of the people. There was a generation of priests associated with the tortoise (Kaśyapa), whose first ancestor had the name 'tortoise', a cosmogonic character standing close to or equal to Prajāpati, the creator of the universe. Prajāpati has created all creatures in the form of Kūrma—another word for tortoise—says a Brāhmaṇa:[95] Kūrma is the same as Kaśyapa. 'Therefore', it is said, "all creatures are children of the tortoise (Kaśyapa).' And in a Buddhist story,[96] a tortoise which has bitten firmly into the vitals of an ape is told: 'The tortoises are Kaśyapas, the apes are Kauṇḍinyas.[97] Kaśyapa, leave the Kauṇḍinya; you have completed the copulation with him.' Is marriage a hindrance only among men and not among their animal cousins?[98] Other priestly families are the cattle (Gotama),[99] calves (Vatsa), dogs (Śunaka) owls (Kauśika), descendants of frog (Māṇḍūkeya). Cows are god-mothers, gods are born of cows. That the human families of 'cattle' or 'calves' have a similar descent is not expressed by the Veda. There was hardly any belief of this sort in the Vedic time. It is, however, possible that it was there in the more distant past. Amongst the generations of princes, we find listed the name Ikṣvāku (cucumber).[100] According to a legend in the epic, the consort of the king Sagara bears upto him a pumpkin, inside which there were 60,000 sons.[101] The father of Saṃvaraṇa, to whom the Kuru-kings trace their descent, was called Ṛkṣa (Bear).[102] The Aryan belief deserves hardly any consideration when a series of Indian folk-races name themselves 'serpents', so also the generation of kings of Chūtiā Nāgpur derive their origin from serpents.[103] It appears, in spite of the Brahmanic tinge, which the story of the serpent-ancestors of this house has, that we have to do here with the ideas of non-Aryan in character. Here, one may refer further to the Vedic injunctions[104] regarding eating and also to the sacred customs such as covering oneself with the skin of the black antelope prior to preparations for a sacrifice, as a mark of ascetism, etc. Similar observances appear elsewhere in connection with totemism.[105] Something of that sort—and that is also valid for the family-names of animals mentioned above—*can* be explained from the point of view of totemism, but by no means a *must*. The absence of convincing traces of totemism amongst the other Indo-European folks, so also the system of relationship free of totemistic trends which the Indian Aryans have in common with them[106] makes it in general rather impossible to accept a totemistic background behind the Vedic culture.

Lifeless Objects as Symbols of Gods

We shall add here examples in which a lifeless object is used to represent god in cult-practices to the cases mentioned above in which an animal was used for this purpose.[107]

The following verse of the *Ṛgveda* (IV, 24, 10) is well known: 'Who for ten milch-kine purchases from me this Indra who is mine when he has slain the foes; let the buyer give him back to me.' An image of Indra working wonders is thought of, perhaps rightfully; but also a fetish-stone untouched by fine arts may have served the same purpose. It is certain that one cannot think here of anything beyond the rudimentary nature of images of the gods during the Vedic age. It is also for sure that such rudimentary elements, present in cult practices described by the Vedic liturgic texts, cannot have played any role.

Very often *symbols of the sun* are used in the cult. Besides the horse discussed above, there appears first the wheel[108] closely comparable with the sun in union with its circular form and its self-propulsion. So, in the *Vājapeya*-sacrifice, the pole meant for tethering the sacrificial animals has a circular wreath made of wheat-flour. A ladder is put up, and the sacrificer speaks to his wife. 'Come, wife, let us climb to the sun.' He climbs up and holds the circular wreath with the saying; 'We have reached the sun, O you gods!'[109] Another sun-symbol appears in the solstice celebration (Mahâvrata). A Vaiśya and a Śūdra—i.e. an Aryan and a representative of non-Aryan powers in heaven and on earth—fight for a white circular piece of hide. The Śūdra leaves it and runs away. The other strikes him down with the same piece.[110] Often gold is a symbol of the sun in the ritual. So we see it sometimes with yet another symbol of the same meaning in the instructions for the sacrificer who has missed the right time for drawing water, i.e. before sunset: when he draws water he should hold a firebrand over it or gold, 'so that his form will be produced who glows in it'.[111] One who has not taken care of timely removal of sacrificial fire which is to be done before sunset 'may bind yellow gold to *Darbha*-grass and say that one should hold it in the direction of the west so that his form be produced, who glows there.[112] When the fire-altar is built a gold plate is placed: 'The gold plate is that sun.[113] We also have to see the sun-symbol in the earthen pot, which is called the 'great hero' (*mahāvīra*) and is meant for carrying the warm drink of milk for the Aśvins.[114]

When the fire-altar is built, the golden figure of a man is also immured. It appears that it is to be understood as the embodiment of Agni.[115] Gold[116] points out to Agni, and a series of verses are addressed to Agni while the sacrificial butter is poured over this figure.[117] How the idea of the dangerous powers of fire were thought of as inherent in the figure originates from the injunction; 'One shall not go past it from the front, so that one is not hurt by this Agni.'[118]

The Animal-sacrifice perhaps furnishes a further case of representation of the deities through material objects; yet, it deals with a view for which I don't wish to lay claim to some degree of probability. Manifold rites in this sacrifice move round a post (*yūpa*) to which the animal is tethered. The post is anointed and tied around with a grass rope decorated to a certain extent.[119] Does it mean that it represents a human or superhuman being? The head-piece (*caṣāla*) of the sacrificial post[120] would correspond to the head of this being. It is not seldom that the Brāhmaṇa-theologians equate this sacrificial post with the Lord of the Sacrifice. Should it have meant originally a deity?

One is reminded of the Ashera of Semitic sacrifice, of a pole beside the altar, which appears to be anointed and turns out to be a representative of the deity.[121] The objection is obvious that the sacrificial post appears only in Animal-sacrifice where it has a clear purpose, namely, the tethering of the animal to it; the presence of deity would, however, demand its expression in every other sacrifice with the same right. This difficulty is hardly insurmountable; it is conceivable that the fetish-post, when its meaning was no more comprehensible, disappeared generally from the sacrificial ritual, surving only in Animal-sacrifice, where a secondary purpose connected with it protected it. Yet as already remarked, it is by no means my intention to see in the post anything more than a most uncertain supposition. I think a more probable explanation for the anointing and decorating of the post results from the fact that it was considered as a tree—really it is addressed continuously in the *Ṛgveda*[122] as lord of the forest; so a relic of the old tree-cult appears to adhere to this tree, bound up with the sacred act.[123]

To sum up, we find, just as in the observation of the animal-fetishism, nowhere or hardly anywhere the material object as a permanent representative of a god revered continuously in the cult. Magic that affects things by making use of their images or related matter influences the whole life as also the cult and for whose purposes it uses, instead of the real sun, his images of the wheel and the firebrand. In the whole Vedic cult, however, these images of a magical nature common to all times and folks do not have more substantial meaning; they have little to do with the progressive tendencies of the Vedic religious thought.

THE PLURALITY OF GODS

Various Sources of Plurality of Gods

It needs hardly to be stated emphatically that the plurality of the Vedic gods rests, to a great extent, indeed to the maximum extent, upon the plurality of nature-beings and other substrata of mythological form underlying them. The god Fire, the god Thunderer—or the original Thunderer—Indra, the goddess Dawn and further the gods 'Impeller', 'Archer' and 'Lord of Prayer' had to place themselves side by side on their own as a plurality of mutually totally independent forms.

So also it is clear that other more external factors could come together in creating the plurality of gods. Linguistic synonyms could result in synonymous gods. Wind is *vāyu* or also *vāta*. Perhaps, the Wind-god was called in one place with one name, in another with another name. In the Veda and even in Indo-Iranian beliefs, the gods Vāyu and Vāta stand next to each other, in no way interchangeable, emphasizing the basic nature with clear nuances of meaning.[124] The god 'Lord of Prayer'[125] is called in the *Ṛgveda*—there even without any distinction—now Bṛhaspati, now Brahmaṇaspati, with two characteristic names, obviously synonymous to each other, and distinguished only quite superficially by additing or by not additing an unimportant suffix (*-man*) to the same root (*brah-* or *bṛh-*). There developed in the later Vedas a differentiation from that: one has to sacrifice to Bṛhaspati on certain occasions, on certain other occasions, to Brahmaṇaspati.[126]

When such quite clear cases illustrate how linguistic differentiation can lead to mythological and cult differentiation, one should, I think, be wary of exaggerated beliefs about the spread of this occurrence. To reinterpret as nature-deities, like the Sun and the Moon, those gods who according to their names represent certain types of action or mastery over certain functions and areas of life, can be done with ease but, as I believe, it is fraught with danger. Then the god 'Stimulator, is turned into the Sun-god. The Sun here is named as 'stimulating' all life, all movement! The god 'Lord of prayer' is represented as the Moon-god and as the god of magical fire representing (presumably) the Moon: the Moon may be considered here as closely connected with the spirit ruling over prayer, magic and conjuration. As against that, I believe that one must stick to the fact that the nature of these gods in reality corresponds to what the names denote ('Stimulator', 'Lord of Prayer') and that here, there are no mythological synonyms of something else (e.g. the sun, the moon). For that I refer to what is quoted above.[127]

There is an instance, where religious possessions of different families, races, perhaps nations[128] intermingle. That is different from what these apparent synonyms say, of Sūrya ('Sun') and Savitar ('Stimulator'); both these expressions must have belonged originally to the circles of the same worshippers. That some such thing may have played a role in the prehistory of the Vedic religion—in fact, must have played a role—is obvious. In the days of prehistoric migrations, foreign elements must have entered into the Aryan belief. Later in the section on Ādityas, a supposition in this regard will be placed before the reader, which explains, if correctly, the double of the Sun and Moon gods Sūrya and Mās on the one hand, and of the original—Sun-god Mitra and the Moon-god Varuṇa on the other hand. Further, the belief of the aborigines of India must have exerted their influence.[129] And ideas, common amongst the different Aryan tribes, must have intermingled with one another. As the Vedic language shows traces of the mixing of dialects, it would surely show us more such traces, if we had had from ancient India as also from old Greece, epigraphic traditions about the appearance of the dialects. So also, we could no doubt find traces, say, of religious and mythological differences in dialects in greater abundance than is the case now, if only the traditions were there which make our task easy to recognize such traces: traditions which would have confirmed local peculiarities of the cults in Greece or Egypt, so also in India and in this way they made it possible for us to clarify the convergence of all that came from different sides. But these are just the traditions we miss. But[130] for a few exceptions, the image of the Vedic belief and cult lacks all local and native features. We do not hear anything about the cult of Pūru or Turvaśa tribe, but only about the cult of the Aryans in general. It appears that the Brahmanic singers and singer-families had not, as a group at least, grown very steadily, but practised their art at one place or the other depending upon the changing course of time. Under these circumstances, it is understandable that the differentiation of the factors originating from one or the other side is possible only with great difficulty within the total complex of the Vedic religious life. Perhaps, I am judging too pessimistically the future prospects, which are open here for research. In any case, I consider the attempts made in this direction less successful[131]. When, for example, honey was brought to the Aśvins and not *Soma* as to Indra, it would be highly adventurous to employ here observations based on a later grammatical text 'that folks were distinguished in India according to drinks... that the gods to whom the drinks were dedicated were different like the national drinks'.[132] Now in the case of the Aśvins, the contributions of different nations must have merged long before Vedic time; one may think of the dates of the Avesta and the discoveries of Boghaz-köi. But can one conclude with any degree of conviction that nationalities varied according to drinks? Cannot, within the sphere of ideas common to a nation, the different nature of two gods, say, their connection with different natural phenomena, bring about that they take different drinks, just as they eat different sacrificial animals—the wild Thunderer drinking the stormily heady drink, and the dew-bearing morning gods drinking honey which is similar to dew in its nature? So also, I have strong doubts, when one tries to localize the 'worshippers of Pūṣan' geographically, or when certain elements of the Vedic cult are derived 'from the circles of Viṣṇuites'.[133] Really the conception of Pūṣan or of Viṣṇu may, in the last instance, date back to a certain circle of worshippers, indeed to definite individuals. But what a wide step from there to the belief that such first worshippers of Viṣṇu are now 'Viṣṇuites' and have not been also the worshippers of Indra and Varuṇa, and which leads further to the conviction that a special position of the followers of the one or the other god reaches up to the horizon of the Vedic world and quite into it, and that conclusions can be drawn about 'the actual seat of the Pūṣan-cult'[134] from the appearance of a couple of Pūṣan hymns more or less within individual books of the *Ṛgveda*. It can certainly be understood that against the Vedic tradition so poor in reference to the historic, the desire of the researcher is strong enough, not to overlook even the improbable. But I fear that this desire can appear to us rather too easily as a trace of historical occurrences. But I do not think that it really deserves this name.

Groups of Gods and Divine Pairs

The question about the sources from which the plurality of the Vedic gods originates gives rise to a further question as to how this plurality appears to the worshippers and how it adjusts itself to their conception.

Of course, it has only a schematic meaning that the number of gods is given several times as thirty-three or as three times eleven, which should be distributed among the three empires of heaven, earth and water,[135] even if there be a certain priority of heaven with reference to the 'heavenly race' of gods, the deities of lower regions are also indeed not missing. One may have to ignore the different versions of the particulars mentioned just now, so also other attempts belonging essentially only to the Brāhmaṇa period to bring the mass of gods into a system.[136] There emerges incidently an idea that an earlier race of gods has preceded the present and that the lords of the world of the present have got their power through the conquest of an older group of rulers.[137]

Frequently, the gods are connected with each other in relationship, namely, as parents and children, because the immortals are in no way free of birth. Thus, Rudra is the father of the Maruts, Aditi the mother of the Ādityas. These connections have been tagged on mostly later to the image of the respective deities.[138] The gods are thought of as friendly to one another, for it cannot be otherwise among them who are friends of human beings and to whom all inclination towards righteousness and goodness is common. 'All gods of one heart, of one mind wander with one will with a single purpose' (*Ṛv.* VI, 9, 5). This general agreement does not naturally exclude specific friendship between individual gods. On the other hand, some frictions appear here and there: thus Indra scares away the Dawn and breaks her chariot; he is angry with the Maruts for Agastya's sacrifice. The individuals have in the scheme of the whole less distinct obligations which easily coincide or merge with one another. Inferior deities in groups form the retinue of a superior god. However, the gods often appear in pairs, especially as common executors of the same feats and recipients of the same sacrifice and praise. It is probable that this distinctive pair of deities, oft recurring both in the poetry and in the rite, was created through a single such pair, homogenous by nature. Other combinations of deities were put together arbitrarily, and they were modelled after this type. This model may be presumed to exist in Mitra-Varuṇa, in one of the most significant and inseparably connected of such pairs[139] in the *Ṛgveda,* for which also its extreme antiquity speaks; it may be dated back to the Indo-Iranian time, as also its probable connection with the most distinguished of all the relevant natural beings for such a pair of parallel gods, namely, the Sun and the Moon. The ectypal pairs[140] show mostly Indra in bond with another god, whom one worships, in that one admits him to the communion of the most powerful gods. One single hymn or a hymn-conglomerate is dedicated to the pair, which gets a special significance in the later Vedic literature, where the speculations about the sacrifice are always biased: the pair Agni and Soma, the sacrificial fire and the distinguished sacrificial-offering, the twin divine patrons of sacrifice.[141]

Indra and Varuṇa as the Most Superior Gods

The divine world does not have a recognized superior head; or there are at best only indications for such an idea.[142] Now the one god, now another assumes more power, more superiority—we shall come back later to these fluctuating concepts: but there are particularly two gods who tower above the others, Indra and Varuṇa. If it is in itself quite understandable that the figures of the gods are elevated so powerfully from the different spheres of nature that for none of them a lower place than the first appears to be sufficiently high, then perhaps a special factor has to be considered to explain the rivalry between Indra and Varuṇa,[143] if the suppositions about the prehistory of Varuṇa to be discussed below should hold true. Besides Indra, inherited from the Indo-European prehistoric time, stands Varuṇa, hailing from a foreign land; the belief of different peoples had credited one of these gods with such an abundance of might that they as rivals had to contest their primacy the moment they met. This meeting took place in Indo-Iranian times and so the older phases of the contest that must have taken place during this period remain obscure for us. What we see is this: that in Iran, Varuṇa—Ahura of the Avesta—has carried away the victory which could not but be his, the highest Lord of Law and Purity, particularly in Zoroastrian teaching. In the Veda, on the other hand, Indra stands in the foreground. Of course, many a word exalts Varuṇa in the songs addressed to him to the greatest heights, and many comparisons between both the gods—above all, their verbal exchange that precedes the battle, which we shall discuss soon—show that one looks at Varuṇa above all others as the rival in greatness with Indra. But the centre of gravity of the cult and of the religious poetry shifts to the side of Indra. During the sacrifices of the war-mongering princes, for whom the singers wrote verses, the prayer for power and victory, for the gifts of Indra had to outcry the desire for forgiveness of sins, for the grace of Varuṇa. And the liturgic poetry applies primarily to the *Soma*-sacrifice; the great *Soma*-carouser is, however, Indra. So, besides Indra's value, the thought of the greatness of Varuṇa comes, for the Vedic poet, only in a particular moment to the foreground, for example, where the contemplation about the hierarchy of the world engages him or the feeling of being pursued on account of the anger of the god, the punisher of sins.[144]

The verbal exchange between the two gods[145] mentioned just now begins with the speech of Varuṇa:

I am the royal ruler, mine is empire, as mine who sway all life are all immortals. The gods follow the will of Varuṇa. I am the king of men's most lofty cover (of the world).

I am king Varuṇa. To me were given these first existing high celestial powers. The gods follow the will of Varuṇa. I am the king of men's most lofty cover (of the world).

I Varuṇa am (real) Indra. In their greatness, these the two wide deep fairly-fashioned regions,[146] these the two world-halves have I, even as Tvaṣṭar knowing all beings, joined and held together.
I made to flow the moisture-shedding waters, and set the heaven firm in the seat of Law. By law, the son of Aditi, the friend of law, has spread abroad the world in threefold measure.

Now speaks Indra:

Heroes with noble horses, fain for battle, selected warriors, call on me in combat. I Indra excite the conflict; I stir the dust. Lord of surpassing vigour.

All this I did. The God's own conquering power never impedes me, whom none opposes. When Soma and lauds have made me joyful, both the unbounded regions are affrighted.

The poet will have imagined a final reconciliation of the gods at battle. He says: 'Purukutsa's wife has worshipped you, Indra and Varuṇa, with sacrifice and prayer. You gave her the king Trasadasyu, the killer of enemy, the demigod.' Thus, both the gods have accepted common veneration, and united have they granted the hero's son to the queen. Thus, the final verse of the hymn also invokes them, to bestow together their pardon on the worshipper.

Incidentally, the Veda hardly carries out any such idea to its logical conclusions there, where it addresses a god definitely as the highest, whose will others have to follow. Neither do the stories about the majesty and glory of the king of gods, much as we find them illustrate this. Nor do the cult orders point to it. The thinking of the age, with which we are dealing here, has only superficially touched upon the idea of the highest world-ruler. It was not given to India's prehistoric time to grasp its fullest depth.

Intermingling of Different Types of Gods

As we find everything full of uncertainties in the questions discussed here, one can say generally of the gods of the Veda, that the outlines of the individual gods tend to become blurred, almost disappear. The fantasy of the Vedic poets and the Vedic people fails to recognize the mystery of the power of form that has given the gods of Homer their vivid outward form. It would be too much to say that Agni or Indra would not have possessed, for the Vedic poets, their own individuality, but the special features of their nature were often almost shrouded by that, which is common to all the gods and makes them all alike with the uniform garb of might, light, goodness and wisdom, which the Vedic poets are not tired of praising in much the same stereotyped phraseology. Many things are added to mix and disfigure the individual forms of particular gods. Several of them are seen at various times in the same functions. Help against harmful demons is given by fire that burns them—what is also achieved by the wielder of the *Vajra*-weapon who smatters them and many other gods. So, Agni and Indra overlap one another in a series of features, and the partial concurrence present once, has naturally then the tendency to extend beyond its original limits. The poet falls from one track of routine comparison of gods into another that leads him further into shorter or longer stretches. Here the inclination of the Veda to combine gods into pairs mentioned above must also have had its influence. While one worshipped Indra and Agni together as heroes, one extended the feature ascribed to one god to the other: Agni, who is otherwise not a *Soma*-drinker, became one in the company of Indra; he became the killer of Vṛtra and wielder of *Vajra*; he became, like Indra, the liberator of cows and waters, of the sun and the dawn. Thus, the myth wanders from one god to the other; the researcher must take care, not to emphasise both alike. He must distinguish much more between the original and the transposed. Besides, there are certain activities which are mythologically, so to say, more or less without any doer, oscillating between one deity and another. So the praise for having stretched the expanse of the earth, for having secured the heights of the heaven with its pillars, is showered on Varuṇa as the Lord of all Order, and then on Indra as the strongest, then again on Viṣṇu as the measurer of all space; and the poet, accustomed to ascribe to this or that god the fame of such feats, does not allow the other gods to be relegated to the background.[147] Further the intermingling of the types of gods are promoted in such a way that the same natural beings appear in connection with different mythological groups of ideas. The water is at first animated by the demons who are just water-inhabitants. But the water also shows itself, one can say, through scientific observations which later became a source of myths, as the place of origin of fire: in the depths of the water lives the fire. So the infant of waters (*apāṃ napāt*) for all purposes, a water-related demon, referring originally to water alone, enters into it to merge with Agni. Agni on the other hand, falls into the sphere of thoughts related to the sun, while the earthly fire is understood as identical with the heavenly sun-fire. In many spheres, but nowhere so marked as in Agni-mythology, the same idea recurs again and again; the reflection over the natural connection of various beings reveals one as present hidden in the other. So, a known tendency of identification of all apparently different types of things becomes more and more significant, gradually adding their naturally increasing vagueness to certain extent. While one seeks to unfold the hidden character of a god in his whole depth and variety, one would like to indicate more and more that one god is identical with the other. Even the most superficial contact—and sometimes lesser still—is sufficient to make the singer say:

You at your birth are Varuṇa, O Agni. When you are kindled, you are Mitra. In you, O son of Strength, all gods are centred. You are Indra to the mortal who brings oblation. You are Aryaman, when you are regarded as having the mysterious names (i.e. the mysterious beings) of maidens, O Self-sustainer. As a kind friend, they balm you with cows,[148] when you make wife and lord one-minded (V, 3, 1-2).

All such play with ideas promotes mono-theistic and pan-theistic tendencies which in turn encourage actively such play. The idea strives to reach the point where every single personality, every existence limited in itself, appears only as a foam-bubble upon the ocean of the universe. But it is not our task here to follow the path from the belief in the Vedic gods to the teachings of the Brahman.[149]

REFERENCES

1. To be exact, one may substitute here Indra's pre-Vedic predecessor, for Vedic Indra is not a proper Storm-god.
2. Or also of a divine animal which was later replaced by an anthropomorphic god.
3. Or eventually, originally in all the stronger similarity with the animal.
4. Also when Agni is introduced as a messenger between heaven and earth, it does not mean that he (Agni) is separated from the sacrificial flame striving heavenwards, going up into infinite heights, with his glow, lustre and smoke. Compare, e.g. Ṛv. VII, 3, 3.
5. Ṛv. VII, 1, 1; III, 29, 13,5.
6. Compare Bergaigne, *Religion védique* I, 19. One may note, say, Ṛv. III, 29, 7, where

it is said (verse 9), 'This is Agni, with whose help the gods have overcome the foes', when fire is freshly produced. The new fire is identical with the old.

7. *Āpastamba Śraut.* V, 10, 12; *Taitt. Brāhm.* II, 5, 8, 8.

8. The hymn is obviously not composed for this occasion, but for producing the sacrificial fire again (therefore: 'bring *again* for the gods') which one had 'to make climb' into the fire sticks by a definite action, and while one rubs them, one 'makes' it 'climb down' from them (compare: *Śāṅkhāyana Śr.* II, 17, 8; *Āpast.* VI, 28, 12). As the same hymn mentions the production of fire by attrition, the idea of 'climbing down' could not be anything else than that.

9. *Vāj Saṃh.* XI, 72. More about the relevant ritual, see *Indische Studien* XIII, 227.

10. *svam asuṃ yan.* It may be noted that the hymn originates probably from the composer of the 'Songs of the Dead' X, 14ff. He likes to move in the sphere of ideas about the death and the other world; he uses, therefore, the expression *asunītim ayan* for the days in 12, 4.

11. In case of the Dawn, however, as it is known, the Veda fluctuates between the idea of one goddess returning every day and the idea of new, different Dawns.

12. Is the female sex of Āpas responsible for the fact that here a homogeneous ideal being has been developed upon the image of Sūrya, etc. as it is not in the case of Agni ?

13. Incidentally, besides the divine type (the Āpas) which has remained closely connected with the natural element, waters also show the type *Apsaras* (nymphs, originally water-nymphs) which has advanced to freer personification. The *Apsaras* having the form of beautiful divine women can leave their element and experience many types of adventures with human beings: that for such an activity gets the character of a certain homelessness and water remains their real home is shown by the story of Undine (mermaid) Urvaśī, the Melusine of India. Besides, a hymn from *Ṛv.* (IX, 78, 3) identifies them completely with their element: the Apsaras flow to *Soma*, i.e. *Soma* is mixed with water.

14. I refer to the discussion on these gods in Chapter II.

15. Conversely, we find the Avestic *Soma* appearing before the prophet busy at the fire-altar as a man of the greatest beauty in the whole of the physical world (*Hōm Yast* 1). On the whole, it is at least a more dissociated Soma from the natural object than the Vedic *Soma*. Also, e.g. Agni of the later Vedic and the post-Vedic literature is, in this context, noticeably different from the one of the *Ṛv* essentially more free with respect to the element.

16. Compare the section on Varuṇa and Mitra in Chapter II.

17. I refer to the relevant section in Chapter II.

18. The occurrence can be described more exactly as under: it is unthinkable that the older period which understood the deeds of the god from storm must have spoken only of mountains, of waters and rivers, which the god inaugurated or liberated and never directly of clouds or of rain. Therefore, both the expressions run parallel to each other, the real and the metaphorical, the latter, incidently, depending finally upon the belief in substantial identity of mountains and clouds (compare Pischel, *Ved. Stud.* I, 174) and of celestial and terrestrial waters. Now the metaphorical expression (mountain, river) suggested a new series of ideas: source of the rivers on the mountains. It had something clearly evident in the case of the identity of celestial and earthly waters (one may think, e.g. of the identity of fire and its different forms of appearance. See the section on Agni) alluded to just now and more vivid to that age than to us, that the latter had to be liberated by the same god and with the same deed like the former. This series of ideas alone survived, because the tribes wandering through the land flowing with rivers were bound to be especially attached to rivers; no one now spoke of clouds and rainfalls, but only of mountains, waters and rivers.

19. The view 'that the Vedic myths of gods have not come directly from the perception of nature, but initially from the ritual, the individual ceremonies of which were compared first with the events in nature' is, according to me, quite wrong. Gruppe (*Die griech. Kulte und Mythen* I, 296) attributes this view to Bergaigne, I think, not quite appropriately, and explains its justification as confirmed. This is, of course, not the place to discuss this much talked-of question in detail (compare R.M. Meyer, *Ritus und Mythus*, *Internat. Monats-*

schrift, 1914, 951ff.). I think, it is hardly possible for the Veda (resp., one may add, for the sphere of pre-Vedic philosophy reflected in the Veda) that a myth like that of Vṛtra-killing had grown from the actions of the cult like the *Soma*-sacrifice handed down to us. If a myth narrates how the god fought waters, and the rites move him to do this or some other similar heroic deed for the worshipper, then the main motive behind the rites for such purpose is that one gives to the god food and strengthening, intoxicating magic drink, one worships him, one brings him laudation. Such a procedure is hardly related to the special appearance of the deed coming just from this god. If the Aśvin-myth makes both the gods sprinkle honey, and the rite causes them to do it generously by the offering of honey (or a substance understood as 'honey'), there is no preceptible reason to explain the mythical conception from the rite, and certainly not the rite from the mythical conception, but rather to explain from the conception of nature (i.e. the dew-fall). There are rites in the Veda which imply a certain—strongly stylized—imitation of a mythical occurrence; for example, Sautrāmaṇī corresponds to the story which narrates how the Aśvins and Sarasvatī freed Indra from the effect of unhealthy drinking: apparently, the story has in this priority over the rite.

20. I refer here to the apt remarks of Bloomfield, *JAOS*. XV, 185. About the myth of the guards protecting the *Soma* mentioned in the following, see *ibid*. XVI, 24.

21. See in the section on Indra in Chapter II.

22. Indra and Aśvins represent the both most important forms of divine interference in the fate of human beings; and thus, the divine-human events in the *Ṛgveda* appear to be so much exclusively linked with these deities that nothing much has remained for the others.

23. Colourful mixing of all sorts of elements is usually present in the complicated structures of a story like the never-ending frequent combination of something that was not the part and parcel of the original. But it is quite obvious how this is to be judged like the reasoning of Jacobi (*Das Rāmāyaṇa* 131) with reference to the legend of Rāma. In the epic, Sītā is the wife of Rāma: 'Since she is the wife of Indra, resp., Parjanya, in the Gṛhya texts, Rāma must be a form of Indra-Parjanya.' It is something like deducing in grammar from the appearance of two forms of different periods at the same place of a paradigm that the more recent is the offspring of the older form in accordance with the phonetic laws. And in the history of myths and legends, a much greater importance is to be given to the probability that new forms have entered than in the history of form-system in grammar.

24. This is shown in detail in the depiction of the cult.

25. See Darmesteter, *Études iraniennes* II, 196, note 1.

26. The *Mahābhārata* lets the haters of Brahmanas become Rākṣasas after death (Hopkins, *Position of the Ruling Caste* 157; and the like, very often; Manu XII, 60 and other texts speak of Brahmarākṣasas in whom certain sinners are embodied). The Buddhists have the concept of Yamarākṣasas, i.e. of the evil dead operating as Rākṣasas (Freer, *Avadāna Śataka*, p. 491). Kinder souls are to be sought in the gods 'coming from the house of men', *Āpastamba Dharm*. I, 3 , 11, 3 as also in the 'gods by virtue of their deeds' which *Śatapatha Bṛ. XIV*, 7, 1, 34. 35 distinguishes from the 'born gods'.

27. *Brāhminism and Hinduism*, 239. Compare Lyalls' remarks in *Revue de l'hist des. rel.* XIII, 364 (the book itself is not at present available to me); Grierson, *Bihār Peasant Life*, 397; *Encycl of Rel. and Eth.* IV, 602f.

28. *Ath. Veda* XVIII, 2, 28.

29. *Kauśika Sūtra* 87, 16.

30. See, e.g. *Kauś. Sūtra* 88, 1; *Taitt. Ār*. VI, 9, 1.

31. It is enough for me to quote here from the Buddhistic literature of Yakṣas and Bhūtas living on a burial ground, *Petav*. III, 5, 2, and also of the different Yakṣas living in Caityas (*Udāna* I, 7; *Saṃyutta Nikāya* I, 10, 4-vol. I p. 208).

32. *Petavatthu* II, 9, 13.

33. *Ibid*., I, 4, 1.

34. His companions, the Aṅgiras can hardly be different from the priest-predecessors, who have risen to dignity which can only be similar to that of the gods; see p. 81f. above.

35. Speyer's 'Eene indische verwante van de germaansche godin Nerthus', *Handel. Maatsch v. Ned. Lett*., 1901-02, p. 3ff.) combinations on the last names do not appear to me

to be happy. One can find a difference, at least in many cases between these and the *tar*-gods in the fact that, e.g. the god 'Protector' protects himself, but the goddess 'Speech' governs over the speech of human beings. But all that gets merged in many ways.

36. Yet the gap is obviously not unbridgeable. It will soon be mentioned that each of the abstract gods have shown that they are capable of taking a considerable concrete substance. It may be mentioned here that Pūṣan in his original nature a more obscure, perhaps basically a more concrete god has been developed to something more than what he is emphatically called, the 'path-lord' (*pathas pati*): resembling entirely the example of the type discussed above. The gods of the first type take a sort of a middle position between the type Indra and the types Dhātar or Vāstoṣpati, as far as they are provided with the nickname of the second type. The same is the case in the *Ṛgveda*. I would not like to bring a case like Agni Vaiśvānara (Agni 'belonging to all men') in this formula; the nickname here is of different nature; but one can, of course, think of, e.g. 'heat consuming Maruts' (VII, 59, 9), 'flesh-eating Agni' (X, 16, 9f.), 'Agni, bestower of wealth' (I, 96), etc. Such cases are prevalent in the later Vedas (see, e.g. *Taitt.* S.I, 8; II, 1f.): there Indra is the giver, the donor, Varuṇa, the Lord of Order, etc. Of course, they are not each time exceptional divine personalities, but common gods in whom an extra-ordinary quality is given prominence, in order to associate them with a definite cultic purpose. Here 'Indra, the Protector' appears along with the independent 'God Protector'. There is, therefore, no reason to consider this to have been separated from that manifestation of Indra. On the contrary, it will be unadvisable for this common type which is craving for recognition of its independence by its association with the god 'Protector'.

37. Compare Usener, *Götternamen*; Schrader, *Reallexikon der idg. Alt.* 679f.

38. It belongs to the group characterized by nouns ending with the suffix *-tar* mentioned on p. 33. It is futile to date this god back to the Indo-European period and classify him with Saturnus. I have justified my conception of Savitar in detail in *ZDMG.* LI, 473ff.; LIX, 253ff. V. Schrader, *Arische Religion* II, 7, note 2 mentions only my *Rel. d. Veda* concerning my view on Savitar. I have dealt with Savitar only cursorily in this book. I may once more refer to my detailed research notes mentioned above. That Savitar is invoked today as Sun-god will say very little to the question, if we think of the original concept. I categorically question the view that the sacredness of Sāvitrī-verse has anything to do with the sun-worship (compare v. Schr. 9, 101) in so far as it concerns the origin of this sacredness.

39. It may be noted that it is due to the nature of Savitar as 'Impeller' that one who started learning the Veda, addressed his prayer first to this god, 'who may bring forward our thoughts'. And that is why the fame of the much-celebrated Sāvitrī of the Savitar-verse which opened the study of the Veda (*Ṛv.* III, 62, 10).

40. 'Prayer' is only an approximate translation. *Brahman* is more exactly a sacred (magically empowered) formula and aura of magic power filling it (compare below the section on magic). See Bergaigne I, 299ff., on Bṛhaspati; Hillebrandt, *Ved. Mythologie* I, 404ff.; small ed. 60ff.; O. Strauß, *Bṛhaspati im Veda* (1905); my Essay in *Nachr. der Gött. Ges. d. Wiss.* 1915, 196ff. Now *NGGW.* 1916, 715ff., on the concept of *brahman.*

41. Compare verses like those in the *Atharvaveda* V, 18, 8. 9., where the spiritual magic power of a Brahmana is compared with the equipment of an archer: 'The tongue of the Brahmana is the bow-string; his voice, the arrow-neck; he carries sharp arrows; what he shoots is not in vain' with the power of his asceticism and fury, he storms after the enemy and shoots him down from afar.

42. See the section on Indra in Chapter II.

43. Compare Hopkins, *Epic Mythology*, 12ff. on divine animals and related matter.

44. Compare particularly Winternitz, *Der Sarpabali, ein altindischer Schlangenkult* (Vienna 1888).

45. This serpent-cult which has the stamp of the serpent-land, India, is possibly the legacy of the aborigines. The absence of the traces in the *Ṛgveda*—any connection with the Vṛtra-myth (Winternitz, 20ff) is to be rejected—and the strong expansion of the serpent-cult of all types is, of course, not decisive in the case of non-Aryan Indians (Winternitz,

36ff), although it speaks for that assumption. The disposition to a cult of this type does not, therefore, belong less also to the Aryans.

46. *Kauśikasūtra* 116. The worms are similarly treated when the milch-cow has worms at the Gharma-sacrifice (*Taitt. Ār.* IV. 36).

47. *Ind. Studien* XIII, 250; *Vāj. Saṃh.* XIII, 31.

48. VIII, 101, 15.16 shows how even in the *Ṛgveda*, the real cow was considered as permeated by the goddess standing behind her: 'I say it to Rudra's mother, to Vasu's daughter, to Ādityas' sister, to the navel of immortality—to one who understands: 'Do not kill the innocent cow, the Aditi, the knower of the speech who raises her voice, who after her worship with all kinds of prayer has come from the gods, the goddess cow...'. It is said to the cow in the *Yajurvedas* for whom the Soma is bought: 'You are Aditi...goddess, go to the god' (*Soma*). (*Vāj Saṃh.* IV, 19, 20).

49. That is, viz. shown by Pischel (*Ved. Stud.* I, 124). Compare also Ludwig IV, 79. V. Bradke, *ZDMG-XLVI*, 447. Different in V. Henry, *Album Kern* 5ff. Reference to Horse-sacrifice (Hillebrandt, V.M.III, 402) does not seem to me to be possible. I cannot conclude with Keith, *JRAS*, 1907, 934 from *VS*.XXIII, 32.

50. Yet Dadhikrāvan himself appears to be identified with Aditi. Compare my note on the reference (IV, 39, 3).

51. Or they have human-animal mixed form like Dadhyañc with the head of a horse.

52. The answer to the question why the universe does not collapse is that a goat carries it with one leg as a pillar. This answer is completely in the style of primitive cosmology. We can scarcely know how a goat was thought of. So also we have a very little clue to interpret this goat as a solar-being. I think it is illusory to say that the *Atharvaveda* XIII, 1, 6, renders this interpretation (V. Henry, *Les hymnes Rohitas* 25; compare also the same in French translation of the work before us p. XVIIf).

53. Compare the material in Bergaigne I, 323ff; in addition to *Śatapatha Br.* I, 8, 1, 7 and the relevant remarks below in the depiction of the cult (see the section on the meal-participation of the sacrificer.)

54. Compare the section on Varuṇa and the Ādityas.

55. Yet, this change is not attested by the text of *Ṛv.* X, 17, 2, but only by accompanying explanations.

56. The comparison of the sun-horse (see p. 41) is obvious for the horse-figure of the morning star and the evening star. We shall try to show that this concerns the two Aśvins. The humanization must have already been completed in the Indo-European period.

57. Bergaigne, II, 220. 223.

58. See the section on Demons and Magic.

59. Vedic Vṛtrahan, i.e. Indra.

60. *Yašt* XIV, 19f.; M.A. Stein, *Zoroastrian deities on Indo-Scythian coins* 5: it must be rejected, I think, that the bird who brought Soma is rather Agni (Bloomfield, *JAOS*. XVI, 1ff.) or Viṣṇu (Johansson, *Solfogeln*, 28; it does not follow from IV, 18, 11ff)).

61. It must be left undecided, whether it is at all important that in *Kāṭhaka* (and also in *Ṛv.* X, 99, 8?) Indra really takes the form of an eagle in the robbery of *Amṛta* resp. *Soma;* Compare Kuhn, *Herabkunft des Feuers* 144, Bloomfield, *JAOS.* XVI, 8f.

62. See below the section on the Ritual of the Funeral.

63. *Kauśikasūtra* 129: *Ṛv.* II, 42, 2; Hiraṇyakeśin G.I. 16, 19f., 17, 1f.; *Taitt. Ār.* IV 28f. The belief in corpse-magic plays a role in the last reference.

64. In the *Atharvaveda* (IX, 4, 9), it is said to the bull: 'You are called Indra.' The bull appears also in *Yašt* XIV (§7) under the incarnations of Verethraghna, the Avestic Indra.

65. Hillebrandt, *Ritualliteratur* 117.

66. *Śatapatha Br.* II, 5, 3, 18. Also compare *Maitr. Saṃh.* I, 10, 16; *Taitt. Br.* I, 6, 7, 4; *Āpastamba* VIII, 11, 19.

67. No contradiction may be found in the bull-Indra against the eagle-Indra mentioned above, p. 39; even this diversity is characteristic of the theriomorphism.

68. *Śatapatha Br.* II, 1, 4, 17; *Kāty* IV, 8, 25. 26; *Āpastamba* V, 10, 10; 14, 17; Baudhāyana quotes in the commentry to the last reference. See also Hillebrandt, *Rituallit.* 106f.

69. *Śatapatha* l.c. 22.24; *Kāty* IV, 9, 13f. 16.

70. *Āpastamba* V, 10, 9.

71. *Ibid.* V, 13, 7 (*Maitr. Saṃh.* I, 6, 2). Perhaps, one must have thought of the Agni-nature of the horse; when carrying Agni to the east led by the horse, it is said: 'March to the east, O you, knower; O Agni, may Agni be there before Agni' (*Āpast.* V, 14, 5; *Maitr. Saṃh.* I, 6, 2). The hymn comes in any case from a different ritual-context to which this interpretation does not apply.

72. *Āpastamba* V, 7, 17; 15, 1; *Śatapatha Br.* II, 1, 4, 3. More often there is talk of the special affiliation of goat to Agni or its identity with the god, e.g. *Atharvaveda* IX, 5, 6. 7. Compare also Charpentier, *Kleine Beitr. zur Indoiran. Mythologie* 64ff.

73. One can also point out to the production of the clay-pan (*ukhā*) in a primitive way without the potter's wheel. 'The ritual introduces here a workshop of pre-historic ceramics and lets the pots appear before our eyes, remotely similar to those which are brought to light from the graves and ash-hills of pre-historic times'. See Hillebrandt, *Rituallit.* 9.

74. Weber, *Ind. Studien* XIII, 220f.; Hillebrandt, *Rituallit.* 162. One may compare also the practice of sending a horse and a goat ahead to the place where clay is to be buried in the *Pravargya-celebration*; ZDMG, XXXIV, 327.

75. *Vāj. Saṃh.* XI, 12.

76. *Ṛv.* X, 1, 2=*Vāj. Saṃh.* XI, 43.

77. As it is well known, the common name of Agni.

78. *Vāj. Saṃh.* XI, 45.

79. Nickname of Agni. The commentator says here: 'Agni named as goat-hair.'

80. *Vāj Saṃh.* XI, 53.

81. *Śatapatha Br.* VI, 3, 3, 22; 4, 4, 15.

82. *Ind. Studien* XIII, 247; Hillebrandt, *ibid.*, 163.

83. *Śat. Br.* VII. 3, 2, 10. 16 (there reference to the sun), *Kātyāyana* XVII, 3, 20.

84. *Kāty.* XXV, 4, 4ff (here the masculine *aja* is sexually indifferent; *Taitt. Brāhmaṇa* III, 7, 3, 1f. (here feminine).

85. Compare *Taitt. Saṃh.* VI, 6, 11 6 with *Ṣoḍaśin*; *Āpastamba* XIV, 3, 1f; *Kāty.* XII, 6, 1; *Pañc. Br.* XII, 13, 26; *Lāṭy.* III, 1,4.

86. So it is said in *Ṛv.* VII, 77, 3 of the Dawn that she leads the white horse—naturally the sun. It is said of the sacrificial horse that it is prepared by the gods from the sun (*Ṛv.* I, 162, 2). Compare in addition *Ait. Br.* VI, 35, etc. as also the *Brāhmaṇa* passages collected by Weber, *Ind. Stud.* XIII, 247, note 3 and Winternitz, *SBE. L*, 280.

87. *Hiraṇyakeśin* G. II, 8. Compare *Āpastamba G.*VII, 20; Hillebrandt, *ibid.*, 84; Hubert and Mauss, *Année Sociologique* 1898, 93f. I have reservations about their view.

88. See p. 44. We would link up here itself the discussion of these cases in which the wheel, etc. plays the same role as a horse or a bull, if the limitation of the present discussion on the relationship of animals to gods was not opposed to that.

89. It may be mentioned here only in passing that there is a belief in transitory metamorphosis of the gods and beings similar to gods into animals of all types (compare Indra and Eagle p. 39—and naturally also into human beings—following in the course of one or the other adventure besides the relationship of the different gods to animals related in their nature to them. As this ability to take such forms is attributed to a human magician, it naturally falls on also to gods whose similarity to human beings means the similarity to human beings, who are at the height of their magical art.

90. *Vāj S.* XXX, 8; *Śat. Br.* XIII, 2, 4, 2; Hopkins, *Ep. Mythol.* 12.

91. Not attested for the most ancient period. The suspicion that the belief in these human serpents as also the serpent-totem (Page 43) originates from the Indian aboriginal tribes cannot be suppressed.

92. *Vinaya Piṭaka*, Mahāvagga I, 63; Winternitz, *Der Sarpabali* 17. One who wished to receive ordination as a Buddhist monk was asked with reference to such beings: are you a human being? (Mahāvagga I, 76). As in European legends, the swan maiden is made to stay on in human form by robbery of her swan-shirt, so also in an Indian story (Benfey, *Pañcatantra* II, 147), it is the Nāga by burning of the serpent-skin.

93. The section on magic may further be compared, concerning the magical acceptance of animal form, and the section on life after death, concerning the entering of souls of the dead into animals.

94. I refer here to the discreet discussion of Keith, *JRAS*. 1907, 929ff.; *Veda of the Bl. Yajus School* CXXI.

95. *Śatapatha Br.* VII, 5, 1, 5.

96. Kacchapajātaka (*Jātaka* vol. II, p. 360).

97. Another Brahmana family. That its name means ape is not, as far as I see, otherwise known.

98. The commentary on the hymn is different.

99. The word 'cattle' (*go-*) appears here with the superlative suffix.

100. Compare Lassen, *Ind. Alt.* I, 597 note 1.

101. *Rāmāyaṇa* I, 38.

102. There is a man named Ṛkṣa in the *Ṛgveda.*

103. Winternitz, *Der Sarpabali* 19f. The members of this princely family wear turbans in the form of a serpent curled together; the seal of this family is a cobra with human face. More about the traces of totemism amongst the aboriginal tribes, see Keith, *ibid.*, 948f. and above all, Frazer, *Totemism and Exogamy* II, 218ff., who comes to the conclusion that totemism was widespread amongst them.

104. Compare below the section on cult-observances.

105. See A. Lang, *Myth, Ritual, and Religion* II, 73. 106. 213; Sayce, *Hibbert Lectures* (1887), 285. Henry (Caland-Henry 481ff.). contemplates about the totemistic character of the *Soma*-sacrifice.

106. Only the exogamy of the Indians asserts itself in the opposite sense. Compare for all that, Frazer, *ibid.*, IV, 13.

107. We do not take into account here the cases, where it concerns the relation of the god animating an object in nature in accordance with his whole character and of this object in nature (Agni and Fire, etc.).

108. Compare the sun wheel of the Celts (Gaidoz, *Le dieu gaulois du soleil et le symbolisme de la roue*), of the Teutons, etc. As the Indo-Europeans knew the chariot, it is possible, though, of course, it cannot be proved, that this symbol of the sun is older than the separation of peoples.

109. Weber, *Über den Vājapeya* 20. 34f., who by mistake uses 'heaven' instead of 'sun'. One comes across the sun wheel also in the foundation of the sacrificial fire; see below the section on Agni.

110. *Lāṭyāyana* IV, 3, 7. 14. 15 (compare Hillebrandt, *Sonnwendfeste in Altindien* 43). 'The hide should be white and round: that is the shape of the sun' *Kāṭhaka* XXXIV, 5.

111. '*Śatapatha Br.* III, 9. 2, 9. 'He, who glows there' is a very common expression in the Brāhmaṇa texts. We may mention here the instruction that the Veda should not be studied in the night in a forest 'where there is neither fire nor gold'. *Āpastamba Dh.* I, 3, 11, 34.

112. *Śatapatha Br.* XII, 4, 4, 6.

113. *Ibid.*, VII, 4, 1, 10. Compare also Negelein, *JAOS*, XXXIV, 242.

114. See the section, 'The Individual Sacrifices and Festivals' and compare Hillebrandt, *V.M.*, small ed. 11, note 2.

115. Weber, *Ind. Stud.* XIII, 248f. Hillebrandt, *Rit. Lit.* 163. *Śatapatha Br.* VII, 4, 1, 15 explains the man as Prajāpati, Agni and the sacrificer.

116. Gold in its relation to Agni plays also a rôle in the foundation of the sacrificial fire. It is thereby not defined really as a form or image of Agni, but Agni's sperm which has been transformed into gold (found in the rivers) after it was poured into waters (*Śatapatha Br.* II, 1, 1, 5; *Āpastamba Śraut* V, 2, 1). It is different in *Maitr. Saṃh.* I, 6, 4 where gold is explained as 'Agni's glow'.

117. *Vāj Saṃh.* XIII, 9ff.

118. '*Śatapatha Br.* VII, 4, 1, 24. Similarly, one should not carry the *Soma* very near to the *Dhiṣṇyas* (the sacrificial places of the priests), for they represent the Gandharvas, who are greedy after the *Soma* (Hillebrandt, *Mythologie* I, 443f.)

119. Schwab, *Das altindische Tieropfer* 68ff. Compare *Ṛv.* III, 8.

120. Schwab, p. 9.

121. Rob. Smith, *Religion of the Semites* I, 171 f., 175, note 1, 187; Stade, Gesch. d. Volkes Israel I, 461. —Generally, one may compare Lippert, Kulturgeschichte II, 376 f.

122. III, 8 and in the Āprī-hymns.

123. Compare in the text the discussion on spirits of trees and forest. 'The staff embalmed with perfumes and wrapped with a cloth or thread', which should be kept between the newly-weds in the first nights after marriage to be spent in chastity, is like the enwreathed and embalmed sacrificial post, but having a distinct fetish-like nature (*Āpast. G.* III, 8, 9; compare Winternitz, *Altind. Hochzeitsrituell*, p. 88). A commentary explains this staff as a symbol of Gandharva Viśvāvasu; In fact, when it is removed, a verse is chanted to it; 'Move away from here, Viśvāvasu', etc.

124. Compare below the section 'Other Deities'.

125. Compare above p. 35f.

126. Compare, e.g., *Taitt. Saṃh.* II, 1, 7, 2. 6 and 8, 2 with one another. Compare also *Nirukta* X, 11. 12; *Bṛhaddevatā* I, 122; II, 2. 3.

127. See p. 35 and literature cited in note, 38 and 40 above.

128. A passing reference was made to this possibility in the case of Vāyu-Vāta. Hillebrandt has pointed it out repeatedly and emphatically.

129. I cannot, of course, find the attempt of T. Segerstedt (in her Essay 'Les Asuras dans la religion védique', *Revue de l'hist des religions* LVII) to prove such an intrusion in the wider context as fortunate.

130. I think here of something like the role played by the river Sarasvatī and the goddess Bhāratī which refers to the tribe of Bharatas (see the section 'Other Deities').

131. I refer here to the remarks put forth by me in *Nachr. der Gött. Ges. der Wiss.* 1915, 373f.

132. Hillebrandt, *Ved. Myth.* small ed. 45 with reference to *Kāśikā* III, 2, 81.

133. *Ibid.*, *V.M.* III, 353, 372.

134. *Ibid.*, 366. Contrary to Hillebrandt, I wish to be rather more frugal in accepting the difference between the mythology of different books of the *Ṛgveda.* One cannot deny in principle their possibility (it is sufficient to remember the well-known fluctuation between Tanūnapāt and Narāśaṃsa in the Āprī-hymns). But when it is claimed, for example, (V.M. III, 290, note 1) that the 5th book does not know the Vṛtra-legend, and that rather Śuṣṇa has come in place of Vṛtra, then it would be difficult to express adequately how this version must appear utterly strange, a version which would be altering the very foundations of the Vedic world of ideas; only its existence is not just not confirmed by the text; it is, in fact, refuted in the most clear terms (see my essay in *Nachr. Gött. Ges. d. Wiss.*, *ibid.*).

135. Sources: Bergaigne II, 146, note 2; Macdonell *Ved. Myth.* 19.

136. Compare Hillebrandt, *V.M.* III, XIIIf.

137. Namely, X, 124 (see my notes on the hymn and in the section on Asuras). Compare also Macdonell 17.

138. This is, of course not in the case of Aditi, who, as it appears, has been created to be the mother of her children.

139. Beside it perhaps in Dyāvā-Pṛthivī (heaven and earth)?

140. One should not allow oneself to be deceived in identifying such pairs by the case recognizable presently with approximate certainty that two hymns addressed to different deities are put together to form a purely apparent unity by those who classified the Vedic text.

141. Hillebrandt's *V.M.* I, 461, (compare Gött. *Gel. Anz.* 1890, 401) surmise about the origin of Agni-Soma cult from a tribethat brought with itself the Animal-sacrifices in the Brahmanic ritual' appears to me to be completely unfounded. The Animal-sacrifices have been ever since well established in the Brahmanic ritual; nothing shows that they belonged to a particular tribe. The available data, however, show with greater probability the process with reference to the pair Agni-Soma which had almost disappeared from the *Ṛgveda,* but which returned later with all the greater force. Somewhere, perhaps (on account of *Ṛv.* I, 93) in

the circle of Gotamas, one hit upon the idea of uniting both these divine patrons of sacrifice into a pair. The idea found favour, and it so happened that Agn*i*-Soma were addressed in most or all sacrifices as patrons of every sacrifice. In the sacrifice in which baked things were offered both received 'butter-share' (*ājyabhāga*); the Animal-sacrifice preceding the Soma-sacrifice was either introduced for them or transferred to them.

142. I differ from the view of L.v. Schörder ('Über den Glauben an ein höchstes gutes Wesen bei den Ariern', *Reden und Aufsätze*, 363ff.)

143. See the section on Varuṇa, Mitra and the Ādityas.

144. The view expressed by some research scholars that Varuṇa and the Ādityas have been the highest gods of an older period and Indra has later pushed them aside appears to me to be going beyond something that can be proved. The conditions of the Avesta, completely shifted to the old state of affairs, in fact, of the whole Iranian religion, do not speak for it. Or is it perhaps the sequence of gods in the documents of Boghaz-köi (compare above p. 13)? Then it would be a narrow basis for that hypothesis. It is hardly possible that only the Indian national belief has elevated Indra to his Vedic greatness. The least, I can find in the hymn depicting the battle for primacy between Indra and Varuṇa (see p. 49), evidence for a sudden change in the position of gods in the order of sequence. What is there is only that every god boasts of his might against the other, and then, as it appears, a balance is reached by their getting equal importance as a result of a plea made to both of them.

145. IV, 42. For details, compare my notes and the literature mentioned there, to which now Hillebrandt, *Lieder des Ṛv.* 87f., may be added.

146. The lower and the higher air-region.

147. An example shows how far it has gone here. A later poet, who prepared the *mantras* for an amulet of *darbha*-grass, speaks of this grass that as it was born, it has made the earth firm and has propped the atmosphere and sky'. *Ath.* V. XIX, 32, 9.

148. i.e. with the butter coming from the cow.

149. Only briefly the theory of the Vedic 'Henotheism' may be considered here (M. Müller, *Ursprung und Entwicklung der Religion* 312ff.; *Physical Religion* 180ff.; of the subsequent literature I prefer Hopkins in the *Class. Studies in Honour of H. Drisler* 75ff.), of the 'belief in individual gods appearing alternatively as the highest gods'. The Vedic poet may—at least in the major layers of the texts—put everything for a moment to a god whom he just addresses, all that can be said of a divine character; every god is one after the other the most independent, the highest, extremely divine. I cannot refrain from expressing my misgiving against this idea of the Vedic singer in getting engrossed in belief in alternating, every time, the highest and the unique deities. I do not want to speak of the numerous songs to 'all gods' in the *Ṛgveda*, in which all the main deities and groups of inferior deities are lauded one after the other. I only point out to the fact that the large mass of Vedic songs are written for a definite ritual purpose, for the Soma-sacrifice which includes the worship of approximately the whole old Pantheon in its wide structure. The poets, who extoll Indra or Agni with that apparent henotheistic ecstasy in adoration of always the one god, knew exactly, as the experienced technicians of sacrifice that they really were, to which place of the sacrifice, before and behind which other gods, the god worshipped by them thus belongs. To my mind, the characteristics of the Vedic poetry evoking the appearances of henotheism are explained, on the one hand, by that indefiniteness of outlines characterized above, which are peculiar to the Vedic figures of gods, and on the other hand, by the understandable politeness of the singer or priest towards that of the heavenly lords with whom he has for the moment the honour to talk.

CHAPTER TWO

The Individual Gods and Demons

AGNI

The Pre-Vedic and the Vedic Fire-god[1]

IF WE try to inquire into the prehistory of Agni, the Vedic Fire-god, we have then access only to the meagre and vague ideas about the mythological and religious validity of fire with reference to the Indo-European period. It may be possible that the myth about the origin of fire from its abode in heaven dates back to that period. It may be further possible that the obvious care taken for the continuous preservation of fire was even at that time surrounded by certain cult forms. It seems, however, doubtful whether the real sacrificial fire together with the magic fire which drove away the demons, belonged to the Indo-European period.[2] It is certain that there is a custom amongst many peoples of this race to give sacrificial alms to the fire. When so many different types do appear in history like the female form of Hestia-Vesta as against the male fire god of the Asians, one must have tried to conclude that, in the Indo-European period the personification of the power inherent in fiire—quite different from, say, that of the Storm-god—must have been vague in nature: a questionable conclusion in view of the fact that the old sphere of ideas was often obscured by the new; this intermingled with the old, and often displaced it.[3]

The picture that offers the comparison of the Veda with the Avesta for the Indo-Iranian age is more definite. A highly developed cult revolved around the fire at that time. It (the fire) was personified as a strong, pure and wise god. This god is well disposed to the house where he is worshipped with joy, he gives fame and livelihood to the friends of the worshipper, he gives cattle, sturdy progeny and spiritual power; but he is the destroyer of enemy. That period also appears to have been busy in differentiating the forms and places of the abode of fire—like the fire from lightning, the fire inherent in the wood of the trees, enticed from them by rubbing, etc.

If we now turn to the Veda, we see that Agni takes the first place immediately beside Indra in the cult and in the religious poetry; the priestly thinking had obviously elevated him, the sacrifical god, to that position. It can even be said that Agni has a decisive superiority over both those gods, having almost the equal place in the *Ṛgveda* outside the sphere of the Soma-sacrifice—with which the Ṛgveda has almost exclusively to do—and outside the great cult exercised excessively in the name of the warrior-nobility. There is a perceptible difference of character between him and Indra. The invincible strength stands out more and pushes aside all else in the case of Indra; it is wisdom in the case of Agni. The former is the great warrior, the latter, the great priest.[4] So, also, there is really only a slight difference in shade in the benevolence expected from both: on the side of Indra: more power, victory, triumph; on the side of Agni: well-being at home, granting of children, quiet prosperity.

The Veda may have all the tendency to give more importance to Agni. But here and there it appears to sound from the expressions of the hymns that this demon, who chooses to carry out his activities on earth in the homes of men, was not wholly equal to the real gods, the heavenly creatures.[5] This view must have been, in fact, no doubt, a view of the very old period. Whenever he is called the messenger of the gods, whenever it is said that the gods have placed him in the homes of men and appointed him for the sacrificial service, giving him eternal youth in return for it, or whenever expressions are used such as that he, the son of the gods, has become their father,[6] he appears to have an exceptional position in comparison with the compact mass of the 'gods'. Above all, it is remarkable, however, that Agni has as good as no part in that most excellent drink of the gods, Soma. As often as it is said of him that he blesses the man who brings him firewood, sacrificial butter and devotion, so also is it a rare exception when it is said that the pious are preparing Soma for him.[7] Should not one then take it for granted that the basic arrangements of the Soma-sacrifice were already confirmed prior to Agni attaining his complete divine importance?

Different Births of Agni

The myths of Agni in contradiction to, above all, those of Indra narrate little about the deeds of the god. This is due to lack of clarity in his less pronounced anthropomorphic form as already emphasized. The speculations with which Agni-hymns deal mainly, apart from their main theme of the appearance and the deed of the god as the sacrificial fire in those forms which are the most contemporaneous for the priest, are concerned with the variety of Agni's different births, his forms of appearance and his places of abode. Considerations of this type are not as suggestive in the case of the other gods as with him. His strange birth from fire sticks and his similarity in nature in the celestial forms, besides the terrestrial in the hidden or in the obvious, had eventually to engage the attention of the Vedic priests with their penchant for mystifying things. This strange birth also serves as a popular theme for the praise of the god.

Sometimes two of the births or forms of Agni will be named, sometimes the favourite triad; even longer lists are found. The designation very often attached to him as the 'twice born' refers to his celestial and earthly nature. 'We want to serve you, Agni, in your highest birth; we want to serve you in the lower place with the hymns of praise.' 'May Agni hear us with his familiar faces, may he hear us with the heavenly faces, the never-tiring Agni.' 'He has his seat in broad plains here below, and in the high lands far away.[8] The expressions which name Agni—with or without emphatic comparison of Agni kindled by human beings and Agni kindled by gods—are associated with the same notion.[9] Also when it is said 'whether you are, Agni, heaven-born or water-born, or born of strength, we invoke you with prayers' (VIII, 43, 28), the same duality[10] of the celestial and earthly fire appears to be indicated. We shall see in our discussion of Agni's birth from the waters that one was mainly thinking of the earthly waters.

The oft-quoted triad of Agni's forms or births[11] is not always understood in the same way. The reference to the heaven, waters and fire sticks is quite clear in the following verse: 'At first Agni was born from the heaven, secondly from us Jātavedas[12] was born; for the third time in the waters...' (X, 45,1). It is said elsewhere: 'They cherish three origins of Agni: one in the ocean, one in the heaven and one in the waters' (I, 95, 3). It is strange that ocean and waters are differentiated here, and there is no mention of Agni's birth through human efforts.[13] I shall cite a few more verses which speak of different births or forms of Agni without emphasizing a definite number. 'You, Agni, the burning one, you are born from heaven, from the waters, from the stone, from the forests, from the plants, you Lord of men, you are born as possession of men in glory.' 'Offspring of the one who is standing, offspring of all that moves; [one worships] him even in stone, in the homes of [men?]: like the Region-lord[?] of regions, the immortal one, the one full of wisdom.' 'Agni, your lustre which is in the heaven and on the earth, which is in the plants, which is in the waters, o you, worthy of worship with which you have encompassed the wide air...'[14]

What is meant now by Agni's heavenly birth and what is meant by his birth from the water? With heavenly Agni, the sun, so also the lightning can come into question. As far as the lightning is concerned, it can be understood as originating from the heavenly as also from the watery realm: its home is, of course, the cloud. We shall, however, see that for the Vedic idea fire is present in quite a different sense in all the waters, in the earthly as well as the heavenly, besides the lightning. Where now the heavenly Agni and Agni from the waters are named beside each other, I believe on the whole,[15] that the former is to be understood as the sun and the latter in the sense: 'just now briefly mentioned to differentiate it from the lightning.' The lightning, however, recedes from view for the present,[16] as it is to be discussed further. Anyway it must be admitted that the meaning which is associated by every single verse with the different forms of births of Agni becomes sometimes doubtful; the more important thing, however, is the positive aspect of how these forms themselves are introduced. Let us observe them one by one.

Agni and the Sun

The similarity of Agni in nature with the Sun, to be more exact, the validity of the sun as a phenomenon of Agni, is undoubtedly a Vedic dogma. Agni 'stands with his lustre there, as the Sun spreading the men over their dwelling places'. 'Agni, shining bright, radiant as the Sun; he resplends like the Sun in the sky.' 'Agni, your rays, which are in the Sun spread themselves across the sky with the rays of the sunrise', etc.[17] But this side of Agni's nature is mentioned comparatively rarely. It belongs, so to say, to the completeness of the form of address used for him, just this form of address used for worshipping him in other forms as well as the form of the heaven-born Sun: usually Agni, the earthly fire, is compared more with the sun in heaven than equated with him (the sun). 'In the heart', it is said, 'Varuṇa created the will, in the water the Agni, the Sun in the heaven and on the fields the Soma' (V, 85, 2): it is seen how far, to the poet talking without bias, the sun is one being and Agni another, put by the creator in another place. The sun was too much of a power by himself to have had a more substantial significance by being conceived as fire.

Besides a few other rites,[18] especially, the morning fire-sacrifice appears to be referring in the ritual to the connection between the sun and the fire: around the time of the sunrise—so also around the time of the sunset—the sacrificial fire[19] was kindled and milk was offered. It may be presumed—and parallels outside India support the presumption—that this act, which, on the one hand, obviously represents the regular maintenance and service usually due to the holy fire, has been simultaneously, on the other hand, at least in the old period, a magic concerning the sun.[20] Perhaps, at least a trace of this idea may be seen in the *mantras* which the later Vedas prescribed for the morning and the evening service of the fire: 'Agni is light, Light is Agni' in the evening; 'Sun is light, Light is sun' in the morning; a parallelism of both the beings of Light, which can very well be the remnant of a closer and more concrete connection that is thought of between them. A Brāhmaṇa[21] also says quite explicitly:

> While he sacrifices in the morning before the sunrise, he causes him[22] to be born; growing into lustre, he rises aglowing, really, he would not rise, if he does sacrifice this offering in him.[23]

For the older periods, however, hymns in the *Ṛgveda*[24] testify to the same view quite explicitly. So it is said: 'Let us Agni, O god, kindle your heavenly, eternally youthful (flame), so that your glorious lustre[25] may shine in the heaven.' 'O Agni, you have made the Sun, the Eternal Star, to mount the sky, bestowing light on men'.[26] The latter verse appears, as it so often happens, to turn the process repeating daily into a happening belonging to the creation of the world. Similarly, then, the sphere of ideas that engages us here, has been added to the myth of Indra obtaining the sun. This myth of how the Aṅgiras split the rocks asunder and joined in the lowing of the cows, 'when the sun became visible as Agni was born',[27] will be discussed later.

Agni and the Lightning

After the Sun-Agni comes the form of Agni as lightning in question. The preference for the storm that dominated the mythological research for a long time has led to the fact that one has read too much into the text for this concept of Agni.[28] Of course, it cannot be denied that the fiery nature of lightning or the relationship of lightning to the fire has been alluded to by the Vedic poets here and there briefly. So Agni is called once[29] 'the luminous thunder present in the expanse of light'. But that is just only, so to say, a casual fringe decoration.[30] When he is named together with the lightning, he is usually compared with it—or the lightning is compared with him—and thereby distinguished from him. Rightly has it been remarked[31] that the nature of the lightning is not favourable for its development into a deity. Surely it is not impossible that it can also become a god. But the most natural thing is that it can become a weapon or a tool in the hands of god. It is in the Indra-myth with the *Vajra* and not in the Agni-myth that we mainly hear of lightning.

The idea of Agni staying in the waters 'covering himself with the waters of the ocean', 'vitalising the semen of the waters' emerges, however, then in the whole Veda. In a verse already mentioned above Varuṇa is seen creating 'the will in the heart, the Agni in the water and the sun in the sky'. That is, water is seen in the same way as the real home of Agni, as the heaven is the home of the sun.[32] It is also felt that the poet has expressed here a thought, which is alive in him and which is vivid for him and does not repeat anything that has become incomprehensible. So it has to be an idea other than that of lightning which had suggested itself to the Vedic people primarily, when considering water as the home of Agni.

It appears to me that the connection of 'waters and plants' which had already become[33] common in the Indo-Iranian period shows the way for ascertaining this aspect of nature of waters, by virtue of which they represent the home of Agni. Like the waters, so also are the plants—the fire sticks from which the fire is produced by friction—the home of Agni, and the Veda likes to put together waters and plants or waters and woods, with reference to Agni's dwelling places.[34] In few verses, there are clearer indications about the nature of this relationship.[35] 'The offspring of waters has entered the fruit-bearing plants.' 'In the waters, Agni, is your abode, you climb up in the shrubs.' 'When he is brought from the highest father, he climbs...up the plants in his abode'.[36] The water comes down from the 'highest father', the heaven; the plants suck their food from the rain and from the water of the earth. This water is in its nature similar to the rain. The plants are indeed the 'first-born essence of waters', 'water is their nature'.[37] Therefore, the power must have remained latent in water, and it breaks forth as fire from the wood of the plants. If the fire then returns to the heaven as smoke, i.e. as cloud, the circle is completed, which is clearly described by a verse in the Veda; 'The same water goes up and down in the course of the day: the downpour (of rains) swells the earth; the flames of Agni swell the heaven' (I, 164, 51). It runs parallel to these ideas and illustrates them when *Amṛta,* the life-extending strength living in the plants and which is given to the sick man with the juice of the plant, is derived from the seed of Parjanya, the god of rains.[38]

One should not deny the probability that these thoughts about the connection between water and fire have been strengthened through the phenomenon of lightning springing forth from the clouds. It can be supposed that there mus t have been still one more natural process at play: the extinguishing of fire in water which appeared to mean the entering of fire into it, and thereby its latent stay in it—'it hisses in the water sitting down like a swan'—so it is said of Agni.[39] The result, however, was that all water was thought of as containing Agni in itself, primarily, of course, the waters of the earth, the rivers and the ponds, for they drew the immediate attention of the Vedic poets.[40] It is said of the earth in the *Atharvaveda*:[41] '...on whom were the Agnis that are within the waters.' In the later liturgic texts there is several times the invocation of Agni living in the concerned waters and also in his different forms in the ceremonies which refer to a pond or simply to a water-pot. The pupil, who takes the ceremonial bath after completing his studies, draws water with the *mantra* through which he seizes the lustrous form of Agni, leaving behind the other fires gone into the water and which spoil the body and disturb the mind. Similarly, the sacrificer gives offerings to all forms of Agni,[42] living in waters at the time of the dedication of ponds, wells or lakes. The priest who consecrates the king by pouring water says: 'To all Agnis living in waters'.[43] Here one may point out to the ceremony connected with the ritual of the building up of the fire-altar performed to appease Agni's destructive glow. Certain objects which suggest moist coolness—reed, she-frog, etc.—are attracted to the altar with the *mantras*; one of them invites Agni to choose his path beneath the reed and in the rivers—'you are Agni, the bile of water'[44]—where perhaps bile, in accordance with the views of later medicine, is considered as a heat-engendering principle. The relevant rites and *mantras* may be comparatively modern. Doubtless, the concept of the relation of Agni to the waters underlying these rites and *mantras* is identical with the Ṛgvedic view.

It follows from the conceptions depicted above that in many verses, which one was accustomed to relate earlier to storm-bearing clouds and lightning, interpretation will now have to give way to those that refer to common water including the waters of the cloud, insofar as no lightning is produced; on the other hand, insofar as the soil is fertilized; and also to those that refer to fire latent in water.' The following verses from a hymn (*Ṛv.* III, 1) may be considered. This hymn engrosses itself with great relish in Agni's secret existence.

The gods discovered beautiful Agni in the midst of waters with the sisters' labour (i.e. of the waters). The seven virgins (the rivers) had brought up the blessed one, who comes to the world in white, and who is red, when waxen mighty. They ran to him like mares to their new-born youngling. The gods gaze in wonder at Agni at his birth.... He sought those who do not eat, the infallible ones, the young daughters of the heaven, who do not attire themselves and yet, not naked. There received him as the one embryo the old, the young, the ones that sprang forth from the same womb, the seven notes.[45] Disseminated in the river of mead were his all-embracing forms crowded in the womb of butter. There stood the milch-kine with udders bursting full, the Wondrous Parents, the Mighty Pair turned to face each other. Carefully cherished (in the mother's womb), Son of Strength, you shone assuming lasting and refulgent beauties and juice descended there, where the Mighty one grew strong by wisdom.

I cannot discover here a convincing reference to the cloud and the lightning. The Vedic poet, who speaks of these, uses other expressions.[46] I think only that Agni lingers in the waters which are considered as seven earthly rivers and sucks the strength from them; then when the seven notes of the holy song resound, he is lit for the sacrifice at the places where butter and sweet drink flow.

Apāṃ Napāt

The concepts of Agni as the one sprung from waters have led to a contamination of this god with a being who is originally altogether different from him. This being is the 'infant of waters' (*apāṃ napāt*). This demon is to be traced back to the Indo-Iranian period. We find him in the Avesta as a spirit of waters in whose depths he lives, and he is invoked together with them constantly. He is called: rich in swift horses[47]—these must be originally the hastening waves—governing the distribution of waters across the earth. But also in the Veda, his original nature as a god of waters[48] is clearly visible through the features which he has got as a result of his identification with Agni. Of the two hymns in the *Ṛgveda* addressed to him, one (X, 30) refers to the ceremonies which have exclusively to do with waters[49] and not with fire. The ritual use of this hymn is essentially quite certain.[50] When the priests get up to draw water meant for the sacrifice, the following *mantra* is recited:

> You *Adhvaryu*, go to the water, to the ocean; give the offering to the infant of waters. It should give you today its well purified wave; press from it the Soma rich in honey. Infant of waters, you who shine in the waters without the firewood, you who are worshipped by the priests at the offerings, give us waters rich in honey, from which Indra got strength for his heroic might.

And the sacrificial butter is poured into water.[51] One can see that it deals here exclusively with a water-demon who is invoked to give water;[52] only that it 'shines without the firewood' could point out to its resemblance with Agni. This resemblance becomes more clear in another hymn (II, 35) addressed to the infant of waters, but here also the water-nature of the demon is predominant. The demon is invoked together with the rivers; he shines in the water; the water virgins transform him into a young man.[53] Yet, on the other hand, similar to the hymn mentioned above, 'he glitters in the waters attired in the ostentatious dress of the butter'[54] and there is an obvious reference to Agni born in the lightning cloud. 'The infant of waters has climbed the uplifted lap, itself erect,[55] attiring itself with the lightning.' Agni is directly addressed at the end, when he is considered different from the infant of waters[56] in several of the Agni-hymns, but in some other hymns he is emphatically distinguished from the infant of waters.

The course of events at bottom is quite clear. An original water-demon, as it could not be easily avoided, has partially collided with Agni as a result of increasing popular speculation about Agni as descending from water, and under the influence of the tendency peculiar specially to Agni of getting identified with the most different types of gods. He has preserved his own nature for the other part.

Agni present in waters and entering the plants with the water is visible when he breaks forth from the fire sticks: it is one more form of Agni's birth. 'Him varied in his form, the lovely infant of floods and plants the blessed wood has born' (III, 1, 13). The ten sisters have engendered him, the fingers of the one who rubbed: one has to rub with all strength, that is why he is called the son of strength.

There are other forms of birth and existence of Agni, but they are mentioned only in a summary fashion. As he is identified with the sun, he is also identified quite isolatedly with the moon. He lives in the stones, and he is born in the stones.[57] It is obviously the spark coming from the fire-stone. He lives (as animal energy, perhaps also as clairvoyant) in human beings—'Agni with many births looks out of our hearts'—and also in cattle and horses, in birds and wild animals, in all those who have two feet or four feet.[58] He lives on earth which is called pregnant with Agni.[59] Perhaps one did not consider the fire present in the wood as reaching the place with water, but also as climbing from the ground into the trees growing on earth. Finally, this god dwelling in so many places could be conceived of as spreading everywhere as 'the germ of all things that move not and that move', as 'the germ of all that is living'[60] as a life force present in all the things.

Descent and Discovery of Agni

The Vedic myths can report very little about the great feats of Agni, above all about the experiences which depend upon the coexistence of his heavenly and earthly life as also his hidden and visible life. The steady heroic nature of a great yardstick rooted in the myths present in Indra is absent in him.

There is a certain divergence between the concepts of Agni's different births and those of his descent, or what one can say, of his coming down. In the former, Agni is given an earthly birth, equal in every respect with his heavenly birth; and in the latter, his earthly existence is derived from his heavenly existence. In the former, Agni, a god, is born; in the latter—at least in accordance with basic concepts—he is brought down as a passive object. If we could ascribe this concept of bringing him down—basing it in the phenomenon of lightning?—to the Indo-European period, as is made probable by the myth of Prometheus, then this passivity of Agni is as easily understood as that of Soma in the myth of Soma's descent. The element had not risen at that time to its full divine dignity.

The Prometheus of the Veda is Mātariśvan.[61] It is said of Agni and Soma that Mātariśvan brought the one 'from the heaven, and the eagle stole the other from the rock.' 'Mātariśvan brought him to us from far away, produced by attrition, from the gods. He brought Agni wandering at large and hidden from our view. As an envoy of Vivasvant, Mātariśvan brought Agni belonging to all people from afar.'[62] Vivasvant is the first sacrificer, the ancestor of the human race;[63] his envoy brings fire for him from heaven and with that he brings it for the whole humanity; his excellent virtue for the Vedic poet is his efficacy at the sacrifice. This is the sketchy Indian version which was elevated to the world-encompassing tragedy of the myth of Prometheus by the profundity of the Greek mind.

The idea of the initiation of the fire by the Bhṛgus is essentially different from the myth of the bringer of the fire, Mātariśvan. The scene of the occurrence there is basically the universe, though the priest-poetry of the Veda does not disregard, as may be understood, the place of sacrifice, the 'Seat of Vivasvant'; here it is mainly the question of dissemination of the fire, especially that of the sacrificial fire by an old legendary generation of priests in human dwellings. The Bhṛgus do not fetch it from the heaven; whenever there is a reference to the place, where they find the fire, it is called the 'place of waters'. 'Bhṛgus have set you amongst mankind...as a priest (*hotāram*), Agni, as a welcome guest.' 'The Bhṛgus have stirred him up, like the treasure, on the earth, the navel of the world,[64] in his greatness..' 'The pious deeds of service have followed him in his footsteps on the place of waters like the lost cattle. Him the secretly hidden found the Usij,[65] the wise Bhṛgus searching in devotion.' 'Bhṛgus have kindled you with the hymns of praise.'[66] It may not appear strange that the fantasy of the Vedic poets brings together occasionally Mātariśvan as the bringer of fire and the Bhṛgus as his ancient fosterers and propagators, so that it appears that Mātariśvan brings the fire to the Bhṛgus,[67] but it cannot also mislead one about the different nature of both spheres of concepts.

Like the wise men amongst the priests, the gods are, of course, not less interested in letting Agni take active part in the sacrifice. So they seek him, and also find him. The main reference in this respect is one of those dialogues in the *Ṛgveda*, to which a prosaic narration, now extinct, appears to have belonged, as part of a framework of arguments and replies.[68] Varuṇa as the leader of the gods says to Agni after finding him:

We have searched you at many places, Jātavedas, you, Agni, you who have entered into the waters and the plants.[69] Yama[70] has discovered you there, you, brightly shining, as you shone ten days' journey away.

Agni answers:

I was afraid, Varuṇa, of the office of *Hotar*,[71] and went away, so that the gods would not place me there. My forms were laid down in many hiding places. I Agni do not understand that work (of the service of *Hotar*).

And Varuṇa(?) replies:

Come hither. Man is pious; he desires to sacrifice. After you have prepared (earlier the sacrifice) (?), you dwell now in gloom. Make pathways leading god-ward clear and easy, and bear oblations with kindly spirit.

Agni replies to that:

Agni's elder brothers have selected this work, like the one who drives a chariot the way to travel. So, Varuṇa, I fled afar through terror, as flies the buffalo from an archer's bowstring.

The gods now grant him eternal life and participation in the sacrificial gifts to win him over for the sacrificial service:

You all gods, instruct me, how I, elected your priest, must seat me here, and how address you. Instruct me how to deal to each his portion (in the sacrifice), and by what path to bring you man's oblation....

I shall get for you the sacrifice of heroic immortality, that I get, O gods, for you a wide space. I shall put the Vajra in Indra's arms, and he should be victorious in all these battles.

Three hundred [here it is not any more Agni speaking, as it appears, but the narrator] three thousand gods, thirty and nine served Agni. They sprinkled the sacrificial butter upon him and spread out for him the seat of sacrifice; they put him down then as *Hotar*.

Agni as the Father of Human Race

Finally the concept of Agni as the father of the human race must be mentioned in the discussion of the mythical past of Agni.

I think this concept plays a more subordinate role than is credited to it, or perhaps, almost an infinitesimal role. One cannot get more information from the *Ṛgveda*, than it is said of him in a passage which makes him also creator of the heaven and the waters, creator of both the worlds: he has 'produced these races of human beings'.[72] It is clear that this change—in the midst of quite different concepts about the origin of the human race—depicts just only one of those numerous ideas that appear and disappear in the Veda and attribute, at least once somewhere, every deed to every god. One should carefully separate the weeds running riot on the fertile ground of the fantasy of the Vedic poets from the treasure of deep-rooted and lasting mythical concepts. I think it is a waste of time to inquire seriously into the origin of such ideas; and I think it is especially unjust to derive what is being discussed here from the identification of the production of fire by rubbing two fire sticks with the human act of production.[73] The sources only teach that the attrition of fire—as it is apparent—was conceived of as production and birth; conversely, it is said of the fruit in a magic *mantra* meant to promote procreation that 'the two Aśvins have rubbed it from the golden fire sticks'; also the ritual gives the names of the mythical couple Purūravas and Urvaśī[74] to both the fire sticks. This multi-directional comparison of production of fire and human procreation is as yet far away from the conception of fire as a begetter of human beings or as the first-born man, and I at least cannot discover a positive trace of the course taken by the development of these concepts.

The conception of Agni as Aṅgiras, as the distinguished Aṅgiras (*aṅgirastama*), is more firmly rooted in tradition than his conception as the father of human beings. It may appear that this idea of the first-designated is quite obvious. The Aṅgirās are the semi-divine ancestors of the later generations of priests or some amongst these generations: 'our fathers are Aṅgirās', 'our old fathers the Aṅgirās', 'the Brāhmaṇa priests are Aṅgirās'; they have 'first honoured sacrifice's statute';[75] as the companions of Indra they burst[76] with their priestly hymns the rock which concealed the cows. That Agni is named as

Aṅgiras, a noble Aṅgiras, may be due to the fact that he is the first of the ancestors of the mankind. But I do not think that the sense of the appropriate expression is thereby captured. The Aṅgirās are, indeed not the oldest human beings in general, but they are the oldest priests as the ancestors of the historical generations of priests. However, Agni is the priest κατέξοχην, and then naturally the oldest priest. Thus, he must be Aṅgiras. And when he, the noblest Aṅgiras, appears in a verse also as the father of Aṅgirās,[77] it is likewise comprehensible as quite a tiny step distancing itself further from the secure mass of ideas. But this on the other hand, cannot any more be attributed to this mass itself; the real father of Aṅgirās is the heaven.[78]

Agni and Human Beings

Finally, we shall consider Agni's influence in real life and his relationship to the present world and to man.

The function, which is perhaps the oldest cultic function of fire and which appears commonly even amongst the most primitive folks, has survived in the case of the Vedic Agni, i.e. his work as the one who destroys bad spirits and inimical magic by burning and averts them. He sees the hidden demons with his bright and sharp eyes; he catches them with his tongue and his iron teeth; he shoots them with his arrow and destroys them with his heat. We shall discuss in detail the rites in which the belief in this work of Agni appears in our discussion of the cult, particularly of the magic; we have just to mention here that Agni shares the role of the destroyer of demons, above all with Indra, the lord of Vajra.[79] Agni is there, as it is nature of things, more the one who destroys the enemies by burning, and Indra is the one who shatters them. The impression is justifiable that the function in question on Agni's side appears to be more deeply connected with his nature, as it is historically probably older and also more prominent in the hymns of praise. Also, in the ritual connected with the expulsion of the demons, Agni or the fire in the most different forms plays a considerably more important role than Indra; it is understandable that Agni as the god closest to man and whose magic power man has at his disposal is preferred here to Indra coming from a distant height.

The blessing given to mankind by the fire of the house and of the sacrifice is compatible with the activity of Agni in the magic fire for the expulsion of the demons. Characteristically, for the world of Vedic perceptions, the sacrificial fire was most important. For it Agni's most important significance lay in his priestly dignity, in his service as a messenger between men and gods. He is celebrated in countless hymns as the one in whom 'the offerings meet', as the one who quickens the prayers, who leads the gods while seated on the sacrificial straw with them, or also as the one who delivers the oblations, ascending the heavens. The poets of these hymns like to glorify in him the divine counterpart of their own position, and in his power the power of their own art of sacrifice. Sometimes, they take pleasure in attaching the qualities and functions of the various priests of sacrifice to Agni; preferably, however, he is given the role of *Hotar*, the priest for whom the recitation of the hymns lauding the god and inviting him to feast is a duty: because to this priest, who owned the art of poetry, the enticement of gods through persuasion must have appeared a nobler task than that of the sacrificial manual workers who do the actual labour at the sacrifice. It is mostly the *Hotar* priests who monopolized the word in the Vedic poetry. This predominance of the idolized sacrificial fire of Agni, considered everywhere in the *Ṛgveda* as a mystical *Hotar*, is obviously a comparatively recent phenomenon, perhaps more a creation of the priests who belonged to guild-like orders rather than that of the spirit of the people. Given this position of the sacrificial god amongst the gods, claims were laid for the primacy of the caste of the sacrificer; the secret-mongering game of concealing ideas subtly, played already in the *Ṛgveda* with the form of the divine Brāhmaṇa, has its direct descendant in the symbolism of the later liturgic texts with their inexhaustible oddities.

Do we meet there an older layer of ideas, where Agni is celebrated without any special prominence, the idea of sacrifice being given to him simply in his capacity as a guest of men, as a friend and a companion of people, indeed also of domestic animals? Do we have here the echo of an earlier idea, central to which was the fire, above all the fire of the hearth, the focal point of domestic life? And of that fire, in which there appears to be the remnant of a former religious significance and which was called the 'fire of the householder', forming the basis of the well-defined ritual of the three sacrificial fires and from which the two others are repeatedly derived ?

The *Gṛhya* texts, even if remotely affected by the exclusivity of the priestly trend, describe the domestic cult in a more popular form than the one obtaining in the great cult of the three fires. They give a clear picture of how the life of an individual and the family was spent under the protection of Agni, in close dependence upon his guidance. On various occasions, the invocations as under were addressed: 'May he be the gatherer of goods. Do not harm us, neither the old nor the young. Bring luck to men and cattle.' One sacrifices at the marriage with a prayer for the bride: 'May Agni, the fire of the householder, protect her; may he lead her progeny to an old age. May she be of blessed womb, mother of livingchildren; may she experience happiness from her sons!' And when the bridegroom scatters the roasted barley in the hands of the bride, he would call this act as 'union between me and you: may Agni bless it'. If a child was born, one sacrificed on the tenth day after the lapse of impurity caused by delivery with the saying:

> May this splendid Agni bestow life to you today; may our life last long. Grant life Agni, strengthened by the sacrificial meal, with face full of butter, sprung from the womb of the butter. Drink butter, the sweet honey of the cow. Protect the child as a father would protect his son.

In the same way, Agni is worshipped when the growing boy is taken to the teacher who should introduce him to the study of the Veda.[80] The householder returning from a journey worships his fire with the saying: 'This Agni is blessed to us, this Agni is highly blessed to us. May we not be ruined in his worship. May he let us stand high.' This simple conception of Agni of the house untouched by priestly artifice is, of course, not unknown to the Ṛgvedic hymns. The pious man prays, also in the *Ṛgveda*, to Agni that he may bless him 'like the father the son', that he may be his 'closest friend'. He is called the 'never-travelling great householder'; 'the milch-kine return to him, the quick runners return to him, the own mighty horses...the generous of noble birth come together at his place'. 'The cows wake up at his shine when he is kindled': the cows 'whose names Agni knows through the sacrifice'.[81] The singer who has obtained abroad rich reward for his art in the form of cattle, horses and chariots announces his gifts on his return to the domestic Agni.[82] Of course, nothing prevents one here in the *Ṛgveda*, as also in the later texts, from thinking of the same sacrificial fire, which was otherwise usually enmeshed in an intricate web of mystery woven by the priests; or, perhaps, it is almost without doubt that just this fire was supposed as a rule. But with that, the way is not blocked for the supposition that, here, the tone of invocations continues in the same way as once in the address to the fire, less exclusively to the sacrificial fire, the nature of which as a centre of domestic life made an intimacy of language and intercourse possible, and which did not return to the cult of the other gods.

The Vedic Indian perceives this friendship between Agni and man as the one which was inherited by an individual from his ancestors from time immemorial. When there is a reference to such a period of friendship also in the case of the other gods, it appears characteristically nowhere so often, and surely never in such a typical form as in the case of Agni. Indra is praised as a god who has bestowed victory on this or that hero of olden times, and Agni above all as a god who was kindled by the ancestors and worshipped by them. The definite rules of the later ritual are well known, according to which Agni who as a god already belonging to the first ancestors of the sacrificer was invoked together with the mentioning of their names.[83] This custom appears to be in preparation, if not already present, in many hymns of the Ṛgveda. But it does not mean that one should conclude therefrom that there was a direct physical continuity of the sacrificial fire from generation to generation; the ritual of the setting up of the holy fire known in all details excludes this conception, and this conception would also be in contradiction to the idea that the death of the sacrificer pollutes the sacrificial fire and makes it unfit for further use. But if not physical, so to say, at least an ideal continuity of fire respected from the fathers to the sons was felt, a connection in which something concrete was seen, something like the continuity, say, of the friendship with Indra from one generation to the other. It is quite understandable that such a special position, such a sense of growing together with the past of a family was acknowledged only to the god who shared the house of the man, who accompanied his life from day to day and saw his generations grow one after the other. One could hardly have spoken of another god like 'Agni of Bharata'.[84]

INDRA

Prehistory of Indra

The Indo-Europeans[85] probably knew the being which was later developed into the Vedic Indra: an excessively powerful, divine or gigantic hero, blond-bearded or red-bearded, the mighty glutton and carouser, the victorious killer of the dragon. There is no doubt that this figure is affected perhaps—it appears, however, quite uncertain—by foreign influences which must have been effectively active on Asiatic soil in a form which was very close to the Vedic and peculiar to the Indo-Iranian. The Vedic Vṛtrahan (Indra as the killer of Vṛtra) comes again in the Verethraghna of the Avesta, and even if those myths which are so important for the god's counterpart in the Veda are missing in the Avesta, the Armenic killer of the dragon Vahagn (= Verethraghna) shows what may be ascertained without this and what is already noted long back, namely, that stripping the Avestic god of the myth of killing of the dragon is just secondary. We find in the Veda Indra, the killer of Vṛtra, embellished with a number of myths which are attributed to him, no doubt, only subsequently. This may have been perhaps—we need not go into details here—done partially in the pre-Indian period, but the addition of new matter also continued on the Indian soil; no other figure of god as that of Indra attracted one so powerfully to attribute to him, the 'Lord of strength', all the most mighty heroic deeds.[86]

The Victory over Vṛtra

The most noble heroic deed of the god, the victory over Vṛtra and the liberation of waters,[87] maintains its place for ever as the centre of the Indra-myths. His mythological nature consists in its fulfilment.

Vṛtra means in the neuter 'enemy', more exactly 'hostile power', literally 'surrounding', 'imprisoning'; in the masculine, the prisoner of waters, as enemy subdued by Indra.[88] The second meaning of the same being is Ahi 'serpent'; the serpent, and not the human form was foremost in the minds of the Vedic singers.

We shall try to reproduce here a few verses of the most spirited of their hymns (*Ṛv.* I, 32).

I will declare the heroic deeds of Indra, the first he achieved, the *Vajra*-wielder.[89] He slew the serpent, then freed the waters and cleft the stomach of the mountains.

He slew the serpent lying on the mountain: Tvaṣṭar fashioned his thundering *Vajra*. Like lowing cows in rapid flow the waters descended gliding downward to the ocean.

When, Indra, you have slain the serpent's firstborn, and overcome the charms of the enchanters, then giving life to Sun, and Heaven and Dawn, you did not find one foe to stand against you.

Vṛtra like a drunken weak warrior challenged the great hero, the mighty fighter, the storming one. He could not withstand the clashing of the weapons, and was crushed, who was Indra's foe.

Footless and handless still he challenged Indra, who smote him with the *Vajra* in the back. Emasculate, yet claiming bull's vigour, thus Vṛtra lay with scattered limbs dissevered.

Humbled was the strength of her who gave birth to Vṛtra. Indra had cast his deadly bolt against her. The mother was above, the son was under, and like a cow beside her calf lay Dānu.

Rolled in the midst of never-ceasing currents flowing without rest for ever onward, the waters bear off Vṛtra's nameless body. The foe of Indra sank to lasting darkness.

Guarded by the serpents, becoming the wives of the barbarian, the waters stayed like the cows held by Paṇi.[90] But he, when he had smitten Vṛtra, opened the cave wherein the floods had been imprisoned.

Nothing availed him lightning, nothing thunder, hailstorm or mist which he had spread around him. When Indra and the serpent strove in the battle, Maghavan gained the victory of ever.

Whom did you see to avenge the serpent, Indra, that fear possessed your heart when you had slain him? That like a frightened eagle through the regions, you crossed nine-and-ninety flowing rivers?

Indra is the King of all that moves and moves not, of creatures tamed and horned, the wielder of Vajra. Over all living men he rules as a King containing all as spokes within the felly.

Rarely does the poetry of the *Ṛgveda* strike with such impact. There is no effort to narrate the events in their proper order or to portray them in detail; a simple striking apt image only here and there, and again and again, without any fear of repetition, the same joyful laudation of the victorious god.

We shall add here a few more individual features from some other Ṛgvedic hymns.

Vṛtra was lying on the 'seven tracks leading into a distance', on the bed of the seven rivers which he had barred. He lay there in ninety-nine bends. He had devoured the rivers, and as the rivers are in the mountain and spring later from the mountain, this leads even to the horrible thought that 'the mountain was in the stomach of Vṛtra'. 'The gods and the old folks alike turn back' full of fear, 'all gods and friends left him avoiding the hissing of Vṛtra'. They left Indra who did not budge from his place, whom the gods 'have put forth to kill Vṛtra'. Indra drank heroic power from the *Soma*; Of his companions, only the Maruts stood faithfully by his side, and also Viṣṇu, the god who covered the world in three steps. 'Then Indra said, as he wanted to kill Vṛtra, "Friend Viṣṇu, march further". ' It appears that Indra does not go as a chariot-fighter for the Vṛtra-battle in the real form of the myth; such a modern visualization, so to say, is at least originally unknown to the story. As he takes the *Vajra* in his hand to kill the serpent, the mountains, cows and priests cheer him on with a loud cry. As Vṛtra suffers a deadly hit, there is mention of him as the one who is sleeping, but soon his panting (for breath) is mentioned and, as it is said in the hymn mentioned above, there is talk of lightning, thunder, mist and hailstone-weather that he causes. Indra severs his head with the *Vajra* or he breaks his limbs into pieces. The heavens are frightened of the roaring of the injured enemy. Indra's weapon opens the udders of the mountain; the rivers hasten to the ocean like the birds flying to their nest, like the chariots in the chariot-race for the first place. The gods applaud the victor; the consorts of the gods weave for him a song of praise.[91]

And the gaining of the waters extends itself to the gaining of the shining light. As the hymn referred to above mentions the god, when he kills the serpent, as creating the sun, the heaven and the dawn, it is said in another verse:[92] 'When you killed Vṛtra, the serpent with your might, you let the sun climb up the heaven, so that he could be seen.' 'You carried the brazen *Vajra* in your hand, you held the sun firmly in the heaven, so that he could be seen.' And a poet shouts to Indra: 'Kill Vṛtra, get the sun!'

If we survey the features of the myth we have here, the question becomes pertinent as to whether there is really, as many think, the talk of storm and the pouring of rain. I think that it must be denied[93] that the Vedic people thought of these. A god fights with a demon in the form of a serpent and opens the innards of the mountains; the waters of the rivers flow in the direction of the ocean. That is what the hymns say. One should not confuse this simple idea with the explanation that by mountains clouds were meant and by rivers downpour of rain. That was not meant; the mountains were the real mountains, and the rivers the real rivers. If there were to be a mention of clouds and rains, the metaphor of mountains and rivers would not have been repeated constantly without the thing being given the right name at some place. Where the poets mean clouds and rain, they use other expressions than those used in the Indra-hymns. One may refer, for example, to the great hymn to Parjanya, the god of rain and storm (V, 83) for comparison. In it, there is talk of rain, again and again talk of rain, lightning and thunder; the god makes his rain-messengers appear; he creates the rain-cloud; Maruts give rain from the heaven; one requests Parjanya: you made the waters rain, now stop. It strikes the trees, and thunderingly it strikes the evil-doer; the leonine voice of the thunder rises; the lightning flies. A Vedic poet describes the storm in this way; but it is almost never[94] said of Indra in the *Ṛgveda* that he made the rain.[95] The magic actions to get rain are predominantly associated with gods other than Indra. On the other hand, they are the personified rivers, no doubt, earthly rivers, Vipās and Śutudrī (Biyas and Satlaj), which speak exactly in the contemporary idiom of the Indra hymns, of the deed of Indra by which they are freed:

> Indra has opened the path for us, Indra, the wielder of Vajra; he has struck down Vṛtra who had imprisoned the rivers... Indra's heroic deed that he struck down the serpent must be praised again and again. He has struck down the obstructors with his *Vajra*, and eager to course, the waters flowed forth.[96]

According to that, it is clear: for the poets it is not as much the question of the storm in the victory of Indra, but of the fact that the god lets the streams break forth from the cleft in the rock, and they bring blessings to the earth as rivers.

It cannot be ruled out that the original sense of the myth is attained, and that this has come about as an answer to the question of how human beings could partake of the invaluable good of the rivers.[97] Yet it is possible, indeed, as I mean, to a very great extent probable, that we have here much more to do with an original myth of the storm, that in the pre-Vedic period it were the clouds where the serpent was resting, that *Vajra*, according to its original character, was a weapon of lightning. The Vṛtra-battle is quite similar to the thunder-battle in the continuously recurring, significant pattern of so many mythologies. Indra is quite similar to Donar-Thor of the Teutons, who, one would like to say, is related to him; Indra's *Vajra* being similar to Thor's hammer, the weapon of lightning.[98] It need not be asked what natural phenomenon is incorporated in Vṛtra in this explanation of the myth. Vṛtra is the indispensable vanquished one for the story of a victorious battle—the unavoidable hostile guard of the treasure that is to be captured: the popular motive of a dragon guarding the treasure. It can be easily understood that the powerful significance of the rivers for human existence in the Punjab could appear in the concepts of the narrators of the myths in place of the downpour of rain.[99]

Another ingenious explanation of the myth that has been recently advocated may be considered, as I think, to be less probable.[100] According to it, Vṛtra is a winter or ice-giant who has captivated the rivers—of course, not in the Indian climate, but in the northern home of the myth—and Indra is the Sun-god who frees the rivers from the icy bond. This explanation turns the rivers in the myth into real, earthly rivers. But is this preference not outweighed by the factors which are cited above in favour of the hypothesis of the storm? Where do we find in the mythologies such a distinct interest in the phenomenon of ice melting? Does Indra's appearance suit the appearance of the Sun-god? Given the water-enclosing mountain playing such a great role in the history of the Vṛtra-battle and easily explained as emerging from the idea of clouds in the interpretation as storm, would not the mountain be an idle, unintelligible addition,[101] if indeed there was the freezing and thawing of rivers? It would be of significance for the choice between the two hypotheses, if a supposition[102] can be confirmed, according to which the Avestic demon Apaoša (truly *ap-vurta*) could be equated with **ab-vṛt*(*a*) 'imprisoner of waters' and understood as the Avestic Vṛtra. As Apaoša is overcome, clouds and winds spring up; rain, clouds and hailstorm spread themselves over the land (*Yt.* VIII, 33) in other words, the scene of that imprisoning in the Avesta from which Vṛtra has his name, it would be in air and not on earth.

Perhaps there are also, in the *Ṛgveda* at least, remnants and traces of the old conceptions concerning the storm and the downpour of rain, but the fact should not really be overlooked that accidental embellishments and purely transitory ideas of individual poets could assume and had to assume at many places complete identity with such traces. A singer identifying himself with Indra says: 'I gave the rain to the mortals who respected me.' In connection with the liberation of waters the expression 'celestial waters' is used in a later hymn. It is said that whatever is firm and movable trembles on account of his thunder; he has thrown the thunder onto the jaw of Vṛtra; he has produced the incomparable missile of the heaven. Indra has blown the serpent from the wide surfaces and from the empire of the air, driven it from earth and heaven.[103] The importance of the references to the stormy nature of the Vṛtra battle, which can always lie in such expressions, will not be paid undue attention, if their infrequency is considered and thought of in the gigantic mass of Indra-hymns; for often in the *Ṛgveda* the might and deeds of every god are depicted occasionally in features which are foreign to his particular form.

The speculations of later periods have incidentally found no difficulty in rediscovering the atmospheric character of Indra's dragon battle; for the commentator of the Veda as also for the poets.[104] Indra is now the god who brings storm and rain. But this does not alter the fact that he is for the singers of the *Ṛgveda* the one who cleaved the earthly mountains and liberated the earthly rivers.

Subduing the Paṇis and Recovering the Cows

The recovering of the cows is considered by the Veda besides the liberation of waters as the second great deed of Indra, or a great deed in which Indra, at least, had participated.

It is doubtful whether this was Indra's deed from the beginning. Beside the version referring to this god represented predominantly in the *Ṛgveda*, there is a story which appears to be the second form of the same myth. Trita Āptya, encouraged by Indra fights the three-headed Viśvarūpa (the universe-formed), the son of Tvaṣṭar; he cuts his three heads and 'releases the cows'.[105] 'I brought forth[106] the cows to Trita from the serpent's grasp', says Indra; is this serpent identical with Viśvarūpa, or a variation of this?[107] But the conqueror is obviously more Trita than Indra; Indra must have been brought in connection with him only later on as a recognized performer of all the greatest heroic deeds.[108] The presence of the same myth in the Avesta also speaks for that. Thraetaona of the Āthwya family kills the serpent with its three mouths, three heads and six eyes. But what he libetates are not cows but two beautiful women.[109] The Greek myth of Herakles killing the three-bodied Geryones and carrying away his cattle appears to confirm that the killing of the three-headed monster is originally connected with the liberation of the cows attested to by the Veda though not by the Avesta.[110]

The ancient form of this myth now with the added feature of the three-headed monster opposes another more humanized version in the Veda. This more humanized form is infused with the motive of mundane life, especially of priestly life. This version appears to have predominantly Indian character, though it is not improbable that at least its beginning dates back to the Indo-Iranian period.[111]

The enemies appear here as a whole troop; they are called Paṇis. When in the *Ṛgveda* the designation Paṇi appears to be given often to a figure in real life, one thinks of these Paṇis in the myth: they are of the wealthy class, particularly unpopular with singers and priests, for they are stingy and do not offer appropriate gifts to the priests.[112] The Paṇis, so the myth narrates, possess herds of cows kept hidden by them in a rock-cave far, far away beyond the globe-girding river Rasā. Indra's messenger Saramā, the bitch of the gods, tracks out the crevice in the rock and hears the lowing of the cows. She demands the cows in the name of Indra, but is sent back with contempt by the Paṇis. Now Indra himself comes with Aṅgirās or with the 'seven priests', the ancestors of priestly generations. The cave opens of itself, or Indra opens it for the Aṅgirās, or they themselves burst it open 'through their words', 'through their litanies', 'through their hymns', 'singing', 'with enflamed fire.' The idea is apparent that these first priests and their descendants alike sing and recite at the sacrificial fire and open the closed rock through the magic power of this action. It is also said that they have opened the rock 'through the *Ṛta* (i.e. law);[113] in this holy act and in its effects, the law of the eternal world-order manifests itself. Also, Agni appears here and there as participating in it. This is understandable in that the sacrificial fire is not missing beside the ritual hymns, as referred to earlier: it will be doubly explicable, if the whole myth should refer to the acquisition of light; the kindling of fire is a magical act which causes the rising of the sun. Above all, one more divine person is named as acting beside the priestly fathers, i.e. Bṛhaspati, the 'Lord of prayer' or better the 'Lord of the holy word';[114] his role is not different from that of Aṅgirās. He belongs to their family; he, the personification of the power of the holy word and the sacred hymn, opens the cave 'with fire-inflamed hymns'. He smashes it and drives out the cows as one breaks the egg, and takes out the young bird or as one takes out the marrow from the bone. Vala, the demon of the cave laments for the abducted cows like the woods for the leaves which are stolen from them by winter. In this way the cows, and thereby the abundance of nourishment, are obtained for the people, for the priests: the enclosure of the cows is found 'from where the human generations take their food'; the Aṅgirās have found 'all the food of Paṇi'; Indra as the first one 'has found the cows for the Brāhmaṇas', 'made to the *brahman* the cows easily accessible'. The acquisition of light, the dawn and the sun are, however, closely connected with the recovery of the cows; the verses showing this association are numerous. The priestly fathers 'drive out the cows calling forth the dawn'; 'they found the light'.

The dawn became visible through the shining (milk?) of the cow. The restless darkness disappeared; the heaven shone forth; the light of the goddess Dawn arose; the Sun stepped over the wide fields looking at the righteousness and unrighteousness amongst the mortals.'

When Indra went after the cows with the fathers 'he found the Sun resting in darkness'. The fathers who exploded the rock 'found the Day and the Sun and the light of the Dawn.' 'Through law (*ṛta*), they exploded the stone, breaking it into pieces; the Aṅgirās lowed (i.e. sang) with the cows. The men girded the Dawn for their salvation; the Sun became visible as Agni was born.' Bṛhaspati 'found Dawn, Sun and Fire; with his hymns he dispersed the darknesses.' 'He drove the cows out, cleft asunder the cave with his holy word; he hides the darkness and let the Sun be seen.'[115]

If we now ask about the significance of the story, it appears then that the dominating motives of their Ṛgvedic form emerge clearly at first. The main persons, above all, are the human and divine prototypes of priesthood: the ancestors of priestly generations and the deified ideal priest Bṛhaspati. As against them, there are the prototypes of the enemies of priests, who are not prepared to give offerings, and of the misers who gave nothing to the priests. And between both, there is a battle for just that possession which the Vedic priest expects from the rich and which is held back by Paṇi, namely, the possession of the cows. Thus, the story is an illustration of the theme that the gods will not tolerate, if the wealth of cows is denied to the devotees and the sacrificers. Some of the verses from the *Ṛgveda* do bring out the moral of the story quite clearly.[116] 'The gods lead forward the pious; one who loves the sacred word, is chosen by them like a wooer... Free of malice, one keeps your (Indra's) commandments and prospers; your help to the sacrificer, the pourer of Soma, is immense' says a poet and then narrates, as an example of this divine help, how the Aṅgirās who had kindled the fire, did their duty and then got all possession of Paṇi (I, 83, 2ff.). In another verse, it is said about Indra 'hating him who pours not, prospers him, who pours...He gathers up for plunder all the food of Paṇi; excellent health he gives to him, who offers gift' (V, 34, 6f.).

One may ascribe by all means a remote antiquity[117] to this mythical mirroring of the priestly claims on life. But this does not mean that an explanation of the original, i.e. the Indo-European myth, is found.

It is possible, perhaps probable, that this myth was an answer to the question, how the possession of their herds of cattle was acquired for the human beings.[118] A different idea may become apparent to one who looks at the problem—perhaps all too prejudiced—from the point of view of the Veda. It is known how, in the language of the Veda, the image of red cows for the dawns comes alive. And, in a series of verses, the Vedic poets speak of the Dawn, using expressions which unmistakably remind one of the story of the recovery of cows or refer to it quite explicitly. It is said of the Dawn that it 'has laid open the darkness, as the cows their stalls'. 'You have', says the poet, 'opened the gates of the firm rock', 'she (Dawn) tore the rock (to pieces); she gave the red (cows). The cows lowed as they greeted the Dawn.' 'Dawn, who stands on the mountain ridges, Aṅgirās now praise your stalls of cattle. With prayer and holy hymn they burst it open; the heroes' calling on the Gods was fruitful'.[119] Is it possible to date the motive of the Dawn of the Veda back to the very origin of the myth and construe this as the acquistion of the morning light?[120] It appears here that this can neither be proved nor disproved.

Winning of Light

Winning of light, sun and dawn which is connected with the discovery of cows in the myth discussed above, is also often attributed to Indra, independent of this deed. He has fastened the sun to the firmament, has made him shine; he has established the heavens with his support, extended the ends of the earth. Thus he appears as a performer of deeds and a founder of orders which can also be ascribed to Varuṇa.[121] It cannot be doubted that here we come across a much later group of concepts concerning Indra than in the myth of the wild, indomitable deed of the killing of the dragon. All that can be hardly associated with the natural meaning of the Storm-god insofar as he disentangles the dark chaos surrounding heaven and earth in the storm, and gives back to human beings the view of the sun.[122] Probably, it alone is the all-surpassing power of Indra, or mainly Indra's power, on account of which even these deeds are also attributed to him. Should he not have been the strongest of the strong who has wrested the greatest possessions from the enemies and given them to human beings, and who has placed the most powerful natural phenomena like sun and heaven in their right place?

Indra's Victory Over the Dāsas

The deeds of Indra which have been discussed so far, i.e. the victory over Vṛtra and the liberation of the cows, stand isolated, each in itself an incomparable event. Now follow deeds which form a series of examples of the same type. That hardly any of their individual features have survived is not because of the examples themselves but more so on account of the poet's tendency to be satisfied with making cursory references to the deeds, which were for the most part merely enumerated in the process of composition.

We are concerned here continuously with the conquering of the enemies called Dāsa or Dasyu. These are the common expressions used by the Indian Aryans for the dark aborigines. So, from the very outset, it is obvious that here is an echo of historical events: the triumph over enemies in battles, which stretched the might of the people right up to the days of the hymn-composers, appeared as the deed of the god mighty in battle, whose friendship the Aryans alone knew to get. This is not surprising. For the Vedic poets there was no distinction between mythical and historical events, for which we evince such great interest. For them the earthly opposition of the Aryans with the dark Dāsas extended into the world of gods and demons; the hostile demon stood for them on the same level as the hated and despised savage. He was, perhaps, in many an instance, really none but the god of a wild race. And, in the same way, the impressive figure of a leader of enemies could equip itself with features common to the devils in the myths. And, therefore, we will have to be prepared from the beginning for the uncertainties arising out of demarcation, the clarification of which remains purposeless amidst the nebula enveloping the historical as well as the mythical elements of this observation,[123] and given particularly the slender evidences found in the *Ṛgveda*. But here again the research scholar must adhere to set rules, if he still wants to recognize figures and shapes in the nebula of the *Ṛgveda*: a circumstance whose effect is neutralized at some point in this welter of uncertainties must not be disregarded from analysis without much ado; further characteristics that are mixed up with other conflicting traits cannot be regarded as less authoritative in nature. It is important to delimit the fundamentally valid against the secondary alterations and not to juxtapose opposites indiscriminately.

In this way, we can approach the nature of the type of deeds of Indra, with which we are concerned, in the following discussion despite unavoidable limitations.

There are a number of verses in the *Ṛgveda* where Dāsa (Dasyu) are mentioned as opponents of the Aryans.[124] The Indian warrior, himself Aryan, has to do with his Aryan and Dāsa enemies;[125] he prays: 'Dāsa and Arya we will conquer with your aid' (X, 83, 1). 'The godless man, much-lauded Indra, whether he be Dāsa or Arya, who would war with us. Easy to conquer be for you, with us, these foes; with you may we subdue them in battle' (X,38,3). Mostly, however, there is mention of the Aryans as friends and conquerors, and opposed to them stand the vanquished Dāsa foes. 'You (Indra) have tamed the Dasyus; you alone have wrested the land for the Arya' (VI, 18, 3). 'Discern you well Aryas and Dasyus; punishing the lawless give them upto him whose grass is strewn' (I, 51, 8). And in another verse, the best commentary on the foregoing: 'Indra in battles helped his Aryan worshipper, he who has hundred helps at hand in every fray.... Plaguing the lawless he gave up to Manu's[126] seed the black skin' (I, 130, 8). Thus we get acquainted with the Dāsas as having 'dark skin'; elsewhere it is said of Dāsa-women as 'having the black mother-womb' (II, 20, 7); a further peculiarity of Dāsas is that they are 'noseless' (V, 29, 10), i.e. they are snub-nosed.[127] Further, they are called in a number of poetic expressions as 'godless', 'not serving the gods', 'not sacrificing', 'not praying', and 'not offering'.

It is seen that these Dāsas are enemies of a different type than the serpent Vṛtra or the three-headed monster Viśvarūpa. They are human enemies, of whom is said whatever the pious Aryan above all had to say of those savage people: their skin is black and they do not sacrifice. They are the enemies, of whom the old Indian names of the kings narrate: Trasadasyu meaning the one 'who makes the Dasyus tremble' and Dasyavevṛka means the one 'who is wolf for the Dasyu'.

I feel that with the foregoing an interpretation of the stories of Indra's victories over the individual Dāsas has been given. Even though the mythical elements may have intermingled in them, the foundation is still earthly-human. This is at first confirmed in the following features: whereas Indra kills Vṛtra for the benefit of humanity in general, he recovers the cows of the Paṇis for the good of the priestly archetypes, the Aṅgiras. Further, individuals are specified by name when Dāsas are subdued—in so far as it is not generally said that Indra accomplished this deed for the Aryans; it is said that Indra in compact with them and showing mercy on them has flattened the Dāsas. These individuals' names are not, or not primarily, the names of priests' ancestors found in many other wondrous deeds, but obviously the names of the princes and warriors, partly perhaps, the names of the ideal representatives of the princely generations; besides them also, as they appear, historical names like Dabhīti, Ṛjiśvan, the son of Vidathin, above all Divodāsa Atithigva[128], the father of the famous king Sudās. Even numerous Dāsas are specified by names, some of which can have mythical meaning like Śuṣṇa ('hisser', compare I, 54, 5? or 'scorcher'?); others may appear as harmless as possible, but yet could be the names of savage leaders made easy to pronounce by the Aryans, such as Pipru, Ilībiśa, Śambara and other names.[129] An individual Aryan prince has his definite Dāsa enemy, sometimes several such enemies.[130] The Aryans also fight amongst themselves, as we have already mentioned. Evidence of feuds manifests itself, when the same tribe or king is described by some hymn-composers as friendly with Indra and victorious and by others as hostile to Indra, and therefore, overthrown by him. And in the same tone, in the same context of the Aryans at feud with one another, there is talk of the battles against the Dāsas.[131] It is clear that, whether here or there, we are on the same historical ground. What we otherwise hear in detail about the deeds Indra has accomplished in compact with the Aryans against the Dāsa-chiefs fits graphically into a picture of earthly-human events. The Aryan leader or priest invokes Indra before the battle: 'The lauds of Gaurivīti made you (Indra) mighty. To Vidathin's son, as prey, you gave Pipru. Ṛjiśvan[132] drew you into friendship, dressing the sacred food, and you have drunk his *Soma*.'

Śambara

The mountain plays a role in the battles with one of the Dāsas, i.e. Śambara who lives in it. Indra has 'found Śambara living in the mountain in the fortieth autumn'. 'You, Indra, also smote down Kulitara's son Śambara, the Dāsa from the lofty hill.' 'Smote down the Dāsa Śambara from the mountain and blessed Divodāsa with shining blessings.'[133] But the fortresses of the Dāsas which are smashed by Indra and his human companions are particularly mentioned very often. And they are the objects of the battle for which the Aryans and the Dāsas fight, and they correspond differently to historical truth than the rivers of Vṛtra or the cows of the Dawns. Often a fabulous number of such fortresses are named: an embellishment of pious eulogy which, however, does not make the real character of these events doubtful, at least in their essence. 'You smote to the ground the hundred fortresses, impregnable, of Śambara, the Dasyu, when strong with might you helped Divodāsa, the *Soma*-presser, to get treasures, and modest Bharadvāja rich, who praised you.' 'Indra and Viṣṇu, you have smitten the firm fortresses of Śambara, nine and ninety; hundred men and thousand Varcins of Asura,[134] you have killed without a fight.' 'You, O hero-hearted, have broken down Pipru's forts, and Ṛjiśvan when the *Dasyus* were struck down.'[135]

Cumuri and Dhuni

In the case of two Dāsas named regularly together, Cumuri and Dhuni, there is a constant feature that Indra has lulled them into sleep; it must have been a nocturnal attack in which their conqueror Dabhīti succeeded. 'You, with sleep-whelming Cumuri and Dhuni, slew the Dasyu, kept safe Dabhīti. There the staff-bearer found the golden treasure. These things did Indra in Soma's rapture' (II, 15, 9). 'This Indra, was your work in war: you sent Dhuni and Cumuri to sleep and slumber. Dabhīti lit the flame for you, and worshipped with fuel, hymns, poured Soma, dressed oblations' (VI, 20, 13).

Kutsa and Śuṣṇa

Śuṣṇa,[136] one of the Dāsas subdued by Indra, has a strong mythical tinge. But here also I consider it probable that ultimately there are at bottom historical events, which are embellished with supernatural trimmings. Śuṣṇa's opponent and conqueror is Kutsa. In order to help him, Indra has strengthened himself with the potions of the magician Uśanā and got a weapon wrought by him. He has done a wonder relating to the sun in favour of Kutsa. I shall mention here some of the verses which refer to this battle: 'You (Indra) saved Kutsa when Śuṣṇa was smitten down; to Atithigva gave Śambara for a prey. E'en mighty Arbuda you trod under foot: you, since time immemorial, were born to strike the Dasyus dead' (I, 51, 6). Indra stands with Kutsa on the same chariot as Kutsa's pulled by the steeds of the wind like Kutsa himself. Therefore, Indra is addressed in a verse which appears to depict the god returning home together with his human friend as under: 'Come to our home resolved to slay Dasyu. Kutsa longed eagerly to win your friendship. Alike in form ye both sat in his dwelling. May the lady, who knows right, exert herself to know you apart' (IV, 16, 10). Another verse (12) of the same hymn speaks of the battle which they have fought together: 'For Kutsa you as day proceeded(?) did hurl down Śuṣṇa with Kuyava and the thousands. Quickly destroyed the Dasyus with Kutsya;[137] Roll the chariot-wheel of the Sun in the decisive moment.' Then one more verse which praises the proof of Indra's might 'when for the sake of those oppressed, and Kutsa, the warrior, you stole away the Sun's chariot-wheel' (IV, 30, 4).[138] 'You took out one wheel of the Sun, and the other you got for Kutsa to let him go. You slew noseless (mouthless?) Dasyus with your weapon, and in their home overthrew hostile speakers' (V, 29, 10).

Without disregarding the uncertainty present in the explanation of these verses, I think, as already pointed out, that the nucleus of the legendary elements lies in the historical events. It does not necessarily mean that an individual real occurrence was woven into this story, but that the total character of various occurrences could have given the material from which an ideal form was created and embellished with divine miracles. The hero Kutsa, son of Arjuna, is, maybe historically or ideally, the ancestor of a Kutsa family, that he—quite like Divodāsa Atithigva named often together with him—appears[139] at places as an enemy overcome by Indra, strengthens the impression of historical reality. A hero of Light has to be a friend of the singer, and a demon of Darkness, his enemy. One who is a friend here and an enemy there, will be—like Divodāsa Atithigva—a man or an ideal representative of a group of people, who are friendly to the singers and hostile to the others. Kutsa fights with Dāsas, whose real leader or again their ideal representative is Śuṣṇa. At first Kutsa is crowded by the enemies. Perhaps, the result will depend upon the day lasting sufficiently long. As the darkness threatens[140] to break out, Indra pulls out one wheel of the chariot of the Sun, and thereby arrests him. The second wheel—perhaps, the fantasy of an individual poet has extended the story—is given to Kutsa who goes with that to victory; Śuṣṇa succumbs. The myth of Indra who obtains the sun for humanity may have influenced the story; but it is not identical with that. Here the miracle performed with the sun is only an adornment to the picture of historical or semi-historical fights.[141]

Namuci

Another Dāsa is Namuci: Indra conquers him in favour of Namī Sāpya while twisting off his head with a weapon of foam. It is a hopeless endeavour to find out the natural significance of this feature;[142] it serves no purpose to ask whence the story of carousal associated with Namuci originates: the Aśvins help Indra tormented by crapulence, in that they extract 'from Namuci' or out of his body[143] a mixed drink, consisting, so it appears, of a divine and a profane intoxicant, *Soma* and *Sūra* respectively; and further in that they demix it through 'segregating drinking' and thereby, with the active help of Sarasvatī, bring about a cure.

In a story like this, we see the original human and historical type of Dāsa disappearing in the nebula of a myth or a fairy-tale. And when the serpent whom Indra robs of waters, or the six-eyed, three-headed monster fought by Trita, or Vyaṃsa, the demon, who strikes down both the jaw bones of Indra, when that is called Dāsa,[144] then these are further features indicating the infusion of the Dāsa-type with the demoniac nature. But the facts of this type do not upset the view that fundamentally reminiscence of historical facts, even if idealized or embellished with supernatural features, survives in the stories of the victories over the Dasyus.

The Asuras[145]

Some verses attribute the name 'Asura' or 'Asura's son' to the Dāsas conquered by Indra. This word Asura, which denotes in the later Vedic language almost exclusively a being hostile to gods, appears moreover in the older texts, in fact, predominantly, as an epithet of gods. Thus, even amongst the Iranians, the same word appears in the form of Ahura as the name of the highest god. How is this change to be explained, which appears to have turned the meaning 'god' into the meaning 'devil'?

One would like to date back the destiny of the word Asura to a clash of the Vedic Indians with the followers of another belief. It is said that the Iranians became enemies of the Vedic cult with their worship of Asura, and so their gods were treated by the cult as devils. I do not think that this hypothesis is based on concrete evidences in the tradition.[146] The evidence before us points out very clearly in another direction. If the old use of the word Asura for gods which began to fade away later, as we have mentioned, is examined from close quarters, then it can be seen that it is not used for all gods with the same preference; it may be far from the opposite of the word *deva*, yet by no means synonymous with the word *deva*. Much rather, it is the distinction between the gods which helps one to arrive at a definite shade of meaning of the word Asura. And this nuance turns out to be exactly such that it explains the clash of the gods with the hostile beings through common names. The name Asura, as it may be seen, is attributed amongst the gods preferably to those about whose *māyā*, i.e. mysterious supernatural power, there is talk. But precisely *māyā* is as well a characteristic quality of bad enemies, they may be then of human or demoniac nature. With reference to the gods, the name Asura is used in the case of Varuṇa or the pair Mitra-Varuṇa very often in sharp contrast to Indra or Agni.[147] In fact, it is Varuṇa or Mitra-Varuṇa alone amongst the gods about whose *māyā* there is often talk. Here the *māyā* has the character of a great might manifesting itself splendidly in the miracles of the universe, but in itself indifferent with reference to the contradiction between the noble skills and the inferior arts.[148] But not less often the same word is used for the malicious tricks of hostile beings,[149] and this second aspect of its use coincides exactly with the second area where we come across the word Asura. The relationship made probable by the similar connotations of the words *asura* and *māyā* is confirmed in the most appropriate manner by the close links between the two ideas in a series of verses, and, in fact, in like manner, in such verses that refer to divine and hostile Asuras. Thus, it is said: 'I shall declare the great *māyā* of the famous Asurian Varuṇa, who standing in the firmament has meted the earth out with the sun as with the measure' (V, 85, 5). Mitra and Varuṇa send rain 'with the *māyā* of Asura'; they preserve the laws of the world-order 'with the *māyā* of Asura' (V, 63, 3.7; compare X, 177, 1). On the other hand, of an evil foe, 'Indra overthrew the forts of Pipru, of Asura rich in *māyā*' (X, 138, 3).[150]

We see from this that the word Asura, where it is used for gods, does not simply have the meaning of 'god' or 'lord'; rather, it must have meant for the consciousness of the Vedic poets[151] something like the 'owner of a secret power'.[152] And as the secret power in the form of cheap, malicious cunning belongs also to evil beings, the word could have been used from the beginning with reference to these, and, in fact, has been used thus.[153] Therefore, the inimically coloured connotation to which one would have liked to trace back the word through historical events, such as the contact with the Iranians, is contained in reality, according to the potency of the word, in its oldest meaning which we can reach, and it is fused with the other use of the word. But the change undergone consists in the word remaining in use only for the evil beings and in the gradual withdrawal of its use for the gods. This may be due to the progressive systematization which classified the enemies of gods into an uniform and compact group opposed to gods and requiring naturally a name. Also the popular etymology with its explanation of Asuras as enemies of the Sun may have easily made its influence felt.[154]

It cannot be ascertained with definiteness that the idea of a separate class of demoniac beings has been associated with the name Asuras where they appear from the very beginning itself, enemies conquered by Indra or the other gods.[155] If Agni or Indra is called killer of Asura, it is sufficient to understand that he has killed an enemy gifted in supernatural magical powers; these enemies could be as well Dasyus—thus Pipru and Vercin are shown as Asuras—as also demons: thus Svarbhānu who eclipsed the Sun. The idea of the battles and the victories of the individual gods over the individual Asuras has been further developed, as far as I can see, in the later hymns of the *Ṛgveda* than the ones of the older period. In the latter, it is still a strange confrontation of the two large hostile camps of the armies of the good, the friendly and the divine on the one hand, and of the evil, the hostile and the Asuric,[156] on the other. Agni, put up by the gods as their sacrificial priest, seeks the magical word 'through which we Gods may quell the Asuras' (X, 82, 5). Another verse narrates, how the 'Gods came, after they had slaughtered the Asuras, keeping safe their godlike nature' (X, 157, 4). A speculative hymn concerned with the beginnings of existence speaks of 'what is there beyond the Gods and the Asuras' (X, 85, 5). There is mention of the rivalries between the Gods and the Asuras in detail in one of the narrative hymns. The Asuras appear therein to be considered as the rulers of the world in the age which preceded the age of the supreme power of the gods.[157] Agni, who had stayed for a long time in dark concealment, goes over 'from the non-God' into the camp of the gods 'from the side not worthy of sacrifice to the participation in sacrifice'. He renounces 'Father Asura' and thus the Asuras lose their magic power (*māyā*); Indra kills Vṛtra, and the supremacy of gods is resolved.

Historical Events

As in the victories over the Dasyus, the historical events appear also in the other verses of the hymns on Indra; for instance, when Indra is praised as the one who led Turuvaśa and Yadu. These are the eponymous ancestors of two closely interrelated Aryan families who find favourable and at times unfavourable mention—the clearest sign of historical reality.[159] Indra led Turvaśa and Yadu from a distance and enabled them to cross the rivers. 'So sapient Indra, Lord of Might, brought Turvaśa and Yadu, though they could not swim, in safety over' (IV, 30, 17). The Lord of all battles is also the patron of the wayfarers, who moved at that time through the land rich in streams. The battles of the king Sudās reach back well into historical times; Indra has given him victory and let his enemies die in the floods, upon the prayer of his priests, the Tṛtsu, amongst whom the very famous Vasiṣṭha appears[160] to have stood at the head with his relatives (priests). 'As to their goal, to Paruṣṇī, they sped to their destruction; even the swift returned not... Indra at once with conquering might demolished all their strong places and their seven castles' (VII, 18, 9.13). It is seen how the idiom characteristic for the subduing of the Dasyus—castles demolished by Indra—appears here in connection with the undoubtedly historical battles. 'So verily with these (Vasiṣṭhas)', it is said with reference to these and related battles, 'Indra crossed the river, in company of these he slaughtered Bheda; so in the fight with the ten kings, Vasiṣṭhas, did Indra help Sudās through your devotion' (VII, 33, 3). The warriors then addressed their prayer anew to him, the leader of victories in the battles and the one who guides the battles on his chariot drawn by two dun-coloured horses, *Vajra* at hand. It is he 'who is invoked by the valiant men of war and by cowards, by those who conquer and by those who flee' (I, 106, 6). 'Him, verily, the men invoke in combat; in the battle of life and death, they make him the protector' (IV, 24, 3). 'Even with the few', one says to him, 'you kill the enemy strong in number, who is stronger, with your strength, the Mighty, with the friends you have' (IV, 32, 3). I close this compilation with the first verse of a battle-hymn (X, 103) which is sung, according to a later liturgical text,[161] by the majestic high-priest while looking at the king marching into the battle: 'Swift, rapidly striking, like a bull who sharpens his horns, terrific, stirring up the people, with eyes that close not, bellowing, Sole Hero, Indra subdued at once a hundred armies.'

Other Myths and Stories of Indra

Of course, many other myths and stories are attributed to Indra as the most active of the gods. No doubt, only to a small degree, they are associated with the original natural meaning of Indra: lores of various kinds in which a performer of powerful deeds appeared, have been lured out of the sphere of myths concerning Indra.

Indra is the vanquisher of the goddess Uṣas (the Dawn).

You, Indra, Mighty One, did crush Uṣas, daughter of the Sky, when lifting up herself in pride. Then from her chariot Uṣas fled, affrighted, when the Bull (Indra) shattered it. So there this chariot of Uṣas lay, broken to pieces in Vipāś; and she herself fled away (IV, 30, 9-11).

Is here originally a reference to a morning storm, when the flashing god scared away the dawn from the sky? Or did the myth refer once to the fading of the dawn before the over-powerful Sun-god, and the Sun-god in turn being displaced by Indra as the most famous divine victor?

Indra is in conflict with the Sun-god himself in the story of Kutsa, Śuṣṇa and Etaśa. We have referred to it above.

Carousals and Amorous Adventures

It is obvious that carousals and amorous adventures of all sorts have been invented for Indra or transferred to him. Honest astonishment at the mighty reveller, who is, incidentally also a mighty glutton,[162] does not remain without a touch of humour. Friend Agni roasted for the friend Indra three hundred buffaloes, and, in addition, 'Indra drank off at once three lakes of pressed *Soma* of Manu for the slaughter of Vṛtra' (V, 29, 7). But not that every intoxication did good to the carouser: that is shown by the story of Namuci. To one more drinking adventure refers perhaps[163] the half-line: 'The stirring draughts of juice outpoured have made you glad; you Thunderer, have rejoiced with Pūṣan and your spouse' (I, 82, 6). The amorous adventures of Indra in the Veda recede to the background when compared to his carousals. But they have also left their traces. Thus, Indra is invoked in one of the old litanies as 'the consort of Ahalyā, Brāhmaṇa of the Kauśika family, who calls himself

Gautama'; the story is preserved in the Rāmāyaṇa as to how Indra approached Ahalyā in the form of her husband.[164] The oldest period certainly possessed sufficient lores of this type, as we come across them several times in the later texts.[165] Those stories cannot be easily explained away as nature-myths. Do they need an explanation at all? How could the gods have missed the experiences which were natural for human beings?

Indra and Vṛṣākapi[166]

At the end, we may mention one more work in which an episode from Indra's home life is described with uncouth humour. It does not appear to deal here with any widely circulated legend, but with the high-spirited inventions of an individual poet of the later *Ṛgveda* period: it is possible—the final verse could point out to that—that human personalities are ridiculed in the name of the Divine Couple. Unfortunately, the context is not very clear, for we possess only the verses which were in the form of questions and answers and probably enclosed in a prose text. There is a quarrel about Indra's pet animal, his ape Vṛṣākapi (bull-ape), between Indra and his wife.[167] The useless animal has damaged some of the wife's things. She scolds:

Your dear Vṛṣākapi, whom you protect, Indra, should be pinched at the ear by the dog, the chaser of the boar[168]...I shall give him one on the head. The naughty should not escape me unhurt.

But cunning is necessary to catch the cautious animal expecting the worst. The goddess poses as if to stir his love; in very concrete expressions which, however, cannot be reproduced here, she praises to him her charms. He falls in the trap: 'He, ho, you lovable woman! What may happen now—the posterior, leg and head, they are already itching for that!' But his confidence serves him badly. No sooner had he made himself sure than did she attack him. And at the same moment—the clever wife of the god must have arranged it thus—the consort appears in his own divine person. Now all the pleasing words do not help the ape to get away; in the end he must be happy that he escapes, badly beaten. Thus Indra lost his dear Vṛṣākapi and always feels this as more sorrowful. 'Wife, since my friend Vṛṣākapi has gone, nothing gives me pleasure. How nice it was when his watery sacrificial meal came to the gods!' How the story proceeds is still more uncertain than the beginning. Verses full of uncouth obscenity appear to have been exchanged between Indra and the wife of Vṛṣākapi when he visits her and when she entertains the god who takes pleasure in eating. Perhaps there is a suggestion, given on this occasion, by which one may understand that Indra's manly power is at the moment not at its fullest height. But the fugitive Vṛṣākapi can give advice in the matter. He appears to be living alone now in wilderness; he has found there the things which are necessary for curing the god's weakness. Under these circumstances one cannot be angry with him any longer. Even Indrāṇī reconciles: 'Come again Vṛṣākapi; let us make peace.' Thus everything ends in happiness and friendship.

Character of Indra

Our survey of the main Indra-legends concludes with the farce of the useless ape and the obscene stories linking Indra and Indrāṇī. Let us now summarize the image of the Vedic Indra in a few words. He is the greatest of the great, the strongest of the strong like the bull; he is passionate, good-natured, when in the mood, inexhaustibly generous, a carouser and a meddler, noisy; he whirls up the dust, smashing all to bits. He is a friend to his friends, and an enemy to his enemies: the friend above all of the great and the mighty, so long as they give him offerings freely. Indra is not the master, also not the servant of a vast world-plan or of the eternal law;[169] just as little is he an educator of humanity in the fields of order, custom and art. Yet, it is his strong arm that has brought for humanity the highest things: the fertile water, the light, the abundance of food from the cows. He is invoked for valour and victory; he is the central point of the cult performed at the holy fires of the master-priests of sacrifice. We meet Indra also often enough in the minor cult of the daily life, in the actions performed for the prosperity of the house and posterity, of the herds and fields. How else could it be different? But Indra-worship does not have its proper home here. Its element is war and glory of victory and the *Soma*-intoxication of splendid sacrifices with the groups of praying, singing and bustling priests, with rich sacrificial reward of horses and chariots, of herds and gold.

Soma, the Drink of the Gods[170]

The drink that inspired Indra to his deeds was the juice of the *Soma*-plant. The idea of an intoxicating drink of gods appears to date back to the Indo-European period. The drink which proves to be a mysterious, ecstatically stimulating force in man, has to be of divine nature and the special possession of gods: *Soma* of the Red Indians is also called the 'holy shrub', i.e. tobacco, through which they put themselves in the condition of supernatural excitement; even the gods smoke in order to share the same excitement. Heaven appears to have been the home of the divine drink even in Indo-European belief; already at that time, one was accustomed to consider the heaven as the real seat of divine beings, as is shown by the name of gods as the 'heavenly' (*deivo*). The bird of the god or the god himself in the form of the bird fetches the drink from its heavenly place of preservation, or steals it from the enviously protecting demon: the eagle of Indra, the eagle of Zeus, who brought nectar, or Odin who carried away the mead in the form of the eagle. Perhaps —one can make here naturally only suppositions—even before the separation of the peoples, the drink of the gods had been particularly the drink of a god, the great divine drinker and the drunkard, the Thunderer. It may perhaps finally be taken for granted that the idea of the immortality of gods was connected, for the Indo-Europeans, with the drink of the gods (*Amṛta, Ambrosia*). Just as human life is preserved by eating and drinking, particularly by drinking medicines which overcome death at least for the nonce, the existence of the gods depended on the enjoyment of a drink, whose essence is immortality.

The view that gods imbibe the celestial drink, and the story of the acquisition of this drink can be hardly regarded as a nature-myth; or the view that some events taking place in heaven had given a decisive cause for the development of these ideas. On the other hand, the starting point was the intoxicating drink found on earth. Its mysterious qualities made one see in it the drink of the gods. And this celestial drink, which naturally could be brought by no other creature than the bird soaring heavenwards—obviously the strongest and the fastest of birds—came into contact with a very effective characteristic of all mythology, namely, the habit of considering all the highest possessions as having been snatched away from a vigilant enemy. There is no cause for us to suspect the presence of a definite natural being in this enemy or in the stealthy bird.[171]

That does not, however, mean that this sphere of ideas could not have acquired firmer substance, even though occurrences in nature which one held to be associated with a concrete, intoxicating substance. It is possible that there was a honey-mead with the Indo-Europeans which could intoxicate them and to which was attributed the status of the drink of the gods. Thus, the assumption gains currency that the widespread ideas of celestial origin of honey or honey-dew[172] must have exerted influence on the myth of the gods' drink. And further, it cannot be denied that also the moon, the donor of celestial dew[173] that appears[174] to be drunk by the divine beings when she wanes, was considered in very ancient times the seat or the essence of that heavenly substance.[175]

If we proceed from the unstable ground of assumptions about the beliefs of the Indo-Europeans to the consideration of the Indo-Iranian period, then we are confronted with the fact that the juice pressed from the *Soma*-plant had replaced the honey-mead. The pressing and the offering of this drink, systematized and glorified in the complicated rites, has become one of the most excellent, indeed the most excellent celebration of the superior cult. Beside the old mythical celestial home of the gods' drink,[176] there appears now its second real home: the *Soma*-plant grows on the mountains. The Avestic poet praises the clouds and the rains which enable the *Soma* to grow on the peaks of the mountains. A skilful god has fashioned it and put it down on the big mountain Haratī; the birds marked with sacred signs have carried it far and wide. However, the sacrificial drink charged with demoniac power is now further turned into—just like the sacrificial fire—a powerful god: this is the typical characteristic of the priests' art of sacrifice found even in the Indo-Iranian age. The similarities in detail point back to this period, for instance, how the Veda and the Avesta, in complete accord, celebrate the good deeds of this kind god: he gives swift horses and excellent children; he, the king of plants, gives medicines and extripates death and all the evil tormentors.[177]

This is the prehistory of the Vedic *Soma* in its basic features. We shall now turn to the Veda itself.

Soma in the Heaven and on the Mountain

Both the spheres of ideas of the old Indo-European celestial drink and of the later Indo-Iranian *Soma* of the mountain meet one another here quite clearly. In a series of verses, the mountain appears to be the home of *Soma*. It is said of the world-ruler Varuṇa: 'In the tree-tops the air he has extended, milk in cows and vigorous speed in horses, set intellect in hearts, fire in the waters, sun in the sky and *Soma* on the rock' (V, 85, 2). And in the hymn addressed to the two divine patrons of sacrifice, Agni and *Soma*: 'One of you (i.e. Agni) Mātariśvan brought from heaven,[178] the eagle stole the other from the rock' (I, 93, 6). But as surely as here, the mountain, emphatically distinguished from the heaven in accordance with reality, is considered the home of *Soma*. Other verses call the heaven his home. 'Fleet as thought, he storms in and pierces the iron fortress; the beautifully winged bird brought the Soma to the Vajra-wielder flying to heaven' (VIII, 100, 8). 'Bearing the stalk, the eagle speeding onward, bird bringing from afar the drink that gladdens, friend of the gods, brought, grasping fast, the *Soma* which he had taken from those loftiest heavens' (IV, 26, 6).

Fetching of Soma

Spirited verses describe the feat of the bird:

Before all birds be ranked this bird, O Maruts;[179] supreme of eagles be this fleet, winged eagle, because strong-pinioned, with no chariot to bear him, he brought to the man the god-loved oblation.
When the bird brought it, hence in rapid motion sent on the wide path, fleet as thought he hurried. Swift he returned with sweetness of *Soma*, and hence the eagle has acquired his glory (IV, 26, 4. 5).

Another hymn closely connected with the previous one (IV, 27) lets the eagle speak for himself: 'As I lay within the womb, considered all generations of these gods in order. A hundred iron fortresses confined me, but forth I flew with rapid speed of an eagle.'[180]

Now speaks *Soma*: 'Not at his own free pleasure did he bear me. Superior was he in vigour and strength. Swiftly(?) left the Bountiful[181] the envious evil spirits and passed the winds with his might.'

The narrator continues

When with loud cry from heaven down sped the eagle, then hastening like the wind he (?) or they (the gods?) bore[182] the Bountiful, then wildly raging in his mind, the archer Kṛśānu aimed and loosened the string to strike him.[183]
The eagle bore him from heaven's lofty summit like (the Aśvins) from the ocean[184] bore Bhujyu. Then downward hither fell a flying feather of the bird hastening forward his journey.

Now *Soma* reaches the mortals, and they press it for Indra: 'The white beaker, filled with cow-drink, the foaming shining liquid; the first of sweet mead which the priests have offered: that Indra to his joy may drink, the Hero, that he may take and drink it to his rapture.'

Thus far about the bringing of Soma to earth.

Divine Personality of Soma

The divine personality that is attributed to *Soma* recedes remarkably behind, say, that of Indra and Varuṇa, in the free development of the being similar to the human beings. The tangible presence of god at the sacrificial place in the form of the *Soma*-plant and the *Soma*-drink puts a limit to the strikingly vivid fantasy. The poets laud the wisdom and the luminous majesty of *Soma*, but they do not speak of his human-like form or deed. Wherever there is mention of heroic or miraculous deeds, one attributes the inspiring feats of Indra to his intoxicating draught; or they are those colourless deeds which are almost common to all the gods; he has stretched the bounds of the earth, held the firmament aloft. One praises him, saying that he has given joy to men and strengthened them: 'We have drunk *Soma* and become immortal; we have attained the light the gods discovered. Now what may enemy's malice do to harm us? What O Immortal, mortal man's deception?' (VIII, 48, 3). And countless times one thinks of *Soma* completely as the one who befriends and inspires the gods, also as the one filled with whose might Indra performs his tremendous deeds. But *Soma* is invoked almost exclusively in those hymns 'to those who are pruifying themselves', in the magic hymns which are sung to the drink that is filtering through the sieve of the world. There one praises *Soma* who discharges, plunging like mighty buffaloes, into the forest of wooden vats and settling down in it like the birds among the woods. Hastening across the track like race-horses longing for fame, running like the streams into the depths, pouring themselves down upon the earth like the floods of rain, they hasten to Indra. *Soma* attires himself in the clothes of the cow, i.e. the milk that is mixed with him; he wraps himself with the effulgence of the sun and lets the sun shine through his might. The singers sing beautifully embellished hymns to him as the mother-cows low to their calves. A formless maze of images and mystical phantasma. How different from the poetry which Greece had dedicated to the Dionysian intoxicating drink and its god! Here the hollowness of the solemnly pious magic intoxication surrounded by the ritual aura of mystery, and there the irresistible, serene redemption of all depths of the soul inspired by god and wine.

Soma and the Moon

Finally, we must go back to an idea mentioned earlier and whose positive proof is found first in the later parts of the *Ṛgveda:* the identification of *Soma* with the Moon.[185] It is already mentioned above that such an idea about the celestial place for the drink of the gods *may* have been ancient. In the main contents of the Ṛgvedic hymns, its traces appear either to be completely absent or to be of secondary importance.[186] Among the countless speculations of fantasy crowding around the idea of a deified drink in the *Soma* hymns, are a few which *can* be interpreted as the embodiment of *Soma* in the Moon. But this interpretation is just *possible* each time and, therefore, quite unlikely. I believe rather that it has to do really with connexions of another sort. *Soma* is very often connected with the concepts of heaven, light and sun. He causes the sun to rise, he shines like the sun, purifies himself in the heaven, looks down from the heaven, wards off the darkness through his light. Where, there is a reference to a definite light of heaven in addition to the general sphere of concept of Light and Heaven, then it is the sun to which *Soma* is brought in a mystical relationship. This relationship is mainly based upon the fact that this god is like Indra or Agni also a champion of light against darkness: but the highest expression of light is the Sun. And *Soma* has participated in Indra's mighty deed, the winning of the sun, in which he inspired Indra. Where, however, this relationship to the Sun, or the oft-mentioned ancient concept of the celestial home of gods' drink was expressed in uncertain generalities—as this has often happened in the Veda—phrases could easily arise which make the interpretation in terms of the other great carriers of light possible. One has, of course, to observe these phrases, taking into account the equation *Soma*-Moon appearing in the later belief.

However, as already mentioned, this equation is quite explicit in a few of the later hymns of the *Ṛgveda*. Thus above all in the great marriage-hymn (X, 85) in which *Soma* appears as the husband of the Sun-maiden or the daughter of the Sun:

Soma holds his place in heaven...in the midst of constellations has Soma his place. One thinks, when they have brayed the plant, that he has drunk the *Soma:* Of him whom Brahmanas truly know as *Soma* no one ever tastes...When they begin to drink you, then O God, you swell out again. Vāyu is *Soma's* guardian. The moons are those which shape the years.

One sees that the idea of the *Soma*-nature of the moon is expressed here as a mystery to which only the Brāhmaṇas are privy. Has the idea been revived from oblivion? Or is it new? A definite decision appears to be impossible. But the motives which make it comprehensible can be found. There was already talk of such motives, insofar as they may have a bearing upon the drink of the Indo-European gods.[187] It may be here that *Soma,* as we saw, is a heavenly and luminous being fighting the darkness like the moon. The moon waxes and wanes again. So, the ritual knows the 'waxing' of the *Soma*-plant parallel to the 'waxing' of the moon, when the half-pressed stalks are moistened afresh. The moon furthers the growth of plants, is the master and patron-saint of the plant kingdom; but the king of all plants, as the most excellent and holy plant, is *Soma*. The reddish, bright and fiery drop of *Soma* flows into the water, as the bright, fiery drop of light of the moon swims in the waters of the clouds.[188] So, it is comprehensible that moon could appear as *Soma* resting in the heights of the heaven—an idea having the greatest amount of success with the teachers of the ritual and with the poets of India. But that should not misguide us to assess its importance wrongly for the

Ṛgveda. If this idea is at all touched upon, it absolutely does not have the significance of explaining the *Soma*-cult and the *Soma*-poetry, in that it reveals it as the Moon-cult and the Moon-poetry. But the cult and the poetry are valid for the holy and miraculously powerful intoxicating drink. However, in the play of fantasy around this phenomenon, there appears also the Moon-motif as one among many others and having modest validity.

VARUṆA, MITRA AND THE ĀDITYAS

Circle of Ādityas

We now come to a circle of gods, which is as much firmly connected within itself as it stands out sharply from the rest of the deities. In the case of these gods, neither the positive deeds of Indra nor the enormous catastrophes of world-life caused thereby stand in the foreground. Rather, it is the great even character of their existence and of their constant activity: whereby the idea is not absent that the laws within which and according to which they rule are also laid down by them. Two great gods, Mitra-Varuṇa, closely connected with each other, are at the top of the Ādityas, one of them being Varuṇa who is the greatest of all. The total number of the Ādityas according to the oldest concept, is quite probably seven,[189] but the *Ṛgveda* does not count anywhere the seven names. When it is, in any case, possible to combine the series of names found at various places into a list of seven, the fact that one is forced to follow this procedure is characteristic of the uncertainty informing the individuality of the less important of the Ādityas. This impression is further strengthened by the superficially allegorical character of a few of these names like Aṃsa (portion) and Dakṣa (competence).[190] In fact, we scarcely hear anything about many of these gods; they have a collective character repeating only those features attributed to Varuṇa and Mitra on a larger scale. To all appearances, their number seven does not rest upon the fact that just seven of the individual divine personalities present were considered to be Ādityas but upon the fact that this number formed a fixed framework which was filled up by fitting individual gods into it; or, one could even say that scarcely an attempt was made to fill it up.

Character and Physical Attributes of the Ādityas

The character of Varuṇa and, in fact, of the Ādityas in general is summed up in the idea of a celestial kingdom which rules over all the world-order and whose physical appearance possesses the attributes of the highest light, particularly of sunlight. 'Luminous magnificance', it is said once succinctly and significantly (I, 136, 3). The title 'king' (*rājan*) or 'prince' (*kṣatriya*), though not exclusivẹly attributed to these gods, is conferred on them more often than on the other gods; there is mostly talk of princeliness, beautiful princeliness and most sublime princeliness in their case.[191] We shall soon speak in detail of their special relationship to the *Ṛta*, the physical and the moral world-order. The nature of these gods stands out perhaps most clearly, when we put them beside Indra. One thinks one can discern here the gods of a higher civilized world beside a god of the barbarians. There a most valorous hero, who has something of a divine brawler in him; the most inscrutable carouser, but not without humoristic tinge. Here, the serene radiant sublimity of a sacred kingdom which punishes the sins and preserves the order of the cosmos. 'The one kills the enemies in battles; the other always protects the order', says a poet of Indra and Varuṇa.[192]

Yet, we have to dwell on the physical attributes of these gods. They can be generally summarized in the words: Heaven—Light—Sun.[193] Mitra and Varuṇa look at the world from distant heavens. They mount their chariot in the highest heavens. They climb their throne at the flash of the dawn, at the rising of the sun. The sun is the eye of Varuṇa or the eye of Mitra and Varuṇa. 'The big eye of the both, Mitra and Varuṇa, opens, the lovely, the infallible.' 'Hail to the eye of Mitra and Varuṇa .. visible everywhere, the lustre born of gods, hail to the son of the heaven, singing to the sun.' Mitra and Varuṇa make the sun climb up in the sky; Varuṇa has opened the paths for him; there is often talk of the sunrise in the hymns praising the Ādityas.[194] Indeed, the sun is called Āditya in the *Ṛgveda* itself as it is done in the later literature.[195] It appears that once,[196] when both the white (eyes, servants?) of Varuṇa looking far and wide are understood as the sun and the moon, there is talk of the moon and the stars as if obeying the command of Varuṇa in the verse; 'Whither by day depart those bears[197] that shine at night, set high above there. Infallible are Varuṇa's laws. And through the night, the moon moves on in splendour.'

Besides this undiscriminating connection made out by most of the texts between Varuṇa, Mitra and even the Ādityas, on the one hand, and the Light and the Sun, on the other, there are evidences of another view which fixes a limit between the kingdom of Mitra and the kingdom of Varuṇa. Mitra rules over the day and the sun, Varuṇa over the night.

In fact, the only hymn of the *Ṛgveda*,[198] addressed to Mitra, is full of general expressions without any evidence of concrete features which hint at such a distinction.[199] But we read in the *Atharvaveda* (XIII, 3, 13), unfortunately, and we cannot conceal it—amidst a maze of old mythological fragments and modern speculations the following expression made with reference to the highest god living in all beings: 'In the evening, he will be Varuṇa, Agni; in the morning, he will be Mitra rising.' That is, the god identifies himself in the evening with the nightly carrier of light, Agni, at the same time with Varuṇa, whom we have come to know here and in the other verses to be discussed below, as the ruler of the night; but then, in the morning, how can the being on the ascendant called Mitra be other than the sun? I do not know of any verse from the Veda in which Mitra's identification with the sun appears to be so definite as here. There are many expressions which distinguish the rôle of Varuṇa and Mitra, simply according to the antithesis between night and day' or night and morning. Thus, in the *Atharvaveda* (IX, 3, 18): 'What was pressed together by Varuṇa be opened up by Mitra in the morning.'

And then there are a number of passages throughout the whole of the Brāhmaṇa-literature which repeat the same idea that Mitra belongs to the day and Varuṇa to the night, that Mitra created the day, and Varuṇa the night.[200] It coincides with the fact that the features of the gloomy, the eerie and the perilous are predominant quite often and in different forms in the case of Varuṇa in contrast to Mitra.[201] In agreement with that is a rule we very often meet in the ritual, that one should offer a bright-coloured sacrificial animal to Mitra and a dark-coloured one to Varuṇa, or to both the gods together an animal having two forms'.[202]

It would be a routine affair, if one were to conclude from the comparatively recent age of these verses that it deals here with the secondary idea in contrast to the spheres of the Ṛgvedic thought. It may be noted that the incorrectness of this procedure has been exposed time and again at numerous points in the field of research on the Vedas. It cannot be discerned where exactly in the spheres of the old ideas, if we recognize only those proved to be old in the old texts, the new took root. In addition, the direction in which the later age has developed the concept of Varuṇa is, as is well known, quite different from the one related to the deity of the night.

Before we now try to determine, on the basis of these facts, the original nature of the deity with which we are preoccupied, we have to consider the correspondences in the Avesta which can prove it.

Avestic Parallels

The equation between Mitra and the Avestic Mithra thrusts itself upon us without further ado.

Just as Mitra and Varuṇa appear in the Veda in a constant union—whose age has been confirmed by the divine pair *mi-it-ra u-ru-w-na* of Boghaz-köi although one hardly needs any proof from outside of India—so too we find Mithra in the Avesta as a member of a pair, in whose case, as in the case of Mitrâ-Varuṇâ, the form of a dual compositum signifies an essential and a lasting union.[203] It is the pair Mithra-Ahura or Ahura-Mithra,[204] both great gods, from whom danger is removed and who are friends of the *Aša.* No reader of the Veda can consider the Avestic passages without feeling the immediate impact of the equivalence of this pair on the Vedic Mitra-Varuṇa, both lords of the *Ṛta.* In fact, it is Varuṇa who constantly bears the name Asura (Iranian Ahura) over all the other Vedic deities. Thus follows the correspondence between Varuṇa and the great Ahura of the Zoroastrians, i.e. Ahura Mazda.[205] How could one expect it to be otherwise? While Mithra showed such a life-force in Iran, should his companion Varuṇa disappear without any traces? And, on the other hand, should the great Ahura Mazda of Iran be a creation born out of nothingness, without a foundation in the old belief? Whence did this belief acquire a form, which was just predestined to evolve into the form of Ahura Mazda like Varuṇa? The features convincingly merge into a clear figure; what the whole situation allows us to anticipate is confirmed by the positive evidences.

And, indeed, both the Veda and the Avesta are full of evidences suggesting the image of Varuṇa to be similar to that of Ahura Mazda in all features. A few hints here may suffice.[206] Both are the masters and the highest representatives of the world-order, the *Ṛta-Aša*. Infallibly, without sleeping, they pierce everything, the open and the hidden deeds of human beings. They have set the world in order, marked out the course of life of all beings.[207] 'Who is the creator, the father of the *Aša*, the first one? Who has paved the way for the sun and the stars? Who is it that makes the moon wax and wane?' asks a Zoroastrian poet while thinking about Ahura Mazda. The Vedic poet says: 'Varuṇa opened the path for the sun. The ocean-waters of the streams hastened, the steeds (waters) like pouring effusion, following the *Ṛta*.' 'Infallible are Varuṇa's commands. The moon moves through the night in splendour.'

I, further, consider it extremely likely that one has to add one more aspect to the similarities between the Veda and the Avesta discussed so far. It is the similarity between the entire circle of the Ādityas and the circle of the Zoroastrian Amesha Spentas discovered long back by Roth and Darmesteter.[208]

That, further less important Ādityas belong to the pair Mitra-Varuṇa is as much a fact rooted in the Vedic tradition as the failure of every motivation for it within the Vedic sphere of concepts: it is clear that we have to do here with a part of inheritance that dates back to the distant past and which can be explained from the concepts of that period.[209] This can be concluded from the Veda alone independent of the Avesta, and this knowledge would be sufficient for the research worker on the Veda. But it is difficult here to leave the fact unheeded, that there is really a group of such gods in the Avesta, in whose stead the Veda hints at the presence of a number of smaller deities in prehistoric times. They are the six Amesha Spentas,[210] the retinue of Ahura Mazda, and with him, and very closely united with him, they give the number seven. These are deified abstractions like 'the best *Aša*', 'the good thought', one would like to say, attired in the pale clothes of the Light. One cannot, of course, take the connection of these Amesha Spentas with the Ādityas for granted in the sense that the contents of the concept appearing on both the sides could be more or less identified.[211] But the concurrence in the number of the deities, their fusion with one another and with the self-same highest guide, Varuṇa or Ahura Mazda, speaks for the fact that the Zoroastrian teaching had built its new creations at least upon the traditional outline and in that sense has preserved a certain relationship with the old sphere of ideas, although more of it has been preserved in the Veda.[212]

And even if this should be wrong, the equation Mitra-Varuṇa = Mithra-Ahura remains as a definite feature of the Indo-Iranian period. In addition to that, there is, it appears, the association of five lesser similar gods with both the great ones, which is also ancient and dates back to the same period. If one succeeds in relating a single element of this system of gods to a being in nature, then one can hope to have found the explanation for the whole.

Mitra is obviously the deity, in whose case such an association can most certainly be proved. The Avesta knows Mithra as a God of Light, 'the one who rides the horses, the ones spiritual, white, radiant, shining, holy, skilful, casting no shadow, flying through the heaven's space'. He appears always most closely connected with the sun. And thus one could unwittingly attribute the slight distance, at which Mithra is from the sun, to the common tendency which strives to place the god independently beside the natural object. To the straightforward concreteness of prehistoric thinking, often no god can stand so near to the sun as Mithra, without himself being the Sun-god. That is why the Avesta itself agrees with the old evidences, when it is said there, as it appears, that the Dawn leads his (Mithra's) chariot, i.e. of the luminous Sun-god;[213] further we have the cuneiform documents, which, in case the combinations are correct, should lead there to the similarity of the Sun-god Dul-azagga with Mi-it-ra.[214] Among the later evidences, as is known, the traditions of the classical world of antiquity takes one to the same result, from Strabo's ἡλιον ὁν καλοῦ σι Μιδρην down to the innumerable inscriptions which are set for the *Sol invictus Mithras*.[215]

Mitra and the Sun

But there is a certain confirmation of Mitra's sun-nature in the convincing simplicity and transparency of the consequences ensuing therefrom. The sun forming a pair with the moon corresponds to that oldest and most prominent feature interlinked with the nature of Mitra, namely, his forming a pair with the second god.[216] With that we arrive at the explanation of Varuṇa as Moon-god.[217] It shall be confirmed by an evidence present in the cuneiform characters.[218] At the same time, we think of the original[219] nature of the god and not of the concept of Varuṇa[220] which was actual for the Vedic Ṛṣis, and still less, the concept of Ahura Mazda for the Zoroastrian theologians.[221] The facts mentioned above agree most appropriately with this view. These facts connect the relationship of Mitra and Varuṇa to the contrast between day and night, bright and dark, or attribute in one form or the other the features of the mysterious to Varuṇa in a manner other than the one for Mitra. He is a great being of light with a special relationship to the night. Does not then the idea about the moon force itself on us of its own accord?

If we now maintain further the estimate of the Ādityas, we defended above, to seven, then a further consequence, it appears, ensures thereform. There are five small Ādityas besides the two great ones. Similarly, there are five planets[222] besides the sun and the moon. One may not like to accept the contention easily that this circle of gods has really an Indo-European heritage. So strongly accentuated is the agreement between India and Iran in this field, equally pitiable is the case of comparisons concerning the larger Indo-European field.[223] One may compare with that the relationships existing amongst the old inherited figures like Indra, or the Aśvins, or the old elements of *Soma*: one cannot resist the impression that one can anticipate amongst prominent deities, like Varuṇa and the Ādityas, surer traces of their existence outside of India and Iran than is actually the case. So, we shall take it for granted that the Indo-Iranian people have either created these gods themselves or accepted them from outside. It may now be considered that these people possessed from olden times a Sun-god and a Moon-god which, as such, were characterized in the most obvious manner and were called 'Sun' and 'Moon'. Here appears now a second Sun-god; here appears to be a Moon-god whose natural significance was apparently forgotten or almost lost amidst the ethical attributes in the Indo-Iranian period. Here figure, so it appears, in this circle of the highest Lords of the world, the gods of the five planets, who have likewise become incomprehensible in their original nature. The Vedic as well as the Avestic people did not care[224] very much for these gods; further, they are classed with the evil powers in the Iranian belief. Is it not probable that the Indo-Iranians have borrowed them—borrowed from the beginning as something only half-understood[225]—perhaps from a people superior to them in the knowledge of the starry heavens, that is from a people who belonged,[226] according to suppositions, to the Babylonian sphere of culture? And if one then surveys the world of the Vedic gods, does not one get in reality the impression that this compact circle of luminous beings distinguishes itself as something peculiar, something strange, from the rest of the Vedic gods? Is not Varuṇa, besides Indra, the sovereign of the world and the strong, thirsting meddler—we have already referred to this contrast above—the representative of an older, higher culture, a witness of a lively contact between peoples, standing at that time at the threshold of India, with the culture of the western nations? It appears they had matured to the earnestness of the view of life earlier than the Indo-European people. Is it an accident that this is perhaps just the place grazed by the influence of this view, where the belief in the powerfully influential forces of nature takes a decisive step towards the ethical?

Whether this loan-theory is correct or not, whether the five planets have played the role presumed here or not: we do not miss the convincing facts about the understanding of the changes in which the original Moon-god is elevated to the heights of Varuṇa and Ahura Mazda.[227] The Sumerians saw in Nannar, the Moon-god of Ur, 'the Lord and the Prince of the gods'; they prayed to him: 'Who is the highest in heavens? You alone are the highest. Who is the highest on the earth? You alone are the highest.' Amongst the Red Indians, the moon has the superiority over the sun; and besides, the concepts referring to him have an evil, mysterious touch about them. 'The moon', say similarly the Finlanders, 'has a strange, manifold appearance. Soon she is thin, soon too broad in her face. The dreadful fellow moves in the night and rests during the day.[228] Do we not have here a key to that emergence of the Moon-worship? The celestial wanderer of the night, who carries out his activity thoughtfully in the dark, who with such an art—here the favourite word *Māyā* used in connection with Varuṇa fits in exactly—knows to change his appearance continuously and make himself completely invisible, is obviously a much more dangerous magician than the sun, who rules in the same form over the bright day. It is, therefore, quite understandable that progressive development has attributed the mastery over the law and the world-order to this night-god. As the greatest magician, the Moon-god was, by preference, enabled to rule over the artistic movements of the universe. And he, whose eyes look through the night, spotted above all other gods, the sins hiding in the dark; and that is why, the particularly urgent need to have a divine night-watchman is felt. However, there took place an operation in the case of this god, that made the elements of concepts emerging from the views of the natural life to be pushed into the background by those concepts concerning human existence. The idea of the moon faded away of its own before the urgent need of society for a god, who would protect the law and punish the sin. It must have been the slow powerful changes in human thought and endeavour over millennia that allowed the tricky and dangerous magician Moon to climb to the status of the Asura Varuṇa of the Indo-Iranians and of the Indians; the Moon, the skilful ruler of the world-order becoming the resplendent and serene ruler of all, whom Zoroaster taught to worship.

The Ṛta

The consideration of the role of Varuṇa and the Ādityas as the masters of the world-order and also as the highest patrons supervising the right and the wrong makes it necessary to clarify above all the relationship in which these gods stand to the idea of the *Ṛta* ('Law', 'Order'). So a few remarks may be added here about the significance of this idea in the Vedic observation of things, natural and human.

Even in the Indo-Iranian period, the thoughts about a dominant world-order, about the determination by a higher force of what must and should take place, had been connected by choice to the ideas of the *Ṛta* (basic meaning, say, 'disposition'?, 'course'?).[229]

The events in which the *Ṛta* appears is a highly diversified event spanning across the whole world.[230] To us—understandably not to the Vedic poet themselves—the influence of the *Ṛta* is separated mainly in nature. The events, whose permanent equipoise or whose regular recurrence awakens the idea of the order, are obedient to the *Ṛta*, or their happening is the *Ṛta*. 'The rivers flow to the *Ṛta*'. 'The heaven-born Dawn has shone according to the *Ṛta*. The world-ordering Fathers 'have carried up the sun in the heaven according to the *Ṛta*', the sun himself 'is the bright, visible face of the *Ṛta*', while the darkness of the eclipse, which envelops the sun after breaking through the order of nature, carries on its activity 'against the order' (*apavrata*). Around the sky runs the twelve-spoked wheel of the *Ṛta* that will never be old, i.e. the year. The power of the *Ṛta* will be especially visible there, where the odd, the apparently contradictory, becomes a fact that is repeated again and again. Like that wonder which procures food for the man, that the dark cow gives the white milk, the raw one, the finished product. All these are praised by the Vedic poets as 'the *Ṛta* of the cow guided by the *Ṛta*'. Agni living mysteriously in waters and plants, the fire breaking forth from the fire sticks, is called the offspring of the *Ṛta*, the one born in the *Ṛta*. The *Ṛta* functions as the moral law governing the actions of men. It is the law—to use the expressions emphasized by the Vedic diction—which imposes truth and going on the straight path. 'The *Ṛta* and truth' is a lasting bond. Often the *anṛta* 'what is not the *ṛta*' is used as an opposite of 'truth'. The honest man 'who strives for the *Ṛta*' is opposed to the man who harms his fellow-men by his deceit or guileful magic. 'One who follows the *Ṛta*, his path is smooth and thornless.'

The cult, however, stands out particularly among the fields in which the *Ṛta* manifests itself. I think one gives rather a too narrow expression to the idea, when the *Ṛta* is thought of in this cnnection only as the technically correct procedure for fulfilling the rites of the cult. Rather, it is the idea that the great cosmic-orders are present in the proceedings of the sacrifice. As the rivers flow, listening to the *Ṛta*, as the Dawns repeat themselves at their hour, so also it is 'under harnessing of the *Ṛta*' that Agni is kindled for the sacrifice, 'the offspring of the *Ṛta*', 'who does his work with the *Ṛta*'; he brings the sacrificial meal to the gods 'on the path of the *Ṛta*'. And, at the same time, the sacrifice is touched by the moral side of the idea of the *Ṛta* in as much as it is there as an embodiment of the truthful and the lawful in contrast to the intrigues and magic associated with the evil spirits. The fathers have founded the statute of the sacrifice, 'announcing the *Ṛta* and thinking of what is right (*ṛju*)'. 'I invoke gods pure of magic; I do my work, I get my thought, with the *Ṛta*'. If the importance, accorded in the Veda upon this connection of the *Ṛta* to the sacrifice, can appear extraordinarily significant, then we must consider that here the priests are talking of their priestly tasks which are in the focus of all their thinking and doing; but, in reality, it has to be a settled fact, that the most important in the idea of the *Ṛta* is the concept of the physical and the moral world-order, and that the sacrificial significance of the *Ṛta* rests upon the fact that the sphere of the cult appeared and had to appear as permeated especially forcefully by the currents of this world-order.

The Ṛta and the Gods

The *Ṛta* is not personified. Those phenomena, reaching far and wide through the Universe and held togeher among themselves by broad internal similarity which have led to the view of the *Ṛta*, could have, of course, been associated—we shall come back to that soon—with the finished forms of the gods; but they had rather to create from out of themselves the concept of an impersonal force. Of course, a hint of concreteness is attached to the *Ṛta*.[231] There is a tendency of localizing, though vague: the Dawns come awakened from the seat of the *Ṛta*; or the sacrificial place is introduced as a seat of the *Ṛta*. There are paths of the *Ṛta*—an especially popular idea, understandably so, since indeed the *Ṛta* just expresses a direction of the happening; there are charioteers of the *Ṛta*, ships of the *Ṛta*, cows and milk of the *Ṛta*. But one neither brought offerings to the *Ṛta* nor did one pray to him.[232]

But then, the concept of the *Ṛta* ruling over the world must have been brought in the Vedic belief—or more correctly in the belief of the Indo-Iranians—in harmony with that of the sovereign might of the gods 'beyond the statute of whom none lives, even had he hundred souls' (X, 33, 9) just as in the case of Homer, who brings the might of Moira in concord with that of Zeus. Above all, it was Varuṇa and the Ādityas whose imperial character brought it about, that an influence similar to that of the *Ṛta* was attributed to them. In their sovereign splendour, they appear above all other gods[233] as the founders and the guides of all lawfulness in nature and in the life of human beings. It is once said that the Dawns shine according to the *Ṛta*; another time the poet makes them, who appear the same today and tomorrow, follow the great statute (*dhāman*) of Varuṇa. We have already quoted this verse above: 'Whither by day depart those bears[234] that shine at night, set high above there. Infallible are Varuṇa's laws. And through the night the Moon moves on in splendour.' The Ādityas have regulated seasons, moons, days and nights, sacrifice and the *mantra* of sacrifice. The pious one follows the orders of Varuṇa or the orders of Mitra and Varuṇa, yet it is the way of humanity to violate the orders of Varuṇa day after day, just like the subjects breaking the orders of the king. Yama, who appeals to the *Ṛta*, as he refuses Yami's forbidden love, also speaks to her of the 'great statute of Mitra and Varuṇa'. In this way, the contents of the idea of the *Ṛta* coincide with the statutes (*dhāman*), the commandments (*vrata*) of Mitra and Varuṇa. And, thus, it may also happen that expressions can be found in which the *Ṛta* is understood as the creation of Varuṇa, or also such expressions which make Varuṇa, so to say, the highest servant of the *Ṛta*. One also finds expressions which understand the *Ṛta* as a world-embracing power without reference to a deity which could have founded or ruled it (see, e.g. IV, 23, 8-10). A majority of conceptions, which, like the fluctuating Homeric ideas about the relationship between Zeus and Moira, represent the natural result of the confluence of different, independently originated series of ideas in the sphere of the Vedic belief, little affected by dogmatic fixations.

'The Aditi's son, the one who maintains order (in the world)', it is said, 'has made the rivers flow; they go their way according to the *Ṛta* of Varuṇa'. Heaven and earth 'promote the *Ṛta* of Mitra'. Here, the poets speak of the *Ṛta* of Varuṇa or Mitra in the same sense as of their statutes or orders; The *Ṛta* is something originating from these gods or something belonging to them, as they are also themselves named as 'the two masters of the *Ṛta*, of the Light'. Again, they are made out to be the accomplishers, administrators, followers of the *Ṛta* rather than the masters, when they are called 'protectors of the *Ṛta*', 'charioteers of the *Ṛta*', 'leaders of the *Ṛta*', or when it is said of them that they 'have grown up in the house of the *Ṛta*'. It can be seen that the shifting nuances reveal the relationship of Varuṇa and the gods to the *Ṛta*; however, yet again these are the gods who are constantly brought into connection with that power of the world-order.

Besides them, obviously standing behind them in importance, there is above all a god, Agni,[235] who plays a similar role. It is indeed true that the most powerful orders of the natural and cultic events are manifest in him; as the next divine companion of human life he, 'the supervisor of all statutes',[236] looks through all the wrong-doing, he distinguishes the good from the evil, and the thing that is done intentionally from the one that is done thoughtlessly; as a friend of the dark, as one who banishes and consumes in fire evil demons, he also burns alive the human evil-doers, the offenders of the orders[231] of Varuṇa and Mitra; and as such he is the champion of law and order.

But just as this side of Agni's nature alone can be illuminated in the context of the total ethical concepts of the Veda, so also our depiction of Varuṇa and the Ādityas must furnish an essential portion of their contents in those discussions, which shall preoccupy us later. There will be talk of Varuṇa's piercing look and the look of his spies, of his anger against the evil-doers, of his fetters and of his tricks; there we shall have to discuss those prayers for clemency, where the anxious heart, visited by misfortune seeks refuge in divine mercy.

Varuṇa as a Water-god

We may make here a few observations, as a supplement to our discourse so far, about one aspect of the nature of Varuṇa which is less important for the Vedic age, i.e. about his relationship to the waters. Varuṇa, or more often, the pair Mitra-Varuṇa causes rain; they belong to the group of gods very often invoked for the rain. It is a very natural function for these celestial rulers from whose lofty realm the rain falls. Perhaps, also in the end, the consequence of the widespread idea that it is the moon who sends the rain.[238] Even if the last-mentioned context was not naturally any more understood by the Vedic poets, their way of expression, nevertheless, suggests at times just the precise original idea. For example, when it is said of the celestial waters: 'Those amidst whom goes[239] Varuṇa, the Sovereign, he who discriminates men's truth and falsehood, distilling mead, the bright, the purifying, here let those Waters, Goddesses bless me' (*Ṛv.* VII, 49, 3). Further, however, Varuṇa's relationship to the waters is as a master of the orders in nature, who shows the path to the rivers. The idea develops from these starting points to the extent that Varuṇa wraps himself with the rivers as robe (*Ṛv.* IX, 90, 2), that the rivers sing to him as the cows low to their calves, that they 'flow in his throat, as if it were a hollow pipe' (VIII, 69, 11. 12). Indeed, the later, so important relationship of Varuṇa, the Indian Poseidon, to the ocean is already found in the *Ṛgveda.*[240] 'The Maruts', so it's said (I, 161, 14), 'move in heaven, Agni on earth; the wind approaches through the air-regions. Varuṇa comes through the waters, the oceans.' This reference is essentially isolated, but it does not appear to be strange considering the little importance of the ocean for the Ṛgvedic period.[241] And, generally, one can find out that the connection between Varuṇa and the waters is remarkably distinct in the oldest part of the Veda from the shining character it gets later.[242] We cannot discuss here in more detail, as to how this character had developed and how on the one hand, the central, world-predominant might of the old Varuṇa faded out and was passed on to new deities, and how, on the other hand, the later period felt more keenly the necessity for an ocean-god, for which exactly this aspect of Varuṇa offered the links.[243]

Aditi

The mother of the Ādityas, after whom she is named, the goddess Aditi,[244] is historically later than her children. They come from the Indo-Iranian period, and she is, at least according to the main aspects of her character, obviously purely Indian. As far as one can see, she is not integrated in the old orders of the cult. She is named in the *Ṛgveda* only in occasional invocations, almost together with her sons and in the cosmogonic speculations; no independent hymns are addressed to her.

Aditi is a personified idea. Her name means 'unbounded';[245] we can translate more easily 'freedom'. The fetters of sin and suffering threaten man; it is above all the Ādityas who control these fetters, and one prays to them to free oneself of these fetters. Thus, as the mother of the Ādityas, a goddess could be introduced who represents and confers the existence free of all fetters; and the one in fetters speaks to her: 'Who shall to mighty Aditi restore us, that I may see my father and my mother' (I, 24, 1).[246] Thus Aditi is invoked together with the deities who free the devotees and free them of sin: 'Agni kindled by this adoration, invite you Mitra, Varuṇa and Indra. Forgive whatever sin we have committed; may Aryaman and Aditi remove it.' 'Redeem us of the wrath of the wolves, you Ādityas, like a fettered thief, O Aditi.' 'Loosen the bonds, O Varuṇa, that hold me, loosen the bonds above, between and under. So in your holy law may we, made sinless, belong to Aditi, O you Āditya.'[247] When the rope is removed with which the slaughtered sacrificial animal is bound, it is said, 'May Aditi loosen these fetters'.[248] It is quite striking that the goddess is invoked, wherever an idea evokes the association prompted by her name calls for it. We do not have the slightest reason to object to the conclusion about her nature that thrusts iself upon us. It is explicit from this nature of hers that we come, particularly often, across the concept of innocence in connection with Aditi: 'May Aditi give us innocence'. 'May Mitra and Aditi, god Savitar introduce us to Varuṇa as innocent!' We read in one verse: 'In innocence, in Aditiship' (VII, 51, 1), or perhaps better, 'in innocence, in freedom from bonds', where, however, the allusion to the name of the goddess cannot be overheard in the expression for freedom. Further,[249] we find Aditi as a redeemer from distress (*aṃhas*), as a leader into the distance, as a mistress of wide plains, wild folds, as the one embracing distance, as the one ruling over the lot of intactness (*sarvatāti*): everywhere, the opposition to the idea of being in the fetters of sin and suffering is clearly visible, and this constitutes the real nature of the goddess.

This concept of unboundedness, so closely connected with the most tangible wishes and cares for one's own life, should not be diluted into that of eternity and make the form of Aditi take root, say, in the striving of fantasy into the realms of the endless expanses of the space beyond the Sun and the Dawn. Just as little can one, I think, interpret Aditi as imperishableness, or with examples from a natural substratum as the heavenly light in its imperishableness, in that the freedom from bonds is expressed in terms of time. If this is done, one would be pushing something to the centre which has its place, at the most, at the periphery. It is correct, indeed obvious at first, that concrete attributes are attached to 'Freedom'; whereas it is personified and tied up in relation with Varuṇa and his group of gods right from the beginning. These concrete attributes corresponded to the luminous nature and the ordering nature of a ruler of those gods, as much as the concepts of light and freedom were closely connected with each other. 'Who prays for the blessing of the Gods today? Who praises Ādityas and Aditi for light?' 'We announce to Aditi, strong in order, light, that does not hurt, and the fame of the god Savitar.' 'Aditi protects us from all distress; may we get sunlight, free of danger'.[250] And further, it had just to be Aditi as the mother of the highest masters of the world, in addition to her being the owner of such an inviting name for all that mystery-mongering, who inclined strongly to come into contact with the mysteries of the beginnings of the world. In the cosmogonic speculations which are there, namely, in the later parts of the *Ṛgveda*, we meet her as giving birth to the gods' father Dakṣa ('competence') and at the same time being born out of him; there is the talk of 'existence and non-existence in the highest heaven at the birth of Dakṣa, in Aditi's womb'. It is sufficient for us to have referred to these features in the image of Aditi cursorily; one will not be misled by them in the interpretation of the hymn in which there is the root of the whole conception.

One may refer here, however, only to one peculiarity i.e. the repeated expression used for the cow as Aditi, and that of Aditi as cow found in the *Ṛgveda* as also in the later texts.[251] 'Do not kill the sinless cow, the Aditi', it is said in a verse used in the ritual, 'when a cow which was to be killed is set free' (VIII, 101, 15). And in another verse: 'O Mitra-Varuṇa, the Milch-cow Aditi streams for the rite (*Ṛta*), for folks who bring oblation' (I. 153, 3). In the later ritual, the form of address Aditi for a cow appearing in connection with the sacred actions is very common. Does the first verse just now cited give a key to this concept? The word 'sinless' indeed refers to a constant Aditi-motif.[252] Does the speaker emphasize its contrast to the killers of the cow (compare verse 16)—the cow has a claim on free life as the one not bound by any sin? One can also think of a similar thing when referring to the second verse: the cow should serve the *Ṛta*, give her milk for the sacrifice; it may be added: one should not captivate her and kill. I am, however, not quite sure that we have therewith at hand the complete motivation for that identification. Several times the deities are enumerated as 'belonging to the water, celestial, earthly, born of cow', or also as the 'celestial, earthly, born of cow, worthy of sacrifice': as against that, it is said elsewhere that they are 'worthy of sacrifice, born from Aditi, from the waters, from the earth'.[253] Is it here the familiar goddess 'cow' belonging to a very low stage of mythical structure-building who was the mother of celestial light, and when in a later age the 'Mother' status was transposed to the new goddess 'Freedom', identified herself with her?

THE TWO AŚVINS

The Aśvins as Morning-deities

It appears certain even at first blush that the two Aśvins,[254] the 'children of sky' (divonapātā) or the 'twin gods', are connected with the appearance of the light at day-break. The *Soma*-celebration is introduced in the early hours of the morning by the recitation of the 'Early-litany' (*prātaranuvāka*). 'O *Hotar*, recite the litany to the gods wandering in the early morning', it is said and then an old ritual text[255] adds the explanation: 'These are the gods wandering in the early morning: Agni, Uṣas (the Dawn), the twin Aśvins.' In a special form of the *Soma*-sacrifice, the same litany follows in the morning after a celebration lasting the whole night. At the end of it, hymns to the Sun recited around sunrise are added.[256] There are clear traces to show that these recitations described in the liturgic texts originate from the period of the oldest poetry of the hymns.[257] Thus the position of the Aśvins is clearly indicated in the course of the natural events through the testimony of the definite ritual-orders. Their workings are bounded by the appearance of Agni which brightens the night and the dawn,[258] on the one hand, and by the rising sun, on the other. And what is constantly repeated by the hymns to these gods is in agreement with that given by the ritual: 'First worship those who come at the early morning....The Aśvins claim the sacrifice at the day-break.' 'Waken them, who yoke their chariot at early morn; may the Aśvin Pair approach.' 'Waken the Aśvins, O Dawn.' 'The Night retires from her sister, the Dawn. The Dark one yields to the Bright (Sun-god) her pathway. Let us invoke you, you donors of steeds and cattle. By day and night, keep far from us the arrow.' 'Agni is wakened. The Sun rises over the earth. The refulgent Dawn has shone with all her light. The two Aśvins have equipped their chariot for the course. God Savitar has stirred the folk to move here and there.' 'When you, Dawn, approach with your light, you shine with the Sun. Then comes this car of the Aśvins on its men-protecting orbit.'[259]

The golden, bright chariot of the Aśvins, swift as thought, drawn by winged steeds or birds, moves in its course (*vartis*) around the sky; the repeated emphasizing of this course appears to show that it is considered as a predetermined path. 'With songs of praise may we call today, O Aśvins, your chariot... that circles heaven with never-injured felloes.' 'Your chariot moves round the heaven and earth in one day'.[260] Thus the word 'surrounding the earth' (*parijman*) is preferably used for them and their chariot. It is also said of them that 'they encompass the Sun in the distance'.[261]

All this means, that one can scarcely avoid accepting the fact that the Aśvins as well as the deities constantly connected with them—Agni, who brightens the night, Uṣas, the Sun—personify a natural phenomenon. All the same, one can feel a certain difference, if the language of the hymns addressed to them is compared with the one of the hymns addressed to the others. Something of the vividness is missing here, when there is talk of Agni illuminating the night and the Dawn awakening the human beings for commencement of their activity. And if one tries to look to the natural phenomenon of day-break, one finds nothing that corresponds to the image of this pair moving across the sky and shining before the sun. It is possible, that a partial coalescence of the original idea must have set in, shifting its individual elements, and the poets repeat what is not understood, what has become incomprehensible on account of that shift. Can a natural phenomenon be ascertained with which, at least, a part of the data provided by the hymns is compatible? And is the part so formed, that even the alteration is not comprehensible, which has displaced the data no longer relevant?

The Aśvins as the Morning Star and the Evening Star

I do not doubt that this natural phenomenon can only be the morning star,[262] which has stirred the myth-building imagination of so many peoples. Beside the fire kindled in the early morning, beside the dawn and the sun, it is only the luminous power to which the fantasy decorating the day-break with divine forms and the cult revolving around the day-break could accord a place, where we find the Aśvins.[263] The time of the appearance, the luminous nature,[264] the flying movement on a definite path around the heaven, around the sun, recurring day after day like the sun and the dawn: all that can be made applicable to the morning star. But certainly, the duality of Aśvins is not compatible with it. But does it not confirm the correctness of our interpretation that the acceptance of the theory needs only an easily understandable shift to bring out the strikingly fitting sense of this feature also? The concept of the morning star cannot be separated from that of the evening star: that is, the second Aśvin.[265] Thus, between the nature and the myth, remains only the discrepancy that the morning star and the evening star are eternally separated; still, the Aśvins are united as two morning phenomena. Cannot this shifting be understood? It is said in one Aśvin-hymn (V, 77, 2): 'Worship at dawn and instigate the Aśvins. In the evening worship does not reach gods; they do not like it.' Could not this preference of the morning to the evening in the cult lead to shifting the concept of the morning and of the evening pair of the gods completely to the morning, though remaining unchanged in all other respects? One may compare with that the significance the Dawn has in the Vedic poetry, although the Dust does not exist at all for it. One can compare with that further the very similar shifting which has transformed the pair Sun-god and Moon-god, Mitra and Varuṇa, into two gods ruling together whose eye is the sun. As a result, it is only the traces which point out to the contrast between the stars ruling over the day and over the night.[266] But traces, however, appear to be preserved, partially of the original independent existence of the two Aśvins and partially of the relationship to the evening. 'Born separately', 'born here and born there', the *Ṛgveda* calls them (V, 73, 4; I, 181, 4), and a fragment of a verse of indeterminable origin explains this: 'One of them is called child of the Night(?), the other your son, O Dawn'.[267] One worries for what Agni will tell 'the earth-circumambient Nāsatya' (IV, 3, 6) about the sins of men. Here we have, as in the Avesta, Nāsatya (Aśvin) in the singular. At several places it is finally said that one invokes the gods in the morning and in the evening.[268]

The myth of the Aśvins and Sūryā appears to confirm what is depicted of the Aśvins in the myths. This myth is quite often mentioned in the texts. A young woman, named Sūryā—the word is the feminine of the masculine word

Sūrya commonly indicating the sun—now as the 'daughter of the Sun' (*sūryasya duhitā*), climbs, won over by the youthful beauty of the Aśvins, their chariot and chooses them as her husbands.[269] 'Two with one Dame ride on with the birds', it is said of Aśvins and the daughter of the Sun in a hymn which characterises, in the form of short enigmatic questions, all the main deities (VIII, 29, 8). Even this connection with Sūryā was, therefore, considered as an excellent experience of Aśvins.[270] 'Observed of all was your rapid vehicle with which you became the consorts of Sūryā' (IV, 43, 6). 'The daughter of the Sun chose your chariot, O Nāsatyas, together with your elegance' (I, 117, 13). Here now the interpretation of the Aśvins, derived above exclusively from Indian sources, appears to be confirmed by the comparison of the myths.[271] One may not like to separate the Heaven's children and the Horsemen of the Veda traversing the heaven with Sūryā from the horse-famous Διóc χου̅ρot of the Greeks and their daughter Helena;[272] and also belong here the 'God's Sons'[273] of the Lettish hymns, who come riding on the horses to woo the daughter of the Sun.[274] One of those hymns appears to say, in which sphere of nature one should seek these sons of God:

The Morning Star had gone up
The Sun's daughter to look up.

Is the Indian-Lettish Sun-daughter the Dusk? Is she the 'Cloud-Maiden?'[275] Or, is she not perhaps the phenomenal form of the sun himself?[276] I put it to the reader. In whatever way one may interpret it, the traits of the myth referring to the morning star and the evening star have the same considerable importance in either case.

The Aśvins as the Redeemers

The Veda celebrates the Aśvins as redeemers from all misery. This characteristic of the divine pair dates back to the Indo-European period as is shown by the comparison with the Dioscuri. The star which proclaims the approaching of the rescuing day-light after the perilous night was greeted as the appearance of a deity bringing succour. The Aśvins were particularly like the Dioscuri, the saviours from the dangers of the ocean.[277] The Veda gives them more often a ship or ships as vehicle; they are invoked to bring treasures 'from the ocean or heaven' (I, 47, 6); it is said to them: 'In the wide space your chariot reaches heaven, coming higher from the ocean' (IV, 43, 5). Thus, they save Bhujyu from the ocean; bad companions or his father Tugra 'had left him like a dying person leaving his property'. 'You wrought that hero exploit in the ocean which gives no support, or hold, or station, what time you carried Bhujyu to his dwelling borne in a ship with hundred oars, O Aśvins (I, 116, 5)'.[278]

And as they save man from the danger of ocean, they also save him from the maladies of all sorts. As physicians, they free man from diseases. They make the blind see[279], the lame walk. They rejuvenate the old, give husband to a young girl growing old in her father's house, and a child to the wife of an eunuch. They protect the weak, the persecuted, the widow; they save the quail from the jaws of the wolf; they soothe one suffering from heat. The hymns addressed to the Aśvins are full of praise for such deeds. Again and again, corresponding to the melody of every hymn, is briefly implied, what everyone knew most vividly. Besides Indra, the Aśvins are the typical heroes of the stories concerning mercy shown by gods. Indra is predominantly there, where it concerns the defeat of the enemies; the Aśvins there, where it concerns rescue without struggle from hardship. These stories should not be interpreted as mythical reporting of the natural phenomena in which the morning star plays a role. The boatman in danger from the sea, the ageing young girl, the wife of an eunuch are human beings, nothing but human beings. And the ingenious pleasure in narration let the mercy of the deities be revealed in their fates. These deities were, for them, above all else the helpers in need and misery.

RUDRA

Character of Rudra

The contents of the Ṛgvedic Rudra-hymns speak, without exception, of the fear of the arrows of the dreaded archer; there is also the prayer that he should spare men and cattle from diseases and death and give to them his miraculous cures.

Invoke the powerful one who is rich in fame, who is young and enthroned and whose attack is like that of a beastly animal. Have pity on the devotee who is praising you. Let armies put down others and not us. May Rudra's weapon fly past us; may the monstrosity of his anger avoid us. Take off the arrows for the sake of our generous friends. Oh, you bountiful giver! Have pity on our children, and grand, grand-children (II, 33, 11.14).

We say hail to the red boar with braided hair and to the dazzling shape. He who carries the best medicines in his hands, may grant us protection, shelter and save us....Don't harm us, O Rudra, harm not either great or small of us, harm not the growing boy, harm not the full-grown man. Slay not the father, slay no mother here, and our own dear bodies (I, 114, 5.7).

That only a few hymns are addressed to Rudra in the Ṛgveda, is to be explained by the fact that, on account of his sinister nature, he did not receive hymns of praise along with the other gods at the Soma-sacrifice.[280] One should not, however, conclude therefrom that this sombre and frightful figure stands in the background, for the older belief. So also, one should not allow oneself to be deceived by the hierarchically graded way of expression of the Ṛgvedic hymns describing the character of wild horrors which were obviously peculiar to the concepts of Rudra from the beginning. The picture got from the later Vedic texts to which we turn now, shows for sure mainly very old features; in most of the contexts, it depends only upon the specific features of the traditions which are seen less in the earlier collections of the hymns.[281]

A Brāhmaṇa-text[282] narrates how the Creator of the World, Prajāpati, in the form of a ram, committed incest with his daughter in the form of an antelope, and the gods searched in vain for someone who could punish him for this sin. 'So they gathered together all the most terrible substances in them; from these substances this god was created'; hence his appearance is horrific. Even the *Ṛgveda* describes him as red.[283] The red colour goes together with death and everything that is horrible:[284] red is the colour of the clothes of one who is sentenced to death; the wreath for the dead is formed of red flowers; red tools are used in deadly magic. It is said in a later Vedic text: 'Blue-black is his stomach, red is his back. With the blue-black, he envelops the enemy and the rival. He hits the one, who hates him, with the red'.[285] In addition, there is mention of the blue-black hirsute growth, the bow and the arrow. His isolated position with respect to the other gods is explained by his dangerous nature and by the reluctance in the cult to invoke him in the same breath with the other friendly gods. A Brāhmaṇa-text[286] distinguishes besides gods, fathers (manes) and men, a fourth special class, 'the Rudras'. The gods attained heaven through the sacrifice (which they performed). However, the god (i.e. Rudra) who ruled over the cattle stayed back here.[287] The precautionary measures which surround his cult, like that of the cult of the Dead, will be discussed in detail, when we consider the portrayal of the cult. It may be mentioned here in passing that the products of the wilderness, not belonging to the village economy, appear very often as the sacrificial offering for him.[288] The verb that is characteristic for the bestowing of the offerings is *nir-ava-dā*. It could be roughly translated as 'compensate', i.e. given him his due, he could go away.[289] The idea of compensation involves also the following: at times, isolated from the rest, some sort of remnants or waste is offered to Rudra in the end, so that he may not go empty-handed. A handful of grass of sacrificial hay is dipped in sacrificial butter or other sacrificial things and is thrown into the fire with the saying: 'Oh you, who are the ruler of our cattle, Rudra, you Bull, wandering near the line, do not harm our cattle. This may be offered to you'.[290] 'After one's own meal, one should pour out for Rudra on clean places in the northern regions what remains stuck to the cooking utensils, so that the place of the house will bring fortune'.[291] This reference shows also what seems to repeat itself again and again: that Rudra's house—separated from the east which is the kingdom of gods—is in the north. To the north of the Vedic land lie the mountains. And, therefore, Rudra has very often the name 'Mountain-dweller', 'Mountain-wanderer' or 'Protector of mountains'; the mountain is also invoked besides the other numerous names of Rudra in a sacrifice for the preservation of the cattle.[292] He lives together with his wife in the mountains. There is often talk of Rudrāṇī, and she plays in the cult a more important role than the other similar sounding names of goddesses like Indrāṇī, etc. who are less important, formless beings. Even his sons are mentioned. 'Bhava and Śarva hasten through the forest, flying like two wolves thirsting for booty'.[293] Above all, his armies attack men and animals, bringing them disease and death; at his command, these armies comprise 'noisemakers, counter-noisemakers, co-noisemakers, disease-makers, hissers and meat-eaters'.[294] One dedicates to them the blood-smeared contents of the innards of the sacrificial animal in the Rudra-sacrifice. It is worth noting, that in the description of this sacrifice, a significant part consists of expressions about serpents, which are unmistakably the names of Rudra-armies. 'He turns towards the north and makes offerings to the serpents with the words: 'hissers, noisemakers, disease makers, winners: you serpents, take this what is for you'. What of the blood that trickles from the intestinal contents is taken by the serpents':[295] characteristic, but as far as I see, only an isolated mention of the armies of Rudra.[296]

While the might of the god is expressed in the disease, there is also the view that the bringer of evil can turn it away or bring about cure. His dart is fever and cough. A *mantra* about the sick man is said as under: 'The arrow sent by Rudra on your limbs and heart, we tear it away on all sides'.[297] Again, he is also 'the best physician of physicians'; he has all the powerful medicines at his disposal, among them—according to the *Ṛgveda* and the later texts—a medicine of special qualities, called *jālāṣa*.[298] Besides men, cattle are also exposed to the attack of Rudra; they are especially subjected to his might. They are considered as reposing in his protection, obviously because it is he, who has the power to harm them. Very often, he is called 'Lord of the cattle'. Sacrifice is due to him in order to drive away diseases from the cattle or to prevent them.[299]

At the end, I emphasize one of the peculiarities of the later Vedic Rudra-type—its traces do not appear in the *Ṛgveda*—namely, the tendency of the god to acquire a vast string of names and also names of places of abode, in order to extend his omnipresence and plurality into infinity. He is celebrated as the great god, the ruler, the lord of the cattle, the merciful, the powerful, the fearful. Names heaped upon Rudra in reality—'thousand terms for thousand Rudras on the earth, in the air and heavens'—make a section of the *Yajurveda* named 'Hundred-Rudra-Chapter' fade into the background. 'His are the names, all armies, all sublimities'.[300] His dangerous proximity is felt everywhere. On a crossway, one should pray: 'Hail to Rudra, who lives on the ways, whose arrow is the wind! Hail to Rudra, who lives on the ways!' In a similar fashion he is worshipped near a dung-heap as Rudra living amongst the cattle; in a place haunted by serpents, as the one who lives amongst the serpents; when there is a whirlwind, as the one who lives in the air; when dipping oneself in a river full of water, as the one living in the waters; in all possible places and situations such as comfortable places of abode, places of sacrifice, big trees, he is worshipped, as the situation dictates, as the Rudra who lives there.[301] If a Brāhmaṇa, who has completed his education, and who is subjected to the strictest rules in all his movements, enters his village on a path other than the main road, he should say: 'Honour to Rudra, the Lord of the place.[302] Rudra appears suddenly at secluded places. 'The shepherds have seen him, the women carrying water have seen him.[303] All wild beasts and birds of the forest belong to him; his power rests on the waters, he rules the fishes and dolphins. He is the Lord of the fields, of the trees. If he makes a weapon himself, he puts it down on the highest tree.[304] He stands in the kingdom of the air and looks beyond the earth with his thousand eyes; his might extends from the eastern oceans to the western oceans.[305]

Original Nature of Rudra

If we ask now about the origin and the crux of the whole concept, then I think that the traditional meaning of this god as the Storm-god is less probable. The physiognomy of Rudra is quite different; the features that must accompany the image of a Storm-god are not seen in him at all, except for a few occasional and individual occurrences which are irrelevant to the inquiry of his nature.[306] It is true that he is called the father of Maruts, and they are, therefore, called Rudras. But this does not prove that he is a personification of the same natural appearance as the Maruts, whose character and appearance, in reality, is completely different from that of Rudra. Apart from this, it may be noted that even the hypothesis of the Maruts being the Storm-gods is not based upon a firm footing. 'No one knows their birth' (VII, 56, 2), so it is said of them. That they are considered as the children of Rudra, must be on account of the fact that they also come from distance beyond reckoning, storming the houses of the people as suddenly as the arrows of Rudra which bring diseases with them. In spite of the fact that Rudra's arrow is called wind, and he himself being called in the 'Chapter on Hundred Rudras'[307] the Lord of rains, clouds, lightning and winds, such expressions lose their significance, as they are used along with countless others which quite similarly relate this god to several other natural phenomena.

Firmer and deeper than the relation of Rudra to wind and weather, is the one which connects him with mountains and forests. Though he is described as the one who is resting at all places, more important—at least in the later Veda texts—are, however, mountains, woods and trees. There lives the wild hunter who is armed with the bow and arrow. Have we then not here an analogue of those European types before us—such as Fauna and Silvans of the wild men, Fanngen of the savages, and similar figures whose characters are so splendidly described by Mannhardt? The spirits of diseases or the arrows of diseases come to the human dwellings from the wildernesses, mountains and forests.[308] These could be the armies of Rudra wandering on the mountains.

This view[309] is disputed on the ground that it is founded just on the *Ṛgveda* alone, in which Rudra is called 'the Asura of the great heaven', 'the red Boar of the heaven', his arrows 'sent from heaven go beyond the earth'. If the character of the source is considered, I do not think that the objection raised is crucial. Yet, it remains a fact that this particular interpretation puts too much emphasis upon the features of Rudra which are valid only beside others, and it is perhaps possible, though I have my doubts, that they came up in later period only beside the others. So, considering the present state of our knowledge, we can only arrive at the basic idea of Rudra being the one who is an originator of disease coming over men and animals from a distance beyond reckoning.[310] Possibly, such a god had finally originated from the concepts of the evil souls who must have flourished in realms similar to those of the celestial gods.[311] It is also possible, that the type of that Mountain-god and Forest-god indicated above is at the bottom of it, or intermingled with it; again, the converse is possible that the uncanny originator of the evil breaking forth mysteriously, had appeared always decisively as the inhabitant of the uncultivated wilds, because one did not want to grant him any place in the peaceful existence of the home. Finally, it is also possible that the first inhabitants of India may have more or less contributed to the building up of this idea. One had pointed out to the remarkable rules of a few liturgic texts that a victim of the cattle-disease should sacrifice through the chief of the aboriginal race of Niṣādas.[312] I can scarcely find a sure trace of the non-Aryan origin of Rudra worship in this single ritual. It could well be an idea that symbolizes Rudra's nature as the one living in the wilderness by a correspondingly characterized sacrificer[313] like through the offerings growing in the wild.[314]

In whatever way one may interpret the questions of the prehistory of Rudra, it is understandable that such a god, strange to the sphere of the sublime, celestial powers, and moreover a horrifying god having the character of crude desoluteness, proved more accessible than the other old deities to the intermingling with the wild fancies of later Hinduism. He has thus handed over the main element of the genesis of the most fearful of all the Indian gods, Śiva.

OTHER DEITIES

The Maruts

After our detailed discussion of the main figures of the Vedic Pantheon, the depiction of most of the rest of the deities may be made essentially briefer.

The Maruts, the god of the wind known as Vāyu and Vāta, also the god of rain and storm Parjanya, deal with wind and weather.

The Maruts, the companions of Indra in the victory over Vṛtra, are the sons of Rudra[315] and the cow Pṛśni, 'the colourful'. All the same, it is risky to see in her the colourful cloud of storm.[316] They are described as a group of handsomely bedecked youths who come travelling in their chariots drawn by spotted mares or antelopes in gorgeous attires with sparkling spears and wearing ornaments of gold on the chest. Storms, downpours of rain and lightnings surround their procession. 'The winds have yoked them as horses in the shafts; their sweat have they made rain, these sons of Rudra' (V, 58, 7). They make the rain open up from the sea and pour down upon the earth; they make the earth and mountains reel in terror; the forests bend low for fear of them marching stormily; they bring darkness on a bright day when they flood the earth with Parjanya's downpour.

The relationship of the Maruts with the storm and the wind, particularly with the monsoons which bring yearly heavy rains, becomes apparent. It is possible, but only just possible, that there is something else in the background as has been presumed several times.[317] The stormy march of the Maruts makes one think of the concepts widespread elsewhere, viz. in the Germanic world, of the raging army, of the wild hunt and of the army of souls marching in the storm and led by Wodan. Of course, in my opinion, there are no clear traces referring to the Maruts as having the nature of souls.[318] And it remains at best a bold venture to see in the Maruts some similarity like the procession of the Maruts with the wild hunt and to take it for granted that this belief has taken a form in a direction which showed the Indian life in the nature. Yet, we may have found the correct answer.

Vāyu and Vāta

Besides these hosts of gods, the Wind stands as a single deity. Its two forms with the names Vāyu and Vāta[319] bring out two phases of development of the same idea.

Both Vāyu and Vāta mean 'wind'; the first word is remarkably rare in the Veda in its appellative meaning, whereas the second is very common in daily usage. Correspondingly, Vāyu is a god of Wind, not very different from Indra, god of Thunderstorm. The reference to the natural phenomenon has faded out; in the same stereotyped expressions he is invited to come with the long rows of his companions (*niyutaḥ*) to enjoy the *Soma*-drink. Its first share is given, according to the old order of sacrifice to the fastest of the gods. It is different with Vāta. The rite does not give him a special place of honour. Instead, the idea of the wind in motion with its bustling freshness clings to him unmistakably.

I praise Vāta's chariot and its power and glory! It goes smashing all with thunderous note. It makes the region red and touches heaven, and as it moves, the dust of earth is scattered.... Travelling on the paths of air's mid-region, no single day does he rest. Holy and earliest born, Friend of the waters, where did he spring and from what region came he? Breath of gods, germ of the world, this god moves ever as his will inclines him. His voice is heard, his shape is viewless. Let us adore this Vāta with our oblation (X, 168).

It is characteristic how the connection of the wind with the thunder and rain is expressed in terms of two pairs of gods. Vāyu appears constantly with Indra: both gods highly lauded in the sacrificial ritual, but with their natural meaning obscured; similarly, Vāta is permanently connected with Parjanya.

Parjanya[320]

Parjanya is the real living Thunder and Rain-god of the Vedic period. We have already remarked above, that the whole sphere of concepts about the thunder, which had grown rigid in the Indra-hymns, thereby indicating that it is no longer understood by the poets, fills the hymns to Parjanya with fresh natural truth.

He smites the trees apart, he slays the demons. All life fears him, who yields the mighty weapon. From him, strong as a bull, flees even the guiltless, when thundering Parjanya smites the wicked. Like a charioteer whipping on his horses, he makes the messengers of rain spring forward. Far off resounds the roaring of the lion, when Parjanya fills the sky with rain-cloud. Forth burst the winds, down come the lightning-flashes. The plants shoot up, the realm of light is streaming. Food springs abundant for all living creatures, when Parjanya quickens earth with moisture....You have poured down the rain: now stop. You have made the desert places fit for travel. You have made herbs to grow for our enjoyment and you have found wisdom for the living creatures (V, 83).

Now follow first some deities which do not—or are at least not recognized by us as such—represent the creatures found in nature or the forces of nature, but definite types or spheres of activity.

Viṣṇu

Viṣṇu plays altogether a secondary role in the Veda.[321] The action standing at the centre of his myth and almost exhausting him is his measuring of the world with three steps and the production of his threefold footprints.[322] 'A god with his might has made his three steps thither where the gods rejoice.' 'Three times strode this god over this earth....Over this earth with mighty steps strode Viṣṇu, ready to give for a home to men...he has made them spacious dwelling.' 'He strode widely spacing with three steps over the realm of earth for freedom and for life. A mortal man, when he beholds two steps of him, similar to the Sun, with restless amaze; but his third step does no one venture to approach, no, nor the feathered birds of air who fly with wings.' 'Within his three wide-extended paces have all their habitation.' 'It is he who verily alone upholds the threefold, the earth, the heaven and all living creatures.[323] The third step leads to the place, where Viṣṇu 'rules beyond this air-space.' 'This highest foot-step is always seen by the generous[324] as if it were an eye in heaven.'[325] The idea about whither the steps led, as it can be seen from the quotations, is not precise. Sometimes, the god has paced across the world thrice; sometimes he went there, where the gods were enjoying; at times, the three steps appear to be related to the three-tier system of the world (earth, air mid-region and heaven).[326] But the concept that the third step is something special, extraordinary, that it leads to the mysterious highest height is predominant.

One would like to believe that Viṣṇu's action of the three steps did not, so to speak, hang in the air, but had a context, was motivated by some events and served a purpose. Later Vedic texts, even the Rāmāyaṇa,[327] suggest the idea that the world was won over from inimical forces through these steps. It is also suggested that the Ṛgvedic period saw in Viṣṇu the apparent dwarf who was imprudently allowed to take what he could cover in three steps; he then grew to a gigantic size and measured the universe with these steps to acquire it for himself and his kind. 'Within his three wide-extended paces have all their habitation'; 'he has strode over this earth ready to give for a home to men'; His steps go there 'where the gods rejoice', it is so said in the *Ṛgveda* (I, 154, 2; VII, 100, 4; VIII, 29, 7). Does it not mean that he got for all the creatures and the gods those dwelling places?

The constant phraseology of the Viṣṇu-hymns and the scarcely doubtful etymology of the name Viṣṇu lead again and again to this idea of striding through the wide spaces.[328] When the poet speaks of the god who gives the earth to the people to live, and who himself lives on high, he is emphasizing that he measured the whole expanses of the earth to give home to the people,[329] that it is the highest height which he climbed with his third step. I think—and the uncertainty about the idea in the *Ṛgveda* strengthens my view—that the three steps did not correspond from the beginning to a concrete idea in nature. The number three owes its position perhaps only to the popularity enjoyed by this number, and it is only the reflection of a general trend of fantasy, when the third appears to be especially mysterious. In this context again, the alliance of Viṣṇu with Indra can be easily understood.

Indra said [it is mentioned] when he wanted to kill Vṛtra, friend Viṣṇu, march further! Heaven, give space, so that Vajra can take a support from you. we want both to kill Vṛtra and make the streams flow; as Indra drives them, may they go freely their way.[330]

There is no doubt about the role Viṣṇu plays here. As the killer of Vṛtra, as the liberator of the streams, he appears in only an assimilation to Indra, which is quite superficial. But as the Vedic poets like to connect the deeds which founded the order of the world and the happy existence of humanity with the victory over Vṛtra, Viṣṇu must then accomplish here, simultaneously with the killing of Vṛtra, a feat which can be called his: he has to stride far and wide and thus set the grand stage for Indra's victory in battle.

Is it now possible to get to the origin of Viṣṇu's form lying deeper via his concept as the traverser of wide spaces? Attempts in this direction are not wanting. One research scholar wanted to find in Viṣṇu a soul and mind, or, so to say, the basic substance of the 'manes'.[331] But I think it is without sufficient evidence or without any context, with the whole rôle of the god described above. Others explain Viṣṇu as the Sun-god. The three steps are supposed to mean the rising, the highest position and the setting of the sun. Of course, it is not impossible that obscurations and displacements really transformed an original solar phenomenon into the Vedic Viṣṇu, but I cannot consider it probable. Definite evidences referring to the sun are absent—relations of some assured age to the course of the day with the morning, mid-day, evening, or to the seasons.[332] In the case of Viṣṇu, the third step leads to the highest height; in the case of the sun, it is achieved by the second step, and the third goes down into the dark.[333] The idea of light plays in the case of Viṣṇu no greater rôle than approximately in the case of every Vedic god.

It is unpredictable which concrete characteristic—it must have been completely obscured in the *Ṛgveda*—other than the original subject of the action of 'striding' could be imagined.[334] But is it then really certain that one must seek such a characteristic? Is it not sufficient to take it for granted that there was a story working with the fairy-tale motif of a giant, who could transform himself into a dwarf according to his liking? As a dwarf, he made the evil spirit promise as much of the world as he could stride across with three steps: there, however, he did his three gigantic steps[335] across the surfaces of the earth and heaven, and, therefore, he is called the 'Lord of the wide surfaces' (vi-snu)?[336]

Pūṣan

Pūṣan is active in various situations: the oft recurring basic feature of his activity is that he knows the paths, shows the paths, leads the paths, protects from being lost or led astray, puts on the correct path the one gone astray, finds back the one who is lost. He is considered the god of agriculture and of the rearing of cattle; he, however, protects fields and herds inasmuch as he guides the furrow drawn by the plough in the right direction, and as he, armed with the goad[337], drives the cows along their paths, so that they are not lost. If the cows are driven on the pastures, one recites the verse: 'Pūṣan, go behind our cows'; if they run around on the pasture, one prays: 'May Pūṣan behind them put his right hand around them; may he bring back the lost to us.'[338] While thus his sphere of activity here is ruled completely by the motive of leading the herds along the correct path, we find the same motif in all its possible variations in his case again, also without any reference to the herds.[339] Thus, he leads the bride on the right path from her parents' home to the house of the husband; one prays, before she covers her way: 'Let Pūṣan take your hand and hence conduct you.[340] He also leads the dead into the other world; one prays to him, who knows all the ways, who does not lose even a single cow, to accompany the dead on their journey from their home on earth, going ahead of them, protecting them on the way, and lead them to their forefathers.[341] One who goes on his business, sacrifices to Pūṣan with the hymn: 'Lord of path, O Pūṣan we have yoked you and bound you as chariot'; one who wants to even a path, sacrifices to Pūṣan, the one who prepares the path; also the one, who has lost his way, turns to Pūṣan.[342] Of the offerings to all the gods and beings spread over the morning and evening, Pūṣan, the Lord of the path, receives his part at the threshold of the house.[343] He drives the evil spirits away from the path, the wolf, the one who obstructs the way.[344] He, the Lord of the path, is himself born on the path. 'On the path of the heaven, on the path of the earth; to both most wanted places of assembly, he travels and returns with perfect knowledge.[345] His consort is Pathyā, the personification of paths.[346] He does errands for the sun, with his golden ships, on the ocean and the air's mid-region.[347] The knower of the way, who protects one from being lost, also finds the one that is lost and hidden and lets the men find it; he found the hidden *Soma*; he found in his search the hiding place of Agni.[348] The form in which he gives treasures to men is the one that he lets men find them; one sacrifices to him, when one wants to recover the thing that is lost.[349] Also, the animal of Pūṣan, the ram—rams draw his chariot—is associated with his mastery over the paths; to the god of the paths belongs the animal, which knows the most inaccessible ways (compare *Av.* IX, 5, 9).[350]

Even taking everything into consideration, it is very difficult to see an evidence of the personification of a natural phenomenon in Pūṣan.[351] It may be said that this clear sphere of Pūṣan's activity is central to our understanding; if at all—what is quite likely—the form of the god has a further prehistory over and above this point. We do not have any chance of penetrating it.[352]

Savitar, Bṛhaspati

I refer to what is said above regarding Savitar, the 'Impeller'; so also about Bṛhaspati or Brahmaṇaspati, the patron of the holy or magically empowered word spoken by the priest.

Tvaṣṭar

I also find Tvaṣṭar the type of a god, in which a certain characteristic manner and sphere of activity assigned to the god yields a framework. Into its comparatively abstract perimeters can then be filled other, perhaps much older mythical sources which the framework itself does not contain. His name, from the same grammatical derivation like Savitar, appears to mean something like 'active agent'. Tvaṣṭar is a craftsman or an artist amongst the gods, the maker of forms (*rūpa*), who is himself universal in form (*viśvarūpa*), 'has adorned all beings with form'[353] (X, 110, 9). He forges works of art like Indra's weapon with which Indra gets victory over Vṛtra; from him originates the goblet of the gods, which then was transformed into four goblets by Ṛbhus to surpass his art. Above all, however, he is the architect of living forms, animal[354] and human. Thus, he rules over creation. Amongst the invocations which introduce the Animal-sacrifice in an old prescribed order, one is addressed to him to obtain the granting of a child to the sacrificer: 'Well pleased with us do you, O god, Tvaṣṭar, give ready issue to our procreant vigour, whence spring the hero, powerful, skilled in action, friend of gods and one who presses *Soma*.[355] As a god of creation, he has close friendship with the women of gods; when during the sacrifice, the woman, the wife of the sacrificer is initiated into the charm to promote fertility, then it is the priest who stands in special relationship to Tvaṣṭar, i.e. Neṣṭar, who has to conduct the relevant ceremony.[356] But the god of fertility Tvaṣṭar is above all himself the father κατέξοχήν: 'Tvaṣṭar created the hero, the friend of gods; the runner, swift horse is born of Tvaṣṭar; Tvaṣṭar has created this whole world.[357] He is the first ancestor of the human race, inasmuch as his daughter, the mother of Yama, of the first man, and Tvaṣṭar himself, the form-giving god, has given form to this darling in the womb of his daughter.[358] One sees in Tvaṣṭar also the father of the most powerful gods. He is the father of Agni;[359] he is, it appears, above all, the father of Indra.[360] Thus, he figures in the myth of the powerful deeds of the child Indra, born just then. This child steals *Soma* from his father, packs him, however, by the feet and kills him. One sees here, how the concatenation of ideas in the different ways they take, leads to the most contradictory rôles of Tvaṣṭar in his relation to Indra; there as a friend, who prepares the weapon for Indra; here the father of Indra, murdered by his just-born child.

Ṛbhus

The rivals of Tvaṣṭar, who compete with him in his artistry, who indeed surpass him, are the three Ṛbhus, in whose name one thought to have rediscovered the name of the Elves, although this is eminently questionable. We have already mentioned how they prepared four goblets from the goblet of gods which was the work of Tvaṣṭar; Tvaṣṭar hides himself amongst the wives of the gods, ashamed at this. They made their aged parents once more young. They prepared the horses for Indra, the chariot for the Aśvins and the universe-shaped cow for Bṛhaspati; immortality was granted to them as the reward for their artistic works.[361] They stayed in the house of the Agohyas sleeping as guests for twelve days. There they prepared—during their sleep—fertility for the fields, led the rivers on to their course, created herbs on the heights and waters in the depths. One thinks one can see in the Ṛbhus the genii of the three seasons, in the twelve days they sleep, the twelve nights around the wintersolstice, in which rests, as it were, the course of the year.[362] Then it would not be far to think of four phases of the moon in the breaking of one goblet into four, a thing especially obvious to the lovers of lunar myths.[363] Interpretations of this sort will have to be taken only as working hypotheses; the little indications present in the hymns that speak of the experiences of the Ṛbhus do not give sufficient proof for a more or less precise judgement. One would find oneself on a hardly negotiable track, if one undertakes to see in them deified human beings in the ephemeral sense, corresponding to the opinions expressed about the immortality conferred on to them.

Goddesses

Divine women and maidens have a very negligible part in guiding the course of the world in the Vedic belief. Of course, there were even from the olden days phenomena connected with the idea of feminine charm and, above all, of matriarchal fertility[364] which led to the divine female personifications like the Dawn, the Mother Earth, River-goddesses, Water-nymphs, etc.,[365] save in the whole cult-belief, these goddesses stand in the background. In keeping with the historical position of the Vedic religion, their personalities are completely unaffected by the quality of sanctimonious prudery. The Dawn who shows her rosy glow to the world is a beautiful maiden going to meet men, revealing her charm winsomely. The Water-nymphs, blessed both with beauty and fertility, are known for their amorous adventures. But the ingenuous naturalness of such ideas does not have anything of that atmosphere of languorous and cunning sensuousness which, for example, surrounded the figure of Astarte: thus the Semitic amalgamation of the sanctum and the brothel remained unknown to the Vedic cult which was nothing less than poor in obscene coarseness both in word and deed.

Uṣas

The old hymnic poems show a greater preference for Uṣas, the Dawn, over all other goddesses. However, this preference is not indicative of her significance in the actual cult. It may be presumed that the circumstances relating to older places of inhabitation have perhaps left their traces; there, Uṣas was a more significant phenomenon than in the home of the singers of the Veda.[366] Hymns not related to the offerings were addressed by these singers to her along with the other deities of the morning—to Agni who illuminated the darkness and to the Aśvins—at the crack of dawn on the day of the *Soma*-sacrifice, even before the birds were astir. These hymns to Dawn waft to us the poetry of the early morn; they steer clear of the mystic sophistries of the sacrificial technique and they have a charm that is wanting in the sacrificial hymns proper. One praised the pious daughter of the heaven, the luminous sister of the dark night, who follows the path of the past Dawns, precedes the coming Dawns, and she is the one who reveals her bosom like a lass aglow with beauty. Red-coloured horses or cows draw her chariot. The Sun-god follows her, his beloved, just like a youth who follows a young girl. I shall reproduce here a few of the verses from one of these hymns (VII, 77):

She has shone brightly like a youthful woman, stirring to motion every living creature. Agni has allowed himself to be kindled by mortals. She has chased away the darkness and made light.

Turned to all creatures, far-spreading, she has risen and shone in brightness with white robes about her. She has beamed forth, the golden-coloured, mother of kine, guide of the days she brings.

Bearing the god's own eye, auspicious Lady, leading her horse[367] white and fair to look at, distinguished by her beams, we see the Dawn who comes forth to all the world with bright gifts.

O Uṣas, nobly born, daughter of Heaven, whom Vasiṣṭhas with their hymns make mighty, bestow on us vast and glorious riches. Preserve us evermore, you gods with blessings![368]

Iḍā, Aditi

Of the other goddesses, we have already discussed earlier the cow-shaped Iḍā, the representative of the abundance of nourishment provided by the cow, and Aditi, who is also at times represented as cow, the mother of Varuṇa and the deities of Light connected with him.[369] Just as to these two goddesses, the feminine gender is attributed to the waters (*āpaḥ*) and the rivers on account of their fertility.[370] We shall have to speak more in detail about them and the *Apsaras* (water-nymphs) further below.[371]

Rākā, Sinīvālī, Kuhū, Anumati

Four goddesses follow who have to do with fertility of the procreation: Rākā, Sinīvālī, Kuhū and Anumati.[372] The later Vedic texts connect them with the course of the moon; it is uncertain whether this view also applies to the *Ṛgveda,* wherein there is no fixed system of four homogenous names, but only mention of individuals occurring in different combinations.[373]

Indrāṇī, Agnāyī, Varuṇānī

Finally, we shall mention here the goddesses, the consorts of the great gods like Indrāṇī, Agnāyī, Varuṇānī, etc.: i.e. goddesses who do not have independent existence and who fit in here, only because they are the divine-majestic consorts of the gods like Indra and Agni. We do not hear of them, except for their names, and besides, they are also not individual names, but they mean only 'Mrs. Indra', etc.[374]

Heaven and Earth, Sun and Moon

Heaven and Earth are, in the Vedic belief, divine powers having only vague meaning; it is rightfully remarked that here there is only a Uranus standing beside Gaias, and not Zeus. Of course, they speak of the Father Heaven and Mother Earth in an expression inherited from the past; they give rich rewards dripping with fat and sweetness to the human beings; Heaven in particular gets the attribute 'wonderfully mighty' (*asura*), with a certain regularity. But Heaven and Earth have not attained live personification of a sure validity in the cult. It is not much different in the case of the Sun and the Moon: we are not speaking of the Sun-god Mitra and the Moon-god Varuṇa, who were perhaps borrowed from a foreign source, and whose relationship to the big stars was no more or hardly any more understood in the Vedic period, and in whose case their development to divine personalities embodying ethical concepts corresponded to the obscuring of the real meaning in nature; rather, we have to deal here with the Sun-god who was called 'Sun' (Sūrya)[375] and the Moon-god called 'Moon' (Mās, Candramās). As far as Sūrya is concerned, he is a benevolent god, who drives away evil spirits with his light; the deadly power of the sun's heat does not give here the decisive motif. But as against gods like Indra, Agni or Varuṇa, Sūrya has a place well behind. The conceptions of his forms are full of variations: sometimes he is the eye of the gods, sometimes a shining horse, sometimes the seven golden mares on his chariot draw him like a homecoming hero; or like a youth in love, he goes after his beloved, the goddess Dawn. Besides him, there is perhaps also a female personification of the sun, the goddess Sūryā, appearing in the myths which depict the sun as the divine bride. We have already mentioned the connection of the Sūryā—here also understood as the 'daughter of Sūrya'—with the Aśvins. But the marriage of Sūryā with Soma, the Moon, is considered as the prototype of the human marriage, sung in a hymn (X, 85), whose recitation is a part of the most splendid embellishment of the marriage celebration: there the Aśvins were the wooers and Agni the one who led the bride; the different parts of the chariot in which the procession of the bride went and the dresses of the bride are equated, in a play of the mystical and the fantastic, with the great powers of the sacrificer and the universe, with which the speculations of the priests were concerned.

A number of verses name other deities together with such divine beings like the Sun and the Moon, but they appear, at first glance, to be less developed than the latter into living forms. 'So may rich mountains and liberal waters, so may all herbs that grow on the ground and heaven, and earth accordant with the Forest-Sovrans, and both the halves of the world (Heaven and Earth) round about protect us.' 'May one far-seeing Sun rise up to bless us. Be the four quarters of the sky auspicious. Auspicious be the firmly-seated mountains, auspicious be the rivers and the waters'.[376]

A closer look enables us, however, to recognize clearly in them the groups of minor, mostly local deities who are rich in forms and filled with life, as against those colourless conceptions of the divinely inspired 'Mountains', 'Waters', 'Rivers' and 'Trees'. It will further permit us, at least, to presume them as those by whom human existence is surrounded. And one also feels, that the daily course of human fates is influenced by them.

Waters and Rivers, Sarasvatī

Let us first consider the Waters and Rivers. The waters are represented as mothers 'which come from heaven, or those that wander, dug out of the earth, or flowing free by nature, bright, purifying, speeding to the ocean' (VII, 49, 2). They contain in themselves all the medicines; they wash away all evil and sin. Filled with life, they meet the man. They watch over his well-being at home.[377] When the priests fetch waters for the sacrifice, they speak to them:

> He who made room for you when imprisoned, who freed you from the mighty imprecation. Even to that Indra, the mead-rich current, the wave that gratifies the gods, O Waters. Send forth to him the meath-rich wave, O Rivers, which is your offspring and a well of sweetness, oil-balmed, to be implored at sacrifices. You wealthy Waters, listen to my invocation (X, 30,7.8).

When a water-barrel is placed, one pours water into it with the *mantra*: 'You wealthy Waters, you control all treasures. You bring auspicious intellect and immortality. You are the queens of independent riches. May Sarasvatī give full life to the singers![378] Of course, rivers of all the waters are glorified. Viśvāmitra, the singer of the race of the Bharatas, says to the rivers Vipāś and Śutudrī, when the Bharatas on a war expedition wanted to cross them: 'Listen, O Sisters, to the singer. I came to you from far with the war-chariot and the train of artillery. Bend down; make it easy for me to cross; do not come up to the axles, O Rivers, with your floods' (III, 33, 9). But in the esteem of the pious people, Sarasvatī among all the rivers has the highest place. On the banks of this river, important places of the cult of the race of the Bharatas must have been situated.[379] This race was obviously quite important for the Vedic religious life. The goddess Bhāratī, i.e. the personified sacrificial gift of the Bharatas[380] and the river-goddess Sarasvatī are invoked together[381] in a fixed verse of the old Āprī-litany which introduces the Animal-sacrifice. 'Best Mother', one prays to her, 'best of Rivers, best of Goddesses, Sarasvatī!

We are, as it were, of no repute. Dear Mother, give us renown' (II, 41, 16). She is the promoter of the prayers.[382] She gave once to the Bharatas the mighty king, to the prince Vadhryaśva, the glorious son Divodāsa.[383]

Gandharvas

Whereas a close contact has been preserved between the deity and the natural substratum in the case of these river-goddesses, the other female water-deities, the Apsaras, are developed into a freer personification, completely detached from their natural character.[384] But the regular association in which the Apsaras appear with the male genii, the Gandharvas, will justify this, if we consider the Gandharvas first, though they appear to have only a secondary connection with the world of waters.

The interpretation of this old type of the Gandharvas, which can be traced back to the Indo-Iranian period[385] in its Vedic name, is extremely difficult. The testimony of the *Ṛgveda* about these characters, appearing sometimes individually and sometimes in groups is obscure and ambiguous; their form has become so colourless, apparently on account of the transposition of the name to various types of mythological creatures, that we get at best an uncertain result.

Like their companions, the beautiful Apsaras, the Gandharvas have numerous places and spheres of activity in the Veda. It may perhaps be taken for granted that the Gandharvas had been originally more definitely localized, as it is perceived in the case of the Apsaras that their character as water-nymphs forms the starting-point for all other things. I would like to presume demons in them who were carrying out their activity in the high regions of the heaven and air-mid-region, one could call them something like elves of the air and the light.[386] The *Ṛgveda* speaks of 'heavenly Gandharva, the diameter of air's mid-realm'; it makes Gandharvas appear 'in the bottom-less air-regions', 'risen high to the heaven's vaults'.[387] Also in the *Atharvaveda,* it is said to the 'heavenly Gandharva', 'whose skin glitters like the Sun' in a verse which gives to the Apsaras the ocean as a home: 'Your place is in the heaven.' Gandharva, whose activities at the marriage centre around the bride, and who is scared away from her proximity, 'has gone away, to his highest place of abode'.[388] In a series of verses Gandharva is identified more or less with one or the other heavenly being of light or heavenly luminous appearance: thus with the stars of the moon's orbit or the rainbow; an enumeration of the Gandharvas is given, in which Agni, Sun, Moon, Wind, Sacrifice and Spirit appear, phenomena of the luminous regions of air and heaven clearly standing out beyond the obvious plays of fantasy. The Fata Morgana is called—though this cannot be proved in the Veda— 'the city of Gandharvas'.[389] Gandharva has something to do with Soma whose home is in the heavenly world; he 'guards his home'; 'he rises high to the heaven's vault, beholding all his (Soma's) forms'; together with Parjanya, the Rain-god, and the daughter of the Sun, the Gandharvas protected the Soma, took him in possession, when the daughter of the Sun brought him, and put sap into him.[390]

But this caring of the Gandharvas for the Soma has its disadvantage; they are also jealous protectors of the precious drink and try to keep it away from gods and men; thus, they assume in the case of the Soma, that typical rôle of the envious and hostile enemy which is played by Vṛtra in the case of waters and by the Paṇis in the case of cows.[391] Brāhmaṇa-texts [392] narrate how the Soma stayed with the Gandharvas, and how the Gandharva Viśvāvasu had stolen him; then the gods and the wise men desire him for themselves, and as the Gandharvas covet women, they buy him from them for the price of a divine woman, the goddess Vāc (speech). It appears that also the archer Kṛśānu who shoots off a feather of the eagle which was stealing the Soma, is to be looked upon as Gandharva.[393]

The Gandharvas are also introduced as ruling over various other areas in nature, besides their ruling over the air and light-region, which we have discussed so far and which apparently forms our starting-point. Namely, in water. Yama says to Yamī, the first man says to his sister, the first woman: 'The Gandharva in the waters, and the water-maiden, they are our highest relations and close relations.' And the Soma that is thrown into the water at the time of his preparation is called 'the Gandharva of waters',[394] i.e. the demon who carries on his activities in the water like the Gandharvas. Is this transposition of the celestial Gandharva to the Gandharva of the waters connected with the identity of the celestial water of the clouds and of the terrestrial waters? Or, is it the love relationship of the oft-mentioned Gandharva to the water-maiden that makes him feel at home in the region of the water? Or, is here finally the idea of the Gandharva in the process of fading out into a minor deity in general, so that he could have a seat both in the water and in the air-mid region?[395]

As beautiful, shining divine youths, the Gandharvas are the natural lovers of the charmingly bejewelled divine women, the Apsaras. A Brāhmaṇa-text describes how a Gandharva sits in the midst of the Apsaras and disports himself on the swing: he points out to one who loves him and says: 'You, there'.[396] The priest speaks of the Gandharvas in the horse-sacrifice; he points out there to the handsome youths who are present in the festival. And he speaks of the Apsaras and points out to the beautiful girls.[397] This leads to one more sphere round which the activities of the Gandharvas revolve; as lovers of women, they have an active sexual life; the female genitals are the mouth of the Gandharva Viśvāvasu.[398] Also here, as in their relationship to Soma, they reveal themselves to be sometimes generous and helpful, sometimes hostile. They and the Apsaras can give or reject fertility; that is why one turns to them to get children.[399] The later period names just that being Gandharva, which emerging from its earlier existence, enters the womb and becomes embryo at the moment of conception. The Buddhistic texts allow the conception to take place 'through the union of three things'; 'Father and mother unite with each other, the mother has gone through the period, and the Gandharva is ready'.[400] But the Gandharva is also the husband's rival, and one must be prepared to displace him. After the marriage, the first nights are spent by the newly-weds in chastity; there is a stick between the two: a symbol of the Gandharva Viśvāvasu, who forbids the husband from taking possession of the wife right away (p. 58 note 123). One prays at the time of marriage: 'Rise up from here, Viśvāvasu; with reverence we worship you. Seek another willing maid and with the husband leave the bride' (*Rv.* X, 85, 22). Thus, also amongst the exorcisms used to drive away harmful spirits from women, particularly from women in child-bed, there is talk in several verses of the banishment of Apsaras and Gandharvas. The plant buck-horn is supposed to scare away the Rākṣasas. The Apsaras are supposed to escape into their rivers and to the big trees, where they have their golden and silver swings and where their cymbals and flutes resound.

I shall tear the testicles of the Gandharva, the husband of the Apsaras dancing up to me with big bushy hair and attack his limb—The one like a dog, one like an ape, a hairy child and with the appearance of a friend the Gandharva lays trap for the bride. We shall drive him from hence with this powerful magic *mantra.* 'Your wives are the Apsarases, you Gandharvas, you are their husbands; run away, you immortals; do not be after the mortals'.[401]

One may not easily permit the notion of the priority of the lower popular belief over the higher priestly mythology, though justifiable otherwise without limits, to make the sphere of such magical exorcisms a starting-point, whence one seeks to construe the whole figure of the Gandharvas. The type of the goblins, which are after women, is really an ancient concept, certainly older than the concept of the Gandharvas. But the latter concept has in all probability a starting-point which is quite different from that belief in goblins; only at the periphery of its sphere of development does it come into the proximity of the regions where this belief prevails; and then this concept does not escape its fate that a tinge of this belief's crude and rude nature remains clinging to it.[402]

Apsaras

Still, let us go back to the Apsaras, the female counterpart of the Gandharvas. We have mentioned them several times in the earlier pages. Their name 'Wanderers of waters'(?) appears to be expressing their original nature: they are water-nymphs, sisters of the swan-maids. 'The Apsaras of the ocean flowed to Soma', says one of the oldest verses which mentions the Apsaras (*Ṛv.* IX, 78, 3) with reference to the waters that are mixed with the drink of the gods. 'In the ocean, I am told, is their seat, from where they move up and down' (*Av.* II, 2, 3). 'Apsaras should go to the stream' (*Av.* IV, 37, 3). Thus, they are driven away from the proximity of human beings. The Apsara Urvaśī swims in a lotus-pond together with her companions when the foresaken husband Purūravas finds her. A poet of the *Ṛgveda* (V, 41, 19) worships 'Urvaśī together with the rivers'. And there are several verses in the later literature which describe the Apsaras as disporting themselves near the forest-ponds, at the banks of the rivers, particularly at the bank of the river Ganges.[403] But like the Gandharvas, the Apsaras also spread themselves into the most different areas of nature from their real home. The water-nymphs climb up on high and carry on their activities in the waters of the air-mid-region and in the celestial world; the goddesses who accompany the Gandharva Viśvāvasu are called 'the Cloudy ones, gleamer, and the Starry ones'; 'the Apsara is smiling at her lover in sublimest heaven'.[404] And on earth, the water-nymphs transform themselves into the nymphs of the trees and mountain-maids.[405] We have already mentioned how the *Atharvaveda* (IV, 37, 4) describes the places liked most by the Apsaras, 'where there are Aśvattha-trees and Nyagrodhas, the big trees, surrounded by foliage, where their swings are, the yellow and the white ones, and where their cymbals and flutes resound'. The mightiest trees like Nyagrodha and Udumbara, Aśvattha and Plakṣa are 'the houses of the Gandharvas and the Apsaras'. If a marriage-procession goes past these trees, one worships: 'The Gandharvas and the divine Apsaras, which dwell in these trees, the lords of the woods, may they have pity upon this young bride; may they not do any harm to the marriage-procession which is coming here'.[406] Later texts speak of mountains as the favourite seats of the Apsaras, where they have their play-fields together with the Gandharvas;[407] they enjoy themselves there in the manner of the Blessed Virgins whom the people's belief depicts as playing and singing in the highest regions of our mountain-ranges.

The Apsaras are embellished with the most bewitching beauty; they are the mistresses of the art of love. The human beings also enjoy their favours, besides their divine lovers, the Gandharvas. That ancient legend, which is prevalent both in Greek poetry and the current folk-belief at home and both amongst the civilized people and the savages,[408] is associated in India with the Apsaras: of the marriage of the celestial woman with the human husband, of Thetis, Melusine, the tree-goddesses, the Blessed Virgins, who live with men in marital communion.[409] The Indian heroine of the story is the Apsara Urvaśī, and her husband is the king Purūravas.[410] As the existence of this divine-human marriages is regularly connected with a condition, i.e. made dependent upon an obedience to some taboo-like injunction, so also the case here. Purūravas should not allow himself to be seen naked by the nymph; indeed, as the parallel stories of other folks let us presume, the transformation of an original version in which it is the goddess who was not allowed to be seen naked in her real form.[411] The Gandharvas, who do not want to leave the Apsaras with the mortals, cause with cunning the breach of that condition. They create nocturnal noises; Purūravas jumps up naked from the side of his wife; there is lightning; she sees him and disappears. While he is wandering in lament, he sees the Apsaras in a lotus-pond swimming like swans and playing with one another, amongst them the prodigal. He implores her to reason, but she asks him to go: 'What am I now to do with this your saying? I have gone from you like the first of the Dawns. Purūravas go home! I am difficult to capture like the wind!" He is in despair; he wants to fall into an abyss; the wild wolves may then devour him. She consoles him cruelly: 'Nay do not die, Purūravas, nor fall in abyss; let not the wild wolves devour you. With Women there can be no lasting friendship; they have the hearts of hyenas.' She promises him that she would send him the son who was born of him;

and finally, his longing for her will also be quenched, if not on this earth: 'Thus speak the gods to you, O son of Iḍā, that Death has got you for his subject. Your progeny shall serve the gods with their oblation, you yourself however shall rejoice in the heaven.[412]

One royal dynasty ascribes its origin to Purūravas and Urvaśī. Thus, more than one royal as well as priestly family[413] in India as in Greece saw its first mother in one of these nymphs who are the personification of the noblest female charm.

Thus, waters and rivers are inhabited by water-goddesses and nymphs. Likewise, ground and floor, mountains, forests and trees house similar groups of gods and demons.

Deities of the Ground

The 'Lord of the place' (Vāstoṣpati) lives in the ground—obviously for every place, there is its own divine Lord: if one wants to move to a new house, one makes him well disposed to oneself.[414] One requests him to banish all afflictions, to increase the possession of cattle and horses, to bestow long life. 'O Lord of the Homestead, banisher of worries, the one who enters all forms, be our friend'.[415] On the field rules the 'Lord of the field' (*Kṣetrasya pati*). One worships him or shows him reverence when the field is ploughed.[416] The field of the fruits (*Urvarā*), 'the one wreathed with threshing-floor', the furrow of the field (*Sītā*) and their divine guardians stand on the boundary between the areas of the demons of the earth and vegetations. Even the mountains are divinely animated, 'manly, resting firm and rejoicing in freshening moisture' (*Ṛv.* III, 54, 20). We hear little about their divinity, but it may be presumed that when the *Ṛgveda* (III, 53, 1) speaks of Indra and Parvata, who travel on their high chariot to the sacrifice bringing blessing and who 'rejoice in freshening moisture', Parvata is also a 'mountain' as in the immediately earlier verse: here a Mountain-god, considered anthropomorphically as a companion of the mighty god, travels on his chariot.[417]

Deities of Plants

But, above all, plants and trees belong to the beings who are divinely animated, particularly the big trees, 'the Lords of the Forest'.[418] 'May the Lord of the Forest be full of sweets for us", one prays. 'The Earth together with Forest-Sovrans protect us', it is said in one verse in which the plants are also invoked besides the heaven.[419] The use of plants and substances extracted from the trees as medicines, amulets, etc. gave one motive for the prayers to the plants and trees.[420] The plant used in this manner is called 'the goddess, born on the goddess Earth'. 'Plants, by this name I speak to you, Mothers, to you the Goddesses: steed, cow and garment may I win, win back your very self, O man'—obviously the prayer of a priest-physician who expected the other said things as a reward for the cure of the sick man. 'The plants', it is said in the same magic hymn, 'hold colloquy with Soma as their king and say: "O king, we save from death the man whose cure a Brahmana undertakes'.[421] I attribute it to the Tree-cult,[422] when one worshipped in the animal-sacrifice the wooden post to which the sacrificial animal was tied; the post represents the tree contained in it, i.e. a divine being. Even at the felling of the trees the concern for the life damaged was expressed. Where one wanted to fell the tree, one put a blade of grass with the saying: 'Plant, protect it', and said to the axe, 'O axe, do not injure it';[423] one poured sacrificial butter on the remaining tree-stump with the saying: 'Lord of the Forest, grow with hundred branches; may we grow with thousand branches.[424] The post that was cut was later embalmed and was tied around with a ribbon plaited from grass.[425] It is indeed the result of a common custom of worshipping trees, i.e. the tree-spirits in them; the post is then constantly called 'Forest-Sovran' in the relevant texts (*Ṛv.* III, 8). The old litany of the Āprī-hymns, in which active genii are invoked at the sacrifice, contains at a certain place a prayer to the 'Forest-Sovran' that he may leave the sacrifice to the gods. This litany belongs to the Animal-sacrifice; here also the post is the Forest-Sovran, and it becomes an animated being, the patron of sacrifice. One who put into use a new chariot took it around a very famous tree, i.e. he worshipped the Tree-deity.[426] One may be reminded here also of the worship of big trees, mentioned above, past which went the marriage procession. When 'the Gandharvas and the Apsaras living in these Forest-Sovrans' were invoked and when—as we saw—the mighty trees were considered as the houses of the Gandharvas and the Apsaras who lived merrily there, an intermingling of the closely related types of the elves—the elves of the air and the water-fins—with the elves of the trees should not appear to be strange.

Just like the single 'Forest-Sovran', the forest as a whole is also animated. There appears in the *Ṛgveda* the Lady of the Woods (*Araṇyāni*), the relative of the Forest-virgins, Forest-ladies, Skogsnufvar, Dames vertes, whom Mannhardt has so excellently described. One hears the sounds of loneliness of the forest whose mystery and horror surrounds the stray wanderer; and the language of the ancient widespread folk-belief echoes in the hymn of the *Ṛgveda*[427] addressed to the Lady of the Woods.

O Lady of the Woods, O Lady of the Woods, who seems to vanish from sight. How is it, you do not look for the village? Are you afraid?

When the loud noise and the chirping of the birds resounds,[428] the Lady of the Woods exults like the prince moving with the tinkling bells.

And, yonder, cattle seem to graze, what seems a dwelling-place appears. Or else at eve, there creaks the cart: that is the Lady of the Woods.

Here one is calling to his cow; another there has felled the tree; at eve, one fancies, that somebody has screamed at the Lady's of the Woods.

The Lady of the Woods does not harm, unless someone attacks her. Man eats savoury fruit and then takes, even as he wills, his rest.

Now I have praised the Forest Queen, sweet-scented, redolent of balm, the mother of all sylvan things, who tills not but has stores of food.

It can be easily understood that very little is said about the Tree and Forest-deities in the *Ṛgveda* as a whole; for the great sacrifice, these minor creatures receded into the background before the hero Indra and the world-encompassing figure of Varuṇa. Yet, it is more significant that the Tree-deities do not play a greater rôle in the Atharvaveda and in the ritual of the domestic sacrifice;[429] indeed, it appears that their validity in the belief of the people which is represented by those texts, has become less significant than is the case, say, in the old Buddhistic literature. But it is quite clear from the material at hand that belief in the deities of this type was not absent even during the Vedic period—and incidentally, it would have been self-evident even without them. Thus it would be proper and useful, if we could round off the incomplete Vedic image of the belief in Tree and Forest-spirits with the help of the data of the later literature. I shall select here the Buddhistic texts: at best a make-shift procedure, but, given the nature of these questions, not likely to succumb to the danger of adding irrelevant features in the places where the Veda has left the image incomplete.

In the Buddhistic lores,[430] the Tree-deities constitute an especially popular method of embellishing; amongst all the deities of lower ranks, these appear to be most closely connected with human life. Partially, it concerns there the deities not identical with the trees, but only accidently and temporarily housed there.[431] But as a rule, the god is firmly connected with the tree (or the creeper, bush, etc.)[432] which forms his dwelling; he is indeed understood directly as a soul of the tree. When a swan speaks to the deity of a *Palāśa*-tree, the verse uses the expression: 'The swan spoke to Palāśa'.[433] It is believed that destruction of a tree would cost the Tree-deity its life: so, the deity of the old tree which has been most worshipped for sixty-thousand years and which should be now cut down, sees it coming.[434] When a new grown tree endangers the existence of an older tree, one says to the deity of the latter: 'That one will break your limbs to pieces'.[435] The deity says to a monk who wants to cut down a tree: 'Do not crush my house, our Reverence, to build a house for yourself.' Finally, on this occasion the arm of the child of the deity is broken.[436] We find here the natural further development, that as soon as the tree begins to be the house of the deity instead of its body, its children also share the house with it. Thus, one also imagines that, when, say, the tree is destroyed by bad weather, the deity takes its children by the hand and goes away, homeless, in search of a new shelter.[437] When the Tree-deity wants to appear before the people, it would as a rule appear in branches, or it can also come out of the tree and will be seen in some form, e.g. as an old Brahmana, wandering around freely.[438] The Tree-deities are, as a rule, friendly to man as long as they are not provoked. One prays to them for the thing one wants and brings them votive offerings: one worships them when one circumambulates the tree, turning right side towards it, when one clears the ground of shrubs around the tree, spreads clean sand and offers sweet incense, wreaths, lights and other sacrificial gifts.[439] Besides the deities, however, which live in the individual trees and animate them, the Buddhistic stories know also forest-creatures of another type: i.e. the giants and wild people living in the forest; they do not embody the friendly life of the tree, but the horror and dangers of the forest, or they are the example of the general, widespread types of evil demons living in the forest. These monsters are after the wanderers in the forest and eat them up. Such a creature appears in the size of a tree, deformed, with black hands and feet; another forest-spirit takes the form of a man searching for honey in the trees; he has put in poisoned honey-food to kill the wanderer; another man-eating forest-spirit has robbed a human woman and is living with her in his cave.[440] Howsoever impossible it may be to claim for any of these details an origin from the Vedic period, it is still quite probable that this faith in savage forest-dwellers in its total characteristics, dates back to the Vedic period, and even beyond that, to distant prehistoric times.

EVIL DEMONS

The countless minor demons who surround the daily existence of human beings are predominantly, if not exclusively, of harmful nature. Friendly spirits rule the fields, sate the corn with abundant nourishment and help at harvest time. We have already mentioned the 'collector', 'heaper' and 'accumulator'. Divine weavers are invoked when the bride puts on her bridal dress; they should clothe her with long life. The girl not finding rest on account of longing is scared away by the god 'Scarer' from her bed. On the battlefield rule the battle-demons, at their head are the Arbudi who carry horror and death into the ranks of the enemies.[441]

It would not serve any purpose to survey these demons completely. Their nature is exhausted in one action that forms their speciality and which is expressed mostly in their name. But the whole mass of evil demons, essentially similar in character, and who threaten above all life and health, threatening and injuring also in many other ways, need a more detailed treatment. These are the spirits which are without relationship to the natural phenomena and powers as a whole;[442] their nature consists in being at the bottom of harm and destruction done to men; it is already pointed out that there are diverse connections between them and the souls of the dead. The evil beings are given mostly the name of the species like Rakṣas, Yātu, Piśāca, etc.;[443] many of them also have individual names. These are sometimes taken—as much as we can understand them—from the nature of the harm caused by the relevant demon, sometimes from the monstrosity of his form or other gruesome characteristics; many of them are obviously nothing but the jumbling of letters, which reflect the gruesome quality of the figure having the name. Very often they appear in groups, quite often in pairs, which are characterized by name as belonging to one another. Thus, the names like Mroka and Anumroka, Sarpa and Anusarpa.[444] They are mortal,[445] sometimes of male, sometimes of female sex;[446] the women play here, amongst this crowd of ghosts and spirits, a greater rôle than amongst the great gods. There are amongst them families and clans. 'The family goes together to the villages', it is said, 'first the father, then the mother...the sister, the night-wanderer looks through the slit into the house. The brother consumption (?) belongs to the demon fever, so also the sister cough, the cousin exanthema. Even kings are present; the groups of the Rakṣasas, who march through the dwellings of human beings are "sent by the Rakṣas-king".[447]

The form of the evil demons is mostly human.[448] That is why there is a talk of their head, eyes, heart, lung, liver, etc. But it is disfigured by some horrible quality or deformity. Thus we come across three-headed demons, two-mouthed, four-eyed, five-footed, fingerless demons, monsters with reversed feet—the toes behind and heels in the front—, demons with the horns on the hands, yellow eye, gut-like mouth, neck of the bear and bucket-like testicles.[449] Some demons have the form of the animals; thus the hound-spirits attack a child with a definite disease (Epilepsy?); there are haunted owls, dogs, wolves and vultures.[450] Many demons appear to be plant-formed.[451] But often they are only the assumed forms, animal or human, in which the spirits appear.[452] They crowd the sacrifice to the deceased in the form of the souls of the ancestors, to the women in the form of their brother, husband or lover; or they haunt them, one like a dog, the other like an ape, like a boy who is fully covered with hair; they become birds and fly around at night.'[453] Of course, their voices and their other gestures correspond to the form they take. There are ghosts who dance around the houses in the evening and cry like donkeys, who make noises in the forest, those who laugh loudly, those who drink out of the skulls.[454] They are to be found everywhere, even in the ocean; one Piśāca flies through the air, the other creeps right up to the heaven, and there is one more hiding in the earth. The falling meteor is an embodiment of a Rakṣas.[455] 'Loose[456] on both ends, the Rakṣas flies through the air.' 'The glow-worms in the water' (i.e., Will o' the Wisps?) are Piśācas. But above all, the ghosts nestle in human dwellings. 'From this village that I enter,' says an exorciser of the devils, 'the Piśācas disappear.' We have already mentioned how they move around in the village and look into the houses. The demons sit even below the fundament of the house; one prays to the 'Lord of the ground' and Indra to drivs them away.[457] Finally, the crossroads are—in India as also in the case of different peoples—visited by the ghosts. They are, therefore, the seat of the most varied assortment of sorcerers. Occasionally, concepts have a rôle in it, for instance: that one wishes to free oneself from some sort of a power of misfortune at the parting of the roads—it should go one way, and the man the other—or that someone of the many passers-by should take upon himself the bad luck lurking there and give thereby peace to the sorcerer.[458] But the main motive in the choice of the cross-roads for sorcery is evident in the fact that the evil spirits live there; and this concept in turn may be traced back—as it is presumed—to the association of the cross-roads with the souls and to their importance as the places of burial.[459]

The evil spirits do their harmful work sometimes of their own accord, sometimes at the instance of people, with whom they are in bond or whom they serve. There is also talk of the 'harnesser of the Rakṣas', the Rakṣas of the 'Yātu-empires' or the 'Yātu of the Yātu-empires' in the *Ṛgveda*; the expression Yātudhana 'container of the Yātu' used for the magician leads to the fact that the evil spirit is considered as living within his human confederate.[460] The rule is characteristic. The one suffering under the spell of an enemy magician should sacrifice to the Agni Yaviṣṭha[461] 'who drives away the Rakṣas from him.' It is seen how significant in such magic is the practice for the magician to send Rakṣas-spirits against his enemy. Thus, one wards off the magic, when one says to the demons: 'Eat the one to whom you belong; eat him, who has sent you; eat your own flesh.[462]

The time of evil spirits is just like the one of the souls, particularly evening and night. In the night Agni prepares a sacrificial cake for the killer of the Rakṣas who is followed by the Rakṣas 'because the Rakṣas go around in the night'. 'It is taught that the night belongs to the Rakṣas'. One addresses the night with the saying: 'You rich in colourful treasures, let me go through you untouched.' Then 'the monsters and the Rakṣas do not find one in the night.' The Rakṣas spoilt (?) the blood of the gods in the night. The Rakṣas kill the one in the night who has completed his consecration to the sacrifice (*dīkṣā*), but Agni, the killer of Rakṣas, guards him. 'The Rakṣas do not have any power in the east, because the rising sun drives the Rakṣas back'.[463] But the new moon belongs especially to the evil spirits. And here also they concur with the souls of the deceased. A *mantra* of the *Atharvaveda* is directed against 'the gluttons(?) who have opened themselves up in heaps on a New Moon-night'; there is another against the eaters of flesh 'who go hunting around the New Moon.'[464]

Harm caused by Them

The harm caused to men by these evil spirits carrying out their activities in the dark is, of course, not very much in keeping with the concepts of the advanced faith in regard to the demoniac and diabolical activities. It deals with something very concrete, namely, harm done to life and health; the greedy spirit stills hunger and quenches thirst with the flesh and blood of man. The usual way of reaching its goal is by entering the man. Thus it is said about a disease-spreading demon: 'Jāyānya flies with the wings; he enters the man.'[465] And one prays to Agni: 'Do not allow the Rakṣas to go into us, not the Yātu of the Yātu-senders.'[466] The mouth appears to be considered as the gate of entrance and exit as well. They push their way in during the enjoyment of food and drink.[467] One washes one's tongue with a string of hemp in a magical act for driving away the Piśāca; in this way the Piśāca should go away.[468] The demons who want to create miscarriage slip through the genitals of a woman.[469] Once the evil spirits are inside, they eat the human flesh, suck the marrow, drink the blood, cause diseases of all kinds. One prays to Agni to get back to the sick whatever the Piśācas have torn off, broken, carried away and eaten. 'We awaken flesh and breath of life in the body.'[470] The Rakṣas cause madness of the mind; they take away the power of speech, so that one is defeated in the wordy duel.[471] They are particularly dangerous during the most important occasions of domestic life like marriage, pregnancy, child-bed and funeral. The numerous rites for chasing the evil spirits away are a common thing for the knower of the marriage ritual; I shall call your special attention to the shooting of a little wand into the air with the saying: 'I pierce through the eye of the Rakṣasas, who are running around the bride stepping towards the fire.'[472] When the young couple is prescribed celibacy[473] after the marriage for a certain period—three nights or longer, then perhaps the original meaning of this ancient and widespread custom—whose real implications were obviously not understood by the Vedic Indians—has to be looked for in the fear of the spirits, who might enter the body of the woman at the time of cohabitation, bringing danger to the offspring, in that they for their part, being obviously lustful, make the woman pregnant;[474] they are led astray by deception indicating to them that the marriage is not consummated.[475] I shall pass over here the customs regarding pregnancy and delivery, which also originate from the fear that the spirits devour the offspring and that they can change the male offspring into a female or cause other maladies.[476]

We come across the spirits stalking the deceased and his survivors in the ritual connected with funeral. The other field exposed to the visitation of spirits is the sacrifice. Even the *Ṛgveda* speaks of the 'Yātu snatching the sacrificial meal to himself'; of the sorcerers (*rakṣásas*) 'who have caused deceit in the divine sacrifice', and the *Atharvaveda* contains the *mantra* of such a magician who tries to make the sacrifice of an enemy fruitless through demoniac deceit: 'The Yātudhānas, Nirṛti and Rakṣas, may they destroy his truth through deceit'.[477] Accordingly, *mantras* and actions referring to the warding off of the demons accompany the sacrifice till the end. The spirits and their instigators cause harm to the cattle, as they do harm to men themselves; they drink out the milk of the cows and eat the flesh of the horses;[478] even the house is attacked by ghostly enemies; if a beam of the house breaks into two, it means that a messenger of death has sat over it.[479] Every moment of life, every action, every possession is threatened by groups of invisible enemies, who are the companions of those who cause harm to the mankind.

It may be finally mentioned that the intermingling of evil demons with another realm of hostile powers takes place unobtrusively at many points amidst a constant state of flux: with the harmful powers and substances thought of as impersonal, but constantly overlapping into the personal. These are diseases, childlessness, sin, etc. which lurk about in the air, fly over to man and contaminate him through touch. It is the main function of sorcery to ward them away from oneself and send them over to an enemy. The depiction of the magic cult to be given below, as it will be supplemented by the discussion of the evil spirits through the description of their prevention, has to deal with the counter-measures against such substances or fluids, and thereby try to explain the way in which they become effective.

ORIGIN OF THE WORLD, HUMAN BEINGS, PRIESTLY HEROES AND WAR-HEROES

Origin of the World

A few remarks about the origin of the world and the relation of the gods to it[480] may be prefaced to the description of the position of the human race in contrast to the gods and demons in the Vedic image of the world. For the poets of the *Ṛgveda*, however, these problems did not stand in the foreground. It may appear to us as obvious that the records of our faith can give us a detailed and definite answer about the origin of the world; but the case is altogether different in the Veda, at least in its older layers. Here, there was a question of glorifying gods and assuring oneself of their favour, and not of piercing into the secrets which may be lying beyond the world of gods, and which are connected in no way with the joys and sorrows of the transient moment.

For the Vedic singer there is not one god whose majesty alone could claim the position of a world-creator, and no one else besides. Not even a single god who would be in a position to be the bearer of the colossal antithesis of god—world. But all these many gods, wielding their might within the world, belong to the world itself. Their influence, which ensures the world-order, is praised; also lauded for having got or produced this or that thing most important for life. But irrespective of such great divine feats, obviously the existence of life not created by the gods but only receiving light and order from them is presumed as self-evident. The way in which they order and enrich this life has no longer the tendency, corresponding to the style in which their own figures are formed, to be described in bizzare forms inherent in so many primitive peoples' myths of creation and of world-order. The images to which the fantasy of the poets of the Veda keeps appear comparatively refined and intelligent. The first images are of the activities of the carpenter, occasionally also of the blacksmith.[481] Both the worlds, the six directions of the heaven, are measured. The earth is held firm with pegs, the heaven is 'carpentered', supported by posts. Then the expression producing or giving birth[482] plays a further rôle; it is often said that the Sun, Earth, Water, Light, Day, etc. were brought into existence in this way. Doubtless, it means, symbolically everywhere, at least almost everywhere, that one thought of procreation in general, without anything being expressed about its exact, so to say, technical nature. But the subjects of all this activity or procreation appear sometimes to be the gods in general, or sometimes, corresponding to the manner of the Vedic 'henotheism', almost all the individual gods in the order in which the singers wanted to praise them, and then in addition to these, also the dead 'fathers'. Indra and Varuṇa stand in the first row, the one mastering the things more with his terrible might, the other ordering them through his wisdom and hidden, wonderful ability. Unavoidably arising collisions betwixt the series of different concepts are felt occasionally, and then, of course, admired as the source of special mysteries. Heaven and Earth are the father and mother of all creatures, and yet Indra has produced heaven and earth; thus one says to him: 'You have generated at the same time the Father and the Mother' (X, 54, 3). On the whole, one cannot, of course, deny the ideas discussed here a certain insufficiency; we scarcely see in them the power of fantasy and the depth of thought. Obviously then, besides all this, there originate myths from the prehistoric period, in the prehistoric style, not suiting the poetry which celebrates Indra and Varuṇa, but preserved occasionally in the later literature, betraying its period through its character. When a Brāhmaṇa-text narrates how the earth was only as big as a span and how the wild boar Emūṣa stirred it up to the height, it corresponds exactly to the style of primitive cosmogony. At least it appears to be such that one is justified in presuming the corresponding origin.[483] One can similarly judge[484] a myth of the origin of the creatures from the thousand-headed, thousand-eyed and thousand-footed *Puruṣa* (man) mentioned in one of the latest parts of the *Ṛgveda* (X, 90). He is a gigantic primordial being. The gods offer him as a sacrifice. The Vedas, horses, cattle, goats and sheep are born from this sacrifice. The Brahmana originates from the head of the *Puruṣa*; the other castes from his arms, loins and feet. Moon and Sun, Heaven and Earth are born from him. The motive of sacrifice may be the last addition of a priestly narrator. But the belief that the world is formed from the body of a gigantic creature cut to pieces, just like the Ymir of the Edda, is found repeatedly in primitive cosmogony, and it must have found its way into the Veda from these regions.

The hymn to Puruṣa takes us from the very hasty and careless remarks about the gods as the rulers of the world to the comprehensive picture about the origin of the Universe. There appear in the later parts of the Ṛgveda figures and problems which were completely beyond the scope of the old hymns of praise. What is it that could be put to order by them and illuminated by them? One preoccupies oneself with the question like: 'What was the forest, (i.e. the wood), the tree, from which they have 'carpentered' the heaven and earth?' And the thought promoted by the monotheistic stimuli surfacing just then is inclined to recognize the producer of this stuff, the great master-worker of the universe in one new, incomparable god: something like the god 'All-Creator' (Viśvakarman; X, 81, 82), or the one unknown, 'who was the one god over the gods', and of whom one knew to ask 'who is the God whom we shall adore with our oblation?' (X, 121).[485] The idea of the independent development of the world-substance also surfaces beside the divine influence. One is inclined there towards monism instead of dualism—the formed and the forming god. But one appears hardly to be choosing consciously between this or that conception, rather one takes to the path chosen by fantasy. Impersonal creatures, abstract things with magical touch coming sometimes from primitive speculation, sometimes from the fringe between myth and speculation, are allowed to be born from out of one another. Betwixt them appear fantastic persons. The existence was born out of non-existence. The world-regions were born after that; it (the existence?) sprang from creatures with the soles of their feet turned upwards (X, 72).[486] This appears to be the description of the position of an ascetic; a very ancient worldly Yogin lets the things be produced from himself. The Dakṣa (intellectual power) sprang out of Aditi, and Aditi out of Dakṣa: the movement coursing back to itself shows that this is the beginning; after Aditi 'gods were born, the glorious, sharers of immortal life'. In another verse it is said:

Order and Truth sprang from glowing Tapas (penance); from it was born the night; from the night, the surging ocean. From that surging ocean the year was afterwards produced, Ordainer of the days and nights, Lord over all who have eyes. Dhātar (the 'Maker') then formed in due order Sun and Moon. He formed in order Heaven and Earth, the regions of air and then the Sun' (X, 190).[487]

Thus, a development, in which first the dark and the fluid is produced from the 'Order and Truth', and from that then, what is bright and clear. A god appears—whence we know not—and his formative work continues the progress.

So we have after all entered the sphere of the budding philosophic speculation which reaches its culmination in that wonderful poem 'Then was not non-existence, nor existence' (X, 129). That is the path we do not have to take here.

Man

It is well beyond the perspective of these spheres of ideas that the development of the world has man as its goal, as seen by the report of the creation given by the Genesis. The man, or also here the Brahmana, there the Kṣatriya, Vaiśya, Śūdra, is only one of the many creatures which fill this world, besides horses and cattle, besides the Vedas and the verse-measures.

The First Man

Often the figure of the first man appears as standing at the top of the human race.

The masses of ideas here are still in flux; thus it is not surprising that different examples of this type are given side by side. We have to speak especially of Yama on the one hand, who goes together with his father (as in the case also in the Avesta) Vivasvant, and of Manu on the other hand.

Yama is above all the ruler of the dead in the Veda; as such, he will occupy our interest further below.[488] This position is due to him, because he 'has died as the first of the mortals, has gone as the first into that world' (*Av.* XVIII, 3, 13 compare *Rv.* X, 14, 2). With that we have to combine further the conclusions, to which a dialogue-like hymn of the *Ṛgveda* (X, 10) leads. There a female counterpart of Yama, Yamī—both the names mean a male, resp. a female twin—tries to lure him into love: 'Those immortals seek it: an offspring of the only mortal.' But he rejects the temptation of the forbidden. It is known since long that this hymn which depicts Yama as avoiding the sin of incest proves just thereby the old belief in incest. Thus the myth lets—we have reasons to ascribe it to the Indo-Iranian age[489]—obviously the mortal human beings be produced by this primordial couple of twins. This trend can be easily understood: if one asked about the first parents, it was not satisfactory to arrive at the one oldest man and the one oldest woman who found her way to him by chance; the last beginning had to be the one beginning, and both belong to each other as twins. How then the rôle of Yama as the first dead one and the Lord of the Dead[490] is closely and naturally connected with his nature as the father of the mortal race is quite obvious.[491]

Yama's father Vivasvant stands beside him as the further example of the type of the first man and the founder of the order of human existence. The Veda and the Avesta and the evidences of contents of various hues and shades are combined to ascribe to him this nature. The Avesta calls him the first mortal who pressed the *Haoma* (*Soma*).[492] Thus, it is Vivasvant in the Veda whose messenger brings from heaven the fire, the ruling power of sacrifice. Agni himself is the messenger of Vivasvant; Vivasvant's prayers make *Soma* flow; the priest names the place where the sacrifice is to be performed as the place of Vivasvant, connecting the present occurrences with its primordial prototype. It is quite understandable that such a first sacrificer is closely connected with Yama.[493] Now a question remains unsolved, namely, whether the figure of Vivasvant was shaped from the beginning in this context and for it, or whether two independently originated forms containing partially related or identical elements were constructed as belonging to each other afterwards in this way.[494] The name Vivasvant, i.e. the 'luminous one'[495] does not answer the question. He may be connected with a feature of the myth which is not preserved. The encounter of so many important circumstances which make Vivasvant as also Yama the representative of the beginnings of human existence will rouse suspicion about attempts to conclude a celestial natural being from that name, as the interpretations then, partly of Vivasvant, partly of Yama, succeeded one another in the usual way in signifying them as the heaven of light, the day, the sun[496] and the moon.

Further Manu or Manus ('man') appears as the first man in the Veda. 'The father Manu' is altogether a living example of this type[497] in the Vedic period, while Vivasvant is at the point of fading away, and in the case of Yama, the concept of the first man recedes into the background behind the concept of the king of the dead—perhaps on account of his connection with the idea of incest. Also in the case of Manu, as is the case with Vivasvant, the sacrificial side of the first man is quite predominant. Like the 'place of Vivasvant', it is the 'house of Manu' where the Vedic priest, who himself functions in the sacrifice, thinks that it is taking place.[498] The sacrifice of Manu is the prototype of the present sacrifice. Indra drinks Manu's three ponds full of *Soma,* in order to strengthen himself for the Vṛtra-battle (V, 29, 7). Agni is the one who is introduced by Manu, who is kindled by Manu; one requests him to rule at the present sacrifice, as he had done it for Manu, when he 'offered the first oblation, with kindled fire, with his (attentive) heart and soul, along with seven priests'[499] to the gods (X, 63, 7).[500]

Divine Origin of Man

The roots of humanity run into the divine world beyond the first man. It does not really appear that the idea of relationship between human beings and gods—in the hymns the worshipper at times invokes those as against the god[501]—could have attained considerable religious importance; and the idea in question was as little fixed in a stable form as the cosmogonic or the theological concepts of the Veda. Sometimes, Heaven and Earth are considered as the great parents of all the beings, as the father and mother of human beings; occasionally, there is talk of Agni as the father of human creations; the twin-couple of the first men, Yama and Yamī, say to each other: 'The Gandharvas in the floods, the Dame of waters—such is our bond, such our most lofty kinship' (X, 10, 4).

Also individual, human races have their own, independent origin from the gods. Sometimes there is a reference to divine fathers, sometimes to divine mothers, sometimes to both. Vasiṣṭha is born in a strange way from Mitra and Varuṇa; the Apsarā Urvaśī is his mother (VII, 33, 11f.). And the poet says, as he speaks of Manu, the father of the whole human race, also of the ancestors of the Brahmana-families like Kaṇva and Atri: 'They are related to the gods; our birth-connections are with them' (I, 139, 9).

The Priestly Heroes

These ancestral fathers of the great Brahmana gentility are the 'Seven Priests'. We have already come across them above as the ones who offered their oblation along with Manu. This is again an example of the type of human founders of the earthly order, so to say, the inaugurators of human life. The system of gentility amongst the Brahmanas is more clearly outlined than in the case of the princely class, and it comprises all within a certain number of families. Thus, the concept of a firm circle of interrelated persons could be developed more easily for the priestly ancestors than for the princely; and the oldest Brahmanas and the masters of the art of sacrifice had to appear in the fantasy of their children all the more in the foreground of the mythical image of ancient history, as it was not the foundation of the affairs of world and state to which their interest was directed, but the establishment of the order of sacrifice and, in addition, the acquisition of such possessions of humanity like light and herds of cattle. And in this the guiding rôle befell the priestly art of sacrifice and magic and not the war-might of the princes. The 'seven *Ṛṣis*' or 'our fathers' or 'the Aṅgiras'[502] have 'arranged these creatures sitting in the air-region which was without the sun (?) and in sunshine (?)', 'found the hidden light, and produced the Dawn with the powerful word'; 'like a dark horse with pearls, the fathers have embellished the heaven with stars; they have set the darkness in the night, and light in the day'.[503] But above all, they exploded the rock with their prayer and kindled the fire. The rock had imprisoned the cows hidden by the Paṇis; thus, they got the blessing of nourishment for themselves and for humanity.[504] It can be said that they preceded those great donors of spiritual salvation as they were later worshipped in the Buddha and in Yājñavalkya as a type of primitive saviours who had not yet attained speculative and ethical heights.

What is narrated about the individual heroes amongst the priests in the old tradition lies to a great extent outside the mythological field. They are predominantly the evidences of priestly art and might, confirmed by historical events or ideal occurrences to which the image of the actual happening was elevated. Of course, the supernatural decoration is not missing. It is narrated there how the seven *Ṛṣis*—here appears the whole group together—'won' for the wife—perhaps the widow oppressed by misery—of the king Purukutsa a heroic son 'Trasadasyu by sacrifice, a demi-god, like Indra, conquering enemies'; this story (IV, 42) is preceded by the conversation between Indra and Varuṇa at the time of their battle. These two rival gods showed mercy to the queen who turned to them along with seven priests after they were reconciled and united. Or, the priestly family of the Viśvāmitras narrated about its ancestor, how he made the river navigable for the chariots and the train of artillery of the Bharatas, how he got for sudās the help of Indra through *Soma*-sacrifice and then arranged the Horse-sacrifice after the war was won. Playing a role, perhaps, in this story, was the deadly enmity, which had separated the rival families of the priests Viśvāmitras and Vasiṣṭhas, and which was attributed by both—correctly or wrongly—to both the ancestral fathers.[505] Besides, there are small images of the spiritual life taken from daily life or at least invented in its themes, but at times, drawn not without amusing malice: such as the portrayal of Agastya who mortified himself because the youthful wishes of his wife came in the way of his spiritual practice; or, the priest-couple of Mudgala and his wife, who distinguished themselves noticeably in a race by driving a vehicle which was not suited for that sport, but finally winning it gloriously with the help of Indra.[506]

The War-Heroes

As amongst the priests, we find also among the kings and warriors many heroes regarded as the founders of their clans. We have already talked about Purūravas, the husband of the beautiful water-nymph, so also about the companions-at-arms and protégés of Indra, who take part in his deeds of defeating Dasyu, like Atithigva. We have sufficiently discussed the position of these persons and their deeds with respect to historical reality.[507] Further, one may be reminded of the passive heroes of the stories of rescue narrated by the Aśvins, and who belonged to different categories; we refer to what is noted above also with reference to them. It has to be left to the future to probe deeper into the older phases of the Indian heroic legends starting from the great epic works of the later period; the primordial forest of the *Mahābhārata* is still waiting for the axe that would clear the way.

It can be maintained that everywhere—even there, where historical reminiscences are out of question—it is the real human world which is the starting-point of the conception of these legendary men. I consider it less probable that the heroes or the patriarchs of the Veda, thought of as human, are to be understood as gods[508] who had shed their divinity and sunken to the earthly sphere or as demons or directly as the embodiment of the forces of nature. The fathers of the human race take part, no doubt, in the victorious deeds which established the natural law, or even accomplished them, such as the gaining of the sun, dawn, etc. But it does not mean that their rôle is that of the natural force; they are not, for example, genii of light, but they are through and through human beings, the concept here being that the strength of the first men have achieved those successes in compact with the gods. Or when king Purūravas, a human demi-god, appears as the husband of the beautiful nymph, he is not to be interpreted as the Thunder demi-god, who has an adventure with an ethereal lady, or as the Sun following the Dawn. It does not concern here a couple of equal supernatural rank, rather it is essentially a man standing before a goddess:[509] he is no one else than a relative of men elevated to the heroic sphere. These men, according to popular belief today, enter into marriage communion with the Blessed Virgins like Fanggen and Skogsnufar.[510]

APPENDIX

GOOD AND EVIL GODS: THE DIVINE AND THE MORAL WORLD

Mercy and Wrath of Gods

The depiction of the individual Vedic gods needs to be supplemented retrospectively. We have to question the relation of these gods to good and evil. This question, however, acquires substance first and foremost according to their useful or harmful character with respect to man.

An optimistic view of the course of the world had to prevail amongst the people marching forward victoriously and living contentedly, particularly, amongst the ruling classes. It is a sort of a faith which sees in the noblest powers of the universe friends, who bring blessings. And, in reality, this friendly character is quite predominant amongst the gods of the Vedic pantheon. Of course, all sorts of evil do come from the supernatural forces, but these are, on the whole, only the army of small demons, goblins, spirits of diseases, etc. to whom such evil is attributed. Corresponding to this notion, diseases and afflictions do not appear to the eye as dependent upon the great and ever reigning beings of nature, but upon the beings at work individually, causing harm through incalculable pranks, so that the ancient type of minor evil demons can remain here on the whole unchanged. But the noble all-prevailing forces of nature, like the sun, fire, storm, form the sure foundations of happy human existence. There is only one god, i.e. Rudra, amongst the great gods of the Veda, in whose case the malefic nature steps into the foreground. Other evil beings like Vṛtra, the envious obstructor of the water-floods, strong enough to oppose Indra on equal terms and to make the gods run at his snorting, are depicted as defeated and destroyed; in addition, they give added substance to the concept of the salutary might of gods, who have rooted out such evil.

The benevolent nature of a god like Indra is, of course, wholly conceived of within the sense and ambit of human benevolence, which needs reciprocity and which is also not unaffected by change and arbitrariness.[511] Indra is the friend of the sacrificer, of the presser of *Soma,* but he kills the miser who does not perform the sacrifice, and he destroys all his worldly goods. Like the Homeric gods, he is not above using cunning and to practice deceit in play against the mortals, when his sensuousness incites him—of course, he is as much subject to it as also to mighty thirst, and occasionally to the effects of powerful drinking-bouts.[512] He gets easily angry; he is inconsistent in his friendship.

> Who lauds him, satisfies him, pays him worship, so that the Lord will bless him always and make him powerful? As one puts the feet forward, the one after the other, he makes the last precede, the foremost follow. He is famous as a hero, tamer of a strong man, ever advancing one and then another. King of both worlds, he hates the high and haughty, Indra protects the men who his people. He loves no more the men he loved before; he turns and moves away allied with others. Rejecting those who disregard his worship, Indra victorious lives through many autumns (VI, 47, 15-17).

One should not give special importance to Indra's word 'hate the high and haughty'. It is usually said otherwise that Indra throws down the insolent, the godless, the wealthy miser; here the poet, who is concerned with the vicissitudes of human life as against the divine force playing with human fates, goes so far as to express the god's hatred of the one who is fortunate: an expression, hardly sufficient, isolated as it is, to ensure a place for the idea of the 'envy of gods' in the Vedic conception of the world.

As against the concept of dangers in the wake of Indra's anger, the confidence in his unfathomable mercy is extensively prevalent, and the pious worshipper feels justified in reposing this confidence in the one who has been friendly with him from olden times. 'He does not diminish the wishes' of the worshipper. 'No one can say, he does not give anything'. 'Indra pours horses and cattle like the pouring of the rains from the stormy heavens.' There is no end to such expressions. But that is also the case, perhaps to a lesser extent, with almost all the rest of the gods in their individual features, corresponding to the nature of the individual gods: thus, in the case of Agni, there is a touch of intimacy about the divine companion of the home. The basic note everywhere is the sure confidence in the abundant mercy of gods which is often put to the test.

The relation to Rudra[513] forms an exception. He shoots the arrows of devastating diseases on men and cattle; in his case, the world of evil forces, otherwise limited to the region of inferior demons projects into the one of the great gods. The cult of Rudra is along the same lines as the cult of the evil demons and of the dead, as far as the precautionary measures of the sacrificer towards the dangerous god are concerned.[514] But the tone of the hymns addressed to him does not corresondingly distinguish itself from the tone of the invocations to the benevolent gods. It is, of course, natural, that the fear of the wicked god is not clearly expressed in what is said to him, but in the things done to him. And Rudra, also the healer of the diseases he sends, does not lack the benevolent qualities which the poet was keen on praising. But all the same, the dangerous nature of the god comes to the fore in the hymns every now and then. One prays to him that he should smite neither great nor small, neither father nor mother, neither one's own life nor the life of cattle and horses; his army may strike down the others; he is fearful like a wild beast. It may be a mistake which makes him angry, or a maladroit invocation, or an invocation made at the inappropriate time, that is, when his attention is taken up by another sacrificer.[515] But, on the whole, the prayers for indulgence addressed to him sound, as if one had expected his attacks even without having given cause or having committed grave sins.

The Gods and the Right

Thus, when the benevolent or harmful action of the gods follows from their character and temperament, it must be specially asked as to what rôle the ideas of right and wrong or of sin play in the relationship between men and gods.

Originating from social life, the ideas of right and wrong, at the beginning, are obviously independent of the belief in god or its primary stages. In itself, it is not clear why the spirits, and particularly those powerful spirits called gods, should be more than human beings, or why they should be actually the friends of the lawful and the enemies of the unlawful. But the historical development extends beyond this separation of both the spheres to the connection of the gods with the law, albeit not an absolute but a predominant connection. They are considered as friends of the law; and as every god is assigned his own sphere of activity in the Universe, the individuals among them can take up their special task of giving authority to righteousness over unrighteousness with the aid of their might.

We are not trying here to trace the older phases of this development, but we are only describing the stage to which it reaches in the Vedic period.

The image of the gods in general have only superficial ethical features. It is most essential for religious conviction that the god is a powerful friend. His strength appears to climb immeasurable heights in the hymns of praise dedicated to him. But that is not the case with his moral sublimity. Of course, the qualities like 'true', 'not deceptive', etc. are attributed to all the gods,[516] but such epithets fall much behind those like 'great', 'mighty', etc.; they show scarcely anything more than the fact that a certain goodness and honesty is a quality of a god as it is a quality of a true man; what is remarked above about Indra illustrates the limitations within which such qualities are to be understood.[517] That the Vedic gods were little interested in acquiring more than a superficial tinge of moral content is best confirmed by the further course of the history of Indian religion. For an age that was so deeply affected by the moral problems like that of old Buddhism, the highest points of ethical perfection lay altogether elsewhere than in the regions of the world of gods; the existence of the Buddhistic god has its purport really only in the fact that he 'enjoys himself in heaven' through immeasurable spaces of time.

But a relation to the moral other than the one which the god as god has can be the one due to him on the strength of his individual character. We have already shown above that from Indo-Iranian times the Ādityas and particularly the greatest amongst them, Varuṇa, were considered as the founders and protectors of the *Ṛta*, of the physical and moral world law. As the gods of the great celestial lights—according to their original nature—they embody the manifested order of all happening most visible on the firmament; all-seeing they know of the most secret of human sins. 'They look through everything that is straight and crooked, all that is near to the kings, even the highest.' 'Who stands and goes, who staggers about, who crawls in stealth and who plunges forth, or what two discuss seated together, that is known to the king Varuṇa as the third party'.[518] The might of these gods piercing through everything is embodied in their 'spies' who never shut the eyes.[519] In contrast to the natural precedence of Mitra (Sun) over Varuṇa (Moon)—an order of precedence confirmed as initially present even by language—Varuṇa (Ahura) is accorded chief importance both in the Veda and in the Avesta. It may be asked in passing whether the reason for this importance does not lie in the role of the Ādityas as discerners of all sin, a role accorded to them in addition to their original natural significance. Of the two great Ādityas, Varuṇa is the ruler of the night. The sins seek the protective cover of the night, and thus it is Varuṇa's lot over that of his companion ruling the day to battle against sin and to protect the *Ṛta*.[520]

If we follow the view about sin and atonement, the juxtaposition and partial intermingling of the same two series of concepts is noticeable everywhere. We already came across that correspondence above in our review of the relation of Varuṇa to the *Ṛta*: the understanding of the sin on the one hand, as the phenomenon which, by virtue of its own nature, brings destruction to the one who is guilty, and on the other hand, as a phenomenon caused by the intrusion of the deity.

Sin

It is necessary to deal with this point a little more in detail in order to study the concepts of the ways in which sins have effect.

First of all, sin has its own independent existence. Just as diseases and similar evil powers are considered as now stable, now as ethereal fleeting substances which can be washed by water, burnt by fire, banished by amulets having magic power or dispelled in many other ways, so too sin (*enas,* beside that *āgas*) is thought of: it is understandable that one comprehends this power bringing evil to the doer according to the model of other evil powers and in the concreteness befalling the rest.[521] Often, in particular, there is the idea of fetters or knots in which the sinner is entangled. Even this idea applies to sin along with other pernicious powers. Thus, one speaks of the fetters of death, of disease; or disease for its part is called the fetter of ruin (*Nirṛti*). Here, of course, the idea of the god punishing the sins is obvious, as of the one who puts the fetters, stretches the knots and the like, but this factor is in no way indispensable; it is enough that the contemplation is directed to the sin as well as to the fetters, which cling to the sinner with their destructive might. Thus one prays to Soma and Rudra for liberation from 'the sin committed by us, still chained to our body'; and one prays to Varuṇa: 'Redeem us from the sin we have committed'.[522] These fetters of sin appear to be thought of as stretched out in the form of a sling in which the evil-doer gets caught. Thus one prays 'to get over' the fetters lying exposed like 'with a chariot and horses'.[523]

It is self-evident that the external, so to say, the material understanding of the sin which we come across here, is also seen in the fact that the subjective factor of the sinful wish is quite far from being decisive; the essential aspect is the objective fact of the sinful act. Also the sin[524] committed unknowingly in sleep is a sin. And further, this whole way of understanding, particularly the conception of sin according to the manner of a substance producing disease leads to the conclusion which appears characteristic for all the lower stages of ethical consideration. It leads to the idea that sin does not attach itself alone to the guilty one but passes over to other persons in various ways.[525] Particularly in the direct way: from the father[526] to the son. When the poet prays for being set free 'from all the sins of deceit we have inherited from our fathers and from those we have committed ourselves' (*Ṛv.* VII, 86, 5), it can be inferred that here both the main possibilities were seen in which the burden of the sin befell one: one's own deed and the one inherited from the father. But one could also become guilty in other ways. The black bird, who carries upon his body the fateful substance of the goddess of destruction (*Nirṛti*), can pass it on to man through the filth he allows to fall. When the sacrificial animal bellows or kicks with the foot, the sin is passed on to the sacrifice, therefrom. The weeping of wailing women brings the guilt of sin into the house. Trita, onto whom the gods have 'wiped' the sin, wipes it in turn onto the man.[527] In the texts referring to sin and to liberation from it, there is throughout the fear of being compelled to atone for the 'sins done by the others'[528]—also those 'done by the gods' belong thereto[529]—and conversely, the constant attempt to impose the sins done by oneself upon the enemy.[530]

Sin causes disease or death to whomsoever it clings;[531] even madness can be caused 'by the sin coming from gods';[532] the substance of the sin brings eclipse by clinging to the sun.[533]

The picture of the concepts referring to the nature of sin will be supplemented below in our discussion of the cult of expiation. It is to be shown there how diverse magic set itself the task of removing that substance, how it was washed away, wiped off, chased, burnt, overcome like a disease cured by medicinal herbs. It may only be emphasized here as to how this view of sin and atonement had to cause serious hindrances to the introversion and the deepening of moral consciousness. Where the sin, just as it could come from without, could also be removed by external means, or where the waters washed off 'whatever evil is wrought, whatever is falsely sworn' (I, 23, 22), it was difficult that more serious feelings could develop than those of a superficially cautious fear of contact with the dangerous substance of sin; one refrained from the need to conquer sin completely in the depths of the soul. With exorcisms similar to the ones used to dispel fever or increase the prosperity of cattle, one ensured Agni's help in order to be put back by him 'among the world of the good', if one 'had promised, what one did not want to fulfil' (*Av.* VI, 119). One prayed to him in a quiet businesslike tone without the least hint of inner emotion. 'If by address, by blame, by imprecation we have committed sin, awake or sleeping, all hateful acts of ours, all evil doings may Agni bear away to distant places'[534] (*Ṛv.* X, 164, 3).

One would really underestimate the diversity of the currents running beside one another in the Veda, if one wanted to believe that the attitude of ancient Indian religious thinking to the idea of sin has been completely and exhaustively expressed in the forms of such outward expiatory magic and the technique of expiatory sacrifice. The expressions of the spiritual poets are, of course, not lacking, wherein the language of the soul tormented by sin is serious and arises from the depths. Such expressions are not used to refer to the removal of the impersonal substance of the sin effected by magic or through the action of a helpful god, but they refer to the reconciliation with an angry god who punishes sins. And thus, we come to speak of the second side of the idea of sin. The sin, which was represented so far as an idea effective by its own strength, is now to be considered by us as the preservation of moral order in its connection with divine anger and divine incidence.[535]

Varuṇa as the Punisher of Sins

As the impersonal physical and moral law of the world (the *Ṛta*) coincides with the 'commands of Varuṇa', so also is sin the violation of Varuṇa's commands or orders. One prays to Varuṇa: 'When through our want of thought, we violate your laws, punish us not, O god for this sin (*enas*).'[536] The fetters or the knots in which the sinner is caught, which themselves represent sin, are at the same time fetters of Varuṇa; he has spread them; he binds the sinful with them. The same poet who invokes the gods Soma and Rudra to free him 'from the sins clung to our body and which we have committed' in a verse quoted above continues: 'Free us from the fetters of Varuṇa'. There are other similar phrases besides this concept of the fetters of Varuṇa. For instance, there is talk of his anger which is most closely connected with the concept of sin. 'I search for my sins, Varuṇa ....The sages give me the same answer: it is Varuṇa, who is angry with you.'[537] In his anger, he sends diseases,[538] abandons the culprit to the beatings of an enemy, shortens the life-span, throws the god-less into the abyss; the sombre, deceitful spirits (*druhas*), which serve him and Mitra, pursue the sins of the human beings.[539]

It may appear that an element of mean craftiness itself is present in this superiority of Varuṇa, who is served by the deceitful spirits and whom even the cunning person does not escape. The Ādityas are called 'unerring, deceiving themselves';[540] one speaks of their 'magic power against the deceitful, their fetters which are opened for the wicked'; one hopes for Agni's protection against the deceit of Varuṇa (*dhūrti*);[541] the word *māyā* (magic power) which appears here is often used for Varuṇa's supernatural wisdom and art as well as for the cunning arts of the evil demons.[542] Was Varuṇa, therefore, portrayed like these demons in their crafty, perfidious way?

This view, which has in fact been advocated[543], appears to me to rest upon wrong estimation of the implications of sentences chosen with bias, of incompletely evaluated expressions. It is to be remembered,[544] above all, that the word *māyā* has just as little inferior as sublime bias. It simply means all secret abilities to perform deeds reaching beyond the general horizon. It is on account of Varuṇa's *māyā* that he sends a succession of dawns, that he measures, standing aloft, the earth with the sun, as with a measure, that the sun moves across the sky and is then concealed by the clouds, that rain trickles, honey-like, down to the earth.[545] It is clear that it concerns in all this here not cunning and deceit, but a secret, incomprehensible faculty. That this faculty could assume the dimension of cunning in an individual case need not be excluded from our consideration; but when that appears in the Veda as the main attribute of Varuṇa, it does not mean that one is justified in saying that cunning and malice alone form the basic character of this god. His might is the friend of the law (the *Ṛta*); it protects the law and punishes the sins of even the strong and the cunning. 'All falsehood you conquer, and closely cleave unto the law', it is said to Mitra and Varuṇa (*Ṛv*. I, 152, 1). And to the Ādityas, 'Gods, you are with the simple ones' (*Ṛv*. VIII, 18, 15). They are called 'strong in law'; 'they have strengthened themselves in the house of the law'.[546] What is said of all the gods also refers to them: 'Auspicious is the favour of gods who wander in righteousness' (I, 89, 2). Wherever the contradiction between the straight and the crooked, between honesty and double-dealing preoccupies the poets, the gods appear everywhere, foremost amongst them Varuṇa and the Ādityas, as friends and protectors of the good.

Only, one should not measure really this compact between Varuṇa and righteousness according to the modern Christian standards. To deceive an enemy was considered by the Vedic Indian as fair and good;[547] it would have appeared doubtful to him to hope for the conquest of the cunning person except through superior cunning. With that, it is clear of its own, in what sense one should understand the expressions mentioned above about the deceitful arts of Varuṇa and the Ādityas. The poets themselves say it: the deceitful spirits of Mitra and Varuṇa pursue the sins of human beings; their slings are spread open for the cheats. But Varuṇa is true and faithful to the good and the pious; whenever he is angry or does harm by his art of deceit, the one pursued by him understands—it is different in the case of the anger of Rudra—that it is the guilt of sin for which Varuṇa is punishing him.[548] And in that he does not try to challenge the god but tries to understand his guilt and to reconcile with Varuṇa, he is confident that Varuṇa will show himself not as a cunning enemy taking pleasure in doing harm but as a kind-hearted god who shows mercy. When we had to talk above about the salvation of the sinner through the magic removal of impersonal substance of the sin, we see here the same influence flowing from the mercy of Varuṇa, which is ready to step in place of anger to loosen the fetters of the sinner. This is similar to human kindness which can be incited by prayer, humility and even by gifts. One sacrifices to the god; one confesses that one is guilty; one shows to him that one has sinned unknowingly, without thinking and in passion; one refers to the old friendship with him; one praises his mercy. 'To gain your mercy, Varuṇa, with hymns we bind your heart, as binds the charioteer his tethered horse' (I, 25, 3).

One of the hymns in which Varuṇa is invoked for the pardon of sins (VII, 86) may be fully reproduced here:

Wise are creatures through his greatness who stayed even spacious heaven and earth asunder. Who urged the high and mighty sky to motion and spread firmly the stars and the earth.

With my own heart I ask myself the question, how Varuṇa and I may be united. What gift of mine will he accept unangered? When may I calmly look and find his mercy?

I search for my sins, Varuṇa; I long to know them. I seek the wise, and ask them. The sages give me the same answer: it is Varuṇa, who is angry with you.

What Varuṇa, has been my chief transgression, that you would slay the friend who sings your praises? Tell me, unconquered Lord! And quickly sinless will I approach you with my homage.

Free us from sins committed by our fathers, from those wherein we have ourselves offended. O King, loose, like a cattle-thief, as from the cord a calf, set free Vasiṣṭha.

Not our own will betrayed us, but seduction, Varuṇa, wine, dice, anger or thoughtlessness! The old is near[549] to lead astray the younger. Even sleep does not remove all evil-doing.

Slavelike may I do service to the Bounteous, serve, free from sin, the ardent God. This Aryan Lord gives wisdom to the simple; the wiser God leads on the wise to riches.

O Lord, O Varuṇa, may this laudation come close to your heart. May it be well with us in rest and labour. Preserve us everymore, you gods, with blessings.

Like the god who triumphs over the cunning of evil-doers by his superior cunning, so too in this hymn, will the man, driven to atonement not by the consciousness of guilt but by the fear of divine wrath, be found wanting when measured against the standards of modern virtue. Can it be of surprise to the historian, if the venerable prayers of the Veda are no longer in conformity with modern ethical standards? The penitent appears before god with measured, dignified calm. There is no passionate outbreak of sorrow or fear; when he speaks, he is calm, almost unruffled. But the earnest awareness of the divine guardian of the Law pursuing sin and, at the same time of the confidence in his clemency towards the penitent, has found here an expression whose simple and deep eloquence, rare in the poetry of the Veda, will be felt even today; and it may make this hymn appear to be one of the pinnacles in the realm of that religious poetry.

Agni and Indra pursuing Sins

Varuṇa and the Ādityas are the most decisive, but, of course, not the only, protectors of the Law and chasteners of sins. The figure of Agni in particular suited the need of the faith to see the world of the Law as connected with the world of gods.[550] This fact was already mentioned above and its obvious reasons were also indicated. Invocations are directed to Agni, similar to those directed to Varuṇa. He is requested to make amends for the sin, not to make the worshipper atone for the sin that is not his, to unclasp the fetters of sin, so that one may stand before Aditi free from sin. The difference between such prayers and those to Varuṇa lies foremost therein that they do not prevail very much over all the invocations of other types in the hymns to Agni, whereas they form the main contents of the hymns to Varuṇa. But apart from that, the special nature of Agni is expressed in a few specific nuances. After Varuṇa, the highest, Agni is to human beings the most immediate discerner of right and wrong and as such, the natural mediator between human justice, human sin and the divine judges: firstly, in that he reports on human beings to the higher gods; secondly, in that he speaks on their behalf to the gods, having become a true friend of man through daily contact. 'Why this complaint to Varuṇa, O Agni,? And why to Heaven? For what is our transgression? How will you speak to bounteous Mitra and to Earth? What will you say to Aryaman, and Bhaga.[551] 'Do you who know Varuṇa, O Agni, put far away from us the God's displeasure....Be, O Agni, nearest us with succour, our closest Friend, while this dawn is shining. Reconcile to us Varuṇa, be bounteous. Come and have pity on us. Be swift to hear us' 'He shall preserve us from Varuṇa's deceipt, from the deceipt of great god'.[552]

I do not want to go through the whole series of deities to collect for every single one, frequent or rare—predominantly, however, fairly rare—evidences of their friendship with the Eternal Law and their hatred for sinners. We may, however, consider briefly only the position of the most celebrated of all the gods in contrast to that of Varuṇa.[553]

Even Indra appears here and there as the pursuer of sins. How can the most powerful of this sphere of action remain completely excluded, how can he not, the mighty vanquisher, the rich donor of mercies, but be the vanquisher of the evil, the donor for the righteous? 'He has smitten all, ere they knew their danger, with his *Vajra*, the grievous sinners.' He says about himself: 'I slay the man who brings no milk oblation, the truth's perverter, the crooked, the hollow': it is indeed remarkable here that the idea of the evil intermingles with that of the one who does not do any sacrifice. Also, in one of the hymns on Indra (IV, 23), there is praise of the *Ṛta* with its strongholds, of the *Ṛta* whose tone also pierces through deaf ears. And Indra is invoked like Varuṇa: 'Slay us not for one trespass, not for two and three, O hero, nor yet for many trespasses.'[554] But the sparseness of such expressions in the gigantic mass of the hymns on Indra points out to the fact, that here, it does not concern Indra's real nature, but only a subordinate embellishment, that it is something carried over from the Ādityas. Indra, the chastener of sin, is not the real Indra; the real is the guardian of the sacrificer, enemy of the miser and the one who does not press the Soma.[555] When it is said that he destroys the insolent braggart, it does not mean that he plays there the role of a servant of the eternal justice, but he is the mighty Lord, who takes offence when another fellow beside him starts boasting. Besides, a series of Vedic expressions which contrast him with Varuṇa show quite clearly that it was not Indra whom one knew as the real Lord over right and wrong. One can reckon up for this point, when Indra is celebrated once as the opponent and destroyer of those who break statutes of Mitra and Varuṇa (X, 89, 8.9): sin is an offence just not against Indra but against those gods, and only after them, the real marshals of the Law, comes Indra, his strong arm then at the disposal of their statutes. But quite characteristic are the expressions given below:[556] 'Aditi, Mitra, Varuṇa! Forgive us, in whatever we have erred and sinned against you. May I obtain the broad light, O Indra, free from peril. Let not great darkness seize us.' 'Far from us still be Varuṇa's displeasure. May Indra give us spacious room to dwell in.' Again and again, Indra stands beside the Ādityas, the wrathful, yet merciful guardians of the Law, in another rôle, as the merciful friend of his worshipper, caring very little for sin and righteousness, the member of a world of gods, which is at first meant to serve the human desire for power and wealth, indifferent to the world of moral ideas and coming in contact with it only gradually and superficially.

REFERENCES

1. Presumptions about the pre-historic development of the Fire-deity, V. Schroeder, *Ar. Religion* II, 582ff.
2. Schrader, *Reallexikon der idg. Altertumskunde* 599f.
3. Compare the remarks of Schrader, *Encycl. of Rel. and Ethics* II, 34f. and of Hirt, *Indogermanen* II, 510.
4. Whereby it is clear that assimilations take place, which, incidentally, merge with the Indra-type. It does not matter, if the Fire-god is stamped as the Vṛtra-killer, but one can hardly name Indra as a sacrificial priest (*Hotar*).
5. Is it because Agni is not mentioned in the documents of Boghaz-köi (see above p. 13)?
6. *Ṛv.* I, 69, 2.
7. Compare I, 99, 1; VI, 16, 16. Agni appears more often as a drinker of Soma, where he finds his place in the company of Indra, in the second line of the Maruts. There, he is to some extent attracted by these.
8. *Ṛv.* II, 9, 3; III, 54, 1; I, 128, 3.
9. Thus, most distinctly in the well-known formula of *Ait. Br.* II, 34. Compare the Ṛgvedic references in Bergaigne I, 103. The concept of Agni kindled by the gods will rest, on the one hand, upon the thought that the heavenly forms of fire—as they are similar in nature to the terrestrial fire—must be kindled like these; on the other hand, upon the idea lying in the divine anthropomorphism that the highest and the sacred activity of human beings must be executed by gods: sacrifice, and therefore, also the kindling of the sacrificial fire.
10. Or a triad with Agni ('born of Strength') produced by rubbing as the third form?
11. See Bergaigne I, 21f., Macdonell 93.
12. Nickname of Agni, 'the one who knows the beings (births)'.
13. The preceding verse has spoken of this. Compare I, 163, 4, for the differentiation between 'water' and 'ocean'. Should 'ocean' refer to the idea of under-sea fire (compare below p. 152 note 40)?
14. II, 1, 1; I, 70, 3. 4; III, 22, 2 (compare my notes for the first verse; is I, 70, 4 to be read as *viśpāḥ*?). In addition, one may take the long enumeration of places of Agni's abode from the later Vedic literature like *Atharvaveda* III, 21, and the short one like *Atharv.* XII, 1, 19f. and in the *mantra* in *Āpastamba Śraut* V, 16, 4.
15. Yet not without restriction; see p. 64f.

16. It does not contradict that, if the bringing down of fire by Mātariśvan (see p. 64f.) from heaven is said to suggest the lightning in its original meaning, for it is quite doubtful, how far this view was still vital for the Vedic poets and thinkers themselves.

17. *Ṛv*. III, 14, 4; VIII, 56, 5. *Taitt. S.* IV, 2, 9, 4; compare also *Ṛv*. X, 88, 6. 10. 11; *Av*. XIII, 1, 11.

18. I quote that, 'the Brahmana sets a chariot or a wheel in motion on the south side, till the wheel has turned thrice' when the sacrificial fire is set up. This is obviously a sun-symbol (see p. 44). I further quote that one should not step at that time between the sun and the fire (*Āpastamba Śraut.* V, 14, 6, 10). Production of fire by rubbing should not be done before the sunrise (*Maitr. Saṃh.* I, 6, 10).—A firebrand as a representative of the sun is found in a ritual, *Śatapatha Br.* III, 9, 2, 9 (compare p. 44).

19. Resp. the sacrificial fires; more details can be dispensed with here.

20. It is futile to ask wheteher this magic is based on the idea of terrestrial fire as an image of the sun or the similarity of fire with the sun: both fairly coinciding for the old way of thinking

21. *Śatap. Br.* II, 3, 1, 5.

22. The sun considered as male.

23. In the sun resting in the sacrificial fire.

24. Bergaigne I, 140f., whose depiction lets the special meaning of this ritual become too much indistinct in the general category of 'action of the earthly sacrifice is based on celestial phenomenon'.

25. Literally 'log of wood'. As the fire rests in the wood, the heavenly fire also presupposes a log of wood. Compare *Ṛv*. III, 2, 9.

26. *Ṛv*. V, 6, 4 (compare my note on I, 30, 9); X 156, 4.

27. *Ṛv*. IV, 3, 11—compare also *Taitt. Saṃh.* IV, 7, 13, 3 where it is said of the old Ṛṣis: 'Kindling the fire, bringing forth the sun'.

28. I agree in this case with Hillebrandt, *V.M.* II, 128ff.

29. *Ṛv*. VI, 6, 2. *Av*. VIII, 1, 11, may also be emphasized. See further in Bergaigne I, 15, Macdonell 92.

30. I mention from the ritual the use of wood of a tree struck by lightning, concerning the relation between Agni and lightning in the rite of the setting up of the fire (*Āpast. Śr.* V, 2, 4, obviously the energy of the lightning-fire should also be made subservient to the rite), so also the expiation to be fulfilled by a sacrifice to 'Agni in the waters' when the sacrificial fire had mixed itself with the fire of the lightning (*Śat. Br.* XII, 4, 4, 4; *Kāty* XXV, 4, 33; *Ait. Br.* VII, 7, *Śānkh. Śr.* III, 4, 7). Of special interest is for this the way of expression of *Ait. Br. ibid.*, 'whose fires mix with the celestial fire: what is the expiation for that? He should offer to the Agni in waters an eight-shelled flat cake'—for which then the verses *Ṛv*. VIII, 43, 9 and III, 1, 3 are prescribed, both mentioning Agni's abode in the waters. It appears to me clearly that the fire of the lightning alone is shown here as a celestial fire. The fire in the waters, distinguished from the fire of the lightning, is, however, so to say, the normal fire. One sacrifices to it to let it overcome the foreign tinge (compare below p. 152 note 40). There follows, incidentally, at the same place, a similar rite to the 'pure Agni' for the case, where the sacrificial fire mixes with the obsequial fire. See below p. 152 note 41 on another sacrifice to 'Agni in the waters'.

31. Hillebrandt, *V.M.* I, 368.

32. *Av*. XIII, 1, 50 may also be compared when the real Agni as the one 'burning in the waters' is juxtaposed with the mystic Agni which 'is set in truth'. See also XIX, 33, 1 where Agni appears, so to say, as the essence of water.

33. As Darmesteter has shown in his script '*Haurvatāṭ et Ameretāṭ*'.

34. Compare *Ṛv*. I, 70, 3; 145, 5; X, 4, 5; 51, 3; 91, 6; *Av*. IV, 15, 10; XII, 3, 50.

35. Bergaigne (I, 17f.) has set an example for me in appreciation of these verses, in fact, of all the most important points mentioned here.

36. *Ṛv*. VII, 9, 3; VIII, 43, 9; I, 141, 4; compare also I, 67, 9. Agni is shown as 'power-abundance of water and plants' in *Taitt. Saṃh.* IV, 7, 13, 2; it is said in *ibid.* IV, 6, 2, 3 that

'the father and the creator of plants has put down the offspring of waters (i.e., Agni) at many places'. See also *Ṛv*. VII, 101,1.

37. *Atharvaveda* IV, 4, 5; VIII, 7, 8.9.

38. *Atharvaveda* VIII, 7, 21f.

39. *Ṛv*. I, 65, 9. It must remain doubtful whether it belongs here, when the sacrificer 'who lets a misfortune-bringing fire extinguish, completes his offerings to Agni in the waters (*Āpastamba* V, 26, 4; compare above p. 150 note 30).

40. Compare *Ṛv*. VIII, 39, 8. 10, where it is said that 'Agni rests in all rivers', that 'the flowing waters surround him—a later Vedic saying names as the 'semen of Agni originating from the waters' the gold, which is, as it is well-known, to be found in the rivers of India (*Āpast*. V, 2, 1). Is the idea of the under-sea fire, especially dwelling in the ocean and which is obviously developed in these contexts, to be ascribed to the *Ṛgveda*? Compare Geldner, Ved. Stud. II, 269ff., Hillebrandt, *V.M.* II, 143 note 3 and my remarks *ZDMG*. LV, 318f.

41. XII, 1, 37. So also *ibid*. VIII, 1, 11 'the Agnis within the waters' are distinguished from the 'Agni of heaven with the lightning; so also in III, 21, 1. 7 'the Agnis in the waters' are different from 'those who follow the path of lightning'. Compare also note 30.—It is, of course, different in the scheme of *Āpastamba* V, 16, 4, where three forms of Agni are distinguished: the Agni in animals, on the earth; the Agni in the waters, in the air; the Agni in the sun, in the sky. Here, therefore, the waters are those of the air-empire.

42. *Pāraskara* II, 6, 10 (*Mantra Brāhmaṇa* 1, 7, 1f.); *Śāṅkhāyana G*. V, 2, 5. More, while discussing Apāṃ napāt, p. 67.

43. *Ait. Br*. VIII, 6.

44. *Taitt. S*. IV, 6, 1, 2; *VS*. XVII, 6. Compare Weber, *Ind. Stud*. XIII, 274. Bloomfield, *Amer. Journal af Philology* XI, 345.

45. The 'seven notes'—i.e., the notes of the scale appearing in the laudatory hymns (compare I, 164, 24; IX, 103, 3)—appear to be thought in mystical unity with the seven rivers (compare Bergaigne II, 132). It is quite doubtful that they have sprung from the thunder sounds of the cloud through the identification favoured by the agreement of the number seven—the development in the meaning of Sarasvatī may be compared—; even if it is correct, the concept becoming independent will leave it always quite doubtful, whether the water, to which one alludes here, is the water of the cloud.

46. V, 84, 3; X, 75, 3c etc., may be compared.

47. 'Swift running' is a popular attribute of the infant of waters in the Veda.

48. By god of water, one should not think of a being similar to Poseidon. Of course, the ocean was not unknown to the Vedic Indians; only it was far.

49. Another hymn VII, 47 referring to the same rite is addressed almost alone to the waters, i.e., rivers, but only incidentally to Apāṃ napāt.

50. Compare my notes on the hymn.

51. In addition to it, a saying in the later Vedas (*VS*. VI, 27, etc.), 'You divine waters, child of the waters! What is your wave...give it to gods', etc.

52. The later Vedic Literature shows Apāṃ napāt in a similar role at a ceremony of the rain-magic (Kārīsīṣṭi, *Taitt. S*. II, 4, 8, 1); Further the sacrifice to be made to Apāṃ napāt may be mentioned when the sacrificial animal was drowned in water (*Kāty*. XXIII, 4, 14).

53. Is the infant of the waters also surrounded by women in the *Avesta*? It is hardly possible; compare Bartholomae *WB* under xša ⊙ rya.

54. What does the ostentatious dress of butter mean? We saw, that the offering of butter was made to the infant of waters.—'Butter is its meal' ' (*Ṛv*. II, 32, 11), only because it feeds the human beings with butter. Because from waters 'which our cows drink' (I, 23, 18), they get the nourishment, which they further give to the human beings (Compare *Śatap. Br*. II, 3, 1, 10). The Rain-god is invoked thus: 'Saturate heaven and earth with butter and let there be abundant drink for the cows' (V, 83, 8). Therefore, one looks upon the butter as originating from ocean and waters (IV, 58, 1; X, 30.13, etc.)

55. The words 'uplifted in the lap, himself erect' are also used in I, 95, 5, for Agni in the waters.

56. I quote here also a verse from the later Vedas (*VS*. VIII, 24, etc.) which belongs to

another rite concerning water at the Soma-sacrifice and in that respect, it is comparable with the hymn *Ṛv.* X, 30. A piece of wood was thrown into the water at the purification-bath following the sacrifice, and the sacrificial butter was offered with the verse, 'Agni's face has entered waters preserving the infant of waters, the wonder-power. Offer the piece of wood house after house. May your tongue stretch out towards the butter.'

57. *Ṛv.* I, 70, 4; II, 1, 1; *Av.* XII, 1, 19.

58. *Ṛv.* X, 5, 1; *Av.* III, 21, 2; XII, 1, 19; 2, 33; *Taitt. Saṃh.* IV, 6, 1, 3.

59. *Ṛv.* VII, 4, 5 (compare 5, 2); *Av.* XII, 1, 19; *Śāṅkh. G.* I, 19, 5; *Hiraṇyakeśin G.* I, 25, 1.

60. *Ṛv.* I, 70, 3; *Av.* V, 25, 7.

61. About this compare particularly Charpentier, *Kleine Beitr. zur indoir.* Myth. 69ff. One cannot get anything much etymologically from the name; compare Macdonell 72, O. Richter *IF.* IX, 247 note 4, Wackernagel, *Ai Grammatik* II 125. 210; Henry, *Journ. as.* 1905, II, 391. I do not think, that the opinion often expressed that M. is nothing but the form of Agni, has no firm basis. The verses which identify him with Agni (Bergaigne I, 53) treat mainly the popular theme that Agni is similar in nature to various gods. This has, of course, nothing to do with the real historical identity (thus I, 164, 46; III, 5, 9; 26, 2; 29, 11). Later mysticism fits into X, 88, 19 and also 114, 1. Then only I, 96, 4 remains, (it may be noted that there in V. 1 Agni is named Mitra) which is too isolated to prove something. That M. is the wind, as the later texts point out, appears to be based upon a secondary speculation by virtue of III, 29, 11? (A later verse from *Ṛv.* fits in perhaps IX, 67, 31.) Hillebrandt, *V.M.* II, 149ff. has a different view.

62. *Ṛv.* I, 93, 6; III, 9, 5; VI, 8, 4.

63. About that see under the section on human beings.

64. That is the place of sacrifice.

65. Another name of legendary family of priests.

66. *Ṛv.* I, 58, 6; 143, 4, X, 46, 2 (compare II, 4, 2); 122, 5.

67. I, 60, 1. Compare also I, 71, 4; X, 46, 9. III, 5, 10 is doubtful. Compare my note on the relevant hymn.

68. *Ṛv.* X, 51-53. See my notes and the literature cited there.

69. When Hillebrandt (*V.M.* II, 144ff., compare 138) explains Agni finding refuge in water as the sun, I cannot follow, particularly, I cannot approve of the role that is ascribed to Agni Vaiśvānara ('belonging to all human beings') as the sun. I think, Agni's refuge in the water depends upon the fact that he was known as hidden in the water from the motives discussed above (p. 65f). I cannot discover in it the connection of the whole to the solstice.

70. As a divine representative of human race who was required for the sacrifice of Agni?

71. See below the section on sacrificial priests with reference to the characteristics of the *Hotar*-priest.

72. *Ṛv.* I, 96, 2 compare 4. Verses like VI, 1, 5 are of course not important.

73. This view represented many times in literature follows in the footsteps of Kuhn, *Herabkunft des Feuers* 69ff.

74. *Ṛv.* III, 29, 1ff.; X, 184, 3; Vs. V, 2. I do not think that Purūravas and Urvaśī are more deeply mythically connected with kindling of fire. They may be owing their name above all to the fact that Purūravas was known as an excellently diligent and, as he begot Āyu, a successful, dutiful husband (*Ṛv.* X, 95, 4f.). That Agni is sometimes named Āyu, may be on account of this connection of the kindling of fire with Purūravas and Urvaśī. Different view in Bloomfield, *JAOS.* XX, 180ff.

75. *Ṛv.* I, 62, 2; 71, 2; VII, 42, 1; X, 62, 2; 67, 2.

76. See under the myths of Indra.

77. *Ṛv.* X, 62, 5. 6.

78. Bergaigne II, 308.

79. See the material in Bergaigne II, 217f. It may be mentioned that this function is occasionally attributed to all important gods; and it is not unusual. It is often attributed to Soma, where the conventional phraseology of the Soma-hymns and the idea that Soma, inspiring powerful deeds is to some extent their performer, appears to me to be more in

play than the profound mythological context. The verses, though they are comparatively numerous, are all almost colourless (also *Ṛv*. VII, 104, a prayer to Indra and Soma, to kill the demons, lets Soma step noticeably behind Indra); so also Soma does not appear to play any important role in the magic ritual in question.

80. It can be said, in the primitive practice of initiation into puberty. We shall show later that this is at the bottom of this Vedic ritual.

81. *Ṛv*. X, 169, 2. How in the sacrifice the cows whose milk was used were named, is shown by Hillebrandt, *Neu und Vollmondsopfer* 12.

82. If my supposition in *ZDMG*. XXXIX, 86 is correct.

83. Compare Weber, *Indische Studien*, X, 78ff.

84. *Ṛv*. VII, 8, 4.

85. Compare above p. 17. One may also refer here to L. v. Schroeder, *Herakles und Indra* (Denkschr. der K. Akad. Vienna 1914).

86. It may be mentioned in brief that a feature of the most powerful gods and heroes narrated amongst various people and agreeing peculiarly in all respects (see A. Lang, *Myth, Ritual and Religion*, I, 183; II, 113f; 244) is also attributed to Indra; i.e., his birth in a way other than the natural. In *Ṛv*. IV, 18, 1-2 the mother (?) says before the child Indra is born, 'That is the well-known way in which all gods were born. In this way he should be born becoming strong. He should not kill the mother in an absurd manner.' But the child answers, 'I shall not go out there. I shall go out from the sides'.

87. It is not said; The conquering of the enemy who is named Vṛtra, Vala, Paṇis etc., and the liberation of waters is a part of the victory over Vṛtra, and the liberation of the cows, that over the Paṇis; i.e., both the myths are conceived as parallel and independent at the same time. They are also independent in their original meaning. This independence is, of course, not due to the occasional intermingling.

88. That the appalative 'enemy' is generalised by the proper name Vṛtra (as we say: a Cato, a Catilina) is not acceptable, on account of the neuter gender of Vṛtra 'enemy'. Besides, the word in the language of the *Ṛgveda*, Vṛtra 'the enemy', is no more a word in current usage. I do not think, that it can ever be used without a side-glance to the demon Vṛtra: that Indra (or one's own men in alliance with Indra) appears as the conqueror of the enemy or enemies, he is then quite predominantly considered as the one who killed enemies, as he had killed Vṛtra. The verb used with it is *han* which also refers to *Vṛtrahan* (compare e.g. VI, 73, 2 where it is said *ghnan vṛtrāṇi jayañ chatrūn, amitrān sāhan*). Without the participation of these suggestions, 'enemy' in the *Ṛgveda* in usual sense,. is *śatru* or *amitra*. The expressions, e.g., in VI, 75 may be noted; A person acquainted with the Veda would definitely feel that Vṛtra would be wrong in place of the words mentioned there.

89. The weapon of Indra, See page 76f.

90. See p. 78f.

91. On the other hand, one also comes across an understandable feature, that after the killing, Indra is afraid of the revenge and flees (I, 32, 14). I think, Hubert and Mauss (*Année sociologique* 1898, 124 note 4) are searching rather too deep for its explanation.

92. I, 51, 4; 52, 8; VIII, 89, 4.

93. With that it is naturally only said that they did not understand the liberation of waters by Indra in this sense. It is of course something different when lightning, thunder etc., (p. 74 f.) appear in the description of Vṛtra's wild behaviour.

94. For exceptions, see Bergaigne II, 184 note 2, Hillebrandt, *V.M.* III, 196 note 3 and compare, what is said on p. 77f. Hopkins (*PAOS*. April 1895, CCXXXVI ff.) amongst others has a different view of the question discussed here.

95. This observation is already made by Bergaigne (II, 184f.). But the meaning which he gives to it—that the verb *vṛṣ-* is only used for 'to rain', where it deals with the act of the divine power without fight—is misplaced.

96. *Ṛv*. III, 33, 6. 7. Compare also VII, 47, 4.

97. This is, as a matter of fact, the view represented by Leyens, *German. Abhandlungen H. Paul dargebracht*, p. 148 f.

98. Hillebrandt (*Ved. Myth.*, small ed. 85) who acknowledges Vajra as a thunder-wedge,

does not certainly want to conclude anything about the myth from this. 'We see the thunder-wedge also in the hand of the Indian Bṛhaspati, the Iranian Mithra and the Greek Zeus'. I wish to speak here only of Indian gods amongst the gods named here. As far as I see, only *Ṛv*. I, 40, 8, *Av*. XI, 10, 12. 13 see also v. 10 (Hillebrandt, *Ved. Myth*. I, 410) can be considered. But is there in the first place (and generally the whole Pragātha concerning this) talk of Bṛhaspati, and not perhaps of the pious amongst the human beings (compare my note on the hymn)? In the second place Bṛhaspati prepared the magically powerful Vajra. The magician of the gods does it. Can such remarks do anything about the fact that Indra and Indra alone, is the master of Vajra? Could it be also said with the same justification in view of *Ṛv*. VI, 16, 14, etc., that the Vṛtra-victory belongs as well to Agni as to Indra?

99. Compare what is said above on p. 52 note 18 about this shifting of emphasis.

100. Hillebrandt, *V.M.* III, 162ff; Small ed. 86ff.

101. Hillebrandt, *V.M.* small ed. 88: 'The mountains...are not the 'castles of cloud' or 'clouds', but the mountains on which there is winter'. The myth, however, speaks of the mountains enclosing water in themselves and therefore cleaved by Indra. Therefore, for the context of the myth they are extremely important. But in the other case, 'the mountains on which there is winter' shows only a background.

102. Of Andreas and Wackernagel. Compare also Hüsing, *Die iranische Überlieferung* 52f; E. Lehmann in *Chantepie de la Saussayes Lehrbuch der Religionsg*.[3] II, 22. On Apaoša, see Wackernagel in 'Aufsätze E. Kuhn gewidmet' 158f.

103. *Ṛv*. IV, 26, 2; X, 124, 9; I, 80, 14; 52, 6; II, 13, 7; VIII, 3, 19. 20; I, 80, 4. Compare above Page 154 note 94.

104. Also the Buddhistic. Thus we read in it that 'the thundering cloud, the hundred-fold wise god (*śatakratu*, i.e., Indra) who fills heights and depths garlanded by lightning and who pours the rain over the earth'. *Saṃyutta Nikāya* vol. I, p. 100.

105. *Ṛv*. X, 8, 8. It is done, however, by Indra in verse 9.

106. Literally 'I brought forth the kine'. *Ṛv*. X, 48, 2. It appears, as if the serpent has eaten the cows and they would be taken out of the dead serpent. Compare *Taitt. S*. II, 1, 4, 5.

107. One may think of the three-headed serpent in the parallels from the *Avesta* (see p. 78).

108. Ṛv. X, 8, 8 Indra incites Trita; II, 11, 19 he subdues Viśvarūpa for Trita (in similar tone moves the verse X, 48, 2 mentioned above). It is different in X, 99, 6 (compare also X, 8, 9). Indra is the only performer in the first half; It may be doubtful whether the deed extolled in the other half belongs to Trita strengthened by Indra in the same context. *Śat. Br*. I, 2, 3, 2 tries to unite Trita's and Indra's roles in killing Viśvarūpa with one another. Even as the killer of Vṛtra, Trita competes with Indra (I, 187, 1); His involvement in this myth appears to be secondary.

109. As it is well-known, the role of guiding the cows back caught by an inimical power has gone over to Mithra in the *Avesta*. *Mihir Yašt* 86.

110. I do not consider this well-known comparison of the Indian myth with the Greek more than only probable; Wilamowitz (*Euripides Herakles*, second edition, I, pp VIIIff.) does not convince me, when it is said, that there can be no comparison. The hiding place of cows in the caves coincides with the Veda in the Roman form of the legend (Hercules-Cacus), in whatever way one may judge its relation to the Greek legend.

111. The agreement of the passage in *Gāthā*, Yasna 51, 5 (*yathā ašāṭ hacā gąm vīdaṭ*) noticed long ago by Darmesteter (*Ormazd et Ahriman* 146) speaks for it in the expressions which are familiar to the *Ṛgveda* (e.g. III, 31, 5; IV, 3, 11; X, 62, 2) for the story of the liberation of cows. It may be noticed that the Avestic passage is in the context, which refers to the claim of the pious to the earthly goods: as in the Veda, the myth appears as the glorification of the claims of the Brahmanas on the gifts of cows.

112. Hillebrandt (*V.M.* I, 83ff.) has shown, that the conception of Paṇis as merchants, is not tenable. But his own view is in conformity with the view of Brunnofer, that they are in inimical race and are the Parners living in historical time at the Ochus (Tedschend) does

not, I think, agree better with the Vedic sources. I refer to my note (compare also *GGA*. 1914, 447) on main reference of Hillebrandt (*ibid*. 97), *Ṛv*. VI, 61, 1.

113. On the similarity of a passage in the *Avesta* to this expression, see above page 155, note 111.

114. Compare above page 35f.

115. IV, 1, 13. 14. 16. 17; III, 39, 5; I, 71, 2; IV, 3, 11; X, 68, 9; II, 24, 3. Few of the verses appear, as if the acquisition of cows was seen as a magic creating the Dawns (One who has the image, gets the thing himself), just like the kindling of Agni, which is discussed in IV, 3, 11 together with the acquisition of cows, is a magic causing the sunrise and appears as such at this place. Compare also my note on I, 6.

116. It is said in *Ṛv*. VI, 13, 3, that through the protection of Agni 'the prince kills with his might the enemy (Vṛtra), the priest runs away with the possession of Paṇi'. As Vṛtra-killing is an ideal of warrior's heroism, so is also, in the same way, liberation of the cows from Paṇi, a distinctive prototype of priestly success.

117. Compare above page 155, note 111.

118. If there, at least in the Veda, the ancestors of the priests play the main role, then it appears to date back to the widely known, and certainly, ancient type of the myths about the ancestors, who have acquired this or that property for humanity: so e.g., in the case of bush-men 'the men who brought *the sun*' (Lang, *Myth, Ritual and Religion*, I, 175) and the like very common.

119. *Ṛv*. I, 92, 4; VII, 79, 4: 75, 7; VI, 65, 5. Compare Bergaigne I, 246.

120. I think, letting the cows of the Greek myth stay in the extreme west would fit very well in it. Therefore, the Dawns, which belong to the east, are to be thought of as detained in the west as long as they are in the inimical power.

121. See the section on this god.

122. At places, the acquisition of the sun appears to be the result of Vṛtra-Victory (compare above page 76), e.g., I, 51, 4: 'When you have slain with might the dragon Vṛtra, you, Indra, did raise the Sun in Heaven for all to see' (more in Bergaigne II, 191). It does not appear to me that in the whole texts the connection of the winning of the light is by far not so firm and predominant with the Vṛtra-victory as its connection with the liberation of cows. I believe, that one cannot think as well of the natural occurrence of the reappearing of the sun after a storm as also rather of a motif of some other type: the acquisition of the sparse things follows the overcoming of the most fearful danger and the most difficult battle.

123. One must bear in mind that the state of research with reference to the Indian heroic legend compared to the German is altogether different: we do not know the national history of old India.

124. Accepting the difference of meaning between *dāsa* and *dasyu* appears to me to be forced in spite of Hillebrandt, *V.M*. III, 276 (I lay stress on IV, 28, 4; X, 22, 8 from many sources). Namely, the interesting hypothesis represented by the same research scholar in I, 94ff., III, 275 in connecting the word *dāsa* with the ancestral name Daer (east of Caspian ocean) may be correct (compare viz. Yašt 13, 144). But I consider this to be extremely more probable that the ancestral name has become specialised in the use of the Iranians from the general meaning than *vice-versa* (see the literature in Macdonell-Keith's. *Ved. Index*. s.v.). I don't go here into the detail of the development of the meaning of *dahyu* (=Ved. *dasyu*) in the Iranian.

125. Bergaigne II, 209; compare below p. 157, note 131.

126. i.e., the ideal representative of the real men i.e., the Aryan. Thus Dāsas are called *amānuṣa* 'inhuman'. It does not mean then that they were not human beings in our sense of the term.

127. *a-nās*. Or 'mouth-less' (*an-ās*), i.e., speaking in an unintelligible language?

128. Hillebrandt (*V.M*. I, 96, 107; III, 268ff.) turns this Divodāsa into a Dāsa-prince. Here Dāsa should stand as a family name in the sense shown in the note 124 above. This statement, which would shake the very historical foundation of the Ṛgvedic poetry, appears

to me to be baseless: a king, who is called 'the servant of the Heaven' (compare Bergaigne II, 209) can, therefore, also belong to the nation of masters.

129. Some such names appear to be un-Aryan in view of their phonetic form.

130. Thus Śambara is the most famous enemy of Divodāsa Atithigva, but Indra has 'killed' Karanja and Parnaya 'with the sharpest wheel-bar of Atithigva, I, 53, 8, compare X, 48, 8.

131. Thus in I, 53, 10; VI, 18, 13; in VIII, 53, 2 it is said that Indra subdued Kutsa for Atithigva, and Āyu for the young king Tūrvayāna, just like the subduing of a Dasyu. There is a mention of the same deed in II, 14, 7 besides the victory over Śuṣṇa, Pipru, Śambara, etc. Compare also IX, 61, 2.

132. This is the son of Vidathin—V, 29, 11.

133. II, 12, 11; IV, 30, 14; VI, 26, 5.

134. See for this word p. 85f.

135. VI, 31, 4; VII, 99, 5; I, 51, 5.

136. Compare p. 82, on the name.

137. i.e., perhaps with the (weapon) of Kutsa (Geldner). Or with Kutsa's *mantra* or *Sāman* (Hillebrandt).

138. At places, the story of the horse Etaśa is added. It is more obscure. Without going into all details and variations, I shall attempt to put together the main features as under: when the Sun moves with his gold-yellow mares (Harit), Indra also drives at the same time Etaśa really belonging to the Sun-god with the horses of wind. There appears to be a rivalry between Etaśa and Harit. Indra strikes down one wheel of the Sun-chariot and checks the run of Harit. Etaśa—as bondsman of the Sun-god? that he finally is-brings back the wheel to him and puts it on the chariot. But he has subdued Harit during this race. Compare viz. Geldner, *Ved. Stud*, II, 161ff. Hillebrandt, *V.M.* III, 278ff., and my notes on *Ṛv.* II, 19, 5; VIII, 1, 11.

139. *ZDMG.* 42, 211; Bergaigne II, 337f. Hillebrandt, *ibid.*, 292 interprets the facts differently.

140. Compare I, 121, 10: 'before the Sun sinks into darkness'. Compare X, 138, 3.

141. It may be a mixing up of the demon-myths that Śuṣṇa is once called 'horned' (I, 33, 12), but it cannot decide about demoniac character of the whole personality; one can as well think of the war-ornaments of a general. A considerable projection of demoniac character can be visible in V, 32, 4. From all appearance, Śuṣṇa is shown as an animal (*mṛga*) in V, 34, 2. Kutsa is finally included possibly in mythical contexts in the verse, X, 138, 1, which is not very clear.

142. Later Vedic texts give, as it is the usual case with them, a more detailed old version of the text. Indra and Namuci had agreed not to attack each other by day or by night, in a dry place or in a wet place. Indra struck him at the crack of dawn, as it was neither night nor day, with a weapon that was neither dry nor wet. This finding of a way out, where every way out is barred, is just like a fairy-tale motif.

143. About this story, see Bloomfield, *JAOS.* XV, 143ff., Hillebrandt, *V.M.*, 255ff., my remarks *NGGW.* 1893, 342ff. and my notes on X, 131.

144. *Ṛv.* II, 11, 2; X, 99, 6; IV, 18, 19.

145. Compare from the literature, *viz.*, Darmesteter, *Ormazd et Ahriman* 269f.; v. Bradke, *Dyâus Asura, Ahura Mazdâ und die Asuras*; Geldner, *Ved. Studien* I, 142; Hillebrandt, *V.M.* III, 430ff.; T. Segerstedt, *Rev. de l'hist. des religions* LVII, 157ff., 293ff.

146. It appears to me to be of doubtful nature, what Hillebrandt (*V.M.* III, 441ff., small ed. 189) understands as the Vedic traces of the Iranian Asura-worship. Compare also p. 86f.

147. Compare the index to the passages in V. Bradke p. 120f. Of course, one has to take into account the very little bulk of hymns addressed to Varuṇa or Mitra-Varuṇa in comparison to those addressed to Indra or Agni.

148. I refer to the section on good and evil gods in which we have to come back to the nature of *māyā*.

149. Bergaigne III, 80.

150. Compare the *Atharvaveda* III, 9, 4; IV, 23, 5; VI, 72, 1; VIII, 10, 22; XIX, 66, 1; *Śat. Br.* II, 4, 2, 5; X, 5, 2, 20; XIII, 4, 3, 11; *Taitt. Saṃh.* IV, 1, 9, 2; 2, 10, 3. Even in the *Rāmāyaṇa*, there is one Asura Māyāvin. One may remember at least the striking name of the Asura Maya of the epic and the astronomical tradition.

151. No matter what is the etymology and the basic meaning of the word. Even if it had finally to do with *asu* (something like 'soul' as the principle of physical life)—besides this possibility, there are other equally important—, nothing would follow from it for the derivation of the Asuras of the Vedic belief, say, from worship of the souls and of the spirits of the ancestors. It results from the evidence of the deciding point of view given here. Upon this is clearly based the name *asura* given to different groups of beings.

152. This interpretation is remarkably supported by the contents of a series of verses. Thus, with reference to Indra VI, 30, 2; X, 96, 11; 99, 2 (there besides *māyāḥ*); for Savitar I, 35, 7. 10 etc.

153. Thus Indra and Agni are called 'killers of Asuras' in verses where one cannot question their remote antiquity (VI, 22, 4; VII, 13, 1). It may be noted that it is said of Indra in the same hymn from which the first of these verses are taken, that he has smashed the one 'having grown great' through *māyā*, he has destroyed all *māyā* (verses 6, 9).

154. Compare Darmesteter 269 and v. Bradke 100, note 2, who correctly refers to *Maitr. Saṃh.* I, 102, 1; 124, 8. Compare also *Ṛv.* V, 40, 5. 9. The view that *asura* gets the *a privativum* is shown, as it is well-known, by invention of the later word *sura*, 'god'. On the whole, it may be noted that Geldner, *op. cit.* and Darmesteter *op. cit.* agree in many respects with regard to the view on Asuras discussed here; It can very easily be seen that I differ from them. As it is well-known, both the 'devilization' of the Asuras in India and of the Devas in Iran has been considered as a parallel occurrence in various ways. I think, there is no serious doubt that the one here and the other there, was accomplished independent of one another, in fact, altogether independent of the mutual influence of the two nations. And besides, essentially in a different way. Great religious revolutions in Iran made old gods appear as devils to the followers of the new faith. Thus the word *deva* was thrown into a negative meaning from the positive. This is different from what happened in India, where the name *asura* originally indifferent with regard to positive or negative idea has been limited on the negative side wihout a considerable change in belief and has survived upon it alone (see p. 85f. in the text).

155. That the name Asura also applies to gods, speaks against the acceptance of such a definite class of beings.

156. That of the Dasyus intermingles obviously with the latter. Compare *Ṛv.* III, 29, 9; X, 54, 1; *Av.* IX, 2. 17. 18; X, 3, 11; *Taitt. Saṃh.* IV, 3, 11, 3, etc.

157. *Ṛv.* X, 124; Compare my notes and the literature mentioned there. Also page 48 above.

158. It is not within our purview to consider the stories of the battles between the Gods and the Asuras varied again and again in the Brahmaṇa-texts and in the later literature. They are in the foreground for the fantasy of these theologians almost like the battles between the rich Ahuramazdas and Anromainyus, between Aesir and giants for the Avestic and the Nordic poets of myths. One may refer here to one feature mentioned often in these stories that the gods are at first at a disadvantage; they then discover this or that trick of the sacrifice and win the battle. I think that one sought too deep for the explanation of this feature when one allowed the 'memory of the old Asura who ruled once the beautiful world' (v. Bradke 106 note 2) or the difference in races (T. Segrestedt, *Revue de l'hist. des religions* LVII, 161ff) to play a role. As those stories end in a victory of the gods and as a rule, are derived from a certain trick, it is a part of an effective narrative technique that the gods were not doing well at the beginning.

159. *ZDMG.* XLII, 220.

160. *Ibid.*, p. 203ff; my notes on VII, 18.

161. *Āśvalāyana G.* III, 12, 13.

162. The Storm-god, right from the Indo-European period, appears to be one or the other.

163. Pischel-Geldner, *Ved Studien* I, XXVII; they think of this verse. Yet it may be dealing there with a situation of the ritual which need not depend upon any story. The oft quoted apparent monologue of the drunken Indra X, 119 is to be denied to this god: it is probably the effusion of the poet intoxicated himself by Soma. See my note on the hymn.

164. Compare viz. Weber, *Sitzungsb. der Berl. Akad.* 1887, p. 903.

165. For example one may refer to the contribution of Örtel, *JAOS.* XXVI, 176ff.

166. *Ṛv.* X, 86. See my notes on the hymn and the literature quoted there.

167. Indrāṇī.

168. Here and at the end of every verse follws a refrain: "Indra, above all!'

169. We shall come back to his contrast to Varuṇa in this respect later (p. 146ff.); compare the section on gods and the moral world.

170. The discussion on Soma in the chapter on the cult may be compared.

171. See on this above pp. 38, 48f. This bird is also well-known to the mythologies of the primitive people.

172. See Roscher, *Nektar und Ambrosia* p. 13ff.

173. *ibid.*, pp. 76, 79, the same Selene 49f.

174. See T. Segerstedt, *Le monde oriental* IV, 60f.

175. Can we also consider the idea of the celestial tree dripping with honey as Indo-European? See Roscher, Nektar und Ambrosia 20f.; E.H. Meyer, *Indog. Mythen* II, 589 and the literature collected by him, *German. Mythologie* 81. As it is known, the original character of Esche Yggdrasil is disputed.

176. Do we have to take for granted for this period the direct proof and identification of the Soma with the Moon (compare p. 91 and p. 93f)? What Hillebrandt (*V.M.*, small edition 76 f.) cites for that, I think, leaves a doubt, when he refers to the 'girdle ornamented by stars' of Haoma, for example. I think, this feature loses strongly its conclusiveness, if it is considered together with all the Avestic proofs for 'ornamented by stars'.

177. The idea of the nourishment of immortality is connected with other substances besides Soma. It can be traced back to this period with more or less certainty. Thus, to water and plants (Compare Darmesteter's work *Haurvatāṭ et Ameretāṭ*); perhaps also to the products of the cow named in the Veda as Amṛta.

178. Compare above p. 68f.

179. Is Indra speaking to his comrades-in-arms, Maruts?

180. The beginning of the verse appears to me to be saying that the eagle, who knew already all the gods in the womb of his mother, must have thought of her in the midst of the friendly fortresses and found the right way. It is just a fairy-tale motif: the being who should perform the great deed is already confronted with the obstacles in the way which are apparently unsurmountable. Compare besides, my note on the hymns and on the nature of the eagle, above p. 55, note 60.

181. One cannot exclude the possibility that the 'bountiful' (*puraṃdhi*) in this and the next verse as also in IV, 26, 7 is an independent person taking part in this air journey. It is of course more probable that the eagle is meant, where then the constant repetition of the same expression may suggest that a proper name is meant.

182. Torn expression. The text is perhaps corrupted.

183. Compare above p. 30 about the episode of the archer and the feather to which, however, one cannot easily attribute a significance in nature.

184. I read (GGA. 1914, 447) *Údrāvato* with Hillebrandt (*Lieder des Ṛv.* 29, note 5).

185. As is well-known, Hillebrandt has made this identification in his *Vedische Mythologie* (vol. I), an object of detailed discussion. He sees in it the basis of the oldest religious life in India. I have expressed my views with regard to it in the first edition of this book and I do not think that it is necessary to repeat them in the second edition. Compare also *ZDMG.* LIV, 57ff.

186. Thus, also the ritual of the Soma-sacrifice is in no way done on the pattern of a Moon-festival. The myth of bringing the Soma down would have definitely appeared different, if the lunar nature had been the main feature of the Soma.

187. One may refer to *Śatapatha Br.* II, 4, 2, 7, *Bṛhad Ar. Up.* VI, 2, 16, *Chāndogya Up.*

V, 10, 4 from the Vedic Literature concerning the idea of the waning moon being consumed by the gods.

188. It is quite clearly said in VIII, 82, 8; 'Soma, which is to be seen in the vats, is like the Moon in the waters'.

189. 'Seven are the Ādityas Deities—with these, O Soma, guard us' (*Ṛv.* IX, 114, 3): quite an unsuspicious evidence; that a later author has placed the verse in *Taitt. Ār.* I, 7 in a worthless surrounding cannot be put forward against him. Seven pegs were dug to chain the Ādityas (*Taitt. Saṃh.* II, 3, 1, 5: *Kāṭh*, XI, 6; *Maitr.* S. II, 2, 1); a more significant rite than the Brāhmaṇa—texts which are ruled on the whole by a belief in the number of the Ādityas as twelve (see below). Here it is then remarked that the Ādityas are 'three times seven' (see also *Pañc. Br.* XXIII, 15, 3). In *Ṛv.* X, 72, 8.9 there is mention of the eighth child of Aditi, 'the one born from a dead egg' (*martaṇḍa*). This was cast away by the mother while she 'went with the seven to the gods'. Whatever may be the meaning of the idea of the eighth child (compare my notes on the verse), it is confirmed also here, however, that the number of living divine children of Aditi is seven. The *Śatapatha Br.* (III, 1, 3, 3) says, while discussing the appropriate *Ṛgveda*-verse quite correctly, that 'eight indeed are the sons of Aditi' (this is according to that verse); 'but what one calls the Ādityas-Deities, they are seven'. Has the number eight a role when in *Taitt. Br.* I, 1, 9 (compare *Ath. V.* VIII, 9, 21) two Ādityas are counted four times with names? *Taitt. Ār.* I, 13, 3 connects, in fact this enumeration quite clearly with the *Ṛv.*-verse. It is significant for the negligible importance of the list that Indra and Vivasvant appear amongst the eight gods. There is a variation in *Taitt. Saṃh.* VI, 5, 6, 1.2. with 4 + 1 Ādityas (Vivasvant is also here). That in the later Vedic texts the number of Ād. is usually given as twelve, obviously depends upon the well-known tripartite scheme which adjusts itself according to the number seven of the main metra: there are 8 Vasus, 11 Rudras, 12 Ādityas: clearly a later adjustment. The number seven emerging as authentic from these facts appears to me to be confirmed further by the Avesta; see in the text. Hillebrandt, *V.M.* III, 97ff. interprets the whole question differently. When he says (p. 103) 'why not five as in VIII, 18, 3 or six as in II, 27, 1', etc., I answer that these verses name five resp. six names without any sign to say that they intended to count the Ādityas completely. When on the other hand, it is found in IX, 114, 3 that Ād. are seven, the evidence has other quality.

190. Bergaigne III, 99 interprets similarly; compare also M. Müller, S.B.E. XXII, 253; Darmesteter *Ormazd et Ahirman* 59 f. Aryaman (compare below p. 420, note 240) is the most concrete figure amongst the smaller Ādityas—but for us not obvious.

191. Thus Varuṇa gets a specially important position in the ritual of the consecration of the king and related ceremonies.

192. We have already referred to above p. 48ff. the circumstances of certain rivalry between Indra and Varuṇa which is expressed directly in the Veda. It may be pointed out here that—as Bergaigne (III, 108 compare 207) has already remarked—the different nature of Indra and Varuṇa or the Ādityas is also in its difference that is asked for: Indra should fight for his worshipper, should give him victory and material possession, Varuṇa should see him through his misery, pardon his sin, have pity upon him.

193. I do not think, that especially Varuṇa's connection to water is important. See p. 104f. about it.

194. Bergaigne III, 109. 116ff. gives the sources.

195. *ibid.*, 107, note 1.

196. VIII, 41, 9. Compare my note on the verse.

197. The constellation—*Ṛv.* I, 24, 9.

198. III, 59, perhaps to be divided into two hymns (1-5, 6-9).

199. Should one perhaps cite here I, 115, 5 from the *Ṛgveda*? Compare my notes on VI, 62, 9; VII, 44, 3; VIII, 26, 15; Bergaigne III, 119 f.

200. For some of the hymns see Bergaigne III, 116 f., Böhtlingk-Roth *see under* Varuṇa, V. Henry on *Av.* XIII, 3, 13.

201. What Lévi, contributes in *La doctrine du sacrifice dans les Brāhmaṇas* 154, note 5 belongs to that.

202. Thus *Taitt. Saṃh*, II, 1, 7, 3f. What is meant is, of course, white and black, as it is clearly confirmed by *Maitr. S.* II, 5, 7. See also Hillebrandt, *V.M.* III, 25, note 2. So also a white and black animal is prescribed (*Āpastamba Sr.* XIX, 16, 21) for the sun and the moon (see about their relationship to Mitra-Varuṇa in the text).

203. I shall reproduce here in part the evidences which I have given in *ZDMG.* L, 45ff.

204. Even from the point of view of the *Avesta*, the first order of the series will be considered as the original, for the other is explained easily as the one decided by the superior position of Ahura (Mazda).

205. One liked to ignore him, despite the fact that the unavoidable equation of both the pairs of deities had to be conceded. One, however, disputed Ahura's identity with Ahura Mazda, albeit standing close to Mithra (Hillebrandt, *V.M.* III, 11 f.; small edition 121). I think, it is arbitrary to see another Ahura in that pair of deities—One does not know, taken from where, and where one should indicate this Ahura proving his existence than to Ahura Mazda who is almost forcing himself on our mind. 'May Ahuramazda protect me, and God Mithra,' prays Artaxerxes Ochus, as if he was commenting on those Avestic *ahura*-passages. In fact, in the Avesta itself, evidences are not wanting which name Ahura Mazda together with Mithra. Besides, Hillebrandt remarks indeed, 'There, where Ahuramazda stands really next to Mithra, he is not equal to him, but he is his Lord and Creator.' As if Ahura Mazda would not be named often enough beside other gods as their equal, albeit considered as their Creator in accordance with the Zoroastrian dogma. It may be remembered that this dual composite appears to be just a vestige from that early period, where these two gods were more on the same level than in the Zoroastrian system.

206. I am reminded of the one already mentioned above p. 95f. What I have discussed here in short is treated by me in detail in *ZDMG.* L, 47 ff.

207. More exactly for Ahura-Mazda: to all the good beings—corresponding to the Zoroastrian dualism.

208. Roth, *ZDMG.* VI, 69ff.; Darmesteter, *Ormazd et Ahriman.*

209. This would be authentically confirmed, if the text of Bogaz-köi—about which I cannot judge—is to be translated: 'The gods together with Mitra; the gods together with Varuṇa' (v. Schroeder, *WZKM*, XXII, 348 f).

210. Even though this collective name does not also appear in the *Gāthās*, the oldest Zoroastrian collection of poetry, I think that this homogeneity of the concerned deities into a composite group just in this number was not subjected to any serious doubt in the *Gāthās.*

211. All the same, it may be mentioned,—as remarked long back—that both the groups of gods coincide in the attributes *sajoṣa* (*sajoṣas*) 'harmonious' and *sukṣatra* 'practicing wonderful mastery' (resp. the Iranian equivalent of these words).

212. A considerable difference between the Vedic and the Avestic sphere of gods becomes immanent: Mitra is one of the two great Ādityas in the Veda; in the Avesta, Mithra does not belong to Amesha Spentas. The discrepancy can be easily explained by the tendencies of abstract spiritualization prevalent in Zoroastrianism. The popular form of Mithra could not find an access to the most holy of the Amĕsha Spentas-beliefs. But on the other hand, the *Gāthā*-poetry confirms Mithra's ancient connection with the highest Ahura.

213. Yt. 10, 143 and in addition Bartholomae *IF.* V, 360, note 1. In the previous, Yt. 10, 68 is quoted. I also refer to the material in Meillet, *Journ. as.* 1907, II, 152 f.

214. Hommel, *Proc. Soc. Bibl. Arch.* XXI, 139; compare also Sayce, *JRAS.* 1909, 1106, who speaks of an Ideogram for Mithra 'the *dawn-completer'*. Of course, I am not competent to judge here.

215. Mitra's role as a protector of contracts and the confederation of friendship which appears in the Veda and in the *Avesta* suits very well his nature as Sun. The all-looking eye of the Sun looks to its fulfilment and preservation. That is why the word *mitra* gets the meaning 'confederation, contract' in the Veda and in the *Avesta*, and gets further the meaning 'ally, friend' in India (on the contrary the god M. has not obviously received his name as 'friend' from this meaning). As regards Meillet's (*ibid.*, 143ff.) view that the god is to be understood as an Iranian personification of 'contract', I can be a party to the counter-remarks of Hillebrandt (*V.M.* small ed. 123). All of it remains unexplained in it. The deri-

vation of the root *mi-* 'exchange' appears to me to be scarcely convincing. We see M. ruling over the alliance of friendship in the Veda, and not over the exchange trade.

216. And not, as one wanted, with the Heaven. Compare my remarks *ZDMG.* L, 62; Hillebrandt, *V.M.* III, 6.

217. Hillebrandt, *V.M.* III, 3ff. agrees with me in this case. He is, as far as I know, the first who has given this solution for Varuṇa's mystery (*V.M.* I, 535).

218. Hommel *ibid.*, 138 according to whom the moon '*was called by his name* Marun (pronounced Varun)' at the appropriate place (*Western As. Inscr.* II, 57, 14a).

219. For the original nature of Varuṇa: Soderblom, *Werden des Götterglaubens* 173.

220. The traces of the view that Varuṇa is the moon may have been, all the same, preserved in the Veda. I refer to *Ṛv.* VII, 87, 6; VIII, 41, 8 (Hillebrandt, *V.M.* III, 9), to ram as the animal of Varuṇa (*Śatap. Br.* II, 5, 2, 16, on account of the horns of the moon?); It appears to me to be really doubtful, whether the bald-headed, yellow-eyed man has to do something with V. at the final bath of the Horse-sacrifice (see below the Section on *Dīkṣā* and Sacrificial Bath; Hillebrandt *ibid.*, III, 32). For this, from the *Avesta* Yt. X, 145 (compare Yasna VII, 13): 'Mithra and Ahura...and Stars and Moon and Sun'?

221. It may be asked here whether, perhaps as it appears, the ancient preference of Mitra to Varuṇa is explained in the linguistic expression from the reference to the sun and the moon. It may appear strange in the face of excessive significance of Varuṇa (Ahura) in the Veda and in the *Avesta*. I am, at least, not sure that this particular position was based upon a purely grammatical rule (compare Wackernagel, *Altind. Grammatik* II, 168). One could consider the metre for the Veda. But the same order has left its traces in the *Avesta* (p. 161, note 204) and repeats itself in Boghaz-köi.

222. One may perhaps add: One of them (Venus) having preference in importance, like one amongst the smaller Ādityas has a preference, i.e., Aryaman's, whose most prominent characteristic is 'Aryaman's path'. The ecliptic in its characteristic as (approximately) a path of a planet? Compare Hillebrandt, *V.M.* III, 80. My note on *Ṛv.* I, 105, 16.

223. The old equation Varuṇa= οὐρανός is subject, as is well-known, to phonetic considerations, which are to be overcome only by forced means of information. Compare at the end Meillet, *Jour. as* 1907, II, 156 f. If the explanation of Varuṇa as an original Moon-god considered above is correct, then the bottom would be completely knocked out from that equation. Does one have to look for the etymology for Varuṇa in the Indo-European field (compare *ZDMG.* L, 60)? It is beyond myself and beyond the sure judgement of everyone to say, whether Aryaman (*Avest.* Airyaman) is related to Airem, the name of the legendary ancestor of the Irish-folk (compare Fick, *Vgl. W.B.*[4] II, 19; Brugmann, *Grundriß*,[2] II, 1, 63), and whether there is a very ancient relationship or borrowing between Iranian *baga* (=Old Indian *bhaga*, name of one of the Ādityas; compare on him my essay, *Nachr. Gött. Ges. der Wiss.* 1915, 361ff.) and the old Slav. *bogu*, whether further, the Phrygian Ζεύς Βαγαιος also belongs to that. Even if the correspondence of these names is correct, it is not assured that the Indo-European gods in question had their original home in such a circle of seven gods.

224. See, however, Zimmer, *Ai. Leben* 354f. and my notes on I, 105, 16; X, 55, 3 about the traces of the Vedic knowledge if the five planets, so also the presumption of Hillebrandt, *V.M.* III, 423 on III, 7, 7 which appears to me to be quite shaky.

225. Will one feel in principle antigonised against such a hypothesis, what was not felt against the recognition of the non-Indo-European origin of the names Apollo and Artemis? I would really not know the reason. One could only wish that the progress of discoveries about the Asiatic wanderings of the Aryans and the contacts they developed may give a firmer foundation to our judgement.

226. I think, it is just an arbitrary presumption (E. Meyer, *Gesch. d. Alt.*[2] I, 2, 821) that only material influence and products of culture could penetrate to the Indo-Iranians from there, but not the gods. Of course, the judgement upon the presumptions put forth here cannot be pronounced, unless the presently disputed doubts about the older Babylonian astronomy are clarified. One may refer to J. Hehn, *Siebenzahl und Sabbat*, Leipz. *Semit. Studien* II, 5 p. 44 ff.; Zimmern in *Schraders Keilschr.* u. A. Testament, third edition, 620 ff.;

Kugler, who writes (*Sternkunde und Sterndienst in Babel* II, 1, 19) 'that the wandering stars as such were known already before thousand and two thousand years (before the seventh century B.C.), is not a scientific fact; this knowledge is rather an absolutely necessary result of the star-cult and the favourable situation of the country over which there is almost a clear sky throughout eight months'. The estimated age of the knowledge of the planets is quite sufficient for my hypothesis.

227. I shall repeat here the comments which are given in my monograph *Aus Indien und Iran* 179 f.

228. The Estonian hymns given by K. Krohn, *Finn.-ugr. Forschungen* III, 22 (1903) may be compared; further Frobenius, *Weltanschauung der Naturvölker* 368 f.; Frazer, *Golden Bough*,[2] II, 159 f.

229. One may compare Darmesteter's excellent interpretation of Ved. *ṛta*=Avest. *aša*, *Ormazd* et *Ahriman* p. 7 ff., further my essay in *Nachr. der Gött. Ges. der Wiss.* 1915, 167 ff. The literal coincidence of both the texts in the expression 'Fountain of the Ṛta' (*khāṛtsya Ṛv.* II, 28, 5; *ašahe xå* Yasna X, 4) is characteristic for the extent to which the agreement between the Veda and the *Avesta* goes. There is no doubt that there would have been more discussion on the *Ṛta* in the Veda, if it had belonged to the old objects of devotion and the sacrificial cult.

230. And, therefore, the Vedic poets like to put after one another various expressions for the glorification of the Ṛta in longer sections.

231. Bergaigne (III, 220) has correctly emphasized this.

232. With infinitely small exceptions.

233. As the Vedic use of the language attaches to them preferably the attribute *dhṛta-vrata* 'upholding the laws'.

234. The constellation.

235. It is seen very clearly, e.g., in *Ṛv.* X, 8, 5 that Agni takes here the second position next to Varuṇa. It is said in all sorts of identifications of Agni with different beings: 'You will be Varuṇa, when you will strive for the Ṛta'. It means that the real administrator of the Ṛta is Varuṇa. Besides, it is quite self-evident that somewhere or somehow practically every god is brought into relationship with the *Ṛta*. Bergaigne has shown III, 249 very aptly for Indra that these connections become less important or remain only at the surface, when compared to those of the Ādityas.

236. *adhyakṣaṃ, dharmaṇām Ṛv.* VIII, 43, 24.

237. See e.g., *Ṛv.* IV, 5, 4; VIII, 23, 14.

238. 'Rain comes from the Moon'. *Ait. Br.* VIII, 28, 15. In *Śatap. Br.* XIV, 2, 1, 21 there is also talk of a 'ray of the Sun giving rain.'

239. Compare in addition I, 105, 1: 'The Moon runs within the waters'.

240. Incidentally, I think that also the concept of Varuṇa as sending dropsy can be traced back correctly to the *Ṛgveda*. This derivation of the water appearing in the human body from the god who rules over the water in the universe is quite in keeping with the old times.

241. I doubt whether the knowledge of the control of the moon over the low-tide and high-tide can be ascribed to this antiquity and to account for it in the Varuṇa-mythology.

242. A hymn like X, 30 referring to the ritual use of water could have been hardly satisfied in the later period with just a cursory mention of Varuṇa as it appears in V. 1.

243. I have tried to prove in *ZDMG*. L, 56 f. the view that Varuṇa should basically be considered as an ocean-god as unfounded. Hillebrandt, *V.M.* III, 13 ff. has also a similar view. Lüders has announced his attempt to defend it again (Sitz. - Ber. Berl. Akad. 1910, 931). His arguments are awaited. Lévi conceived the problem discussed here quite in a different way from mine (*La doctrine du sacrifice* 159 ff.).

244. There is no doubt that the forceful derivation of the word Āditya from aditi is correct. The interpretation of *ādi-tya* as *āditya* ('existing from the beginning') is less correct.

245. Hillebrandt (*V.M.* III, 107) appears to consider it to be shaky. I can consider the formation of the word as especially clear with *ákṣiti ácitti ábhūti áriṣṣti ámati*, etc., standing with that on line as a name of a demoniac being appearing as *árāti* and tracing it back to

the root *dā* 'bind'. The contents of the invocations fit that most exactly as is to be shown soon. It may be noted that the goddess Aditi plays a special role in proximity of the story of Śunaḥśepa (I, 24, 1.2. 15, compare v. 12. 13); he was however *nídita* 'bound', (V, 2, 7). When Agni is invoked there for the sake of *nídita* to untie the fetters, and when the same request for freedom is made to Aditi, then it is clear what *-di-* means in the name of the goddess. So also *dāman* 'bond' derived from the same root is in the same sphere of ideas II, 28, 6; VII, 86, 5 to be considered here. One cannot certainly think of the root *dā-* 'divide', therefore 'Undividedness', 'Wholeness' (Geldner, *Zur Kosmogonie des Ṛv.* 5).

246. Hillebrandt (ibid) finds it striking that, if Aditi means 'freedom', the wind, which would deserve that predicate at the most, does not belong to the Ādityas, her sons. But the bond that is thought of here, is to be understood above all in the sense, which is just indicated by the sphere of concept of the Ādityas: as the imprisonment through sin and through distress which is the result of the sin (I can refer here to the good remarks of V. Schroeder, *Arische Religion* I, 401, note 1). The free speed of the movement of the wind is far-fetched.

247. *Ṛv.* VII, 93, 7; VIII, 67, 14 (see also v. 18); I, 24, 15. The end of the last verse is literally: 'sinless for Aditi'. sinless, so that the liberating goddess may give us her gift of freedom.

248. *Taitt. Saṃh.* III, 1, 4, 4; Schwab, Altind. Tieropfer 108.

249. One may refer to the material in Bergaigne, *Journ. asiatique* 1883, II, 510.

250. It may be especially pointed out that the light is called 'wide' (*uru*): a characteristic word for the sphere of concepts of Aditi. See Hillebrandt III, 108 for the facts concerning this. When the ideals of light and freedom come together in the case of this goddess, I think, her name says clearly enough, what is the first, and what is the second. And the process, how the second is attached to the first, is indeed as clear as it could be.

251. Compare what is noted above p. 38. Only one word can show the identification of Aditi with the earth which has almost vanished in the Ṛgveda. This concept is easy to understand, when one thinks of unlimited vastness in the case of the earth.

252. When it is here *anāgām aditim* ('the sinless, Aditi'), then it is indeed obvious that the vese moves in the sphere of the concept of e.g., *anāgāstvé aditivé* VII, 51, 1 ('In Sinlessness, in Aditiship').

253. VI, 50, 11; VII, 35, 14 (compare also X, 53, 5); X, 63, 2. Of course it is by no means certain that one has to think of Aditi and the Āditiyas while thinking of the cow and its divine children. Also Pṛśni and the Maruts can be considered.

254. Literally 'Horsemen'. I refer to the presumption expressed above on p. 38 f. about the original horse-form of these gods. The Aśvins are also called Nāsatya. This name of underminable meaning recurs in the *Avesta* in singular as a name of an evil demon. Compare above p. 13 about the same name in the documents of Boghaz-köi. This is presumably the older of the two names.

255. *Aitareya Brāhmaṇa* II, 15.

256. *Śānkhāyaṇa Śrautasūtra* IX, 20; *Āpastamba* XIV, 4, etc.

257. Bergaigne, *Recherches sur l'hist. de la liturgie védique* 9. 58.

258. Yet *Ṛgveda* shows uncertainty with reference to the order of the Aśvins and the Dawn. Bergaigne, *Rel. véd.* II, 432. The arrangement of a few sections of the *Ṛgveda* upon which Hillebrandt, *V.M.* III, 382, note 2 depends, cannot be considered here as based upon other principles.

259. *Ṛv.* V, 77, 1; I, 22, 1; VIII, 9, 17; VII, 71, 1; I, 157, 1; VIII, 9.18. More in Bergaigne II, 431 f. Also the idea of the Aśvins as rich in honey, offering honey from the honey-bag lying on their chariot, the whip (kaśā) with which they sprinkle honey goes together obviously with the appearance of the Aśvins in the morning (for material see Bergaigne II, 433 f.). It is certainly not the gift either of the wetness in the clouds or of the Soma; with that the constant appearance of the idea just of honey may remain unexplained. I think, one should think of the morning dew. It may be noted that also the Dawn is the 'creator of honey' (III, 61, 5). I also refer to Vodskov, *Sjoeledyrkelse og Naturdyrkelse* 519 ff.

260. *Ṛv.* I, 180, 10; III, 58, 8. It is said about the Sun-horses in I, 115, 3, almost literally as in the last hymn: They go in one day around the heaven and earth. So also of the Dawn

IV, 51, 5. About Aśvins it is also said IV, 45, 7 that they 'travel through the regions with their chariot in one day'..

261. Ṛv. I, 112. 13.

262. This view is not new. But the solution of the problem solved long back (see namely Mannhardt, *Zeitschr. f. Ethnologie* VII, 312 f.) has not got its due recognition everywhere.

263. One thought of the constellation of Gemini. But they can claim the validity as morning star only for a short time of the year, with the same right as every star near the ecliptic. And besides, in the Nakṣatras, it is not at all Gemini (*Punarvasū*) which can be considered as belonging to the Aśvins, but the *aśvayujau*= β, γ Arietis. Appropriate remarks in Hillebrandt, *V.M.* III, 388 f. about the universal improbability of the Gemini-hypothesis.

264. Aśvins are described as 'reddish-white' (*śyeta*) in *Śatapatha Br.* V, 5, 4, 1.

265. That is indeed an obvious view, as if one wanted to think of the purely accidental and temporary appearance, say, of the Jupiter besides the Venus in the morning sky.

266. It is, one can understand, possible, but it cannot be proved that an impression of a real, human pair like that of youthful princes has concurred in the coupling of the two Aśvins into a pair of youths appearing together. Even the language might have had its influence here. Nāsatya and the other one belonging to him could be indicated by the Dual of Nāsatya (corresponding already in the Indo-Iranian period). On the other hand, one may think of the possibility, that last of all, a belief, dating from the distant past in the peculiar magical forces clinging to the twins, has also played its role (compare J.R. Harris, *The Cult of the heavenly twins*)—Is it the simultaneous growing of the sidereal sphere of the concept with the scheme of the wonderful twins?

267. Yaska XII, 2. The translation of the first word is uncertain. The fragment can hardly be very recent on account of its metrical scheme. Compare *Taitt. Ārany.* I, 10, 2 where the Aśvins are called 'children of night(?), shining'. In the same (§1) there is talk of the radiant (*śukra*) form of the one and the silvery (*rajata*) of the other Aśvin(?); But *rajatam* is a recent and irrelevant transformation of the older *yajatam* (Ṛv. VI, 58, 1). The verse Ṛv. I, 181, 4 referred to above, names further the fathers of the two *sumakha* ('Hero'?; the word appears as epithet of Agni, Indra, Rudra and Maruts) and the heaven. That does not get us anywhere.

268. Bergaigne II, 500; Hillebrandt, *V.M.* III, 385, note 1. Should one remember here also the near and the distant wheel of the Aśvins (Caland-Henry 203; compare VI, 62, 10)?

269. This daughter of the Sun is wrongfully identified with the Dawn; compare my note on Ṛv. VII, 69, 4.

270. Does the preference for number 3 mentioned often in the Aśvin-hymns go together with the triad of these travelling together (Bergaigne II, 500 f.)? Hillebrandt *ibid.*, 383 has a different view.

271. I base my arguments here upon the facts as also upon the conclusions of Mannhardt (*Die lettischen Sonnenmythen, Zeitschr. f. Ethnol.* VII). Compare also L. v. Schroeder, *WZKM.* IX, 130 f.; further the South-Slavonic material in Krauss, *Volksglaube und religiöser Brauch der Südslawen* 4 ff. Bielenstein, *Magazin herausg. von der Lett.-Litt. Gesellschaft* XIX, 4, 240 ff., interprets the Lettish hymn in a different way than Manngardt; according to him, the 'God's sons' of these hymns are the beings found as riders and active forces above and behind the clouds.'

272. In fact, Wilamowitz, *zu Eur. Herakles* 30 denies their original star-nature. The Dioscuri sojourn ἑτερήμεροι in the light and in the nether-world. Is perhaps a shifting seen there appearing like the one in the Veda, contrary to the fact that always only either the morning star or the evening star appears: a defeat of the idea of separation of both the celestial beings against the one of their similarity? But here, the student of Indology may, of course, only ask, he cannot answer. It may be remembered that also a Germanic example is added to the rest of the examples of the concept of Dioscuri mentioned here.

273. Also in singular, so that the stars appear as a unit, while otherwise the God's sons appear in the plural who act just like the Aśvins, whether it is in the evening or in the morning.

274. Sometimes for themselves, sometimes for the moon. Quite in the same way, the two Aśvins appear as wooers also in the Vedic marriage-hymn X, 85 where Sūryā is associated with the Soma and the Moon. v. Schroeder, *Ar. Religion* II, 399 f. thinks differently on the relationship between the Sun and the Sun-daughter.

275. The first is the phrasing of Mannhardt (*ibid.* 295), the latter that of E.H. Meyer (*Indog. Mythen* II, 673).

276. Is it transformed to the Sun-daughter, because the word sun is masculine?

277. This Greek and Indian coincidence deserves to be considered, while discussing the question, whether the Indo-Europeans knew the ocean. Greek material suggests the idea that the Elm's fire played a role in the case of stars rescuing man from the danger of ocean.

278. On the whole, one can say that the Aśvins travel across the ocean, Indra across the rivers. Indra is the protector of the marches of war and travelling in the Vedic land full of rivers.

279. Does this wonder of cure which can be seen as a donation of light have any special connection with the luminous nature of the Aśvins?

280. Was *Ṛv.* I, 122, 1 composed before Rudra's participation in the Soma?

281. Hillebrandt (*V.M.* II, 203) finds that the earlier period, more than the later emphasizes, Rudra's medicinal power, on the other hand, less of the horror originating from him. I think, that this horror is clearly visible in the Ṛgvedic hymns. But the style of the poetry brought a certain poise along with it, which is maintained throughout; the usual tone of invocation otherwise was also adhered to here.

282. *Aitareya Brāhmaṇa* III, 33.

283. And, therefore, Rudra is called red-one though not so correctly. One would expect *rudhra*. Is the word made similar to the word *indra*, perhaps with an effort of avoiding the suggestion of its root *rudh*–?

284. Compare Zachariae. *WZKM.* XVII, 211 ff. and the literature there.

285. *Atharvaveda* XV, 1, 7. 8.

286. *Taittirīya Āraṇyaka* V, 8, 4. 5.

287. *Śatapatha Brāhmaṇa* I, 7, 3, 1.

288. Please see the section on sacrificial meal.

289. See the section: 'The Cult: General Survey'. The use of *ava-dā* in the *Ṛgveda* (II, 33, 5) confirms that this trend of Rudra-cult dates back to ancient period.

290. *Gobhila*, I, 8, 28.

291. *Āpastamba Dh.* II, 2, 4, 23.

292. *Kauśika Sūtra* 51, 7.

293. *Śāṅkhāyana Śr.* IV, 20, 1.

294. *ibid.*, IV, 19, 8.

295. *Āśvalāyana G.* IV, 8, 28. Compare Winternitz, *Der Sarpabali* 41. The feminine form in the address to *sarpāḥ* (masculine) is to be explained as carried over from the phraseology in connection with the *rudrasenāḥ* (feminine).

296. Winternitz, *ibid.*, proves the connection of Rudra and the serpents by the *mantra* with which 'Rudra sitting amongst the serpents', is worshipped, where serpents live (*Hir. G.* I, 5, 16, 10). But this *mantra* is only one of many exactly corresponding to those, which are to be addressed to Rudra as the one living here and there in the remarkable places of all sorts (compare p. 112 f.).

297. *Atharvaveda* XI, 2, 22; VI, 90, 1.

298. According to Bloomfield (*Amer. Journal Phil.* XII, 425 ff.) it is urine. This appears to me on account of *Ṛv.* II, 33, 7; VII, 35, 6 to be improbable. It might have got at the most transformed. Besides, one notices how the essential identity of the Ṛgvedic and the post-Ṛgvedic Rudra gets confirmed in the agreement of such a detailed feature.

299. *Āśvalāyana G.* IV, 8, 40 f.; *Kauṣika Sūtra* 51, 7, etc.

300. *Āśvalāyana G.* IV, 8, 29.

301. *Hiraṇyakeśin G.* I, 16, 8 ff.; compare *Pāraskara* III, 15, 7 ff., where we have in addition Rudra living in the forests, mountains and amongst the fathers (manes).

302. *Āpastamba Dh.* I, 11, 31, 23.

303. *Taitt. Saṃhitā* IV, 5, 1, 3.

304. *Taitt. Saṃhitā* IV, 5, 10, 4.

305. *Atharvaveda* XI, 2, 23 ff.

306. On account of Hopkins, *Proc. Am. Or. Soc.* 1894 CL f. the following may be said with reference to the above that Rudra once (II, 33, 3) holding Vajra in the hand does not prove in reality either his origin as a God of Storm or Thunder, or the author's consideration of him as such. So much less is also proved by his weapon (*didyut* VII, 46, 3): he is indeed the hunter (*astā* Av. XI, 2, 7; a verb preferably used is: *asyati*); *didyut* is of course a part of *astā* (I, 66, 7). His oft quoted medicines should be waters (compare p. 112), namely that of the clouds. Just as Water-creating-god, Rudra is also artist of cure. That water has, according to the Veda, curing power is really as correct, as it is equally incorrect, that curing power was put into the water. I do not find that some expression about Rudra's medicines refers to water; I think, the real fact is contrary to this view. Compare the material in Bloomfield, *Am. Journal Phil.* XII, 426.

307. *Taitt. Saṃh.* IV, 5, 7, 2.

308. Compare Mannhardt, *Wald- und Feldkulte* I, 14. 22f.

309. It was represented in this way in the first edition of this book. Against that Hopkins *ibid.*; Hillebrandt, *V.M.* II, 199f.

310. If the summer, the monsoons and the change over to the autumn mainly bring epidemics to men and cattle, I do not think that it is sufficient to conclude 'that Rudra is the god of horror of the tropical climate from the beginning of the summer...to the autumn' (Hillebrandt, *V.M.* II, 207; in the small edition he incidently adds 'only we should not think to have found his origin thereby'). I think, Rudra's harmful effect is in the centre of his conception and not the season in which, this effect culminates.

311. It need not be proved, that such a god having this nature of a soul must have been obscured for the consciousness of the Vedic period.

312. *Kātyāyana* I, 1, 12; *Āpastamba* IX, 14, 12; T. Segerstedt, *Revue de l'hist. des religions* LVII, 300; Hillebrandt *V.M.* small ed. 163. Compare Weber, *Ind. Stud.* X, 13.

313. Above p. 111. Also it deals with such an offering in the sacrifice discussed above.

314. One may consider the word 'worship the Niṣādas' in the 'Chapter on Hundred Rudras' together with the sacrificer of the Niṣāda race (*VS.* XVI, 27).

315. Compare above p. 113.

316. We cannot easily know about the nature of Pṛśni from Yajus *Vāj Saṃh.* II, 16.

317. I refer namely to L.v. Schroeder, *WZKM.* IX, 238 ff., *Mysterium und Mimus* 121ff.

318. Hillebrandt, *V.M.* III, 317 ff. Small ed. 103 ff. has tried to bring in such traces. But I do not think that he has done it convincingly. The obvious idea of the flying Maruts being compared with the birds is more harmless than understanding them 'from the concepts of the cult of manes'. That 'according to *Śatapatha Br.* IV, 5, 2, 17 the call *Svāhā*, which is not withheld for Rudra, is as less due to them as also to the manes', refers only to a special sacrifice, which is just not the right sacrifice, i.e., the offering of a cow-embryo found in a sacrificial cow which is considered as sterile. One should not speak there *Svāhā*. A general exclusion of the Maruts from the worship with *Svāhā* is out of question. But then it does not really mean, on the other hand, that the Maruts could have been originally the souls of the Dead. The *Svāhā* is also given to the Angiras. Further 'the position of the Maruts similar to that of manes, Rudra or the demons' in the sacrifice (compare also v. Schroeder, *Mysterium und Mimus* 123) prescribed by *Kātyāyana* (XVIII, 4, 23 ff.) rests upon a misunderstanding, which I tried to clear in *Nachr. Gött. Ges. der. Wiss.* 1915, 388 note 3; with the same right which is of course scarcely intended—Agni could be ascribed a position similar to that of the manes. Compare further Nachr. *ibid.*, 224. Can one find a trace referring to the manes-nature on the southern altar, i.e., the altar lying in the area of the manes (Hillebrandt, *Rit. Lit.* 116) in the worship of the Maruts in the festival of Varuṇapraghāsa? I doubt.

319. So also the Avestic Vāyu (for which, as Wackernagel tells me, one can take Vāyu) and Vāta. Compare Charpentier, Kl. *Beitr zur indoiran. Mythol.* 37ff. and above p. 45.

320. The name was traced back to the Indo-European period, though really wrongly

and compared with Litauic Perkunas, and the Nordic god and goddess Fjörgynn, Fjörgyn. According to Hirt, *Idg. Forschungen* I, 481 the meaning is 'Eichengott' (Oak-god). More on Etymology, see Hillebrandt, *V.M.* III 331, note 5.

321. I cannot discover any trace of his 'ancient and deep-rooted pupularity' which must have remained in the Ṛgveda in the background on account of the 'element of sensuousness and erotic' that is attributed to him (v. Schroeder, *Mysterium und Mimus* 56). We should not judge the Vedic Viṣṇu after Kṛṣṇa.

322. Do the three steps of Viṣṇu go together with the three steps paced by the Amshaspands from the earth to the sphere of the sun according to the Zoroastrian belief? Three steps of the priest in the Avestic ritual are made according to these god's steps, just as the sacrificer paces three steps in the Vedic ritual, to represent the three Viṣṇu-steps from the heaven to the earth, or from the earth to the heaven. Compare Darmesteter's French translation of the *Avesta* I, p. 401 and Hillebrandt, *Neu-und Vollmondsopfer* p. 171. f.

323. *Ṛv.* VIII 29, 7; VII, 100, 3. 4; I, 155, 4.5; 154, 2.4.

324. i.e., the blessed ones who enjoy the celestial reward for the generosity shown to the priests.

325. VII, 100, 5; I, 22, 20. 'Eye' is naturally the sun.

326. This idea is predominant in the later Vedas; compare *V.S.* II, 25; XII, 5, etc. For the rest refer to MacDonell, *JRAS*, 1895, 171.

327. See MacDonell *ibid*.

328. Bloomfield's (*Am. Journal Phil.* XVII, 427 f.) derivation from *vi* and *snu=sānu* is extremely probable; compare my remarks *Nachr. Gött. Ges. d. Wiss.* 1915, 374 f. Besides '*vi*' there is a further characteristic catchword for Viṣṇu, '*uru*' ('wide'). Thus the name of the god is *urugāya* 'striding far'; he gives the people *urukṣiti* 'spacious living-place'; He performs with Indra *urum u lokam* 'wide space', etc. for the sacrifice. v Schröder, *Ar. Religion* II, 10 derives the name Viṣṇu from the root *viṣu*. I refer to *NGGW*. 1916, 715ff.

329. So it is also said of the Maruts where they are united with Viṣṇu in a common invocation and as a result are made similar to him, that they 'whose terrestrial dwelling is wide-extended' (V, 87, 7).

330. *Ṛv.* IV, 18, 11; VIII, 100, 12. The second verse obviously gives Indra's words to Viṣṇu.

331. K.F. Johanson, *Solfågeln i Indien* (1910) 8ff. This nature of Viṣṇu is proclaimed amongst other things in the fact that the thumb (without the nail) is put in the sacrificial meal in the sacrifice of manes with a verse and *mantra* dedicated to Viṣṇu (compare Caland, *Altind. Ahnenkult* 57. 117. 141. 188, etc.; even otherwise the thumb plays a role in this ritual; see *ibid.* 24. 26). I do not know whether the ritual with the thumb aims at the prevention of the evil powers (Caland 188; perhaps the thumb signifying phallus, compare Dieterich, *Mutter Erde* 95, note 1 Charpentier, Kl. *Beiträge* 54? Has the phallus, as in Greece, an apotropous meaning? The nail would perhaps impair the similarity of the thumb with the phallus; is it, therefore, without the nail? Or is there a connection with the well-known influence of the sacrifice of the dead to get an offspring?). The role of Viṣṇu in this can be based simply on the known preference of the performers of the ritual of the later Vedas to this god, who was mentioned at a number of occasions without any recognizable reasons. When one incidentally spoke the verse here, 'Viṣṇu has strode here; thrice has he put his foot-prints', then the putting of the thumb in the meal could arouse the thought of the foot-prints stamped on the universe.

332. The 'ninetyfour names' I, 155, 6—if one understands the number containing 4 and 90, thus 360, the number of days in a year—give only quite a vague clue. Also I, 22, 21 can be used only with a very good intention. The identification of Viṣṇu and the sun is complete in the texts of the status of Av. XIII, 2, 31; XVII, 1, 6ff.

333. One should then, if not quite obviously, interpret the three steps of the sun as beginning, middle and full height alone of the path of the sun.

334. One could even think of a god of mountains; but this is also not satisfactory. If such a phenomenon lying at its base could be perceived, one could perhaps find a way to explain, as much I can see, the obscure feature of Viṣṇu that he is called *śipiviṣṭa* (i.e.,

affected with a definite body infirmity). Johansson's (*ibid.* 12f.) discussion of this word, I think, does not do full justice to a portion of the material.

335. Does the fact perhaps play a role here that in the home of this belief, as at so many places of the world, the foot-prints of the god must have been shown to which then the appropriate story could be attached?

336. Of course, as one can subscribe to Hillebrandt, (*V.M.* III, 335) there remain still features in the image of Viṣṇu, which do not allow themselves to be derived from this basic concept, at least with our means. I think, this remnant cannot go beyond the usual measure of insoluble occasional or relatively later plays of fantasy. We must be prepared to face them everywhere in such a case, and Hillebrandt also on his part takes them correctly into account (see *ibid.*, p. 361). Is really besides, as Hillebrandt thinks, the conception of Viṣṇu put forth here incapable of explaining his connections with the manes? The existence of the souls was put in the highest heights: What was more natural than to turn Viṣṇu's *paramam padam* into a mark of their place of abode?

337. This goad (*aṣṭrā*) is called *paśusādhanī* *Ṛv.* VI, 53, 9, i.e., not as Bergaigne II, 424 wants 'creating herds', but—what corresponds more exactly to the nature of Pūṣan—'leading the herds on the right path'. The verb *sādh* is (besides *nī* 'lead') characteristic for Pūṣan (VI, 56, 4.5; X, 26, 4): this fits completely to the god of paths; it may be remembered that *sādhu* is a constant epithet of 'path'. As to *nī*, it is not an accident that Pūṣan was one with Indra just when Indra was leading the waters forward (*anayat* VI, 57, 4).

338. *Ṛv.* IV, 57, 7; VI, 54, 5-7, 10; *Śānkhāyana G.* III, 9.

339. Compare nevertheless below, page 170, note 352.

340. *Ṛv.* X, 85, 26; *Āśvalāyana G.* I, 8, 1. Pūṣan appears also to have been considered as the paver of the way, active in the bridal night, in the concrete sense of the term: *Pāraskara* I, 4, 16, etc.

341. *Ṛv.* X, 17, 3ff, Similarly Pūṣan's goat shows the sacrificial horse the way into the empire of gods, I, 162, 4.

342. *Ṛv.* VI, 53; *Āśvalāyana G.* III, 7, 8. 9; *Śāṅkhāyana Sr.* III, 4, 9.

343. *Śāṅkhāyana G.* II, 14, 9.

344. *Ṛv.* I, 42; VI, 53, 4.

345. *Ṛv.* X, 17, 6. It is a part of Pūṣan's mastery over the paths that he is called *vimuco napāt* "Lord of the place to stay in (on this Bergaigne II, 422 f. makes a mistake); Ṛv. V, 46, 1 (compare III, 53, 5) shows how *vimuc* is connected with the ways and proper guiding upon them. As *vimuc* also may mean absolving oneself, e.g., of the sins, it is clear that Pūṣan is also invoked occasionally by this catchword (*Av.* VI, 112, 3).

346. See the references in Caland-Henry 71.

347. *Ṛv.* VI, 58, 3.

348. *Ṛv.* I, 23, 14; X, 5, 5 (compare my *Hymnen des Ṛgveda* I, 467).

349. *Ṛv.* VI, 48, 15; VIII, 4, 16; *Āśvalāyana G.* III, 7, 9.

350. One characteristic of Pūṣan may be mentioned here which I cannot explain, i.e., his toothlessness. That is why mush is his sacrificial meal. There is a reference to this toothlessness only in the later Vedic literature (*Śat. Br.* I, 7, 4, 7, etc.). *Ṛgveda* (VI, 56, 1) also shows that the modest god is mocked as the eater of mush. Did one think of the toothlessness to explain the sacrificial food, or, is the former based on the other hand on the latter concept?

351. Most recent attempts in this direction: Hillebrandt, *V.M.* III, 362 ff. 1 small ed. 111ff.; Siecke, *Pūshan, Studien zur Idee des Hirtengottes* (1914). The first scholar assumes a Sun-god, the latter finds that it is also 'irrefutably clear that there is in him the old Moon-god' in the case of Pūṣan. The arguments of both the scholars do not appear to me to be convincing. Hillebrandt emphasizes, among other things, Pūṣan's attribute *āghṛaṇi*, according to him 'glowing'. The exact meaning is not very clear, and there is a lot of margin and unfortunately, little support for the surmise about the contexts or the ideas which this attribute might have got for Pūṣan. For example, he could be the one 'going into the glowing fire', say, in connection with a story, for he alone knew, being grown to stand all heat, to cover a path full of fire, or with the point that he leads the evil beings into this fire.

VII, 40, 6 (also VI, 48, 16; 53, 8, compare VIII, 60, 20) could fit in well for this. I think, however, that in no case such an attribute of a completely uncertain implication can question the god's conception which is founded on a broad base. That *Av.* VII, 9, 1 is especially an evidence of Pūṣan's solaric nature (V. Henry), appears to me to be quite unfounded.

352. It must be left to be asked to the research on Greek mythology as to how much light is thrown by Pūṣan upon the nature of Hermes. The bundle, so to say, of the functions is remarkably similar for both the gods: protection of paths and wayfarers (Hermes ὅδιος ὁδοιπόρος πομπός Hermes-pillar as the signboard for the path); Messengership; psychopompy (it is also quite in the manner of Pūṣan when e.g., Hermes leads Persephone to the upper-world;) protection of the herds; bestowing of the findings (ερμαιον). It may further be noted that Hermes is very often shown with the goat, sitting on him or carrying him (Roscher, *Lex. der Myth.* I. Columns 2378, 2398, 2404, etc.). Has the wiglike hair resp. Krobylos shown on Hermes-figures to do something with Pūṣan's *kaparda* (*Ṛv.* VI, 55, 2; IX, 67, 11)? This circle of questions would get another face, if the etymological assimilation of Pūṣan and Pan (παων) holds true as suggested by v. Bradke (Theol. *Lit.*-Z. 1895, 581) and W. Schulze (*KZ*, XLII, 81, 374). Then the probability would incline towards the fact that a shepherd-god is to be perceived behind the god of the path (compare above p. 118), as against the result to be derived from the Veda. But this equation is obviously quite uncertain.

353. The reference of Tvaṣṭar to the 'forms' is characteristic for him both in the later literature (e.g. *Śatap Br.* XI, 4, 3, 3) and in the *Ṛgveda*. The reason for his 'universality of form' may be on account of the fact that he was looked upon as the father of the three-headed monster Viśvarūpa ('Universe-formed' above p. 78) who was overpowered by Trita. Does Tvaṣṭar go together with the Germanic smith Wieland (compare E.H. Meyer, *Amz. f. deutsches Alt.* XIII, 33; *Germ. Mythol.* 300 f.)?

354. *Ṛv.* I, 188, 9.

355. *Ṛv.* III, 4, 9. See ninth resp. the tenth verses of the Āprī-hymns. When the priest prays for the birth of a son to the host of the sacrifice, it is quite understandable that he thinks for himself this son as a hero and a pious sacrificer. We shall not believe Hillebrandt (*V.M.I*, 525) that the hero, the friend of god of this prayer, is the Moon.

356. See in the discussion of the cult.

357. *Vāj Saṃhitā* 29, 9.

358. *Ṛv.* X, 17, 1; V, 42, 13. Compare X, 10, 5.

359. Hillebrandt, *Mythol.* I, 522 f.

360. Bergaigne III, 58 f., Macdonell 57. Vodskov 445 ff. has a different view.

361. Is the myth of Ṛbhus-Elves(?) as the masters of the highest artistry Indo-European? See E.H. Meyer, *Anz. f. deutsches Alt.* XIII, 35; *Germ. Mythologie* 124.

362. However, compare the next note.

363. Compare Ludwig III, 335; Hillebrandt, *V.M.* I, 515f.; III, 115. 140ff. 145; Small ed. 144 f. When Ludwig IV, 160; V, 510 believes to find clearly the validity of Ṛbhus as the gods of season directly in the traditions, then it is based on a misunderstanding. And besides, the arguments we come across here are of highly uncertain nature. That Agohya, in whose house they slept through twelve nights, is explained as the Sun-god Savitar. I think this identity of Agohya and Savitar, Savitar's nature as Sun-god and the presence of twelve nights in the sphere of Vedic concepts is doubtful (compare on the one hand, Hillebrandt *ibid*, and on the other hand, my discussions *ZDMG.* LIX, 253ff., especially 262 f.; Thibaut, *Astronomie, Astrologie und Mathematik* 9f.). The connections which Hillebrandt III, 140ff. finds between Ṛbhus and the festival of Cāturmāsya appear for me to be similarly problematic. The same scholar speaks of the Ṛbhus as 'the gods of a clan which particularly nourished the art of building chariots...and elevated the genii of the seasons to the position of the gods' (Lieder des *Ṛv.* 92, compare *V.M.* III, 152). I think, this interpretation is too bold. See above p. 46 about the tendency of attributing individual clans etc., to the individual gods as devotees.

364. It must have been in many cases the grammatical gender of the word in question (like *nirṛti* 'destruction') which determined the feminine nature of the deity.

365. I do not find in the Veda a goddess who could be understood especially as a 'goddess of women' or as a 'divine representative of women' (Compare R.M. Meyer, *Deutsche Rundschau*, August 1910, p. 283).

366. But on the other hand, I consider it to be wrong, when Weber, *Omina and Portenta* 351 remarks about the Dawn, that this goddess, to whom such splendid hymns are addressed, has disappeared completely into the ritual, 'because she really lost all significance, when the Indians moved further into the southern parts'. I think, that the contrast taken for granted here between an older and a later condition within the Vedic development does not hold true; very clear traces of the hymns agree exactly with the statements in the liturgic texts and show that both in the earlier and in the later Vedic period the position of Uṣas in the Soma-sacrifice was early litanies in which she received praise, but she was not given Soma to drink. Compare also Hopkins, JAOS, XIX, 28.

367. The eye of the god and the white courser are of course the sun.

368. I think that the idea is rather carried into these so obvious facts, and one cannot interpret from them 'that we have to think generally in the Veda, apart from the individual verses, of the morning of the new year, and not of the daily dawn' (Hillebrandt, *V.M.*, small ed. 26; compare *V.M.* II 26 ff.). If the hymns on the Dawn open, as it can be easily understood, the Soma-celebration *Agniṣṭoma*, and if the spring, the first season, is prescribed for this celebration, then it is more than a bold conclusion to interpret the Uṣas-hymns as 'the hymns of the New Year'. 'The verses of Vasiṣṭhas sound like a New Year's hymn: 'Vasiṣṭhas awake to welcome with songs Uṣas; first the melodies with the hymns; her, who divides both the united worlds from each other and shows apparent all Uṣas awoke, creating new life; she hid the darkness with her light. Youthful and unrestrained she comes forward. She has turned thoughts to Sūrya, sacrifice and Agni' (VIII, 80)'. Why should this only look more like a New Year's hymn than simply a hymn of the Dawn? The arguments of H. which are based on the festival Ekāṣṭakā (of the eighth day of the dark half of the month connected with the change of the year) do not appear to me to be convincing. Particularly, the correctness of the statement that 'Uṣas appears in their place—i.e., of Ekāṣṭakā—in the *Ṛv.* and brings again sacrifice, Agni and Sūrya' (small ed. 29) appears to me to be completely unfounded.

369. See above p. 37f, 105f. and on Iḍā under the depiction of the Cult (Section on the participation of the sacrificer in the meal).

370. Yet one may think of the male water-genius Apāṃ napāt (above p. 67 f.). Thus there is a god Sarasvant beside the river-goddess Sarasvatī.

371. So also the mother earth will be mentioned at least cursorily. For the name Apsaras, Wackernagel, *ibid.* 159f. Is the accent not understandable, if the composite of the determinative is taken?

372. The names of the first three are not quite clear; the fourth one means 'agreement'.

373. Material in Weber, *Ind. Studien* V. 228f.

374. See above p. 89 on Indrāṇī's appearance in the story of Vṛṣākapi; On Rudra's wife p. 41. About the validity of these names compare Geldner, *Ved. Studies* II, 1. I think that only his surmise that the real name of Indra's wife in the *Ṛgveda* was Śacī is wrong; so also it is completely wrong to say, that the naming of Śacīs in the plural is explained 'from the Harem-life of the Vedic gods'.

375. In the *Avesta*, Hvare is to Mithra, what Sūrya is to Mitra in the Veda.

376. *Ṛv.* VII, 34, 23; 35, 8.

377. Thus *Hiraṇyakeśin* (*G.* II, 4, 5) prescribes to keep a water-pot near the head of a lying-in-woman with the saying: 'Ye waters, guard the house. As you guard the gods, guard near the woman, who is ornamented with the blessing of a child'.

378. *Ṛv.* X, 30, 12; *Pāraskara* III, 5.

379. I doubt quite decisively that there is mention in the *Ṛgveda* of the non-Indian Sarasvatī in Archosia (Harahvaitī) as also I doubt that Sar is a river of death as concluded from *Ṛv.* X, 17, 7ff.

380. In full form she is called *hotrā Bhāratī* (sacrificial gift of the Bh.). One may compare the invocation of Agni as Bhārata, i.e., belonging to the Bh.

381. Besides them, there is the third goddess Iḍā who is already mentioned.

382. Here lies the tendency of the later identification of Sarasvatī with Vāc., i.e., 'speech' and to her development, so to say, into the muse. Compare Hillebrandt, *V.M.* III, 375, note 3.

383. About the cult use of Sarasvatī-water see, e.g., *Śatapatha Br.* V, 3, 4, 3.

384. Besides the Apsaras probably also those evil demons living in water must not be absent for the Vedic belief as they appear in the later literature, e.g., in the Buddhistic stories. There is often talk of the Rākṣasas who live in the ponds, etc. They have a horrible appearance and they eat all the creatures, who come into their field. Thus, they appear to be the examples of the general type of demoniac evils, who have their dwelling place in the waters rather than the personification of the concerned waters. Yet the Buddhistic stories know, of course, also the water-deities in another sense: thus, the deity of Kauśikī (Gaṅgā) who appears before the ascetic sitting at the bank and says to him that she has her house in the floods; many mountain-caves send to her their waters (*Jātaka*, Vol. V, p. 5); the ocean-deity (Vol. VI, p. 35 f.), etc.

385. It is too much to equate Gandharva=Kentauros.

386. Yet see under note 395 below. I do not think that the tradition gives any basis for the specific consideration of these air-spirits as wind=spirits; if G. are named once (*Ṛv.* III, 38, 6) as having 'wind-blown tresses', it means practically nothing. The traces of appearance of the wind-spirits from the souls of the dead are to be discovered in the role of Gandharvas in a marriage-ritual (see p. 124); but I think it is quite arbitrary (E.H. Meyer, *Indog Methen* I, 219 f.). The spirits of ancestors (Pitṛs) who have come to see the bride are invoked in the procession of the bride (*Av.* XIV, 2, 73); they are supposed to grant children. If the procession goes past big trees, 'the Gandharvas and Apsaras who live in these trees' are requested to show mercy (*ibid.* V. 9; *Kauśikasūtra* 77, 7). I do not understand how one can see in it 'that the Gandharvas have placed themselves in the position of the Pitṛs or beside them'.

387. *Ṛv.* X, 139, 5; VIII, 77, 5; IX, 85, 12.

388. *Av.* II, 2, 1. 2; XIV, 2, 36. *Bṛhad Āraṇyaka Upaniṣad* III, 6: the kingdom of the Gandharvas appears between the air-region and the region of the sun.

389. The 27 stars of the moon's orbits *Vāj Saṃh.* IX, 7. Rainbow probably on account of *Ṛv.* X, 123; compare my remarks there. Enumeration Agni etc.; *Vāj. Saṃh.* XVIII, 38ff. Fata Morgana see *Pet. Wörterb.* under *gandharvapura, gandharvanagara.* It cannot be proved that the connection of this conception with the Gandharvas is Indo-Iranian (Weber, *Ind. Stud.* XIII, 136, E.H. Meyer, *Indog. Mythen* I, 99).

390. *Ṛv.* IX, 83, 4; 85, 12; 113, 3.

391. The Indo-Iranian origin of this feature is correctly taken for granted, because in the *Avesta* (Yt. 5, 38), the inimical Gandharva who conquers the hero Keresāspa carries on his activity in the ocean Vourukaśa, the seat of the white Soma.

392. *Aitareya Br.* I, 27; *Taitt. Saṃh.* VI, 1, 6, 5. Even in the *Yajusmantras* Soma is addressed: 'Let not Gandharva Viśvāvasu catch you; be an eagle, and fly away' (*T.S.* I, 2, 9, 1).

393. *Taitt. Ār.* I, 9, 3, he is shown clearly as such.

394. *Ṛv.* X, 10, 4, compare 11, 2. IX, 86, 36.

395. It may be, besides, noted that also the *Avesta* knows (Yt. 15, 28) Gandharva as the lord of the abyss, living in waters. Does this concept also date back to the Indo-Iranian period, or is it developed independently among both the peoples?

396. *Pañc. Br.* XII, 11, 10.

397. *Śatap. Br.* XIII, 4, 3, 7. 8.

398. *Śāṅkhāyana G.* I, 19, 2.

399. *Pañc. Brāhm.* XIX, 3, 2.

400. Compare against that, Hillebrandt in 84. Jahresber. *der Schles. Gesellsch. f. vaterl. Kultur*, 22. Feb. 1906, though not convincing. The literature about the controversy mentioned here is also given. I really do not find here anything more than a secondary and

subordinate side-development of the concept of Gandharvas. Compare also Windisch, '*Buddhas Geburt*', 12 ff.

401. *Av.* IV, 37, compare VIII, 6, 19. If IV, 37, 8-10 is very clearly observed as to how the type of the Gandharvas mingles with that of the Piśācas; this can be combined with the fact that an old Buddhistic verse (*Saṃyutta Nikāya* Vol. I p. 33) makes a forest be filled by a group of Apsaras—and Piśācas.

402. It does not appear to me to be similar with any of the features connected with the significance of the Gandharvas in nature when demonianism is traced back to them,—as also to the Apsaras (compare the Mannhardt, *Wald- und Feldkulte* II, 36 f.). Thus, in the case of Apsaras their attribute as the friends of the game of dice need not be considered while inquiring about their original nature (compare in addition Henry, *La magie dans l'Īnde ant.* 114).

403. See Holtzmann *ZDMG.* XXXIII, 635, 641.

404. *Av.* II, 2, 4; *Ṛv.* X, 123, 5.

405. Compare v. Schroeder's remarks on Nereid, *Griechische Götter und Heroen* I, 65; Mannhardt, *Wald-und Feldkulte* I, 99 f.

406. *Taitt. Saṃh.* III, 4, 8, 4; *Atharvaveda* XIV, 2, 9.

407. Holtzmann ibid. 640 f.

408. One may compare the view which Wilken, *Revue coloniale internat.* IV, 377 note 1 communicates from Dutch-India.

409. Mannhardt, *Wald- und Feldkulte* I, 69, 103 f., 152 f.

410. Another version of the same legend is the story of the king Śantanu who liberates the river-goddess Gaṅgā narrated in the epic (*M. Bh.* I, 3888 ff.; compare E.H. Meyer, *Indog. Mythen* II, 578). He should not use a single rebuking word to her. As she throws the children born to her from him, one by one, into the river, he breaks the condition, and she forsakes him.

411. So much correctly L.v. Schroeder *ibid.*, 53 f.

412. *Ṛv.* X, 95; *Śatapatha Brāhmaṇa* XI, 5, 1. Compare my notes on Rv. X, 95 and literature mentioned there. According to the depiction of the *Śatapatha Brāhmaṇa* based on the sacrificial-science, Pur. becomes Gandharva after the completion of a definite ritual prescribed to him by the Gandharvas and is united with Urvaśī.

413. About Urvaśī as the first ancestor of the family of priests, compare *Ṛv.* VII, 33, 11-13. The equally famous Apsaras Śakuntalā is the ancestral mother of family of princes Bharatas (*Śatap. Br.* XIII, 5, 4, 13). More in *ZDMG.* XXXIII, 635 f.

414. One may be reminded of the earth-deities appearing in the Buddhistic literature who play a role at the time of the foundation of a city (*Vinaya Piṭaka* Vol. I, p. 228 f.).

415. *Ṛv.* VII, 54; 55, 1; *Śāṅkhāyana G.* III, 4, etc.

416. *Śāṅkhāyana G.* IV, 13, 5; *Āśvalāyana G.* II, 10, 4. *Ṛv. IV*, 57, 1-3, etc.

417. Regarding the mountain-deities and the tree-deities to be discussed below, I refer to the treatment of the material in the *Mahābhārata* by Hopkins, *Jour. Am. Or. Soc.* XXX (1910), 347 ff; *Epic Mythology* 6 ff.

418. The following Buddhistic verse may be compared: 'World-famous and big is this tree, standing at a special place; it appears, as if divine beings are housed in it', etc. *Jātaka* Vol. III, p. 24.

419. *Ṛv.* I, 90, 8; VII, 34, 23.

420. As against that the plant-kingdom falls noticeably into the background as far as it is considered for the cultivation of fields (compare what is said on p. 1 above).

421. *Av.* VI, 136, 1; *Ṛv.* X, 97, 4. 22. The whole hymn X, 97 is an invocation to the medicinal plants. The worship of plants has another context, when an animal-sacrifice is brought to them to get children. It had been the plants which had hindered the birth of children. *Taitt. Saṃh.* II, 1, 5, 3.

422. Yet compare what is said above on page 44f.

423. So also, while cutting the hair and while cutting up the sacrificial animal.

424. Thus in a later sacrificial ritual (Schwab, *Das altind. Tieropfer* f.); we, however,

do not have any reason not to consider this view as old. The last *mantra* is taken from the *Ṛgveda* (III, 8, 11) and was presumably composed for the use in question.

425. Schwab *ibid.*, 68 ff. These rites are old (*Ṛv.* III, 8).

426. *Āśvalāyana G.* II, 6, 9.

427. X, 146. The hymn is undoubtedly one of the latest, but one cannot conclude from that the later age of the concepts.

428. Literally, 'When Ciccika comes to the help of the 'bull, who roars'. ' Both the birds are not known.

429. I mention from this field the worship of an Udumbara-tree to be performed after marriage with good scents, flowers, thrown-away food, clothes and threads; *Baudhāyana G.* I, 13 (Winternitz, *Altind. Hochzeitsrituell* 101).

430. It should not be overlooked that the following quotations (and generally the quotations from the *Jātaka* in this book) refer partially to the prose of the Jātakas. This should be considered, though approximately, as the one reflecting the original intention of the appropriate story.

431. E.g., *Jātaka* III p. 325.

432. *Jātaka* I p. 328.

433. *Jātaka* III p. 209.

434. *Jātaka* IV p. 154.

435. *ibid* III p. 209

436. *Vinaya Piṭaka* Vol. IV p. 34.

437. *Jātaka* I, 328. 442.

438. *Jātaka* I, 169; II, 385; III, 404, etc.—I, 168; III, 23.

439. *Jātaka* I, 259; II, 308; III, 23, etc.

440. *Jātaka* I, 273; III 200. 527.

441. *Atharvaveda* III, 24; 25, 1; XIV, 1, 45; XI, 9. 10.

442. Yet the demons like the Gandharvas, whose concept appears to be originating from the natural phenomena, can develop an effect similar to those and assimilate themselves with them; compare above p. 125f.

443. The terminology used with reference to the evil spirits is naturally not quite distinct. Leaving aside the less important expressions, the relation of the three most important may be mentioned in short; i.e. Rakṣas (Paroxytones) Yātu, resp. Yātudhāna and Piśāca; this may be apart from the evil demons, the Druhas who carry on their activity especially in the ethical sphere. The first of the expressions is obviously fairly common. It is used when one speaks of the evil spirits without more specilization (as it is very often in the Yajurvedas). The words Rakṣas and Yātu (Yātudhāna) are exchanged in the two big hymns of the Ṛgveda pertinent here (VII, 104; X, 87). A few verses speak for the identity of both the ideas. Thus in VII, 104, 16 "The one who says, he is pure, who calls me Yātudhāna though I am not Yātu, or the Rakṣas (Oxytones, i.e., one who is harmful with the help of a *rakṣas*, see p. 131 f.).—where obviously in the second part of the sentence the guilt and innocence are to be understood in the same relation as in the first. Further X, 87, 10, where Agni is invoked to destroy the three "tops" of Rakṣas, to destroy his ribs, to tear the roots of Yātudhāna into three parts: even here, it obviously concerns one creature. When in VIII, 60, 20, one prays for the warding off of the Rakṣas and the Yātus of the Yātu-empires, both the words are separated, but again VII, 104, 23 stands on the side of these words, where there is talk of the Rakṣas of the Yātu-empires, as there is talk of the Yātu of the Yātu-empires. Is this the explanation for these apparitions, that Rakṣas denotes a species, and Yātu only one type? From that we can see as to where the speciality of the Yātus lies. It is, that often the words *yātudhāna* (fem. yātudhāni), *yātumant* and *yātumāvant* (see e.g. the verse VIII, 60, 20 quoted just above) appear besides the word Yātu. Hardly *yātudhāna* can mean anything else than "contents for Yātu", i.e., the magician who is inhabited by the Yātu, takes his services and is identical with him to some extent (compare my remarks on VII, 34, 8). Therefore, it cannot surprise us that there is occasionally confusion between *yātu* and *yātudhāna* (Rv. VII, 104, 16 where *ayātu* is a describing composite). Thus *yātumant* and *yātumāvant* is also obviously the magician who is connected with Y. Thus Yātu is to be

specially understood as the type of evil spirits used by magicians for harmful purposes (compare Avestic *yātu*—magic, magician). Similar action can also be expressed by *rakṣás* (see above Ṛv. VII, 104, 23); the man who is served by a *rákṣas* is called *rakṣás*, *rakṣasvin* or *rakṣoyuj* ("One who harnesses a R."); as it is a common accusation, that either this or that is a *yātudhāna*, so also it is disputed whether someone is pure or a *rakṣas* (*Ṛv.* VII, 104, 23; compare I, 35, 10). The concept of Piśāca is a little beyond the concepts Yātu and Rākṣas in the terminology of the evil creatures. This word is found only once in the *Ṛv.* (in the form *piśāci* in I, 133, 5, besides *rakṣas*, and is obviously different from it). Later the Piśācas are often named and are distinguished from the Rakṣas and Yātu as a rule. Thus in *Taitt. Saṃh.* II, 4, 1, 1 the three classes, gods, human beings and manes are juxtaposed with the three inimical classes of the Asuras, Rakṣas and Piśācas. Compare also *Av.* I, 35, 2; V, 29, 11; VI, 32, 2; *Hir. G.* I, 11, 8; Ludwig V, 421. On the other hand, there is the identification of the Piśācas with Yātu in *Av.* V, 29, 9. The predominant speciality of the Piśācas in causing harm results from the fact, that they are often called *kravyād* (see e.g. *Av.* V, 29, 9; VIII, 2, 12; XII, 3, 43). This word is just the synonym of Piśāca and can be looked upon as the regular name of the concerned creature in the Ṛgveda (VII, 104, 2; X, 87, 2. 19; 162, 2). Charpentier, Kl. Beitr. zur indoiran. Mythol. (1911) 1 ff. has collected the material on P; I do not find his view that glowworms and will o' the wisps are the original Piśācas as convincing. The Asuras (compare above p. 85 ff.) are completely separated from the all these classes of creatures; they are the enemies of gods in their mythical battle, and not of men in their present life. *Taitt. Saṃh.* VI, 2, 1, 5.6 is characteristic for the fact, as to how they were understood, to some extent, as the Rakṣas put back into the prehistoric experiences of the gods. They appear, however, at places as contemporary enemies of men, e.g., *Av.* VIII, 6, 5; *Kauś. Sūtra* 87, 16; 88, 1. On the different classes of evil demons: Hopkins, *Ep. Myth.* 38ff.; Grierson *ZDMG.* LXVI 67 ff.

444. *Av.* II, 24; These pairs belong to the class of the demons Kimī īn discussed by Weber, *Ind. Stud.* XIII, 183 ff. One may think of the "Kimīdin-pairs" named in the *Ṛgveda* (VII, 104, 23; X, 87, 24 cf. v. 13) when considering such comparisons.

445. See *Av.* VI, 32 2 and many other verses.

446. The neuter gender *rákṣas* does not justify the conclusion that these creatures are sex-less.

447. *Hiraṇyakeśin G.* II, 3, 7; Av. V, 22, 12.

448. When Bergaigne says (II, 217) that the Rakṣas-nature is directly attributed to the human beings (that is the *mortels*), I do not think that it is in the verses quoted by him. See note 443 above on the relation of the human beings to the demons who are in league with them. It should not, however, be denied that some sort of intermingling between man and demon can take place (note 443 above).

449. Something like this is particularly found in *Ath. Veda* VIII, 6 and Hiraṇy. G. II, 3, 7 (compare *Pāraskara* I, 16, 23).

450. *Hiraṇy. G.* II, 7, compare *Pāraskara* I, 16, 24; *Ṛv.* VII, 104, 22.

451. That is why Agni and Indra are invoked to destroy the spirits and "uproot" them completely (*sahamūra*, *sahamūla*) *Ṛv.* III, 30, 17; X, 87, 19), or there is talk of their head (*agra*) or their heads and triple roots (*Ṛv.* III, 30, 17; X, 87, 10). But this root is not to be understood figuratively. Because also "those, whose god is the root" (*mūradeva*, *Ṛv.* VII, 104, 24; X, 87, 2. 14) appear in the same surroundings as inimical creatures, as also the woman, "who has a harm-causing root" (*Av.* I, 28, 3): i.e., the root in which the evil spirit is embodied.

452. Of course, it is often doubtful whether the form of a demon is to be understood in this or in the previous sense.

453. Compare *Av.* XVIII, 2, 28; *Ṛv.* X, 162, 5; *Av.* IV, 37, 11; *Ṛv.* VII, 104, 18 (exactly it does not concern here the transformation of the demons, but the magicians connected with them—see note 443 above—into night-birds).

454. *Av.* VIII, 6, 10, 11. 14, *Hir. G.* II, 3, 7.

455. That is why their expiation with the "hymns killing rakṣas" (*Kauś. Sūtra* 126, 9).

456. i.e., not firmly rooted like a plant.

457. *Av.* IV, 20, 9; *Śat. Br.* III, 1, 3, 13, *Av.* IV, 37, 10 (compare Roth, Festgruß an Böhtlingk 97; to be read in the text as *jyotayamānakān*; IV, 36, 7; *Hir. G.* II, 3, 7; *Av.* II, 14, 4.

458. *Av.* VI, 26, 2. Grierson, *Bihār Peasant Life* 407.

459. I shall give only a small selection from the rich material on cross-roads. The magical actions taking place there for banishing evil spirits and diseases, *Kauś. Sūtra* 26, 30; 27, 7. Offerings for Sahasrākṣa *ibid.* 30, 18. Magic for finding the lost *ibid.* 52, 14 (here it may deal with the cross-road as a point from which all directions can be supervised). House of Rudra at the cross-road, *Śatapatha Br.* II, 6, 2, 7; *Hiraṇy G.* I, 16, 8. Fire which becomes impure after a case of death is placed on the cross-road. *Āśvalāyana G.* IV, 6, 3. After the death of a worshipper, what is due to him is thrown on a cross-road (for his soul? or for removing an uncanny substance?), *Kauś. Sūtra* 46, 39. More in Winternitz, Altindisches Hochzeitsrituell 68. I shall take two references from the Buddhistic literature which show the cross-roads as the places of burial. *Mahāparinibbāna Sutta* (*Dīgha Nikāya* vol. II, p 142): "How does one deal with the body of the king ruling over the earth?...One erects a monument (*thūpa*) for the dead king ruling over the earth at the crossing of big main-streets." Dhammapada-commentary p. 309 Fausb: "He lays the remains to rest and erects a monument at the crossing of big main-streets (thūpa)." Compare Samter, Geburt, Hochzeit und Tod 146, so also the article *Cross-Roads* in the *Encycl. of Rel. and Ethics.*

460. Compare p. 175, note 443.

461. Really to the "most recent Agni"; here on account of the rhyme on *Yavayati,* "he drives away". *Taitt. Saṃhitā* II, 2, 3, 2.

462. *Av.* II, 24.

463. *Taitt. Saṃh.* II, 2, 2, 2; *Manu* III, 280; *Śatapatha Br.* II, 3, 4, 23; *Taitt. Saṃh.* II, 4, 1, 1 (for that Geldner, *Ved. Studien* II, 167, note 1; K.F. Johansson, *IF.* III,237); VI, 1, 4, 5; II, 6, 6, 3. *Mahābhārata* VII, 7832 says that the Rākṣasas have special power in the night.

464. *Av.* I, 16, 1; IV, 36, 3. I do not know what is *āgare* and *pratikrośe* in the second verse.

465. *Av.* VII, 76, 4.

466. *Ṛv.* VIII, 60, 20.

467. *Av.* V, 29, 6-8. Do we not have here one of the origins of fasting during holy occasions. i.e. the occasions characterised by the proximity of spirits? The danger should be avoided that the spirits creep into the one who is eating.

468. *Kauśika Sūtra* 25, 28.

469. *Av.* VIII, 6, 3.

470. *Av.* V, 29, 5.

471. *Av.* VI, 111, 3; *Hir. G.* I, 15, 5.

472. *Mānava Gṛhya* I, 10 (Winternitz, *Altindisches Hochzeitsrituell* 60).

473. Weber und Haas, *Ind. Stud.* V, 325 f.; Winternitz *ibid.* 87; compare ploß. *Das Weib* I, 503; v. Schroeder, *Hochzeitsbräuche der Esten* 192 f.; Fehrle, *Kultische Keuschheit* 40; J.J. Meyer, *Das Weib im altindischen Epos. Durkheim,* 235 f. On literature on Tobias-nights: Durkheim, *Les formes elementaires de la vie religieuse* 434, note 1; 446, note 1.

474. Compare *Av.* IV, 37, 11; *Śatapatha Brahm.* III, 2, 1, 40 etc.

475. Or it may be much more—the one does not exclude the other—that the wife is seen in these days as harassed by the spirits against whom the man has to protect himself, or does he have to respect their privilege? Has the Indian concept that the woman belongs to three supernatural husbands (Soma, Gandharva and Agni; *Ṛv.* X, 85, 40. 41) been developed from the taboo of these three nights? Of course, then a further question becomes pertinent, whether also the motif has a rôle, that one should spare and gather one's might which could be at one's disposal and about which one could be more sure.

476. Compare *Av.* VIII, 6. besides Gṛhya-texts.

477. *Ṛv.* VII, 104, 21. 18; *Av.* VII, 70, 2. The Rakṣas disturbing the sacrifice are familiar to the later texts. e.g. *Rāmāyaṇa* I chapter 30 (ed. Bombay), Śakuntalā Str. 93 Pischel.

478. *Ṛv.* X, 87, 16 f.

479. *Kauś. Sūtra* 135, 9.

480. I refer to Lukas, *Die Grundbegriffe in den Kosmogonien der alten Völker* 65 ff.; Geldner, *Zur Kosmogonie des Rigveda* (Marb. 1908).

481. These and others like them are widespread across the earth. Compare e.g. Brinton, *Religions of Primitive Peoples*, 123.

482. The expression is, as Geldner *ibid.*, 3 has appropriately remarked, in the older texts at a place taken up later by the concept of releasing oneself (*sṛj*-, compare my "Lehre der Upanishaden" 82f.).

483. That is remarked by A. Lang in "*Myth, Ritual and Religion*" (Chapter on Indian myths about the origin of the world.) Wild Boar: *Śatapatha Br.* XIV, 1, 2, 11.

484. As also acknowledged by A. Lang (*ibid*).

485. The answer given in the last verse of the hymn which names Prajāpati as the world-creator of the Brāhmaṇa-period is a later addition.

486. "Brahmaṇaspati (above p. 35f.) produced these (births) with blast and smelted them like the smith is before the lines mentioned here. Does it mean that the god existed before the non-existence, existence, etc.? Or does it mean that his action, though mentioned at the beginning, took place in the later part of the events? Perhaps, we are not justified in ascribing to the poet a definite conviction of the one or the other.

487. It may be noted, how the confused diction names the sun twice (first *sūrya*, then *svar*; compare my remarks on X, 189, 1).

488. See the section on Animism.

489. The Iranian Yima-Yimeh corresponds to the twin-couple Yama-Yamī.

490. In the *Avesta*, as the king of a golden era; see below in the section on Animism.

491. Hillebrandt's (*V.M.* I, 495, Lieder *des Ṛv.* 139) view that Yama of the *Ṛv.* X, 10 is to be distinguished from Yama, the god of the dead, is not acceptable. Besides other corresponding reasons, one may note the special nature of the hymn-collection X, 10-19 which is constantly full of clear or concealed (see my remarks on 12, 6; 13, 4) references to Yama. It would be venturing too much to say that there are two Yamas, and who do not have anything to do with each other.

492. The second is Āthwya, the third Thrita ("The Third"). Hillebrandt, *V.M.* III, 343 footnotes, has correctly pointed out, as to how close are the expressions of the *Ṛgveda*.

493. VIII, 67, 20 the god of the Dead is called Vivasvant instead of Yama. Passages on Viv. as the father of the human race: See Hillebrandt *V.M.* I, 488.

494. As he is the father of the first mortal, V. cannot be considered himself as mortal. In fact, one uses the sacrificial address *svāhā* (not *svadhā*) for him which is used for the gods, while for Yama both the addresses are current. *Av.* XVIII, 3, 62 appears to be agreeing with that, but *Ṛv.* X, 17, 2 appears to be really contradicting it. But certain unclarity here should not be surprising. Compare, besides, above p. 167, note 318.

495. Connected constantly with the verb used for the shining of the dawn. I am not inclined to accept Bartholomae's (*WB.* Column 1452) doubt on account of the verses like I, 44, 1; III, 30, 13; VIII, 102, 22.

496. Evidences even of the later Vedas for Viv.=Sun: Hill. *V.M.* I, 488. I, 46, 13 is considered as the Ṛgvedic evidence amongst others (ibid, 486): The Aśvins, "who were living with Vivasvant", should come to our sacrifice. Why with the Sun? Why not with the first sacrificer? As they have visited him, they should visit us; the following *manuṣvat* also speaks for that.

497. Thus Manu appears also like Yama as the son of Vivasvant in the later Vedic period. Perhaps it traces (or the identification of the both) back to *Ṛv.* (VIII, 52, 1; more about the relationship between M. and Viv. see in Bergaigne, I, 88). A Christensen, *Festschr. f. Andreas* 63ff. discusses the Iranian traces of the concept of the first man, Manu.

498. Material in Bergaigne I, 66.

499. We shall come back to them soon.

500. It may be mentioned in short that the legend of the flood is connected also with Manu—when the Adam of the Veda took over to some extent the rôle of Noah—. According to this, Manu saves himself in a ship warned by a fish armed with supernatural knowledge

(see namely *Śatapatha Brāhmaṇa* I, 8, 1, 1ff.). I agree with most of the research scholars that this story, we come across in the later Vedic tradition, is borrowed from the Babylonian sphere. Compare besides, the well-known works of Andree and Usener, and Winternitz, *Die Flutsagen des Altertums und der Naturvölker* (Mitt. der Anthrop. Gesellschaft in Wien Vol. XXXI, 1901).

501. See Bergaigne I, 36.

502. Compare what is said on page 70f. about this name. As we see in the seven priests the helpers of Manu in sacrifice, Aṅgiras are the followers of Yama in the other world. In the sacrifice for the dead, one worships "Yama, accompanied by the Aṅgiras" and prays: "Come, sit on this bed of grass, O Yama, in company with Aṅgiras and fathers." (*Ṛv.* X, 14, 4).

503. *Ṛv.* X, 82, 4 (I presume *niṣattāḥ*, compare my note); VII, 76, 4; X, 68, 11.

504. Compare on this myth p. 79f. above.

505. *Ṛv.* III, 33 (above p. 123); III, 53 (compare Hillebrandt, *Festgruß an Boethlingk* 43; Geldner, *Ved. Studien* II, 158 f.; my notes). See also my remarks in *ZDMG.* XLII, 204, note 3.

506. I, 179; X, 102 (Literature on that in my notes).

507. One may also think of the horse Dadhikrāvan who got the divine respect, p. 37.

508. In connection with this, I refer to the controversy of Gruppe (*Griech. Kulte und Mythen* I, 298 ff.) with Bergaigne.

509. As already pointed out by Roth (*Erläuterungen zum Nirukta* 155).

510. See above p. 173, note 409.

511. See Bergaigne III, 203f. for the evidences.

512. Thus he wooes Āhalya in the form of her husband.

513. To some extent also to the Maruts who are viewed as the sons of Rudra. Bergaigne III, 154.

514. See under the Depiction of the Cult.

515. *Ṛv.* II, 33, 4.

516. The compilation made by Bergaigne III, 199 may be referred to.

517. Thus, there was also a sacrifice for Agni Vaiśvānara, by which one could assure for oneself for one year the possibility of unpunishable infidelity. *Kāṭhaka* XIII, 1.

518. *Ṛv.* II, 27, 3; *Av.* IV, 16, 2.

519. It is possible that the spies are originally the stars, but it is not proved by the references in Bergaigne III, 167. That idea could have been scarcely alive for the poets of the *Ṛgveda* as every connection of the spies to the night, appears to be absent. Besides, it is understandable even without the acceptance of such a natural subtratum that the gods, who should know everything hidden, should be provided with the spies.

520. Besides, Mitra who appears on the whole in the Veda as a double of Varuṇa standing at the second place has—from the Indo-Iranian period—the speciality of being the protector of contracts and the alliance of friendship. That is why the special importance that is got—wherever there is a reference to him—by the expression *yātayati* (show the people the right place in relationship to one another, i.e., to bring them in agreement; *IF.* XXXI, 133). Compare above p. 161 f., note 215.

521. Thus, *enas* is on the same line with sorcery (*Av.* V, 30, 2-4), with dirt, with bad dreams (*Av.* X. 5, 24), with *pāpman* (VI, 113, 1.2) etc. The sin of murdering a Brahmana is taken up by the performer Indra in his hand and is carried around by him for one complete year till he succeeds in laying it off, *Taitt. Saṃh.* II, 5, 1, 2).

522. *Ṛv.* VI, 74, 3; I, 24, 9, Compare Bergaigne III, 161 f.

523. *Ṛv.* II, 27, 16. It also leads to the idea of sling when one prays to the gods, that they should not catch the men like a bird, *Ṛv.* II, 29, 5. Compare also *Av.* IV, 16, 6; VIII, 8, 16.

524. See *Vāj S.* VIII, 13; *Ṛv.* X, 164; 3; *Vāj. S.* XX, 16.

525. This idea has the other side, that even a good deed of the one could benefit the other. Compare *Ṛv.* VII, 35, 4 and the Section on the Life after Death.

526. Also of the mother or another relatives; *Av.* V. 30, 4; VI, 116, 3; X, 3, 8.

527. *Av.* VII, 64; *Taitt. Saṃh.* III, 1, 4, 3; *Av.* XIV, 2, 59f. (Bloomfield *Am. Journal Phil.* XI, 341); VI, 113,

528. *Ṛv.* II, 28, 9; VI, 51, 7; VII, 52, 2.

529. *V.S.* III, 48; VIII, 13.

530. See e.g., X, 36, 9; 37, 12.

531. See e.g., *Av.* V, 30, 4; VIII, 7, 3.

532. *Av.* VI, III, 3.

533. *Av.* II, 10, 8. Often, one comes across the prayer that the one who desires to harm the other sinner harms himself, that the curse returns to the one who curses, or also as already remarked (page 145) that the sin of the worshipper himself clings to the one who desires to harm him (Bergaigne III, 190 ff.); certainly there is in it more or less clear concept in play, that the sin becomes fatal to the man, who is accessible to its infection through its own strength.

534. Even if the liberation from the sin is connected here with the action of a god, the first of the two types of ideas to be separated is obviously present—the sin being harmful through its own nature and by arousing the anger of the god. The god works as the remover of the harmful power. Compare p. 146.

535. It can be said that the first interpretation of the sin has its place predominantly in the *Atharvaveda*, while the second in the *Ṛgveda*. One should also take care here before concluding about the period of the texts on the basis of some concepts. In fact, the difference between *Ṛv.* and *Av.* is completely explained by the different contents of the two collections. The sin indeed has to appear different in the hymns of magic which are concerned naturally with the manifold magic meant to remove sin or its after-effects from the hymns dedicated to the great gods in which their influence is completely in the foreground.

536. *Ṛv.* VII, 89, 5.

537. *Ṛv.* VII, 86, 3, compare p. 148 f. Sin and anger of Maruts are similarly interconnected. "What secret sin or open, stirs their anger, that we implore the Swift ones to forgive us" (VII, 58, 5).

538. Particularly dropsy: compare above p. 163, note 240.

539. *Ṛv.* I, 25, 2; II, 28, 7; I, 24, 11 (Compare VIII, 67, 20); IX, 73, 8; VII, 61, 5, etc.

540. *Ṛv.* II, 27, 3; also Agni V, 19, 4. See Bergaigne III, 199.

541. *Ṛv.* II, 27, 16; I, 128, 7.

542. Compare the discussion on this above p. 86f.

543. Geldner, *Ved. Studien* I, 142.

544. See above p. 86.

545. *Ṛv.* III, 61, 7; V, 63, 4; 85, 5; VIII, 41, 3. Compare generally about the *māyā* of Varuṇa in Bergaigne III, 81.

546. And many similar examples. See Bergaigne, III, 258f.

547. This is a general characteristic of all the ancient moral; it would be wrong to see in it a speciality of the "Oriental".

548. *Ṛv.* VII, 86, 4 (Bergaigne III, 156); see page 148f.

549. A stronger power has driven the sinner into the sin.

550. Bergaigne III, 169 ff. gives the major portion of the material on this side of the nature of Agni.

551. *Ṛv.* IV, 3, 5, The series of gods to whom Agni will speak goes further in the following; even Bergaigne (III, 206) remarks that Indra (p. 149f. on him) does not appear there.

552. IV, 1, 4, 5; I, 128, 7.

553. Bergaigne has set an example for me in his excellent Chapter III, 200-209.

554. *Ṛv.* II, 12, 10; X, 27, 1; IV, 23, 8ff.; VIII, 45, 34.

555. V, 34, 44, says explicitly of Indra: "He does not flee from the sin (of the man)"i.e. he cannot be hindered by the sin in his friendship with the man. It is true, there is also another view, see Bergaigne III, 201.

556. *Ṛv.* II, 27, 14; VII, 84,2; Bergaigne III, 207.

CHAPTER THREE

The Cult

GENERAL SURVEY

The Cult as Practice and Warding off

Man's activity vis-a-vis gods and spirits is directed towards seeking their blessings and help and warding off their malefic influence. This is partially achieved by influencing them, as creatures who are powerful in their personal freedom of action, through the means of cultic practices and through persuasion and offerings, but also partially by coercing them through the art of magic and producing through one's own strength a concatenation of causes and effects corresponding to laws of this magic. And in this respect, they are in the same class as the real or alleged impersonal creatures, whom the magician feels capable of governing according to his own will.

The Vedic cult adopts predominantly the first of these two methods in respect of the great gods. The towering might of the god excludes here the idea of force that is to be exerted against him, or allows this idea to appear as something inconsequential and only of secondary importance. Since the great gods are mainly considered as benevolent powers, only seldom does the worshipper try, in that he worships and feeds the god, to keep him away through amicable persuasion, which is namely, the characteristic peculiarity of the cult of Rudra[1]. The behaviour towards small demoniac powers, amongst whom the malefic are predominant, takes different shape. Man believes that he can match them, not only through the assistance of the benevolent great gods, but also through his own might and cunning. Accordingly, it is warding off with which one is predominantly concerned in the forms of magic[2]. The cult of the Dead shows a double face. The souls of the fathers, kind to their children, but at the same time sinister, receive at times attention that makes them favourably disposed; at times, the magic defence steps in so that they do not harm the living and do not force upon them their proximity beyond time[3]. As already mentioned, one will obviously employ solely magic means against impersonal powers and substances, in whom a kind attitude cannot be induced.

Care of god, from the modest offerings to the minor creatures in the realm of spirits up to the lavish offerings of the well-to-do sacrificer to the highest lords of this realm, consists mainly in the offerings of food-stuffs and of the refreshing, nourishing and intoxicating drink, therefore, in the oblation: in which case, it is understood that this hospitable reception of the god includes or can include certain incidental attentions, like the offering of a comfortable seat and of sweet perfumes, etc. Offerings of clothes—this is remarkable—appear to occur only in the cult of the Dead, but are not meant for the gods, who were considered as being attired; equally rarely do we come across, as far as I can see, offerings of objects like weapons, chariots, etc., which go along with the equipment of the god. And all valuable objects which exceeded the requirements of personal use, do not appear to be dedicated to the god in the Vedic cult. On the one hand, it is based upon the fact that the cultic custom in its basic features dates back to an age where a well-developed idea of private property, i.e., the idea of divine private property was unknown. On the other hand, it may be due to the absence of the houses of gods, where such property could have been stored. Also the fact might have played a rôle, that the Brahmana-marshals of the cult naturally preferred to recommend the giving of generous gifts of, say, gold desired by all, to the priest rather than to the god.

Of course, the alluring and acclamatory speeches, mostly in metrical form, in addition to song and occasionally instrumental music, were a part of the gifts. The dialogues we come across—theological riddles along with their solutions as also conversations of obscene nature—are perhaps also to be considered, at least, in part as meant for the entertainment of gods. On the other hand, other actions belonging to the cult, in which case one could also think of a similar explanation, e.g., chariot-racing, archery, dice-playing, dancing, sexual acts, etc. are not apparently dedicated to the delight of gods, but to the magic acts, through which the sacrificer seeks to assure for himself strength, happiness, fertility of his fields, his wives, etc.

Supplicatory Sacrifice, Sacrifice of Expiation; and Thanksgiving Sacrifice

The sacrifice ought to obtain for man the mercy of god, be it in general or in specific instances; thus it can be termed as a supplicatory sacrifice. The sacrifice of expiation is in some way a special instance of the supplicatory sacrifice. Here, the supplication is directed towards forgiveness of sins, towards non-exaction of revenge for a sin committed, non-doing of threatened harm. Perhaps an image, a part, instead of the original or the whole, that is claimed by god, is sacrificed in the hope that he is satisfied with it[4]. We shall come back to the sacrifice of expiation in a special section on it later. Thanksgiving-sacrifices are completely or almost unknown to the Vedic cult, as the word 'thanks' is unknown to the Vedic language. Rites which could be considered as Thanksgiving sacrifices appear to be almost always supplicatory sacrifices on closer observation. Thus the sacrifice of the first fruits of the soil[5] does not obviously express thanks for the blessings of gods received already, but seeks blessings for the future. It may be incidentally remarked that this appears to be primarily not so much for the hope of future harvests, but for the prosperous enjoyment of what is available[6]. Also the alleged Thanksgiving sacrifice after the birth of a son[7] is in reality wholly a supplicatory sacrifice. There, as is distinctly expressed, it concerns the 'purification' of the new-born 'with the brilliance of the holiness, conferring on him sharpness of wit, the blessing of food, the power of the senses and cattle'. Even then, one could not obviously think of a Thanksgiving sacrifice, even if the custom of the solemn vow which became popular later was already practised in the Vedic period.[8] Gift promised to the god in the event of a definite show of mercy, and offered to him only after its appearance is nothing else but a postdated supplicatory sacrifice. A few further cases of sacrifices which could be comprehended as Thanksgiving sacrifices become doubtful if they are more seriously viewed. An enumeration of kings who are consecrated with 'Indra's holy and great anointment', says of everyone that 'he has marched victoriously around the whole earth and offered the sacrificial horse'[9]. Could then the Horse sacrifice be considered as the Thanksgiving sacrifice for great victories? It might have something of its character. But closer scrutiny of the concerned ritual shows quite clearly, as I think, that there was also here, if not exactly a supplicatory sacrifice, at least originally a magic act directed towards obtaining desired goods (see p. 185), one hoped to obtain from the Horse sacrifice invincibility victory and a government blessed with glory and plenty[10]. And if this rite presupposes successes already achieved, then there is in it much less the element of thanks than the idea that such wishes have no meaning for the weak and insignificant, that such a venture spells danger to the one who toys with the rite without sanction. 'The one who offers Horse sacrifice without the necessary sanction will be washed away'[11]. Further, the sacrifice to the dead celebrated at the occasions of happy events in the family, like birth or marriage[12], does not show in its ritual any sign of showing gratitude to the ancestors as bestowers of happiness. It appears to deal here simply with the recognition of the fact that even the dead relatives of a house had a claim to partake of the joy of the living; perhaps the thought plays a rôle here that just the one who is the partaker of happiness has above all, reason to assure himself of the mercy of those powerful helpers. The sacrifice prescribed in the following lines of a Sūtra text[13] is perhaps the nearest to the semblance of a Thanksgiving sacrifice. 'If the one who has set up the sacrificial fires is stricken with illness, let him depart...It is said, the fires love the village. Longing for this and eager for return to the village, they want to make him healthy, thus it is taught. If he is cured he should make a Soma sacrifice or an Animal sacrifice or a similar sacrifice and live again at the same place. Or without such a sacrifice.' Perhaps, here is an instance of supplicatory sacrifice concerning future health, as one would like to believe, given the analogy of a few of the cases discussed. But one can hardly deny that such a supplicatory sacrifice is very much similar to the Thanksgiving sacrifice, and it may be presumed that just this kind of supplicatory sacrifice could have easily given in the course of its development a starting-point for the Thanksgiving sacrifice.

How Sacrifice is Effective

Now it must be asked further: how does the sacrifice work? In what way does it help the man to get the desired blessings?

The concept prevalent in the Veda is doubtless as follows: The sacrifice goes to god as a gift presented to him. The sacrificer hopes that it will have an effect on the mind of the god not through coercion, but through the awakening of his enormous goodwill in favour of human beings. The same motive recurs again and again throughout the Veda: this sacrificial meal, this drink should satisfy, strengthen and please the god. This is drastically expressed by a story in the Vedic text[14] of a later date. Indra goes to Suśravas and says: 'Do sacrifice to me, I am hungry'. He sacrifices, and Indra goes round with the sacrificial cake in hand. As it can be easily understood, the god loves the sacrificer; he, of course, is lenient to the poor, who can give only very little[15]; but he hates the miser. Contented, he donates his gifts to the generous, as was done him (by the generous) earlier. 'Drink, and wax great!' says the *Ṛgveda*, 'yours are the Soma juices, the pressed, Indra, and these we bring you. Even as you drank, Indra, earlier Somas, so drink today, a new guest, meet for praises...Then bring hither, and let none prevent it! We know you well, the Lord of wealth and treasure. That splendid gift, which is your own, O Indra, vouchsafe to us, Lord of the Tawny Coursers' (III, 36, 3.9). 'Indra, drink Soma, satisfy therewith your longing; then fix your mind upon bestowing treasures' (I, 54, 9). 'The hero never checked by men has gained his strength through Indra, he who presses out and pours his deep libations forth, O Vṛtra slayer, unto you' (VII, 32, 6). 'I became', says Indra, 'the furtherer of the sacrificer; I have conquered in every fight the men who do not offer the sacrifice (X, 49, 1). The sacrificer addresses the god in a phrase of a somewhat later origin: 'Give me; I give you. Put away something for me; I put away something for you. Offer me sacrifice; I offer you sacrifice (*Ts.* 1, 8, 4, 1). And in the same sense, the Sūktavāka formula[16], where the priest says after the completion of oblations, 'God so and so, accepted this sacrifice; he has become strong; he has got greater power for himself.' Thereupon, the one who has arranged the sacrifice says, 'May I also win, following the victory of the god so and so.' It is always the god upon whom the effect of the sacrifice is seen. The reward, which man promises himself, comes from the hands of god. His well-being follows the well-being of the god made possible by the sacrifice. He knows himself in comparison with the more powerful one and relies on the long-standing friendship without a feeling of an endless distance or his own unworthiness. He appeals to this friendship in a tone whose ingenuity often borders on importunity. Thus he brings his present to the god while "seizing his right hand'. The expectation of a return reward hardly intensifies into the idea that the god has become his debtor[17], that an order of the law standing above him demands of him the payment of this debt. But he has all the same the consciousness that the relation in which he stands to god will not permit the god to do anything other than to reciprocate amply the tokens of kindness received by him.

This is the concept that runs across the whole length and breadth of the *Ṛgvedic* sacrificial poetry, as expressed in hundreds, indeed in thousands of hymns and verses. Its recurrent appearance amongst the peoples of the most diverse origin entitles us to consider it as normal for long intervals of human culture.

But the surroundings amidst which this sacrifice exists and the past upon which it rests, are, as we know, full of the conceptions and practices of magic that claims to guide directly the course of events without the aid of external goodwill[18]. And ethnology teaches us to recognise particularly the old and the ancient types of cultic actions, which one would very much like to term as sacrifices and which appear more or less similar to the sacrifices understood in the usual way, but whose meaning is principally different, gravitating more towards magic. Here the question, whether one should apply to it the term "sacrifice", would mean finally a point of dispute about words. There is in the field of totemism the killing—one can call it sacrifice—of the totem animal and the sacramental eating of this animal or of the totem-plant. But there appear also rites independent of totemism whose idea it is to gather magic power, say, in an animal and to set that in action,—may be in the indefinite expanses, or may be in definite directions, in that their container, so to say, is opened by killing of the animal[19]. This is done, say, for the prosperity of the relevant type of plant or animal, for rendering harmless the infringement of a taboo, for the practice of magic upon spirits and gods[20]. Then further, connected with it or independent of it, eating of animal or plant substances, to produce the effect of magic, to give definite powers to the consumer and to establish a communion with the other consumers. In this context, one may mention further the rites of the service of fire and its application in the Sun magic or its use in burning away the hostile powers. One may mention further the giving away of women, servants, animals, food, useful objects, etc., to the dead and burning them with him[21]. Finally, in the sacrifice at the time of construction (of a house, etc.) one immures salubrious substances or living beings in a construction to give it firmness or to put in it the protecting spirits.

Beside all this, the sacrifice wooing for divine pardon stands out as something peculiar, explaining itself through itself on the one hand; however, on the other hand, mutual influences and intermingling had to take place. Original magic sacrifices—if one be allowed this brief expression—and in fact, magic of all types, could cover itself with the top layer of the components of latter as a result of the dominant place the sacrifice of gifts had in the Veda. For instance, the ancient Horse-sacrifice appears to be, as shown below[22], in its original nature, an exemplum, indeed a well-preserved exemplum in the Veda of a magic-sacrifice not ruled by the idea of gift. But the concept that the sacrificial horse is offered to the gods like any other sacrificial animal has spread beyond this, even if only superficially. Conversely, the sacrifice of gifts had to acquire for itself elements of the magic-sacrifice. For example, the enjoyment of a portion of the sacrificial meal on the part of the sacrificer[23], permits, as it appears to me, an explanation also on the basis of the sacrifice of gifts, but it is quite likely that here—in this case long before the Vedic period—older rites of the sacramental enjoyment of food had their influence. And on the whole, it is very clear that the background of the sacrifice of gifts, saturated with the concepts of divine proximity and of the mysterious success, offered a terrain like no other for practicing the art of magic. The attempt to explain the rites of the sacrifice in terms of their incidental peculiarities had to result in discovering in them the influences of the nature of magical effects. Not the least, the sacrificial priests must have promoted and intensified the concept of the magic power obtained by sacrifice in order to demonstrate the indispensability of their own art. Finally, the transformation of an act of sacrifice into an act of magic must have been promoted by a close, parellel occurrence, through the intermingling of the incantation of prayer and the incantation of magic, i.e., of the word that pursuades the god as also the man, and of the word that calls forth influences in the world of objects by virtue of its correspondence with the object or with an occurrence denoted by it, just as the picture stands in magical correspondence with the image of the object. Prayer is a part of the sacrifice: If the prayer adopts something from the effects of the magic-incantation, then the way in which the sacrifice becomes effective must also be modified accordingly to obtain magic coercive power over gods, things and occurrences.

Sacrifice Coercing Gods; Sacrifice and Magic

In fact, it can be clearly understood from a number of verses of the *Ṛgveda* that the sacrifice, which is generally understood as gift and homage, captivates the god through a sort of a magic coercion and subjugates him to the sacrificer. Thus it is said[24], 'While other men than we with kine chase him as groups (of hunters) chase the wild animals, inveigle him with their milch-kine'[25] (VIII, 2, 6). A priest, who invites Indra for his sacrifice, says to him, 'Let no men check your course as fowlers stay the bird' (III, 45, 1). It is once said with reference to Agni whose visible body is indeed subjugated to the power of man, 'May the mortal command over such an Agni, the bountiful, with sharpened teeth' (IV, 15, 5). And finally a verse which places, if not the sacrifice, then the worship (*namas*) as a might which surpasses the gods. A poet who offers his worship to the Ādityas to free himself of the sin, says, 'Mighty is worship. I dispose worship towards myself. Worship has held in place the heaven and earth. Worship to gods! Worship commands and rules over them. I make amends for even committed sin through homage' (VI, 51, 8).

The unusualness of such expressions of the power of man over god in the *Ṛgveda* shows all the same that it is to them, and not to the other conception of sacrifice that the distinction is to be applied,—what the interpreter of the Veda must have always in his mind. This is the distinction of the isolated feature from the one that belongs to the regular inventory of the Vedic thought. How many a time does the poet talk himself, so to say, into the hyperbolic glorification of the god or any other being, he is speaking of at the moment. Thus, one should not take too seriously an expression as the one in that hymn about worship that worship also rules over gods. In the first two quotations, it is no accident that both times, they are the rivals of the speaker, who chase after Indra, lie in wait for him and catch him like bird-catchers. Their efforts directed towards the god are deliberately shown in bad light, and the question addressed to Indra appears to give to understand: will you allow yourself really to be stayed by such people, as if you were a bird and they the fowlers[26]?

The *Ṛgveda* shows that the sacrifice of gifts and homage is endowed with magic power. This is concretized in a rite, and especially clearly shown in the hymn of Devāpi for getting rain (X, 98). 'Sit down for the sacrificial service of the Hotar', the priest is invited, 'pay your worship duly; serve the gods, Devāpi, with oblation.' And the priest 'knowing the god's goodwill' sits down: 'there he has brought down from the ocean above to the ocean below, the celestial waters of rain. Gathered together in the highest ocean, the waters stood, by deities obstructed. They hurried down set free by Ṛṣṭiṣeṇa's son, in gaping clefts, urged onward by Devāpi[27].' It is seen how the idea slips out of the initial direction: the gods were supposed to give the rain at first in their mercy; now, the priest is pouring it himself by the magic power of his sacrificial art.

This priestly art in the later Vedic period has increased beyond measure the rites and the interpretation of the rites, which introduce magic power into the sacrifice or into its individual procedures, to give to the sacrifice magic power even over the gods. The choice of the verse-measure in the litanies, the number of the verses to be recited, every minor feature of the sacrificial gifts, the nature of the sacrificial reward for the priests[28]: all this appears there as a lever in the hands of a knower, a priest, who employs it causing the most powerful effects far and near. But we cannot follow here in detail these views, whose evidence is found in almost every page of the *Brāhmaṇa*-texts[29].

Expiatory Sacrifice and Expiatory Magic

Perhaps a few remarks on expiatory cult follow most appropriately after what has been just said. I must come back to this cult more in detail after what I have pointed out above (p. 182). We shall observe here two trends, corresponding to the difference in the lines of thinking crossing each other in the conception of sin (see above p. 144): trends whose clear, principal separation cannot be invalidated by the fact that they, most understandably, collide with one another in a single act of expiation in many cases.

Pacifying the Gods; Removing the Substance of Sin

On the one hand, if the sin is violation of divine will and thereby provocation of divine wrath, the act of expiation is addressed to the god; he is gratified and pacified through gifts and signs of submissiveness. But, if on the other hand, sin is considered as something clinging to the sinner according to the type, say, of miasm, the expiatory cult consists of magical procedures which destroy these infections or keep them at a distance where they can do no harm, so that the sinner will be free and pure, 'like the sweat-stained person freed of impurity after his bath', 'like the bird flying away from the egg[30]'. Also, this view permits a version, where the god is cast in the rôle of a liberator, i.e., when magic is not directly employed to remove the substance of sin, but recourse is taken to the god's might and skill. Here, the position of the god is obviously a different and more outward one than where the liberation from sin is transposed into the soul of the god, and it is understood as an act of his grace.

Expiatory sacrifices with their prime objective of divine mercy are obviously quite within the sphere of the usual sacrificial cult. They are sacrifices like every other, performed as a rule to appease Varuṇa, the divine guardian of the world-order, the chastener of sins. Thus, the sacrifice—for, it probably concerns one such—which comprises that splendid and moving prayer of the Vasiṣṭhan mentioned above[31] (p. 148 f.). 'When shall I be close again to Varuṇa?'—seeking out his sin, he goes to ask the sages; but they all give him the same answer: it is Varuṇa who is angry with you[32].

A series of other expiatory acts are of different nature than such sacrifices and prayers. The most prominent expiatory act of the regular ecclesiastical calender belongs to the second of the three four-monthly festivals, i.e., the celebration of the Varuṇa-praghāsas which takes place at the beginning of the rainy season. A round flat cake is prepared out of barley roasted in the southern sacrificial fire, the fire of the impure and sinister actions. One cake for every inmate of the house and one more in addition to it, meant for the unborn, as explained perhaps correctly by tradition. The wife of the sacrificer is asked about her paramours: 'with whom do you consort?'—she has to name them or lift as many grass-blades as she has lovers. It is a type of confession of sins as a part of the great expiatory action. 'The woman sins against Varuṇa, when she, belonging to one, consorts with another. He asks her that she may sacrifice without the least twinge of conscience. And the sin will decrease through confession, because the truth prevails. And that is why he asks her. If she does not confess, it would be bad for the relatives' (*Śatapatha Br.* II, 5, 2, 20)[33]. Now the woman is led to the sacrificial fires. She puts the cakes in a basket-swingle on her head and offers it into the fire—again into the southern fire—with the saying: 'What in the village, in the forest, in the hall, in our minds we have committed as sin, we offer all that here!' Amongst further offerings to the same fire, one is to Varuṇa, with sayings which call forth the mercy of the god: he should not be angry, should not cut off the life of the implorer[34]. The rites are brought to conclusion with a bath, apparently meant for washing away of sins, and wherein the sacrificer and his wife clean each other's back and thereafter put on new clothes.

It is seen, how here an action of altogether different nature constitutes the main expiatory act in the ceremony with the cake of barley besides the Varuṇa-sacrifice, wherein one implores for god's mercy. It gets only superficially the character of a sacrifice. The expression 'offer away' (*avayaj*) we come across here and in similar cases points above all to something being thrown away. This has been reinterpreted as sacrificing by the priestly fantasy caught up in the sacrificial ritual. Likewise, burning after the completion of the usual sacrifice of such objects, which cannot be brought into contact with profane life on account of their sacred character, has undergone the same reinterpretation. The sin of the housemates remains attached to the cakes, to every single cake, the sin of one person. With the offering, i.e., with the burning of cakes, the sin is burnt.

A similar burning of the sin is added to the ritual of the Soma sacrifice. The chips of the sacrificial posts are thrown into the fire, one at a time with the following sayings: 'You are the offering for the sin committed by gods. The one by human beings..by the fathers...you are the offering away for the sin committed by oneself. You are the offering away for the sin for the sake of the sin. You are the offering away for all the sin, the sin I have committed knowingly and unknowingly.' It is also clear here: what is called offering away is actually burning away, physical destruction of the sin, without the invocation of divine mercy.[35]

When such expiatory ceremonies are included in the context of the higher cult, one can be so much the more certain to come across them in numbers in the sphere of the lower cult and amongst conjurations and magical actions connected with the casual occurrences of daily life. The magic hymns of the *Atharvaveda* and the relevant ritual instructions of the *Kauśika Sūtra* confirm this expectation. Thus, the expiation of the brothers is described, who have committed an offence in that the younger brother has married before the elder. Fetters of reed grass are put around them near the water, a symbol of the fetters of sin; consecrated water is poured over that; thereupon, some of these fetters are thrown into the foam of the river and allowed to be swept away: 'disappear with the foam of the river', the appropriate saying[36] is addressed to the evil[37]. The one who has spoken a lie, should sip water with the saying, 'Whatever be the falsehood we have spoken in the last three years[38], may water protect from all the disaster, from all the distress[39]'. If someone is touched by a crow or sullied by its filth—the saying we shall soon quote, makes it very clear how far there can be talk of sin—, one washes him or takes a firebrand around him with the saying: 'What the black bird has let fall while flying up, may the waters protect me from all disaster and distress. What the black bird has wiped off here with your mouth, O Nirṛti[40] may Agni Gārhapatya absolve me of the sin'[41].

Thus fire and water are effective as the powers that remove sin—water washing it sometimes, and at other times carrying it away. Other verses from the *Atharvaveda* let the sin and its consequences be destroyed by medicinal herbs (VIII, 7, 3; X, 1, 12) or amulets (X, 3, 8) or charms (V, 30, 4); it is driven away (*apa-sū* VI, 119, 3), wiped off (V, 30, 4) with the help of the plant Apāmārga ('Wiping off')[42], removed above all through a god, particularly Agni[43] who absolves one of it, purifies, or wipes it off. Then, so to say, as correlate of such customs of purification, there are observances whose purpose is, apparently, to emphasise distinctively the impurity of the one who is not purified. The murderer carries like a flag the murdered man's skull; he drinks out of the skull; he wears the skin of an ass or a dog which helps everyone he meets to identify him as the one who is burdened with sin; he lives on alms got by making known the curse he has upon himself.[44] The pupil who has infringed the duty of celibacy wears the skin of an ass and lives on alms; he also makes known his deed.[45] One who has sinned against his wife also wears similarly the skin of an ass and lives on alms, for which he begs with the words: 'Alms for the one, who has sinned against his wife[46]'. It appears that in these prescriptions, there is consideration partially for third persons who are warned against any relationship with the one who is burdened with sin.[47] But I think, there is also another interpretation. The sin which perhaps will be atoned for later, is entitled at first to take complete possession of the person of the sinner. This act of taking possession finds its visible expression in those observances.[48]

Concerning the procedure like burning down, washing off, etc., for the removal of the sin, it is seen that they are the same by which also other diseases are magically warded off. It just concerns the forms of thinking of an age which sees in sin, above all, a clinging of harmful substances and thus, treats it like other pernicious things. Therefore, the term of the Vedic language, next in significance to expiation, *prāyaścitti* or *prāyaścitta*[49]' contains really something more: to this belongs the sacrifice to be performed or any other similar act that is to be performed where there is crime, offence, neglect of sacral duties, knowing or unknowing disruption of the normal course of sacrifice; or where there are other events portending disaster, like, for instance, when a woman or a cow gives birth to twins, or when someone hears of himself being talked as dead, and all those countless portents and similar occurrences[50]. In treating them, the fantasy of the Brahmanas, no doubt to their own advantage, vied with the fantasy of their western collegues.

THE PARTICIPATION OF THE SACRIFICER AND THE PRIESTS IN THE SACRIFICIAL MEAL

Man's Enjoyment of the Sacrificial Meal

The Indian sacrifice has an important feature which is common with that of many other peoples. It is, that human beings also enjoy a part of the sacrificial meal besides the god. The organiser of the sacrifice enjoys it, if he as a Brahmana is qualified for this enjoyment which spells danger to the uninitiated[51]; also besides him or in his stead, his sacral representatives, the priests. The appropriate formula in its extant form fairly modern, dates back certainly to very ancient times, if one considers its contents: it is the "invocation of Iḍā" (above p. 37f.), i.e., the deified cow and the abundance of nourishment contained in her. It is said there: 'Iḍā is invoked...May Iḍā call us. Cows with milk are invoked. The milk that is added to the Soma; may cows with milk used for the Soma call me. The milchcow is invoked with the bull. The cow whose foot-marks are butter is invoked. May the cow whose foot-marks are butter invoke me"[52] etc. It is a litany of pastoral origin, pointing to a form of sacrifice dealing with the means of nourishment provided by the cow or, perhaps, with the cow itself as the gift dedicated to the gods. After reading this litany, the priests and the organiser of the sacrifice enjoy their part of the sacred meal.[53] This share is cut off at the time of the offering of the sacrificial cake, as in the Animal sacrifice and essentially according to the same rules; it is clear that the significance of the action is the same everywhere. Also in the Soma sacrifice, the priests and the sacrificer receive their share of the sacred inebriating drink.

Magic Influence of the Enjoyed Sacrificial Meal

It was already remarked (p. 185f.) that one could suppose in all this the influence of ancient rites which had preceded the type of the Vedic gift sacrifice. The enjoyment of the sacred repast invested with magic was a part of these ancient rites and also fitted in easily into the framework given by that type itself. Human beings savour of the food the gods have enjoyed, for it is considered to be filled with a blessed quality, imparted by divine proximity and nearness. It is considered a "powerful medicine" which man —of course the man equal to this enjoyment[54],—imbibes through the food[55]. Thus, the priests address the barley mixed with the Soma and offered to Indra's horses, "Whatever joy comes from you who bestows horses, who bestows cattle...that I enjoy" (*VS.* VIII, 12). And in the sacrifice of the boiled drink of milk, 'Your honey drink, Lord Gharma[56], sacrificed in the fire that's Indra's equal, we are thirsting to enjoy. Hail to you! Do not harm unto me!" (*ibid.* XXXVIII, 16). "They drink it with relish; thus they put the glow into themselves", comments a *Brāhmaṇa-text*[57]. "Were he not to enjoy his share," says another text (*Ait. Br.* VII, 26, 2), "he would keep away from the sacrifice; because the sacrificer's share is the sacrifice". In other words, the portion of the sacred meal eaten by the sacrificer, signifies the manifest transference to him of the divine blessing contained in the sacrifice, in a manner most appropriate to the perceptions of olden times.

A series of related customs can be cited here to confirm this perception of the "medicinal" nature of the sacrificial meal. The sacrificer's wife who wants a son, partakes of the flour-dumpling offered in sacrifice to the spirits of the ancestors (*Gobhila* IV, 3, 27 and other literature): thus she wins over, through the sacrifice, the favour of the ancestors who grant the blessing of children. The person suffering from a grave illness also partakes of the same meal in the sacrifice to the Dead. He will then either recover soon thereafter or die (*Aśv. Śr.* II, 7, 17). While accepting a pupil for education the teacher gives the remnants of the sacrificial meal prepared on this occasion with the saying: "May Agni put wisdom in you", etc. (*Hiraṇyakeśin G.* I, 4, 9). The newly wed couple, on entering their new home, first partake of sacrificial food that has been consecrated by *mantras*; the relevant *mantra* is: 'With the tie of the sacrificial meal, the amulet, with the thread of life, the colourful, whose knot is the truth: with that I bind your heart and spirit. What is your heart, should be mine. What is my heart should be thine. The meal is the tie of life, and I bind you with that!" (*Gobh.* II, 3, 18 f., *Mantra Br.* I, 3, 8 f.). Here, in the conclusion of a bond that unites life, what matters most is the partaking of food which creates this bond. But the effect is intensified in that the sacrificial gift charged with mystical power, is chosen as the food. The sacrificer enjoys later the butter touched simultaneously by the priest and the sacrificer before the Soma sacrifice,— signifying obviously a type of an oath of allegiance. Thus the sacrificer takes within himself the substance which guarantees the mutual loyalty of all those who participate in the sacrifice.[58] The Brahmana pupil bound by celibacy sacrifices an ass when he violates his oath. The idea here is to replace by the lascivious ass whatever he has lost by way of virility[59]. The sacrificer puts on the skin of the ass[60]; the piece of the sacrificial animal which he is to enjoy, is cut from its penis ((*Kāty*. I, 1, 17). It is indeed a drastic expression for receiving the special effect of sacrifice into the person of the sacrificer.[61]

In some other cases the medicine present in a part of the sacrificial meal is applied externally; here, the idea is basically the same. Anointing of the hearts of the bridegroom and the bride with the remnants of the sacrificial meal can be done instead of a shared food (p. 191) after the marriage.[62] The remnants of the expiatory offerings sacrificed on the fourth day after marriage and which are supposed to ward off evil powers are poured together. The bride will be annointed with them from top to toe[63]. If a part of the carriage is damaged during the journey of the young couple from the house of bride's parents, a sacrifice is offered and the damaged part is annointed with the remnants of the sacrificial butter[64]. At the Soma sacrifice, the Hotar anoints his eyes with butter that is poured over a certain sacrificial offering[65]. In the Vājapeya sacrifice, the priest sprinkles the sacrificer with the sacrificial meal mixed with water, milk and various nutritive substances. A similar thing is done at the time when the fire-altar is built[66]. The sacrificer is covered with the remains of the offering made to the two Aśvins, Sarasvatī and Indra, in the Sautrāmaṇī sacrifice, after the offering of a series of gifts intended for the cure of infirmities; for that the saying: 'I pour over you the medicines of the Aśvins, for glory and for holy fame! I pour over you the medicines of Sarasvatī for power and abundance! I pour over you Indra's Indra-might for strength, happiness and glory![67]". In the Vājapeya, the horses smell the sacrificial meal, both before and after the race which is a part of this feast, in order to get power and speed[68]. The smoke emanating from the sacrificial fire as well as the aroma of the sacrifice are considered as effective carriers of the power of blessing contained in the sacrifice. At the time of the stoking of the holy fire, it is moved from one place to another in such a way that the sacrificer inhales its smoke[69]. It is prescribed for the prosperity of herds in a sacrifice: "One makes the cows stand around the fire so that they can smell the sacrificed food"[70]. Also, contact with things belonging to the sacrifice gives the man the power of the sacrifice: thus the sacrificer establishes his connection with sacrifice by touching the sacrificial animal[71]; one touches in the Sākamedha-festival the remnants of sacrificial cake thrown into the air for Rudra, and "thereby gets cured[72]".

Thus we find in the various forms the concept, that the substance present in the sacrifice imparts power to men, even to animals and inanimate things, when it is eaten, smelt, or smeared on oneself. The power imparted is the one implied by the nature of the particular sacrifice.

The resulting explanation that the sacrificer partakes of the sacrificial meal is best confirmed by the exceptions to the rule.

Avoidance of the Sacrificial Meal

The Greek sacrificial ritual forbade, on the whole at least, the enjoyment of the offerings made to the manes or to the chthonic deities; the offerings were made here as holocausts. Apparently, at bottom is the idea that the otherwise curative enjoyment would become in this case dangerous, more so on account of the contact of such an offering with sinister deities.

It is quite the same in the ritual of the Veda. Offerings to sinister beings like the souls of the dead or Rudra are surrounded by various precautionary measures amongst which avoidance of the enjoyment of sacrificial meal is quite predominant. "He does not enjoy anything from that. . so that he turns it into something that is dedicated to the ancestors", says a *Brāhmaṇa*[73]. It is in fact prescribed in the ritual of the offering of the flour dumplings made to the manes that the dumplings given to the manes are later on kept in a dish and the sacrificer smells them instead of eating of them: "that is the participation of the sacrificer (in the sacrificial meal)", says a *Brāhmaṇa*[74]. Apparently, this smelling represents a compromise between the fear of eating a meal touched by the dead and the rule that the sacrificer should enjoy from the sacrificial meal[75]. Something similar is found in a sacrifice through which someone, wishing death for himself, attains his goal. Here it is prescribed that, from the opening consecration onwards, one may only smell what would have been otherwise meant for enjoyment[76]. Also here, it is the reference to death which rules out the enjoyment of the sacrificial meal. Occasionally, there is also the view that, what the adept dares to enjoy, may only be smelt by the uninitiated. Thus, for instance, in the offering of sour milk[77] which is affected by sacred sinisterity, and which therefore, is connected with the *Pravargya*-celebration that is handed down to us as esoteric knowledge. While the priests who have received the *Dīkṣa*-initiation eat from the remnants of the offering, limitation to the "enjoyment of breath" i.e., smelling of the meal, is left to the others, though not imposed[78]. It is prescribed for the offering of the cattle to Rudra, the god who brings danger: "He should not eat from it. One should not bring anything of that into the village"—the sacrifice is performed at a place not visible from the village—, "because this god persecutes the beings. He should keep his people away from the neighbourhood of the sacrificial place[79]". The reason for not enjoying from the sacrificial meal cannot be more evident; the relevant abstinence is just one amongst many precautionary measures which are necessitated by the dangerous nature of certain beings that receive sacrifice, just as, for instance, the transfer of the sacrifice to Rudra to a place not visible from the village, i.e., to a place from where the village also was not visible to Rudra.

In this context, there are further customs particularly of the cult of the Dead, the Rudra-cult, as also the worship of Nirṛti (destruction), which I shall touch upon briefly: holding the breath during a rite; touching the water after the completion of a rite[80], above all, the injunction against looking at some one[81] and also against looking around oneself, when one returns home after the completion of a practice which is dedicated to sinister powers[82].

MAGIC FIRE, SACRIFICIAL STRAW AND SACRIFICIAL FIRE: THE THREE-FOLD SACRIFICIAL FIRE

Ethnology informs us that besides the use of fire as sacrificial fire, there was apparently an older use for it, for which the expression magic fire is recommended: harmful substances and evil demons are burnt or driven away with the aid of fire.

The Magic Fire

The magic fire coincides in the Vedic cult with the sacrificial fire, and to distinguish between the two types is for us all the more difficult, for they had blended together, no doubt, in many ways fairly early, even for the ancients themselves. At the bottom of those cultic practices overladen with diverse sacrifices, there lay the consequence obviously in the performance of a rite in front of the burning fire. This consequence was, that, at least as a rule, all offerings were made in this fire. The rites of many primitive races, which do not know the sacrificial fire, give us a clue for the interpretation of the use of fire. There, all the most important acts were usually performed in the presence of fire. A fire burnt beside a woman giving birth to a child protected her and the child from the persecution of spirits. The ceremony through which the adolescent boy is taken up into the circle of men, various customs, like cutting of hair, etc., offerings to gods and spirits, and finally the funeral: all require the proximity of fire so that the spirits do not harm. Whoever is familiar with the widespread use of fire the world over, will recognise in many instances the same fire, even where the ritual prescribes the offering of sacrificial gifts. Like the segregated quarters of the woman in childbed (*sūtikāgṛha*[83]), so too does the Indian custom of the woman-in-childbed-fire (*sūtikāgni*) have much in common with that of primitive peoples. "The sacrificial fire of the house", says *Hiraṇyakeśin*[84], "is carried away and the fire of the woman-in-childbed is brought. That is used only for warming up (of vessels, etc.)". Above all, of course, it is used for magic, besides its practical purpose. The author continues: "Besides fumigation, no other holy actions are performed with it. He fumigates the child with the small corn mixed with mustard-seed"—and then follow *mantras* against evil spirits sent by their king, wandering through village at night and drinking out of skulls. Agni shall burn their lungs, liver and heart.

As in the case of birth, the fire also guards the other most important stations of life. One may consider say, the description given by *Śāṅkhāyana*[85] of the ceremony of the cutting of hair, known also as a particularly significant rite in the ritual of numerous primitive peoples. A fire is set up, the vessels are placed with good-luck charms, and necessary utensils like mirror, scissors, etc. are put down. The hair of the boy is moistened with lukewarm water, and then his hair is cut, while verses are recited that would bring him the blessing. But one does not mention here the use of that fire for the presentation of a sacrificial offering. One could be tempted, seen alone from the point of view of the Veda, to explain the presence of fire as caused by other similar rites where there was a sacrifice and, therefore, a sacrificial fire; but the facts of ethnology make us recognise here clearly the magic fire meant to drive away the demons.[86]

The same fire appears also in the rite of acceptance of the pupil (*upanayana*), i.e., in the ancient solemnisation on attaining puberty, which was remodelled according to the conditions of the Brahmanic pupildom. Teacher and pupil "both step behind the fire, the teacher with his face towards the east, and the other one towards the west"[87]. And the teacher invests the pupil with the girdle, the sign of "being born for the second time'. Here, however, a sacrificial offering is mentioned, but this conceivable addition cannot eclipse the original meaning of the fire. The lesson in the Veda connected with the ceremony of acceptance has a similar description[88]. "They sit to the north of the fire, the teacher facing towards the east, and the other one towards the west". The texts are then recited, and for every hymn, water is sprinkled into a pit—is it an offering for the dead poets of the hymns resting in the depths?—but there is no mention of the sacrificial offerings for which the fire is supposed to be meant. The nearness of a fire is most emphatically prescribed for the chanting of especially sacred hymns, i.e., of those fraught with danger: "If they (hymns) are recited without the means of appeasement, the god brings death to the creatures"[89]. We shall speak of the fire in the initiation (*dīkṣā*) of the Soma-sacrificer at some other place[90]; this fire also is unmistakably a magic fire. In the sacrifices of the grand ritual carried out with the three fires, the third fire or the southern fire, may be understood, so I think, in the context of its original meaning, as the magic fire meant for driving away malific spirits. For, it is from the southern direction that the souls of the dead and related demons approach, bringing peril in their wake[91]. The use of fire in the sacrifice to the dead as a fire driving the demons away, is quite predominant. Apparently, it was believed that evil spirits, precisely in the company of the dead, could press forward towards the sacrifice quite easily. Here a brand was taken from the southern sacrificial fire and put down in the southern direction with a *mantra*, which invited Agni to drive away all the Asuras who may be present here and there in various forms[92]. Finally, we may mention the fire carried into the battle (*senāgni*)[93], and the fire with which the survivors, after the funeral, kept away the death-bringing powers from themselves[94]. This brief survey will suffice to show how the use of the magic fire was firmly rooted and at the same time widespread in the Vedic cult.

Sacrifice without the Sacrificial Fire; The Sacrificial Straw

The most predominant use of fire in this cult is, as it is well-known, a different one: as sacrificial fire, it carries offerings to the gods. Of course, not every offering was handed over to it. In certain cases—namely, where the offering was meant for water-deities—one offered into the water[95]; pits covered with grass were places of its reception in the sacrifice to the dead[96]; offerings made to Rudra and the demons similar to Rudra were[97] thrown into the air, burried in mole-hills or hung on trees, etc. But on the whole, it can be maintained that the Indian ritual in its present form rests mainly on the use of sacrificial fire.

In its present form: because, as I mean, there is evidence of another condition; it shines quite clearly at places where really fire is used, of course, apart from the cases of sacrifice in water, etc. just cited above. We may refer here to Herodot's[98] description of the Animal sacrifice of the Persians. When the Persians wanted to sacrifice, he says, they did not erect any altars or kindle any fire. The sacrificer "cuts the sacrificial animal to pieces and cooks the meat; he spreads out the tenderest grass, mostly clover, and puts the meat all over it. When he has done that, a magician standing there sings a theogony—this is, according to them, an accompanying song—because without a magician, they are not allowed to perform a sacrifice. The sacrificer then takes away the meat after a short time and does with it what he likes". It is quite obvious that this ritual of the Persian Aryans is closely related to that of their Indian kinsmen. The singing magician is the Hotar of the Veda (Zaotar of the Avesta). The spread out grass appears in the Veda as *Barhis*[99] (compare the Baresman of the Avesta)[100]. The only difference is that this grass is, to the Persians, the place, where the gods receive the offerings (to be more exact, the essence or the soul of the sacrificial offering; its insignificant body is taken away again by men), whereas at the Indian sacrificial place, fire burns beside the *Barhis*, the mouth of the gods, as the *Ṛgveda* so often says, with which they consume the sacrifice. The comparison of the Persian custom with the Indian suggests the idea, that in the Indian coexistence of *Barhis* and the sacrificial fire, one can recognise on the one hand traces of an old primitive form, in which one was accustomed to hand over the offerings to the god, and on the other hand, an innovation embedded in it. The way in which the Vedic poets speak of the *Barhis* is in fact as characteristic as the rites concerning the *Barhis*. Once, one thought of this bed of grass above all as the soft seat filled with mystical power upon which the gods sat to enjoy the offering. "Spread yourself as soft as wool", the *Barhis* is addressed (V, 5, 4), "the sacred hymns have sung to you; bring gain to us, you beautiful sacrificial grass!"[101]. "Spread out the sacrificial grass for the sacrifice...Like the children coming from here and there to their mother, let the gods sit upon the grass's summit" (VII, 43, 2, 3). "He on whose *Barhis* with gods you sat, to him, O Agni, are the days propitious" (VII, 11, 2)[102]. For this purpose, there is the rule of the ritual: at the same place where the gods are sitting for the sacrifice, the offerings are placed according to the usual custom. These offerings are then given to the fire[103]. If now, this placing upon the sacrificial grass is compared with the placing, similarly, on the sacrificial grass described by Herodot in the sacrifice of the Persians, then it can be considered probable that the Indian custom signifies the residue of the rite clearly preserved by the Persians: once the offering meant for the gods, but not handed over to them at that time through fire[104], was placed upon the seat of the gods, i.e., on the sacrificial grass, and it was accepted by them there[105]. The nomadic clans of the shepherds could not believe that the presence of their gods was bound to the immovably fixed signs of nature; we get acquainted here with the holy place of their cult, the carpet of grass as soft as wool and which can be spread everywhere equally with ease. The presence of god called to sit upon it sanctifies it, i.e., makes it dangerous for profane contact. That is why, the Indian sacrificer throws the *Barhis* into fire after completing the act, of course, in its original sense, i.e., to make it harmless[106].

Fire used to remove Substances and the Sacrificial Fire; The One and the Three Sacrificial Fires

In the act of consigning to the flames, discussed here[107] and appearing on diverse occasions, of the objects which have been affected by the contagion of sacred or uncanny powers, in sacral rites or elsewhere, one of the factors—even if certainly not the only one—could be found that led from the sacrifice involving only the placing of the offering to the sacrifice involving the sacrificial fire[108]. What should be done to the offering placed thus, whose inner essence, one thought, was enjoyed by the gods? What the god had seized, spelt danger to man. We saw how one tried to ward off this danger by burning. The burning took away the material object, belonging to god and feared by man, upwards amidst the whirling smoke to heaven, where the most noble deities had their abode. Thus, the transition from the removal through fire to the offering through fire is understandable. In one way, however, this transition gives rise to a contradiction. One thought earlier that the gods alighted upon the *Barhis* to enjoy the offering, but now one sent the sacrificial meal to them in their heavenly abode. It is unquestionable to me that the first side of this dilemma represents a way of conceptualising whose roots run deep. But not in few verses of the *Ṛgveda* does one come across other conception also[109]. The contradiction emerges perhaps never so distinctly as in the verse in which a Vasiṣṭhan poet says, "Agni, call forth the gods so that they enjoy the sacrificial meal. With Indra leading, let them be happy here. Convey this sacrifice to the gods in heaven. You gods, preseve us evermore with blessings" (VII, 11, 5). A contradiction, as it inevitably has to be, where a series of ideas of so many different origins collide with one another[110].

Let us now turn from these presumptions about the pre-history to the actual conditions and customs governing the Vedic sacrificial fire[111]. One must first mention here the contrast between the sacrifices involving one fire and those involving three fires. Beside the simpler mode of sacrificing with one fire, there developed early[112] a more artistic way of sacrificing requiring three fires. The interest of the sacrificing artist, the ever increasing priestly artfulness, was directed preferably to sacrifices of this kind, notably to the Soma sacrifice pertaining to them. Originally,—in this case, one can only make surmises—it must have been such, that a constantly maintained holy fire of the simpler sacrifice was divided into three for the needs of these complicated rites. But in the ritual before us, the one fire, i.e., the fire of 'the house' and the three fires stand side by side independently. Every head of the family maintains one fire and fulfils the cult connected with it; it befits the high-ranking and the well-to-do to lay three fires and found therewith a larger cult-centre. Many gather in the house of the host who does the sacrifice, Brahmanas, sacrificial priests and others[113]. Certain principal ceremonies are common to the rituals of the one fire and of the three fires: the daily sacrifice in the morning and in the evening, the celebration of the New Moon and the Full Moon are performed in both ways, concurring in the essentials—a sacral duplicate that may be held to be non-original. Other customs fall only within this or that field; thus the consecration pertaining to domestic life is done with one fire, and the Soma-sacrifice with three[114].

On close verification of the three fires[115], one[116] may state with certainty, that there is in them an obvious intermingling of three different fire-services. This idea is obvious, but I cannot discover anything in the actual conditions of the Vedic ritual that confirms it, not even the traces of such distribution of the holy acts to different fires, so that the performances associated with each one of them could be imagined as a sacral special possession of any one group of priests[117]. Rather, it concerns apparently a concurrence of all the three fires in the same rites, in such a way that in the rôle of every single one, a definite characteristic governs or at least dominates. At the head is the *Gārhapatya*-fire ('Householder's Fire'), obviously the representative of the old fire of home and hearth; it alone is always kept going, and both the other fires are taken from it, when desired[118]. The person going out of town takes leave first of the *Gārhapatya*-fire and then of *Āhavanīya*-fire (see immediately below); the person returning home greets at first the *Āhavanīya*- and then the *Gārhapatya*-fire. The *Gārhapatya*-fire is considered to some extent as standing in the centre, for one takes leave of it first and returns last to it[119]. The second fire referred to here, the *Āhavanīya*-fire, ('Fire of Offerings') is laid towards the east. A *Brāhmaṇa*[120] refers to the distinction between the two[121] in the following words: "That is the *Āhavanīya*. It is not there, that one may cook in it what is not cooked. Rather, it is there, so that what is cooked, is offered in it". Thus the *Gārhapatya*, the fire of practical, human use, serves for preparations like the preparation of the sacrificial meal, the warming up of vessels, etc.; the *Āhavanīya* is the flame in which the gods receive the offerings[122]. Finally the third fire, the *Anvāhāryapacana* ('Fire for the Anvāhārya-necessity')[123] or the *Dakṣiṇāgni* ('Southern Fire') stands, as its place in the south shows, in special relationship to the manes and evil spirits. We have already expressed our guess above (p. 195) that this was meant to ward off imminent disturbance during the sacrifice.

But at the same time, it served to accept the offerings directed thereto. The *Gārhapatya* 'belongs to the sacrificing householder as his deity', the southern fire 'belongs to the hostile rival'[124]. The *Gārhapatya* protects against the danger coming from the fathers (manes)[125]. At the consecration of a king, a brand is taken from the southern fire and a certain offering is made in it in order to ward off evil spirits; the appropriate *mantra* reads: 'The demon is killed'.[126] A firebrand is similarly taken from the southern fire in the sacrifice and offering is made in it to the goddess of destruction, Nirṛti[127]. But the main occasion for the use of the southern fire is, as already indicated, the Manes-sacrifice which centres around this fire and the pits dug beside it in the ground. Regulations for the monthly manes-sacrifice on the new moon day, as also the yearly sacrifice connected with the festival of the *Sākamedhā*, give predominance to the southern fire in the same measure.[128]

Founding of the Sacred Fire

As for the foundation of the cult through the setting up of one or many holy fires, it is not important for us to explain them in detail, either according to the Vedic schools or according to the distinction in regulations differentiating the one or the three fires. It may be sufficient to remark that the renewed kindling of fire by attrition and fetching of the available fire from certain places like from the house of a rich owner of cattle or from a great sacrificer stand side by side; in the one case, the emphasis is on the untouchability of the freshly kindled fire, in the other on the happy omen of the blessing connected with the old available fire. The most common instruction is the recommendation to keep the fire going on also as domestic fire. It is in this fire that the sacrificer consigns the piece of wood for the last time as Brahmana pupil, in keeping with his duty as pupil; or again, the piece of wood used in performing his marriage ceremonies. We have already spoken, in another context, about the fetish-like incarnations of Agni as a horse and a he-goat, which play a rôle in the setting-up of the fire according to the ritual of the three fires.[129]

On certain occasions of the ritual, new fire is kindled by attrition and united with the old *Āhavanīya.* This is an obvious act of reviving and strengthening, perhaps also the residue of a way of handling the holy fire other than the traditional one, and its repeated replacement from time to time.

Allowing the old fire to die and eventually after some interval, laying the new fire was considered necessary; if the old had brought no luck to the sacrificer, then the ceremony of 're-setting up' (*punarādheya*) was performed.

SACRIFICIAL MEAL AND DRINK

Even the Vedic sacrifice confirms the natural principle that man offers to god what is welcome to himself as food.[130] This is obviously the rule though there may be exceptions to it. If one may presume the impact of old magic rites for augmenting food resources or for warding off the taboo attached to them, on the arrangement of the sacrifice, then it has to follow, if viewed from this angle, that the sacrificial gifts were precisely those foodstuffs so important for economic life.

Vegetable Substances, Milk, etc.

If we do not consider at first the Animal sacrifice and the Soma sacrifice, then we come across the use of all the major products of agriculture and cattle-breeding as sacrificial foodstuffs. At the top is milk in its different forms (sour milk, etc.), butter and both the excellent cereals, barley and rice[131] which are used in the preparation of different cooked and baked dishes. It is unmistakably clear that greater sanctity and mystic significance was attached to milk products than to agricultural products. Offerings of water meant for the thirsty souls, characteristic of the cult of the Dead, may also be mentioned here.

We shall speak more in detail in the Animal sacrifice of the tendency of offering the food to the individual god in accordance with his special nature. Here some phenomena are to be considered from the same point of view; thus, for certain occasions in the cult of the Dead or a cult to be practised in the name of a dead person, the milk of a cow is prescribed, whose own calf is dead and that is nursing the calf of another cow[132]; for Nirṛti, the goddess of destruction, the sacrifice of the grains[133] fallen aside while preparing another sacrificial meal is mentioned or that of the black rice[134]; for the goddesses Night and Dawn—the black one and the bright one born of the former—the milk of the black cow that has a white calf[135]. Rudra living in the wilderness enjoys on a series of occasions—with a characteristic transgression of the limits of the sacrificial gifts to only economic products and which are otherwise quite common—wild sesame, wild wheat, milk of deers, in short, things growing wild or originating from the forest[136]. The sesame seeds have a special relationship—I do not know why—with the dead[137]. Finally, we must refer in this context to the rôle of the numbers, sacred to different gods, at the time of the offerings. Eight pieces of sacrificial flat cake are prepared for Agni and eleven for Indra[138], and so on: an artificiality, certainly not dating back to remote antiquity[139].

The Animal Sacrifice

The Animal sacrifice[140] shows corresponding conditions. Of animals, mainly cattle and goats[141], in addition to sheep, were eaten. 'The cattle are called over here, called over here are goats and sheep': these set phrases are used in the consecration at the time of construction of a house[142]. It is precisely these three animals that are commonly used as sacrificial animals[143]. Amongst them again, the goat appears to have been regularly used for the frequent minor sacrifices addressed to a long series of gods; cattle was too expensive for that[144]. Animals meant for human consumption, not regularly but only secondarily, were excluded at least from normal use in the sacrifice: thus game[145], birds and fish; above all, of course impure animals: pig, dog, etc.

One cannot seriously consider among the exceptions the vast number of sacrificial animals of all kinds which are prescribed for the Horse sacrifice as attendants of the main Host[146]. Here, it is hardly the original cult practice, rather the priestly artfulness. More important than the transgression of the otherwise valid limits in the choice of sacrificial animals, is the sacrificial horse itself. This is not to be interpreted as the relic of an age, for which horse-meat was a common means of subsistence[147]. An old magic ritual, about which we shall speak later, must have been at the bottom of it[148]. Similarly, it is less important in the Ass sacrifice meant as expiation for the infringement of celibacy (see above pp. 190, 192) whether the ass is fit to be enjoyed by the deity; what matters more is that man can best conjure back out of the animal's excesses what he has lost by way of virility. Also, it is more magic than sacrifice when the fish-otter appears[149] as the sacrificial animal for the water god Apāṃ napāt in the rain-magic. We come across many such things at various places.

The correspondence between the qualities of the god and the offering brought to him, already mentioned in the Non-Animal sacrifices, is more clearly distinguished in the Animal sacrifice. There is a tendency, even if remotely not unexceptional[150], to make the sacrificial animal match the god's sex, colour and other qualities. Even as food imparts to the eater its special qualities[151], so will the god, whose strength the sacrificial meal is to increase, experience the utmost increase of substance in that quality required of him, by the eating of the animal most like him, or the animal viewed in ancient times as identical with him[152]. We find that the bull is a common sacrificial animal for Indra, whose essential nature is defiant manliness, and who is named bull a number of times in the hymns; Indra also eats the buffalo[153] with which one also likes to compare the powerful god. In certain sacrifices, besides Indra's bull, there is a goat, reddish in colour, for the Aśvins—"because the Aśvins are also reddish in colour", it is said,—and a female sheep of certain qualities for Sarasvatī[154]. For Agni, surrounded by clouds of smoke, there is the sacrifice of a goat with a black neck; the Sun and the god of Death, Yama, get two goats, white for the one and black for the other[155]; it is important in the sacrifice to the manes, who were robbed of their life-force and the power of creation, that a wether is offered to them and not a ram[156], etc. When a piebald (*pṛśni*) cow is offered to the Maruts[157], the sex is not correct, but the reference to the piebald (*pṛśni*) cow, the mother of Maruts, is unmistakable. The *basta* (goat) of Tvaṣṭar[158] must be connected with the *basta* that the Ṛgveda (I, 161, 13) lets appear in the neighbourhood of the Tvaṣṭar myth. Incidentally, the specific determination of the animal and the choice of its genus may be due to the influences of magic; thus, at the offering of a black sacrificial animal to get the rain: "it is black, because this is the nature of rain; with the nature it has, it will get the rain for itself"[159]. A blood-red animal is offered by the priests, who put on red clothes and red turbans, when an enemy is to be killed[160]. This is not the priestly hair-splitting of later origin. It has the stamp of antiquity.

The sacrificial animal was killed with the expressions, common to other peoples, of efforts to free oneself from the sin of a bloody deed and from the impending revenge. It was told: "You are not dying, you are not harmed; you are going to the gods along beautiful paths" (I, 162, 21). The killing was called euphemistically "to get the consent of the animal". The killing was effected by suffocation or strangulation without spilling blood; one tried here to prevent the animal from crying; the main persons involved in the sacrifice turned their backs till the animal died.

Plexus of the Sacrificial Animal

The parts of the sacrificial animal offered to the god fall into two separate lots. Their offering amounts to two separate acts of the ritual. If the animal is killed, then the plexus (omentum), one of the fattest parts, is at first taken out, cooked and offered with all solemnity[161]. After this act, the ritual-texts prescribe presents to the priests and purifications[162]; it is clear, that here a portion is cut. Afterwards, the rest of the animal is cut to pieces[163]; the pieces of meat are cooked and after the offering of a cake of rice, portions of individual pieces are offered to the god[164]. The priests enjoy the other portions. What is left over, is distributed amongst the priests, the sacrificer or the Brahmanas who desired to share it[165], save the last piece of the tail which is preserved for the closing ceremony and is meant mainly for the wives of the gods. Thus, the offering of the plexus and of the appropriate portions of the remaining parts of the body, are two separate acts. I shall quote a few sentences from the description of the *Aṣṭākā*-animal-sacrifice given in the *Áśvalāyana*[166]. "He kills the animal according to the instructions for the Animal sacrifice...takes out the plexus and offers it with the verse, 'Take the plexus, O (Agni) Jātavedas, to the fathers, to where you know they are living, far away. May streams of fat flow to them. May all these wishes be fulfilled. Svāhā!' Then, from the cut portions (of the remaining parts of the body) and from the cooked meals, with the verses,"—etc.

Do we find here the vestiges of a practice of giving the plexus—I shall not say exclusively—to the god alone, but of burning it separately? Strabo[167] says of the closely related Persians, that they do not offer the sacrificial animal into the fire, but distribute it amongst themselves. They give only the soul to the gods. Only a small piece of the plexus (ἐπιπλου τιΜικρόν) is thrown into the fire. In the sacrifice for remission of sins[168] of the Old Testament, the kidneys together with the fat and the plexus—thus pieces of fat somewhat greater in quantity than in the Indian ritual, but essentially of course a corresponding part—were sacrificed on the fire-altar of the sacrifice, but the remaining part of the body is burnt outside the sacrificial area, i.e., destroyed, as it is laden with the sin to be atoned for or with divine anger. Pieces of fat were offered on the altar, in the sacrifice for the sin[169], and the remaining was eaten by the priests. Pieces of fat were offered on the altar in the Thanksgiving sacrifice[170], "that is the sweet-smelling fire for the Lord to smell"; the remaining was partially given to the priests, and partially consumed by the sacrificer and his relatives. The native witnesses examined by Callaway[171] describe the sacrificial customs which are valid amongst the Zulus today as under: The sacrificial bull is killed and skinned. Then something of the fat of the plexus is taken and burnt with incense; the house is filled with the smell of the burnt plexus, and one thinks that one has created a sweet smell for the spirits of one's people. The meat of the animal is, however, put down; the spirits come and eat of it. One finds it untouched in the morning, but the spirits have licked it[172].

How come the plexus has a special position? Is it considered the bearer of soul and life[173], and thus by choice as the part of the animal that is holy for sacrifice? But statements made in the *Brāhmaṇa*-texts, which point in this direction[174], are subject to doubts; in order to explain what one wanted to have explained, the authors could invent reasons all too easily. Or, is here a question of smoking the fat for the god, as suggested by the expression "the sweet smell for Him" of the Old Testament[175]? The burning of the plexus could then be understood within the context of the sacrificial technique, as in the case of the old Persian burning, further perhaps also in the case of the Indo-Iranian period (p. 196). Here, the actual food meant for the god was only put before him, and not transmitted through fire.

The blood of the sacrificial animal was poured out for the Rakṣas (evil demons) in the Vedic ritual[176]. It appears that, as in the offering of the baked food, where the chaff was thrown to the Rakṣas[177], so too blood was considered as waste matter, with which one came to terms with the inferior folk of the world of spirits[178]. Here also, the idea of these beings harming life and health as blood-suckers, must have played a rôle.

Human Sacrifice

We must also refer to the question of the existence of Human sacrifice in the Vedic period in relation to Animal sacrifice[179]. We must first of all mention here, that among the instructions for the building of the fire-altar (*agnicayana*) which is, as is well-known, surrounded by special ceremonial pomp, there is an instruction that five sacrificial animals—man, horse, cattle, goat and ram—are to be sacrificed to different gods. The bodies (except that of the goat) are thrown into water from which clay is to be taken for construction. It is said, that this action gives firmness to this clay; the five heads are, however, immured later in the lowest layer of the walls[180]. All this is characterised in the *Śatapatha Brāhmaṇa* as the custom of the past, but by no means of the distant past[181]; at present, substitute rites are said to be in vogue. The way in which the appropriate instructions appear is quite unsuspecting. What has remained preserved here, in connection with the ritual construction of the altar, in the tradition, was presumably once for the constructions in general, as far as they possessed the corresponding importance[182]. Thus, we recognise here a belief spread over all the world, that a building can get solidity through a sacrifice at the time of construction, particularly a Human sacrifice[183]. But the customary meaning of this rite as sacrifice does not obviously correspond to its actual meaning, in so far as one understands 'sacrifice' in the usual sense of the word. The main issue here is clearly one of giving firmness to the construction, in that one drives into it a human soul and the magic power clinging to the human corpse. Therefore, magic carried out by killing of a man, but no Human sacrifice in the usual sense: even if the magic has acquired the form of a sacrifice in the course of time[184].

What otherwise is cited to prove the existence of the Vedic human sacrifice[185], does not seem to me to rule out all doubt. When the old books of the ritual describe[186] in all details the 'Human sacrifice' (*puruṣamedha*) in a special chapter after the Horse sacrifice, the whole appears to be a product of fantasy, copied after the Horse sacrifice and exaggerating grossly the colossal conditions of the Horse sacrifice. Even if this show-piece among the large priestly collection of models had once roused a pious prince to its execution, it would still remain an irrelevant accident for the consideration of the real Vedic cult[187]. But no definite traces—as much as I can see now—are to be discovered in the Vedic India of the real Human sacrifices which either date back to the cult of the cannibals or represent the surrendering of human life for other forfeited or endangered human lives as an expiatory sacrifice, as magic for increasing human fertility, as the sacrifice for the first-born[188]. It is doubtful, what importance can be given to the fairly old legends describing such sacrifices[189]. It is of course quite possible that this widespread practice was at home in this cultural area too.

The Soma

The excellent sacrificial gift of the Vedic cult is the Soma. Man stills in the sacrifice, not only the hunger and the thirst of the god, but he also helps him to an intoxication in which he himself later on takes part[190]. It was already remarked in another context that the idea of the intoxicating drink of the gods, particularly of the Storm-god, and particularly in connection with it—as can be certainly concluded—the use of such a drink in the cult, can be dated back in all probability to the Indo-European period and be referred to the honey-mead, an intoxicating drink of that period (p. 91). We saw that the juice-extract of the Soma plant took the place of the honey-drink in the Indo-European period[191]; it was mixed with water and milk. The Soma-drink is called *madhu* (honey) variously in the Veda; the obvious speculation has been made, that here the Indo-European name of honey-mead (*madhu*) has been passed on to the modified drink, just as with the Greeks, who shifted from mead to wine, but retained the old name (μέθυ) for the latter. This may be correct, but I think, another explanation is possible, even probable for that particular name of Soma. The Vedic poets are very familiar with words like honey, honey-rich and the like for liquids which are considered as sweet or pleasant. Honey is present in the cow, i.e., sweet milk; butter is called honey-rich or even honey; even water waves and air are called honey-rich. Diverse plays of fantasy are associated with the substance of honey, the excellent carrier of sweetness. Accordingly, it can be understood from the Veda alone, without calling to aid the Indo-European honey-mead, when Soma is called there honey or honey-rich; whatever be its taste, the pious way of expression had naturally to accord it a sweet taste. It was completely valid for that Soma that was mixed with really sweet substances like milk and honey, and also where the special mythological or ritual qualities of the deity drinking Soma, led the fantasy of the poet to the idea of honey[192]. Methinks, it is rather an instance of the poet's fanciful manner of speech than the retaining of an age-old expression. This shows that the name Soma as *madhu* appears to have not had a place in the old set terminology but mainly, with regard to the distribution of the name among the deities, in the cult of the Aśvins: but the Aśvins, in all likelihood, are related to the Soma-cult in a much more superficial way than, for instance, the Storm-god[193]. It may be noted above all that the Avesta, which is quite close to the Veda with regard to the terminology of Soma, does not know the equation Soma = *madhu*[194]. Here, one does not meet the Vedic poet's fondness for playing with the idea of honey. Thus, the expression in question must be a neologism of the Vedic period; further, the mixing of honey with the Soma must represent a simple sweetening like with milk whose connection with the pre-historic honey-drink of the gods is extremely doubtful.

Was the Soma at any time a popular drink in the daily life of the Aryans? I doubt very much[195], and in saying this, I don't believe, I am contradicting the basic principle, that man gives the god as offering, what he himself likes to enjoy. One must bear in mind, that on the one hand, the drink could have come into question not only because it is pleasant, but also because of its magic properties; yet on the other hand, the rôle belonging to the Soma in the cult was, at first, apparently not invented for it. It received that rôle from the drink of an older age, entered into a perfect, hieratically defined situation. This means, that there was no need for it to have had at any time real validity for profane life. For the Veda, it is clear that Soma was nothing less than a popular common drink, and I think, that Avestic testimonials do not teach us anything else. The actual inebriating drink of ancient India was Surā[196].

Inedible Sacrificial Offerings

I conclude this survey on sacrificial meals and drinks with the remark that here and there—this was referred to already in the context of the Ass sacrifice and Horse sacrifice—non-edible esp., potable substances were also offered as sacrificial offerings or added to these. I think, there is, in such cases, a mixing of sacrifice in the usual sense and of magic. Magic manipulations performed with an object can be turned into a sacrifice at the hands of a diligent sacrificial artist; the sacrifice can be considered as a means of magic to get a substance into the hands of the sacrificer or into other beings, or, otherwise, in their possession. One who wishes long life offers hundred nails of Khadira-wood on a full moon night. This is done perhaps as the nailing down of life through the hundred years one wishes for oneself; one who desires the possession of deadly weapons, sacrifices iron nails. The offering of thousand gifts of calf-dung gives large cattle, and sheep-dung, small cattle[197]. Offerings of the hairs of wolves, tigers and lions are mixed in the *Sautrāmaṇi*-sacrifice[198]; thus, the sacrificer gets the might of these animals. In order to destroy ants, poison is mixed in the offering[199]. But the principle, that the god is given the offering which is also enjoyed by man, does not become invalidated by such exceptions.

THE SACRIFICER AND THE PRIESTS

The Sacrificer

We have to deal with the subject of religious activity, with the sacrificer and with the assistants and helpers employed by him, the priests of the sacrifice.

Does the social and state system appear, in the sacrifice, as subject beside the individual?

The direction in which the development of this system in the Vedic period proceeded is that of the caste. The significance of the genes retrogresses in the face of caste. It is seen very clearly, in the history of Vedic literature and Vedic sacramental customs, how the individualities of the old families of singers faded increasingly; their collection of songs were integrated into the one corpus of the *Ṛgveda*, the work of the whole Brahmanic class, upon which a common ritual utilizing at random all those collections, was built; the gentilic classification receded behind that of the 'threefold knowledge'[200] and behind the branches of the schools. The bond of Brahmanism maintained by the mutuality of minds striving for the same goal and by common interests is stronger than the disruption of this unity through individual rivalries. As against that, the tribal system—one may not like at all to use here the word 'state'—gets a subordinate position. Its structure is very loose. The only constant element in it is the king. The Brahmana hardly belongs wholly to his tribe, his people. He moves hither and thither, without regard for tribal boundaries, and practises his spiritual art, wherever profit and honour beckon him. Thus, the higher religious way of life depicted by the Veda, is essentially the affair of the Brahmanas on the one hand, and on the other, first of the kings and then of the aristocrats and the wealthy. There, the learned ones, possessors of mystic power; here, the mighty employers capable of paying money, not in fraternal union within a religious community, but opposed to one another, rather as rival wooers for divine mercy. For the general public, the masses, remained only the rôle of spectators. We should not really discard the incompleteness and one-sidedness of our tradition. It is indeed possible that, say, villages or guilds (*śreṇi*) did not altogether lack sacra. They hardly go together with the scheme of the sacral character given in the Veda; it must be left to future research to find out whether more recent traditions lead here to any clues, which also permit one to speculate on the like obtained in olden times[201].

It is clear from all these circumstances that the centre around which the Vedic sacrifice revolves, is nothing but the sacrificial fire or the three sacrificial fires of the individual. The 'sacrificer' (*yajamāna*) or the 'master of the sacrifice' (*yajñapati*)[202] is this individual and not the gentilic or political union. When it is said in many verses of the *Ṛgveda* that 'the Vasiṣṭhas are praying to Agni', or that 'Indra is praised by the Bharadvājas with the Soma-extract', etc., it does not refer to the gentilic sacra of those families, but only means that the Brahmanas from the house of the Vasiṣṭhas or Bharadvājas have taken part in the sacrifices organised by the wealthy, presumably by kings, and have composed hymns for them. Of course, there belonged, naturally to the person of the sacrificer, certainly often a large entourage. We have to think of him mostly as the head of the 'whole family', which consists of parents and children, brothers and step-brothers, and which can be stretched to the ascendants and the descendants and the distant relatives from several generations[203]. They are present at the time of the sacrifice. At a certain place of the rite, they touch the wife of the sacrificer—and she, the sacrificer himself, and the sacrificer, the *Adhvaryu*-priest[204]; thus they express the participation of the whole family in the sacrifice and the blessing expected from it. Therefore, the real subject of the sacrifice is the *Yajamāna*. There are sacrifices which, according to the circumstance, are offered for the general welfare, also for the welfare of the entire people, with a very wide circle of people participating.[205] But, there also, an individual, the king is the organizer of the sacrifice in the technical sense. Thus in the Horse sacrifice[206], a characteristic prayer shows, that it concerns not only the well-being of the king, but also of the people. The *Adhvaryu* prays, 'May the Brahmana be born in holiness, in full glow of holiness. May prince be born in imperial might, a hero, an archer, a perfect marksman, capable of handling the chariot; may cow be born rich in milk, the draught animals strong enough to haul, the horse fleet of foot, the woman fertile, the horseman victorious, the youth ready-witted at the assembly. May a hero's son be born to this sacrificer. May Parjanya give us rain at all the times as desired. May the corn ripen to fruit. May work and peace be blessed to us[207]'. A prayer, as one can see, for the land and people, and if not for the people, at least for the Brahmana and the warrior: as for the third class of people, the common man himself is not named, but the farmers and the shepherds about whom the master is more concerned. But the form in which one could have prayed and sacrificed in the name of the people is missing; the Horse-sacrifice is and remains the king's sacrifice.

In an observation of the circumstances governing state and private law in ancient India, it would be appropriate to elaborate these brief hints. However, I may be allowed only to refer to what, in my view, is the sole and perhaps insignificant exception to the rule, that the sacrificer is the individual. It refers to those complex systems of the Soma sacrifice extending over a long period, over a year (*Sattra*, sittings) and for which purpose numerous Brahmanas gathered together, apportioning amongst themselves the usual priestly functions in such a way, that each one of them was considered as the master of the sacrifice, somewhat on the basis of the following agreement: 'What we want to get through this celebration, through this Animal sacrifice, that belongs to us all. Good deed belongs to us all. But, if someone does something evil, that is his alone'[208]. Whether such Sattras, reference to which in a later hymn of the *Ṛgveda* (VII, 33, 13) is doubtful, are of recent origin, or whether one may see in them a vestige of the old gentilic sacrifice, is very difficult to decide at this stage.

The Priests

The priests, who are appointed by the offerer of the cult, and who act on his behalf, stand at his side, as already mentioned. His position besides them is two-sided. On the one hand, if one may say so, his personal right to property is clearly seen in the sacrifice. It is he and his consort, who are raised to an almost god-like position by the *Dīkṣā* (see below); but the sacrificial priests do not do this.[209] They practise their function solely on the basis of his choice, his contract[210]. Numerous *mantras* uttered by the sacrificial master express clearly that, whatever is to be achieved through the sacrifice, belongs to him. For example—among many formulas—the address to the sacrificial altar (*vedi*): 'Let me milk from you for me, the sacrificer, what I wish'. Over the sacrificial gifts, he speaks the words, 'through this (sacrifice) we would like to attain Indra's friendship, immortality[211]'. And the rule is made: 'All the requests that are made by the priest in the sacrifice belong to the sacrificer alone'[212]. But on the other hand, it is made emphatically clear, that the sacrificer, save for a minor part that belongs to him and his wife, depends upon the priests for all the chief aspects of the sacrifice, by they of manual or liturgical nature. Vedic India was after all quite far from the ideal state of freedom, where each one, as his own priest and without the mediation of others, would have felt called to and also qualified to approach the deity. The Vasiṣṭhas, Viśvāmitras, Bharadvājas—in fact only those families from among whom the Brahmana-class was formed[213]— are the sole repositories of the art and craft of the right sacrifice and prayer, as technically schooled experts and participants in the potency of the *brahman*. One who wants to sacrifice carries over the functions of the priests[214] to the members of those families in the feeling of pious faith (*śraddhā*).

We are not trying here to give a picture of the social position of these Brahmana families; but the rôle that has befallen their members within the cult, must be considered by us in detail.

Let us first try to explain the immediate consequence of the statement made above that the Vedic Indian did not know *sacra publica*. There were, of course, also no *sacerdotes publici*. Notably, the type of priestly collegium, like the pontifices or the saliī of Rome, is absent altogether, though this can be easily accounted for. Such a continuity of the repositories of a certain priestly knowledge or ability, authorised by the state, would have to presuppose the organisation of public life on a scale unknown to the Vedic people.

Remotely comparable with those colleges is perhaps, what may have indeed formed their prototype: the naturally created priestly family circle or clan like the Vasiṣṭhas and Viśvāmitras just mentioned. An essential difference, however, is that each of those ancient corporate bodies had, as sole possessor or as an exclusive authority, a well-defined portion of the sacral functions. In contrast, the Vedic priestly families practised, concurring in the main features, in general the same cult, principally the same Soma-cult. There were, of course, differences between the families, and the more we go back in time, the greater they would be; and thereby, probably,—besides the common main cult—different special cults and rites in possession of individual families would come to be known[215]. But obviously, as already remarked, the whole development proceeded towards the disappearance of these special features. On the one hand, the association of the cult with the individual holy places and individual sacred objects, the whole spirit of the cultic local traditions adhering to the soil, if not absent, then rather ill-developed, must have contributed to this disappearance. But on the other hand, a general compensation must have been encouraged by the absence of a system of state, which, as it happened in ancient communities, would have placed the cultic specialities at the service of the whole, and preserved thereby their individuality. Thus finally, as can be presumed, with the increasingly distinct withdrawal of the priestly family communities all importance fell, on the one hand, upon the great totality of the class or caste, and on the other hand, upon the individual. It was his affair to determine which part of the common class property was to go to him, what spiritual knowledge and skill he wanted to acquire, what application he wanted to find for them in the service of the sacrificial masters bestowing rewards. And in the place of the old, there cropped up a new difference, essentially though of another sort, but only in so far as the increasing dimension of the ritualistic science brought in its wake unavoidable specialisations, as that 'threefold knowledge' of recitation, singing and performance of the sacrifice separated itself. Here then, it was left to the individual to choose his subject of study.

The relationship between the sacral principal and the priest employed by him showed two main forms; the priest functioned either as the household priest (Purohita) or as the sacrificial priest (Ṛtvij), i.e., he had either the orders to manage, on behalf of the royal master, the administration of the cult performed in his name, or he had to fulfil, for an individual sacrifice, one of the definite priestly rôles which were prescribed for every sacrifice.

Purohita

Purohita[216] in the normal sense of the word is to be understood clearly as the one in the service of the king, and *vice versa*, the king as the one who employes a Purohita. 'Now about the position of a Purohita', says a Brāhmaṇa-text[217], 'the gods do not eat the food of a king, who has no Purohita. If a king has to sacrifice, he should appoint a Brahmana as Purohita so that the god can eat his food'. Occasionally, there is talk of Purohitas in a wider context: thus the rule, that at that point of the sacrifice where, for a sacrificial master of the Brahmana caste, his ancestors were named as sacrificers blessed by Agni, one must, if the sacrificial master is of the second or third caste, introduce the names of the ancestors of his Purohita into the relevant formula[218]. This will have to be understood to the effect that even apart from the royal household, the Brahmanas as spiritual trustees held an established position among the important households akin to that of the royal Purohita. Our tradition, in any case, lets the royal Purohita appear throughout as the actual bearer of this title who stands in the foreground of all matters. It also gives us—particularly when we supplement the references given in the Vedic texts on ritual and laws through the rich extra-Vedic sources like the Buddhistic narrative literature and the great epics[219]—a clear picture of the position of such clerical and courtier-like bearer of dignity.

The king appoints the Purohita[220] who appears to hold office as a rule till his own death or the death of the king. Often the stories let the son become the Purohita after the father's death; thus, a sort of hereditary tradition appears to have developed, though more factual than legal. We do not have to go into the matter to find out whether it was also the case in the Vedic period itself. The relationship between the king and the Purohita is compared to marriage, the nominating act of the marriage, since for him, the same *mantra* is prescribed with which the bridegroom holds the hands of the bride: "I am that you are, you are that I am; I the heaven, you the earth; I the melody of the song, you the word of the song. So let us make the journey together[221]". And the Purohita enters into a similar proximity to the king when denoted as his Guru[222] or when he, the king's consort and son are compared with the three sacrificial fires. He is then compared with the foremost and the most prominent[223]. "He (the king) should follow him, as the pupil the teacher, the son the father, the servant the master": this is what is said in the old manual of statecraft[224]. The narrative literature illustrates amply the fellowship between the king and the Purohita. It depicts the Purohita as sitting behind the king and riding solemnly on the state elephant through the town with great pomp—the Purohita as accompanying his king and queen fleeing the besieged city with a servant—the wicked Purohita slain along with his wicked king by the mob; everywhere, the Purohita stands close to the king in glory and riches. No doubt, such glory came to the Purohita in the Vedic period; in that age itself, the Brahmana striving for the highest goal had such dignity; but the loftiest height was reached by the one—testified in several instances—who united in himself the Purohita-status of two or three royal households: a position which is unimaginable without the overpowering cultivation of a priestly prestige that towered over individual weak kings. It is in the very nature of things that such goals were reached first by the cleverest and most unscrupulous intriguers and that their achievement predestined the lucky winner to play a leading rôle amidst the bustle of courtly cabals.

The Ṛgveda places the entire prosperity of the kingdom upon the Purohita, 'the guardian of the empire', as he is called in one of the sayings; 'the king rules safely in the beloved home; where a Brahmana leads the way, there is always plenty for the king, and his subjects are obedient', says that the Veda (IV, 50, 8) with a clear reference to the Purohita as the one 'who leads the way'. The picture given by legal texts and stories of the political, and in general, of the public activity of the Purohita, does not have well-defined outlines. This is quite natural for the administration of the state in ancient India always in flux and not bound by definite norms. The Purohita ought to be well-versed in law and administration and be at the helm of all affairs of the state, he should advise the king, and the king should act accordingly; we find him teaching the king, particularly the holy texts, acting in the name of the king, imposing penance and arbitrating property disputes; in difficult conditions prevailing at the time of succession, at the time of change of government, he can step in and take necessary action.

It should suffice here to deal briefly with the duties and the rights of the Purohita[225]. Detailed reference may, however, be out of place. We have to deal mainly with the sacral aspect wherein the source of their power lies. It may not be too much to say that the Purohita is the *alter ego* of the king in matters sacral. The invocation of Agni was mentioned wherein one named the ancestors of the Purohita at that place where the ancestors of the sacrificial masters were named. The king should, at least in the view of some preceptors, perform certain offerings with the sacrificial fire of the Purohita in the Horse-sacrifice[226]. The Purohita should participate in the fast through which the king has to atone for the errors in the maintenance of law and order[227]. But of prime importance is, that the chief arrangements for all the royal sacrifices and other cultic and magical acts have to begin with him. It is narrated in the ritual texts with diverse variations as to how the gods, when they were faring badly in their battle against the demons, turned to their Purohita, the god Bṛhaspati: 'Find out for us a sacrificial act, by which we can get victory over the demons'. A Buddhistic Sūtra[228] tells us similarly how a king of pre-historic times decides to make a great sacrifice after splendid victories. 'It (the sacrifice)', he says, 'may suffice me as blessing and joy for a long time to come'. He then calls his Purohita to get instructions about the sacrifice to be celebrated, who imparts them to him while using the opportunity for several moral and educative reflections[229]. Even in the *Ṛgveda* (X, 98) we find the Purohita, Devāpi, who acquires a magic prayer to create rain and uses it in a sacrifice. The *Atharvaveda* (III, 19) shows a Purohita using magic meant for battle. A Buddhistic text[230] reports how the Purohita reads the omen to the king and indicates what is needful for its expiation. Doubtless, we must imagine also the Purohita as the real active person in the great mass of sacred acts concerning the domestic cult, in the magical acts and atonements done in the name of the king[231]. He is the true successor to the medicine man of the savages who performs all magic for his chief[232].

If we now find in the regular sacrificial cult, like the Full moon and New moon sacrifices, the Soma-sacrifice, etc., a series of sacrificial priests with clearly defined functions, the reciting Hotar, the singing Udgātar, the Adhvaryu pressing the Soma and doing the offerings, the Brahman supervising everything—we shall deal with these priests later—, then it must be asked here: what is the relationship of the Purohita to these sacrificial priests[233]? I think, it is in the very nature of things that this supreme director of the royal cult could well take up wholly the rôle of one of these priests, but none of these rôles necessarily fell to his lot. As far as I can see, it is entirely confirmed by tradition. It considers the Purohita as apart from other sacrificial priests, where the religious personae of the court are specified[234], though it knows no rules. And such rules could scarcely be missing, given the detailed treatment of such questions by the ritual-texts. These say that the Purohita had to perform, generally or in some cases, the functions of one of these priests[235]. But we find in many cases that the Purohita really functioned as a sacrificial priest. An in fact, as his high position appears to bring with itself, chiefly in the most distinguished of the relevant functions. If I understand correctly, I think, a change took place here in the course of time. In olden times, as long as the poetic creativity adorning the sacrifice was alive and in full bloom, the most distinguished priest was the one who could recite the poetic work of art and the one who certainly must have created it himself, i.e. the Hotar. Later, when the creative activity ceased and one was content with repeating the creations of the old poets, this highest position went over to the priest who had newly emerged, as it appears, around this time[236], i.e., it went over to the Brahman who was supervising the sacrifice in all aspects. In accordance with it, I think, it is preferably the Hotar[237] in the older literature and the Brahman in the later, in whose functions we see the Purohita emerge. The *Ṛgveda* (X, 98) gives a classical example for the Hotar in the case of Devāpi already mentioned by us, 'When as chief priest for Śaṃtanu, Devāpi chosen for Hotar's duty, prayed beseeching, graciously pleased Bṛhaspati vouchsafed him a voice that reached the gods and won the waters'. Thus, Agni is the divine Purohita of men[238], at the same time the Hotar χάc΄ εζοχήν [239], and both the 'divine Hotars' invoked constantly in the Āprī-litany are called at the same time 'both the Purohitas[240]'. Instructions in a *Brāhmaṇa-text*[241] point out more to the Brahman than to the sacrificial priest whose function was taken over by the Purohita[242]. These instructions state that the sacrificial meal is to be handed over to a Brahman if the sacrificial master is a Kṣatriya and, therefore, not qualified to partake of it. 'For the position of the Purohita is occupied by a Brahman in the case of Kṣatriya; the Purohita, is, however, half the ego of the Kṣatriya.' And the story of another *Brāhmaṇa-text*[243], of how Indra disclosed certain secret *mantras* to Vasiṣṭha ends with the words: 'that is why the creatures who have Vasiṣṭha as their Purohita, continue to propagate. Thus a Vasiṣṭhan should be made a Brahman: thus one can propagate[244]'. Thus, Bṛhaspati, the Purohita of the gods, is also their Brahman[245], as present in the later Vedic literature. All that proves no more than the fact that this age felt the acceptance of the function of the Brahman by the Purohita as natural, but not that it was a definite rule. It is, therefore, not surprising that the Purohita appears occasionally in quite a different rôle, in that of a singer[246], at the sacrifice.

We may conclude these remarks on the Purohita with the reference that the entire existence of the Brahmana caste with its monopoly of the cult has been sought to be derived from the privileged status of these priestly officials. But this view can be hardly deemed correct. The separation of a hereditary class of priests, at least in the main, had taken place, as we saw, before Ṛgvedic times, perhaps long before that. Then it could have been derived, if at all, from the dominating influence of the pre-Vedic, probably pre-Indian Purohitas: and there it is neither provable nor probable that the influence of such royal sacral-officials has made more than one among many contributions to that naturally developing hereditariness of priestly knowledge and skill and thereby to the development of the Brahmana caste. But for the Vedic point of view, the Purohita-status is represented not so much as the source but as the outcome of the existence of the Brahmana-caste, as the result of the clause that the birth within certain families alone qualifies one to supervise the cultural affairs. Further, it is quite probable that those influential court officials have played an important rôle in the gradual intensification of Brahmanic caste-arrogance and Brahmanic claims.

After the Purohita, let us consider the second type of persons engaged by a sacral-Yajamāna: the sacrificial priests (*ṛtvijas*) who are to be chosen for individual sacrifices, who are supposed to appear in a certain number and who have to perform well-defined functions.

The Sacrificial Priests: The Old List of Seven

We may find the oldest list of the sacrificial priests[247] in a verse of the Ṛgveda (II, 1, 2); In it Agni is identified with them in order of preference: 'Yours, Agni, is the Hotarship, yours the Potarship duly timed; yours is the Neṣṭarship; you are the Agnīdh of the pious; yours is the Praśāstarship; you do the Adhvaryu service, you are the Brahman and Householder in our home[248]'—thus, if we leave out the 'householder' (organiser of the sacrifice), then there are seven priests, probably the 'seven Hotars', often mentioned in the Ṛgveda (i.e., the Hotar and the six others)[249], whose number can be linked with the seven Ṛṣis, the ancestors of the great Brahmana-generations.

The same number seven is retained in several passages in the later sacrificial rituals, directly or transparently, in the formulas and in the rituals. Thus, the proclamation of the priests, made by the Adhvaryu while pressing the Soma in the morning[250], is extended to include the Hotar, the two Adhvaryus, the Praśāstar, the Brahman, the Potar, the Neṣṭar and the Agnīdhara. If we omit the second Adhvaryu as an addition to the original[251], we have seven priests. In his request for permission to imbibe the Soma along with others, the Acchāvāka, a priest of obviously later addition (see below p. 218), addresses, 'The sacrificial lords, Hotar, Adhvaryu, Agnīdhara, Brahman, Potar, Neṣṭar, Upavaktar[252]'. Our list of priests also tallies almost with the list of priests who are accorded their own fire-altars (*dhiṣṇya*) in the Soma-sacrifice and their own Soma-cups (*camasa*)[253]; the slight deviations give scarcely any cause to doubt the view of the seven priests as an inventory of priests of the most ancient times.

We must also refer here to the connection between this list of priests and that of the old-Iranian Soma-sacrifice[254] comprising eight priests. The identity of one of the most prominent Vedic priests with the most prominent liturgist of the Avestic ritual is an important and a well-established fact: the Vedic Hotar on whom the grand recitations devolved corresponds to the Avestic Zaotar who recited the Gāthās in the Iranian Soma-sacrifice. Also the names and the functions of the remaining Avestic priests refer completely to the sphere of the acts important in the Vedic Soma-celebration, to the washing, pressing and sifting of the Soma, to its mixing with milk, to the fetching of water necessary for the sacrifice and to the maintenance of the holy fire. Given the shifting to which names and, as we shall see, functions of the individual priests were subject, it is understandable that a direct identification of the Vedic and the Avestic priestdom can be tried only at few places, and that too as a conjecture: thus one would like to compare Ātrevakhš' 'the fire-guardian' with the Vedic Agnīdh ('kindler of the fire'), Āsnatar ('washer'), who has to wash the Soma and strain it with the Vedic Potar ('Purifier'). The Avestic list is important not only because of its contents but also because of what it does not contain. Besides Zaotar, the reciter of the litanies, there are no other singers: a fact meriting special attention in the context that the three singers of the usual Vedic rituals are likewise missing from the list of the ancient Vedic priests just discussed above.

What concrete contents are linked with the names in the list? What traces of the gradual development of the cult can be discovered in them?

Let us consider first both the priests who appear prominently in the list and who stand at the head in the prose formulation: Hotar and Adhvaryu. Their difference is clear and simple: the former has to recite and the latter has to look after the actual arrangements for the sacrifice.

The Hotar

The name Hotar which denotes the performer of the sacrificial libation[255] appears to refer to the period when it was the duty of the same priests to speak praises of the god, to invite him and to pour out the offering. In the minor offerings, this unity of the priestly function remained; in the major[256] offerings, there came about the separation of the speaker and the real doer of the action so that he became the speaker who—not in agreement with the etymological meaning of the word—assumed the old name of the person speaking and acting as priest. It was then his duty to recite at the individual main stages of the sacrifice the poem which celebrated the deeds, the might, the splendour of the god revered each time, which invited him for a drink and commended to him the wishes of the sacrificer—poems (*uktha*) connected with the recitation of the 'intoxication' (*mada*)[257] even in Ṛgvedic times, prosaic invocations containing here and there disjointed verse-fragments which, enumerating their honorifics, invited the gods to get inebriated by drinking the Soma[258]. The later ritual often lets the Hotar accompany the offering with two individual verses; the typical content of the first (*puronuvākyā*) is an invitation to the god to take part (in the sacrifice), and the second (*yājyā*) to enjoy the offering. It appears, the second of the two verses took shape first, for sequences of such verses meant for certain fixed series of offerings belong to the characteristic stock of the *Ṛgvedic* sacrificial poetry[259]. The relevant initial verses are missing there; their type appears to be present only in few opening verses of the *Ṛgveda*[260]. It needs to be hardly mentioned that other incidental recitations devolved on the Hotar besides the ones mentioned above: thus, in the Soma-sacrifice, foremost the grand morning litany to the deities of the morn and many shorter recitations accompanying the individual phases of the action[261]. The poets of these various litanies must have been principally the priests who recited them: thus, there is no doubt that we have to think of the Ṛṣis of the *Ṛgvedic* poetry in the first place as the Hotar-priests or as the ones who inspired its creation when they functioned as Hotar-priests. There is no doubt also that the priest who had to contrive and to express artistically just and effective word for the god, was supreme sacrificial priest in the consciousness of the age: how then was chosen the Hotar alone amongst all the priests as the human countertype of Agni, the priestly god?

The Adhvaryu

The Hotar is praised as 'smooth of tongue', the Adhvaryu as the one with 'smooth hands'. As a rule, he has to speak only in such a way that his dedicatory *mantra*[262] for success and for warding away evil accompanies the individual acts of his manifold routine. He split this routine with other priests, particularly with Agnīdh, whom we shall discuss soon, in such a way that in this distribution, considerations of convenience were of more importance than any fixed principles. On the whole, however, it is he who occupies the centre of the actual sacrificial rite as the chief guardian of the sacrificial fire and the straw, as the marshal and purifier of the tools and utensils, as the bestower and provender of the sacred cakes and as the one who presses the Soma.

Agnīdh

Among the rest of the priests mentioned in the list together with these two main persons, we have to consider at first Agnīdh, the 'kindler of fire' mentioned just above. A *Brāhmaṇa-text*[263] says of him that 'he kindles the fires'. Actually, there are a series of functions under his control having a connection with the sacrificial fires, their purification, piling of the burning wood and the like[264]: on the whole, he is the helper of Adhvaryu[265]; in some minor sacrifices carried out by a small number of priests, Adhvaryu and Agnīdh act together as priests, whereas the Hotar only speaks[266]. A feature in the

New moon and the Full moon sacrifices, where the Hotar touches Adhvaryu with one hand and Agnīdh with the other on the shoulder, and whereupon both sit down[267], expresses significantly the similarity of the two[268].

Praśāstar

The priest appearing under different names as Upavaktar ('invoker'), Praśāstar ('administrator of orders'), Maitrāvaruṇa ('priest of Mitra and Varuṇa') does not appear in the minor sacrifices like the New moon and the Full moon sacrifices; he is present in the Animal-sacrifice and in the Soma-sacrifice, in addition to those already mentioned. His functions are of two kinds. He is above other priests in giving numerous orders (*praiṣa*) as his first two names suggest; even in the *Ṛgveda* (IX, 95, 5), it is said of Soma that he urges on the flow of speech, 'like the Invoker that of the Hotar[269]'. Then he has to take up on his part a series of recitations, and in this respect, he is the only one[270] in the Animal-sacrifice, but one amongst many assistants of the Hotar in the Soma-sacrifice. He forms a homogeneous pair with the Hotar in the Animal-sacrifice; thus the invocation to 'the two divine Hotars' in a litany[271] pertaining to this sacrifice cannot be understood as anything other than the counterpart of precisely this pair of priests transposed to the divine world. His third name Maitrāvaruṇa is associated with recitations to Mitra and Varuṇa that devolve on him in the Soma-sacrifice. His special relationship to these gods is clearly seen from the little data provided by the *Ṛgveda*[272]. Probably, his rôle as the 'administrator of orders' is connected with his relationship to Mitra and Varuṇa, the divine commanders[273].

Potar and Neṣṭar

The remaining three priests belong especially to the Soma-sacrifice. Of these, Potar and Neṣṭar disappear altogether in the later Vedas. The former name means 'purifier' of the Soma, and the latter the 'leader', i.e. the one who leads forth the sacrificer's wife to the sacrifice. It may be presumed that the 'purifier' of the Soma, accorded the place next to the Hotar, must have once played a great rôle in the ritual of 'Soma purifying himself' (*S. pavamāna*). In the extant orders of the sacrifice, he appears to have been reduced to a pattern; he occupies his traditional place amongst the other priests without taking any important part in the performance. Neṣṭar, in special relationship to Tvaṣṭar, the god of fertility, comes to the foreground only once in the Soma-sacrifice. The offerings to the consorts of the gods[274] gives an opportunity for the sacrificer's wife to take part in the ritual where, of course, the magic of fertility has to be induced. The priest, Agnīdh, who has to partake of the said Soma-offering, does this seated on Neṣṭar's lap. Then Neṣṭar leads in the consort who requests the chief singer (Udgātar) ogling at her to grant her the semen; besides, she pours repeatedly water over her bare thighs[275]. The significance of the last act is clear; but the enjoyment of the Soma by the priest seated on Neṣṭar's lap may also have related significance;

it may have to do with the transfer of vigour from the priest, who drinks the magic potion of the Soma dedicated to the divine consorts, to the one who is about to lead in the mortal wife to the sacrifice[276]. The obscene slant to the rites (of course repulsive more to the modern man than to the Vedic Indian) connected with Neṣṭar makes one believe[277] that this priest originates from the cult of the non-Aryan barbarians. But I think, this is without basis: that there is a priest in the Soma-sacrifice who is connected with the sacrificer's wife and thereby to the fertility-magic, is as inconspicuous as it is obvious that this magic has just that slant that is in keeping with its nature. This holds good for the Aryans as well as for the barbarians.

The last of these seven priests, the Brahman (later Brāhmaṇācchaṃsin) is mainly occupied in the Soma-sacrifice with the recitations to Indra in accord with the Hotar to whose assistants he belongs[278]. We shall refer to him once more later (p. 218).

Singers

Several priests, of great importance to the historical ritual, are missing from our list of priests. We believe, we can recognize in them the priestly circle of ancient times[279]. Missing from our list above all, are the singers numbering three[280] of the later as well the Ṛgvedic period. They did not participate in the minor sacrifices, but had to recite during the Soma-sacrifice, individually or together, different verses of the sacrificial songs interspersed with interjections, exultations and magic words[281]. These songs can be divided into two major groups. On the one hand a song or a complex of song-recitations to the Soma (*Soma pavamāna*) strained and refined through the sieve of goat-hair, was part of every Soma-pressing ritual that took place on the sacrificial day at morn, at noon and in the afternoon. These songs are of a quite different type[282] from those in the *Ṛgveda* with the invitations to the gods. It may be said that the note of cheer of the priests at the emergence of the intoxicating, divinely animated drink meant to scare away demons has been developed into songs which are directed to Soma in hundredfold repetitions throughout the whole of the *Ṛgveda*: Stream forth purified; mingle with the milk of cows; strengthen Indra and the gods; drive away every wicked enemy; bring us light and salvation. But the singers recited the second large group of sacrificial hymns to the usual sacrificial gods, on the whole such that the more prominent deities, who were given the offerings after the regulation governing the three pressings of the Soma and to whom the litanies were sung by the Hotar, also received their praise in songs[283]. There those—among other magic connections—may also come to the fore that, that song celebrated in the myth, was repeated along with its miraculous effect by which the priestly ancestors gained the imprisoned cows (p. 80): the song similar to the lowing of the cows (*Ṛv.* I, 62, 3; IV, 3, 11, etc.) has magic effect, with the cows submitting themselves to the singers. But are these hymns to be denied a place in the ritual of the ancient priest-circles? The absence of the singers in the old enumeration of the priests (p. 214)[284] as in the Avestic Soma-ritual appears to suggest this view. But one cannot overlook the possibility that the hymn may be older than the existence of the singers themselves; one could even think that in olden times the recitation of hymns was, for example, more important to the Potar, 'the purifier' of the Soma than the process of purification. But one cannot say anything here with certainty.

Brahman

A further important priesthood of later period which has to be denied to the old period, I think, is that of the Brahman. The Brahman is the supervisor of the entire sacrifice in the ritual of the later Vedas. He should know all the three Vedas; his work compensates the work of all other priests; he rules over the sacrifice with the thought; over the priests with the word. He sits on the Brahman-seat beside the most important of the three fires, faces it, solemnly stretches his folded hands, but utters not a word in the midst of all the noise. He is the 'physician of the sacrifice': all the mistakes committed in the welter of sacred actions and recitations are to be announced to him, and he has to make them good 'as one joins limb to limb, or as one ties with a lace straps and belts or something else that becomes loose'.

But there is clear evidence that this priesthood was not known in very ancient times: above all, the absence of the Brahman in the list of priests discussed above (p. 213), besides the lack of definite references in the *Ṛgveda*[285], though of no moment by itself. As for this list, the state of affairs more precisely is—I think, the argument acquires thereby greater conclusiveness—that in fact there appears therein a priest with the name of the Brahman: but it can be proved that this priest does not correspond to the Brahman of the later ritual, but to another priest, who recites mainly in the honour of India, the Brāhmaṇācchaṃsin[286]. Even if we are aware of the term Brahman used in olden days for other technical purposes, it certainly could not have had at that time its later meaning. Finally a tradition[287], which appears credible, refers to the relatively recent origin of this priesthood, according to which formerly only one member of the Vasiṣṭha-family could become a Brahman; a certain litany, one of the few, the Brahman has to say during the sacrifice, was supposed to have been known once to the Vasiṣṭhan and, as the legend goes, would be revealed only to the Vasiṣṭha. It can be seen that, here, one has to deal with an innovation originating from the priestly practice of an individual family—an innovation of a later date—if we may regard the quite modern look of that litany as a standard. This innovation then began to prevail generally, obviously favoured by the same tendency, to which it also owes its origin, namely the increasing meticulous care for painstaking correctness of the least detail, whereupon the success of the sacrifice was considered to depend[288].

DĪKṢĀ AND SACRIFICIAL BATH

Dīkṣā

The initiation of the sacrificer and his wife precedes the Soma-sacrifice; to it correspond rites which cancel this initiation once more at the end of the holy act. The initiation is called Dīkṣā, a desiderative form which perhaps means 'the desire to serve god'[289]; the concluding act is called Avabhṛtha, i.e., 'carry downwards'; the sacrificer carries the squeezed Soma-shoots and other objects used in the sacrifice down to the water[290]; he purifies them, and he himself takes bath with his wife and the priests.

Dīkṣā as Magic Rite

The Dīkṣā, introduced through a sacrifice to Agni and Viṣṇu[291], is performed in a sacrificial hut[292] where the sacrificer—this also applies to his wife—is shaved, bathed and anointed, dressed in new clothes. He clasps the holy girdle and sits down on the black skin of the antelope spread near the sacrificial fire[293]; his head is covered; an antelope-horn is tied to the lapel of his dress. He has to scratch himself with that when necessary. Thus he sits silently till sunset; he drinks boiled milk which builds energy appropriate to the Dīkṣā, and he keeps awake throughout the night, or he sleeps in his hut, entrusts himself to Agni's care, so that the god protects him from the persecution of evil spirits[294]. This initiation which is related to many an observance—e.g., obligation to stammer in speech, to keep three last fingers of the fist closed—lasts according to the view of various persons for a brief or a lengthy period, according to a few, till complete physical exhaustion sets in[295].

The *Ṛgveda* does not appear to mention the Dīkṣā save for a few places of doubtful authenticity[296]. The poets were interested only in praising the gods, not the magic customs which were meant more for men than for the gods or wholly for any one particular god. The Dīkṣā is obviously one such magic custom of an ancient type. It is to be placed alongside the rites common among various primitive races, which aim at establishing contact with gods or spirits by inducement of ecstatic states. Several means are available towards this end: contemplation in a lonely spot, secluding oneself and hiding oneself from disturbing apparitions, all kinds of self-mortification, steam-baths and chiefly, fasting for 'one cannot espy the hidden on a full stomach' as a Zulu-saying[297] goes. Fasting[298] and physical exhaustion are then, as already mentioned, the main elements of Dīkṣā. It is said[299] that the respiratory functions cease, if the Dīkṣā is carried too far. 'It is taught: when the one initiated to Dīkṣā becomes lean, then he will be pure for sacrifice. When the skin and bones droop, he will be pure for sacrifice. He undertakes Dīkṣā when fat, sacrifices when lean' (*Āpastamba Sr*. X, 14, 9, 10). Besides the other factors mentioned earlier, heating played a rôle at least originally, in Dīkṣā, although this is not mentioned in the extant descriptions of the rite. Clothes and also nearness of the fire must have caused some heat; in fact a special *mantra* is indicated for the initiate when sweat breaks out[300].

Dīkṣā and Tapas

The most important and central to the aspect of heating is the explicit understanding of Dīkṣā as Tapas (penance) which has been expressed diversely[301]. As a kind of mystic substance, the magic power of this Tapas is present in the person performing Dīkṣā. If he is defiled by a forbidden sight, 'the Dīkṣā disappears from him, also his blue-black darkness (*nīlam*), his arresting power (*haras*).' If water from the sky falls on him, then 'it destroys his power, his strength, his Dīkṣā, his Tapas', and in order to make good the damage, one has to say to the water, 'You moistening waters, give me power, give me strength, give me power. Do not destroy my Dīkṣā, my Tapas'[302]. In this context of the concept of Tapas, Dīkṣā is seen as part of the observances which commence with the use of heat for obtaining supernatural success. Actually, the reference to heat as the vehicle of penance is in the fore in earlier times, whenever various forms of penance are understood by the name Tapas. In fact, Tapas is nothing but heat. 'Order and truth were born from the inflamed Tapas', it is said in the *Ṛgveda* (X, 190, 1). The priest warms the potsherds upon which the sacrificial cake is to be cooked, in that he puts burning coal atop them and says, 'Become hot (*tapyadhvam*) through the Tapas of the Aṅgiras, the Bhṛgus'[303] (*Vāj. S. I*, 18). We often come across the Tapas of the 'fivefold heat' in the later literature: heating by four fires which surround the ascetic after the four directions of the world and by the sun. A Jain text describes the ascetic who 'lets himself burn, rigid as a pillar, face turned sunward, on a place exposed to the fiery sun'[304]. Enlightenment and supernatural power of various types—similar to the power as it was later attributed to the historical successor of the old Tapas-performer, the Yogin—were considered as the result of this heating and other related acts of self-torment, like fasting, keeping awake, holding the breath[305], etc. 'The gods have entered them', says the *Ṛgveda* (X, 136) of those in a state of trance or ecstasy, and alludes thereby to a way of conception that has played a significant rôle from the lowest to the highest forms of religion. It is a poet of the *Ṛgveda* (VIII, 59, 6) who sees the old creations of the ancestors, of the first sacrificers of the most ancient human stock, in the vision attained by Tapas. The dream is born from the soul replete with Tapas and 'speech pleasing to the gods is born of Tapas'. One who has performed great Tapas reaches the sun; Indra conquered the sun after practising Tapas. One reminds the king who has taken the wife of a Brahmana, of the seven Ṛṣis, the ancestors of the Brahmanas, 'who had sat down for Tapas'; the magic power of the Tapas that belongs to the Brahmana shall bring evil to the offender. Tapas gives the strength for the mightiest of creations; the goddess Aṣṭakā, performing Tapas, gave birth to the greatness of Indra; the Ṛṣis are born of the Tapas[306]. In numerous legends of the *Brāhmaṇa-texts*, Prajāpati, the creator of the world, does Tapas and gets the power to release the world and the beings from themselves. Once he performed such a Tapas, that lights came out of the pores of his body; they are the stars[307]. In many verses of the *Brāhmaṇa-texts* there is talk that either this or that mythical being was helped by Tapas to get enlightenment in which some secret of sacrificial art revealed itself to him. It is said of the sacrificer, who remains awake on the night before the laying of the holy fire—again a situation where the Tapas is a preparation for an especially sacred act: 'Thus he turns to the gods. United with the gods, spent, but richer for it in Tapas, he lays the fire' (*Śatapatha Br.* II, 1, 4, 7). The Buddhistic texts give a visual picture of how one expected to attain visionary enlightenment during the Buddha's days by fasting and sweating, by mortifying oneself and by straining the body to the utmost.

These phenomena we come across in India are clearly examples of a type spread over the whole world; promoting ecstatic communion with spirits is particularly characteristic for the inferior forms of religious life. Thus, it should be obvious, even without such positive expressions of the *Ṛgveda* adduced here that the entire sphere of ideas of ancient Vedic times must have played a rôle, and that it is not a case of new constructs of later origin. This rôle must have been more significant than what can understandably appear within the extremely limited horizon of real hymnic poetry. I refer here further to one more hymn of the *Ṛgveda* (X, 136), which, though it does not mention the word Tapas, is within the sphere of ideas closely connected to the concept of Tapas: the same hymn from which we inferred above (p. 220) the expression of the gods entering the person in a state of ecstasy. This lively hymn describes the orgiastic drive of the old Vedic world still not ennobled by the thirst for redemption that motivated the ascetics of the Buddhistic period, but yet not wholly cast in the mould of those crude forms of the savage medicine-men. The hymn speaks of those 'enraptured ones with long hair' (*keśin, muni*) dressed in brown ḍirt, who moved around as the wind blows when the gods have gone into them, who drink with Rudra poison[308] out of goblets. 'In drunken ecstacy we have mounted the chariot of the winds. You mortals, can see only our body...Horse of the wind, friend of the Storm-god, the ecstatic one is motivated by god. He lives in both the oceans, the east and the west[309]. He wanders on the paths of the Apsaras, Gandharvas and the wild animals.' The Vedic sacrificial cult had wholly refrained from this doing of possessed miracle-men; the sober activity of the ritual secret-mongering and of its official technicians was tuned to a different note. But in various traces and remains, the system of Tapas is projected inṭo the cult of the Vedic world, and it would not be a mistake to give the rite of Dīkṣā a prominent place amongst these remnants, if we were to compare the performer of this initiation, who sits covered in antelope-skin, hungry and vigilant, beside the exorcising magic-fire with the types of priest-magicians, so familiar to ethnologists, who try to become possessed through mortification.

The Motif of Rebirth

Another motif, the motif of rebirth appears to be present in the Dīkṣā though compatible with the motif of Tapas. It may even be said that this supersedes that.

'The priests', says a *Brāhmaṇa-text*[310], 'make the person, in whom they have performed the Dīkṣā, go into an embryo again...the Dīkṣā-hut is the womb to the Dīkṣita[311]: Thus they allow him to enter into his womb; they cover him with a cloth. The cloth is amnion for the Dīkṣita: thus they cover him with the amnion. A black antelope-skin is placed over it. Chorion is outside of the amnion: So they cover him with chorion. He clenches his fists. With clenched fists the embryo lies inside. The boy is born with clenched fists....He climbs down for the Avabhṛtha-bath after removing the antelope-skin (below): therefore, the embryos are born redeemed from the chorion. He descends with his cloth on; the boy is, therefore, born with the amnion.'

It is, however, strange that this conception of Dīkṣā prevalent throughout in the *Brāhmaṇa-texts* is not expressed in the *mantras* themselves which accompany it. Yet I think it has its justified status. For it agrees exactly with the views and the customs in which inferior cultures the world over depicted the ascent of man to another, higher state. Such an ascent is experienced by the Dīkṣita: 'One who performs Dīkṣā turns verily to the gods; he becomes one of the gods', says a *Brāhmaṇa*[312]. 'It must be made clear that the original thinking of man does not know the concept of development, but conceives of natural processes of change as also religious change, of say a 'conversion' of any type, as an unique act of the transformation of man, as the origin of a new man...One dies and another is born'[313]. The widespread initiatory customs represented typically as re-birth suggests that the depiction of the death of the old man must have been a part of Dīkṣā as its first act. It is not so surprising that it is now lost[314]. But from what is preserved, traces of the motif of birth appear quite clearly. Thus, the clenched fists[315] are sure evidences corresponding to the verse in the *Brāhmaṇa* mentioned above. Thus, the stammering of the Dīkṣita can perhaps be explained[316]—if the shift of the idea from the embryo to a small child is assumed.

The Sacrificial Bath

For the final ceremony[317] corresponding to Dīkṣā at the end of the sacrifice, one has to descend into water from the sacrificial place. The sacrificial utensils coming in contact with the Soma, including the pressed Soma-shoots, are dipped in water, as also the antelope-skin used in the Dīkṣā and many other things. Finally, the sacrificer, his consort and the priests get into the water. Husband and wife clean each other's backs. They put on fresh clothes on coming out. The offerings and the *mantras* accompanying these rites are addressed, above all to Varuṇa, the redeemer from sin; the request for redemption is present in diverse forms. 'You have hundred and thousand physicians; O king! Your mercy is said to be wide and deep. Drive away hatred and destruction. Absolve the committed sin from us. 'And in a *mantra* addressed to the purificatory bath itself now personified: 'You have taken away the sin committed by gods and the one committed by men. O god, protect us in your immensity from harm.'

Is purification from guilt and sin really the original meaning, is Varuṇa, the liberator, from the beginning the god of the sacrificial bath? It can be seen that these references, though in no way connected with the true nature of the rite, could quite easily be brought into the rite by theologians, who interpreted the sacrifice and embellished it with their own inventions. Water made them call to mind Varuṇa, the lord of the waters, and they gave him offerings, paid him reverence. Ablutions were known as the means for removal of impurity and guilt, and Varuṇa was after all the liberator from sin. Thus, these features could be easily added on to the rite of the sacrificial bath. The original nature of the ceremony is, however, to be looked for elsewhere. It is common belief that a man is not permitted to take over into daily life traces of dealings with supernatural powers that remain attached to him and his possessions as a sacred, yet dangerous substance[318]. That dealing began with Dīkṣā; it is concluded here. The ritual clothes and utensils which were given to man and wife are put aside. But a bath is needed for complete removal of the precarious substance. A *Brāhmaṇa-text* (*Maitr. S.* III, 6, 2) says in this context: 'When he gets into the water for the sacrificial bath, he takes back the Dīkṣā into the water', and in the *mantras*, there is an expression which gives the precise meaning of the action: 'The pure waters, the absolving waters, the absolvers of Dīkṣā and Tapas' (*Āpastamba Śr.* XIII, 21, 3). Correspondence of Dīkṣā and the sacrificial bath discussed here and confirmed clearly by the rites leaves really no doubt that in the original meaning it is not sin and impurity but the still remaining traces of supernatural powers from which the bath was to absolve one[319].

We may incidentally refer here to a ceremony very similar to the sacrificial bath. The later Vedic texts acquaint us with it: the bath or the ablution marks the end of the instruction in the Vedas by a Brahmana-mentor. The relationship of this ablution to the initiation, which begins the studies is exactly like the one between the sacrificial-bath and Dīkṣā. The youth has taken an oath at the beginning of the studies which have brought him very close to the divine powers, produced in him the condition of the Tapas, which is also characteristic of the performer of Dīkṣā[320]; now he casts aside this oath; the bath washes away all traces of that (divine) contact. Like usages in both instances refer to each other: 'Agni, Lord of the oath, I shall take the oath'—afterwards: 'Agni, Lord of the oath, I have practised the oath'[321]. The holy attributes of the priestly pupil taken up at the beginning of schooling, viz., the girdle, the staff and the antelope-skin are taken off and cast into waters[322]; new clothes are put on. One observes how exact parallels can be drawn from these rites and the sacrificial bath and how they mutually explain one another[323].

CULT OBSERVANCES

The Dīkṣā is, in the Vedic tradition, the most prominent example of a complex of observances which prepare the completion of a sacred act. Thus, the earlier section can serve us as an introduction to the attempt to survey now in a broader context the different kinds of such observances which are partly incumbent on the performer of certain rites and which are also partly associated with entry into a certain stage of life or with the learning of certain parts of the Vedic curriculum. The concerns here vary; sometimes, as in the Dīkṣā, the aim is to fill man with certain magical qualities, sometimes it is to ward off, at least originally in the rites, evil powers: for the person prepared for sacred actions or for receiving especially sacred knowledge, enters a realm prone to attacks by spirits and, therefore, in need of enhanced precaution. Those positive and these negative measures get mixed up at several places, and the interpretation in individual instances, as it can be obviously expected, is often subject to doubts which cannot be easily overcome.

Fasting, etc.

The most common precautionary measures against harmful and hostile powers[324] appears to be fasting, resp., avoiding certain foods, avoiding sexual intercourse, remaining awake or sleeping on the floor, finally silence, or, with an ethicising re-interpretation betraying the spirit of a later age, avoiding untruthful speech. Thus, the one who has to set up the sacrificial fire must observe silence and spend the night before without sleep[325]. The performer of the New moon and Full moon sacrifice has to abstain from eating meat and from sexual intercourse; he is permitted to have wild fruits and plants for his supper, but he is forbidden to take the food he is to offer the next day. He has to sleep on the floor with his wife during the night[326]; there is also a rule[327] that man and wife should spend at least a part of this night without sleeping and telling stories, etc.[328]. He must speak only truth. The young couple must sleep on the floor in the first three nights after the marriage, observe chastity and avoid all salted and spicy dishes[329]. The Brahmana-pupil is ordered to avoid sexual intercourse and elevated resting place[330]. After the celebration of his acceptance as pupil, he has to stand the rest of the day in silence, and for three days, he is not to eat any salted food[331]. Before an especially sacred lesson is taught, he has to abstain[332] from food for three days, or a day and a night, and he has to remain silent 'with eyes bound[333]'. Even the teacher is ordered to observe 'chastity for a day and night and eat no meat'[334] before the completion of the rites connected with the teaching of such lessons. The man offering Śabalīhoma lies for twelve nights on barren ground, drinks only sweet milk, speaks only what is necessary and observes chastity[335].

It is the task of ethnology to write the pre-history of these observances whose essential features can be found the world over[336]. It would have to investigate, particularly with reference to fasting, how the motif of abstaining from all food, so that food is available for the gods, defines itself from the motif of fear of harmful spirits threatening at close quarters especially the celebrant and, attracted by the food, capable of entering man along with it, if care is not taken. It would have to investigate also how the motif of abstention defines itself from the motif of fear of equally harmful impersonal substances, further from the motif of going hungry in order to induce ecstatic states and from other motifs considered here[337]. When in the Vedic ritual, fasting appears often in the special form of an injunction against spicy or salted food—thus when a pupil goes to the Ashrama, in a marriage or at a funeral—or also as an injunction against meat-eating, then it must be noted that the superstitious abstention from eating salt is widespread, whatever be its significance[338]; the origin of abstention from meat-eating is obviously there, because of the fear of the soul of the killed animal and the substance of death clinging to its body[339]. From the point of view of Vedic theologians, fasting is, on the one hand, the main form of ascetic exertion (Tapas)—'that is the whole Tapas, the abstention from eating', says a *Brāhmaṇa*[340]; on the other hand, however, fasting is understood, as far as it precedes a sacrifice, above all as a duty, so to say, a social obligation, towards the gods one would like to entertain: 'That is not in order, if someone wanted to eat first, while others are not eating, how would it be, if someone were to eat first, while the gods do not eat?'[341].

The following remarkable rite is also to be mentioned in connection with fasting. Anointing or, rather, sprinkling the sacrificer with water took place in the Vājapeya ('The drink of strength') celebration, in the manner of king's consecration, with the purpose of getting for the sacrificer strength and superiority. For this ceremony, water with milk was poured in a vessel, as also seventeen different types of food[342], according to some, and according to others, all kinds of food one could think of, with the sole exception of one kind of food. 'The one he does not take, he should give it up and should not enjoy it lifelong. Thus, he does not go to the end[343]; thus, he lives long'[344]. A similar rite is found when the Agni-altar is built. The ground where the altar is built, is ploughed, and all kinds of seeds are strewn over it. 'They are all plants. That is all food, all plants. With that, he puts in him (the priest in the sacrificer) all the food. He should take away from it one type; he should not enjoy it lifelong'[345]. For the Vedic marshal of the ritual, there may be ethical overtones in the thought, that aspiring for all enjoyment brings disaster, but the one, who gives up, at least, one enjoyment in wise self-control, is closer to one's goal. The consideration of widespread regulations of the primitive folks makes one assume that we are dealing here with the echo or an imitation of very ancient taboo-laws.

Avoidance of Various Dangers, Particularly of coming in contact with the Dead

When we turn from fasting and similar customs to the other observances mentioned above (p. 219), we see there clearly the original motif: the fear of attacks by spirits. On account of their fear, the person setting up the sacrificial fire did not dare to sleep or to speak. If the pupil accepted by a teacher spends the rest of the day in silence, or if the pupil who is to commence study of an especially sacred lesson remains silent and binds his eyes, then it is done obviously not to see the fearful apparitions about him; so too does the youth spend the day in solitude, who, on completion of his studentship enters adulthood accompanied by solemn ceremonies[346]; also sleeping on the floor appears to belong to the same context: one wants to get away from enemies who could surprise one in one's habitual resting place at night. That in sexual abstinence, there is also a similar precaution at play, shall be confirmed in our discussion of the funeral rites[347]; another significance of this observance will be discussed below (p. 231).

The motif becomes very clear in a number of regulations we have to mention here: avoiding all things connected with death or the dead. The Brahmana who has taken a bath at the end of his schooling (Snātaka) should not go to any place of execution, let alone to a funeral ground; he should not see a pall-bearer. The teacher who goes out into the forest to recite to the pupil the secret teaching banned in the village, should not see blood or a funeral place, not, see any 'corpse-shaped' animal[348], as it appears in a rule of uncertain import. From the reference to the dead, I would like to explain also, at least the second part of the rule that the Snātaka should not climb a tree and or descend into a well—according to another version, he should not even look into a well[349]; the depths of the earth belong to the dead[350]. We may also include here the rule which forbids one to sit on the bare floor, etc.[351]. The same appears to be valid for observances, wherein fear of the use of earthenware comes to light. One who wants to learn the Jyeṣṭha-sāman, should not 'eat or drink out of earthenware' from the beginning of the instruction in an observance[352]; similarly, there is the express rule that the vessel in which water is to be used while reciting the secret texts, should be of metal[353]. Similarly, the rule of not drinking out of earthenware holds good for one who wants to learn the secret of the Pravargya-sacrifice[354]. These customs go together obviously with the directives that the vessel with milk for the New moon sacrifice (Sāṃnāyya) must not be covered with earthenware[355], that the one who dedicates himself to the Soma-sacrifice must not take out of earthenware the milk that nourishes him[356], that the sacrificial butter of the tānūnaptra-rite in the Soma-sacrifice must be covered with a vessel not made of clay[357]. In one place, the tradition of the *Brāhmaṇa-age* attributes the rejection of clay to the fact that 'the falsehood uttered by man on the earth gets mixed with it immediately[358]'; it approximates to the original meaning in as much as it deals here really with the impurities located in the ground, the place of origin of earthenware. The ethicing slant alone, given to this impurity by the reference cited above, is of obviously secondary import. Other references from the Brāhmaṇa-literature, I think, lead us precisely to the correct import. Several *Brāhmaṇas*, for example, refer to the injunction against covering the milk with earthenware in the New moon sacrifice: 'If he were to cover it with something earthen, the fathers (i.e., the dead) would become the deity to whom it belongs[359]'. The earthen substance is in constant touch with the dead and belongs to the dead; 'the abode of the earth[360]'; it is said in the Ṛgveda, be it the grave or the earthen funeral urn. Thus, the observances relating to the avoiding of earthenware appear to be quite similar to those discussed above, and they must have been caused by the fear of contact with the sphere of the dead.

If a Snātaka is enjoined upon not to go to another village in the evening and not to enter it by a secret path[361], then keeping oneself from the dead, from women-in-childbed, etc., belong to the same or related categories; indeed a similar impurity clings to them as to the dead. We may dispense with the collection of further details of this kind; on the whole, the essence of these observances which concern avoiding of some sort of danger or the other should be clear.

Infusing Oneself with Magic Substances

But there are, besides them, as pointed out earlier, other observances of a contrary nature, whose discussion must be included here: namely, those observances aimed at infusing the one who practises them with some sort of a substance[362], as it were, and also at establishing and maintaining for him the compact with some supernatural powers. Rain and storm, heat and sun appear particularly as those substances around which magic of this kind revolves.

The Rain Substance

To the curriculum of the Sāmaveda belongs the Śakvarī-song. Embodied in it is Indra's weapon and the symbol of omnipotence, the Vajra, through which, as said in the *Ṛgveda*, the Vasiṣṭhas, to the accompaniment of deafening noise, infused strength into Indra[363]: it is, therefore, one of those texts whose study was confined to the forest alone on account of their holy, awe-inspiring character. The pupil who wanted to learn this song was prescribed observances to be kept for periods ranging from twelve to nine, six to three years—according to some, only for a year. Amongst them the following are found[364]: he has 'to touch the water' three times a day; he has to wear black clothes and to enjoy black nourishment; if it rains, he has to sit down, but must not seek shelter; he must say to the pouring sky: 'Water is the Śakvarī-song'; if there is a lightning, 'Śakvarī-song looks like that'; if there is thunder, 'The great one (is it the cloud?) is making a loud noise'. He should not cross the running waters without 'touching the waters'; he should board a ship, only if there is danger to his life and only on 'touching the water', 'because, it is said, the excellence of the Śakvarī-song dwells in the water'. If the pupil is to finally 'learn to sing the song by himself', a vessel with water is kept, into which plants of all types are put; he must dip his hands in it'. It is said of these observances, that 'Parjanya will send rain at the behest of one who lives thus'. It is clear, how all rules aim at bringing the Brahmana in contact with water and making him at the same time an ally of the water-powers, so that he is safe from their enmity. Even the black clothes and black eatables have this meaning. They refer to the rain-bearing clouds; it may be remembered that a black sacrificial animal is used for obtaining rain. 'It is black, for this is the nature of rain'; in another magic rite to get rain, it is explicitly said: 'He puts on a black dress with black trimmings, because this is the nature of the rain'[365]. Thus, it may be taken for granted that here, old magic customs, which prepared and sanctified the rain-magician for his office, have been preserved and fitted into the spheres of concepts and regulations governing the Vedic school curriculum. Perhaps, it is in the same context that the rule appears, amongst the observances incumbent on a Brahmana (Snâtaka) at the close of his studentship, that he should walk through the rain uncovered[366] and not run[367]: it appears that, as a man who has taken it upon himself to exert influence on the rain, he should not shirk from contact with it in anxious haste[368].

Sun Substance

Another observance related to the school curriculum of the Sāmaveda is the 'Sun-observance'; everything in it is arranged in such a way, that the Brahmana comes into contact with the sun. 'Those who perform this, wear only one garment. They do not allow anything to come between them and the sun except trees and shelter-huts. They get into the water not more than knee-deep except when instructed by their mentor'[369]. Similarly, in an observance of the *Yajurveda* for one who learns or performs the sacrifice of boiled milk (Pravargya, Gharma): 'He has to observe the following. He should not cover himself in sunlight.—'I shall not be hidden from him (the sun)'. He should not spit out in sunlight. 'I shall not spit at him'. He should not urinate in sunlight—'I shall not dirty him'. How far his light reaches, that far will he reach—'I shall do him no harm through those things'. He should eat at night by light: so that he makes an image of the one, who glows there[370]'. This passage, however, ends with words which reflect the spirit of other age: 'Thus, however, spoke Āsuri: there is only one principle by which the gods live: the truth. Therefore, he must speak the truth alone.'

To this compilation, I add the directives which are valid for the second, intensified initiation[371] of the Soma-sacrifice. The initiation (Dīkṣā), as shown above[372], represents originally a state of magic connected with heat. In the second initiation the sacrificer clenches the fists more tightly and pulls the sacred sash more firmly (see above p. 220 f.). It is now said here[373]: 'He takes the heating-observance[374] upon himself (i.e., he drinks only hot milk for food). He wipes (his hands) with boiling water. Because Agni is extinguished with the cold: he does thus to keep it inflamed'. It can be seen how the observance is directed towards infusing in the sacrificer the substance of power of heat.

Further, there are observances meant to arrest the loss of such power:

for instance, the injunctions against bathing, cutting the hair, trimming the beard, (clipping the nails, etc.).

Bathing as well as cutting the hair are found, with a clear parallelism between the two, in a wide range of contexts in the rituals. It may be useful to have a look at them.

The Bath

The bath[375] with its power of removing a substance clinging to man must be avoided or taken, according as it brings good or bad. Thus, we come across it in the ritual very often as an act of purification to be completed before commencement of a sacred action. Before the Soma-sacrificer enters into Dīkṣā, he bathes with a saying wherein the waters are invoked as the power that purifies and takes away all impurities[376]. The bride and the bridegroom have a bath before the marriage, or they perform ablutions. A woman must bathe before magic can be used to counter her barrenness, likewise before parting her hair, when pregnant, etc. But in contrast, the one who subjects oneself to practices which impart special holiness or sanctity, should not bathe before the end of the period during which this special character is present in him. In turn, this period during which bathing is forbidden, concludes with a bath that washes away that special character and prevents it thereby from the danger of being carried over into profane life. We have considered above (p. 223 ff.) the distinctive application of these views to the offerer of the Soma-sacrifice, in the correspondence of the Dīkṣā imparting him sanctity and the Avabhṛtha-bath taking it away. We have also referred there to analogy related to the customs to be observed by a Brahmana-pupil. Here, a purifying bath[377] precedes the acceptance-ceremony which establishes the character of sanctity peculiar to it. The bath, that concludes the studentship, takes away this character. It would follow therefrom, that in the intervening period bathing must have been forbidden. This would border practically on infeasibility and would not have been practised, at least during the epoch of the ritual-texts under consideration[378]. However, during the year-long period of initiation analogous to the studentship of the Brahmana-pupil, and which is associated[379] with the trimming of the beard (*godāna*) of the growing lad and it is expressly forbidden 'to bathe, to comb, to brush the teeth and wash the feet[380]'. It is part of the ascetic practices related to the celebration of the festival of seasons (*cāturmāsya*) not to 'enter the water before a purificatory bath (*avabhṛtha*)[381]'; here the intimate connection between the ban on bathing for a period and bathing at the end of it becomes quite clear. In a verse that describes one's striving to submit oneself to asceticism (*tapas*) as useless[382], it is said, 'What is all this dirt, this skin, the beard, what is this asceticism?' The dirt, i.e., obviously the avoidance of bathing, is characteristic of one who wants to acquire special magic power through Tapas. It appears that this way of thinking is also applied to the animal that is integrated into a sacred act: the sacrificial steed, which is consecrated before being offered and then set free for a year, had to be kept away during that time 'from waters where it is possible to bathe[383]'.

Shaving

Like the rules for bathing mentioned above, there are rules for *shaving*[384]. The custom of shaving is an ancient one, especially in initiatory ceremonies held for the child one year or some years after birth and later for the adolescent—here, the hair is done after the fashion distinctive of any one family, and later, even the beard is cut[385]. This rite is considered as a purification of the head and also as an act leading to longevity and happiness, connected particularly with the propriety of gentilic norms[386]. Undoubtedly, the purification from the taboo associated with hair is also at least implied here[387]. Even elsewhere, shaving, like bathing, appears as an act of purification, particularly preparatory to the commencement of a sacred deed or a consecration or prior to entry into any new situation in life. Thus, one who solemnizes the New moon or Full moon sacrifices shaves his hair (except the tuft which is the mark of distinction of a family) and his beard[388]; even the clipping of nails is mentioned. The Soma-sacrificer, who as we mentioned above, bathes on his entry into Dīkṣā, also has his hair, beard and nails cut[389]. One saw in it the doing away of that which is not pure in the body, of the 'dead skin'[390]; there may also be the intention of making the family mark of distinction visible as far as possible during the sacrifice, though not expressed explicitly anywhere. Further, shaving and clipping the nails are also apparently acts of purification, done after a death by the survivors along with ablution, rekindling of the fire and the procurement of new utensils[391]: the old hair which had come in contact with the powers of death should not accompany one in one's new life. Doing the same to the dead before funeral does not have obviously any meaning[392] other than the riddance of the impurity caused by death to the old existence, prior to the quasi-sacrifice of cremation and the entry of the deceased into a new existence.

But in contrast, we come across instances—corresponding to bathing—where the cutting of hair is forbidden.

If a person is fully infused with a curative substance, then it is considered to be spread all over the body inclusive of hair and nails. Thus, it is said of one who recites for himself the Veda-texts, in full knowledge of their mystic significance, that he 'is filled with Tapas (asceticism) upto the tips of his nails'[393], even if he is resting, anointed and bejewelled, in a comfortable place. On the fourth day, after the marriage, before cohabitation for the first time, the newly wed girl is annointed 'including hair and nails'[394] with water mixed with the remains of sacrificial offerings which can dispel evil. Even earlier, we came across a verse wherein Tapas is embodied in the dirt of the ascetic and in the skin he wears and also in his beard[395]: he is infused with the magic substance upto his beard. It follows naturally that a person is not allowed to get rid of the hair and the beard as long as he has to preserve the corresponding power in them; perhaps, on account of the misgiving that the shorn hair may carry the dangerous substance to an inappropriate place and give even enemies a chance to do harm to the person who is consecrated. Thus, the verse mentioned above shows that the ascetic lets his beard grow. The injunction against bathing, also against the cutting of hair is equally valid for the year-long observances at the time of the trimming of the lad discussed above (p. 229)[396]. Consecıation of the king is followed by a year's observance. In this period, he is allowed to rub his body clean, but is not allowed to bathe, he may cut his hair short, but is not supposed to shave it[397]. A *Brāhmaṇa-text*[398] gives clearly the reason for it: 'That is the collected power and the juice of the waters in which he is bathed (at the time of consecration): when poured, it reaches first his hair. If he were to cut his hair, he would let this glory miss the mark and disappear: he, therefore, does not cut his hair, for the observance lasts a year.'

Such an observance is naturally concluded with a hair-cut, like not-bathing with a bath. For the king who has celebrated the royal consecration, one does after a year the 'Soma-sacrifice which marks the conclusion of this observance with a hair-cut in name only[399]'. We found, if not for the studentship itself, then at least for a like observance the injunction against shaving besides that against bathing: in the ceremony (*samāvartana*) at the close of studentship, shaving of hair and beard, hair on the body and dipping of nails go together with the ritual bath[400]. The Soma-sacrificer who has had a bath and a shave before the introductory consecration puts aside the character of the consecration through a fresh bath and shave[401].

It may also be mentioned that even smiling, like shaving, was considered as the loss of power. The old Vedic comparison of lightning and laughter is well-known; the idea being that one who smiles gives out to a certain extent some light-energy. Therefore, the rule was drawn that the Dīkṣita, the recipient of the Soma-consecration, must keep his hand in front of his mouth while smiling 'for preserving the radiance[402]'.

Celibacy

Finally, it becomes quite obvious that the idea of avoiding the loss of energy or substance, plays some part in it, even if not the only motif as in the injunctions against bathing and shaving as also sexual intercourse. Where prescribed that the sacrificial horse must be kept away from waters meant for bathing as also from the mares[403], the close parallelism of both the rules with those that prescribe men abstinence from bathing and sexual intercourse on certain occasions, is obvious. A *Brāhmaṇa-text* which prescribes an expiatory offering for an act of copulation by the sacrificial horse, explains the effect of this offering through which the sacrificer 'puts seed by means of seed into the horse'[404]. The flaw is in the loss of consecrated substance. Likewise, there are *mantras* for the loss of semen suffered by the Dīkṣā-initiate or by the Brahmana-pupil, also for the man who has visited a woman not supposed to be touched by him, etc.[405]. Here, the idea of power or energy lost and replaced is clearly evident.

THE PRAYER[406]

Spontaneous Prayer and Fixed Rites

The sacrifice was accompanied by prayer. We have already described how it became a part of sacred action[407]. This is the appropriate place to make a few more remarks about the form and content of prayer, as also about the views of the Vedic poets on the nature and power of prayer.

Of course, besides the ritually prescribed prayer, there was spontaneous prayer, according to exegency and wish. 'The merchant, always on the move, has reached the shore' through his prayer. 'As Atri, when descending into the cavern, called on you loudly like a wailing woman, you came to him O Aśvins, with the freshest and most auspicious fleetness of an eagle[408]'. The spontaneous prayer of this age could have been hardly different from, say, the naming of an individual concrete desire associated somewhat with expressions which commended with warmth to the deity the wish and the person of the worshipper; one cannot think of a prayer here, which could have been the expression of a sensitive inner life in constant communion with the deity. Besides, the spontaneous prayer directed to a specific wish was to all appearances essentially confined by precocious development of a ritual art, which had more or less foreseen every wish, and had fixed for it an offering, howsoever small it be—most often offerings of sacrificial butter—together with the appropriate *mantra*. For a sick man, one sacrifices the six offerings of cooked rice with the hymn: 'I set you free through the sacrificial meal, that you may live'; one who desires rich stock of cattle, sacrifices thousand offerings of the dung of a pair of calves; one who desires luck in commercial venture, offers bits of the wares with a formula invoking divine blessing meant for the trade[409]: everywhere, there is a finished liturgic form; and even if it does not concern here the tradition of the ancient Vedic age, we have good reason to date back to it the furthering of rituals with a pronounced tendency towards rigidness. It is questionable whether, at that time, the spontaneous immediacy of prayer was accorded in essence greater freedom.

The Liturgic Prayer

Prayer in liturgic form appears mostly, though not always, in connection with the sacrificial acts. Those prayer-hymns unaccompanied by offerings display some measure of independence towards the sacrifice. They are addressed to the deities of the morn in the early hours of the day of the Soma-sacrifice: to Agni illuminating the darkness, to the Dawn and to the Aśvins.[410] Another example of a prayer without offering is the 'twilight devotion'; according to *Śāṅkhāyana*[411], a Brahmana-pupil does this 'in the forest, holding a piece of wood, sitting day by day in silence till the stars appear, in that he utters after the twilight the mighty words, the Sāvitrī[412] and the benediction. Likewise, in the morning, facing the east, standing, till the disc of the sun is seen'. Such a prayer could be naturally strengthened by gestures of adoration like the Upasthāna, the act of standing in veneration before an object of worship, e.g., in front of the sacred fire or sun. A *Brāhmaṇa-text* says about the beneficial effect of such an Upasthāna directed towards one's sacrificial fire[413]:'the supplicant finds a donor, but the preserver may overlook even the one he is to preserve. When he says (to the fire): 'I am to be preserved by you; preserve me!', then the fire knows him; then it remembers that it has to protect him.'

The prayer, determined by the ritual—or anything similar to the prayer—could also take the form of a mere thought. In the liturgic recitation of the verse, where the word 'rich in strong sons' occurs, the priest is supposed to think of a strong son, if the wife of the sacrificer desires one; likewise, he should think of the foetus, if the wife of the sacrificer so desires; if he prepares himself to crush the Soma-shoots with a pressing-stone, he should think of his enemy in order to direct the crushing blows at him; elsewhere in the ritual, the sacrificer should think: 'Agni, Vāyu, Lightning, Moon! May I attain communion with you'; or anything else he desires[414]. Incidentally, the interpretation of such a thought prescribed by the ritual as prayer, is, in our sense of the word, inaccurate. It appears, it is not concerned so much with the articulation of a desire to the gods as knowers of human thoughts, but rather with guiding or influencing, in a definite manner, a procedure endowed with magic effects, through the magic power of one's own thought.

Contents of the Prayer

As we explained earlier[415], the liturgic prayers for praising and invoking the god in a sacrifice are mainly in poetic form. In contrast, the *mantras* for the consecration of the sacrificial utensils, of the individual manipulations are in prose-form. Thus, several prayers in prose-form are to be found, on occasion even within the central features of sacrificial ritual[416]. For instance, the prayer pertaining to the Horse-sacrifice referred to earlier (p. 207), which extends beyond individual interests into the domain of public life. In the New moon and Full moon sacrifices, the Hotar says a different prayer: 'O sacrificer, may both heaven and earth be kind to you at this sacrifice. They bring salvation to the family, they let trickle fresh dew, fearless and silent, they cover the broad meadow and bestow security; they make the skies rain and the waters run, they bring salvation, give comfort, they have juice and milk in plenty; it is good to approach them and live upon them he (the sacrificer) implores them for longevity, for the prosperity of his progeny, for wealth, for dominant status among his kindred, for a plentiful spread of the sacrificial meal, for heavenly life, for all love. May he obtain, what he has sought through this sacrifice and find joy therein. May the gods give that to him. That which the God Agni gets from the gods, we men get from Agni[417]'.

These prose-prayers not lacking in power and dignity have yet little of warmth and fervour, of the solemn sublimity of those prayers where the Old-Testament-like devotee implores the gods for his welfare and the welfare of his people. In a modest, matter-of-fact tone, the priest enumerates the goods that can be promised from the sacrifice to the sacrificer, eventually also to the people, or more precisely to the higher echelons amongst them—all quite within the sphere of positive earthly goods: long life, riches, respectable rank, favourable weather, finally even an abode in heaven; there is no mention of spiritual or ethical good[418].

Those ancient prayers meant partly for recitation and partly for singing, particularly in the Soma-sacrifice, are connected with those mentioned last. They form the collection of the Ṛgveda, and therewith the main bulk of the Vedic prayers, and are a level with those prose-prayers mentioned just now. But they deal mainly with praise of the god besides expressing the desires of men; they glorify his greatness and might, his mysterious being and his deeds; I have already characterised the tone predominant in these glorifications (p. 2f.). It is briefly joined by the request for gifts from the god who is satisfied by such praise[419]. 'We have wishes, the Lord of the dun-coloured horses', it is said to Indra, 'you are liberal; here we are; here are our prayers'. And Indra himself speaks to the pious: 'While pressing the Soma, ask riches from me[420]'. These riches are expressed mostly in broad and general terms, given less individualistic traits of that liturgic poetry. One asks for gifts, treasures, blessing, protection and victory over temptation. If the language of the devotee is more precise, then there is usually talk of longevity and healthy progeny, of cattle and horses, of chariots and gold. Further it is said of enemies, misers and Brahmana-haters that evil should befall them; that the god should take away their belongings and give them to the pious. There is hardly talk of goods like rightful thinking or of not doing things that invite divine punishment; in the atmosphere of contentedness prevalent here, the prayers for reconciliation with the angry god, for liberation from the fetters of sin[421] recede well behind the prayers of the rich and the fortunate for power and victory. One supports one's prayers by remembering one's own zeal or the old familiarity with the god and his earlier benevolent deeds—it is more a question of such remembrance than giving real thanks; the god is given to understand that, if one were to be like him, and he likes man, favourable hearing and granting of opulent blessings will not be long in coming. The note of passion, of humble devotion of the striving after lofty aims of mankind are unknown to the superficial nature of these prayers.

Effect of the Prayer

The Vedic poets[422] see in the prayer, in 'this oblation fashioned in the heart'[423], a means to delight and to invigorate the god and whose efficacy is hardly secondary to the actual sacrifice. Of importance is naturally the element of praise upon which rests the efficacy of the prayer; the god finds pleasure in them; he gets pleasure in doing new things from memories of the old. Special preferences of the individual prayer intensify the effect.

Soon the poet recommends his hymn as the one preserved by, as the one inherited from his forefathers; soon he commands to the gods his 'new and beautiful prayer, coming fresh, newly born.' But, above all, the hymn must have immaculate, artistic beauty. The singer has fashioned it 'as an efficient, diligent man fashions a chariot', he has freed it of all flaws 'like the one who cleans the corn with a swingle', like 'purified butter'. 'A new, shining, beautiful prayer is prepared for Agni Vaiśvānara, as one purifies the Soma.' Such prayers, 'born from the thoughts as the rain is born from the clouds', run to the gods as the rivers flow to the ocean, like the cows to the pen. They lick him and low at him like the mother-cow does to the calf. They coax him and embrace him like the wives their husbands, the beloveds the lovers. They strengthen him like the Soma-drink. 'The donors of the Soma magnify Indra's might through their hymns.' 'Great he is, may his body become greater, the one praised in song and hymn.' 'The priests, having elevated Indra through their songs have made him great, that he may kill the snake.' 'They harness, with the hymn to the swift god, dun-coloured horses to the broad, broad-yoked chariot, the horses that drive Indra, those horses harnessed by the word.' The effect of the hymn and the song on the divine listener, to give him pleasure and to narrate to him the wishes of men alludes here to the independent magic effect, resting of its own upon the original power of the consecrated word. Again, we meet here the intermingling of the word of prayer and the word of magic, to which we had referred in another context (see p. 186) as the exact counter-image of the intermingling of the sacrificial act and the magic act[424].

THE INDIVIDUAL SACRIFICES AND FESTIVALS

The Sacrifices of the Course of the Day, Month and Year

In surveying the individual sacrifices of the Vedic cult we shall give first preference to those recurring at regular intervals: for, a calendar of festivals had developed long since out of the disorderliness of worship that was dictated by momentary needs[425]. The evidence of the Ṛgveda fails here, apart from a few clues here and there: it is to be expected, given the predominance of the old hymnic poetry in respect of the Soma-sacrifice. But if all facts are taken into consideration, even this sphere of the regular sacrifices can be dated back in all probability to the most ancient times or at least their basic features.

The Fire Sacrifice

Sacrifices accompany the course of the day, month and year. Of course, it is doubtful, whether the actions of the morning and the evening '*Fire-sacrifice*' associated with the day were, in their original intent wholly valid sacrifices; it appears to be more appropriate to understand them in the first place as a regular, and obviously, as a cultic embellishment of the service of the sacrificial fire so necessary for its preservation[426]. Besides the fire-sacrifice, oblations were made to all creatures in the morning and in the evening. One gives thought to the gods and the genii ruling in and about the house; food is placed adoors, on the mortar, on the bed and in the water-barrel. Offerings for the souls of the dead are placed in the south where the heavenly abode of the dead lies. Feed is thrown for dogs and birds. Pregnant women, boys and the aged are fed.

The New Moon and the Full Moon Sacrifices

The New moon and Full moon sacrifices follow a monthly course. An annual pattern is followed mainly by the three festivals held at an interval of each on full moon days at the beginning of spring, of the rainy season and of the cold season. In the simple order of the Veda, the customary festival days are the two main aspects of the lunar month, the full moon notably, and next to them in importance, the waning mid-half of the month. There was no calendar which, like the fasti of ancient Rome, could have converted, without any distinction, days into festival days at any given time of the month; further, there were no traces of steady growth and coalescence of elements originating from here and there. Priestly assiduousness that felt increasingly the claims of numerous deities to a share in the regular sacrifices, did not, however, satisfy them by organising more festivals, but by conferring validity on the ancient, ever numerous gods. None of the customary Vedic sacrifices, at least in that stage of development evident in the ritual-texts, is dedicated to a single god[427].

Perhaps, besides Agni, Indra is to be seen as the most important god in the cake-offering of the New moon and Full moon sacrifices, which is shared, according to the ritual-texts amongst various deities. Not that there is anything in his nature that has to do with the phases of the moon; the moon just indicates the time to pay respects to the most powerful of the gods. I think, this sacrifice in its frequent recurrence is to be considered as the main feature of the regular cult[428]. The new moon, or generally the waning moon, was also the period for the souls of the ancestors to receive their monthly feeding.

The Four-monthly Festivals and Śunāsīrīya

Whereas the ceremonies related to the course of the day and the month mentioned above appear as essentially identical in the sacrificial ritual of the one as well as the three fires (p. 197ff.), the three festivals alone, that accompany the seasons of the year corresponding to the natural tripartite division of the Indian year into hot, wet and cold periods, belong to the major rituals, the view must have been prevalent that the person who maintains only one fire at home, is not capable or worthy of its celebration. Besides the ritual tripe dished out by the later Vedic organizers of the sacrifice, there is a series of old rites which have retained the unalloyed characteristics of popular cult-life. The Maruts are particularly in the foreground in each festival. They would not have got prominence in this manner so easily in the post-Ṛgvedic period. In the second celebration held at about the beginning of the rainy season, the offering of Karīra-fruits thrown on the sacrificial offerings represents a rain-magic corresponding to the cultic use of these fruits elsewhere[429]; the seasonable commencement of rains is to be furthered. A *Brāhmaṇa-text*[430] says explicitly 'that Karīka-fruits are taken to get rain, to get the blessing of food'. Sacrifice is to be made to Varuṇa on the northern side of the sacrificial place, and on the southern, to the Maruts. Figures of a ram and a sheep made of barley-flour and pasted with wool, with the sexual organs displayed prominently, are added to the offerings. The major expiatory sacrifice pertaining to this celebration, the burning of the barley-cake and the penitence of the consort of the sacrificer has been already discussed above (p. 223). A bath similar to the Avabhṛatha (p. 188) concludes the celebration. The association with fertility is clear from the ram and sheep. Does it concern here the fertility of the herds because of the ram and the sheep? Or does it concern the fruitfulness of corn because the figures are made of barley-flour, the animals being then the representatives of the corn-demon[431]? A customary First fruits-sacrifice is out of question here; for spring would be the right time for barley[432]. But it appears that, as in the rest of this festival, the idea of the warding off of sin, calamity and the wrath of the gods dominates; here also, the desire for fertility appears with the special expression for appeasing Varuṇa's displeasure[433]: Varuṇa's cereal is the barley, his animal the ram. Both point to this god who also plays a rôle in the expiatory rites mentioned above[434]. It is understandable that a celebration which has to do mainly with the supernatural, has to end with a bath.—A big feast for the dead, a sort of All Souls Day, is tied up with the third of the three festivals of the seasons: the ancient winter commemoration of the Indo-European period[435] can be said to have fitted itself at this juncture into the frame-work of the Indian rituals. Besides the commemoration, there is a sacrifice to Rudra Tryambaka, the dangerous god skilled in the use of the bow, whose attackes one wants to ward off for the good of oneself and the cattle, whose power of healing one wants to have for oneself. One offers to him sacrificial flat cakes, one for every member of the family at the crossroad, the abode of the sinister gods; an additional flat cake[436] is buried in a mole-hill: 'That is your share, Rudra; mole is your animal': 'with that, one assigns to him the mole amongst the animals: thus he does not harm the other animals', explains a *Brāhmaṇa*[437]. One chants, 'We have given Rudra his share, the god Tryambaka, so that he may let us prosper, that he may make us happy and lead us on to a suie goal. You[438] are medicine: medicine for the cattle, medicine for horse and man, prosperity to the ram and the mother-sheep.' One goes around the fire three times towards the left, clapping the hands on the left thigh, and three times towards the right, clapping the hands on the right thigh; even the unwed girls of the house go around with other members of the family, and they pray to Tryambaka who grants a husband to a virgin, 'I would like to loosen myself from here like the cucumber from its stalk, not from there', i.e., from the parental home, but not from the husband's house. At the end of it, the remaining pieces are flung into the air, retrieved and hung[439] in two baskets at the ends of a cart-beam, as food on the way for Rudra, so that he may go afar without harming the man.

These are then on the whole three seasonal sacrifices with their popular customs. The fourth one, the Śunāsīrīya, is associated with these festivals purely due to the artificed theoreticians of the sacrifice. The name tells us, that it is dedicated to the genii who bless the plough. If this festival of the plough, for the sake of conformity with the three other festivals spread over twelve months, is now linked with a thirteenth month, an intercalary month for adjustments of differences in the lunar and the solar calendars, then it is pure fancy that has imported an interpretation into the nature of this festival[440].

Solstice Customs

Amongst the rites concerning the seasons of the year, there are also vestiges of customs connected with the solstice, to be more exact, the customs of the winter solstice[441]. Traditionally, they appear in the context of the cycle of Soma-sacrifices spread over the year, and concurrent with the sun's movement. Thus, they are woven into the frame-work of the Soma-ritual and, albeit superficially, exclusively with its priestly ceremonial. 'The drums are beaten; (The priest) beats the earthen kettle-drum. The noise-makers make noise'[442]: this refers obviously to the frightening away of the spirits and the souls of the dead which are powerful especially in the darkest season of the year. An Aryan gets into a scrap with a Śūdra for possession of a white, round hide, explained[443] correctly by tradition as the image of the sun; the Śūdra has to let go of it and run away; the other strikes him down with the very same hide. The import is clear: the sun is in danger of falling prey to the dark powers, but one succeeds in preserving him for the Aryan folk. That one of the priests has to sit on the swing[444], refers perhaps to the sun which is called in the *Ṛgveda* (VII, 87, 5) 'the golden swing in the sky'. With the span of his right hand, he touches the swing-board and the earth and says, 'The great united with the great': one misses the object[445], but there is a vague suggestion here that the sun has reached his perigee very close to the earth. And added to it are other customs not directly connected with the sun's movement. One cohabits on an enclosed spot on the sacrificial place. One shoots arrows through a cowhide. Girls laden with pitchers of water dance around the fire. They finally empty the pitchers into the fire and sing:

'How sweet the cows smell, hurrah!
Here is sweet sap!
Pleasant smell the cows exude!
Sweet is the sap!
The cows are mothers to the butter!

Sweet is the sap!
In our care, may they multiply!
Sweet is the sap!
We shall bathe the cows!
Sweet is the sap!', etc.

Obviously, it has to do everywhere with the fertility of man and nature. The sexual rite is directed towards that end. The arrow-shots, it appears, ought to pierce through the occluding clouds; the vital winter-rains must fall; there must be water for the cowherds. The crude palpableness of the old folk-customs has retained itself completely, and it stands out against the ritual artifices in whose midst tradition has placed them.

Linked with the course of the year is the festival, rather the festivals of the first fruits[446] depending upon the different species of fruits: an attempt was made to establish a firm, if not a complete, connection with the new moon and full moon phases, once felt as customary festival periods.[447]

Finally, there are a few rites associated with certain dates, to be performed only with the domestic sacrificial fire, and having no part in the ritual of the three fires: thus, a sacrifice for the prosperity of herds[448] to be performed on the full moon of Āśvayuja (around the beginning of autumn); further, the rites of the serpent-cult[449] which are probably part of the rites of a comparatively later period: the rites pertaining to the serpent cult are performed both at the beginning and the end of the period where the threat from the serpents is greater (on the full moon of Śrāvaṇa [July-August] and of Mārgaśīrṣa [November-December]). Finally, there are the celebrations of the three Aṣṭakās[450] to be performed during the winter months. Their timing—the last quarter of the moon of the relevant months—is compatible with the meaning which appears to emerge from the uncertain and vague references in the texts: in the first place, they are obviously the manes to whom the Aṣṭakās are intended so that a similar meaning could be arrived at for those celebrations of the domestic sacrificial ritual, like for the feast of the souls in the ritual of the three fires, that is tied up with the sacrifice of the third season of the year (above p. 237)[451]. The manes were offered dumplings and an animal, both customary in the cult of the Dead. 'Even if he (the sacrificer) is without any means, he should celebrate the Aṣṭakās with an animal. Or he should prepare a sacrificial cake. Or he should throw fodder to a cow. Or he should kindle brushwood, in the forest, and say: 'That is my Aṣṭakā'. But he should not fail to do something'[452].

The Pravargya Celebrations

In attempting to proceed to the Soma-sacrifice from the sacrifices which make up the regular Vedic ecclesiastical calender, we may mention first a rite that appears traditionally to be part of the Soma-sacrifice, rather the preparations for it, but which probably must have been originally an independent rite: the sacrifice of boiled milk to the Aśvins (Pravargya, Gharma)[453].

A vessel, finger breadth in height is heated. A silver plate is kept below it and a golden plate above. Cow's milk and goat's milk are poured in it and offered to the Aśvins; the sacrificer partakes of it from the vessel. The ritual-texts prescribe the repetition of this celebration, daily in the morning and in the afternoon, over a number of days preceding the Soma-sacrifice; only the morning-celebration appears prominently in the *Ṛgveda* corresponding to the nature of the Aśvins. 'Agni makes the face of the Dawns glow; the singers' pious voices have ascended to the gods. Borne on your chariot, Aśvins, turn hither, and come unto our full and rich libation'—thus begins a hymn (V, 76), and another speaks of the glowing draughts that accompany the Dawns (VII, 33, 7). I think—if I may hazard a guess—that here is a case of magic referring originally to the sun[454]. 'They have brought the Gharma from the sun', it is said in the *Ṛgveda* (X, 181, 3). The heat of the glowing draught represents the heat of the sun; the sacrifice should assure it, strengthen it, but above all, for the benefit of the sacrificer. Of course, the proof of this can rest only upon the later Vedas which is understandable, given the sources at hand. But in the actions as also in the *mantras*, they allow the concept of heat to stand out as the leitmotif; further, a series of references point out especially to the heat of the sun. Earlier (p. 228), we mentioned the observances connected with the secret percepts: it was forbidden, for example, to go covered in the sun, to spit or to urinate: this shows very clearly that the offerer of Gharma is considered as having a special alliance with the sun. From the *mantras*[455] belonging to the Gharma-celebration, I quote here the invocation to Savitar: 'whose upward surge, in its impetus, has made the light shine; the wise one, whose golden hand has created the sun.' 'I saw the watchman, not taking rest, going up and down on his beat'—obviously, this refers to the sun[456]. The following among the *mantras* of the *Yajurveda* allude to the boiling cauldron, or speak of it[457]: 'The fire glows, hailing together with the fire, with the god Savitar, with the sun.' 'To the heart you, to the spirit you, to the heaven you, to the sun you.' 'I sacrifice you to the sun-ray, to the rain-giving one'[458]. 'Set aglow the sun's glow.' 'Sun you are, give me sun.' 'Singing, they composed the great song[459]; thus they held fast the sun, made him shine.' And wholly in the sense of these verses do the *Brāhmaṇas*[460] offer explanations for the individual sacrificial actions, which state frequently that the Gharma-celebration or the boiling cauldron used therein is the sun[461]. As for the milk contained in the cauldron, it can be said that the white fluid is the symbol of the sun's brightness. 'Radiance you are, light are you', the priest says to it[462], and a verse of the *Ṛgveda*[463] aligns it with the feats of Indra by stating that the god 'has awakened the finished in the raw one (i.e., the milk in the cows) and led the sun up to the heavens.' In that one makes the milk scalding hot, one gives heat to the sun: and if, in accordance with the tendency emphasised many times, magic assumes the form of the sacrifice enjoyed by gods, which of the deities would then have the right to receive this sacrifice, like the Aśvins who rule over the morning before the appearance of the sun?

The Soma-sacrifice[464]

The Soma-sacrifice is beyond compare among all the other cult-practices of Vedic lore. It is questionable whether it had in real life the pre-eminence it had in the tradition. The relatively close circles of the priestly schools were attracted to the Soma-sacrifice by material interests; further, it provided an avenue for their poetic fancy and their propensity to subtle trumpery. The high esteem with which the priests, therefore, regarded the Soma-sacrifice, does not prove that it enjoyed similar esteem in the religious life of the common people. Only a few must have been able to perform the Soma-sacrifice; when celebrated, it could have had at best, for the masses, the character of an incomprehensible play that was witnessed passively. In fact, it plays no significant rôle in the descriptions of old Indian folk-life not pertaining especially to the Vedic sphere, for instance in the Buddhistic literature.

The Soma-sacrifice was not fixed by the calendar, at least, not with the same rigidity that determines the celebrations discussed above. As for the rule found in the later texts, that it is to be performed in spring or every spring, it is really doubtful whether this originates from an older period; thus, the rule appears to recommend the spring only as a favourable period without assigning the sacrifice surely to it, as is the case with the full moon-sacrifice on full moon day. The character of the Soma-sacrifice as an extra-ordinary act of liberality towards the gods and priests practised by the rich and the elite is not nullified by that regulation.

The Soma cannot be offered like the sacrificial cake or animal to this or that god depending upon the exigencies. According to the fixed order of pressing the Soma three times a day (morning, noon and afternoon), and added thereto the nightlong rites during "Atirātra'[465], the Soma is offered to a series of deities, which admits of individual additions but otherwise with fixed main features, comprising in its intent all deities[466]: the more important are named individually and the inexhaustible bulk of minor gods share the offerings made to 'all gods'. Thus, the Soma-sacrifice is a general drinking festival for gods and priests.

Indra as its Principal God

Indra enjoys the most important position of honour amongst the divine guests. This ritual also gives him the lion's share of the songs and sacrificial *mantras* which celebrate him above all other gods as the drinker of Soma, as the god to whom the eagle brought the Soma and as the god who performed valorous deeds inebriated by the Soma[467]. He also receives amongst other gods, alone as well as with his divine companions, offerings and laudations when Soma is pressed at morn. But then, the noon-pressing belongs to him alone, forming apparently the acme of the whole sacrifice[468]. Here the most excellent melodies—Bṛhat and Rathaṃtara—are sung to the texts glorifying Indra.

The Gods and the Three Pressings

According to the ritual of the later period, a great Indra-litany is assigned to each one of the four priests in charge of spoken recitation.[469] To the pressing of the Soma belongs the pompous recitation of a priest who was not occupied during the celebration at morn, namely the Grāvastut, the 'Extoller of the pressing-stone'[470]: it is not an accident that he appears only when Indra has the main part in the Soma. Thus, everything here is full of high praise of this one god. Finally, Indra gets afresh his share in the third pressing along with other gods[471]. It is said in the *Ṛgveda* (IV, 35, 7), 'Lord of Bay Steeds, at dawn the juice you drank: Yours, only yours, is the noon-day libation. Now drink with the wealth-bestowing Ṛbhus, whom for their skill you made friends, O Indra.'

It is difficult to decide here whether the preference given to Indra is to be explained by the fact that the sacrifice of the intoxicating drink which is meant in the Avesta and in the Veda for all the deities was intended for the Storm-god according to its recent origin; it is very difficult to arrive at a definite solution of this problem which dates far back into the Indo-European period.

As for the other deities participating in the Soma-sacrifice, besides Indra, at a secondary level, we must first consider, as main documentary evidence, the litany occupying a prominent place among recitations of the Hotar at the morning libation[472], i.e., the 'litany of the fork-thills' (Prayoga-śāstra). We can trace this back with certainty to the *Ṛgveda* which contains several detailed examples of this litany though divergent from one another[473]. The order of priority of the gods is—apart from those deviations—as under: Vāyu—the wind, who perhaps as the fastest of the gods has established claim to the first drink of the Soma, then the pairs, Indra and Vāyu, Mitra and Varuṇa, the Aśvins; further again Indra, all the gods and finally Sarasvatī. If we find litanies recited by the three assistants of Hotar to Mitra-Varuṇa, Indra and the pair Indra-Agni in the ritual of the later texts at the morning pressing, then these data add on Agni to the list of the deities enumerated above, of course, not as an independent deity, but along with Indra; several *Ṛgvedic* hymns suggest the probability of the ancientness of this pair of deities as the receivers of the Soma[474].

We have already referred to the mid-day pressing which exclusively belongs to Indra, with the Maruts entering the picture only as his retinue. According to the ritual of the later Vedas, the evening pressing includes the drawings of the Soma for the Ādityas, for Savitar, for all the gods, for Agni as the one accompanied by the divine consorts; afterwards, for Indra as the lord of the bay steeds. The order of the litanies departs from it to some extent; two are recited: to all gods—with the main sections devoted to Savitar, Heaven and Earth, the Ṛbhus and all gods—and to Agni together with the Maruts, which litany, among its motley components, contains also a few verses to the divine consorts[475]. I have no doubt that these orders deviate in their essentials from those of the *Ṛgvedic* period. According to the data of the old collection of hymns, the Ṛbhus, or the Ṛbhus with Indra, got apparently the major portion of the evening Soma; they have been pushed to a relatively subordinate position in the later order[476]. The participation of the Ādityas[477] in the Soma-sacrifice, the peculiar link between Agni and the Maruts[478] for which there is little to suggest, given the nature of the concerned deities, is recorded so rarely by the Ṛgveda, that one may presume here an instance of the peculiarity of individual family-rituals which had not yet attained in those times universal recognition. The *Ṛgveda* lets also the divine consorts partake of the Soma. Likewise, the approach of Indra's steeds together with Indra himself accords fully with the *Ṛgvedic* views—irrespective of whether it took place at one particular place and in one particular form, as in the later rituals. But I think it probable that the offering of the Soma to Savitar does not date back to olden times; for otherwise references to the Soma offered to him could hardly be absent in the *Ṛgvedic* hymns to this god[479]. It is significant that one had to choose, rather, to compare a non-*Ṛgvedic* verse[480] as a specific verse to make the offering (*yājyā*) to Savitar, so that one could refer therein to the Soma-draught of Savitar.

We had to dwell on these details a little longer so that the relationship of the Soma-sacrifice to the older and the younger ranks of the Vedic world of gods could be brought out. A deity like Prajāpati, the creator of the world, so important to the later Vedas, could get a place in Soma-sacrifice, in the subordinate rituals, only in easily discernable additions to the original ritual; this deity has, however, stayed away from the authentic basic elements of that sacrifice. And what is valid for Prajāpati has at least near validity for Savitar. Savitar, celebrated in so many songs of the Ṛgveda, is doubtless much older than Prajāpati, but everything points to the fact that this god with an abstract name (the 'Stimulator') and abstract character[481] belongs to the later forms of the Vedic world of gods. Obviously, the Soma-ritual must have stood firm, at least in the Vedic period, to deny entry to this god[482]. Thus, Agni also—we have thought of this fact in other context too (p. 162)—is excluded in a sense from the sphere of the Soma-drinking deities. He drinks of the Soma, rather in a subordinate position, as member of a long line of gods, on the basis of his relationship to one of the priests, to whose lineage the lineage of the gods are linked[483], or in the company of Indra[484], whose characteristics he shares to some extent, but not of his own right and with respect which would be equal to his significance in the Ṛgvedic world of ideas. We may see in these orders of the Soma-sacrifice, vestiges of an age, to which Agni, lacking still his later significance, was only a servant of gods, but not a god, with equal rites like great heavenly gods.

The Soma-Sacrifice as Rain Magic

We discussed above (p. 185, etc.) how both concepts, i.e., sacrifice as an act of liberality to win over the goodwill of gods, and magic that influences directly the course of events, cross each other in diverse ways within the Vedic cult. Thus, it is not surprising that a secondary effect, magical in nature, is attributed to the Soma-sacrifice: it is a rain-magic, not obviously, or not primarily, in so far as it prompts the mercy of the rain-giving gods, but not directly influencing the rain. The outgush of the Soma-juice from its cavity in the plant, the rustle of its trickling through the strainer were occurences quite similar to the customary practices in rain-magic, wherein a sort of image of rain or the moistening of the earth or the plants is made, in the expectation of a performance like from nature. Thus, the Soma dripping through the sieve, is also a rain-giver, being himself a son of Parjanya, the rain-god, whose fecundity has made him grow. 'He is in compact with the seed of heaven rich in milk', it is said of him. 'He creates the waters; he makes the heavens rain.' 'May the rains descend upon us from on high.' 'Clarify yourself into rain for our sake, let the rains surge upon us from the skies'[485].

General View of the Soma-Sacrifice

The texts dealing with the Soma-sacrifice portray vividly and in rich detail, the activities at the place of such a sacrifice; and at least with respect to their main characteristics, this picture can be certainly traced back to the Ṛgvedic age. Priests and lay spectators throng together[486] the sacrificial place located on a grass-plot at a commanding height. Here burn the three fires, with the sacrificial grass strewn about[487]. Betwixt them, very close to the eastern fire meant for the offerings, lies the hollowed out, grass-strewn surface of the Vedi, an elongated square with scalloped sides. Here and there one can see the various sheds, to the poles to which sacrificial animals are tethered, the seats and fire-altars of the individual priests, the vessels for spring water and holy water of all types, the pressing equipment, buckets and bowls for the Soma. In the midst of it, the flock of priests going about their work in quiet or lisping *mantras,* with numerous servants and helpers at their side; the sacrificial master himself with his consort, emaciated by the privations of the preparatory observances. The action, preceded by diverse preparations over many days, begins in the early hours of the morning with the litany to the deities astir early. It is soon followed by the preparation and offering of the sacrificial cake, then by the sacrifice of the goat to Agni or of the eleven sacrificial animals to the different deities, thereafter by the pressing of the Soma-plant, by the purification of the extracted drink through various emulsions by emptying it into and out of different vessels, and finally by the offering of the Soma to the gods and the enjoyment of the priest's share of it. In between, priests give out orders to one another, call out to one another, lend a hand to one another, pay reverence before the fire-altars, consecrate the vessels or their own body by touch, distribute among themselves the presents of the sacrificers,—presents of cattle, horses, gold, clothes. The purification of the sacred drink with the sieve of goat's hair is accompanied by a monotonous song of the three priest-singers who sit there, gazing steadfastly towards the horizon. The reciting priests recite seated. Seated opposite is the Adhvaryu, the first of the performers of the actual sacrificial act or an assistant of Adhvaryu who responds with a solemn note of cheer. These are the recitations, wherein shines forth many a thought of ingenious poetry, many a word of audacious beauty among the stereotype usages and artifices riddled with mysteries, addressed to the invisible listeners, who are thought of as sitting on the sacrificial bed of straw: the scores of gods and their consorts, above all the god Indra, who has come down astride his bay steed, undeterred by the call of other sacrificers, to enjoy the inebriating draught beckoning him. Thus the performances and recitations go on through the day after the three pressings at morn, noon and eve. There are motley invocations to the gods, some of the creation of the Indian spirit, some of Indo-Iranian or Indo-European origin. Here, we have on the one hand, at least in the picture presented by the later texts, superimposed concepts of a comparatively modern way of thinking that tries to apprehend man and nature rationally; on the other hand, lurking behind everything are ancient notions, magic actions, with their still faintly recognisable crude imprint of a remote, savage past.

Rites concerning Family life

We shall survey further the more important of the cult-practices surrounding the events in the life of a family. We shall try—as far as it is possible—to avoid any discussion of family laws which lie actually outside the pale of our study, but consider only the cultic side of these practices.

Marriage

It is quite likely[488] that the Indian marriage has retained many Indo-European rites. While, at best, questionable evidences point to the ancient custom of marriage by abduction, the Vedic nuptial rites express rather the union of man and woman, regulated in peace and solemnly, often brought about by the purchase of the woman[489], or at least influenced by vestiges of such a practice. In this marriage, the woman is subordinate to the husband, but held beside him in esteem, though she may not always be the sole companion[490]. The nuptial rites deal further with the driving away of all the evil powers, the summoning of happiness to be shared over the years and prosperous progeny. On the whole, the nuptial rites as well as other related ceremonies belong understandably more to the realm of magic than to the sacrificial cult[491]. The joining of hands signified the handing over of the bride to the groom; the stone she stepped on, imparted to her its firmness; the seven steps she had to take, led by her husband[492], and the common partaking of the sacrificial meal established the bond of friendship and togetherness. The bride was brought from her parental home to her husband in a cart[493] driving over two strings that had been laid out, one red and the other blue in colour. On entering her new home by stepping over the threshold[494], she was made to sit down on the skin of a red bull, and on her lap was placed the son of a woman who had borne only male living children. If all this was observed, the bride could hope for abundant blessings and healthy male progeny. The worship of god in these rites recedes more to the background. It is clearly directed towards Agni, the god[495] who is intimately associated with the life of the individual and the family. Thus, bride and the groom go three times round the fire[496], the divine witness to the marriage, who then has to accompany the young couple through life in his capacity as the family fire. Diverse sacrificial offerings were also made. But it is quite clear that at least, on the whole, there was no well-entrenched relationship to deities who blessed the marriage. For example, a *mantra* to be said by the bridegroom to one of the most prominent offerings, the sacrifice of roast corn out of the cupped hands of the bride reads: 'This woman speaks, strewing corn: 'May I bring luck to my relatives! May my husband live long!'[497]. This is just a common blessing wherein there is no trace of the feeling of being bound to real, personal powers that guide one's fortunes.

The nuptial rites are interespersed with numerous verses and *mantras* which invoke fleetingly this or that god, which confer this or that magic blessing. But one can hardly assert that these verses and *mantras* are of a higher order than this benediction, from whose tone departs most, in the least agreeable sense, the actual marriage hymn, the Sūryā-hymn[498] recited by a Brahmana at the marriage ceremony. This hymn, which rose in the later Vedic period, is about the marriage of Sūryā, the sun-maiden, with the Soma—that mystical Soma 'known only to the Brahmanas, partaken of by none': a song full of vacuous priestly trumpery, bereft of all poetry which could have brought the shining image of the divine couple into a meaningful association with human hopes of domestic joy. Thus, in accord with the mood pervading Indian spiritual life, the Vedic nuptial rites depart from those of the Indo-European past, taking us neither to those spheres of untrammelled beauty of the Greek marriage ceremonial nor to the regions of the sober legalistic attitude of the Romans[499]. It is a confused mass of pretentious priestly verbiage, ready to conceal all and to drown increasingly expressions of natural human feeling.

The marriage is followed by a period of abstinence lasting three nights, in India as well as in many other lands; we have already referred to it above (p. 134). Offerings of atonement (expiatory sacrifice) on the fourth day mark the end of this period; they dispel all the destructive powers inherent in the woman: the woman who kills her husband, who is childness, who causes harm to the cattle.

Rites for Pregnancy, Delivery, Childhood

The rites to be performed during *pregnancy,* later after *birth* and during *childhood* for the welfare of the child, have the same predominant magic character like the nuptial rites. The actual sacrificial acts recede also here into the background. A medicinal powder strewn into the nose of a pregnant woman makes the embryo grow into a male child. In the fourth month[500] of the first pregnancy, 'parting of the hair' is done: the hair of the woman is parted[501] with a porcupine-quill in three places[502]. Raw udumbara fruits are tied around her, no doubt, the symbol of the immature life inside the womb, to which is to be imparted the juicy richness of the udumbara fruit. Then, there are rites after the birth of a child, to give it life-force, inter alia by infusing breath; also rites to give it the power of understanding, to consecrate the food it is to eat, and above all, the naming-ceremony, held, probably as in the Indo-European custom[503], on the tenth day after birth, i.e., at the end of the period of impurity. It is mentioned that two names are to be given; one of them remains secret, obviously for protection against evil magic. In the third year[504], the ceremony of cutting the hair[505], full of religious sanctity, also common among other primitive peoples, is held along with the fashioning of a distinctive family hair-style. While vessels filled with substances like ox-dung, various species of corn, etc., which bring prosperity, are kept beside the fire, the child's hair is moistened, a few blades of grass[506] are placed, and then it is cut, in four steps on the right, and in three on the left side. The hair so cut is mixed with ox-dung and burried with it in a shrubby place or near water or in the cowshed[507]. In the same way, the ceremony of shaving the beard is held for the sixteen year old lad.

The Upanayana

The most important initiatory rite for a growing boy or youth is the Upanayana, the initiation into knowledge by a preceptor[508]; we must consider it in detail.

The Upanayana is to be performed corresponding to the three castes, in the eighth, eleventh or twelfth year counting from conception; it can, however, be postponed, respectively to the sixteenth, twentysecondth or twenty-fourth year: figures, contrived no doubt to accord with the number of syllables in the metres corresponding to the three castes and their deities.

The teacher stands near the sacred fire[509], the boy between him and the fire, bathed and bedecked, with hair shaven. The teacher twists the girdle around him three times from the right. The girdle as the accompanying mantra says, 'protects from the evil word, like a clearing agent, it purifies for us the colour, it obtains strength for us with every breath: the kind deity bringing us luck'[510]. Just as the bridegroom holds the hand of the bride in the nuptial rite, the teacher holds the hand of the pupil. Then he makes him turn from the right and places his hand on his shoulder so that it touches the place where his heart lies; the relevant *mantra* says that he takes thereby the pupil's heart into his will: 'May your thought follow my thought; may you rejoice in my word with all your heart; may Bṛhaspati join you to me'[511]. It was customary for the teacher to give his pupil an additional name which referred to his genealogy or was derived from the name of a god or a constellation. This name was to be used for exchanging greetings on solemn occasions[512]. Finally, the teacher instructs him: 'You are pupil (*brahma-*

cārin); put the faggots into the fire; drink water; do your service; do not sleep by day; control your speech till you put the faggots into the fire.' Thus the boy begins his studentship. During this period, he has to observe strict celibacy, not to eat certain foods like honey and meat[513], he has to put wood into the sacred fire of the teacher, both morning and evening, and to go begging through the village for his food. But above all, he has to learn the Veda, first the Sāvitrī. which introduces him to the study of the Veda, the verse wherein the god Savitar is requested to stimulate man's thoughts[514].

One who has received the intitiation of the Upanayana, is 'twice-born'; a rebirth follows the earlier, physical birth. 'The teacher', says a *Brāhmaṇa*[515], 'when he places his right hand on the boy, he becomes pregnant; the Brahmana is born on the third day to the recitation of the Sāvitrī[516]'. From now on, the boy is considered capable of eating the remnants of sacrificial meal[517].

The Upanayana described here is not mentioned in the *Ṛgveda*. Accordingly, one could be inclined to consider it as a new construction of later origin, risen from the ground of the Vedic scholastic institutions, and then interpret it in that context alone. It is nonetheless instructive to note how extra-Vedic sources place the whole in an altogether new light; we are transported from the sphere of the Brahmanic teaching to the prehistory of the Upanayana among the institutions of the primitive past.

Even the Avestic girdling of the sacred thread, by which a fifteen year old is accepted into the community of the Zoroastrians[518], guarantees, in revealing its common origin with the Upanayana, the pre-Vedic character of this custom. Further, we find essentially similar rites the world over among the primitive peoples. Here, it celebrates the acceptance into the community of men of a youth on his attaining puberty[519]. The idea of the second birth is found to be linked with this act also among the various tribes as in the Vedic Upanayana[520]. Rites show, that the former life vanishes, the boy is killed[521]. Then begins a new life. Very often, a new name is given to the one who is initiated. Reborn, he gains access into the knowledge of mysteries of adults. In many ways, this initiation is bound by taboos of different types, in regard to the consumption of food as in India; wearing the girdle is again, as in the Vedic ritual, wholly a part of the initiation into puberty; also, instructions concerning rules of conduct is a widespread trait, as in the Vedic Upanayana.

After all this there can be no doubt—this has already been acknowledged by ethnologists[522]—that the Upanayana is nothing but a specific Vedic form of the ancient initiation of a youth. The acceptance of the boy into the company of men and their activities became, in the spiritual atmosphere of the Brahmana-class, the acceptance of the sacred knowledge of the Veda, and corresponding characteristics find expression in the rites; more so, because it concerns the establishment of a certain form of companionship for life between teacher and pupil,[523] there are rites which have been imported there from the marriage ceremonial that aims at establishing a similar companionship. But behind these innovations, the original core of the rite cannot lie concealed, for only thereby does it align itself with the initiation of boys common to African, Australian and American primitives.

The Samāvartana

Corresponding to the Upanayana, there comes at the end of the studentship the Samāvartana, 'the return'; the main part of this rite is a bath, discussed earlier (p. 223). This is apparently considered as washing away the quality of the Brahmana-pupil.

Finally, we should speak here of the funeral rites. But it would be more appropriate to deal with them later, in the context of belief in life after death and the cult of the Dead.

Rites Concerning Public Events

Before considering a few prominent rites concerning public life, we must remember (see p. 207 above) that it was only the individual, and individual alone, in this instance solely the king, who counted as the acting subject in these rites, as the offerer of these sacrifices, and not the tribe or the people as such. Here recur chiefly those conditions obtaining in the nuptial rites discussed earlier: it is rather the magic rites that stand in the foreground, than the sacrificial rites in a limited sense. This is natural in ceremonies meant not just to awaken the mercy of the gods, but much more, to obtain for man definite powers and successes, and therefore, the efforts to attain that goal have to be given, as far as possible, immediate and concrete expression.

Rājasūya

A solemn function, or to be more exact, sprinkling with water (*abhiṣeka*), initiates the king into his office; a further act, king's coronation (*rājasūya*)[524] elevates him to the plenitude of power. Both ceremonies, not mentioned in the older tradition, must have received their exclusive distinctness only in the later Vedic period; but the magic acts, constituting their main aspects, appear to be of an altogether older origin. The celebrations are associated with the Soma-rites; may be, it was an old custom to have the divine drink at royal feasts of this kind. The king receives the function seated on a couch made from the wood of the udumbara—fig-tree—a tree which is the symbol of abundance to an Indian. A tiger-hide is spread over the couch. A goblet also of udumbara-wood, contains a liquid made of diverse things with benefic properties like butter, honey, water from rain that falls on a sunny day, etc.; this liquid is sprinkled over the king. There is a similar consecration[525] in the Rājasūya and a series of other rites assuring the king of success in all walks of life. Thus, there is a raid on a herd of cows, according to other version, arrow-shooting and looting of the less powerful relatives of the king, further a game of dice with a cow as a stake, where the king must be thought of obviously as the winner[526].

Vājapeya

The Vājapeya ('The drink of strength')[527] is considered as more sublime and effective than the Rājasūya. Here, the chariot-racing was at the fore. Of course, the sacrificer has to win: obviously a magic act, meant to impart to him swift strength (*vāja*) most visibly represented by the swift horse. It is followed by the ascent to the sun (see p. 44), i.e., to a circular wreath made of wheat-flour representing the sun. This is placed atop the pole for tethering the sacrificial animal. The sacrificer, who comes down again, receives then an unction like in the celebrations discussed above[528].

The Horse-Sacrifice

The highest sacral expression of royal might and splendour is the Horse-sacrifice (*aśvamedha*)[529]. 'He has marched around the earth victoriously and presented the sacrificial horse': this is the constant refrain of a text[530] on the greatness of the legendary kings. As mentioned earlier (p. 183) this is not actually a thanksgiving-sacrifice for successes already had, but rather one that is permissible only after such successes and intended for the fulfilment of all the lofty desires of a king. Where the gods appear in their totality, with special emphasis on Prajāpati[531], as recipients of the sacrifice in the ritual texts, then it is clear that the vestiges of another concept have been preserved at the same time: verses narrating[532] about the Horse-sacrifice of old kings mention at several places, that the sacrifice is to be made to Indra, the killer of Vṛtra—and besides him, of course, to 'the gods'[533]. We shall come back to it again. We must first describe the main features of the sacrifice.

At the bathing of the sacrificial horse dedicated for the purpose, a man of contemptible extraction had to kill a 'four-eyed dog', i.e., a dog with eye-shaped spots below the eyes—obviously a symbol of evil powers[534]—with a club[535]; it was made to swim beneath the horse standing in the water. 'The one who seeks horse's life shall be plagued by Varuṇa', so goes the *mantra* with it. After the horse was consecrated, it was set free to roam about in the open; a retinue of armed youths accompanied it and watched over it. Meanwhile, several sacrifices, relation of solemn stories, song and lute-concerts took place at home; both young and old, rich and poor took part in the celebrations full of show. Finally, after the year had passed, the horse along with countless sacrificial animals[536] was led in amidst the splendour of three days long Soma-celebrations. The chief queen had to lie down by the dead horse; woman and animal were covered with the same cloth; it is clear that thereby the fertile procreative instinct was roused and infused with the blessing emanating from the Horse-sacrifice. There were facetious exchanges between the priests and the royal wives accompanied by their retinue—is it an instance of people's high-spiritedness acquiring later a ritual substance? Or the farcical conversation of the gods who were invisibly present? Or,—this is the most probable—also a part of the magic of fertility? Exchanges of a more serious nature took place among the priests. Conundrums regarding priestly wisdom were found and solved[537]. What plenitude of blessing was thought of as inherent in this sacrifice, the barbaric, grandiose show piece of the Vedic cult, was seen from the magic power attached to the water used for the sacrificial bath after the completion of the Horse-sacrifice. The water has received the sacred power inherent in the sacrifice: 'after the sacrificer steps out, enter the evil-doers, who have not kept any observances: they are considered as purified by the Horse-sacrifice'[538].

There suggests itself indeed a reference to Indra in such a ceremony which moves wholly within the realm of martial heroism. We have encountered him above (p. 250) as the deity of Horse-sacrifice in historical or semi-historical reminiscences. But it is remarkable that Indra hardly plays the part one expects of him, either in the verses and *mantras* of the Horse-sacrifice or in the two great hymns of the *Ṛgveda* (I, 162. 163) pertaining to it. It is constantly said in the Soma-texts, 'Indra, drink the Soma; let it strengthen you.' But there is no matching statement here: 'Indra, eat the horse and may it give you swiftness and strength.' To me, it is obvious, that the interchange of deities in the Horse-sacrifice (p. 250) in favour of a relatively later and vaguely outlined deity like Prajāpati, is indicative of an inconsistent development of an old lasting relationship to a deity. Does it not have to do here more with a magic sacrifice than with a sacrifice of gifts to the god (comp. above p. 186)[539]? The horse incorporates royal might and majesty[540]. Consecrations intensify this potency inherent in it to the utmost. Its roaming about for a year (see below) brings the whole land in contact with it[541]. Finally, the animal is sacrificed; through that the magic power flows into the sacrificer in extreme concentration on the one hand; and on the other hand, its effect is spread world-wide. 'May this steed with our oblation gain us royal might.' Thus the *Ṛgveda* (I, 162, 22) expresses appropriately the import and the purpose of it all[542]. It is, therefore, not surprising, that the concepts of the Gift-sacrifice have clung to this magic sacrifice, though according to me, they are only superficial; rather it is just that which can be expected, given the facts of the case[543].

MAGIC AND THE LIKE[544]

Sacrifice and Magic; Magic—Permitted and not Permitted

The sacrificial cult described here was found to be constantly interpersed with magic acts; therefore, it is necessary to consider the elements of the Vedic magic in this context.

The well-informed will know that the magic rites are essentially the same, both among developed and less developed peoples. And what follows here, will confirm, though such a confirmation is hardly needed—that even the Indian tradition provides an example of a type prevalent the world over. We have probably reached here a highly primitive stratum—this question may be left out here—of the pre-religious concern of man for his well-being.

In any case, long before one worshipped Indra and Varuṇa, evil spirits were kept away with the aid of water and fire, noise and drum-beats; the enemy was destroyed by destruction of his image or of his hair that had been cut off; and rain was conjured up by creating an image of rain and water kingdom.

The cult of the sacrifice and the worship—as far as it is there—is, understandably, most closely connected with the operation of magic at the lowest levels of culture, the priest is more often than not a magician than priest. But further development had to draw apart the two spheres one of them being elevated increasingly in the course of powerful historical currents through the progressive development of ideas and, not the least, through the ethicizing of religion; the other sphere, persisting in its inertness being given the character of un-culture and backwardness. Is this separation of cult and magic, one can almost say, of belief and 'superstition', already present in the Vedic period? The counter-poising of the prayer-literature like that of the *Ṛgveda*[545] and the magic-literature of the Atharvaveda could appear to be speaking for that. But I think, a closer look will show this appearance to be wrong. The sacrificial invocations had established themselves fairly early as an independent type, and those prayers to the great gods offered then very little room for mentioning magic practices. But magic-hymns were *brahman*[546] indeed as much sacrificial hymns[547]. The ritual of the same sacrifices for which the prayer-hymns were meant is described to us in the remaining Vedic texts as permeated from the beginning to the end with magic customs whose practice devolved on the sacrificial priests. And as we saw, there are rites associated with certain occasions or directed towards certain goals, like marriage initiation of a boy, annointing of a king. These rites, in so far as they promote a more pronounced appearance of magic elements, depict indeed complete patterns of diverse kinds of magic, which are found mostly in forms that carry the stamp of remote antiquity. Are we to assume that the *Ṛgvedic* sacrificial priests and the poets of the hymns lived as if on an island unaffected by magic in the midst of this realm of magic dating back on the one hand to the past and on the other hand, reaching again through the priestly literature of the later period? Certainly not. On the contrary. In the *Ṛgvedic* period, the priest was at the same time a magician—which of course, does not mean that he was the only magician. We would be having a false idea of the ambience of Vedic belief, if we were to ascribe only to the most advanced minds an enlightenment that would have explained the way of sacrifice and prayer done as practicable, but rejected magic as ineffective or objectionable superstitution. Doubtless, who ever had need for magic and could use it, be it priest or layman, took recourse to it. It is in the nature of our sources that we hear less of the petty practices of private magicians than of the magic approved officially by the priest-schools. The person suspected of perfidious magic harmful to all in compact with evil spirits, was naturally regarded as disreputable person; the Vedic poet[548] complains indignantly about his enemy who calls him, the pure one, a magician and a companion of evil spirits, as also about the magician who says: 'I am pure': "May Indra slay him with his mighty weapon; let the vilest of all creatures perish." The contradiction can be well understood, if we encounter such magic, so harshly upbraided here, or similar magic equally evil in our opinion, among the customs accepted and persued unhesitatingly by the pious. Against the one who sacrifices with evil intention the alliance of 'the magician, of the destruction, of the evil demon' is invoked: 'May they destroy his truth through injustice'[549]. Whenever of the two men, who have sworn to be faithful to each other, deceives the other first, offers a certain magic-sacrifice; after that he can continue to deceive without inviting Varuṇa's wrath[550]. The ritual-texts are full of directions for the one who wants to harm one's enemy and for the priest who wishes to give the sacrifice a magical twist and thereby cause harm. And if the Law-book of Manu classified evil magic amongst the reprehensible acts, it is the same text also that says that a Brahmana should not complain to the king against an evil-doer, but throw him down with his own might: the magic formulae of the Atharvaveda are the weapons of the Brahmana which he may use against his enemies without hesitation[551].

The Magic Substance

The forces which should be made to act through magic for or against man's well-being are represented only in part as gods or spirits: whereby the gods withdraw behind those extremely perfidious and malefic spirits we discussed above (p. 137 ff.). Magic employs beside the spirits—perhaps preceding them for the stage of the Vedic development—, another class of beings: impersonal or scarcely personal substances and powers which, with the most diverse modes of influence, exist independently, or are inherent in other beings, affect human beings or their belongings in various ways and bring them good or bad fortune. The most common expression for such beings is 'body' (*tanū*). Hunger and thirst are bodies[552]; in a woman of evil disposition dwells the 'husband-killing body', 'the body of son-lessness', 'the body of herd-lessness'[553]. Or these substances are expressed neutrally: 'What is fearful in you'—'that on account of which you miscarry'—'the badly-sacrificed in the sacrifice', which lives on as a dangerous force in the sacrificial post and enters the man who touches this post[554]. Such a being is the *brahman*, the sacred-sinister substance or power of the world of the Veda which elevates the knower and the owner of this word, the *brahman*, over the layman[555]. Comparable kinds of powers are numbers, syllables, times of the day, seasons, times of the waxing and waning moon, the directions of the sky. Right and Left, and indeed, the power of thought aimed steadfastedly at a goal. If such a power and substance is embodied in some being, like the invincible, tiger-like strength in the tiger, the abundance of nourishment in cow, then it is there in all its parts, in everything that belongs to it or that is similar to it, and which comes in contact with it or had come in contact with it: not only in the flesh of the animal, but in its skin, in its hair, in the horn, and the like, and in roots, stalks, leaves, buds and seeds of plants. The characteristics of water live in water plants or aquatic animals like frog[556], the power or nature of the boar in the earth that is stirred by him[557], the power of the lightning in the wood of the tree struck by it,[558] the characteristics of the native land in the clod of the native earth which the prince driven from his land uses in the magic to aid his return[559]. The man is connected with the earth by his footprints through a magic association[560]; the image, the name contains part of that which it represents and is named after it[561]. Everywhere is seen the strong awareness of the unlimited significance of associations, of mutual dependences, indeed of a certain identity of all the beings connected in truth by howsoever weak a bond. This is characteristic for all the interior stages of culture, a way of viewing things, which goes together with the ancient strength of gentilic feeling, now hardly comprehensible to us; or to be more exact a way of viewing things which encompasses this feeling in itself as a special instance.

The influential substances can as physical beings, move about hither and thither, settle down here and there, or take this or that form. Like in the Avestic text where the royal splendour of the Yima escapes from him visibly in the form of a bird[562], a Buddhistic story[563] shows the splendour (*śrī*) of the pious Anāthapiṇḍika fluttering from one place to another, from the crest of a white cock to a jewel, and from there to other objects. In a story of the later Vedic period,[564] the keenness (*tejas*) of the smiling Makha leaves him, escaping[565] with the smile; the gods mix it into the plants: thus shoots up the millet[566]. Substances to be manipulated can be transferred from one object to another by touch: therefore, inducing or avoiding touch plays a main rôle in magic. Those substances enter the body mostly through food and drink: here we have one of the root causes for fasting that is prescribed often in the ritual[567]. In the latter-day Vedic epic of the bird Garuḍa[568], Tārkṣya drinks the half of the ascetism (*tapas*) along with the magic power attached to it which the wise Vālakhilyas have acquired: thus he gets the power to beget Garuḍa. But the fluids can also take to more airy ways. They can be inhaled: sufficient reason, to hold the breath on several occasions. They can be transmitted through look; the one who looks can transmit them to the others through one's look, one may, however, take them up in oneself in the same way and get infected by them: reason, not to look in a particular direction on several occasions or not to look around oneself. Restrictions stand in the way of these various types of movement or transmission of the substances—we refer here only to the important ones—like through water, fire, mountains, narrow holes: a brief hint is sufficient here, as further examples of different magic acts of the movements as also of the restrictions of the fluids will give a more complete and vivid picture.

But it must be emphasized here that the boundary between those impersonal substances and the personal demons is not a clear-cut one. The harmful spirits and the magic contagions that cause the same harm, intermingle with one another in the twilight zone of this magic. Thus, the evil substances called *pāpman*[569] are referred to as neutral substances, but sometimes also as evil demons: one speaks of the 'deities with the name *pāpman*', of the 'thousand-eyed immoral *pāpman*', who are invoked to commiserate the afflicted man and to leave him[570]. It must finally be added that all these magic substances and the acts of magic warding-off related to them are in no way limited as against real harmful beings and the real measures to counter these. We have already mentioned in another context (p. 36f.) how serpents, ants, worms, etc., which are to be driven away, are addressed as demoniac beings: just as the cow, to whom one owes one's food, is animal and goddess at the same time. Thus, there is no principal difference if one tries to remove, say, field-vermin through really or apparently effective means of practical nature, or if one makes use of similar means against substances or demons carrying diseases. Just as superstition and magic cannot be limited against belief and cult on the one hand, there is, on the other hand, particularly in the most ancient state of things, a good part of original natural science and hygiene which can scarce be separated from the sphere of religion and superstition even by the dividing lines of our systems; in truth it was never really separated therefrom.

Important Types of Magic

After these preliminary remarks, it will be easy to describe the more important types of magic acts. It may, however, be presumed that the rule is valid for the magic as well as for the sacrifice: 'Pure may the acts be performed with cleanliness[571]'. One fasts, takes a bath, puts on fresh garments. Also preparatory consecrations are prescribed which, similar to *dīkṣā* in Soma-sacrifice—but in a more simple form—, gather and increase the magic power in the performer of the act[572]. One now tries to reach one's goal in most cases by warding off demons or magic substances from oneself or others, and in another set of instances by guiding them towards oneself or others. Besides that and in close connection with it, there is the procedure—, events which cannot be caused directly—natural events not under human control; where one is too weak or not in a position to influence the others, the effect is achieved through stimulation, aided by an image which is intended to produce or influence[573] its archetype. What is done to a part or to a specimen is to influence the whole thereof or the species it represents. In view of the long-standing, strongly felt, substantive link between the image and the archetype, part and the whole, it is obvious that this form of magic cannot be separated in principle from the process of guiding of a magic substance to the being it is to influence. One likes, in all this, to combine several processes directed at the same goal for strengthening the effect and for greater safety. Wholly alike those procedures that operate with the image of reality, there is one more important type of magic to be discussed here, i.e., the magic of divination, which procures the knowledge of that which cannot be directly known, say, of future event by a roundabout way. The most common procedure is to make an image of the event in question or of such an image already available—particularly within the sphere of the sacrifice saturated with mystic significance—and then to conclude about that, which one wants to know, from the thing thus observed. Just as the earlier procedure of magic consisted in causing an event by creating its image, here the main event is known from the observation of such an image.

Warding-off of Malevolent Beings

Let us now illustrate the types described here briefly through examples, beginning with the exorcism of malevolent beings: whereby, even if, the same means are used, on the whole, against demons as also against impersonal substances, combating those personal enemies reveals understandably in individual cases a unique form.

The warding-off of the evil demons does not assume in all circumstances the form of open hostility; one tries to escape their persecution even in a friendly way, through expressions of worship, through offerings[574]. They are requested to go away and to take pity on man; 'May worship be yours', 'we want to serve you worshipfully with sacrificial offerings'[575]. It is explicitly clear that the demon is within rights when he harms man; to the spirit of diseases that attacks the child, one says: 'It is true that gods have granted you a wish. Why then, choose this child'[576]. Sacrifices to evil demons are frequently mentioned;[577] they get their share in the sacrifices of the common cult, though of course in the form of a scanty settlement, the chaff, blood, stomach and excrements of the sacrificial animal[578]. The expressions of reverence are often tied up with defensive words or acts. One hurls a firebrand at the jackal which is considered as possessed by powers of death, but at the same time a reverential attitude is shown to it by reciting *mantras* of praise[579]. One pays homage to the serpents and in the same breath declares one's intention to destroy them, to smash them together, tooth for tooth, jaw for jaw[580]. One tries first to reach one's goal by fair means, but if it fails, then one resorts openly to counter-measures. If the ants do not go away despite sacrificial offerings and *mantras* of praise, then one makes a poisoned offering accompanied by symbols of hostility, and invokes the gods to destroy the ant-eggs and all their progeny[581].

Now the attempts to deal with evil spirits in a friendly manner fall well behind combating them, behind the forceful repulsion of harmful substances. This warding off is at the outset a sort of precaution: one avoids what they could bring about; one makes the access difficult to them. We have already discussed above the significance of observances like fasting, celibacy, holding the breath, silence, seclusion, etc., aimed at this end[582]. Just like one's person, one also hides from the evil-doers even such wastes of one's own body, which could offer them points of attack. For instance one conceals or buries the child's or the boy's hair that is cut at the initiation ceremony, beard, nails[583]. Further, every contact is avoided with the elements wherein dwell dangerous spirits or harmful substances: thus, after delivery, to touch the mother during the ten days of her impurity is dangerous; the stones to be laid for the erection of the Agni-altar, for the goddess of destruction (Nirṛti) are brought to their respective places without touching them[584]. Not-hearing impure sounds and not-touching go together, above all, not looking of impure or dangerous persons and objects: thus not-looking at the offerings given to the dead, Rudra, etc.[585] Further, we also come across the common custom of not-looking-around-oneself in India and elsewhere, in the regions of advanced as well as primitive culture, when leaving the place of sinister practices, for example, after rites which have to do with the dead, with evil demons, Nirṛti and Rudra.[586] If one approaches the dangerous spirits, care is taken not to come too close to them: the priest carrying the Soma is not supposed to go very near to the places of fire where the greedy Gandharvas live; they await the Soma with open mouths.[587] One conceals from the spirits or the dangerous souls the way by wiping out footprints or by avoiding the correct door, etc. Thus the branch of a tree is bound to the dead on the way to funeral. This wipes off the footprints.[588] The priest carrying the sacrificial fire is followed by another priest who wipes off his footprints.[589] The sacrificial fire of a dead person which has become on account of his death a seat of powers bringing death, is removed by a different way and not through the door. The boy possessed by the 'dog-demon' (epilepsy?) is brought into the assembly-hall, where the magic for driving away this demon is to be performed,[590] through an opening made in the roof. Just as one tries to hide the way from the spirits, one also tries to block it. One makes use for that of fire which is placed beside the person or the locality to be protected, one lustrates it.[591] Water has a similar effect—it is said that 'the Rakṣas cannot step over the waters',[592] so also the stone, the symbol of the mountain breaking up, a meadow or any other shrubbery.[593] We have already mentioned above that keeping awake helps against the spirits that threaten the person who is asleep, and that one keeps awake throughout the night, if need be, by relating stories.[594]

If one is seized by spirits or attacked by other harmful elements, washing counts as the chief remedy of removing them. All curative powers live in the waters; they drive away all harmful elements—is said in the *Ṛgveda* itself (I, 23, 19ff.). Thus one washes away all the evil powers from the new-born;[595] on all festive occasions one takes a clean bath; bathing and washing plays an important rôle in expiatory ceremonies (p. 188 f.); the sacredly dangerous substance inherent in the sacrifice is removed by a sacrificial bath at least after major sacrifices, in order not to carry it over into profane life.[596] It would be pointless to present a larger collection of material in respect of the bath which plays such a clear rôle in the cult and in the magic;[597] only the practice need be mentioned that after the recitations of *mantras* to sinister elements—Rudra, evil demons, the dead, etc.—, one has to purify oneself with water from the contact made with these thereby.[598] If in India and elsewhere[599] the urine of the cow appears to be a valuable means of purification, it can be presumed that it is based upon the efforts to use a substance for washing that could bring to man at the same time the abundance of nourishment inherent in the nature of the cow.[600] Wiping-off has also a rôle to play besides washing or along with it. The impurification caused by bird-droppings which brings ill-luck is wiped off and washed away. The face is wiped off after a bad dream.[601] Harmful substances are wiped off with a black woollen cloth[602] and also with lead, which is often referred to in magic acts disparagingly. As a means of purification and cure, the plant *apāmārga* was used in the most diverse ways. Its name was interpreted as 'wiping off' perhaps only in popular etymology, and it is said of it, that the gods wiped off the harmful powers and demons with it (compare above p. 189).

A further means of getting rid of harmful enemies is by burning. After all that is said about Agni as the killer of demons and its use to prevent the approach of evil elements,[603] there is no need to elaborate here. Fumigation is next to burning in importance; the new-born child is exposed to the smoke of mustard, to drive away all evil from it.[604]

Further, the hostile elements are beaten up or shot at.[605] A man goes in search of a bride,—his bow and arrow at the ready.[606] When the priests beat the king during the consecration (*rājasūya*) and say: 'I am leading you away that you may not be beaten up', one can only read meaning into it. The significance of the custom is expressed more appropriately in another expression pertaining thereto: 'We are knocking away the evil from you'.[607] Beating-away of evil powers may be seen in the practices at several places in the rites where one walked around in a circle—particularly around the fire—beating upon one's own thighs.[608]

Here we come across the rôle accorded to the staff in diverse aspects of the ritual. The Veda-pupil (*brahmacārin*), who is prone to attack by the spirits, particularly due to the observances imposed on him, is given a staff together with the announcement of his duties during the solemn act of his admission; he has to carry it constantly and he should not allow any gap between his body and the staff.[609] At the celebration on completion of his studentship the staff along with the girdle put upon him at the time of admission and other especially sacred objects are 'sacrificed into the water'.[610] At the same time, upon entering a new stage of life as a Brahmana subject to new observances, he gets a new staff of material other than the one he carried as a pupil. A *mantra* spoken in its different versions shows the purpose of the staff: 'Protect me from all sides'—'protect me from all sides from all the powers of destruction'—'beat away the swarming enemies, as does Indra, the donor of treasures'; here, besides human enemies and malevolent creatures, animals, Rakṣas and Piśācas are also mentioned.[611] We have mentioned in another context (p. 223) that the consecratedness of the Soma-sacrifice is comparable with that of the Brahmana pupil: here as well as there, a condition distinct from profane existence and characterised by special observances, which is brought about by an act of consecration, is concluded with a bath that washes away this consecration. This confirms our notions that the staff used to drive away dangerous spirits is an attribute of the Brahmana-pupil and also of the performer of the Soma-initiation (*Dīkṣā*). The rule is given: 'Handing over of the staff to the dīkṣita or the brahmana-pupil';[612] but the meaning of the staff used in *dīkṣā* is explained by a *Brāhmaṇa-text*:[613] 'the staff is a thunder-wedge (*Vajra*) to drive away the Rakṣas.'—The staff of the performer of *dīkṣā* passes into the hand of the priest, the Maitrāvaruṇa, during the further course of the sacrifice[614]. When he stands near the seat of the reciting priest during the offerings, the body leaning forward, supporting the staff on the sacrificial altar (*vedi*),[615] this posture can no doubt be interpreted as a sign of readiness to ward off the approaching hostile spirits.[616] Another staff, called *sphya* which appears in various practices of the sacrificial ritual, has in many contexts the same significance of a weapon used to drive away demons. The priest addresses it: 'You are the right hand of Indra, with a thousand edges, with a hundred sharp points'; he throws it on the earthen sacrificial altar (*vedi*) and throws the earth thus stirred up on the heap of the rubbish with the *mantras* that call this earth the enemy, the demon Araru: he should be kept in chains far away from the place of the sacrifice to gods.[617] In the sacrifice for the dead, one wipes the altar with the *sphya* and says: 'the Asuras and the Rakṣas sitting on the altar have been beaten away'.[618] It can be seen how the same ritualistic feature repeats itself in different forms.

A further remedy for removal of evil elements consists in the use of odour—thus the sweet fragrance of bdellium (*guggulu*), which appears often in the ritual, used to scare away spirits that bring diseases and curses.[619] They are also repulsed by noise: kettledrums are struck and noise made at the festival of the solstice (*Mahāvrata*), apparently to drive away the spirits that increase in strength around the time of the shortest day; pots are broken at the burial; a gong is struck when the 'dog-demon' (epilepsy?) is to be driven out of the boy.[620]

Thus we come across throwing-away, shaking-off and stripping-off of the hostile elements or substances in diverse ways. The black antelope-skin used in the sacrifice is shaken off with the words: 'the Rakṣas is shaken off; the enemies are shaken off.' After the feeding of the souls, the lappet of the garment is shaken off to remove the souls clinging to it. The branch that is used to wipe away the footprints of the dead (p. 257) could, as a result, acquire dangerous powers; it is, therefore, thrown away. The clothes are changed after sinister duties like the funeral. The impurity in the hair of the bride—this is to be certainly understood above all in a magical sense—is combed away with a reed-comb having a hundred teeth[621]. The custom of pulling through a narrow hole common to the superstitions of so many races is also found. I think, this is done to strip away the element that is to be removed. Indra pulls the Apālā who is suffering from a skin ailment 'through the hole of the wheel-cart, through the hole of the yoke'; the god 'makes her skin golden purifying her three times'. I think, it has been correctly understood as the traces of a similar purification when the hole of the cart-yoke is placed atop the bride at the marriage.[622] The removal often also takes another form. The element to be removed is carried over to the objects (also to animate objects) coming in contact with it in one way or the other, and these are then removed or dispelled by *mantras* or symbolic acts as far as possible to the most distant places and thus rendered harmless. The hostile element is allowed to go across to the other side at a cross-road.[623] The cloth used to wipe away the impurity of the bride is hung in the forest; so also the dangerous substance in the clothes of the bride is banished to a pole or a tree, which is then attired with those clothes.[624] For the woman who has miscarried, ceremonies are arranged one after the other in three huts to drive away the unpropitious element dwelling in her; she is made to stand on lead or the like and is washed; the black clothes worn by her are taken off each time, and the hut where a part of the evil element remained is burnt down[625]. Against headache and other ailments, one covers the head with a braid of muñja-grass, and one goes out strewing empty fruit-seeds with a strainer. Then the strainer and the braid together with a bow-string are placed on the spot where there is attack of the pain.[626] The meaning seems to be, that the spirit of disease goes out from the head to the braid; it is enticed to leave the body with the help of seeds; it is then put down where its presence is manifest and the bow is drawn to kill it or to arrest its return. The venom is led into a blade of grass or a firebrand and it was thrown on to the serpent, letting it return thus to its origin.[627] Fever was removed by tying a frog under the bed of the sick man, water was then poured on the sick man and allowed to fall on the frog; finally the frog was probably removed. Similarly jaundice was dispelled by washing the yellow substance applied to the sick man in such a way that it fell on yellow birds—parrots, thrushes, etc., that were tied under the bed with a yellow string; it appears that the birds had to fly away finally from there.[628] A person suffering from feverish thirst was made to sit with a healthy man on the branches of a tree. A pap was stirred atop the head of the sick man and then given to the other person, 'so that he may carry over the thirst to the other man', says the text. The sick man is then given water to drink, and finally both eat the same pap, dressed in the same clothes: obviously a new expression for transmitting the suffering to the healthy man.[629] A scented preparation mixed with butter was applied on a person possessed by an evil spirit. At a cross-road—where the spirits dwell—a similar substance was put into a basin full of burning coals which was placed on the head of the sick man. Thereafter, the sick man went into a river and scattered that stuff with his face towards the current; another person sprinkled him from behind with water. Finally, the substance referred to was hung in an unburnt clay vessel near a bird's nest.[630] We have here, side by side, the most diverse ways of removing evil: the dangerous element is blended with a mixture of scents, burnt with fire, washed away by river water or given over to the birds;[631] all done to repel them. We shall conclude this survey of Vedic magic procedures to get rid of harmful powers with a reference to the idea of banishment of anger beneath a stone, of attaching the poison to the sun, of driving away the hostile magic across the ninety rivers, of banishing Takman, the demon of disease to strange, distant peoples like the Gandharvas and the Magadhas, of the idea of banishment of an evil deed or an evil dream across vast expanses to Trita Āpatya.[632] A few tools used to drive away evil did not get their due in the discussions so far; they shall be discussed further below in particular: thus amulet and medicine, magic-*mantra*, and magic sacrifice.

Transmission of Spirits and Substances

The magic transmission of spirits and substances, both benevolent and malevolent, to oneself and to others, to friend and foe, is in contrast to their expulsion. As already mentioned in some another context, the hostile magician is often considered to be harbouring (p. 132 f. above) an evil spirit, and if some one suffers on account of hostile magic, it is regarded correspondingly as a normal occurrence occasioned by his opponents letting loose such spirits upon him. Thus the Ṛgvedic magician sends the demon of disease *apvā* (dysentery) against a hostile army: "Bewildering the senses of our foemen, seize their bodies and depart, O Apvā, attack them, set their hearts on fire and burn them; so let our foe abide in utter darkness." Magic acts are usually associated with such *mantras*, just like the shooting of a "white-footed" arrow (?) which contained the forces of disease against the hostile army.[633] The magician could also—so too the spirits serving him—take the form of an animal and bring harm to the enemy in this form. The belief in such metamorphosis was characteristic of the Vedic magic and especially so of magic of almost all races. Thus the person pursued by such magic invokes the Maruts "to search and to seize among the villagers the magicians hostile to him, who turn into birds and fly about at night".[634]

Substances with magic powers that are to be directed to oneself or to others are transformed mostly through touch[635] as mentioned above (p. 254). They can, however, appear in various forms depending upon the nature of the body which is the carrier of the concerned substance. "Anoint yourself with the one; make an amulet of the other; wash with the one, drink the other of those things", it is said once with reference to magic substance.[636] Yet again it is an immaterial touch, so to speak, that goes out, e.g., from a favourable or an unfavourable star in which the moon is just then in conjugation. The same touch goes out also from the waxing or waning of the moon or from the day's length: Present in these conditions is a magic power that affects human beings or actions.

The following excerpt from a ritual-text[637] speaks of the effect of contact. Here, the pure logic of the sacrificial magic gains expression. Should the sacrificer touch the animal to be sacrificed? "It is said: the sacrificer must not touch it, because it is led to its death. He should, therefore, not touch it; he should, however, touch it. The animal led to the sacrifice is not led to its death; therefore, one must touch it. He would exclude himself from the sacrifice, if he would not touch it." Thus, the ritual is full of instructions that a person doing this or that should touch another person or an object; the blessed power inherent in the sacrifice is thus transferred. Those who take part in courting a girl touch a water container into which flowers, fruits, corn and gold have been put;[638] thus they receive the propitious powers inherent therein. In the same way, one sits on a bull's hide in order to fill oneself with fertility, and the like.[639] Or on an antelope skin[640] to acquire the sanctity attached to this animal, on a goat-skin[641] for food in plenty, and on a tiger-hide[642] for its invincible power. The solidity of the stone is imparted to the bride who is allowed by the bridegroom to step upon it with the *mantra*: 'Come, step upon the stone; be firm like the stone; put down the enemies, conquer the adversary'.[643] The abundance of water and food associated with the ants is led to the three sacred fires and through that to the sacrificer by placing a portion of the ant-hill[644] in the places meant for these fires.

Just as the act of wiping-off is meant to ward off hostile substances, so too can they be introduced by the acts of wiping-on, anointing, sprinkling with water, etc. Guilt of a sin, the dangerous substance of a wicked dream can be wiped on to a man.[645] Bamboo-shoots are sacrificed to destroy an enemy after one has applied one's own sweat on them.[646] This act signifies that one directs against the enemy, weapons saturated with the power of one's own inner heat, with one's own *tapas*. The same is the case with the king's consecration, the anointing or sacrificing of the war chariot,[647] etc. The purpose here is to impart a substance replete with magic power.

Obviously, eating plays an important rôle amongst the means for transmission of such a substance. I discussed earlier the power ascribed to the eating of the sacrificial food—of the strength imparted to man through the blessing embodied in the sacrifice; I also mentioned the custom of giving a child to eat for its first meal the substance which represents each time that especially desired quality that is to be imparted to it.[648] I may mention further that a mixture of the milk of a cow having a calf of the same colour like itself, dung-heap, bdellium and salt is eaten in order to let the draught-oxen prosper.[649] At the ceremony to get male progeny, the woman has to eat a barley corn and two mustard seeds or beans placed on both sides of the barley corn and an image of the male genital organ[650] so that she may give birth to a male child. Communal eating by several persons of the same food promotes community feeling and commits them to mutual loyalty. Originally, it was obviously intended to make the person who causes harm to another aware that he would thereby bring harm to himself.[651]

I shall mention here besides eating or making someone eat, also rubbing into someone's nose, making the horses sniff, and breathing.[652] Even a glance has a good or bad influence, according to the situation, on the one looking at someone, or on the one who is looked at. The person who has completed a certain ceremony of purification purifies the whole society of men by his mere look.[653] The benedictory power of the look is implied, when the performer of the sacrifice demands of the priest: 'Look at me with the eyes of Mitra', and when the guest who is honoured, says to the sweet food offered to him, 'I look at you with the eyes of Mitra'.[654] But the evil look,[655] for example, of a serpent brings harm to the one who meets it; the bridegroom protects the bride at the marriage from an evil eye by rubbing her eyes with an ointment and praying: 'Be not be with evil eye, no killer of the husband'.[656] On the other hand, the effect of the one looked at on the one who looks is revealed in many injunctions. For instance, the Brahmana who has completed his studies with a solemn bath, should not see an enemy, an evil-doer, a pall-bearer, urine and refuse; or the teacher, who has to instruct his pupil in a most sacred Vedic lesson, should not see a Caṇḍāla, a woman in child-bed or a menstruating woman, etc.[657]

Often the transmission of a substance is made most effective in India and elsewhere by burying or by any other way of hiding a magic object; thus, the effect takes place in secret and is out of reach of the opponents who want to thwart it. The *Atharvaveda* is full of *mantras* which express concern against magic, 'which has been buried in the sacrificial straw, in the graveyard or in the open'; also against that which is hidden in a well, that which has been carefully equipped like the bride bedecked for her marriage procession; further, against magic whose parts are joined together like Ṛbhus (see above p. 120), who put together the parts of a chariot.[658] Such magic is described in the *Kauśikasūtra*:[659] belongings of the person who is to be harmed—a wreath, hair, the twig used for cleaning the teeth—are placed in the opening of a mortar, the symbol of crushing, and buried beneath three stones along with unpropitious objects like the uterus of a cow that has been sacrificed at a funeral or a cow that has died of an epidemic. But the good luck of a person endangered by such a magic can be restored, when the buried object is exhumed with the *mantra*: 'Your good luck, which is buried under the three stones and the four stones, I dig it out again together with the blessing of progeny and riches.' There used to be a special ceremony[660] in the Soma-sacrifice which represented the exhuming of the buried magic of an enemy or a rival. Even propitious magic could take the form of burying; we have mentioned below (see note 649) the burying of the mixture of milk, dung-heap, bdellium and salt by which the prosperity of cattle is promoted. And whenever the snipped-off hair, nails, etc., were buried in a cow-shed or in any other place which could bring luck, there is at bottom the clear intention:—besides other purposes—to let the object in question become saturated in secret with the propitious substance.[661]

Finally, it must be mentioned that utensils of all description in which the relevant power was embodied, were used in the manipulations to be undertaken. This was considered to be also effective in transmitting substance or power. The banished king was given enchanted food to eat in order to restore him to power; it was cooked with wood that had grown out of the stump of a tree which had been clipped off, thus signifying the restoration of the destroyed existence.[662] In a sacrifice with the same purpose of restoring the power of the banished person, the place of fire was strewn with earth from his native land or other materials coming from his country;[663] oblation was made to remove ants; one used a sacrificial spoon of *Bādhaka* wood;[664] *Bādhaka* means 'remover'. Thus the power of removal is set in action. In the sacrifice for victory in battle the earth stirred up by a wild boar and wherein lay, therefore, its strength was used for the sacrificial altar.[665] It is clear, how everywhere the substances required for the appropriate occasion were made to act effectively in favour of the person who is to be influenced by magic.

Magic with the Help of an Image and the like

We shall now describe a few cases of the magical procedure already detailed above (p. 255). Here the anticipated event is induced by producing an image of the event. The superior cult of the three sacrificial fires is replete with rites, which have similar significance or which approximate their original meaning.

We have seen how the kindling of the holy fire at dawn is a magic to make sun rise, or how Soma-juice trickling through the strainer represents rain-inducing magic.[666] The chariot race at the royal sacrifice of *Vājapeya*, where the king who does the sacrifice, wins, is a magic meant to give him victorious power and swiftness:[667] the sole success, artificially produced for him is a reproduction of general, true victoriousness. So also, solemn game of dice which figures[668] variously in the ritual and represents clearly a magic that gives the sacrificer luck and victory. At the solstice-celebration where an Aryan fights with the Śudrā for a white, round piece of hide and tears it away from him,[669] the sunlight is freed from the menacing powers of darkness. Sexual acts on the same occasion[670] are an image or a model of the fertility one wishes women to acquire. The *Sautrāmaṇī*-sacrifice, it appears, is to be considered as magic that can be repeated, albeit through a very loose and crude reproduction of a mythical event with beneficial results for the sacrificer.[671] The Aśvins and Sarasvatī cure Indra who has taken ill after an excessive bout of Soma-drinking: so too shall the sacrificer suffering from some sort of misfortune be raised to greater strength, better luck. Are we mistaken in perceiving here the origins of religious and dramatic presentations in those remote times?[672]

The type of magic which has occupied our attention here, is often found in the rain magic in a context having a special bearing on all the older rituals. An arrow is shot through a hide in solstice-celebration (p. 239): probably the hide illustrates the canopy of the sky that is to be pierced. Similarly, girls with pitchers of water dance around a fire; they empty the pitchers and sing a song which refers to the washing of the cows (p. 238 f); this has obviously to do with rain-magic. When the Agni-altar is arranged in layers, jugs of water are emptied, 'so that the rain starts there'; then the corn is sown in the ground made fertile by this rain.[673] After an otter is cast into the water, it rains abundantly.[674] The one who wants rain, throws shrubs into the water, submerges them and then lets them float in it. He fastens the head of a dog and, of a goat, hair and old shoes to the end of a beam and 'lets them fight' (strikes them against one another?)[675] Should the ram open the canopy of the sky or the dog tear it to pieces?[676]

We may also mention briefly a few more examples of magic acts of this type.[677] An enemy is destroyed when his image or shadow is pierced through the heart or a chameleon representing him is killed.[678] One destroys worms by trampling upon twentyone *Usīra*-roots and burning them saying, 'I split with the stone the heads of all worms, male and female alike, I burn their faces with fire'.[679] In order to obstruct a person, for example, a slave, one pours around him, when he is asleep, one's own urine from the horn of a live animal, thereby building an imaginary wall around him.[680] In order to remove misfortune, one gets rid of old, used objects which represent the substance of misfortune; one burns an old pair of shoes and an umbrella.[681] To remove the field-vermin *tarda*, a Tarda is buried head downwards and its mouth tied with a strand of hair so that it may not eat the corn.[682] In order to nail down evil spirits, an odd number of pegs are driven into the earth; one who wants to thresh the

Soma-shoots to prepare the Soma for the sacrifice, thinks of his enemy so that the threshing can be directed at him[683]. We conclude this with the magic by which the river is led into a new bed. One pours water on the course the river is to take, reeds are planted and representatives of water like the frog and the water-plant Avakā placed in it:[684] this image of acquatic life developed here will become then reality.

Divinatory Magic[685]

We have already pointed out above (p. 255 f) that magic—at least to a large extent—to ascertain the hidden, particularly the future rests upon the magical correspondence between image and reality. The expert knows, say at the sign of an omen or a portent, to understand correctly and, if need be, to bring about himself the imaging process which shows the true event that is to be represented.[686] Significant images of reality are presented notably by those spheres replete with magic power, for example, those pertaining to the dream, the sacrifice, the death and the funeral. The movements of the sacrificial animal, the path taken by the sacrificial smoke, the appearance of the dead[687]—all these give one a peep into the future. Apart from divination with the aid of significant images, one also receives knowledge of the future from the superhuman knowledge of the gods and the spirits. Both methods have got mixed with each other in many instances. The latter method can be seen particularly in the interpretation of the gait, the flight or the voice of those animals which have a special relationship with the gods and the spirits, like the owl, crow, hyaena, etc. (above p. 39).[688]

We shall confine ourselves to few details.

One who wants to know whether a girl would make a good wife, should let her choose from different clods of earth taken partly from lucky soil—from a furrow, a cow-shed, etc.—and partly from unpropitious soil like a burial ground or a cross-road.[689] Her choice indicates her nature and her fate. If one wants to know whether the child that is to be born is a boy, the descendant of a Brahmana is asked to touch a limb of the pregnant woman: if the limb has a masculine name, then it will be a boy.[690] Fire kindled in a certain manner before the battle between two armies shows, from the direction of the smoke, the result of the battle.[691] Also three cords woven out of sinews are placed on coals: the middle cords stands for death; the other two, the two armies.[692] After the rite for obtaining a husband is over, the girl's suitor will come from the side whence the crows come.[693] The direction taken by the cow at a certain point of the sacrificial ritual is indicative of the sacrificer's fortune.[694] If the fire burns brightly at a particular sacrifice, the sacrificer gets twelve villages; if smoke comes, he gets at least three villages.[695]—Depending upon which one of the three fires seizes the corpse first at the funeral, one may conclude whether the soul belongs to the heavenly, the ethereal or the human-world.[696] The hyaena gives out its significant cry 'upon being urged or of its own will'; the owl 'flies to the house of the gods'; One says to it, 'Fly around the village from the left to the right and herald good fortune oh owl!'.[697] The experts interpret the heavenly constellations, the physical features, say of a girl, whom one courts, and above all dreams.[698] Forecasting weather is a speciality of the ancient Brahmanas, who are called 'cow-dung-smoke prophets' on account of the method used by them.[699] This is based, however, on a doubtful view. Just as such prophets exact information about certain events from external signs, so too does one believe that spiritual personalities have an insight into the future by virtue of the magical power of *tapas*[700] (see above p. 220ff.) and the like[701] or on account of their inner enlightenment. Their knowledge of the hidden and the future is partly based on expert observation of the auguries; it is also arrived at in part independently. The wise man who can read the future is quite often met in narrative lore. For example, Nārada who foretells the death of Satyavant; and the Buddha, who predicts several future events. It is certainly in keeping with the tradition of the ancient and common folk-belief when a king says before battle:[702] 'The spiritual ascetics know all. Who knows who will win and who will lose? I shall ask the hermit'. Yet, in the instructions of the Vedic texts on how to read the future, the observation of omens and portents described above is preferred over individual gifts of clairvoyance. Especially the belief in knowledge obtained by supernatural means was not developed in ancient India into institutions comparable to the oracles of ancient Greece.[703]

Amulets and Medicines[704]

We must complete the description of the Vedic magic-practices by adding a few remarks on the effectiveness of several magic agents which have already been mentioned above, namely, amulets and medicines, charms and magical sacrifices.

We have already mentioned above (p. 261) that a transmission of power or substance can be transmitted effectively through inner as well as external application, by eating and drinking, by anointment or by wearing an amulet. The magic medicine or amulet comes in principle from a substance—preferably, it appears, from the plant-kingdom. It embodies whatever effect is to be achieved, even it be only through the sound of the name. Obviously other, mostly magic processes of production and consecration of the relevant magic object also play a part. The concept of the amulet as the seat of a spirit, resp. of a soul by which the effect to be achieved is performed, does not appear to be there in the Veda:[705] what works effectively is usually the substance inherent in the amulet in the sense mentioned above (p. 253 f.).[706] Expectation of help from such a power must be naturally harmonized somehow or other with hope of help from the god. Thus, the magic *mantras* are full of diverse expressions that derive the effectiveness of amulets, medicines, etc., from the divine world[707] in one way or the other. These magic means are soon said to be of divine origin, or they are identified with the gods; soon it is said that the gods have given them to man, that they have invigorated them, cast a spell on them, imparted their seminal power to them, that they work in unison with them; but above all, it is often said that the gods themselves achieved their successes by using magic that was prompted by the occasion. Indra used it against the Asuras to conquer them, Tvaṣṭar gave it to Aditi that she may became the mother of the gods' sons, etc.

Magic Formula[708]

The magic power of the word can be seen in the magic effects produced by the name[709] and in ominous expressions, both propitiatory and unpropitiatory, so too in many senseless, but magically significant strange-sounding words like *khat phat*, etc. The magic power of the word reaches maximum intensity in magic formulas, curses and oathes. In India and elsewhere,[710] the commonly found type of propitiatory dialogue is based on the belief in the benefactory power of the word: the answer to the question pronounces the omen; although the answer appears to be fortuitous, it has in fact been agreed upon earlier. The wife asks the performer at the ploughman's festival, 'Have you ploughed?' He replies, 'We have!' She asks further, 'What have you got from it?' He answers, 'Property, happiness, prosperity, children, cattle, food and its enjoyment!' The husband asks his pregnant wife when her hair is parted, 'What do you see?' And she answers, 'Progeny!' In the rite to obtain a male child, the husband asks his wife after giving her a magic potion, 'What are you drinking?' She answers, 'Birth of a son!' The young couple asks a Brahmana-pupil during the rite performed on the fifth day after marriage, 'What do you see?' He says, 'Sons and cattle!'.[711]

The actual *magic formula* is mostly[712] in verses, —though occasionally still in prose,—in that prose with its dull, at times meaningful, at times meaningless rhythm of invocation—. The formula comprises often verses hastily put together or old verse compositions, originally of different import but which were later degraded to magic formulas to meet the most superficial contingencies.[713] The formula is uttered mostly in gentle whispers.[714] Its power is often increased by repeating it three times. Often gods or a series of gods and demons are invoked;[715] one calls by name or says, for example, 'Oh, night, your nine and ninety wakeful spirits, eighty-eight, or are they seventy-seven?'[716]: they are to help and to protect; it is clear that prayer and the actual magic are constantly mixed. The magician gives commands in his own capacity or makes threats; he gives expression, as it were, in narrative form to the course of events he is to conjure up. Just as uttering the name exerts magic power over the thing named after it, so too does the naming of the desired event bring about the event. The power of the magic is strengthened by comparison of the desired effect with the natural or divine events; these similes used repeatedly in magic formulas are not obviously chance poetic embellishments, but contain a magic factor: the beings or events named in the simile are supposed to attract their counterparts in the situation at hand. 'As the rising sun robs the stars of their brilliance, I rob the power of all women and men hostile to me.' 'The cows have rested; the birds have gone to their nests; the mountains stand rooted to their spot: I have made the kidneys stay in place firmly.'—'Just as the wind agitates the lotus pond from all sides, your embryo shall stir; it shall come forth in ten months'.[717] The magic *mantra* is related to such similes where it narrates how the gods succeeded once by using the same magic that is being performed now, by using the same amulet being used now (compare p. 266 f.); the long-standing power of magic becomes effective anew this time. The oft recurring features of the magic are as follows: The entire range of possibilities to counter by all means the evil spirit, the seat of evil or that which is to be countered at the given moment, is expressed in detail: I am driving away the disease from the eyes and the nose, from the ears and the head, the neck, the back and the arms—if you belong to Soma, I shall buy you for king Soma; if you belong to Varuṇa, I shall buy you for king Varuṇa; if you belong to the Vasus, I shall buy you for the Vasus;[718] if one knows the spirit which is to be driven away, then it is made to feel: this is your name, we know your birth; this is your father, this is your mother.[719] The objects from which magic influence is expected, are described as these or those substances contained in them, or originating from them; the drum, for example as originating from the lord of the forest, stretched over with the cows (*Av.* V, 20, 1), i.e., made of wood and mounted with leather: this again is not purely a rhetoric device; it is meant to attract the magic qualities of the relevant substances to assist in the magic.

Curse and Oath

A special case where the word appears as the main vehicle of magic power, is the curse inclusive of the oath. The gods curse the trees which offend them. 'You should be struck down with a club made of you, as if with a thunderbolt'—'That is why the trees are struck down with a club made out of them, as if with a thunderbolt, for they are cursed by gods'.[720] Agni curses the fish which has betrayed his hideout in the waters. That one should kill it by all means of subterfuge: 'that is why the fish is killed by all means of subterfuge, for it is cursed'.[721] It is but natural that the cursing the enemy plays also a rôle in the actual life of the Vedic age. This is confirmed by numerous *mantras* to avert the curse or to turn it back to the one who places the curse. 'May the curse turn to the one who curses. We crush the eye and the ribs of the evil *mantra* with the *mantra* that is kind to us' (*Av.* II, 7, 5): it appears that the curse takes on here a personal touch and moves back and forth in its spiritually concrete form between the magician and his opponent who send it against each other. The evil power of the curse can be strengthened by further magic ceremonies: 'If one's wife has a lover and one hates him, one should then lay the sacrificial fire in an unburnt pot and scatter the sacrificial straw of reeds towards the right direction;[722] then one should offer three reeds coated with butter to the right direction accompanied by the *mantras*: 'You have sacrificed in my fire; I take from you all hope and prospect, N.N.!' Here he utters his name. 'You have sacrificed in my fire; I take away your children and cattle, N.N.!'—here he utters his name. 'You have sacrificed in my fire. I take away your breath, N.N.!'—here he utters his name. The person cursed by a Brahmana who is adept at it, leaves this world, bereft of power, bereft of the blessing of his good deals'.[723]

Oath[724] is a curse directed against oneself if one breaks one's word or tells a lie.[725] One's own life,[726] life of the next of kin, one's possessions in this or the other world—if need be, also some of these possessions—are pledged for the verity of one's own word. Gestures or symbolic acts representing the magic that produces the hostile powers can be connected with the formula to invite disaster upon one's own person. The priest who performs the great royal consecration makes the king take an oath[727]: 'All my honours achieved through sacrifices and gifts from the day of my birth to the day of my death,[728] my place, my good deeds[729], my life, my progeny, shall belong to you if I deceive you.' An old Vedic verse mentions the names of the god Varuṇa, the cows and the waters[730] in this context; in the later literature, there are rules that say, for example, that the Kṣatriya should swear by his comrades and weapons, the Vaiśya by his cows, corn and gold, the Brahmana by the truth.[731] In a story, girls swear that they will take to husband an old man or no one at all if they tell a lie.[732] A queen swears that she wants to be reborn as a demon if she betrays her husband.[733] The person who swears, takes upon himself and his own life the evil powers by the gesture of touching himself, by touching his head or his heart. Satyavant swears in an epic that he will not be able to survive any misfortune befalling his parents: 'with this truth, I touch myself[734]—and it is said elsewhere in a similar context, 'thus I touch my head'.[735] Apparently, this touching is referred to by a rule in a Sūtra-text[736] which prescribes cleaning oneself with water, if a *mantra* is spoken to Rudra, to the evil spirits 'or if one has touched oneself'; also in the act of touching oneself, there is the idea of involvement with sinister powers that needs purification. Of course, if the oath is broken, punishment follows: when the Moon-god did not keep his oath to Prajāpati, Rājayakṣma (phthisis)[737] seized him.

Magic in the form of Sacrifice

We have already seen in many passages above the compounding together of the sacrifices done to honour, to entertain or to seek the favour of the gods by magic that guides the course of things through secret force:[738] the imagination which is accustomed to the idea of magic transposes its effect to the sacrifice; the imagination native to the sphere of concepts of the sacrifice resorts to the form of sacrifice to couch in it the magic acts.[739] The sacrifice forces the demons or magicians to come out from hiding and reveal their identity; the sacrifice drives out demons; the sacrifice can help a woman to surpass her rival; it can help the outlawed prince to return and to victory over his adversaries.[740] There are two very common types of magic acts. Magic character is lent to an action which is mostly in the form of a sacrifice by choosing the sacrificial animal, or offerings which have a bearing on the specific purpose of the concerned action, or by giving special shape to some other objects of the sacrificial act;[741] and on the other hand, one offered objects suited for magic manipulations as sacrificial gifts in order to achieve a particular goal. Every page of the ritual texts[742] contains evidence for the first procedure; as for the second, it may not be out of place to give a few examples and to remember those mentioned before.[743] Ants are driven away by sacrificing poison.[744] An enemy is destroyed by sacrificing bamboo tips anointed with one's own sweat—with the power of one's Tapas.[745] One who desires cattle, sacrifices the excreta of two calves, for sheep, the excreta of a pair of sheep, etc.[746] One who desires long life, nails down, as it were, life for a hundred years by sacrificing one hundred nails of Khadira wood.[747] The practice of sacrificing through a hole has been developed in a similar fashion, obviously on the basis of the method of stripping off the harmful substances (discussed above p. 259), by pulling them out of the affected persons through a hole.[748] From all this, the intermingling of the spheres of ideas of sacrifice and magic becomes as clear as daylight.

REFERENCES

1. The constant verb used always with reference to Rudra and similar beings in the sense of "giving him his share and thereby satisfying and passifying him" is *ava-dā*, *nir-ava-dā*, compare Ṛv. II, 33, 5 and material with reference to this collected in the Sacred Books XXXII, 430; also *Taitt. Saṃh.* II, 6, 6, 6; *Taitt. Ār.* V, 8, 9, etc.; compare also *Pañc. Br.* IX, 8, 3.

2. In this case, it is not excluded that one tries amicable means like offerings and expressions of reverence also against evil spirits. We shall come back to that in the section on magic.

3. We shall exclude the cult of the Dead from the following depiction of the cult and consider it in a separate section together with the ideas about the life after death.

4. Here, really, the wish addressed to the god is represented at the same time as magic (see in the course of discussion p. 187). An image or part of it is, to magic, identical with the original or the whole. When that is offered, the god is put in the possession of it.

5. See thereon B. Lindner in Festgruß àn O.v. Böhtlingk, p. 79 f.; Hillebrandt, *Ritual-literatur* 85. 119 f., who finds here an original Thanksgiving-sacrifice. Frazer gives the ethnological information in *Golden Bough*2 II, 459 ff.

6. Expressed in the tone of the primitive system of the cult: one was afraid of the wrath of the spirits, if one did not satisfy them right at the beginning of the enjoyment of the fresh harvest. References to such thoughts are also found in the Veda (thus *Śatapatha Br.* II, 4, 3, 1 ff; 5, 2, 1 ff.). It is instructive that the person who sets up the sacrificial fire, should not enjoy anything of the corn before the offering of the first-fruits, also, he should not eat any meat before the Animal-sacrifice (*Śāṅkh. Śr.* II, 3, 26; Hillebrandt, *Rit. Lit.* 121): both are clearly parallel rules resting upon the same idea. The relationship of the offering of the first-fruits to wishes, which concern above all these and not the harvests to come, is confirmed by the relevant *mantras*. "He is speaking about the meal that is to be tasted: 'I hold you, with a gift for Prajāpati, for my luck, my fame, for the blessing of my meal'. With the *mantra*: 'You gods, you have led us from this good to the better! We want to reach you through this food. So go into us, O juice, giving refreshment; be good to us, man and cattle', he tastes it sprinkling the water over it three times". *Śāṅkhāyana G.* III, 8, *Kauś. Br.* IV, 12., however, prescribes the offering of the first-fruits generally for "the one, who wishes for himself the enjoyment of food".

7. *Taitt. Saṃh.* II, 2, 5, 3; Schwab, *Altind. Tieropfer* p. XIX note 6. It is not much different in TS II, 2, 1, 3. The sacrifice of the one who possesses thousand cattles (*Taitt. Saṃh.* II, 1, 5, 2) is to be judged like the offering of the father; compare below note 11 on special achievements as a prerequisite for a sacrifice.

8. Thus one promised Agni an offering in the name of a madman, if the sick man's health improves (*Av.* VI, 111, 1). It is said in *Taitt. Saṃh.* VI, 4, 5, 6: "He should say (to the god): 'Kill so and so, then I shall sacrifice to you'. Then (the god) kills that person and demands the sacrifice." The Śunaḥśepa-story gives an example of a vow from the Vedic literature. The childless king "turned to the king Varuṇa: let a child be born to me, and I shall sacrifice to you". *Ait. Br.* VII, 14.

9. *Aitareya Br.* VIII, 21 f.

10. Compare Hillebrandt in *Festgruß an Böhtlingk* p. 40 f.

11. *Taitt. Brāhm.* in Hillebrandt *ibid* 41. The idea that a certain sacrifice or a certain, especially important form of a sacrifice can be attempted only by a powerful or a fortunate person is also found elsewhere. The sacrifice that is to be brought to the "great Indra" instead of Indra, is only possible by the person at the peak of his good fortune (*gataśri*) (Weber. *Ind. Stud.* X, 150).

12. See Caland, *Über Totenverehrung*, p. 36 f., *Alind. Ahnenkult* p. 37 f.

13. *Āśvalāyana G.* IV. 1, 1 f.

14. *Pañc. Brāhmaṇa* XIV, 6, 8.

15. See the reference in Bergaigne II, 227.

16. Hillebrandt, *Neu und Vollmondsopfer*, 144.

17. It may be at the most quite isolated. Bergaigne perhaps explains correctly (*Rel. védique* III, 164) ṛṇa VIII, 32, 16, '*the claim that the priests and the sacrifices have on the gods until their sacrifice has been rewarded*'. But the material collected by him in II, 229 f. furnishes hardly any proof for that idea. When it is said of the god "nobody can say of him that he will not give", "Soma is never drunk without atonement", or when the man often reminds the god: "If I were you, and you were me, I would give you amply"—then it is the language of firm confidence, and an urgent reminder, but I do not find in it the view that makes just precisely the god to be man's debtor.

18. When here and repeatedly below, the two spheres, worship of the gods and the magic, are treated as being to some extent opposed to each other, it does not mean—and it need hardly be emphasized—that we are prejudiced to the train of thoughts of Marett and others—thoughts much beyond the horizon of considerations occupying our minds—which point out finally to common interests lying at the bottom behind that contrast.

19. This is also true of the theory of sacrifice which Hubert and Mauss have developed in their excellent *Essai sur le sacrifice* (*L'année sociologique* 1898). The rise and fall of a curve in the consecration. It reaches the peak with the killing of the sacrificial animal ("*one can drive away the energies that this consecration has aroused and focused on it* (*i.e., the victim*), *some towards the beings of the sacred world, others towards the beings of the profane world*"). Then the curve drops. But I think, it is the mistake of the authors when they believe to have described thereby the common Vedic Animal-sacrifice. Here the punch line is not, so to say, in the equation of a corresponding movement of a curve, the main thing is that the animal is eaten by the god and the worshipper.

20. The Ṛgvedic poets did certainly think of rites of this type, and hardly of a sacrifice bringing gifts and veneration—as far as one can ascribe to them here a definite idea—, when they said something like: "Atharvan broadened the paths at first through the sacrifice" or "the gods have sacrificed the sacrifice through the sacrifice: these regulations were the earliest", and the like.

21. One can conceive this—there is no need for dispute—as a sacrifice in the classical sense.

22. In the Section: Individual Sacrifices and Festivals.

23. See in the text the section on this enjoyment.

24. These verses are the most characteristic, perhaps the only really characteristic verses from the detailed collection of Bergaigne II, 231 f. I think, in the case of most others, the vigour of exegesis ignores the carefree breadth of the poetic metaphor and reads into it the concept "*that the sacrifice deals with the god according to his liking.*" Thus, when the priest calls Indra for the sacrifice "like the cow for milking" or, when it is said that he "makes" the god "flow like a fountain of riches", etc. Compare my remarks in *Gött. Gel.* Anz. 1890

p. 413 f. on Geldner's (*Ved. Studien* I, 139 ff.) view that Vedic sacrifice is like a ensnaring net in which the priest catches the gods.

25. i.e., according to the usual Vedic use of the language (p. 3) with milk, which is to be considered here as bait (Geldner *ibid.* 145).

26. A verse similar to the verse VIII, 2, 6 refers to the speaker himself: "Even as hunters pursue the elephants, we bringing oblation, call you (the Aśvins) down at morn and at eve" (X, 40, 4).

27. The last word is doubtful; to be exact it is: "in the one provided with scrapers" (in the brooks which scratch the ground).

28. As it can be easily understood, this is treated as always important. As Agni receives life through the wood of the trees and the plants through water, sacrifice receives life through the sacrificial reward (*Kāṭhaka*, XI, 7).

29. In connection with this, I refer chiefly to S. Lévi, *La doctrine du sacrifice dans les Brāhmaṇas* (1898).

30. *Atharvaveda* VI, 115, 3; XIV, 2, 44.

31. Really, the idea of the sin as a substance that clings into one or more exactly as fetters is also in the same prayer, and Varuṇa is asked to remove them (Verse 5).

32. Satisfying a god or a spirit which pursues man without such reason and solely on account of his destructive nature is essentially quite similar to the appeasement of the wrath a god provoked by mortal sin (compare above p. 143). The appeasement can also take the form, that one offers to the god, instead of the man whose life is endangered by the god or the spirits, a representative part of man's nature or an image. But cases of this type are very rare in the Vedic cult. Perhaps one can include here the sacrifice of the hair to the dead (compare below the Section on the cult of the Dead). I do not think that the plate-shaped cake in the *Varuṇapraghāsas* (see in the text) is an image meant for substituting the fallen man, but rather a receptacle for the substance of sin (see the text). It is also not correct, I think, that the sacrificial animal offered to Agni and Soma 'means buying one's freedom' (*Taitt. Saṃh.* VI 1, 11, 6). Equally little do I think, that the ass in the Ass-sacrifice dies as the proxy of the sinner who has violated celibacy (p. 192); see below p. 274, note 59 for my interpretation of this sacrifice. Compare also Lévi, *La doctrine du sacrifice* 130 ff.; Keith, *Veda of the Black Yajus School*, CVI. Eitrem, Opferritual und Voropfer 136 sees in the rite discussed here more of a real sacrificial offering than burning away of the sin. I am not convinced.

33. When the Brāhmaṇa-text on the obligation to confess sin (compare *Sāmavidhāna Br.* I, 5, 15) gives an ethical interpretation similar to a modern concept (compare also *Manu* XI, 227 f.), one may doubt whether one meets the original meaning of the obligation in the context of the old magic ritual. Perhaps the idea was: the effect of magic which removes sin may leave unaffected the sin one keeps concealed. By confessing it, the effect of magic is guided to the relevant sin. See p. 189 f. about one more significance of the confession of sin.

34. *Ṛgveda* I, 25, 19; 24, 11 (see *Āśvalāyana Śr.* II, 17, 15); *Śāṅkhāyana Śr.* III, 14, 5).

35. Sources in Caland-Henry, *Agniṣṭoma* 388. One can speak of 'sacrificing away' here as a magic act (so too in connection with the sin or other dangers in many other references, e.g., *Taitt. Br.* III, 10, 8, 2: 'the thousand fetters...We offer them all away through miraculous power of sacrifice'; compare *Ār.* IV, 11, 1 f.; 14, 1; V, 9, 1). Correspondingly, in the sense discussed above, the god's inclination to punish or to cause others harm can be appeased and his favour obtained. I would like to understand in this sense, when it is said in *Ṛv.* I, 133, 7 that the one who presses the Soma offers away all the hostility of the gods, or when Agni is invoked in IV, 1, 5, 'to offer away to Varuṇa' or when (with the expression *ava-īmahe*, which is close to *ava-yaj*) it is said in I, 24, 14: 'We implore away your anger, Varuṇa, through devotion, through sacrifice and gifts'.

36. *Av.* VI, 113, 2. In addition, the ritual *Kauś. S.* 46, 26 ff. (Caland, Ai. Zauberritual 153). The characteristic verse *Vās. Dharm* I, 18 can be compared where amongst the 'sinful' (*enasvin*) men also those appear who have misshapen nails or black teeth.

37. From the ritual of the three sacrificial fires, one may compare the flushing away

of a pot together with the magic-food in *Sautrāmaṇī*-sacrifice, with verses which express the doing away of all sins. *Vāj Saṃh.* XX, 14 f; *Kāty.* XIX, 5, 13.

38. An oft recurring feature: the magic extends its effect upto a definite time. 'Whatever sin he commits within a year, he sacrifices it away'. *Taitt, S.* VI, 6, 3, 1.

39. *Av.* X, 5, 22; *Kauś. S.* 46. 50.

40. The goddess of destruction. It appears to mean: wiped off from itself, wiped off from me.

41. *Av.* VII, 64; *Kauś. S.* 46, 47 f.

42. This plant owes to its name (or to the interpretation of its name?) its manifold use in magic for 'wiping off' evil of all kinds. Compare Zimmer, *Altind. Leben* 66; Henry, *La magie dans l'Inde antique* 181.

43. *Av.* VI, 119 (*Agni Vaiśvānara*), VII, 64, 2 (*Agni Gārhapatya*, see above); XII, 2, 11.12; XIV, 2, 59 ff. (together with Savitar); see also *Ṛv.* X, 164, 3. The Maruts *Av.* VII, 77, 3; Viśvakarman II, 35, 3; Pūṣan VI, 112, 3; 113, 2; all gods VI, 115; etc.—Agni and Varuṇa are in the foreground in the ceremony of 'atoning for everything' (*sarvaprāyaścitta*) (*Kāty*, XXV, 1, 11; compare *Hiraṇy G.* I, 3, 6).

44. *Āpastamba Dharm.* I, 9, 24, 11; 10, 28, 21 f.; *Gautama* XXII, 4. *Baudhāyana Dh.* II, 1, 1, 3; *Manu* XI, 72. Several of these texts prescribe that the sinner should carry the leg of the bed as a staff (compare also *Manu* XI, 105); also this must be—doubtful for the same reason—a sign of being burdened by sin. Compare *Pañc. Br.* XXI, 3, 5 about the ass and dog as impure animals; *Āpastamba Dh.* I, 3, 10, 17. Because evil demons were represented as drinking out of skulls (*Hiraṇy G.* II, 3, 7), the murderer, perhaps, should also confess to being a Rakṣas himself to some extent, for he also did the same thing.

45. *Gautama* XXIII, 17 f. *Pāraskara* III, 12, 8; *Manu* XI, 12, 2. See page 192 where further material is mentioned.

46. *Āpastamba Dh.* I, 10, 28, 19.

47. As also isolated living, withdrawing oneself from human contact, etc. which are considered as a duty of the sinner (*Āpastamba Dh.* I, 9, 24, 13; 10, 28, 13; 10, 29, 1; *Manu* XI, 47, etc.).

48. If wearing the skin of the ass or a dog, as it appears in these regulations, looks like an expression for acknowledgement of guilt by the sinner and its announcement to all those whom he meets, then the assumption is consistent with the fact that the custom could have emerged from the wearing of hide of the sacrificial animal—in this case, that of an animal in the expiatory-sacrifice—(compare R. Smith, *Religion of the Semites* I, 416 f.). In fact, a pupil who has infringed celibacy has to make a sacrifice of an ass (compare with what is said on page 191 f.).

49. Not yet in the *Ṛgveda.* According to the meaning of the word 'concern for satisfaction'. Compare, for this term, v. Negelein, *JAOS.* XXXIV, 233.

50. The gods accomplish a *prāyaścitti* for the sun at the time of the solar eclipse. *Kāṭhaka* XI, 5.

51. Whether this restriction appearing in the later Vedic texts, was also valid for the Ṛgvedic period, cannot be asserted; I think so, in view of the present state of things.

52. The goddess Iḍā originated, according to *Śat. Br.* I, 8, 1, from the sacrifice of butter and similar substances offered by Manu.

53. See Hillebrandt, *Neu-und Vollmondsopfer* 122, 125 ff.; Schwab, *Tieropfer* 148.

54. Compare above p. 190. The idea of the necessity of a special precaution during this enjoyment of the share of the meal is specifically mentioned in a section denoted as Prāśitra. I am not able to explain its special position. Here the rule, obviously as a measure of precaution, is valid that it must be gulped without being chewed. The mouth is afterwards washed. A *mantra* says that it should not be mixed with other food and should settle down above the navel. Compare Hillebrandt, *Neu-und Vollmondsopfer* 119 ff., 130 f.

55. I prefer this formulation to the one that says that a substantial communion between god and man is created through the food. I do not think, that the expressions of the Vedic

poets and theologians refer to one such communion. Also compare Keith, *JRAS.* 1907, 939 f.; *Veda of the Bl. Yajus School* CVII f.

56. The personified hot drink.

57. *Taitt. Āraṇyaka V*, 8, 12.

58. *Ind. Studien* X, 362 f.; Hillebrandt, *Ritualliteratur* 127; Caland-Henry 61 f., 72.

59. Compare *Vaitānasūtra* 12, 9; *Baudhāyana Dharm.* III, 7, 12; IV, 2, 11 and the material collected by Pischel on ass and Ass-sacrifice in *Ved. Studien* I, 82 f., as also my note on *Ṛv.* X, 86, 18.

60. Can one see in the clothing of oneself with the hide of an ass a means through which the power of the ass is carried over to the one who is to atone for his sin? One may refer to what is said above on p. 190 and p. 273, note 48. Compare also—although I am not wholly convinced—Keith, *ibid.* 942 f.

61. I may also quote that according to *Śāṅkhāyana* (*G*, I, 27, 11) the mother enjoys the remnant of the first solid food that is given to a child accompanied by the observation of solemn ceremonies: probably, to direct the same blessing of nourishment which is assured to the child through the rite, to the future children of the same mother.

62. *Āśvalāyana G.* I, 8, 9.

63. *Gobhila* II, 5, 6.

64. *Gobhila* II, 4, 3.

65. *Āśvalāyana Sr.* V, 19, 6.

66. *Kātyāyana* XIV, 5, 24; XVIII, 5, 9; *Ind. Studien* XIII, 285.

67. *Kāty.* XIX, 4, 14; *VS.* XX, 3; *Ind. Studien* X, 351.

68. Weber, *Über den Vājapeya* 28. 31.

69. *Kāty.* IV, 9, 11. Compare also the healing of sick cows and horses through the sacrificial smoke, *Sāmavidhāna Br.* I, 8, 14f.

70. *Hiraṇy. G.* II, 8, 10.

71. *Śatapatha Br.* III, 8, 1, 10; *Taitt. Saṃh.* VI, 3, 8, 1. 2.

72. *Śatapatha Br.* II, 6, 2, 16. Compare *Kāty.* V, 10, 20.

73. *Śatap. Br.* XII, 5, 1, 12.

74. *Śatap. Br.* II, 4, 2, 24; Compare *Kāty.* IV, 1, 20. The sources in *Kāty.* V, 9, 13 ff.; *Śatap. Br.* II, 6, 1, 33; *Āpastamba Sr.* VIII, 16, 3, 12 referring to the same context may be compared.

75. 'He smells it: that is as much as not enjoyed and also not unenjoyed', is said of the sacrificial meal of the sacrifice to the dead in *Taitt. Brāh.* I, 3, 10, 7. Yet, the enjoyment of this meal has also been retained despite the misgivings described here, mostly, on the side of the sacrificer's wife who gets a son through it. Compare above p. 191; Caland, *Altind. Ahnenkult* 13. 191; Ada Thomsen, *Arch. f. Rel.* XII, 489.

76. *Kāty*, XXII, 6, 2.

77. Dadhigharma. See *Ind. Stud.* X, 382.

78. *Kāty.* X, 1, 26.

79. *Āśv. G.* IV, 8, 31 f. The sentence does not lose in value, when it is said further: 'He may eat from it, however, by order (from whose side?), because it is salubrious.' Compare also *Pāraskara* III, 8, 14.

80. The rule is laid down: 'When he has spoken the *mantra* to Rudra, to the evil demons (Rakṣas), to the manes, to the Asuras or a curse and when he has touched himself (as a sign of oath), he touches water' (*Śāṅkhāyana* G. I, 10, 9, compare *Kāty.* I, 10, 14). A short summary of the most important sinister factors in the cult.

81. As an example, I shall quote the offerings for the ancestors (manes) and for Rudra prescribed in *Śatapatha Br.* XIV, 2, 2, 35. 38. In the case of the former, he looks to the north; it is well known that the south is the heavenly direction of the manes. In the case of the second, he looks to the south while the offering is thrown to the north, the direction of Rudra. 'That he does not look at it, happens, lest Rudra should do him harm.'

82. 'They return without looking around, so that Varuṇa does not follow them.' (*Maitr. S. I*, 10, 13). Likewise even in modern superstition, compare e.g. Wuttke's *Deutscher Volkasaberglaube*, Register under 'looking around'.

83. On segregation of the place of delivery which is very common amongst all the peoples, compare the *Encycl. of Rel. and Ethics* II, 636.

84. *Gṛhyasūtra* II, 3.

85. *Gṛhyasūtra* I, 28.

86. A characteristic confirmation of this interpretation of fire in the ceremony of the haircut, is given by the fact, that the same ceremony is found as a part of other rites, also in the ritual of the three fires (see in the text). There, its performance is prescribed 'to the west of the southern fire' corresponding to 'to the west of the fire' in the domestic ritual (*Kāty*. V, 2, 14, compare *Pāraskara* II, 1, 5). It will, however, be shown, that the southern of the three fires has the function of driving away the demons.

87. *Śāṅkhāyana G.* II, 1, 28.

88. ibid, II, 7.

89. *Pañc. Brāhmaṇa* XXI, 2, 9.

90. See the Section 'Dīkṣā and sacrificial bath'.

91. *Śatapatha B.* IV, 6, 6, 1.

92. *Kāty*. IV, 1, 9; *Vāj. Saṃh.* II, 30.

93. Weber, *Ind. Stud.* XVII, 180.

94. See the Section on Funeral.

95. *Kātyāyana* I, 1, 16; IX, 3, 7; X, 8, 24, etc.

96. Compare the Section on the cult of the dead.

97. *Kātyāyana* V, 10, 13, 18; Weber, *Ind. Studien* X, 342; Hillebrandt *V.M.* II, 190; *Hiraṇyakeśin G.* II, 9, 5.

98. I, 132, Compare Strabo XV, 3, 13. 14.

99. The etymological meaning appears to be 'cushion'; compare *upabarhaṇa*; *upabarbṛhat Ṛv. V*, 61, 5; *upa barbṛhi*, X, 10, 10.

100. The Avestic Baresman, as is well known, consisted of the branches of a tree tied around with a ribbon (Darmesteter, *Le Zend-Avesta* Vol. I, p. LXXIII f.). They (branches) rested, during the sacrifice, partly on a pillar (figure, ibid. Plate VI), and were partly held in the hand (ibid. 386. 391; *Vend.* XIX, 19, etc.). The Baresman was touched in various forms during the consecrations and the offerings pertaining to the sacrificial ceremony; the offering was brought near it or poured out over it; the different places of the Baresman resp. the right and the left side, represented thereby different deities: the right side the souls, in complete agreement—and which is perhaps not at all accidental—with the Vedic meaning of the right side (the south) as the region of souls. The original identity of this Baresman with the Vedic Barhis appears to me to be hardly doubtful. Both words, though different in suffix, belong obviously to the same root (*baresman* has hardly anything to do with *brahman*; same interpretation by Osthoff, *Bezz. Beitr.* XXIV, 143 f.). Both indicate a vegetable element figuring in the sacrifice, here branches, there grass; both in the Veda and in the *Avesta*, it is a bearer of a special sanctity or proximity of god. A ribbon that is tied around, plays a role in Barhis (Hillebrandt, *Neu und Vollmondsopfer* 8, 64) as also in Baresman. It is, however, particularly important that the verb *star* resp. *fra-star* 'spread out' (compare the Vedic *prastara*-bundle belonging to Barhis; Hillebr. 64) is used. (it may be noted, that also the Avestic *barezi*ꞷ 'cushion' which corresponds exactly to the Vedic *barhis*, has also the verb *star*). The Avestic pious man is called *steretōbaresman* ('the one who has spread out the Baresman'), like the Vedic *stīrṇabarhis*. It may also be noted that in the *Avesta*, fire and Baresman, Fire-Baresman and Haoma, Libation and Baresman, are so solemnly named beside each other as the main elements of sacrifice and holiness, as in the Veda the kindled fire and the spread-out Barhis, or Fire-Barhis and Soma, or Barhis and the sacrificial offering; compare *Vend* 3, 16, etc.; 9, 56, *Visp.* 2, and on the other side *Ṛv.* IV, 6, 4; X, 21, 1; *Vāj. Saṃh.* XV, 49; *Ṛv.* V, 37, 2; 2, 12, etc. I must leave to the student of Iranian Studies to examine in which way the transition of the sacrificial grass resting on the earth into the sacred branches detached from the earth and becoming mobile was accomplished, as known to the Avesta, or whether the old Barhis has merged with an element originally different from it. For other information on Barhis and Baresman, see E. Lehmann, *Zarathustra* I, 131 f.

101. This verse is in the so-called *Āprī*-hymns; the constant invocation to Barhis in these hymns speaks of the sublime holiness that is ascribed to the Barhis.

102. Thus a straw of grass similar to the Barhis was spread out for the serpents in the serpent-sacrifice. *Śāṅkhāyana G.* IV, 15, 5.

103. Hillebrandt, *Neu und Vollmondsopfer* 71; Schwab, *Tieropfer* 64 f. 115, etc. (compare *Ṛv.* VII, 13, 1; X, 15, 11, etc.). Sitting on the Vedi and on the Barhis amounts to the same; Vedi is just the place covered by Barhis. We may refer here to the rule that what fell on the Barhis was not considered as having fallen from the sacrificial offering (and thus depriving the god of that). *Taitt. Saṃh.* VI, 3, 8, 3.

104. The assumption favoured here, that the prehistory of the Vedic sacrifice dates back to a type of sacrifice without the sacrificial fire (compare for that E. Lehmann, *op. cit.*, I, 126 ff.; Schrader, *Reallex.* 599 f.),—which is then to be ascribed later to the Indo-European age?—should not prejudice the ethnological estimation of the age of the sacrificial fire (compare Ada Thomsen, *Arch. f. Rel.* XII, 479). I may refrain from going into this problem.

105. That, to which Lehmann, *op. cit.*, 128 f. draws our attention, is clearly preserved in the sacrifice to the dead; see its description in the text.

106. One cannot be misled on this quite evident view by the fact, that the present form of the ritual of burning has acquired the character of an offering. Hillebrandt, *ibid.*, 169.

107. Like the sacrificial grass, many other tools used for the sacrifice are burnt. Thus, the wooden logs placed around the sacrificial fire, the wooden span named *avaru*, which plays a rôle in the erection of the sacrificial pillar, the branch which serves to drive away the calves of the cow at the time of the milking of the sacrificial milk, the spit used in the Animal-sacrifice, the jar of ointment used to anoint the *Agnicayana*-sacrificer, etc. (see Hillebrandt, *Neu und Vollmondsopfer* 145. 148. 169; Schwab, *Tieropfer* 121. 155 ff; Weber *Ind. Stud.* XIII, 285). Besides burning, there is burying: often where the sinister element plays a role. It is characteristic for this, that the rest of the spits is thrown into the fire in the animal sacrifice, but for the heartspit, a different treatment is prescribed: the priest should keep it without touching the others or himself with it; it cannot be placed on the earth or in water (*Śatap. Br.* III, 8, 5, 9 f; *Kāty.* VI, 8, 3; *Āpast.* VII, 23, 10); finally, it is buried at a lonely place, at the edge of a pool, etc., or hidden under the earth; one returns from that place without turning around (Schwab 161 ff.). The special treatment of this spit rests upon the fact, that the heart is the seat of life (a *mantra* spoken on the heart removed from the spit, appears to express this: Schwab 135); the suffering of the killed animal enters into the heart-spit, it is said in *Śatapatha* (*ibid.* §8); most probably, the original sense is that something of the substance of the soul of the animal is attached to it. Other cases of burying, in the context of cult practices like sorcery, are common; the Buddha, facing death, instructs Cunda to bury the remnants of the last meal offered to him and enjoyed by him (*Mahāparinibbāna Sutta*). One may be allowed to consider this as an echo of sacral burying. One cannot draw a firm line between burying and burning; it is not only the treatment of the human corpse, in which both practices are in vogue side by side (compare *Pāraskara* III, 8, 12 in the ritual of the cattle-sacrifice to Rudra: 'the entrails smeared with blood are thrown into fire, or they bury it in the ground'). Besides burying and burning we would have to mention finally washing away by the water, which is used at the same time for removing impure, ghostly substances causing diseases, as also for the removal of the fluids which cannot be separated from it, and which have in them the holiness coming from the gods and, therefore, dangerous; one may refer to the discussion on sacrificial bath (*avabhṛtha*) (in the Section on '*Dīkṣā* and Sacrificial Bath').

108. Robertson Smith has arrived at the same assumption on the basis of Semitic sources (*Religion of the Semites* 1, 367).

109. Bergaigne, *Rel. védique* I, 71 gives the material.

110. My interpretation here is different from Ada Thomsen *ibid.*, 479.

111. We are considering only the important types of the sacrificial fire and these, only in their basic relationship.

112. It can hardly be doubted that this process occurs, in substance, before the *Ṛgvedic* age.

113. *Śatapatha Brāhm.* II, 1, 4, 4.

114. As both the Cake-sacrifice and Animal-sacrifice permit one fire or three fires, and as the Soma-sacrifice alone is bound to the three fires among the main types of sacrifice, it may be presumed that this is the starting-point from which the use of the three fires developed (similarly Knauer, *Festgruß an Roth* 64).

115. For the following, compare Hillebrandt *V.M.* II, 88 ff.

116. Ludwig III, 356.

117. One must reproach Ludwig's argument cited in the preceding note for leaving out the factual distribution of the functions of the three fires, while discussing their origin.

118. I do not go here into the details of irrelevant fluctuations in the concerned regulations (Hillebrandt *V.M.* II, 89).

119. *Śatapatha Brāhmana* II, 4, 1, 3 ff.; Compare *Śāṅkhāyana Sr.* II, 14. 15.

120. Compare on this Weber, *Ind. Studien* X, 327, note 5.

121. *Śatapatha Br.* I, 7, 3, 27; III, 8, 1, 7.

122. With that, the most prevalent, and as it appears to me, the original relationship is expressed. (Details with regard to practical usage have indeed been observed), compare *Śat. Br.* I, 7, 3, 26f; Kāty. I, 8, 34. 35; Hillebrandt, *Neu und Vollmondsopfer* 65 not: 4, etc.

123. The sacrificial reward in the New Moon and the Full moon sacrifices (Hillebrandt 44. 133). It is prepared over the fire named after it (*Kāty.* II, 5, 27), perhaps only because it appeared to belong as *dakṣiṇā* to *Dakṣiṇāgni.* Hillebrandt *V.M.* II, 91, note 1 interprets differently.

124. *Śatapatha Brāhmaṇa* II, 3, 2, 6.

125. *Śāṅkhāyana Śraut.* II, 14, 3; 15, 4.

126. *Vāj. Saṃhitā* IX, 38; *Śatapatha Br.* V, 2, 4, 15 f.

127. *Śatapatha Br.* V, 2, 3, 2.

128. Compare *Kātyāyana* IV, 1, 2.3. 8; V, 8, 6. 16. 21, etc.

129. See p. 40.

130. Of course, apart from the rare case when the offering is made to a being not thought of as anthropomorphic: Indra's horses get horse-meat. It does not contradict the principle laid down here, if there is, on the other hand, the idea that there must be a certain distinction between that which is given to god and to man. 'Do not make the cake too broad. If he made it broad, it would be too human. Varily, what is human, is flawed in the sacrifice'. *Śat. Br.* I, 2, 2, 9 (Oltramare *La role du yajamāna* 22).

131. Latter missing or less important in the oldest Vedic period.

132. *Agnihotra* in the name of a dead person: *Ait. Br.* VII, 2; *Śat. Br.* XII, 5, 1, 4; *Āśv. Śraut.* III 10, 17; *Kāty.* XXV, 8, 9. Manessacrifice; *Taitt. Saṃh.* I, 8, 5, 1; *Kāty.* V, 8, 18, etc.

133. *Taitt. Saṃh.* I, 8, 1, 1; *Śat. Br.* V, 2, 3, 2; *Kāty XV*, 1, 10.

134. *Taitt. Saṃh.* I, 8, 9, 1; *Śat. Br.* V, 3, 1, 13; *Kāty.* XV, 3, 14.

135. *Vāj. Saṃh.* XVII, 70; *Kāty.* XVIII, 4, 2.

136. *Indische Studien* XIII, 272.

137. See e.g. *Baudhāyana* Dh. II, 1, 2, 27; *Śāṅkhāyana G.* IV, 1. 3. It is characteristic, that the rule for the propitiatory sacrifice offered to the deceased, in which many peculiarities of the cult of the Dead are dropped, says: 'Barley represents the sesame' (*ibid,* IV, 4, 9).

138. Corresponding to the number of syllables in *Gāyatrī, Triṣṭubh,* etc.

139. The distribution of the metres amongst the deities, upon which rests the ritual validity of the numbers, is seen in the *Ṛgveda* only in the beginnings.

140. I refer here to the detailed and useful discussion of Hillebrandt, *Tiere und Götter im vedischen Ritual* (83. *Jahresbericht der Schles. Ges. fur vaterl. Kultur*).

141. Compare *Śatap. Brāhmaṇa* III, 4, 1, 2.

142. *Śāṅkhāyana G.* III, 3, 1.

143. Compare *Kāty.* XIX, 3, 2. 3; XX, 7, 19.

144. *Ait. Brāhm.* II, 8, 5: 'The (sacrificial substance) stays the longest in the goat; that is why he is the most common of all the sacrificial animals'.

145. A Brāhmaṇa-text (*Taitt. Br.* III, 9, 1, 2 f.) says: 'If he were to conclude the sacrifice with the forest animals, father and son would quarrel...bears, man-eaters, robbers, beasts of prey and thieves would appear in the forest. It is said: the forest animals are no animals. If he were to conclude (the sacrifice) with the forest animals, the sacrificer would soon be carried away dead into the forest'.

146. The forest animals amongst these should be, incidentally, set free. *Ind. Studien* X, 348; *Taitt. Br.* III, 8, 19, etc.

147. The enjoyment of this meat was, of course, present in historic India, but formed an exception. See e.g. *Vinaya Piṭaka, Mahāvagga* VI, 23, 11.

148. See in the Section 'The Individual Sacrifices and Festivals'.

149. *Kauśika Sūtra* 127.

150. I shall be content to give a few of the exceptions to the rule about the sexual correspondence between the god and the sacrificial animal. Mitra and Varuṇa get a *vasā* at the end of the Soma-sacrifice (Hillebrandt, *Rit. Lit.* 134).—Ram for Sarasvatī (ibid, 125). Mother-sheep (or rather its image) for the Maruts (*ibid.*, 116; *Kāty.* V, 5, 17 f.). *Vasā* for the Maruts, see p. 201 with note 157 below. Many such cases can be explained by the fact that the once firmly rooted sacrifice of a certain animal got transferred to another deity by some coincidence.

151. That is why one selects, for the first consumption of meat by a child, meats of different animals, according to the special qualities which one wishes for the child (*Pāraskara* I, 19, etc.).

152. Compare Keith, *JRAS.* 1907, 936 f.

153. Hillebrandt *V.M.* I, 231, note 2.

154. *Śat. Br.* V, 5, 4, 1.

155. *Vāj. Saṃh.* XXIV, 1. Likewise, more often for Agni, e.g., *Taitt. Saṃh.* II, I, 2, 7.

156. *Rāmāyaṇa I*, 49, 9 ed. Bombay.

157. To be more exact, a cow, not pregnant and also not yielding milk. *Kāty.* XIV, 2, 11. Yet in *Taitt. Saṃh.* II, 1, 6, 2 a male piebald (pṛsni) sacrificial animal for the Maruts.

158. *Kāty.* VIII, 9, 1.

159. *Taitt. S.* II, 1, 8, 5. Exactly the same way, the rain-sacrifice of the Zulus: *The heads of villages select some black oxen, there is not one white among them...It is supposed that cattle are chosen because when it is about to rain the sky is overcast with dark clouds* (Callaway, *The Religious System of the Amazulu*, p. 59).

160. *Kāty.* XXII, 3, 14. 15. Certainly the colour of Rudra has its influence here; the animal is offered to Agni as the one accompanied by Rudra.

161. Schwab, *Das altind. Tieropfer* p. 112 ff.

162. *ibid.* 121 f.

163. And also in such a way, that every individual part remains intact and the bones are not broken (*Ath. V.* IX, 5, 23; *Ait. Br.* II, 6, 15, etc.; Compare Kohler, *Arch. f. Rel.* XIII, 153 f.).

164. In addition to this, an invitation-formula, in which it is said, according to *Taitt. Br.* III, 6, 11, 1. 2 (compare *Vāj. S.* XXI, 43; Schwab 144)—the formula is laid down for the sacrifice of the goat to Indra and Agni-: 'May Hotar honour Indra and Agni. Of the sacrificial meal of the goat, they eat today the fat cut out from the middle portion before the demons and human enemies could seize it. Now they should enjoy them (here follows the praise of the pieces which are to be offered)'. Compare also *Āpastamba Dh.* I, 6, 18, 25 for the special place of the plexus-sacrifice.

165. Schwab 149.

166. *Gṛhya* II, 4, 13. 14.

167. XV, 3, 13 (732). Compare also Vendidad 18, 70 and (where Darmesteter refers to this verse) Catull 89.

168. Levit. 4.

169. Levit. 7.

170. Levit. 3.

171. *The Religious System of the Amazulu*, p. 11. 141. 177.

172. More on the distribution of offering, see in Ada Thomsen, *Arch. f. Rel.* XII, 462f.

173. Compare Wundt, *Völkerpsychologie* II, 2, p. 10 ff.

174. They are collected by Hubert-Mauss, *L'année sociologique* 1898, 79 note 2, Compare also 80 note 4.

175. Thus *Rāmāyaṇa* (I, 14, 37 ed. Bombay) also lets 'the smell of the smoke of the plexus' be inhaled in the description of a sacrifice.

176. Schwab 132.

177. Hillebrandt, *Neu-und Vollmondsopfer* 171.

178. In its favour is the fact, that the stomach and the excrements of the sacrificial animal, which were apparently to be considered as waste, were similarly treated with blood (Schwab *ibid.*). Different view in Keith, *JRAS*, 1907, 940 f.

179. See Hillebrandt, *Ritual-Lit.* 153 and the literature mentioned there, Keith *ibid.* 943 ff., *The Veda of the Bl. Yaj. School*, CXXXVII ff. For Human-sacrifice compare Eggeling *SBE.* XLIV, XXXIII ff.

180. See Weber, *ZDMG.* XVIII, 263 ff.; *Ind. Stud.* XIII, 218 f. 251 f.; compare also Hillebrandt. *Ritual-Lit.* 162 f. One may mention incidentally that 21 beans were thrown when the human head was brought. Is it a sacrifice to the dead for the killed man? Was the bean a part of the dead even from the Indo-European period? Compare L.v. Schroeder, *WZKM.* XV, 187 ff.

181. The last one who practiced this was Śyāparṇa Śāyakāyana (VI, 2, 1, 39); whose name goes back to the period which can be called historical.

182. We find, like the Construction-sacrifice, a custom of burying an embalmed stone, while constructing a house, under the central pillar as a symbol and vehicle of dripping abundance (*Śāṅkh. G.* III, 3, 10). Compare also *Āśv. G.* II, 8, 14.

183. See Taylor, *Anfänge der Kultur* I, 104 ff; M. Winternitz, *Mitteilungen der Anthrop. Ges. in Wien*, Sitz.-Ber. 19th April 1887; *Mélusine* III, 497; Sartori, *Zeitschr. f. Ethnologie* 1898, 1 ff.

184. Even cremation of widows (see the section on Funeral) mentioned in the Veda is certainly not a Human-sacrifice; the wife is sent through fire into the other world with the dead man as his possession.

185. See Weber *ZDMG. ibid.*

186. The Buddhists count the Human-sacrifice together with the Horse-sacrifice: *Saṃyutta Nikāya* Vol. I, p. 76.

187. Although the Jātaka-commentary (Vol. III, p. 44) among the Buddhists mentions a great sacrifice of always four sacrificial animals of the same type, amongst them also of four sacrificial human beings, this is to be judged as an excogitated artifice of the sacrifice, if not as a pure creation of imagination, and nothing of popular reality can be ascribed to it.

188. A further possibility is the surrender of the human life forfeited by sin, which is represented as a sacrifice. It does not appear, that this could have any reference to India. Indian literature on law knows, of course, of cases, where purification carried out for the good of the sinner appears as his killing; the gravity of the sin needs the sharpest remedy: death or procedures that bring about death. But such killing is no sacrifice and does not revolve around the forms of the sacrificial rite. If at all, there is an exception to this (*Āpastamba Dh.* I, 9, 25, 12; compare *Vasiṣṭha* XX, 25, 26), then it ought to be the frequent instance of transformation of a procedure obtaining elsewhere into a sacrifice. Compare my remarks in Th. Mommsen, *Zum ältesten Strafrecht der Kulturvölker* 83 f.

189. Like the story of Śunaḥśepa, the Buddhistic story of sacrificing the imprisoned kings to a tree-deity (*Jātaka* vol. III, p. 160; more in Cambridge Jātaka-Index under *Sacrifice* [*human*], etc). The well-known Śunaḥśepa story narrates how a king indebted to Varuṇa—he had promised his son to him as sacrifice—is persued by the gods' wrath and undertakes to sacrifice a young Brahmana in his stead: he should be sacrificed as a sacrificial animal in the *Rājasūya*-sacrifice. The gods who are invoked by the aggrieved youth, give him freedom; but Varuṇa turns his anger away from the king. This story should be

read to the king who offers sacrifice by the priest at the celebration of *Rajāsūya*, so that he may be freed from all sins, from the fetters of Varuṇa (Weber, *Über den Rājāsuya*, 52). Weber (*ibid.*, 47) assumes—perhaps appropriately—that the real significance of this recitation at the *Rājasūya* lies in spelling out the termination of the old custom of human sacrifice.

190. It is doubtful, whether Soma-sacrifice can be considered as the 'sacrificing of the god', as understood by Hubert-Mauss (*Année sociol.* 1898, 129). Soma is offered, so that the god is intoxicated, strengthened. And because highest powers are present in the Soma, it is itself considered as god. But it is not sacrificed, in as much as it is god. Its occasional playful identification with Vṛtra appears to me to be meaningless.

191. Compare Hillebrandt, *Vedische Mythologie* I, 3 ff. and the literature quoted there in addition to Macdonell-Keith, *Ved. Index* II, p. 475 concerning the botanical question.

192. It concerns the Aśvins in whose sphere of ideas honey plays a main rôle, and who perhaps really received the offering of honey in olden times (Hillebrandt *V.M.* I, 239 ff., Small, ed. 44, 100).

193. Hillebrandt *ibid.*, 239.

194. Thus correctly, Hillebrandt *ibid.*, 238.

195. Henry has a different view in Caland-Henry, *Agniṣṭoma* 471 f. Compare also Oltramare, *Le rôle du Yajamāna* (Muséon 1903), p. 20 f., sep. note. Keith, *Veda of Black Yajus School* CXIX f.

196. The *Surā* found sacral application in the ceremonies of *Sautrāmaṇī* and *Vājapeya*. In both cases, the ritual appears to have the character of priestly subtleties, so that the possibility of old, really popular Surā libations cannot, naturally, be denied. Compare Geiger, *Ostiran. Kultur* 233 about the sacral application of the corresponding Avestic drink (*hurā*).

197. *Gobhila* IV, 8, 11. 12; 9, 13. 14.

198. Weber, *Ind. Stud.* X, 350; Hillebrandt, *Rit. Lit.* 160.

199. *Kauśika Sūtra* 116.

200. The knowledge of the three priestly classes that is laid down in the *Ṛgveda*, *Yajurveda* and the *Sāmaveda*.

201. Thus, it remains questionable for the time being, in which form the popular festivities mentioned by the later sources and called as *samāja* (*Pāli samajja*) (compare Hardy, *Album Kern* 61 ff.; compare also his *Archiv f. Rel.* V, 132 ff.) contained cult elements, especially of the sacrificial cult, and how far they date back to the old period.

202. I refer to the fine essay by Oltramare (see note 195 above) on the *Yajamāna*; also refer to my remarks in *Arch. f. Rel.* 1904, 221 ff. I am not particularly convinced by *Hillebrandt V.M.* II, 121 ff.

203. Jolly, *Recht und Sitte* 77.

204. *Āpastamba Śr.* XI, 16, 14, Compare Hillebrandt, *Rit. Lit.* 128.

205. Even beyond the people, the whole universe is considered to be interested in the right accomplishment of the sacrifice, particularly in the priestly speculations of the later Vedic age. I refer to the good remarks made by Oltramare *ibid.* 11 f.

206. Compare Hillebrandt, *Nationale Opfer in Altindien* (*Festgruß an Böhtlingk 40 ff.*) I refer specially to the story of *Kūṭadanta Suttanta* (*Dīgha Nikāya* V) from the Buddhistic literature.

207. *Vāj. Saṃh.* XXII, 22.

208. *Śatapatha Brāhmaṇa* IV, 6, 8, 13. This is not contradicted by one among these sacrificers taking over the specific and typical functions of the householder.

209. Is it because these, as Brahmanas, are already in the state of holiness demanded of them (Hubert-Mauss, *L'année socilogique* 1898, 53)? I doubt very much. The organizer of the sacrifice as such needed the Dīkṣā, even though he was a Brahmana. The idea seems to be, that the venture to donate Soma to the gods has its own claims on the employer which are not valid for those giving help alone. Thus, the washing away of the holy substance is a more decisive procedure for the sacrificer and his wife than for the priests (Caland-Henry 401 f.).

210. Of course, certain personalities or the members of certain families have a right,

on the basis of the things that happened earlier, to expect such a contract, and may express in word and deed their vexation at not being awarded it. But, it is finally the sacrificer who makes the choice.

211. *Āpastamba Śr.* IV, 5, 1; 8, 4.

212. *Śatapatha Brāhm.* I, 3, 1, 26.

213. Compare Zimmer 186 ff., my remarks in *ZDMG.* LI, 273, note 2 and note on *Ṛv*, X, 98; Macdonell-Keith, *Vedic Index* under *Varṇa* and the vast literature mentioned there about the much discussed question whether the sacral special rights of these Brahmana-families had been clearly laid down even in Ṛgvedic times.

214. If he himself belongs to the privileged circle, he can, on his part, function as a sacrificial priest; compare below p. 282, note 237.

215. Such a speciality, which we can in fact recognise, is mentioned in the text; p. 212.

216. Compare in general Macdonell-Keith, *Ved. Index.* see note 213 above.

217. *Aitareya* VIII, 24. *Śatapatha Br.* IV, 1, 4, 5.6 also shows characteristically that *Purohita* was considered invariably as part and parcel of the king.

218. Weber, *Ind. Stud.* X, 79.

219. Compare Hopkins, *Ruling Caste in Anc. India* 151 ff. for the *Mahābhārata.*

220. According to the norm, apparently one; the only evidence about several *Purohitas* I can mention (Sāyaṇa on *Ṛv.* X, 57, 1; compare Geldner, *Vedische Studien* II, 144) is in a story of a very fictitious character; these four Purohitas mentioned in it were, incidentally, brothers.

221. *Ait. Br.* VIII, 27. It is said in the marriage-*mantra*: 'So let us do the marital journey'.

222. Bloomfield, *The Atharvaveda* 30.

223. *Ait. Br.* VIII, 24.

224. *Kauṭilīyaśāstra*, I, 5.

225. It would be a rewarding work—what we cannot undertake here—to pursue the history of this status and its limitations, if at all there were any, as against the purely temporal, highest offices of the state.

226. *Śatapatha Br.* XIII, 4, 4, 1.

227. Vasiṣṭha 19, 40 f.

228. *Kūṭadantasuttanta* (*Dīgha Nikāya*), already mentioned on p. 280, note 206.

229. Among these, the discussion on this aspect is interesting that it is improper to sacrifice, if public opinion can say something against the virtues, wisdom, etc., of the king and the *Purohita:* a new illustration to prove how these two important persons stand next to each other on such occasions.

230. *Mahāvagga* (*Vinaya Piṭaka*), X, 2, 6.

231. Compare *Vasiṣṭha* 19, 3f. and Bühler's note on *Gautama* 11, 17.

232. Thus, a claim is made in the literature of the *Atharvaveda* which deals mainly with magic, that the *Purohita* is an *Atharvavedin* (Bloomfield, *The Atharvaveda* 29f.; 32ff.; compare also the *Kauṭilīyaśāstra* I, 5). Compare below page 282, note 242.

233. Compare the treatment of the same question in Geldner, *Ved. Studien* II, 143 ff. I do not fully agree with his view. Compare also the references in Bloomfield *SBE.* XLII, LXVIII, note 3.

234. *Manu* VII, 78; compare IV, 179. *Ṛv.* I, 94, 6 could itself give the impression that the Purohita 'had been a proper *ṛtvij*, i.e. the sacrificial priest' (Geldner *ibid.*, 144); if one were to consider this reference in the light of what we know otherwise, then it can be shown, that the poet should not be understood so rigidly. He identifies Agni with different *ṛtvijas* one after the other, and calls him also Purohita, which position is sufficiently related to that of the *ṛtvijas* to be named besides them. Then he continues: you know the qualities of *ṛtvijas*. A poet could speak like that without counting the Purohitas amongst *ṛtvijas* in the strict sense.

235. Thus, we can understand a reference like *Ait. Br.* VII, 26 as such a rule; I refer to page 212f. It may be noted yet, how certain functions are accorded to *Adhvaryu* or *Purohita* in the consecration of the king (*Śat. Br.* V, 4, 2, 1; 4, 4, 15; *Kātyāyana* XV, 5, 30):

Another *Ṛtvij* with his technical designation as such, e.g. the *Brahman*, would have been named beside *Adhvaryu*, if it had been a matter concerning such a person and not exactly the *Purohita* had been incommensurate for these designations.

236. On this, see p. 218.

237. The sacrificial master, as far as he functioned as *Purohita*, took over the position of the *Hotar* himself. It appears to be the position of the *Hotar* as a rule. *Āpastamba Śr.* XII, 17, 2, *Gobhila* I, 9, 9.

238. Amongst the gods, Bṛhaspati is also the *Purohita* besides Agni in the *Ṛv.* (II, 24, 9; IV, 50, 7). The only difference is, that Agni is the *Purohita* of men and B. that of gods.

239. Agni is Hotar and Purohita at the same time, *Ṛv.* I, 1, 1; III, 3, 2; 11, 1; V, 11, 2. His designation as Purohita is connected with technical expressions referring to *Hotar* VIII, 27, 1; X, 1, 6.

240. *Ṛv.* X, 66, 13; In 70, 7, there is even talk of *purohitāv ṛtvijā* in short, where the standing technical expression *hotar* is left out.

241. *Aitareya Br.* VII, 26.

242. Compare Bloomfield, *The Atharvaveda* 32 f. Obviously, this relationship depends upon the relationship between the position of the *Purohita* and the *Atharvaveda* (p. 281, note 232).

243. *Taitt. Saṃh.* III, 5, 2, 1.

244. Geldner (*Ved. Studien* II, 144 f.) has correctly considered both these last sources, though I think, he goes rather too far in connecting the ideas of Brahman and Purohita. A part of his sources appears to me to be suffering from the blame that *brahman* is understood by him rather partially as the technical designation of a priest (comp. below p. 284, note 285). Thus, the reference (not considered by G.) in *Taitt. Saṃh.* I, 8, 9, 1, which specifies *brahman* and *rājanya* in the same context in which *Śatap. Br.* V, 3, 1, 2, names *purohita* and *sūyamāna*, does not appear to me to prove anything.

245. We shall come back to the position of the priest-god Bṛhaspati in the older texts on page 284, note 285.

246. *Pañc. Br.* XIV, 6, 8. Here is also a reference to the difference between the *Brahman* and the *Purohita Āśv. G.* I, 12, 7.

247. Weber, *Ind. Stud.* X, 141. 376 has already collected material in connection with these lists and duly evaluated them.

248. Other hymns of the *Ṛgveda* in which one or several of these names are missing, but which complement one another alternatively, confirm this list; see Weber, *ibid.* X, 141 with note 4. The songs are to be noted for the *ṛtudevatās* mainly; compare my note on *Ṛv.* I, 1, 1 (also *VS*, XXIII, 58); see also IX, 114, 3 and the note on VIII, 72, 7).

249. Thus, Henry (Caland-Henry 478).

250. *Kāty.* IX, 8 8ff.; *Ind. Studien* X, 376; Caland-Henry 186f.

251. The second *Adhvaryu* is the *Pratiprasthātar*, nowhere mentioned in the very first sources; I shall try to prove (p. 215 f.) that in the older period, another priest, *Agnīdh*—he is mentioned in the list above—was considered as the second *Adhvaryu*. If two *Praśāstar* appear in the wording of the formulas, also this can be explained easily as parallels to Mitra-Varuṇa; *Praśāstar* is also called Maitrāvaruṇa (see p. 216).

252. The last name is the second synonym of *Praśāstar* (compare earlier note). Corresponding form in Caland-Henry 221 may also be compared.

253. Amongst the possessors of *dhiṣṇya*, *Adhvaryu* is missing from the seven priests discussed here; *Acchāvāka* has come in his place. In fact, from the point of view of the ritual-texts, these are the seven 'Heralds' (*hotrāḥ*; Caland-Henry 3.349, Compare 211 ff. 287; Weber, Ind. Stud. IX, 375). Was it considered necessary to take up *Acchāvāka* who is similar to *Hotar* in character, and to remove *Adhvaryu* who is obviously too much unlike to him?

254. See Darmesteter, *Le Zend-Avesta*, vol. I, p. LXX F.; Henry, Caland-Henry 477 ff.; Keith, *Veda of Black Yajus School* CXIX.

255. The derivation of *hu-* ['pour (the sacrificial-cast)'] is considered by me to be probable for grammatical reasons. In this regard I agree with Wackernagel *Ai. Gramm.* II,

189. Yet the origin of *hu-* ('call', thus the meaning: 'caller') cannot be unconditionally excluded: in this case, whatever is said here about the history of the word will have to be modified. Hotar as 'sacrificer'; seven Hotars. Compare Weber, *Ind. Studien* X, 139. See also p. 215.

256. We have to deal here with the distinction of the *juhotayas* and *yajatayas* (Hill. *Rit. Lit.* 99) so called in the systematic sacrificial texts of the Veda; in the former, *Hotar* speaks and *Adhvaryu* acts; in the latter, the old individual priest functions, for which the name *Adhvaryu* is used, corresponding to the substantial part of his duties.

257. See Hillebrandt, *Bezzenbergers Beiträge* IX, 192 ff.

258. One should like to believe that these invocations which are also called *nivid* ('*taking into account*'), represent the original essence of the great recitations; the ways of primitive man to invoke the '*laudatory names*' of the beings to whom the offering was made, have been really preserved in them. But it is disputable whether the nivids are of ancient origin in their extant form, as Haug (*Ait. Brāhm.* Introd. 36) presumes.

259. Compare my remarks *ZDMG.* XLII, 243 f. In the later ritual, even the great Soma-recitations which have taken the place, to a certain extent, of Puronuvākyas correspond regularly with Yājyā verses (compare Geldner, Ved. Studien II, 152).

260. *ZDMG. ibid.*—Bergaigne (*Recherches sur l'histoire de la liturgie védique* 13 ff.) appears to me to have gone too far in assuming such beginnings.

261. I have given more details in *ZDMG, ibid.* p. 242 f. Compare also Bergaigne, *Recherches sur l'histoire de la liturgie védique* 15ff.

262. The whole in prose; the type discussed above p. 7 f.

263. *Kauś. Br.* XXVIII, 3.

264. See for example Hillebrandt, *Neu-und Vollmondsopfer*, 32.82.135; *Taitt. Saṃh.* VI, 3, 1, 2. *Vaitānasūtra* 18, 1. *Āpastamba* V, 13, 8, etc.

265. Look up for example, the situation described by Hillebrandt p. 68. One may also mention here how Adhvaryu and Agnīdh carry out the recitation of the sacrificial *mantra* in one of the most common types of the sacrificial offerings (e.g. Hillebrandt p. 94). *Adhvaryu* says to *Agnīdh*: 'Om! Let him hear!'—i.e., *Hotar. Agnīdh*: 'May it be! May he hear!' And now Adhvaryu to Hotar whose attention has been attracted: 'Recite the sacrificial *mantra*!'

266. I disregard here *Brahman*, the supervisor of the whole, the fourth priest of the smaller sacrifices; compare p. 218. on him.

267. Hillebrandt p. 90 f.

268. When there is a reference once to 'both the *Adhvaryu*' in the *Ṛgveda* (II, 16, 5; compare I, 181, 1; X, 52, 2), then it may be asked while describing the parallel between *Adhvaryu* and *Agnīdh*, whether, in olden times these two are to be understood in place of *Adhvaryu* and *Pratiprasthātar* in accordance with the later conditions. This supposition is supported by Ṛv. X, 41, 3 and above all by the verse in *Śāṅkhāyana Śr.* I, 6, 3 (in other form, however, *Āśv. Śr.* I, 3, 24; *Āpast. Śr.* XXIV, 12, 7).

269. One may compare Schwab, *Altind. Tieropfer* 90 for illustration: 'Maitrāvaruṇa steps in front of Hotar to the right side of his seat, puts his staff down in the Vedi, and standing, with his body bent a little forward, he directs his Praiṣa to the Hotar for the recitation of...the sacrificial verse'.

270. See e.g. Schwab 96. 114. 117. 132 f. 137. 144 f. He distributes the work with Hotar variously in such a way, that of the two verses pertaining to an offering (above p. 215), he says the first and Hotar the second.

271. In the *Āprī*-litany.

272. II, 36, 6, cf. I, 15, 6.

273. *pra-śās* is often a verb for royal rule and the royal ruler κατ᾽ ἐξοχήν are after all Mitra and Varuṇa. Compare *varuṇa-praśiṣṭāḥ*, Ṛv. X, 66, 2.

274. More exactly: to Agni as the one accompanied by the divine consorts.

275. Caland-Henry 368. 371 f.

276. '*Agnīdh* donates semen to the Neṣṭar, the N. to the wife', says the *Taittīrya Saṃhitā* (VI, 5, 8, 6). Compare also *Śatapatha Br.* IV, 4, 2, 18.

277. Hillebrandt *V.M.* I, 250. 261, note 2.

278. Of course, not in the later, quite artificial distribution of fourtimes four priests (*Ind. Stud.* X, 143 f., Caland-Henry 2).

279. The following refers often to the explanations of Haug, *Ait. Brāhm.* Introduction p. 17 ff.

280. There is a clear allusion to two of them (*Prastotar* and *Udgātar*) in *Ṛv.* VIII, 81, 5; it may be by chance that Pratihartar is not mentioned in the *Ṛv.*

281. On this, compare my remarks *GGA.* 1908, 723 f.; Konow *Sāmavidhānabrāhmaṇa* 22. I also refer to Bloomfield *WZKM.* XVII. 156 ff.

282. It is well-known, that the order of the *Ṛgveda* emphasises them.

283. And at least according to the later ritual, so that the recitation of the hymn preceded the reciting litany. Incidentally, the rule implemented in the ritual-texts, that the hymns and the litanies must be present always in the same number and individually belong to one another, appears to be an artifice of relatively recent origin. The songs addressed to the Soma that purifies itself, have no real connection with the litanies of the Hotar; yet, one insisted on this connection and tailored every thing to match of the hymns and litanies. This led to arbitrary constructions, as mentioned in *Ind. Stud.* X, 385, note 1 (compare also 374, note 3).

284. If the singers also participate in the enjoyment of the Soma-cup (*camasa*), one may, however, consider its peculiar isolated position in the ceremony. See Schol. on *Kāty.* IX, 12, 3; Caland Henry 219.

285. The main difficulty we have here is that the word *brahman* can mean the Brahmana in general as well as the priest of sacrifice Brahman in the technical sense. Geldner (*Ved. Stud.* II. 145) wants to understand in *Ṛv.* mainly 'in the specific sense of the main priest of sacrifice or Purohita'; a view which does not appear to me to be tenable after considering the appropriate references. A tendency, which is generally justified, to explain the *Ṛgvedic* words according to their later technical sense cannot be applied indiscriminately to all cases. All the same, there is no dispute when in X, 141, 3—a much later passage—there is a reference to 'Bṛhaspati, the Brahman' where the word can have its later special sense. This I consider to be impossible for II, 1, 3; X, 52, 2 may be more appropriate. If Bṛhaspati in IV, 50, 7, 8 also appears to be identified with the *brahman* who precedes the king, then verse 9 must be taken into consideration where *brahman*, in contrast to *rājan*, signifies undoubtedly the Brahmana in general. Thus it is quite possible that the god Bṛhaspati before he became the Brahman of the gods in technical sense, was simply understood as the Brahmana, the priest amongst the gods: and which concurs therewith, that in the formula *Bṛhaspatir ukthāmadāni saṃsiṣat* (*Ait. Br.* II, 38, etc.), he carries out the technical functions of the *Hotar* and not of the *Brahman.* Compare my notes on *Ṛv.* VII, 33, 14; X, 88, 17.

286. This is to be called in solemn language *Brahman* as is expressly prescribed (*Kāty,* IX, 8, 11). The introduction of the *Brahman* in its later sense which seized for itself the name, could have been the cause for the change of name. Both the meanings of Brahman have been mixed up, with a certain deliberateness in *Śatapatha Br.* IV, 6, 6, 5. Compare *NGGW.* 1915, 207, note 4 for Brāhmaṇācchaṃsin. Also *NGGW*, 1916, 731 ff.

287. See the material in Weber, *Ind. Stud.* X, 34, 35.

288. I do not intend here to go through all the subordinate priestly offices. Yet, we may mention *Acchāvāka* ('Addresser'—called so because of *Ṛv.* V, 25, 1, compare *Kauś. Br.* XXVIII, 5, Caland-Henry 220 f.), who appears in the Soma-sacrifice as the third assistant of Hotar (beside Maitrāvaruṇa and Brāhmaṇācchaṃsin.) constantly in the later Vedic lore. I cannot discover any reliable traces of the existence of this in the old lists of the missing priests (Bergaigne has a different view, in *Rech. sur l'histoire de la liturgie védique* 47); References in e.g. *Kauṣītaki Brāhmaṇa*, XXVIII, 4-6 (compare also *Ait. Br.* VI, 14, 8; Kaṭh. XXVI, 9; Hillebrandt, *Rit. Lit.* 130 at the end) appear to me to refer directly to its addition at the relatively later age.

289. The derivative from *dah-* 'burn' (Whitney; Hillebrandt Mythologie I, 482; Charpentier, *Desiderativbildung* 67), I think, is wrong on account of factual reasons; the

voluntary death by fire of the sages like Kalanos, referred to by Hillebrandt, is not known to the Veda and does not suit the context in which *Dīkṣā* is understood. Should one think, with Weber (*Ind. Stud.* X, 358 note 1), with myself (*ZDMG.* XLIX, 176, note 1) and Güntert (*IF.* XXX, 98 ff.), of the root *dāś-* (=*dāś*), so that the word expresses the wish to serve the gods? It is possible that the derivative of *dakṣ-* (*Pet. Dictionary*) is more appropriate. Though we, for our part, would hardly express the mystic and magic properly to be obtained by *dīkṣā* as *dakṣa*, such an idea could have easily suggested itself to the ancients. It may be seen, how there is talk of *dakṣa* precisely in the *mantras* of the *Dīkṣā*-ritual (*Ts.* I, 2, 2, 2,; 3, 1): in addition even outside of this field, the use of the word family *dakṣ-* which can lead to assumptions in this direction: thus *Ṛv.* VI, 48, 1; VII, 16, 6; 32, 9; 97, 8, etc. I do not want to give much importance to the play upon words in *Śat. Br.* II, 2, 2, 2. Different opinion on *Dīkṣā*, v. Schroeder, *Ar. Religion*, II, 249, note 2.

290. This carrying down to the water is technically called *abhy-ava-har* (with the accusative *apaḥ*), just as the climbing down of the sacrifice thither is called *abhy-ava-i* (*ava-i*). Accordingly, one need not doubt in the case of the well-known connections of the verbs *har* and *bhar*, that *Śatapatha* (IV, 4, 5, 1) has a right to say *tad yad apo 'bhyavaharanti tasmād avabhṛthaḥ*. Removal of some sort of impurity is not implied by the word.

291. Compare above page 20, note 21.

292. Compare, on the following, B. Lindner, *Die Dikshâ* (1878); Hillebrandt, *Rit. Lit.* 125 f; Caland-Henry 11 ff. 66, 393 ff.; Lévi, *La doctrine du sacrifice* 102 ff.; Hubert-Mauss, *L-année sociologique* 1898, 48 ff.; Keith, *The Veda of the Black Yajus School* CXIII ff.

293. The black antelope-skin which plays a significant rôle in the sacrificial ritual, is considered as an embodiment of sacred being (*brahman*) in the Brāhmaṇa-texts. Sitting on this skin and clothing oneself with it will thus mean, for the Vedic period, infusing the sacrificer with the substance of holiness, just as sitting on the skin of the potent he-goat is considered as infusion of potency (compare *Śat. Br.* V, 2, 1, 24). Thus, *Atharvaveda* (XI, 5, 6) describes the *Brahmacārin* 'clothed with the antelope-skin dedicated (*dīkṣita*), with a long beard'. Also the antelope-horn (see the text) gets apparently similar holy resp. protective power against dangerous influences: that is why, it is used also in the anointment of the king, to be stroked over the moistened body (*Śatapatha Br.* V, 4, 2, 4; *Kāty.* XV, 6, 8). This may be compared with the use of shoes made from the skin of the black antelope *Taitt. Saṃh.* V, 4, 4, 4. Does the sacral significance of the black antelope date back to the repeated use of black colour (black clothes, etc.) in the primitive cult, where the concern is to make man invisible to the pursuing evil spirits? Throwing the waste of the sacrifice to the demons under the black antelope-skin would also concur with it (Hillebrandt, *Neu- und Vollmondsopfer* 171); should there be a darkening enclosure between them and the human beings? Different opinion on the black skin, Eitrem, *Opferritual u. Voropfer* p. 387, note 4.

294. *Taitt. Saṃh.* VI, 1, 4, 5 f. About remaining awake: *Maitr. Saṃh.* III, 6, 3, *Āpastamba* X, 12, 6, etc.

295. Analogies of this preparation for the Soma-sacrifice are also present in other contexts as preparations for such a holy act. Thus, the pupil who has violated an oath, has to spend the night near the fire covered in the black antelope-skin, before the purification ceremony necessary on that count. He then creeps out of the skin in the morning (*Baudhāyana Dh.* III, 4, 4). It is quite similar to the *Dīkṣā*, *Kauś Sūtra* 47, 12 ff. describes a *Dīkṣā* for the one who wants to practise sorcery. Observances like fasting, etc., as a preparation for holy acts are quite common; see pp. 219 ff.

296. VII, 33, 13? Compare my note on this verse; also on I, 164, 36; IV, 17, 15. Perhaps IX, 83, 1 may be considered where it is said: 'the raw (not the ready one), whose mass has not been heated, gains not this (Soma).' [On *Dīkṣā* as inner inspiration (burning), see text]. The sacrificial bath (p. 219), in close relation to the *Dīkṣā*, is mentioned, incidently, in VIII, 93, 23. We have no reason to doubt, that the word *avabhṛtha* is used in the same sense as it was used so often later (compare Ludwig V, 186); This is expressly proved, though somewhat redundant, by *nicumpuṇaḥ*, a word which has a special relation to the ideas concerning the sacrificial bath (*Vāj. Saṃh.* VIII, 27), whatever be its other meanings (is it related to *cupuṇikā*, *TS.* IV, 4, 5, 1?).

297. Plentiful information on this is to be found in Taylor's *Anfänge der Kultur* (German transl.) II, 411 ff.; compare also Lang, *Myth, Ritual and Religion* I, 111ff.; Ed. Lehmann, *Mystik* 9ff. etc. It may also be mentioned that amongst the coastal inhabitants of North-west America, the magician (Hametze) inspired by god, prepares himself for the festival, by starving and shutting himself off in the darkest corner of his house, before attending a celebration, because custom requires that the holy man should appear pale and lean (Ausland 1890, 269). The Vedic *Dīkṣā* is quite similar. Also amongst the Scots it is found that *a person was wrapped up in the skin of a newly slain bullock*; the concerned person, who is put down at a wild, lonely spot, gets then inspirations (Lang, *ibid.* I, 107). Retiring to a dark corner, enwrapping oneself in the skin of an animal, etc., belong to those so endlessly frequent precautionary measures of the primitive cult, through which one tried to protect oneself on particularly festive or dangerous occasions against the evil spirits. Thus, amongst the Red Indians, the menstruating woman is confined with her face painted black under a leather tent-cover (Ploß, *Das Kind*[2] II, 434), and many such customs. Wilken has collected them in his essays on the hair-sacrifice (*Revue coloniale intern.* III, IV). See also *Encycl. of Religion and Ethics*, V, p. 761f.

298. Compare also *Śatapatha Brāhmaṇa* IX, 5, 1, 1ff.

299. *Śatapatha Br.* XIII, 1, 7, 2.

300. *Āpastamba Śr.* X, 14, 1. The provision made for scratching, needs a special explanation (antelope-horn, see above p. 575 with note 293, p. 748, compare also *Anguttara Nikāya* vol. II, p. 207). The North-American Red Indians youth, before he becomes a complete warrior 'is forbidden to scratch his head or any other part with his fingers; he has to take a piece of wood for that' (Ploß *Das Kind*[2] II, 429). Further, I refer to the material given by Frazer, *Golden Bough*[2] I, 319 (see also p. 85 and register under *Scratch*). One may also compare a similar injunction against the use of one's hands while eating under certain circumstances (below p. 288, note 337). Is there in the hands of certain persons. or in certain situations such considerable power that touching with a tool capable of driving away evil powers (respectively with other hands while eating) seemed to be more advisable than with one's own hands? We have here an instance of the state of taboo in which a person becomes dangerous to himself. This is discussed by Edv. Lehmann ('Die Anfänge der Relig.', in *Kultur der Gegenwart*, 2nd Ed. 18).

301. See e.g. *Vāj. Saṃh.* IV, 2, 7; *Āpastamba Śraut* X, 6, 5 (compare also 12, 3); *Āśvalāyana Śraut* IV, 2, 3. Henry, *Journ. as.* 1905 II, 390 ff. understands *Tapas* differently.

302. *Taitt. Saṃhitā* III, 1, 1, 2 f.

303. Priestly families of prehistoric times.

304. *Bhagvatī* II, 1, 65 (Weber. Abh. der Berliner Akad. d. Wiss. Phil. hist. Klasse 1866, p. 286.)

305. Holding the breath was an important form of the *tapas*; it was taken for granted, that heat was created thereby (see e.g. *Baudhāyana Dh.* IV, 1, 24, and compare Buddhistic evidences like *Majjhima Nikāya*, vol. I, p. 244). Compare also my 'Lehre der Upanishaden' 261.

306. *Av.* XIX, 56, 5; *Taitt. Ār.* V, 6, 7; Ṛv. X, 154, 2; 167, 1; 109, 4; *Av.* III, 10, 12; *Ṛv.* X, 154, 5.

307. *Śatapatha Br.* X, 4, 4, 2.

308. Medicines inducing ecstasy?

309. Thus it is said of the Brahmana-pupil filled with *tapes*: 'In a moment he goes from the eastern to the northern (?) ocean' *Atharvaveda* XI, 5, 6.

310. *Aitareya Br.* I, 3.

311. The recipient of *Dīkṣā*.

312. *Śatapatha Br.* III, 1, 1, 8. Thus the *Dīkṣita* says at the beginning to Agni: 'My body is in you; your body is in me', and conversely at the end: 'My body, that was in you, is now mine; your body that was in me, is now in you' (*TS.* I, 2.11, 1.2; 3, 4, 3). The *Dīkṣita* 'has gone away from this world, yet has not arrived at the other' (*Kāṭh.* XXIII, 1). He does not stand up before anyone, he greets no one; all have to wish him (Caland-Henry 21). The king who wants to do the Horse-sacrifice is praised at first along with the

kings of antiquity, but from the *Dīkṣā* onwards together with the gods (Hillebrandt *Rit. Lit.* 151).

313. These are the sentences of Dietrich, *Mithrasliturgie*2, 157. Rich collections of ethnological material is to be found there and particularly in Frazer, *Golden Bough*2 III, 422 ff., in addition to Lévy-Bruhl, *Les fonctions mentales dans les sociétés inférieures* 417ff; Schurtz, *Altersklassen und Männerbünde* 102 ff.; *Encycl. of Rel. and Eth.* VII, 317 f.

314. Is there in *Jaim. Up. Br.* III, 11, 3 a slight trace of the relevant idea?

315. The rite for the one believed to be dead and buried *in effigie*, who returns alive and is introduced anew to life through embryonic state and birth is discussed by Caland, *Altindische Toten- und Bestattungsgebräuche* 89 (compare also the same, Urquell, N.F. II, 193 f. [1898]; C.H. Raabe, *Bijdr. tot de kennis van het hind. doodenritueel* 50 f.) is an interesting confirmation of the fact, that this is indeed the meaning of the clenched fists (Caland, *Arch. f. Rel.* XI, 128 expresses actually a different opinion about the clenching of the fists).—See in Lévi *loc. cit.* on further connections of the *Dīkṣā*-ritual to the parturition—is it not perhaps too much?—.

316. The presence of the motif of rebirth in Dīkṣā is also confirmed by the clear appearance of the same motif in *Upanayana* which can be compared in many respects with *Dīkṣā*. See p. 223—What particularly concerns the stammering, is reported of Congo in the context of related rites: '*Sometimes they carry on the pretence of talking gibberish*'. Of the African west coast north of Congo: '*It is amusing to see their affected simplicity.*' Of the North American Red Indians: '*They must pretend to have forgot the very use of their tongues, so as not to be able to speak*', (Frazer *ibid.*, 426. 429. 431.).

317. Henry (Caland-Henry, p. 477, note) compares it with the water-rites of the Avestic ritual at the end of the Yasna.

318. Compare amongst others Robertson Smith, *Religion of the Semites*, Vol. I, p. 405. 432 f.; Eitrem, *Opferritus u. Voropfer* 132.

319. Water which has taken up these potencies, gets thus special magical power. It is said of the sacrificial bath of the great Horse-sacrifice: 'Once the sacrificer has come out, the evil-doers get in, who do not have to practice any observances before. They are said to be purified by the Horse-sacrifice'. *Kātyāyana* XX, 8, 17. 18. It may be mentioned here, that as part of the ceremony of this sacrificial bath, a crippled, bald and yellow-eyed man (according to some texts from the family of Atri) was led into the water till it came up to the level of his mouth; then the offerings of 'Embryo-killing', etc., were sacrificed on his head; he was then set free and chased away (*Śāṅkh.* XVI, 18, 18f.; more in Hillebrandt *V.M.* III, 31 f.; see also *Śat. Br.* XIII, 3, 6, 5 and other texts). He is considered as an incarnation of Varuṇa. *T. Ār.* I, 2, 3 also confirms this view. I doubt whether it is correct; Could the god have been driven away without any respect? The person on whose head an offering of 'Embryo-killing' is sacrificed, must be representing this most serious sin, perhaps the most serious sins in general. Chasing away the man, means its removal. Weber, in *ZDMG.* XVIII, 268 is not convincing: the real sense of the ceremony is in the Human-sacrifice and it is said to be the death of the deformed Atri (who in fact does not die), upon whom rests the power of expiation of the Horse-sacrifice *Avabhṛtha.*

320. Compare *Atharvav.* XI, 5, 1, 2. 4. In *Manu* XI, 122 the mystic holiness of the pupil is denoted as 'Brahma-like sharpness'.

321. *Hiraṇyakeśin G.* I, 7, 8; 9, 8.

322. *ibid.*, I, 9, 10.

323. These parallels are also expressed in Manu II, 169. Also, when in *Av.* XI, 5, 6 the Brahmana pupil is called *dīkṣitaḥ*, it is because the Upanayana is a sort of a *Dīkṣā*. I refer here to the next section (p. 229 ff.) in which we have to discuss once more the ritual meaning of the bath.

324. It is quite clear in *Baudhāyana Dh.* I, 11, 21, 18. 19 with reference to the new moon and the full moon period: 'He should not eat meat; he should not go to any woman. Because around new moon and full moon, the Rakṣas and Piśācas hover around; thus it is taught'. We may refer to Winternitz's Index (*SBE.* L) under *Abstinence*, *Animals* (e), *Chastity*, *Fasting*, *Food*, *Sleep*, *Speech*, in respect of the particulars given in the text.

325. *Āpastamba Śr.* V, 8, 1f.

326. Hillebrandt, *Neu- und Vollmondsopfer* 3. 6. 14.

327. *Gobhila* I, 6, 6.

328. Compare Frazer, *Journ. of the Anthrop. Institute* XV, 82, about relating stories, etc. as a precautionary measure to ward off evil.

329. *Gobhila* II, 3, 15 and often. Compare above p. 338.

330. *ibid.*, III, 1, 17 f.

331. *ibid.*, II, 10, 45. 47.

332. *ibid.*, III, 2, 37.

333. Similarly, looking at the couldron filled with the substance of the sun (p. 228) in the *Pravargya*-sacrifice is considered as dangerous and liable to cause blindness; the sacrificer's wife and no uninitiated person should see it. *Kāty*, XXVI, 2, 3, 4. Compare 4, 12; *Taitt. Ār.* V, 3, 7.

334. *Śāṅkhāyana G.* II, 11, 6.

335. Material in Weber, *Ind. Studien* V. 440, 446.

336. We have to do away here with more detail, but we may illustrate, with at least two examples, both referring to Red Indian tribes, the similarity of the relevant Indian orders with those of distant peoples. Before the fulfilment of any kind of rite '*to prepare themselves all the people fasted two days, during which they did neyther company with their wives, nor eat any meat with salt or garlicke*' (Acosta in Lang, *Myth, Ritual and Religion* I, 283). Preparatory observances before the puberty-ceremony of the girl in California: avoid meat for three days, live in a distant hut (Ploß, *Das Kind*² II, 432).

337. The article *Fasting* in the *Encycl. of Rel. and Ethics* may be compared. The rule mentioned above could refer to the first of the viewpoints that one should not eat from the food to be offered on the evening before, and to the second, the way, how fasting appears in the funeral rites (see below the Section on this and the parallels there from outside of India. Without entering into detail about the whole complicated question here, I may refer to a characteristic observation Wilken makes about the people in Newfoundland (*Revue colonials internationale* IV. 399): the one who performs the ceremony of the hair-cut should not partake of the food himself; he must be fed by others (Compare also Frazer, *Golden Bough*² I, 373; III, 205. 207; Jevons, *Introd. to the History of Religion* 70). In play here is apparently the fear of dangerous substances which are present in the hands of the person himself who is eating (compare above p. 286, note 300). But a series of cases of fasting in the Vedic ritual appear to be similar to this fasting at the time of the hair-cut. For the sake of completeness, we may also refer to fasting before partaking of a sacred meal in order to have its pure and unalloyed effect (Indian evidences which expressly state this purpose of fasting are not known to me); also to fasting after partaking of forbidden food, till the bowels are empty (*Āpastamba Dh.* I, 9, 27, 3; *Gaut.* XXIII, 23).

338. See the material in Frazer, *Totemism and Exogamy* IV, 223 ff.; compare Hehn, *Das Salz* p. 14. According to *Āpastamba Dh.* II, 6, 15, 15 salted things (as in the case of the Greeks, see Hehn *ibid.*, 25) are excluded from sacrifice. We cannot undertake here an examination of this custom; as a tentative attempt at explanation, we may put forth the suggestion that the infertility of saline ground, the unpalatability of the saline sea-water made salt appear as the carrier of desoluteness and death; Or do we have here the preservation of the custom of a saltless age (Schrader, Reallex. under *Salz*)?—Besides, salt is considered in the Vedic ritual as the representative of the abundance of food and cattle; see e.g. *Śatapatha Br.* V, 2, 1, 16); compare v. Negelein, *Traumschlüssel* 37, note 2 (but different opinion on p. 163). One may also refer to Eitrem, *Opferritus und Voropfer* 309 ff.

339. The injunction against recitation of certain especially sacred Veda-sections 'while enjoying meat, at death- and birth- feasts', *Śāṅkhāyana G.* VI, 1, 7, is characteristic of the impurity or of the danger of eating meat.

340. *Śatapatha Br.* IX, 5, 1, 6.

341. *Śat. Br.* I, 1, 1, 8.

342. The number 17 which is sacred to Prajāpati is repeated again and again in the *Vājapeya*-ritual.

343. That means, he is not guilty of immoderate attempt to appropriate all food to the last for himself. And at the same time: he does not die prematurely.

344. *Śatapatha Br.* V, 2, 2, 4; compare IX, 3, 4, 4. See Weber *Über den Vājapeya*, p. 36.

345. *Śatapatha Br.* VII, 2, 4, 14. Compare Weber, *Ind. Studien* XIII, 245. Here, reference is to be made also to Gobhila's rule for learning a certain, particularly sacred hymn (III, 2, 58) which, presumably, can be translated as under: 'May he avoid any one kind of corn, any one place, any one dress' (incorrect in *Sacred Books* XXX, 76). All the same, it is comparable with the injunction against eating mutton mentioned above (p. 41) or against sitting on Kuśa grass for the person who has used the sheep or the grass as fetish of the sacrificial fire. Likewise, one was forbidden from eating again in a rich man's house from where one had fetched one's sacrificial fires for the sake of the good omen (*Āpastamba* V, 14, 2); all these would have implied approximating the sacred with the attendant danger to one's well-being. Hereto pertains also, so it seems, the injunction against eating of birds which applied to the person who erected the Agni altar representing a symbolic bird (*Śatapatha Br.* X, 1, 4, 13).

346. *Śāṅkhāyana G.* III, 1, 12.

347. See also above p. 134.

348. *Śāṅkhāyana G.* II, 12, 10; VI, 1, 4. 5.

349. *Śāṅkhāyana G.* IV, 12, 27f. (Compare 7, 34. 35); *Āśvalāyana G.* III, 9, 6, etc.

350. Compare under the Section on Life after death—cannot one explain the rule about climbing the tree similarly? Compare the rôle of the tree in funeral in the Section on Funeral-ritual.

351. e.g. for the *Snātaka*, *Śāṅkhāyana G.* IV, 12, 21. Compare Frazer, *Golden Bough*[2] III, 202. 234. 463 ff.; According to him, the power of the holy person should be prevented from being discharged into the earth.

352. *Gobhila* III, 2, 60. 61.

353. *ibid.*, III, 2, 35. The same rule for the pot with honey, when the guest is honoured. *Pāraskara* I, 3, 5.

354. *Śatapatha Br.* XIV, 1, 1, 30. *Pāraskara* (II, 8, 2) repeats this rule, as also the whole sphere of regulations to which it belongs, for the *Snātaka* who is to observe them on the first three days after completion of his schooling. In the *Pravargya*-sacrifice, the role played by sacred clay vessels (*Mahāvīra*), will also attract this injunction.

355. Hillebrandt, *Neu- und Vollmondsopfer* 14.

356. *Kātyāyana* VII, 4, 33.

357. *Kātyāyana* VIII, 2, 1.

358. *Śatapatha Br.* XIV, 1, 1, 30. The *mantra* in *Kāty.* XXV, 5, 29 is also characteristic of the idea of the clay-vessel as a piece of earth.

359. *Taittirīya Brāhmaṇa* III, 2, 3, 11; *Maitrāyaṇī Saṃhitā* IV, 1, 3; *Kāṭhaka* XXXI, 2.

360. The same word *mṛnmaya* is used in the references mentioned above. *Ṛv.* VII, 89, 1. Compare Caland, *Ai. Toten-und Bestattungsgebräuche* 108 and note 395, for the vessel which is also called *mṛnmaya* in which the bones (remains) of the dead are put.

361. *Gobhila* III, 5, 32. 35.

362. 'He sharpens his glory with it'. This is said in *Taitt. Ār.* V. 8, 13.

363. *Pañc. Br.* XII, 13, 14; *Taitt. Saṃh.* II, 2, 8, 5, etc.; *Ṛv.* VII, 33, 4.

364. *Gobhila* III, 2.

365. *Taitt. Saṃhitā* II, 1, 8, 5; 4, 9, 1; above p. 201.

366. *Pāraskara* II, 7, 7.

367. *Gobhila* III, 5, 11 and often elsewhere.

368. To these remarks on the Śakvarī-observances, compare the notes of Frazer, *Golden Bough*[2] I, 93f. They affirm what is said here most appropriately. See also *NGGW.* 1915, 379.

369. *Gobhila* III, 1, 31 ff.

370. *Śatapatha Brāhmaṇa* XIV, 1, 1, 33. The same regulations are repeated for the *Snātaka* in *Pāraskara* II, 8.

371. *avāntaradīkṣā*, compare Caland-Henry 66.
372. See page 220f.
373. *Taitt. Saṃhitā* VI, 2, 2, 7; Compare *Āpastamba* XI, 2, 2f.
374. Compare *Śatapatha Brāhmaṇa* XIV, 1, 1, 29.
375. Compare Winternitz' Index (SBE. L) under *Bath*. See also Eitrem, *Opferritus und Voropfer* 76 ff.
376. *Vāj S.* IV, 2 (Ṛv. X, 17, 10); *Kāty*; VII, 2, 15.
377. *Hiraṇyakeśin G.* I, 1, 7.
378. See *Āpastamba Dharm.* I, 1, 2, 30 (but compare 28); i*Baudhāyana* I, 2, 3, 39; *Gautama* II, 8 (but compare 13); *Manu* II, 176.
379. This period of initiation and the disciplehood is opened with an act called 'intro duction', and is similar to the initiation of the Brahmana-pupil. Also here, it is constant duty to wear the girdle, to go out to beg alms, to place faggots in the sacred fire, etc. *Gobhila* III, 1, 10, 27.
380. *Gobhila* III, 1, 20. 21.
381. *Kātyāyana* V, 2, 21.
382. *Aitareya Br.* VIII, 13.
383. *Kātyāyana XX*, 2, 13.
384. See particularly Frazer, *Golden Bough*[2] I, 368ff. and Winternitz, Index (*SBE.* L) under *Hair*. As far as I see, the Vedic ritual has preserved a real Hair-sacrifice only in the cult of the Dead (see below the relevant section). That a lock of white hair growing between the horns of a ram is thrown on the *uttaranābhi* in an Animal-sacrifice (Schwab 36; compare also the rite of the *Varuṇapraghāsāh*, Hillebrandt, *Ṛit. Lit.* 117), should not be understood as such (compare Eitrem, *Opferritus und Voropfer* 407ff. on the specially representative, vigorous nature of the hair on the forehead).
385. Hillebrandt, *Ritual-Literature* 49. 50.
386. It is said in the corresponding *mantras:* "With the knife, with the *Dhātar* ("the creator") Bṛhaspati's, Agni's and Indra's hair was cut for the sake of long life: I shave with the same for your long life, for good fame and well-being."—"Purify his head, do not harm his life." Thus the barber is told. See *Āśvalāyana G.* I, 17, 12. 16; 18, 5 and the parallel references. Compare also *Gautama* XX, 5.
387. I refer to Frazer, *ibid*, 387.
388. Hillebrandt, *Neu- und Vollmondsopfer* p. 3f.
389. The Shaving at the Three Seasons' sacrifices (*cāturmāsya*) appears also to belong hereto; Observances commencing with shaving were connected with these. Compare *Śatapatha Br.* II, 6, 4, 5ff., *Kāty*, V. 2, 13f. 21, *Āśv. Śr.* II, 16, 22ff, etc.
390. *Śatapatha Br.* III, 1, 2, 1; *Maitr. Saṃhitā* III, 6. 2.
391. *Āśvalāyana G.* IV, 6, 4.
392. *Āśvalāyana Śr.* VI, 10, 2; *Gṛhya* IV, 1, 16.
393. *Śatapatha Br.* XI, 5, 7, 4.
394. *Gobhila* II, 5, 6.
395. *Ait. Br.* VII, 13, above p. 229.
396. *Gobhila* III, 1, 22.
397. *Kātyāyana* XV, 8, 28; *Lāṭyāyana* IX, 2, 18. 21. Even the manes of the horses in the kingdom should not be cut (*Lāṭy, ibid.*, 26).
398. *Śatapatha Brāhmaṇa* V, 5, 3, 1, Compare 6.
399. *Śatapatha Brāhmaṇa ibid.*, 2; Compare *Lāṭy* IX, 3, 1 ff.
400. *Śāṅkhāyana G.* III, 1, 2; *Gobhila* III, 4, 24.
401. *Āpastamba* XIII, 23, 16. Also in the bigger sacrificial complex, *Śāṅkhāyana Śr.* XVIII, 24, 19; *Kātyāyana* XIII, 4, 6.
402. *Taitt. Ār.* V, 1, 4. A little different in *Taitt. Saṃh.* VI, 1, 3, 8. Compare also *Āpastamba Dh.* 1, 2, 7, 6. 7.
403. *Kātyāyana* XX, 2, 12. 13.
404. *Śatapatha Br.* XIII, 3, 8, 1, Compare *Taitt. Br.* III, 9, 17, 4f.
405. The person initiated into *Dīkṣā* requests: "what he has lost from the juice unknow-

ingly, may invigorate him again' (*Vaitānasūtra* 12, 9; Similarly in §8 also for saliva that trickles out). It is said about the Brahmana-pupil who has suffered loss of semen, that his breath has escaped to the Maruts and his energy to Indra, etc.; he prays: "May Maruts anoint me, may Indra and Bṛhaspati, may this Agni anoint me with long life and energy" (*Taitt. Ār.* II, 18). *Taitt. Ār.* I, 30: "May to me return the power of the senses, life and blessing, may return to me the Brahmanahood, in my possession. The seed which has escaped to the earth from me, escaped to the plants and waters. I take them back again in me for long life and glory'. Also compare *Āśāvalāyana G.* III, 6, 8; *Kātyāyana* XXV, 11. 21 and the remarks above p. f92. on the Ass-sacrifice of the Brahmana-pupil.

406. See Winternitz' Index (*SBE.* L) under *Prayers.*

407. See page 214 f. Compare also p. 47 f, 2 ff.

408. *Ṛv.* V, 45, 6; 78, 4.

409. *Āśvalāyana G.* III, 6, 3 (*Ṛv.* X, 161); *Gobhila* IV, 9, 13; *Hiraṇy. G.* I, 15, 1.

410. See above p. 106f. 121.

411. *Gṛhyasūtra* II, 9.

412. The 'great words' are the three words, which had not yet combined in the Ṛgvedic period to form the solemn combination of *bhūr bhuvaḥ svaḥ*. The first is "earth", the third "sun"; in the second I see the combination of the first half of *bhūḥ* and the second of *svaḥ*: thus the whole formula would express the union of the earth and the sun or the movement from the former to the latter. On Sāvitrī see p. 54, note 39.

413. *Śatapatha Br.* II, 3, 4, 7.

414. *Śāṅkhāyana Sr.* V, 9, 19; 14, 12; *Śatapatha Br.* III, 9, 4, 17; *Śaṅkh.* IV, 8, 4. 5. The verb constantly used in this combination is *dhyā.*

415. See above p. 2f.; 7f.

416. Of course not in the thoroughly poetic *Ṛgveda*, i.e., also not in a version of the oldest Vedic period. One has to remember here also the Nivid-forms discussed on p. 214f.

417. *Āśvalāyana Sr.* I, 9, 1. 5; *Śatapatha Br.* I, 9, 1, 4 f.; Hillebrandt, *Neu-und Vollmondsopfer* 143 f.

418. When it is said in a prayer of the Horse-sacrifice "The Brahmana is born in holiness", then the word "holiness" (*brahman*) is, of course, not to be understood in the ethical sense; what is meant is the mystical power and art, so to say, the magic substance, inherent in the office of a priest.

419. Quite according to plan: "First the devotee tries to make the god be well-disposed towards his desires. Then he recites these desires to the god in the actual prayer" (Wundt, *Völkerpsychologie* II, 3, 661).

420. *Ṛv.* VIII, 21, 6; X, 48, 5.

421. I refer to p. 146 ff. about these prayers particularly addressed to Varuṇa.

422. See the material in Bergaigne I, 277 ff.; II, 267 ff., compare also Zimmer 337 ff.

423. *Ṛgveda* VI, 16, 47.

424. See the section on magic, for the form of the magic *mantras* and the type of effect ascribed to them.

425. One may think here of the classification of the holy actions in the later doctrines: *nityakarmāṇi, naimittikakarmāṇi, kāmyakarmāṇi*, i.e. 1. constant actions, 2. those, which are called forth on definite occasions (e.g. in case of a birth), 3. those, which are directed towards the attainment of a definite wish (examples for this are referred to on pages 182 ff.; refer especially to Caland, *Over de "Wenschoffers"* (1902).

426. *Ṛv.* IV, 2, 8, VII, 1, 6 suggests that this morning and evening rites date back to the Ṛgvedic period. See p. 64 on kindling of fire at morning as magic to bring about sunrise.

427. The extraordinary sacrifices made in the case of certain wishes are different: they are usually directed to one god who is supposed to fulfil just that wish.

428. If the ritual-texts let Agni-Soma at full moon alternate with Agni-Indra at new moon, then the dates of the *Ṛgveda* (compare above page 48) make it improbable, that even in the oldest period one of the most prominent sacrifices was made to Agni-Soma. In all probability, the original condition obtaining here has been shifted to this divine pair through

the well-known preference of the priests who belonged to a much later period, whereby the identification of Soma and Moon must also have played a role.

429. See e.g. *Taitt. Saṃh.* II, 4, 9, 2; and compare Caland, *Over de 'Wenschoffers'* 6 f.

430. *Maitr. Saṃh.* I, 10, 12 at the end.

431. Thus Hubert-Mauss, *L'année sociologique* 1898, 110f, Could both points of view be valid at the same time?

432. Hillebrandt, *V.M.* III, 35.

433. *Śatap. Br.* II, 5, 2, 1ff. narrates that the creatures ate in the beginning the barley of Varuṇa. He punished them. Prajāpati helped them with this sacrifice and redeemed them from Varuṇa's bond.

434. As Varuṇa and also the Maruts taking part in the festival are donors of rain (Bergaigne II, 185), it is possible, though it cannot be proved, that Varuṇa, originally as such, had reached (one may think of the Karīra-fruits) this position in the calendar of festivals (similarly Hillebrandt, *V.M.* III, 34). Later, as the chastener of sins, he brought along the celebration of atonement herein, introducing the character of atonement into the corn-rite. Yet, the connection of the agricultural rite with the countering of evil, which is seen here, is also observed in other literatures (Frazer, *The scapegoat*, 134ff. 225).

435. Caland, *Über Totenverehrung bei einigen der idg. Völker* 78 f.

436. As in the celebration for atonement mentioned above, apart from the additional cake, one cake each that takes the sin into itself is prepared for every member of the family (see p. 188).

437. *Śat. Br.* II, 6, 2, 10.

438. Rudra appears to be addressed.

439. And besides at such a height, that no cattle can reach it-so that Rudra's possession is undisturbed? See *Kauśika Sūtra* 7, 11 for a similar stipulation.

440. Compare Hillebrandt, *V.M.* III, 221ff., for Śūnasīrīya. There are, on the whole, less characteristic customs connected with agriculture besides this and the festivals of the first fruits mentioned on p. 239; see the sources collected by me in *Sacred Books* Vol. XXX p. 304 under Nr. 23-25 as also the *Kauśika Sūtra* 20; 24, 1.2.

441. Compare the creditable research of Hillebrandt, *Die Sonnwendfeste in Alt-Indien* (Roman. Forschungen Bd. V). I do not, however, consider as successful his attempts to demonstrate shifts which would result in the festival under consideration being classed as midsummer festival. I further refer to Friedländer, the *Mahāvrata* section of the *Cānkhāyana Āraṇyaka* (1900); Keith, *Aitareya Āraṇyaka* 26 ff., *Veda of the Black Yajus School* CXXX f., my remarks in Nachr. Gött. Ges. d. Wiss. 1915, 386.

442. *Śāṅkhāyana Sr*; XVII, 14, 10f. The 'earthen kettledrum' consists of the skin of the sacrificial bull stretched over a hole in the earth; it is struck with the tail of the same bull.

443. Compare above p. 44 with note 110 on p. 57.

444. Compare with that V. Schroeder, Lihgo (Mitt. der Anthr. Ges. in Wien XXXII), p. 2 f., Frazer, *Golden Bough*2 II, 451. For swing in Mahāvrata compare v. Schroeder, *Ar. Religion* II, 137f., compare 150. 345. He quotes Frazer, *Golden Bough*2 II, 449 ff.

445. Compare v. Schroeder, *ibid.*, p. 3., note 1. Is *saṃdhām* perhaps to be added (Friedländer, *Der mahāvrata-Abschnitt* 41, note 2)? Then it would give "contracted union". The *Śāṅkhāyana Āraṇyaka* (See Friedländer *ibid.*) explains the *mantra* in a sense different from the one understood here.

446. Compare above page 182f. Lindner im Festgruβ an Böhtlingk 79f., Hillebrandt, Rit. Lit. 85 f., 119 f.

447. See *Kauṣ. Br.* IV, 12; Paddhati on Kāty p. 346 f. ed. Weber. The meaning of the stipulation is clear, that the relevant celebration follows the New moon sacrifice if celebrated on new moon, and precedes the Full moon sacrifice, if celebrated on full moon; the sacrifice should fall under all circumstances during the propitious period of increasing light.

448. I mention here the cattle-sacrifice for Rudra (*sūlagava*) and setting free of the bull (*vṛṣotsarga*) among the other customs related to the cattle-rearing: see for these and related customs, the *Sacred Books* XXX p. 304, sources collected under 26 and also *Kauśika Sūtra* 19; 21, 1 ff; 24, 19 ff.; 51. I have to desist from a more detailed treatment of these rites and

the agricultural customs. All sorts of magic pertinent here are discussed by Henry, *Magie* 102 ff, 106 ff.

449. See above p. 36 and Winternitz, *Der Sarpabali, ein altindischer Schlangenkult* (Vienna 1888).

450. See Caland, *Altindischer Ahnenkult* p. 166 ff., Hillebrandt, *Rit. Lit.* 94 ff.

451. Ideas concerning the course of the year and its sanctification are connected with the veneration of the dead, particularly in the so-called *Ekāṣṭakā*, which is related to the winter solstice and the turn of the year; see *Ath. V.* III, 10; *Ind. Studien* XV, 145 f., XVII, 219 f, etc.

452. *Gobhila* IV. 1, 18 ff. As the fire burned, an omen indicated good or bad luck (*Taitt. Saṃh.* III, 3, 8, 5). Do we have here a custom related to the solstice? Igniting the underwood is also done during the rite, to satisfy a believer who is no more. (*Kauśika Sūtra* 46, 40).

453. See particularly Garbe, *ZDMG.* XXXIV, 319 ff.; Eggeling, *SBE.* XLIV, XLVI ff.; Hillebrandt, Rit. Lit. 134 ff.; Compare also my remarks, Nachr. Gött. Ges. d. Wiss. 1915, 387. 389 ff.; Keith *Veda of the Bl. Yajus School* CXXIII ff.

454. Different in Geldner, *Ved. Stud.* II, 135 on account of *Ait. Br.* I, 22, 14. I see in the explanation there of the rite as a *devamithunam,* one of the numerous arbitrary notions of Brāhmaṇa-theologians; if the matter were correct, it would have been expressed differently in the rites and in the pertinent *mantras.*

455. *Āśvalāyana Śr.* IV, 6, 3; *Ṛv.* I, 164, 31.

456. The tradition of the Brāhmaṇas explains this *mantra* clearly thus; *Śatapatha Br.* XIV, 1, 4, 9; *Taitt, Ār.* V, 6, 4.

457. *Taittirīya Āraṇyaka* IV, 7, 1.2; 8, 4; 17, 1.

458. On this aspect of the matter, compare note 461 below.

459. The Angiras. See *Ṛv.* VIII, 29, 10.

460. e.g. *Taitt.Āt.* V, 4, 8; 9, 2; 11, 5; *Śatapatha Br.* X, 2, 5, 5. 15; XIV, 1, 3, 6. 17; 2, 1, 3; 2, 2, 12.

461. I also point out here to the *dadhigharma* interwoven into the Soma ritual which has a clear ritual association with the Gharma (*Ind. Stud.* X, 382; Caland-Henry 283); there emerges also the connection with the sun's course or sun's orbit: 'the sun has reached the midst of his path', it is said in the Ṛgvedic hymn (X, 179, 2) referring to this sacrifice. A verse of the frog's song is also important (Ṛv. VII, 103, 8.9). The frogs which raise their voice every year during the rainy season, are compared with the priests who conduct a ceremony that stretches throughout the year, with 'the Brahmanas offering Soma', with '*Adhvaryus,* who sweat at the cauldron'. 'They preserve the divine order of the year divided into twelve parts; these men do not miss the right time. When the rainy season arrives in the course of the year, the heated cauldrons are laid down to rest'. The later ritual prescribes the day before the commencement of the Soma-pressing for doing away with the cauldron. (*Indische Studien* X, 365). One may have the impression, that the cauldron of the celebrating frogs is related to the blazing sun's heat during the hot period which precedes the rainy season. Thus, our presumption that the milk-sacrifice represents magic directed at the sun with its heat, is confirmed by the Ṛgveda. But when the Ṛgveda further refers to the fact, that the connection to the blazing heat of the sun also relates it further to the rain relieving it, then this is in full agreement with the invocation cited on p. 240 which is addressed to the 'sun's ray, the one who gives rain', and equally to the following verse of the Brāhmaṇa: 'They look to the glowing cauldron; the rain-god sends the rain from the glowing sky: thus the rain-god grants rain; the creatures prosper' (*Taitt. Ār.* V, 6, 11). Also, the application of the Ṛgvedic verse (X, 139, 4; compare *Taitt. Ār.* IV, 11, 7) takes us to the same sphere of ideas. It is pertinent to this sacrifice and relates how Indra goes after the waters and sees thereby the outlines of the sun.

462. *Taitt. Ār.* IV, 12, 1.

463. VIII, 89, 7; there, the heating of Gharma is also alluded to.

464. I refer above all to Caland-Henry, *L'Agniṣṭoma* 29.

465. This extension of the tripartite day-celebration through a night-celebration (*atirātra*) was known already in the Ṛgvedic period. Also the connection of several, possibly numerous

days for Soma-sacrifice with a larger complex at festivals, at least in the beginnings, dates back to the same period.

466. With the exception of a sinister god like Rudra; compare note 482 below.

467. This scarcely needs further explanation in respect of the *Ṛgveda*; VIII, 2, 4; 3, 20, or within hymn I, 139, the special tone of the 6th verse may be compared. I shall mention a *mantra* from the ritual of the purchase of Soma to show how Indra is singled out in the ritual *mantras* with reference to Soma: 'May (Soma) enter the right thigh of Indra, willingly into the one who is willing, happily into the one who is happy' (*VS.* IV, 27). A *mantra* for the inaugural touching of Soma: 'Shoot for shoot, God Soma, may you get strength for Indra, the winner of treasures. May Indra strengthen himself for you! Strengthen yourself for Indra!' (*VS.* V, 7). The other *mantras* at the time of preparation of Soma which single out Indra as the recipient of the sacrifice, are VS. VI, 30, 32. Subramaṇyā-litany may also be referred to (Caland-Henry 65).

468. Only that its first part refers to 'Indra who is accompanying the Maruts'; thus, in a way it refers also to the Maruts, but only as the retinue of Indra. But I think Hillebrandt's assumption, *V.M.* III, 211, 322 that this appearance of the Maruts is a speciality, particularly of the ritual of the Viśvāmitras, is wrong. Compare my notes on *Ṛv.* VIII, 36 and series of evidences of the *Ṛgveda.*

469. Also to the Hɔtar, the litany mentioned in the previous note on Indra accompanied by the Maruts.

470. Caland-Henry 268 f.

471. The formula in *Kātyāyana* X, 5, 9 which puts Indra ahead, may be compared.

472. It is the second of the two great litanies (*śastra*) of the Hotar; the first is addressed to Agni who is not, as is otherwise the case in these litanies, invited to the Soma-drink, but called as the god who performs the sacrifice.

473. Compare the detailed discussions of Bergaigne, *Recherches sur l'histoire de la liturgie védique*, 31ff. and my notes on I, 135. 139.—I doubt, however, that traces of the Vedic tradition as collected by Hillebrandt, *V.M.* I, 258, are to be ascribed to the prehistory of the relevant orders. If e.g. in *Vāj Saṃh.* XIX, 26 'only the Aśvins' are said to be named as the recipients of the early offering-which is also not quite correct-then the consideration of the *Sautrāmanī*-ritual to which that verse belongs, shows, how the Aśvins came to take up their role which is of no interest to us.

474. The row of deities mentioned here, which results from the litanies of the *Hotar*-priests, agrees principally with that series to which the *mantras*, to be recited by *Adhvaryu* at the drawing of the Soma portions, are addressed (*VS.* VII, 1 ff. etc.). -I add to the above information on the morning libation and its deities, that there belongs one more series of twelve Soma-drawings which dates back to the Ṛgvedic period (*Ṛv.* I, 15; II, 36. 37) and which corresponds to the six priesthoods of *Hotar*, *Potar*, *Neṣṭar*, *Agnīdh*, *Brahman* (i.e., *Brāhmanācchaṃsin*; compare above p. 218), *Praśāstar*, and simultaneously, it appears to the twelve months: their deities in turn, corresponding at first to the six priests, are Indra, the Maruts, Tvaṣṭar, Agni, again Indra, Mitra-Varuṇa; then four times 'those granting wealth' (Draviṇodas), the Aśvins Agni—I would like to attach, in part, more superficial significance to the combinations of the priests with the deities than in Hillebrandt *V.M.* I, 262.

475. In the later ritual, a portion of the Soma drawn in the morning is given to the combination of Agni and the Maruts at the evening libation; compare Caland-Henry 167 f. 381.

476. The traces of its one time validity have been preserved in the song-recitation pertaining to the purification of Soma in the evening libation and is called the song of 'Ṛbhu-purification'.—Compare also Hillebrandt *Ved. Mythol.* I, 257; III, 144.

477. See *Ṛv.* VII, 51.

478. *Ṛv.* V, 60 and hymn III, 26 do not mention the Soma drink; see my note with reference to this.

479. Hymns like *Ṛv.* IV, 34, 8 or IX, 81, 4 cannot be recognised as fully valid.

480. *Śāṅkhāyana* VIII, 3, 4; *Āśvalāyana* V, 18, 2.

481. Compare above p. 34 f.

482. Exclusion of Rudra which is taken for granted, is at least to be interpreted differently

(yet compare *Ṛv*. I, 122, 1, Caland-Henry 210): it rests upon the fear of proximity of the dangerous god. The *Aitareya Brāhmaṇa* (III, 34) speaks of a recitation of a verse to him, by which one should come to terms with him. But just in this recitation, the fear, which one has of him, is seen; the word 'hither' and the name Rudra occurring in the verse, were changed so that he was not called forth.

483. See above p. 294, note 474.

484. With reference to Maruts, see p. 150, note 7.

485. *Ṛv*. IX, 74, 1; 96, 3; 39, 2; 49, 1. There are many such examples; compare also *Taitt. S.* II, 4, 9, 2, Bergaigne *Rel. védique* I p. XII. 214 f., Henry in Caland-Henry 486 f. Is there not a magic meant for the possession of water, milk, etc. in the admixture of water, milk, etc.? Compare e.g. *TS*. III, 2, 8, 4 f. (Caland-Henry 336 f.). The magic significance is also clear, when water from a river which breaks through a mountain, is used in the Soma-sacrifice (Hillebrandt *V.M.* I, 212): the effect of the liberation of the river through Indra should be assured to the sacrificer. The form of sacrifice called *Ṣoḍaśin*, shows, that the Soma-sacrifice can also be changed into a magic for getting light; compare Hillebrandt *V.M.* III, 217; my notes on Ṛv. I, 6 (p. 5).

486. 'One who receives gifts at the Soma and one who does not, both may come here; they come here to see that splendour'. *Śatapatha Br.* II, 2, 3, 1.

487. I cannot venture upon a definite judgement as to how far back in time the use of brick-altar in the Soma-sacrifice can be dated. The construction of this brick-altar has been made by the more recent Vedic theology into the main showpiece of ritualistic secret-mongering (Weber, *Ind. Stud.* XIII, 217 ff. Hillebrandt. *Rit. Lit.* 161 ff.). However, see my explanation *NGGW*. 1916.

488. I refer above all to L.v. Schroeder, *Die Hochzeitsbräuche der Esten und einiger andrer finnisch-ugrischer Völkerschaften in Vergleichung mit denen der indogermanischen Völker* (Berlin 1888). *Schrader, Ṛeallexikon der idg. Altertumskunde*, under 'Heirat'; —Winternitz, *Das altindische Hochzeitsrituell* (Vienna 1892), and the same in the *Transactions of the International Folklore Congress* (London 1892), 267 ff.; specific Indian sources in Hillebrandt, *Rit. Lit.* 63 ff.

489. On the one hand, there was obviously marriage by abduction; on the other, protests against purchase of women are found quite frequently in the literature on law. Compare thereon Jolly, *Recht und Sitte* 49 f., 51 f.

490. Jolly, *ibid.* 64.

491. I distinguish according to these categories rather than distinguishing according to those of the 'civil act' and the religious acts with Winternitz (*Hochzeitsrituell* 57.)

492. On the seven steps as the establishment of the bond of friendship, compare Hass, Ind. Stud. V, 321; Winternitz, *Hochzeitsrituell*, 53; *Transactions* 270.

493. Compare on this Zachariae *WZKM*, XVII, 144 ff.; Samter, *Geburt*, *Hochzeit*, *Tod* 167 ff.

494. Compare Crooke, *Folklore* XIII, 238 ff.

495. Compare above p. 72.

496. At least, in the perception of the Vedic period, worship made to Agni; originally, apparently, magic of lustration.

497. According to the Version of *Śāṅkhāyana* (*Gṛhya* I, 14, 1). Also *Āpastamba G*. V, 6; *Hiraṇyakeśin* I, 20, 4. Somewhat different *Āśvalayana* I, 7, 13; *Pāraskara* I, 6, 2; *Gobhila* II, 26 f.-(compare above p. 72.

498. Compare above p. 94 and my notes on Ṛv. X, 85.

499. I think that Leist, Altarisches *jus gentium* p. 154 has gone too far in his attempt to reduce the Indian conditions into sharp juristic concepts.

500. According to some texts, at later stages.

501. What does this parting mean? Is it a variant of the change of hair-style at the time of marriage so common among many people? This is evidenced in the case of India by *Kauś. Sūtra* 79, 14 (cf. *Av*. XIV, 1, 55 f.; Ind. Studien V, 405f; compare Schroeder, *Hochzeitsbräuche der Esten* 144 f.) Was it originally the idea, that the woman would be made unrecognisable to the threatening spirits by the change of hair-style (compare Frazer, *Journal of the Anthrop.*

Institute of Gr. Britain and Irland XV, 98)? Or should the evil powers be warded off which could enter the head and body through parting (compare *Av.* IX, 8, 13)? Should the entry impeded by the hair be made easy for the child's soul (compare *Aitareya Upan.* I, 3, 12)? Henry accepts the latter supposition (*La magie dans l'Inde ant.* 139). It is reported of the Celebes island, that the woman should not wear her hair loose during pregnancy (Ploß, *Das Weib* I, 486).

502. Compare *Kāty.* V, 2, 15; *Kauś.* p. 29, 12.

503. Kaegi in *den Philol. Abhh. für Schweizer-Sidler* 65, note 60.

504. This, the most common; I am not listing variants.

505. Compare above p. 230.

506. I can see here (unlike Kirste, *Indogerm. Gebräuche beim Haarschneiden* [from the *Analecta Graeciensia*; 1893]) nothing other than the fiction that the hair is not hurt but only the grass. The *mantra*: 'grass, protect him' is addressed to the grass; and to the razor: 'Axe, do not hurt him': two *mantras,* which are found in the felling of the stem meant to be the sacrificial pole (Schwab, *Tieropfer* 6) and at the time of the first incision into the body of the slain sacrificial animal (*ibid.* 111f.), in both the cases, obviously with the same intention to ward off the odium of injury by the performer. Compare *Śatapatha Br.* III, 6, 4, 10; 8, 2, 12.

507. This is naturally to avoid harm being done to the child, say, through magic by means of the hair, compare Frazer, *Golden Bough*² I, 379 ff.); magic of fertility is connected with it.

508. *Compare Encycl. of Rel. and Ethics,* VII, 323.

509. Compare p. 195 for its significance in this action.

510. The *mantra*-literature attaches special mystical power to the girdle. See e.g. *Atharvaveda* VI, 133 where the connection between the girdle and studentship is quite clear; the last verse runs thus: "You, whom the old Ṛṣis, the creators of beings, have bound around themselves, bind yourself around me, o girdle, so that I can live long.' The girdle is also prominent in *Dīkṣā* which is closely connected with studentship (p. 219; compare also the minor Dīkṣā prescribed for witchcraft *Kauś. Sūtra* 47, 14. 22 and my comments in ZDMG. LXII, 594). Perhaps different motives have got mixed here. One should think first of the assumption of the dress of elders, in the initiation of the pupil. But the *Dīkṣā* (especially also the tying of the girdle tightly for a certain period prescribed there; see Caland-Henry 66) suggests the view that the girdle had to be tight to arrest the mystic power in its wearer (is it also thus with the ribbon of the Barhis? In the wrapping-up of the sacrificial post, see Schwab, *Tieropfer* 72 ff.?). Further, it must be taken into account that the rôle of the umbilical cord must have been given to the girdle in the course of the conception of *Dīkṣā* as an act of birth, compare *Maitr. S.* III, 6, 7 (twisting the girdle around the navel in *Upanayana*: *Hiraṇy. G.* I, 4.4 f; when in a relevant *mantra,* the power of the girdle is connected with 'inhaling and exhaling', it is linked with the navel, the 'knot of the breath-power', on whose two sides, inhaling and exhaling are distributed (*Kāṭh.* XIII, 10). Further, one could think of the separation of the pure upper half and the impure lower half of the body with the girdle (*Taitt. Saṃh.* VI, 1, 3, 4). What Frobenius, *Weltanschauung der Naturvölker* 327 ff. gives to understand would lead us in a different direction altogether (cords, strings, etc. through which the spirit climbs into the human being).

511. Also in marriage (*Pāraskara* I, 8, 8), only that there Prajāpati, the god of progeny, is named, and not Bṛhaspati, the god of Brahmanic wisdom.

512. *Gobhila* II, 10, 23 f.

513. *Śatapatha Brāhmaṇa* XI, 5, 4, 18; *Āpastamba Dharm.* I, 1, 2, 23; *Gautama* II, 13, etc.

514. Compare above p. 54, note 39.

515. *Śatapatha Br.* XI, 5, 4, 12, compare *Atharvaveda* XI, 5, 3. It is different in *Śat. Br.* XI, 2, 1, 1, where the explanation given for the second birth is 'when the sacrifice favours him' (on that, compare *Taitt. Br.* I, 1, 2, 8).

516. The third day after the *Upanayana* was chosen by many for the recitation of Sāvitrī.

517. *Kāty.* V, 6, 30 comments; *Gobhila* III, 8, 12.

518. See Geiger, *Ostiranische Kultur* 238.

519. Lippert, *Kulturgeschichte* II, 340 f; Frazer, *Totemism and Exogamy,* I 36 ff; Ploß,

Das Kind[2] II, 411 ff.; Kulischer, *Zeitschr. für Ethnologie* XV, 191 ff. H. Schurtz, *Altersklassen und Männerbunde* 95 ff; *Enc. of Rel. and Ethics* VII, 315 f. and other excellent ethnological sources.

520. I remind you of the remarks I made above (p. 222) on the occasion of *Dīkṣā*.

521. This part of the rites has not been preserved, as far as I see, either in the Veda or in *Dikṣā*.

522. See Lippert, *ibid.*, II, 349.

523. Both these are the only principal persons. That this celebration has such a completely private character is characteristic for the fading away of gentilic and political togetherness, in any case in the later Vedic period which forms our sources.

524. Weber has dealt in detail the material concerning the *Abhiṣeka* and the *Rājasūya* in *Über die Königsweihe, den rājasūya* (Abh. der. Berl. Akademie 1893). See also Keith, *Veda of the Black Yajus School* CXI ff.

525. It is clear from the numerous instructions that, here, it is a question of drowning the whole body with the appropriate substance. The king must smear the liquid with a horn of a black antelope (compare above p. 219f.) for one year, he should not have his hair cut which has been touched at first and for the most part by the liquid (Weber, *Rajasūya*, 53.89).

526. Weber *ibid.* 56f. 132. 69.

527. See Weber *Über den Vājapeya* (Minutes of the meeting of Berl. Akad. 28th July 1892); Keith, *Veda of the Black Yajus School* CVIII ff. This celebration was not performed by kings alone, but also by persons of the princely and the Brahmana castes.

528. On the injunction against food connected with it, see above p. 225.

529. Compare namely Hillebrandt, *Nationale Opfer in Alt-Indien* (Festgruß an Boehtlingk 40f) and the same *Rit.-Lit.* 149 ff; Eggeling *SBE* XLIV, XVff., v. Negelein, *Das Pferd im arischen Altertum* 90 ff.

530. *Aitareya Br. VIII*, 21 f.

531. Whose role cannot be obviously very old.

532. In the section, *Śatapatha Br.* XIII, 5, 4. *Kaṭhaka* X, 9 speaks of 'Indra with the horse-sacrifice'.

533. Has Varuṇa been once the god of Horse-sacrifice as has been presumed? I do not find convincing evidence; *VS.* XXII, 5 or *TB.* III, 9, 16, 1, etc., is no evidence.

534. Yet see note 535 below.

535. 'Four-eyed dogs' (four-eyed obviously as an expression for enhanced power of vision) appear also as dogs of the god of death. They are found in Iran as also among other Indo-European races (see E.H. Meyer, *Deutsche Lit. Zeitung* 1892 column 1105) as animals who scare away or scent spirits (compare *Atharvaveda* IV, 20, 7, where the magic herb makes one capable of seeing ghosts, is called 'the eye of the four-eyed bitch'). Probably, the killing of this dog in the consecration of the sacrificial horse had originally the purpose—deviating from the interpretation attached to it in the present ritual—of giving the horse protection from being persecuted by spirits; that is why it had to swim up to the horse. Compare, in addition, my remarks in *Arch. f. Rel.* VII, 226, note 1. Compare also Hommel, *Aufsätze E. Kuhn gewidmet*, 442.

536. These sacrificial animals may be a later embellishment; the *Ṛgveda* (I, 162, 2-4; 163, 12) knows only of the goat of Pūṣan (compare above p. 118) who announces the sacrifice to the gods. But the enumeration of the priests *ibid.*, 162, 5 shows, that the Soma-ritual was connected with the Horse-sacrifice even at that time.

537. Refer to Frazer, *Golden Bough*[2] III, 69, note 1 about the ritual game of riddles.

538. *Kātyāyana* XX, 8, 17. 18. Compare above p. 287, note 319.

539. I refer to, say, Frazer's Chapter '*Killing the Divine Animal*", *ibid.*, II, 336 ff.

540. 'The steed is the royal might, the other animals are subjects', *Śatap. Br.* XIII, 2, 2, 15. 'Horses are the attributes of king's dignity', says a Buddhistic text which forbids the enjoyment of horse-meat. *Mahāvagga* (*Vinaya Piṭaka*) VI, 23, 11. The feature mentioned above p. 290, note 397 is characteristic.

541. Is it to be compared, that amongst the Giljakes the bear which is to be sacrificed is carried from door to door in the village? Frazer, *ibid.*, II, 380.

542. *Ṛv.* X, 56 (see my note on the hymn) mentions perhaps a Horse-sacrifice pertaining to the cult of the Dead. Has the horse accompanying the dead into the other world taken here the form of the solemn Horse-sacrifice or does it only resemble this?

543. I would hardly like to believe that. In contrast, it is much more a type of gift-sacrifice at bottom and that the magic character stepped in later; both the Horse-sacrifice hymns of the *Ṛgveda* themselves make it improbable. Of the divergent concepts of the Horse-sacrifice I emphasise the following new literature: Hillebrandt, *V.M.* III, 32, note 3; Eggeling *SBE* XLIV, IX ff. and Keith *JRAS.* 1907, 934. 938, *Veda of Bl. Yajus School* CXXXII ff. Further E. Lehmann (*Chant de la Saussaye*, Lehrb. der Rel. gesch.[3] II, 37) according to whom it is the question of the sun or the Light-gods being provided with a new horse for their chariot; I do not see any evidence for this argument. The views of Charpentier, *Kleine Beiträge zur indoir. Myth.* 45 ff., and in many respects also of Negelein *ibid.*, 90 ff. 111 ff. are close to the opinion expressed here.

544. Of the pertinent literature, I emphasise Hillebrandt. *Rit. Lit.* 167, ff. Caland *Altind. Zauberritual* (1900); V. Henry, *La Magie dans l'Inde antique* (1904) and the works of v. Negelein. An essay of Hubert and Muass, *Esquisse d'une théorie générale de la magie* (*Année* sociologique 1902-03, 1ff.) rich in ideas, deals with the general foundations of magic. As for me, I hope to be able to come back to the relationship of magic to the Vedic Cult in more detail at a different place.

545. It may be remembered that the magic hymns in this Veda appear almost in the appendices, outside the oldest strata of collections.

546. See above p. 54 note 40.

547. I refer to my discussions in *NGGW.* 1916, 715ff.

548. *Ṛgveda* VII, 104, 16.

549. *Atharvaveda* VII, 70, 2.

550. *Taitt. Saṃh.* II, 2, 6, 2.

551. *Manu* XI, 63. 32.

552. *Taittirīya Ār.* IV, 22.

553. *Śāṅkhāyana G.* I, 18, 3.

554. *Kauśika Sūtra* 102, 2; *Atharvav.* III, 23, 1; *Hiraṇyakeśin G.* I, 16, 16. I am reminded here of the expressions *lakṣmī alakṣmī pāpman* which are close to these spheres of ideas.

555. To be more exact: the Brahman, originally only the holy word (the holy formula or the hymn) itself, has been hypostatised very early as such a power. Compare *NGGW.* 1916, 715 ff.

556. See the material collected by Bloomfield *Am. Journ. of Phil.* XI, 344 f.

557. *Varāhavihata* appears often in magical use.

558. e.g. *Kauśika Sūtra* 48, 37.

559. *Kauśika Sūtra* 16, 31.

560. Dust of the footprints of an enemy in the magic directed against him: *Kauśika Sūtra* 47, 45. (Similar in Hillebrandt, *Rit. Lit.* 173). The Zulus find their lost cattle again through the earth from their footprints (Callaway, *Religious System of the Amazulu* 345). Further collections on magic with the footprint amongst different people see A. Lang, *Myth, Ritual and Religion* I, 99 f., Caland, *Wenschoffers* 10, Frazer, *Lectures on the early history of the Kingship* 79 ff, *Griech. Mythol.* 883, etc.

561. *Kauśika Sūtra* 29, 27 gives recent evidence of such a concept, characteristic of priestly magic tricks, where the partaking of a meal is prescribed cooked on the fire of birds' nests to ward off evil spirits. This is explained from the fact that Indra who drives away the evil spirits is invoked in the relevant *mantra* (Atharvav. VI, 2, 2) 'in which the Somajuices enter like the birds settling down in a tree'.

562. Yašt 19, 34.

563. *Jātaka* vol. II, p. 410.

564. *Taitt. Āraṇy.* V, 1, 3.

565. Compare above p. 231.

566. A pun is meant here (*syāmāka* and *smayāka*—millet and smile).

567. Compare above p. 224f.

568. *Suparṇādhyāya* 2.

569. The word (masculine) means 'evil being', 'evil power'.

570. *Atharvaveda* XI, 8, 19; VI, 26—It may be observed how in the hymn *Av.* IX, 8, the idea shifts constantly between the demons and the impersonal beings; and the observations of Grohmann (*Ind. Stud.* IX, 383) about this vacillation in case of disease resp. Takman, the demon of disease, may be compared.

571. *Kauśika Sūtra*, 7, 29 f.

572. Thus the case discussed in *ibid.*, 47, 12 ff.

573. If observed more carefully we can distinguish the following possibilities: one accomplishes the act in question on the image of the person to be treated, or on an image of that act on the person to be treated, or an image of the act on his image.

574. Compare the discussions of Grohmann, *Ind. Studien* IX, 413.

575. Compare *Atharvaveda*, I, 12. 13; V, 7; VI, 13. 20, *Hiraṇyakeśin*, *G.* II, 7, 2, etc.

576. *Pāraskara* I, 16, 24.

577. e.g. *Baudhāyana Dh.* II, I, 32.

578. Hillebrandt, *Neu-und Vollmondsopfer* 171; *Schwab Tieropfer* 131 f., above p. 203.

579. *Hiraṇyakeśin G.* I, 16, 20 f.

580. Winternitz, *Der Sarpabali* 11.

581. *Kauśika Sūtra* 116.

582. See above pp. 219 f. 224f.

583. *Hiraṇyakeśin G.* I, 9, 18; II, 6, 12; *Pāraskara* II, 1, 23; *Śāṅkhāyana G.* I, 28, 23; *Gobhila* II, 9, 26, etc. If burying is prescribed, in a place which brings luck (e.g. the cowshed), then the intention of hiding is identical with that of introducing a lucky substance.

584. *Gobhila II*, 7, 23. *Ind. Studien* XIII, 243.

585. *Śatapatha Br.* XIV, 2, 2, 35. 38 (above p. 274, note 81).

586. Of the extremely rich materials, I shall mention only a few: *Maitr. Saṃh.* IV, 8, 5; *Śatapatha Br.* V, 2, 3, 4; XII, 9, 2, 8; XIII, 8, 3, 4; *Kātyāyana* XV, 1, 11; 2, 8; *Kauśika Sūtra* 7, 14; 140, 20; *Āśval. G.* IV, 6, 4; *Ind. Studien* X, 342; XIII, 243; Weber, *Über den Rājasūya* 11 (where there is a wrong explanation of the custom). See also above notes 81 and 82 p. 274; Samter, *Geburt, Hochzeit und Tod* 147 ff.

587. *Śatapatha Br.* III, 6, 2, 20; Hillebrandt *V.M.* I, 444.

588. I refer to the relevant chapter below in this instance and on the whole in the following for features concerning the funeral ritual.

589. Schwab, *Tieropfer* 32.

590. *Hiraṇyakeśin G.* II, 7, 2.

591. For e.g., moving around of a firebrand kindled at both ends around the sacrifice for the dead to keep away hostile souls, *Kauśika Sūtra* 87, 30; Lustration of the sacrificial animal, Schwab, *Tieropfer* 96 f.; and the like frequently. Compare also above the remarks on the magic fire pp. 71, 194 f., as also Caland, *Een Indogermaanach lustratiegebruik* (1898).

592. *Maitr. Saṃh.* IV, 8, 5.

593. I refer to the crossing of ditches filled with water in the funeral ritual, the pouring of water done between oneself and the stone meant for the goddess Nirṛti (*Ind. Stud.* XIII, 243), the stone or the clod of earth taken from a boundary and, therefore, gifted with special power of demarcation, which separates the living ones from the dead in the funeral ritual, the mat (*Kauś. Sūtra* 86, 14) which is similarly used there (with the saying: 'This is kept in-between to ward off misfortune'). The wood kept around the sacrificial fire 'to beat away the Rakṣas' (*Taitt. Saṃh.* II, 6, 6, 2; Compare *Gobh.* I, 7, 16, *Hir.* G. I, 2, 1, etc.).

594. See above p. 224.

595. *Hiraṇyakeśin G.* II, 3, 10.

596. See above p. 223.

597. I may refer particularly to what is said above p. 229 f.

598. Above p. 274, note 80.

599. For e.g., *Kātyāyana* XXV, 11, 16. Compare Darmesteter (*Le Zend-Avesta*) with Vend. 19, 21.

600. Similarly, one prefers to use water which has taken up the power of the curative

plants and which is consecrated through *mantra* (*śāntyudaka*, Henry, *La magie dans l'Inde antique* 49).

601. *Hiraṇy. G.* I, 16, 5; *Kauś. S.* 46, 9.

602. *Kauś. Sūtra* 71, 16. 17=86, 19, 20; *Av.* XII, 2, 1 compare 19 f.

603. See above p. 71. 194 f. The obvious, common case of gods or demons being set in motion to drive away or destroy evil elements, does not really need any more explanation.

604. *Hiraṇy. G.* II, 3, 7, Compare *Pāraskara* I, 16, 23, *Petavatthu* III, 5. About mustard, compare also Benfey, *Kleine Schriften* III, 13, note 1.

605. Also castration of the concerned creature is found there: *Atharvav.* III, 9; *Ind. Studien* XVII, 216.

606. *Kauśika Sūtra* 75, 13; compare also 25, 14; 35, 3 (*Ind. Studien* XVII, 285).—We have described above p. 134, how the eyes of the hostile, threatening spirits are shot out at the marriage.

607. *Kātyāyana* XV, 7, 6 (Compare *Śatapatha Br.* V, 4, 4, 7; Weber, *Rājasūya* 63; I don't think, one can attach a tinge of Canossa to the rite).

608. e.g. *Pañc. Br.* IX, 8, 9; *Kauśika Sūtra* 84, 10; *Ind. Studien* X, 342.

609. *Gobhila* III, 1, 14. 27; *Śāṅkhāyana G.* II, 13, 1. 2.

610. *Śānkh. G.* II, 13, 8; *Hiraṇyakeśin* I, 9, 10.

611. *Āśv. G.* III, 8, 20; *Pār.* II, 6, 31; *Hir.* I, 11, 8, Compare *Gobh.* IV, 9, 17.

612. *Kauśika Sūtra* 59, 27.

613. *Śatapatha Br.* III, 2, 1, 32.

614. *Taitt. Saṃh.* VI, 1, 4, 2; *Kāty.* VI, 4, 6. Schwab, *Altind. Tieropfer* may be referred (p. 88) for the Animal-sacrifice in which the Dīkṣitā did not have the staff in hand.

615. Schwab 90. *Āśvalāyana Sr.* III, 1, 20.

616. Compare Haug. *Ait. Brāhm.* Introduction p. 15.

617. *Vāj. Saṃh.* I, 24ff; Hillebrandt, *Neu- und Vollmondsopfer* 50 f.

618. *Śāṅkh. Śraut.* IV, 4, 2; Compare also *ibid.* 14, 8.

619. *Atharvaveda* XIX, 38.

620. Hillebrandt, *Sonnwendfeste in Alt-Indien* 39, Compare above p. 238; *Kauśika Sūtra* 86, 15; *Hiraṇy. G.* II, 7, 2.

621. Hillebrandt, *Neu- und Vollmondsopfer* 28, etc. *Kauś. Sūtra* 88, 27; 71, 21; *Āśval. G.* IV, 4, 10; *Atharvaveda* XIV, 2, 68, compare *Kauś. Sūtra* 76, 5.

622. *Ṛv.* VIII, 91, 7; Winternitz. *Altind. Hochzeitsrituell* 43 ff; Compare *Kauś. Sūtra*, 15, 4; 72, 16. I also refer to Frazer, *Golden Bough*[2] III, 398, ff. Caland, *Altind. Zauberritual* 31, note 5 has another interpretation of this pulling through than the one discussed here. Compare also Zachariae, Z. des Vereins f. Volksk. XX (1910), 154 ff.

623. *Atharvav.* VI, 26, 2; compare above p. 132.

624. *Kauś. Sūtra* 76, 1f; 79, 24; *Atharvav.* XIV, 2, 48-50. Compare also the banishment of diseases or other evil powers to the trees or mountains, *Atharvaveda.* I, 12, 3; II, 25, 4.

625. *Kauś. Sūtra* 34, 3 ff. On lead compare note 602 above,

626. *Kauś. Sūtra* 26, 2 ff.

627. *Kauś. Sūtra* 29, 6; 32, 24.

628. *Kauś. Sūtra* 32, 17 (*Atharvav.* VII, 116); 26, 18 (*Atharvav.* I, 22; Ṛv. I, 50, 11 ff.); should we not read in Sūtra 19 *prapātayati* (compare say, *Ṛv.* X, 97, 13; *Av.* VII, 115, 1 and also *Kauś. S.* 18, 16)? Also the Semites removed the miasmata and other forms of impurity by letting the birds fly away with them (R. Smith, *Religion of the Semites* I, 402).

629. *Kauś. Sūtra* 27, 9ff.; *Atharvav.* II, 29, 6.

630. *Kauś. Sūtra* 26, 29 ff.

631. Compare above p. 260.

632. *Atharvav.* VI, 42 2; *Ṛv.* I, 191, 10; *Ath.* VIII, 5, 9 (compare 7, 15); V, 22; *Ṛv.* VIII, 47, 13 ff. Particularly about *Trita*: Bloomfield *PAOS.* 1894, CXIX ff.

633. *Ṛgveda* X, 103, 12 (compare *Kauś. Sūtra* 14, 21); *Kauś. S.* 14, 22. The commentators take a white-footed sheep for granted. Reference to arrow, see Caland, *Altind. Zauberritual* 29, note 7.

634. *Ṛv.* VII, 104, 18.

635. Therefore, the common rule of not touching, for which examples are given on p. 256.
636. *Atharvaveda* XIX, 45, 5.
637. *Śatapatha Brāhmaṇa* III, 8, 1, 10.
638. *Śāṅkhāyana G.* I, 6, 5.
639. Very often in the domestic sacrificial ceremonies.
640. Compare above p. 219; *Ind. Studien* XIII, 285.
641. *Ind. Studien*, ibid.
642. Weber, *Rājasūya* 62. 135 etc.
643. *Śāṅkhāyana G.* I, 13, 11. An extension of this rite is, e.g., in *Hiraṇy. G.* II, 3, 2 where an axe and gold is put beside the stone to assure firmness, courage and riches to the new-born child.
644. And similar related magic objects like a mole-hill earth stirred up by a boar, etc.—See *Atharvaveda* VI, 100, 2; *Śatapatha Br.* XIV, 1, 1, 8; *Taitt. Ār.* V, 1, 4; 2, 9; 10, 6; *Āpastamba* Sr. V, 1, 7; 9, 8; Weber *Ind. Stud.* XIII, 139 f; Bloomfield, *Seven Hymns* 17 f., *SBE.* XLII, 511 about the ants as finders of water, being in contact with the hidden life-juice of the earth and having curing power. Compare also Frazer, *The Scapegoat* 33. As in case of setting up of the fire, the ant-hill is used in making the layers of Agni (*Ind. Stud.* XIII, 220) and in Pravargya-sacrifice (*Śat. Br.* XIV, 1, 2, 10); it plays also a role in *rasakarman* (*Kauś. S.* 21, 23), the sacrifice against poisoning (*ibid.* 31, 26), etc.; one should not urinate over it (*Manu* IV, 46)—Does the ant-hill have a different significance, when, on several occasions, the remnants and waste of the offerings, spoilt, over-cooked sacrificial food is thrown over it (*Taitt. Br.* III, 7, 2, 1; *Kaṭhaka* XXXV, 19; *Āśvalāyana Sr.* III, 10, 23; Weber, *Rājasūya* 12, 104, note 2, 109, note 1; Compare Krauß, *Volksglaube und relig. Brauch der Sudslaven* 158)? First of all, it belongs obviously to the category of removal of dangerous substances (see above p. 197.). Thus, amongst the Zulus (Callaway, *Relig. System of the Amazulu* 315) the disease is buried in an ant-hill; the ants build their hill again and thus shut off the dangerous object. Does the curative effect of the ant-earth also play a role in these Vedic rites? Should this power be made effective at the same time with the barring of that object? Compare further Hillebrandt *V.M.* III, 337; Henry, *Magie* 53 f.; v. Negelein, *Traumschlüssel des Jagaddeva* 208 f.; also Gruppe, *Griech. Mythol.* 800 f. and the *Encycl. of Rel. and Ethics* I, 501.
645. See above p. 145.; *Atharvaveda* XVI, 7, 8.
646. *Kauśika Sūtra*, 47, 44. Compare the relevant verse *Atharvav.* II, 12, 1.
647. Above p. 249; *Ind. Stud..* XIII, 286. See *Kauś. Sūtra* 8, 23-9, 11; Henry *La magie dans l'Inde antique* 49 on *śāntyudaka*, the water filled with the power of plants and dedicated amidst recitation of several texts.
648. See above p. 190 ff.; Page 278, note 151.
649. *Kauś. Sūtra* 20, 25. The same mixture is buried for an act done for the prosperity of cattle (*ibid.*, 19, 19): the substance causes each time the same effect whichever way it is used.
650. *Hiraṇy. G.* II, 2. 2, 3; *Āśv. G*, I, 13, 2, etc.
651. I refer to the king and the priests eating together at the anointing of the king (Weber, *Rājasūya* 140 f.), to the bride and the bridegroom after the marriage (above p. 192), and also to the ceremony creating harmony in *Kauś. Sūtra* 12, 8.
652. The pulvarised Paidva-insect (on account of the mythological significance of the serpent-slayer, the white horse Pedu) is rubbed into the nose (*Kauśika Sūtra*; see Bloomfield's *Introduction* p. XLIV); also to the woman in child-bed, a substance which effects a male child-birth (*Śāṅkh. G.* I, 20, 5).—Then letting the horses sniff; Weber, *Vājapeya* 28—breathing of the new born: *Śāṅkhāyana G.* I, 24, 2, etc.
653. *Baudhāyana Dh.* III, 5, 7, if Bühler's (*SBE.* XIV, 297) translation is correct.
654. *Vāj. Saṃh.* V, 34; *Āśvalāyana G.* I, 24, 14.
655. Caland, *Zauberritual* 79, note 27 lists sources on the evil eye.
656. *Aitareya Br.* VI, I; Ṛv. X, 85, 44 (*Śāṅkh. G.* I, 16, 5).
657. *Śāṅkhāyana G.* IV, 11, 3f.; 12, 19, II, 12, 10.
658. *Atharvaveda* X, 1, 1. 8. 18; IV. 18, 5; V, 14. 31. XIV, 2, 65, etc.
659. 36 15f. Compare Bloomfield, *Seven hymns*, 8f., Henry, *Magie* 125.

660. The rite of Uparavas. Compare *Śatapatha Br.* III, 5, 4; *Taitt. Saṃh.* V, 2, 11; Caland-Henry 100 ff.

661. Compare above p. 299 note 583.

662. *Kauśika Sūtra* 16, 28. The rite mentioned above p. 298, note 561 can be compared. Here it is a question of the choice of fuel. Compare also *Kauś. Sūtra* 48, 37. 38.

663. *Kauś. Sūtra* 16, 31 f.

664. *Kauś. Sūtra* 116.

665. *Kauś. Sūtra* 15, 2.

666. See above p. 63f. 243f.

667. See above p. 250. Weber, *Über den Vajapeya* 27ff. The significance of the act is clearly expressed in the relevant *mantras.*

668. See e.g. *Āpastamba Śr.* V, 19, 2f.; 20, 1f.; Weber, *Rājasūya* 69 f.

669. Above p. 238.

670. Above p. 238. I am also recalling here the obscene actions in the Soma-sacrifice and the Horse-sacrifice (p. 216 and p. 250 resp.).

671. Compare my essay 'Indra and Namuci' NGGW. 1893, 342 ff. and my notes on Ṛv. X, 131.

672. v. Schroeder, *Mysterium und Mimus im Ṛgveda* (1908), goes too far in assuming such presentations. Compare on the other hand, my discussion of this book *GGA.* 1909, 66 ff.

673. *Śatapatha, Br.* VI, 2, 4, 2.13.

674. *Kauśika Sūtra* 127, 10. 11.

675. *ibid.*, 41, 1 ff.

676. Other attempts at interpretation: Henry, *Magie* 110. Compare Zachariae *WZKM.* XVII, 137 f. about the old shoes; Samter, *Geburt, Hochzeit und Tod* 195 ff.; Eitrem, *Opferritus und Voropfer* 368. Further materials on getting rain are in *Taitt. Saṃh.* II, 1, 7, 3; 1, 8, 5; 4, 7, 1 ff.; Hillebrandt, *Neu- und Vollmondsopfer* 142 f.; compare also the above on the second of the four monthly festivals (p. 236f.), on Śākvarī observance (p. 227 f.), on Gharma-sacrifice (p. 293, note 461). It would be easy to increase this collection at will.

677. It is not unequivocally certain in all these acts, that they can be classified in the rubric assumed here. It is quite understandable that the outlines become blurred sometimes, or that different concepts concur. For example, the striking of the pegs to destroy evil spirits, can be placed alongside the acts discussed on p. 258f. above.

678. *Kauś. Sūtra* 47, 54 f; 39 f.

679. *Kauś. Sūtra* 29, 24; *Atharvaveda* V, 23, 13.

680. Perhaps more exactly: Does one place the essence of one's person present in one's urine around him?—*Hir. G.* I, 14; *Pāraskara* III, 7 (compare Pischel, *Philol. Abhh. Martin Hertz dargebracht* on page 69 f.).—Why the horn of a living animal?

681. *Kauś. Sūtra* 18, 10 ff.

682. *Kauś. Sūtra* 51, 19, compare *Atharvaveda* VI, 50, 1.

683. *Kauś. Sūtra* 25, 24; *Śatapatha Brāhmaṇa* III, 9, 4, 17.

684. *Kauś. Sūtra* 40, 1 f.; compare Bloomfield, *AJPh.* XI, 348 f.

685. Compare particularly Hillebrandt *Rit. Lit.* 183 f. 186; Henry *Magie* 59 ff.

686. But the development tends apparently in diverse ways to become an independent omen, consequent upon the original image surrendering more and more of its real likeness. Also, the possibility of different associations between the omen and that which is interpreted through it, and finally also the frequent connection of the two through pure arbitrariness at the auguries, should not be completely ruled out by removing the relationship between the image and that which is being represented.

687. They, of course, mean death for the person who sees it; *Jaiminīya Up. Brāhmaṇa* III, 29 (compare in the text the discussion on ghosts). Yet, the arrangement of this omen under the heading 'Image of reality' can be contested.

688. Also divine judgement is a part of the category of inquiry into the hidden with the help of superhuman influence (Fire-test, e.g. *Pañc. Br.* XIV, 6, 6; water-test, etc.). Its origin from the Indo-European period is considered probable by Kaegi (Festschr. der 39. Philologenversammlung 1887, p. 40 ff. Compare also Schrader, Reallex, under *Gottesurteil*).

The word 'divine judgement' used here cannot imply, incidentally, how far the influence of divine will and divine justice can be read into the original, apparently purely, magic occurrence (compare R. Lasch, der Eid 1908). In the first place, the point is not very clear whether the element should punish the guilty, or testify through its behaviour to guilt and innocence. The procedure is much akin to the oath, in which one takes the punishment upon oneself by cursing oneself for the falsehood (see p. 268f.). As a matter of fact, the Indians place divine judgement in the category of *śapatha* (curse, oath) (see Jolly, Recht und Sitte 144f. and the literature mentioned there).

689. *Gobhila* II, 1, 3 f. The inspection of the building site can be compared in *Āśv. G.* II, 8, 2 ff. Incidentally, it appears to have more practical than magic character.

690. *Kauśika Sūtra* 33, 19 f.

691. *ibid.*, 14, 31.

692. *ibid.*, 15, 15 f.

693. *ibid.*, 34, 24.

694. *Śatapatha Br.* IV, 5, 8, 11.

695. *Gobhila* IV, 8, 15 f.

696. *Āśv. G.* IV, 4, 2 f.; Compare *Śatapatha Br.* XII, 5, 2, 9 f.

697. *Hiraṇyakeśin G.* I, 17, 1. 3. Two hymns of the Ṛgveda II, 42.43 are known to deal with voices of birds. The direction from left to right is quite favourable in an omen, the opposite one unfavourable; see Caland, *Een Indogerm. lustratie-gebruik* 46 f.

698. In the *Ṛgveda* (VIII, 47, 15; Pischel *ZDMG.* LX, 111; see also X, 164 with my note; Sammlungen aus Atharvaveda, etc. : Pischel in v. Negelein [see below] 378). Compare further *Ait. Ar.* III, 2, 4; *Chānd. Up.* V, 2, 8, 9; *Ath. Parisiṣṭa* 68. More in Hillebrandt, *Rit. Lit.* 184; Winternitz, Index (*SBE.* L) under *Dreams.* For the more recent period: J. v. Negelein, *Der Traumschlüssel des Jagaddeva* (1912). There on p. 40 ff. (compare *Ath. Pariś.* 68, 3, 5 ff.), also materials on intentional, ritual induction of prognostic dreams (incubation). Finally compare Bolling in the *Ency. of Rel. and Eth.* V, 38 ff.

699. Bloomfield, *Seven Hymns of the Atharvaveda*, p. 19 f; *SBE.* XLII, 532. Deviating from this Caland, *Altind. Zauberritual* 175; compare also Henry, *Magie* 69.

700. Thus it is said in the *Mahābhārata* (III, 16870 ed. Calc.) 'By this Tapas I know the desires of others.'

701. For example, through the power of the plant Sadampuṣpā, which gives one the capacity to understand all magicians and evil spirits. One speaks to it: 'Show me the Yātudhānas, men and women; show me all Piśācas; With this intent, I take hold of you, o herb!... Whichever flies through the air, whichever creeps across the sky, and whichever hopes for protection from the earth: let me see that Piśāca.' *Atharvav.* IV, 20; *Kauśika Sūtra* 28, 7. From the old Buddhistic literature: Rhys Davids, *Dialogues of the Buddha* I, 24.

702. *Jātaka* vol. III, p. 4.

703. The question of the oracle of the dead is alluded to below in the section on Belief in Life after Death. Compare also p. 55, note 63.

704. Hillebrandt, *Rit. Lit.* 178; Henry, *Magie* 89 ff.

705. Yet, compare above p. 132 on evil demons appearing in the form of plants—When for e.g., a serpent's head is immured in the altar of Agni (*Ind. Studien* XIII, 252; Hillebrandt, Rit. Lit. 163; compare generally on construction-sacrifice above p. 203f., then it could hardly have been in the Vedic period, the seat of a soul-like serpent-demon. It could only have been the carrier of serpent-power, so to say, of the substance of serpent. 'He puts on a serpent's head; thus he adopts the swiftness inherent in the serpent', says *Taittirīya Saṃhitā* (V, 2, 9, 5).

706. Thus it can be agreed—the opposite indeed would be odd—that there is talk of a certain animation given to the arrow and the drum, the plough and the dice (p. 23), and sometimes also to amulets (see e.g. *Atharvav.* X, 6, 5). In the case of plants, the idea of the plant-soul plays its part to the full.

707. And then of such natural powers like heaven and earth, water and fire, lightning, etc., corresponding to their eminence in the place of the old gods (compare p. 10f.).

708. Compare Hillebrandt, *Rit. Lit.* 169 f. I shall come back later to the relation

between the magic formula and the magic act, discussed by Marett in his fine essay '*From Spell to Prayer*' (*Folk-Lore* 1904).

709. Calling the name of a person alone is not the only thing in magic directed to it but also the belief in the magical effect of the things and acts corresponding to their names. 'The plant Apāmārga wipes off all evil, because it appears that its name means 'wiping off' (above p. 189 f.; Ants are removed through a sacrifice with a wooden spoon made of Bādhaka ('Remover' above p. 263); The game of dice drives off the dog-demon (*Hir. G.* II, 7, 2) which brings disease, obviously, because the player is called 'dog-slayer' (*śvaghnin*), etc.

710. See e.g. Mannhardt, *Aberglauben* p. 53; p. 84, note 26.

711. *Kauśika Sūtra* 20, 16 f.; *Gobh.* II, 7. 10; *Āśv. G.* I, 13, 3; Baudhāyana in Winternitz, *Altind. Hochzeitsrituell* 101. Compare also Caland, *Zauberritual* 53, note 8.

712. At least from the end of the Ṛgvedic period; compare above p. 4 f.

713. Thus, for example, the beautiful verse of a speculative Ṛgvedic hymn (X, 121, 2) which celebrates the unknown god as the bestower of life and power, as the ruler honoured by all gods, has become a magic *mantra* against the miscarriage of a cow (*Kauś. S.* 44, 1). This is probably because it is considered as directed to Prajāpati, 'the Lord of progeny', as composed by the poet 'Gold-fruit'.

714. I refer particularly to Caland, *Zauberritual* 87, note 2.

715. Compare above p. 10f.

716. *Atharvaveda* XIX, 47, 3 f. Similar numbers VI, 25. Compare A. Kuhn, *KZ*, XIII, 128 f.; Wuttke, *Dtsch. Völksaberglaube* §109. 480, about the preference for numbers of this type found in magic also elsewhere.

717. *Atharvaveda* VII, 13, 1; 96, 1; *Ṛgveda* V, 78, 7. It is shown on p. 298, note 561 as to how similes can be converted into ritual acts.

718. It is well known, that the same feature is seen in magical sayings of various peoples; compare Krauß, *Völksgl. der Südslawen* 38, 136; Ploß, *Das Kind*[2] I, 141, etc.

719. Compare Weber, *Omina und Portenta* 408; *Ind. Studien* IV, 395.

720. *Pañc. Br.* VI, 5, 11; what is meant is the wooden handle of the axe.

721. *Taitt. Saṃhitā* II, 6, 6, 1.

722. Often the inversion of the right course in different contexts appears in evil magic in India as elsewhere. Thus, word for word, the formulas in reverse order: *Āpastamba Śr.* XIV, 15, 1.

723. *Śatapatha Brāhmaṇa* XIV, 9, 4, 11. With reference to the belief in the effects of curse, it is to be mentioned that it is considered much more as dependent upon the disposition of a person against whom the curse is made, i.e., whether the person has a receptive disposition. The Brāhmaṇa-texts often warn against some ritual flaw, not by saying: 'This and that misfortune will follow from it', but: 'if someone says then: 'This or that misfortune will result therefrom', then one would be exposed to it' (*Śatap. Br.* XII, 4, 1, 4; and many more examples): the pertinent flaw makes one disposed towards succumbing to the effects of the curse.

724. Compare Jolly, Recht und Sitte 144. See p. 302f. note 688 for divine justice connected with the oath.

725. Correspondingly the same verb (*śap-*) means 'curse' in the active voice, 'swear' in the middle voice, i.e., to curse oneself. The magic procedure present in the oath, tends naturally to develop along ethical lines (compare *Chānd. Up.* VI, 16). However, I feel that v. Schroeder, *Ar. Rel.* I, 146 ff., 156 ff., (different is the case with R.M. Meyer, *Arch. f. Rel.* XV, 435 ff.) has given its foundations excessive ethical and theological slant.

726. Thus in *Ṛv.* VII, 104, 15, where the one who swears says, 'May I die today, if I am a Yātudhāna (above p. 174f. note 443) or if I have burnt the life-force of a man'. Where the stanza then continues accordingly with the cursing of the person who has illegally wronged the speaker, then the similarity between the oath (self-curse) and curse becomes clear.

727. *śāpayitvā 'bhiṣiñcet. Aitareya Br.* VIII, 15.

728. Similar in *Baudhāyana Dh.* I, 10, 19, 10; *Nārada I*, 224.

729. This is an expression which is often used in swearing (compare *Manu* VIII, 256;

Nārada I, 248; *Rāmāyaṇa* II, 34, 48 ed. Bombay, etc.). As the deeds decide about the fate in the other world, it implies roughly, that one swore upon the happiness of one's soul.

730. *Taitt. Saṃh*, I, 3, 11, 1 (compare *Atharvaveda* XIX, 44, 9; *Śatapatha Br.* III, 8, 5, 10). The usage, to hold the water with the hand, is also mentioned while cursing; such water is then filled with the magic power of the curse and brings forth special results where it is poured (*Rāmāyaṇa* VII, 65, 29 f). Even today, an Indian swears with the water of the Ganges in his hand—it may be noted here, particularly on account Varuṇa's name being mentioned, how the invocation of a divine witness begins to play a rôle in the procedure of magic.

731. *Manu* VIII, 113. It means, of course, that one brings bad luck upon one's comrades, etc. if one forswears oneself. Swearing upon truth (*satyam*; parallels outside of India: Hirzel, *Der Eid* 136) is a relatively modern spiritualization of oath; *ṛtam amīṣva, ṛtam āmīt* Taitt. S. II. 3, 5, 1 (compare *NGGW*. 1915, 176, note 2) appears to be close to it. In the epic and in the Buddhistic stories, etc. the oath-like appeal to truth (in Pāli *saccakiriyā*, amongst the northern Buddhists *satyavacana*) appears also to be a popular means of miraculous doings. It is said: when otherwise this and that is true, this and that should happen by the power of such truth. See e.g. *Jātaka* Vol. I, p. 214. 331; *Divyāvadāna* 27 (p. 417 ed. Cowell-Neil, compare my 'Buddha' 6, 342) etc.; *Mahābhārata* III, 2208; XIV, 2029 ed. Calc.

732. *Jātaka* ol. III, p. 138.

733. *ibid.*, p. 502.

734. Compare above note 731.

735. *Mahābhārata* III, 16847; V, 5991 ed. Calc. The touching of the head goes together with the curse: 'His head shall split apart' e.g. *Chānd. Upan.* I, 10. 11; *Śat. Br.* XIV, 6, 9 28), 'his head shall split in seven pieces' (often amongst the Buddhists, e.g. *Saṃyutta Nik.* Vol. I, p. 50. 51).

736. *Śāṅkhāyana G.* I, 9, 10; above p. 274, note 80.

737. *Taitt. Saṃh.* II, 3, 5, 1 f. (compare with that Aufrecht, Rhein. Museum 40, 160).

738. Compare mainly pages 185, 205f.

739. Similar to what we have seen above p. 188, 197, that burning of harmful or dangerous substances has turned into a sacrificing, eventually a 'sacrificing-away' (*ava-yaj*).

740. *Atharvav.* I, 8; *Hiraṇy.* G. I, 15, 5; *Ṛv.* X, 159, 4; 174. Similar things are quite common.

741. Most of the magic acts of *Kauśika Sūtra*—according to an interpretation which appears doubtful to me—are to be enlisted in the usual New moon and Full moon sacrifices (Caland, *Altind. Zauberritual* VI f.; compare also Bloomfield, *GGA*, 1902, 495 ff.; Henry, *Magie* 39 ff.). The rule, as long as it is right must be credited largely to the artificial, priestly stilisation.

742. See also above p. 201ff. 263.

743. See namely p. 205f.

744. *Kauśika Sūtra* 116; above p. 256.

745. *ibid.*, 47, 44; above p. 262.

746. *Gobhila* IV, 9, 13, 14; compare above p. 205.

747. *Gobhila* IV, 8, 11.

748. *Kauśika Sūtra* 72, 16; compare 15, 4.

CHAPTER FOUR

Animism and the Cult of the Dead

THE SOUL, HEAVEN AND HELL

The Soul

The ideas of the Vedic Indians about death and life after death are based on animism which the Indo-European people brought with them from their primitive stages of development. This concept finds expression in references to an air-shaped or shadowy being, namely the soul, that dwells in the body. It can leave the body which then sinks into unconsciousness, whereas it itself roves about far and near. It parts permanently from the body[1] in death and continues to lead its own existence for some time or for ever assuming visible or invisible shapes.

It is no simple task to answer questions regarding the specific form wherein these ideas can be called as characteristic of the Vedic age or those regarding the nomenclature of the soul.

To begin with, there are passages which speak of the dispersion of the parts of the living being after death. This also includes the psychic components, i.e., those understood by us as psychical in nature. Thus, one spoke to the dead at the time of cremation, 'The Sun receives your eye, the wind your Ātman, (p. 333, note 8). Go as your merit is, to earth or heaven. Go if it be your lot, unto waters; go, make your home in plants with all your members' (*Ṛv.* X, 16, 3). Likewise, in the case of the Animal-sacrifice: 'The sacrificer should let the eye of the sacrificial animal go to the sun. He should release his breath to the wind. His Asu to the air (see below). His ear to the world-regions. His bones to the earth' (*Ait. Brāhm.* II, 6, 13)[2]. But this dispersion of individual elements must not be construed to exclude the belief in the continuity of a disembodied universal personality[3]. At the funeral or at the Animal-sacrifice, significant expressions are directed to the dead or the sacrificial animal whose being was described just earlier as being dispersed through the universe. These expressions addressed to the 'You', to the personality of the man or the animal, predict or wish this or that fate for them in the other world. For example, one speaks to the sacrificial horse: 'May you take the easy paths unto the gods' (*Ṛv.* I, 162, 21). To the dead man: 'Thither let God Savitar away transport you, where dwell the pious who have passed before you' (X, 17, 4)[4]. There is no doubt that the one who leaves the corpse in death, to which this 'you' of the sentences refers, is identical with the being that escapes, in Indian and in non-Indian belief, from the body in a dream and hovers about freely. When a person who is asleep, is rudely awakened, this being is in danger of not finding its own way back[5]. This is identical with 'the man, a thumb's length tall' (*puruṣa*) who dwells, according to a passage of the Upaniṣads, within a person (*ātman*) as the lord of the past and the future[6]. It is also identical with that 'man, a thumb's length tall' whom the god of death, in that epic story, draws out and takes away with him from the lifeless body of Satyavant that has been left behind.[7]

As for the expressions used to name this being in the texts discussed here, it is uncertain whether the expression *puruṣa* (man) cited from the later texts is missing just perchance in that particular sense; given the available ethnological evidence, we cannot doubt the ancient origin of the idea of the soul as a tiny man living in man, as expressed by this phrase. Beside other less important names in the Veda, there is talk at times of *asu*, the breath of life, at times of *manas*, the mind[8]. Among these expressions, *asu* denotes obviously first a force pertaining wholly to the realm of physical life.[9] Nothing indicates, whether thinking, feeling or wishing could be connected with *asu*. We often find expressions like 'the living asu has reached us', '(Agni) creating the highest *asu*, the living, the unsubdued' (*Ṛv*. I, 113, 16; 140, 8)! The concept of *asu* as the life-giving force, found in the later Vedic texts[10] along with the later forms of usage, does not appear to be contradicted anywhere. *Manas* on the other hand, is the mind, the seat of thought and intellect of wish and will, of joy and fear. The concept of *manas*, as residing in the heart, which is expressed later very often in clear terms, belongs probably to the oldest Veda[11]. *Manas* has departed from the sick man lying unconscious; it flies, swift as thought[12], far away to Yama, the god of death[13], to heaven and earth, ocean and mountain, sun and dawn: but the priestly art of magic and of healing tries to make it return 'to life, to live here' (*Ṛv*. X, 58)[14].

Often, life and death appear to depend upon the remaining or the going out of *asu*, or *manas*, or at times of both. We read[15] in the hymns of the *Atharvaveda* which seek to ward off death from the sick man: "May this man remain here with his *asu*, in the kingdom of the sun, in the world of immortality.' 'May not breath and power forsake you; we are summoning your asu.' 'May your *asu* not leave your body.' 'Stay here, do not go away. Do not go to the fathers. I bind your *asu* with a firm knot.' 'May not the *manas* go there; may it not hide. Do not depart from the living; do not follow the fathers:' 'I hold fast in you what is your *manas*:' 'Do not stay here with the manas averted.' 'Let your *asu* be here, here your breath (*prāṇa*), here your life's span, here your *manas*.' Finally, let us refer to the expressions *asunīti*, *asunīta*, literally 'asu-guiding'; they obviously indicate movement of the souls guided by Agni, the psychopomp. They can be directed from the here to the beyond, and from the beyond to the here whence the manes descend, led by the god to enjoy earthly sacrificial meal[16].

The alternating appearance of the one or the other, of the physical or the spiritual power, in the rôle of the psyche may appear strange. As the attention was focussed separately now on this, now on that aspect—if, say, the term, *puruṣa* was not accepted even in this antiquity (comp. above), the whole aspect was not given its due. If only we could ask the Vedic poets, or if there was an old story like the Homeric Nekyia which could give an answer[17], then it could be presumed that *asu* and *manas* of the dead person unite and cling to each other in the other world[18]. But in no way is the idea of a total personality embracing these elements is lacking, as referred to earlier. The invocations in the numerous and comprehensive ritual texts pertaining to the cult of the Dead are never addressed to *manas* or *asu* of N.N. but always to the N.N. himself, to the father, the grandfather, the fathers, the Vasiṣṭha, etc.: a clear expression that the true ego of the departed one was considered as existent in the kingdom of the souls[19]. Thus, the rôle of *manas* depicted here will make us recognise right away that the Vedic idea of the soul living in the other world must have been far removed from the Homeric one, in so far as the psyche of the Veda could hardly resemble that insensible phantom bereft of all thought and will, as depicted in Homeric poetry. As the *manas* has gone to the other world, the functions of intellectual life characteristic of *manas* on earth, will have remained with the 'fathers' over there.

Besides, the body also has a certain share in the existence in the other world. This is shown in the *Ṛgveda* (X, 16, 6) by one's concern for the bodily injuries caused by a bird or any other animal[20], further, in the *Atharvaveda*, amongst other things, by one's request to the fathers to set right the limbs not in position (XVIII, 2, 26), also by giving away clothes to be worn in the world of the souls, etc. But at the same time, the body going to the other world is to be understood certainly not as a crude substance, but refined by the power of Agni, who sends it across, something akin to the 'fine body' of later speculation[21].

Heaven

When the Vedic Indian speaks of immortality as something unattainable in this world, he means in reality a long life. 'One who lives for a hundred years or more, he attains immortality.' 'A hundred years: so great is immortality, the infinite, the boundless'[22]. If the goal has been reached sooner or later, to which place of action does the existence of a pious man shift? What is the substance of this existence?

Well-known verses (*Ṛgveda* IX, 113, 7 ff.), the prayer of a Soma-sacrificer to the sacred drink, show the form taken by cherished hopes of the Ṛgvedic man of piety:

'O Soma Pavamāna, place me in that deathless undecaying world, wherein the light of heaven is set, and everlasting lustre shines. Flow o drink for Indra's sake[23].

'Make me immortal in that realm where dwells the King, Vivasvant's son[24]. Where is the secret shine of heaven, where are those waters young and fresh. Flow o drink for Indra's sake.

'Make me immortal in that realm where they move even as they list, in the third sphere of inmost heaven where lucid worlds are full of light. Flow o drink for Indra's sake.

'Make me immortal in that realm of wish and desire, the radiant region (of the sun-courser?), where spirits' food[25] and repletion are found. Flow o drink for Indra's sake.

'Make me immortal in that realm where joys and delights, where enjoyment and enjoying linger, and desires of the wish are fulfilled. Flow o drink for Indra's sake.'

These verses praise, though not justly, the profound apprehension of future life. Besides heavenly light in the physical sense and the unhampered movement, repletion from spirits' food is also desired, namely, the food given to the souls in the sacrifice to the dead; in addition, one desires 'joys and delights, enjoyment and enjoying' : these are but vague words which can at best awaken a semblance of true spirituality, but in truth, one will have to think of very base pleasures[26]. One does not get to feel here the keen, ferocious battle-eagerness which fills the other world of the Nordic heroes; everything in this Brahmana-heaven has the character of metaphysical and physical enjoyment.

Yama, Lord Over the Dead

Ruler in the empire of the dead is Yama[27], the son of Vivasvant. The *Atharvaveda* says of him that he 'was the first mortal to die and first to enter the other world' (XVIII, 3, 13). Here is an instance of oft recurring mythical type of the chief of the souls found among the various races of the world. I think it is altogether wrong to allow this type to evanesce among the various personifications of natural phenomena like the setting sun or the moon. As it was shown above, after a myth of Indo-Iranian origin, the human race was born of the 'twins' Yama and Yamī (Indo-Iranian Yima and Yimeh). This father of all mortals was then presented in Iran, and may be in the Indo-Iranian period as well,—of course the Veda is not aware of it—as the king of a golden age which knew neither old age nor death, heat nor cold, scarcity nor passion. And, as in Hesiod's legend of the five world-ages, the men of the golden race become extremely powerful demons after their death. In the Avesta this kingdom of Yima, lives on as the kingdom of the blessed wise men transposed into a wonderland far away from the world. We are overstepping empirical confines, yet within rights in presuming behind all these ideas, the belief of the Aryan age that the souls of those who lived in the golden era with Yama on earth also stand close to the king in the other world, forming a sort of a nobility of the dead.[28]

Place and Characteristics of Life in Heaven

As we have seen above, the *Ṛgveda* transfers the scene of blissful life with Yama to heaven. Not all fathers live there—we shall come back to it—, but this is the choicest dwelling-place of the fathers. There is talk of the highest regions of light (see above), or of the highest heaven (*Ṛv.* X, 14, 8), or of the centre of the heaven (15, 14), or of the lap of ruddy dawn (15, 7). The *Atharvaveda* also speaks of the highest world (XI, 4, 11); the third firmament (IX, 5, 1. 8; XVIII, 4, 3), the back of the firmament (XVIII, 2, 47), the luminescent world (IV, 34, 2). It describes the location of the fathers' world in detail in the following verse (XVIII, 2, 4): 'Rich in water, the lowest heaven is called thus, the middle one the *pīlu*-empire[29]; the third is called the upper-heaven in which the fathers sit.' There are specially favoured places in heaven as the reward for the highest achievements. Thus, especially the sun[30]. 'High up in the heaven abide the Guerdon-givers: they who give steeds dwell with the sun for ever' (*Ṛv*. X, 107, 2). 'Those who have advanced to the sun through asceticism. . Skilled in thousand ways and means, the sages who protect the sun' (X, 154, 2. 5).

The verses to Soma mentioned above (p. 309 f.) have already given us a few features for further portrayal of heavenly bliss. Other expressions of the *Ṛgveda* and also the *Atharvaveda* fully concur with them. Earthly imperfection is done away with: that does not mean inner elevation to ethical ideals, but the removal of physical infirmity; the dead 'have left the diseases of the body behind; they are not weak, their limbs are not weak, their limbs are not twisted'[31]. They are on friendly terms not only with Yama, but also with the gods of heaven. 'There shall you', so it is said to the dead at the time of cremation, 'look on both the kings enjoying their sacred food, Yama and God Varuṇa' (*Ṛv*. X, 14, 7)—Varuṇa, may be as the most prominent of the gods who rule over the heavenly regions of light, or may be as the supreme knower of the guilty and the innocent. Elsewhere, there is talk of the blessed ones who accompany Indra and the gods on their chariot (*Ṛv*. X, 15, 10). Yama banquets with the gods under a leafy tree; there resound song and flute (*Ṛv*. 135, 1. 7); the blessed ones have to be certainly thought of as participants in this festivity; some of them drink the Soma, others honey or molten butter (X, 154, 1).

A chief source of their enjoyments are the offerings made at the time of funeral or at later celebrations for the dead, like food and drink, clothes and salves;[32] another source accompanying them to the other world is the reward for works done on the earth, for their sacrifices and pious gifts (*iṣṭāpūrta*). The *Ṛgveda* (X, 14, 8) lets the blessed ones find once more in the other world their 'sacrifices and gifts', and the *Atharvaveda* is full of descriptions of the streams of blessings that will flow in the beyond to the giver from the offerings made to the priests on earth[33]. There was a characteristic rite which symbolised heavenly reward associated with the offerings of a particular porridge to a Brahmana. 'With pools of butter, with shores of honey, with brandy instead of water, full of milk, water, sour milk: honey-sweet shall such rivers flow surging towards you in the heavenly world. May lotus-ponds surround you on all sides': a sort of concrete instruction is given to the generous donor after receiving these rewards by making in the porridge little pools and rivers containing the aforesaid liquids after the different directions of the sky[34].

We may complete this description of the Vedic paradise with another prospect that presents itself in the other world to the donor of this porridge: 'Fire[35] does not burn their limbs, many women await them in the heavenly world...Lord Yama does not rob them of their seed.'

As far as we can see, the idea of an ultimate, world-encompassing, universal perfection did not get associated, in pre-Buddhistic India[36], with the concept of such heavenly existence for a favoured few. In olden times, one did not pay, understandably, sufficient attention to the whole. This might have enabled one otherwise to envisage one such conclusion of the course of the life of the universe. The imagination took a different course in the wake of concepts like metempsychosis and redemption.

Hell

Is the hell opposed to the heaven of the Vedic belief? At the outset, it is clear that for the *Ṛgveda*, the heaven is the world of the pious (*sukṛtām uloka*), of those 'who reached the sun through mortification'[37], those valiant heroes who scoffed at death[38], the sacrificer, the generous donor. In other words, it is barred to the evil-doer. 'Thither let God Savitar transport you, where dwell the pious who have passed away before you' (*Ṛv*. X, 17, 4), said one to the dead. Once the concept of life after death had been developed with emphasis on other worldly rewards for earthly virtues, then the idea of punishment, meted out in the other world for earthly sins, had to surface. This was an unavoidable consequence. One may recall here—not to speak of other distant races—how the Avesta concurs precisely with the Veda with regard to the fates of good and evil souls, to the way that leads to heaven or to hell. One may be tempted to proceed from individual details to the well-known tendency of Avestic theologians to arrange evenly and schematically the two cosmic halves of light and darkness; however, this mode of visualization is essentially the inevitable result of an inner logic. It is possible, though at best a guess, that it originates from the days of common Aryan heritage. One also tried to avoid all concepts of hell and punishment by interpreting the teachings of the oldest Veda in such a way that immortality was regarded as a free gift of heaven; thus, to the one, who does not accept this gift, corporeal death is the end of all existence.[39] This appears misleading. It is not Yama or any other god who gifts life after death to the mortal; continuity of life is but a matter of course[40] according to the concepts which go back to the most primitive times; one could only express the hope or fear that the gods would exercise their mercy or wrath respectively on the soul that lives on.

Therefore, we must accept without hesitation the Vedic belief in hell. What do the texts have to say about that? There can be no doubt about the later Vedas; that belief is clearly present in them; there may be doubts only with respect to the *Ṛgveda*. But here too, evidences are not altogether lacking, as emphasized by many others[41]. Of course, much importance can hardly be given[42] to the concept of Yama's two four-eyed piebald dogs guarding the ways, past whom the dead are wished a safe journey at the funeral (*Ṛv*. X, 14, 10.11). It is possible that these dogs were to keep away, in the fancy of the Ṛgvedic poet, the wicked from the kingdom of the blessed. They can also be understood in terms of a conceptual sphere that allows the dead to assemble in a common Hades without any distinction between good and evil: in this case, they were part of the whole apparatus of spectral horrors that accompany the transition from earthly life to the world of darkness[43]. But a few other evidences of belief in hell in the *Ṛgveda* cannot be removed without doing violence. 'Indra and Soma cast the wicked into prison[44], plunge them in darkness[45]; that has no support, so that not one of them may ever thence return: so may your wrathful might prevail and conquer them' (VII, 104, 3)[46]. 'May all the three earths press him...who in the day or night would fain destroy us' (*ibid.*, verse 11). And of the wicked magician (enchantress): 'She who wanders like owl (?) at night-time, hiding her body in her guile and malice, may she fall downwards into endless caverns'[47] (*ibid.*, verse 17). The expressions here are too positive to be interpreted as mere destruction. A verse of the *Atharvaveda* (II, 14, 3) can be placed side by side with the last of the *Ṛgvedic* verses mentioned above. This verse curses all the enchantresses away into 'that *house* there below'. They must have thought of a dark abyss from which the rejected ones wanted to escape to the light: but the firm enclosure and the intense anger of the gods weighing heavily restrain them. Less clear are a few other verses which let the sinners or those haunted by misfortune or divine wrath fall in the 'pit' (*karta*): it can hardly be proved that this means anything more than a terrible end. The verses are as follows: 'Protect us, God[48]; let not the wolf destroy[49] us. Save us, o gods, from falling into the pit' (II, 29, 6). 'The guardian of Law, most wise[50], he beholds all creatures that exist. He drives into the pit[51] the hated riteless ones. The thread of the Law is spun in the cleansing sieve,[52] on the tip of the tongue by Varuṇa's art. This, by their striving, have the prudent ones attained: he who does not have this power shall sink into the pit.' (IX, 73, 8.9). The least reliable evidence is the invocation of such verses like the one directed to Indra 'to send down the foe to the nether darkness' (X, 152, 4). Anyone who wanted his foe's destruction could speak in this way. Let us compare this verse with the *Atharvan* hymn meant for the protection of the sick person: 'They do not die there, they do not go to the deepest darkness; cattle and horse, man and animal, all live there where this holy word is spoken, a weapon that protects life' (VIII, 2, 24. 25); here it is no doubt the question of protection from death, and not from hell. Thus, we have no right to relate the *Ṛgvedic* invocation to the darkness of the hell.

It can be seen that we hear very little about the belief in hell during the *Ṛgvedic* period[53]. It appears, that it was left, on the whole, to a later age to unsettle the imagination by frightening descriptions of the torments of hell, which the Buddhists were fond of doing. The *Atharvaveda* (V, 19, 3) gives a foretaste of it in the picture of the sinners sitting in streams of blood and devouring their hair[54]. One saw in the gods, who were accorded, by the old Vedic poetry, places of honour in the sacrifice, more of donors of earthly goods than rulers presiding over otherworldly suffering. In our main sources for the proof of belief in otherworldly life, namely the *mantras* said at the funeral of a pious sacrificer, there is clear evidence that one had no occasion to think of hell; for one felt safe from it due to one's good deeds. Perhaps, these verses could have dealt with the major final judgement to be made about the soul's otherworldly fate, if one had thought of it in terms of a trial by a court whose decision is final. But it is doubtful whether such a formal Last judgement was accepted in ancient times without contest[55]. It is said in a later Vedic text (*Taitt. Ār.* VI, 5, 13): 'Where dwells Yama, the son of Vivasvant, men are divided: those who are faithful to the truth here below and those who did not speak the truth': it is possible that this division was the result of a trial but it need not be made explicit[56]. The gods know the innocent and the guilty and they send every one of them to the appropriate place: perhaps, this simple concept was sufficient for that period.

General Characteristics of the Vedic Belief in Immortality

Let us try, with the benefit of a total view, to find an expression for the character of the Vedic belief in immortality as far as we have understood it, and to assess the impact of its hope of heaven and fear of hell on cult and life.

The goods one knows are material goods-health, enjoyment, riches, the might of the individual and of the race. Therefore, the other world cannot bring anything but material joys and woes to the soul, which does not lose its corporeity even in death and to which, therefore, cling all the wants and habits of the material life. Of course, the imagination has used the wide scope of the other world to heighten the sufferings of hell and the joys of heaven, particularly the latter which claimed its most urgent attention. But this picture, given the heavenly ideal of the Veda hardly goes beyond the limit of a utopia that has been transposed to a luminous world with inexhaustible brooks of milk and honey and with equally inexhaustible joys of the harem. The removal of all imperfection that one anticipates, signifies solely ridding the outwardly body of all infirmities and with that, the restoration of the full capacity to enjoy; the union with the gods signifies delightful intercourse to the accompaniment of music and drinking: joys and desires for the distant future which are obscured by the tangible joys and the urgent immediate desires of daily life. Apart from the sections which refer to the funeral and cult of the Dead, the Veda speaks only occasionally of the other world, where then the motif of heavenly reward for generous patrons of the priests stands in the foreground. In the prayers, we find that one wishes death to one's enemies, but to oneself the life of a hundred summers. Apart from prescribing the gifts for the priests, the cult is also concerned, at the time of the funeral with the welfare (of the soul) in the other world[57]; for instance the trifling concern that Agni should not harm the body, that he and Soma should make whole the injuries done to the dead by the crows and ants, that the rite be completed befittingly to make the soul reach the right place. What a transformation from here to the mood that dominated in the old Buddhistic India, where life was preparation for death, illumined by the thought of the triumph of eternity over all the transitoriness.

OLDER FORMS OF ANIMISM

Souls living in the Depths; The World of Fathers

It is not unlikely, that the Vedic concepts described by us so far, of a heavenly world with rewards for the pious and of the darkness of hell, hail essentially from the common Indo-Iranian past along with the priestly-theological slant given to belief, apparently even in those times. We have no reason[58] to date back still further and to presume in them a common property of the undivided Indo-Europeans. Besides, they represent, as a matter of fact, a comparatively more recent form of thinking about afterlife, although they appear to carry a stamp of spiritual infancy, if measured by the yardstick of highly developed religious teachings. As we know from experience, it is true of all religious concepts and customs, especially those concerning death and afterlife, that at no time or anywhere, was religious life dominated by innovations which were not built upon the substratum of older concepts. Aren't these conditions, so true of Homeric Greece, equally true of the Veda[59]? I think, the question can be answered in the affirmative, in fact much more can be asserted. Not just evident here or there, but visible in a broad spectrum are other layers of concepts, much older than what the reader encounters at first in the *Ṛgveda* or what we have observed thus far.

If I am not mistaken, the concept of the 'world of the fathers' (*pitṛloka*) comes first. This, however, does not appear in the *Ṛgveda* under this term. In the later Veda texts, the world of the fathers is given an equally rightful place by the side of the world of gods, or of the world of gods and men. It is identified with Yama's empire (*yamarājya*); it is far away from us, 'the third world from here'[60]. If it is occasionally transposed to divine heights[61], it is then hardly the original concept. The opposite of the world of gods points in another direction than to a shared heavenly existence with the gods. The world of gods is in the north, that of the fathers in the south. Its gate is located south-east.[62] To all appearances, it is considered as a general empire of the dead which can be termed neither as heaven nor as hell[63]. And there are several references to show that this empire is to be found more at a depth than at a height, for example, the expressions which concern the path of the dead in their future existence. In many passages, this path is understood indeed as leading upwards, which is but natural for the faith in heaven. Thus, the *Atharvaveda* (XVIII, 2, 22) lets the Maruts, who storm through the air, carry the soul upwards. But such passages are in opposition to others wherein the path taken by the soul—here, of course, there is no question of the souls of evil-doers—is thought of more or less clearly as leading into the depths. I think, it can be reckoned from the expression *pravat* used often to indicate this path. This word which really means 'forward leading path' appears to be associated especially with the idea of downward movement, for paths leading downwards aid easy forward movement, like the forward movement of water caused by the downward direction[64]. It is said of Yama, the one who first went into that world, that he 'travelled along the wide *pravat*, showing the path of many' (*Ṛv*. X, 14, 1), that he 'was the first to go to the *pravat*' (*Av*. VI, 28, 3). 'They come to the fords[65] across the wide *pravat*, where the sacrificers, the pious go' (*Av*. XVIII, 4, 7). Does this of trepeated expression, probably inherited in this context from the past, seem to point to ideas which looked upon Yama's empire not as a heavenly world, but as an under-world akin to the Homeric Hades?[66] The *Āśvalāyana* (*Gṛhya* IV, 4) goes further in its depiction of the cremation-rite: 'If the dead man is burnt by one who is in the know, he goes together with the smoke (of the pyre) to the heavenly world: this is well-known. May one dig a knee-deep pit to the north-east of the *Āhavanīya*-sacrificial fire and plant an Avakā, i.e., Śīpāla-plant[67]. (Soul) departs from there and goes to the heavenly world together with the smoke: that is well-known.' Thus, a hint of the depths of the earth, of the underworld has built into the idea the upward movement of the soul[68]: this may be a vestige of a belief in the underworld stretching further afar. Does not the reference 'deep paths where the fathers dwell' (*Av.* XVIII, 4, 62) belong to the same context? And does one not feel, that the picture of the fearful, dark way where Yama's dogs lie in wait for the souls (e.g., *Av.* VIII, 1, 9.10) is part of another scene than that ascent to the shining firmament?

In this context we have also to consider the *Yajurvedic* appellation of the pit in the sacrificial ritual as the 'seat of the fathers' or as 'the world where the fathers are sitting'[69], wherever it appears in the ritual; so too, what is said in a magic prayer for rescuing the person nearing death: 'I have tipped you out of the lower earth to the upper: may Aditi's sons protect you there, both the sun and the moon' (*Av.* VIII, 2, 15): thus, the place of abode of the dead is considered here as the 'lower earth', which is not lit up by the sun and the moon. We have already shown above (p. 313) that the world of the dead—without any reference to hell or its punishments—was called the 'lowest darkness': After considering the whole range of evidence given here, one would be inclined to link such expressions with the view of Yama's empire as a subterranean shadow-world and not as the heavenly world of the blessed ones[70].

Probably, this concept of the other world was, in reality, more important than the notions of heaven and hell, for the belief of the *Ṛgvedic* period than for the *Ṛgvedic* texts. The funeral *mantras* of the *Ṛgveda* are written for persons of high estate, for whom the well-rewarded priests are busily trying to obtain a place of honour and glory in the other world. Even then, they did not miss the opportunity to keep ready torments of hell for the enemies of such a person and also their own enemies. But the mass of the dead people is thought of neither as so greatly blessed nor as condemned to the lowest depths[71]. In their concept of existence, there predominated the sad feature, which for man's natural attachment to life, cannot be easily separated from the idea of death. Death appeared after all to be an 'evil' (*pāpman*), as it is often termed in the later Vedic texts.

Thus when over this empire of the dead an existence of heavenly salvation is built, this occurrence could perhaps be expressed thus: that these highly favoured dead are at the same time favoured by gods as they have become heavenly beings or something similar. The wishes for power, happiness, splendour of the deceased fathers and for power, happiness, splendour of one's soul after death grow in the same proportion with the work of fantasy in these problems. The belief in the bliss of heavenly gods had indicated how the hopes of the human psyche could find contentment; the thought of the rightful claim of pious works to reward, raised desires to demands; in addition, the funeral rites of cremation and burial gave one to understand that the way downwards was also the way upwards. Is it not then clear, that thus the empire of the dead—at least the empire of the noble dead—has ascended from the depths of the nether world to the heavenly height[72]?

Sacrifice for the Dead

Our interpretation so far was based mainly upon the forms of prayer, which in Vedic antiquity, accompanied the customs associated with death and the dead. We shall now speak of the customs themselves. It appears that a very important evidence of extremely old concepts of afterlife has survived persistently in the rites for the dead which are on the whole different from the rites for the gods in the Vedic cult.

I shall now describe the sacrifice for the dead in its main features, as depicted in *Gobhila* (*Gṛhya*, IV, 2. 3)[73]. This sacrifice is repeated partly on certain days—around new moon—and partly on special occasions.

'In the south-east mid-region,[74] they[75] partition a place whose length extends in the same direction. Precisely in that direction, they must turn their face when they fulfil the rites.' Then it describes how the sacrificial fire is brought to the place, and how the food meant for the dead is prepared out of a mixture of rice and meat[76]. Then, three pits are dug, one span long, four-fingers broad and as much deep; darbha-grass is strewn over it. Brahmanas in odd numbers sit down[77]; with their permission, the sacrificer gives offerings to Soma, the one united with the fathers, and to Agni, the patron of offerings to the dead. A firebrand is placed beside the pits to drive away the evil demons, who might have crept in along with the fathers. The text then continues: 'Thereupon he invokes the fathers: 'Come you fathers, you friends of Soma, upon your deep, old paths. Give us here fine possessions, let us have riches and unharmed male progeny'. Then he should put down the water-pots near the pits. He should hold one water-pot with the left hand and empty it from right to the left over the Darbha-grass in the eastern pit and call the father by name: 'N.N. Have a wash, and those who follow after you and after whom you follow. Let these offerings be made to you!'[78]. After he has touched the water[79] he does it similarly for the two others[80]. He should hold the sacrificial spoon with the left hand, remove the third part from the food that has been blended together and put it down near the eastern pit, taking it from the right to the left over the darbha-grass and calling the name of the father: 'N.N. that is the dumpling you and for those who follow after you and those after whom you follow. This offering to you!' After he has touched the water, he does the same for the other two pots. If he does not know the names, he should put down the first dumpling with the words: 'Let this offering be for the fathers who sojourn on earth!', and the second dumpling with the words: 'Offering to the fathers who sojourn in the air!', and the third with the words: 'Offering to the fathers sojourning in heaven![81]. After he has put it down, he mutters: 'Here, you fathers, rejoice, rush forward with ardour to take your share!' Then he turns back[82], and without taking breath he murmurs: 'The fathers have rejoiced; they rushed forward and took their share with ardour!' (Then he offers in the same way salves, sesame-oil and fragrances to the fathers). Upon that he requests them to let him go. He places both his hands over the eastern pit, the palm of the right-hand turned upwards with the *mantra*: 'Hail to you, oh fathers, to your life, hail to you, oh fathers, to your voices!' Over the centre pit with upturned left palm, he says the *mantra*: 'Hail to you, o fathers, to your fecundity! Hail to you, fathers, to your life-giving sap!' Then, over the last pit, with the hollow of right hand turned upwards, he says the *mantra*: 'Honour to you, fathers, to your spiritual nourishment, O fathers, to your anger!' Then he murmurs with folded hands: 'Honour to you, fathers, o fathers, honour to you!' He looks at the house: 'Give us a house, o fathers!, He looks at the dumplings: 'May we have, o fathers, what we offered to you[83]'." It is mentioned finally that he offers[84] to the fathers as their clothes, new pieces of a fabric,—like the dumplings earlier, other texts mention also hair from the sacrificer's body. If he wants sons, his wife should eat one of the dumplings accompanied by a verse in which the fathers are invoked to bestow male progeny. The other dumplings are to be thrown into water or in the sacrificial fire or given to a Brahmana or thrown to a cow.

There is not doubt, that in this ritual also, there are elements of later origin. Thus, we have reason not to assign to the older *Ṛgvedic* period[85] the offerings to Soma and Agni who are paired off in endless repetitions in the later Vedic texts. Also, the Brahmanas who assist is the celebration, receive food and presents, though not explicitly stated in the description above. They must have gained this rôle much later[86]. But if we separate these innovations, there remains the picture of ceremony with the features of remote antiquity, namely the feeding of the souls, which recur essentially in the same form among all primitive races as a part of the heavenly abode of the souls; the gifts are not sent above to them through the sacrificial fire. They are located in the earth: the soul lives in the depths of the earth, or also on the earth, near the human dwellings[87]. It waits for the living beings to satisfy its hunger and clothe it. It comes for a meal, sits at the place that has been prepared for it[88] or slips into the water-vessel[89]; it enjoys the heat of the food that is given and leaves behind the substance that has turned cold[90]. Once the soul has received its share, care is taken to see that this uncanny guest does not stay longer. In the instance cited below, it will have to be understood as the last vestige of the material types of exorcism, like beating the air with a club, etc. Like the Athenian θύραζε Κῆρες, οὐκέτ' Ἀνθεστήρια, the Indian sacrificer who has at first invited the souls ('You fathers, rejoice'), says later, 'the fathers have rejoiced'. This is expressed more clearly in other descriptions of the ritual[91]: 'Go away, you fathers, you friends of the Soma, upon your deep old paths. But return to our houses after a month to eat the offerings, rich in progeny, rich in men.' Even dusting of the hem of the garment finds mention[92]; no doubt, it means shaking away of the souls.

We know all this from sources which are of later origin, in fact considerably later than the *Ṛgveda*. But this cannot prejudice our belief in the ancient origin of these rites. The simple offering of edible dumplings placed before the dead, was not accompanied by hymns and songs to the mighty gods as they were invented in the Soma-sacrifice: therefore, it is understandable that there is no reference to this ceremony in the book of hymns. Its whole appearance, however, would be incomprehensible, if it had originated at the same time as these texts which report upon them. It does not correspond with the thinking of this age, but much more with the thought and expression of a stage of the culture still far removed from the deities of *Ṛgvedic* poetry.

Belief in Ghosts and the Like: The One Who Just Died

We must refer here to a few practices which appear to suggest that the dead person does not unite with the other flocks of souls immediately after death, but continues to live apart for a while, in proximity to human beings and, therefore, of danger to them.

It must be mentioned above all that the regular monthly *śrāddhas* intended for the father, the grandfathe- and the great-grandfather of the sacrificer were not performed for the dead person in the period immediately following his death. He was honoured solely through a single *śrāddha,* and, as a rule, was admitted in the company of his fathers only after a year. In that event the new entrant displaced the most removed of the three preceding ancestors, who then went over to the indeterminate general crowd of the fathers. Apparently, the idea at bottom is, that the dead man takes his due place amongst the ancestors after some time, but till then he remained in an in-between situation. This can be perhaps confirmed by a few differences between the *śrāddha* of an individual and the general *śrāddha*. The dead are not summoned. At the end, when the fathers are allowed to go ('go away, fathers', etc. p. 318) it is said here: 'May one rest in peace'[93]. Instead of the prayer that the gifts donated to the fathers may belong to them for ever, one prays only that they be there for the dead[94]. The idea expressed in these variations suggests that the dead man lingers on during this period in the proximity of the living, and that this is purely as a temporary as opposed to the later, permanent state. All the later literature[95] distinguishes also clearly between the ***Preta***[96], and ***Pitaras***[97]. ***Preta,*** who is honoured separately, means literally the one who has gone over, it has also the meaning of 'ghosts'. The ***Pitaras*** ('fathers') are the fully privileged ancestral spirits. And even if there be in the ***Ṛgveda*** an opposite idea—of the smoke from the pyre transposing the dead directly to the fathers—I think the weighty evidence of the ritual concurs sufficiently with inner probability leading one to believe that the later texts actually preserve here ancient belief[98].

Just now the difference between the provisional and the definitive *śrāddha* discussed above appears to point to a change in the condition of the dead, so too does the difference between the provisional and definitive funeral. It is proven custom[99] with many peoples to let a definitive funeral, associated with a great feast for the dead, follow a provisional one, at a later date, often only after a number of years; the period of mourning for the dead—i.e., in the original nature of things the need for special precaution against being haunted by the dead—extends, according to the norm, upto this ceremony though one often finds that this period of mourning is curtailed[100]. We shall discuss later that this difference between the provisional and the definitive funeral was also common to the Vedic ritual; here we make only a passing reference in so far as it appears to suggest an incomplete naturalization initially of the dead into the other world. It is quite clear that a magic effect upon the existence of the soul had to be ascribed to a ceremony like the definitive funeral, and that this effect must have been thought of as the transfer of the soul into a lasting condition far away from the world of the living. We find in fact that this magic effect is regularly associated with that rite in the belief of the primitive races.

Strictly speaking, it is to be expected that the transition from the individual veneration of the dead person to his participation in the general cult of the dead coincides with the definitive funeral, but the ritual-texts portray these processes quite independent of each other. Yet, in reality, it is strange to observe how both the ritual expressions for the entry of the dead person to his eternal place of rest, have ultimately assumed independent existence, obscuring any connection between the two. This may be due to the fixing of the period for the *śrāddha* of an individual to one year.

We have already mentioned that the expression *Preta* was used for the one not yet taken up amongst the 'fathers', also meaning 'ghost'. The existence of the dead man still roaming about the living world acquires ghost-like character; only a proper funeral has the power to give peace to the ghost.[101] That does not mean, however, that all belief in ghosts depends upon the funeral not or not yet completed[102]; it could have also emerged regardless of funeral practices or could have become independent of them subsequently, such that the belief in retribution took part in it and ghost-like existence instead of an inadequate funeral became the punishment for sin. But it will be appropriate here to survey the main features of the ancient Indian belief in ghosts.

The *Ṛgveda*, though lacking in specific references to this belief, speaks at least once (X, 15, 2) of the fathers 'who have sojourned in the earthly ethereal region or in well-protected habitats[103]'. This almost reminds one of the ghost-like existence led by the dead in the vicinity of the living. A later Vedic text adds to it the factor of sin and punishment: one who spills the blood of a Brahmana shall 'not get to see the world of fathers[104]' for as many years as the blood moistens the grains of sand.

The Vedic texts seem to offer little material for a closer description of the existence of the ghost-like souls which are excluded from the world of fathers[105]. The story of a *Brāhmaṇa-text*[106] of the king Uccaiśśravas Kaupayeya is interesting, though not exactly concerned with the ghost in the sense indicated just earlier. He dies; his close friend, his nephew takes to hunting to dispel his sorrow. He sees, between himself and the gazzele the king Uccaiśśravas. 'Have I lost my senses, or do I see well' 'You have not lost your senses. You are seeing well. I am the one whom you take me to be.' 'O Illustrious one, it is said that if a (dead person) appears, the others (to whom he appears) go into his empire (they also die). How could you then appear to me?' " 'Yes'—thus he spoke—'when I met the ruler of the other world, I have appeared before you (with his permission) to drive away your sorrow and to educate you'." The living being wants to embrace the dead man. But he evades him 'as though one nears smoke or wind or ether or fire's glow or water, and he cannot be held embraced.' He speaks: 'Your form is the same as the one earlier, and yet I cannot hold you and embrace you.' 'Yes,—thus spoke the other one— a Brahmana well-versed in Sāman sang for me the Sāman; he has shaken off my corporeity through the unsubstantial Sāman; that person for whom the Sāman-knower sings a Sāman, reaches the kingdom of gods.' The folk-belief in the dead appearing to the living is quite evident here despite the theological slant. But as far as I can see, this is the only such story in Vedic lore. That is significant, but also easily understandable. Heaven and hell enjoy preference in religious fantasy driven to the extreme, particularly with the belief in metempsychosis becoming increasingly alive. In popular belief the ghost-world was just but a rudiment existing outside of the lively, contemporary modes of thinking: it is said[107], 'the living and the fathers do not appear together.' Thus, in the literature of the *mantras* meant to ward off evil demons and pests, we meet creatures who spread diseases or cause trouble, but they are not ghosts. It is probable that these Rākṣas, Piśāca, etc., originate[108] to a large extent from the evil souls of the dead, but for the Atharvan poets this context had become long since obscure, and those types independent. Only in the old Buddhistic texts, we hear again of ghosts.[109] Here, stories of ghosts who are punished for their sins on earth are popular as salutory examples; they also urge one to be generous to the pious monks; for one can soothe the sufferings of the dead in the other world by gifts given in their honour. If we leave aside this particular point, then the Buddhistic belief in ghosts gives probably, in essence a true picture of the direct information almost held back from us by the Vedas; there is no reason to think of any innovations here.[110] It is, therefore, appropriate to review the Buddhistic concept on ghosts. That the Buddhistic texts consider these ghosts not merely as a poetically-educative staffage, but take them seriously, is seen by the fact that the communal law, in its invariably sober tone, discusses a case where a monk, despite the law forbidding sexual sins, keeps company with a female ghost; it also discusses a case where a monk, in spite of the law forbidding theft, has appropriated a ghost's belonging. This was considered like the belonging of an animal as ownerless.[111] In the stories, the ghosts are found often at lonely spots, where a traveller meets them; they also accost the monk who has withdrawn in solitude. The king of Surāṣṭra while returning to his country from the capital of Maurya, reaches at noon a path that runs into a swamp; an eerie smell pervades the air, terrible sounds are heard.[112] He notices that he is close to the people from Yama's kingdom and a man looking like god approaches him under a mighty Nyagrodha-tree, beautifully embellished who is recognised as a ghost (*preta*) and narrates to him of the evil life he led.[113] Other ghosts turn up on the bank of the Ganges, in a field of sugarcane-field on a dung-heap in front of the city Vesālī.[114] They are not invariably tied to the place where they appear. The husband invites his wife whom he meets as a ghost, and asks her to come home and see her children.[115] Another ghost goes into the royal city of Rājagṛha to the king to show him how it can be redeemed.[116] When friends and relatives give food to the ghost, it lives on it; if it is not present, then other friendly or related ghosts take it; their absence is, of course, ruled out.[117] A strange text[118] describes how the human dwellings are surrounded by the ghosts of the dead members of the family: 'They stand behind the walls, at the boundaries and cross-roads; they stand at the door post; they return to their house;—one who is sympathetic, gives them food and drink; ghosts wish them long life.' 'There, fields are not cultivated, cattle are not looked after; there is no trade, no commerce. The dead and the departed live on the things given to them from this world. Like the rain-water that falls on the heights and runs down to the depths, what is given to the dead is for their benefit.' Here, it appears that it was the normal lot of the dead to sojourn ghost-like near their old home. Usually, however, ghost-like existence appears to be an exception, as a punishment for guilt accompanied by torments of all kings. With a monstrous stomach and a very narrow mouth, naked or covered with one's own hair, persecuted by heat, against which water, shadow, wind offer no shelter, starving or eating refuse, thirsty in the midst of Ganges-water, turning what is desired into blood, tumbling about like madman, like game in flight: thus the Buddhists describe the ghosts, suffering more themselves than causing harm to the human beings they meet.

Finally, we may stress upon a peculiar feature of these Buddhistic stories: the ghost relating his story to a man he meets, says repeatedly[119] that it would 'die' in so many months and go to this and this hell. Speaking in terms of the belief in metempsychosis, does the earlier notion surface there that ghost-like existence is but a transitory stage before the soul proceeds to its final destination?

Of course, one cannot venture to judge how far such individual, concrete features of the later belief in ghosts can be dated back to the Vedic period, like the ghost-city of Divyāvadāna,[120] or the islands of the Jātaka[121] inhabited by ghost-women or the eerie, grave-side scenes of horror (for example, in the drama *Mālatīmādhava*, the story of the sun-umbrella with the five sticks).[122] But we shall be justified in using the total picture of those concepts in their approximate sense, only to fill up a gap left by the Vedic tradition in our knowledge of the ancient Indian views on life.

Embodiment of Souls in Animals, Plants and Stars

I may remark in addition that the traces of the widespread belief in the embodiment of the souls of the dead in animals, as far as I see, appear only sparingly in the older literature. Of course, the most important evidence is the rule of a law-book[123] that a dumpling, as the manes receive it, must be thrown to the birds: 'for it is taught that the fathers come down taking the form of birds.' The sources for the belief in the embodiment of souls in serpents[124] provide insufficient basis to arrive at conclusion with regard to old Aryan India. The burial-ritual contains perhaps a feature that points to animal embodiment;[125] the narrative literature would have given more information if the innovations of the belief in metempsychosis had not got inextricably mixed up with the remaining vestiges of such old concepts. Or could advances in research here succeed in making a distinction? For example, there is the story of a mother who dies while her son is away. Out of love for him, she turns into a she-jackal and accosts him on his way so that he may not enter a forest where he is likely to meet with misfortune.[126] This story may have to do with old folk-belief that the souls of the dead can enter animals. If this be correct, do we not then have here a characteristic of the concepts which paved the way for the belief in metempsychosis? And will this belief not lose more and more of its character of an unmediated innovation for advancing research?[127]

We may further ask whether one did not believe also in souls entering plants; about that, one may refer to a few remarks to be made when we discuss the burial-ritual.[128] After all, embodiment in stars is also not alien to ancient Indian belief.[129] A well-known passage of the great epic[130] speaks of the 'starry figures glittering like lights, small at a distance, though really very big'; : they shine 'of their own, having got their light by their good works'—royal sages, fallen war-heroes ascetics who have reached the heavenly world through mortification. But this idea appearing here in the epic dates back to the Vedas. A Vedic law-book[131] says: 'The beings of the sages who have done good can be seen glittering on high', and a *Brāhmaṇa*[132] explains the stars assigned for women and then for 'the light of those who have reached heaven by their good works'. Should not one understand in the same sense, when the *Ṛgveda* says: 'High up in heaven stand they, who have given sacrificial reward?' Or, when it speaks of the heavenly existence of 'the Ṛṣis rich in mortification and of poets who guard the sun'?[133] Or, when the *Atharvaveda*[134] lets the unmarried ones, who have departed childless, 'ascend to heaven and shine at the back of the firmament'? Can we not consider as a vestige of the belief in the star-souls the naming of the Great Bear as seven Ṛṣis, or the naming of the Pleiades as Arundhatī, the symbol of fidelity, or the concept of the Kṛttikās as the consorts of the heavenly Bears?

THE DEAD AND THE LIVING

Intrusion of the Dead in the Existence of the Living

The existence of the cult of the Dead goes to show that the souls—unlike the inhabitants of the Greek Hades—are capable of coming into contact with the living and influencing their final destination. The cult of the Dead is deeply interwoven with the laws regulating family life. It extends[135] throughout the year, preferring new moon days or the waning-half every month, also the hour of fading daylight, the afternoon. Besides, it makes out certain periods to be particularly sacred for the manes—the festival of the Sākamedhās (p. 237), the Aṣṭakās in winter, towards the end of the year (p. 239) and also on a set date during the rainy season. This belief is, of course, found only in the later texts, but concurs with the ideas of related peoples. It lets the souls leave Yama's house at certain periods and visit their progeny on earth, demanding food: happy the one who satisfies them.[136] Like the epics with the frequent references to the appearance of the dead, so too does the Vedic collection of hymns and *mantras*[137] reveals in diverse forms an active relation between the dead and the earthly fates. Mostly the 'fathers' are invoked in general, but occasionally the Brahmana sacrificer directs his prayer to the individual ancestors of the priest-generations by names, to Kaṇva, Kakṣīvant and to the whole class of patriarchs; or, the poet from the house of the Vasiṣṭhas invokes the departed Vasiṣṭhas.[138] One asks, just as one asks the gods, generally for blessings and that one's prayer be answered; but one also asks for specific favours like rain or the gift of successful speech in open court. One also requests that the dead give the needy on earth in exchange for the oblation, or that the collected merit of the sacrifices and gifts of the fathers may aid the worshipper in destroying his enemy.[139] Before the battle, one prays to the fathers who conquered with their lances and mighty arrows, the hostile legions[140]. In the Pravargya-sacrifice, besides the gods the fathers also give their consent to the sacrificer.[141] But it is particularly the continuation of the family lineage that is in the care of the ancestors. 'Give me strong sons, you great-grandfathers! Give me strong sons, you grandfathers! Give me strong sons, Oh you fathers!' This is the prayer at the *śrāddha*.[142] One of the dumplings prepared for the manes is given by the sacrificer to his wife, if she desires a male issue, with the mantra: 'Give an embryo, you fathers, a son, lotus-crowned, that man be here'.[143] The sacrificer moistens his face with the water left over from the offering to the fathers, if he wants to have a son.[144] Dumpling is offered to the fathers before marriage,[145] obviously to effect progeny, and one believes that they come to see the young bride, when the bridal procession is made to halt.[146]

Certainly, one believed also that the dead can come to the aid of the living with their supernatural knowledge. We may include here—after stripping it of the trappings of the belief in metempsychosis—the feature one often found in the Buddhistic stories[147] that a 'deity related by blood' can give good advice to the man.[148]

There is little mention of the evil done by the dead to the living. One cannot expect it to be otherwise, given the contextual character, to a large extent, of the concerned Vedic texts, namely the burial-ritual and the *Śrāddha*. Sufficient evidences clearly prove that the idea of souls causing harm is not absent. In the *Ṛgveda* itself (X, 15, 6), there is a prayer at the time of the sacrifice to the dead: 'Do not harm us fathers, if we have committed a mistake against you in our human way.' It is said in one of the later Vedic texts:[149] 'What they take for themselves, is the share of the fathers.' Their own fathers will become angry and do harm only if provoked by neglecting them or by withholding offerings due to them. Probably, the souls spell danger more to a stranger; one may recall the invocation to the fathers (p. 324) to put to use the merits of their good deeds for the destruction of the supplicant enemy: the priest's emphasis on the merit of the good deeds is not important here; most important is the belief in the souls of the fathers who destroy their progeny's enemy. In a like context, 'the Dasyus[150] who have infiltrated among the fathers in the guise of relatives' are warded off during the *Śrāddha* with a firebrand lit at both ends.[151] The souls of unborn children are considered especially evil—in India and elsewhere; they are considered as bloodsuckers.[152] On the whole, the various precautions found throughout the entire ritual for the dead, point to the belief that the souls approach more easily the person who does not protect himself.

However, the concept of souls causing harm had lost its intensity in the Atharvan age. We have already said (p. 321) that in this Veda they are not really souls—at least for the consciousness of that time—but other types of demons like Rakṣas[153] who appear as causers of disease and misfortune.

THE FUNERAL[154]

We have often referred to the funeral customs in earlier sections; now we have to come back again to them in the present context.

Various Types of Funeral

It appears that cremation, though by no means the universal practice in the Vedic age, was at least common among the higher circles of society. Later authors describe the burial grounds as full of decomposing bodies that had been thrown away, when the law-books[155] rule that infant corpses are to be buried or thrown away, 'left exposed like a piece of wood in the forest'. The great epic[156] says that the dead body is 'burnt or buried or done away.' Here, it can be said that these different funeral or non-funeral practices were obviously known to the Vedic age. The *Ṛgveda* speaks of the dead (X, 15, 14)—not, say, of ordinary people, non-Aryans, etc., but of the pious ancestors living blissfully in heaven,—'those consumed by fire and those not consumed by fire', and in the *Atharvaveda* (XVIII, 2, 34) is a similar verse which invokes Agni though more concretely: 'Those buried, thrown away, cremated or set up: Agni, bring them all here, the fathers, so that they can partake of the oblation.' It may be doubtful, who these 'set up' (*uddhitāḥ*) are. Another verse where the expression is used, cites an instance of an unborn calf coming to light at the sacrifice of a cow which has not been allowed to get pregnant. 'Thereupon one says: whither shall he set up the calf? One should set it up on a tree (*uddadhyuḥ*). ...As against that, one, however, says: Whoever places the curse on him: 'One will set him up on a tree, when he is dead', that it may be fulfilled' (*Śatapatha Br.* IV, 5, 2, 13). The custom of tying the corpse to a tree to keep the living away from the dead, is common to many peoples: we have to understand thus this Atharvan expression 'setting up' the dead.[157]

The burial which thus actually occurs amongst the Vedic Indians, is not discussed in the ritual-texts, apparently because it is considered as not normal. And the attempt made by many[158] to cull out descriptions of burial ceremonies from the Ṛgvedic hymns to the dead (X, 18) can hardly be justified. It is said to the dead man there: 'Betake yourself to the lap of mother Earth'—'Cover him, as the mother wraps her skirt about her child, O Earth'—'I place the earth above you.' But it should not be overlooked that all this fits as much into the ritual of cremation as also that of the burial. The mortal remains not completely consumed by fire are lowered into the earth: that the text does not refer to this act, but the burial of the whole body cannot be maintained with certainty.[159] As a matter of fact, the later ritual-texts include the verses in question in the description of their funeral—which is, of course, the cremation—by giving them precisely the same term.[160] And the same interpretation is rendered likely in the case of the *Ṛgveda* too, if we consider the fact that the sections comprising these verses whose contents and authorship unmistakably go together, contain a cremation ritual, which would be incomplete, were it not for the *mantras* detailing the burial of the bones: a gap filled up to precision by the text in question.[161]

Thus only the cremation remains as better known of the various kinds of funeral. We shall now present its main aspects.[162]

Cremation

The Aryan dies, not in bed, but near his sacred fires, on the ground, cleaned with cow-dung and strewn with grass.[163] He is washed; his beard, hair and nails are cut; he is anointed, garlanded and given fresh clothes. One will have to imagine the corpse—like at the scene of cremation and burial later[164]—being accompanied by the wailing of women, with hair unkempt and dishevelled, dancing about and beating themselves upon their breasts and thighs.[165] Then the corpse is carried to the place of burning or carried on a cart, preceded by the sacrificial fire[166] and the next of kin, and followed by the cow to be sacrificed; the distant relatives follow with unkempt hair. The branch of a tree tied to the dead man wipes out the footprints so that death does not find the way back to the living beings. The following verses of the *Ṛgveda* are meant for this stage of the ceremony:[167]

The dead person is addressed.

'Go forth, go forth upon the ancient pathways, whereon our sires of old have gone before us. There you shall look on both the kings enjoying their sacred food, God Varuṇa and Yama.

'Meet Yama, meet the Fathers, meet the merit of free or ordered acts, in highest heaven. Leave sin and evil, seek anew your dwelling,[168] and bright with glory wear another body.'

The evil spirits are driven away from the path of the dead:

'Go hence, depart ye, fly in all directions: this place for him the Fathers have provided. Yama bestows on him a place to rest in, adorned with days and beams of light and waters.'

And again to the dead:

"Run and outspeed the two dogs,[169] Saramā's offspring, brindled, four-eyed, upon the happy pathway. Draw nigh then to the gracious-minded Fathers where they rejoice in company with Yama.

'And your two dogs, Yama, the watchers, four-eyed, who look on men and guard the pathway,—entrust this man, O King, to their protection, and with prosperity and health endow him.

'Dark-hued, insatiate,[170] with distended nostrils, Yama's two envoys roam among people; may they restore to us a fair existence here and today, that we may see the sunlight.'

Then the dead man is kept on the pyre which according to later sources, is surrounded by the three fires in the case of a person who performed the cult of the three fires. His wife is asked to lie next to him, but soon she is asked to get up. 'Get up, O woman, to the world of life. Gone is your life's breath with whom you lie; come here! You have come up to this marriage here with the husband who is holding your hand and who is wooing for you[171].' Like the wife, the dead warrior is separated from the symbols of his warriorhood. The bow[172] which is provided him, is taken out of his hand: 'I take the bow from the hand of the dead so that the mastery, power and strength may remain with us. There you may overcome, like we here, every attack of hostile legions' (X, 18, 9).[173] According to later texts, all the sacrificial utensils are kept on the funeral pyre of a sacrificer. They are placed upon and around the corpse; only those which cannot be burnt—the vessels made of clay, metal or stone—are thrown into the water, or they are given away to a Brahmana: A text[174] actually objects to it—it mentions explicitly only earthenware and stoneware—: 'the one who accepts these things is considered to be pall-bearer'.[175] The Ṛgveda (X, 16, 8) appears also to hint at the giving along of the sacrificial utensils. The fire is invoked: 'This vessel, O Agni, do not destroy. It is dear to the gods and to the donor of Soma. Let this drinking vessel go to gods. Let the immortal gods inebriate themselves from it.' Probably, this refers to the Soma-vessel kept on the funeral-pyre.[176] Further the *Ṛgveda* (verse 4) mentions the goat burnt together with the dead; Agni is told: 'Your portion is the goat: with your fire consume him; let your fierce flame burn him. With your auspicious forms, Jātavedas, bear this man (the dead) to the region of the pious.' The dead man himself is told (verse 7): 'Put on the armour of cows[177] against the flames of Agni, cover yourself with fat and marrow, so will the Bold one, eager to attack you with fierce glow fail to girdle and consume you.' The later texts supplement these interpretations when they speak of a cow which is slaughtered as a 'shielding animal'; limb for limb the dead body is covered with the parts of this animal; the face with the fatty retina, the hand with the two kidneys as protection against the dogs of the god of death; the whole body with the skin along with the head and feet. Then the funeral pyre is set alight;[178] invocations implore Agni for the safe passage of the dead to the fathers. A goat is tethered loosely near the funeral pyre with a cord so that it can easily free itself.[179] Surely, offerings took place here, even in ancient times,[180] although the *mantra* which accompanies the most important of the offerings is missing in the *Ṛgveda*.[181] 'You (Agni) are born from him (the dead); may he be born again from you': the fire which the living had once kindled gives new life to the dead.

The mourners cleanse themselves before and after returning from the cremation ground. They step beneath a yoke made of branches of the *parna*-tree which has a cleansing effect; they take a dip in the water from which an offering is dedicated to the dead; they change clothes; they avoid looking around themselves on the way;[182] they touch on entering the house purifying and propitious substances like water, fire, cow-dung and barley corn.[183] The fire used for the cremation is not taken out by the door but through another exit[184] and put down on a barren spot.[185]

Impurity of the Survivors

The first days after the death of a person are considered impure for the survivors. They avoid the accustomed bed and sleep on the ground; they observe chastity; they do not cook at home, but live on food bought from or given by others.[186] The period of impurity is shorter or longer, depending upon the nearness of kinship; namely, a three day and a ten day period. 'Or the observances', says a text,[187] 'go on till the mortal remains are collected': perhaps, the original practice; it is but natural that these customs incumbent on the living, depend upon the rites which concern the remains of the dead person and thereby, implicitly, his person too.

Collection of the Relics

On the third day[188] after the cremation the relics are collected. Rites at the cremation-ground are mentioned—they recur also in other contexts. They describe mostly the extinction of fire and the coolness following in its wake. Water-plants and a she-toad are brought there: 'Cool down, Agni, and refresh the spot which you have scorched and burnt, here let the Kiyāmbu grow, panic grass and Vyalkaśā. Full of coolness, you cool plant, full of fresh moisture, fresh herb, come hither with the female frog: fill with delight this Agni here'.[189] Other texts speak of sprinkling water and milk over the place of fire.

Burial of the Relics; Erection of a Mound

Now the bones are collected, put into an urn[190] and covered with fragrant substances. The various sources give different accounts about the burial-place of the bones[191]. I reproduce here the description of the *Āśvalāyana*.[192]

'After they have been carefully collected and cleaned with a sieve, they should be buried[193] in a pit at a place where no other water except rain-water flows, with the verse: 'Go away to the mother earth, to the wide space of the friendly earth. Soft like wool is she, the virgin to the generous one. She protects you from the womb of destruction'.[194] He should throw earth upon it, with the verse: 'Open yourself Earth, do not press on him. Let him go in happily, creep in. Cover him Earth as the mother covers her child with her skirt'. After throwing the earth, he speaks the next verse: 'The Earth shall open up, stand firm. Thousand pillars shall rise. Let it be your house, dripping with butter; let it be your permanent place of refuge.' He places a covered bowl upon it with the verse: 'I pile up the earth around you. May no harm come to you as I put down this lump of earth. May the fathers hold these pillars for you. Yama shall prepare a seat for you there.' Then they go away, without looking around themselves, take a bath and prepare a funeral repast for the dead man'.[195]

A few texts describe the erection of a mound over the grave, as the concluding rite: a special honour not shown to all the dead.[196] As a *Brāhmaṇa*-text[197] recommends, one must wait for that till one does not know how many years have passed since the death: just as elsewhere in the ritual, sinister occurrences remain concealed from the living in terms of space, this happens here in terms of time. 'He should do it after a long time,' explains the *Brāhmaṇa*, 'thus he conceals the death. When one does not remember any more even the years, one removes the death from earshot.' The mortal remains are brought from their place of rest.[198] If they are not to be found, one should take instead dust from that place or 'one should spread out a cloth at the water's edge and call N.N. (the name of the dead man). If then an animal sits upon it', it is said to represent the place of the mortal remains:[199] an important rite, apparently independent of the theory of metempsychosis in the usual sense of the word, that shows the soul of the dead as incarnated in an insect or the like, and hovering about the burial ground. At night one goes around the mortal remains, fanning them with a cloth or with a fan.[200] Music of all kind is played; 'celebrate the fathers', it is said. Metallic cymbals are struck;[201] one plays the flute; wailing women with unkempt hair go around the mortal remains three times, turned towards them from the left and striking themselves on the right thigh:[202] all this in order to avoid contact with the substance of the death. All this happens first at nightfall, then around midnight, and later around the morning; this can be repeated several nights. Finally, the mortal remains are brought around the morning[203] to the place where the mound is to be erected, to a pleasant spot, but not visible from the village, away from the road—the living have to be secure from the nearness of the dead. This spot is located in a thicket free of thorns but full of roots: obviously, the idea is that no thorn should injure the dead, and as a *Brāhmaṇa*[204] says, 'the fathers slip into the roots of the plants'. Is this an instance of the belief in dead souls living in plants and trees?[205] Such a place is furrowed, water is sprinkled and seeds of all types are sown.[206] After several other rites, the mortal remains are finally emptied and so arranged that they form a human body. Memorial made of stone and earth is set on it. Flat cakes and barleycorns are given as food.[207] While going away, all means are used to prevent the death from following the person returning into life. The texts mention the fire that drives away all the evil powers, the wiping away of the foot-prints, the crossing of ditches filled with water, the placing of a stone or a lump of clay from a boundary which is considered as having the power of demarcation—here between life and death. Even the *Ṛgveda* alludes to such a symbolic dividing wall: 'Here I erect this rampart for the living; let none of these, none other, reach this limit. May they survive a hundred lengthened autumns, and may they bury death beneath this mountain' (X, 18, 4). It is said just there (verse 3): 'Divided from the dead are these, the living; now be our calling on the gods successful. We have gone forth for dancing for laughter, to further times prolonging our existence.'

The Funeral Rite on the whole; Effect of Cremation

Thus far, the details of the funeral-ritual; let us survey once more the whole. The most prominent feature is the use of fire to transport the soul to the heaven. This belief does not apparently assume the form that the soul remains attached to the body till it is burnt, and that it is separated from it only by fire: all indications pointing to such a thought are missing in the *mantras* of the ritual; though they would have been scarcely avoidable; also the view referred to above that even in the case of serious illness or in the unconscious state of approaching death, the soul has gone already to Yama's kingdom would be in direct contradiction with this belief. Really it should not be overlooked that even this view does not fit into the concept of Agni as the transporter of souls to Yama's kingdom, the concept of the cremation as the time of this transportation. Obviously, the discrepancy is explained from the development of the whole set of concepts. The interpretation in question of the cremation has nothing to do with the original nature of this type of funeral. Burning of the body, originally in India and elsewhere, which appears as the equivalent of burial, goes together apparently with other instances in the ritual where a dangerous substance is either burnt or buried.[208] The actual impurification coming from the body, rather dangers arising from the attachment of the soul to the body, the substance of death inherent in it and the magic that can be linked with the dead body, ought to be removed. Burning of the corpse in this sense may be much older than the belief in the heavenly life of the soul. Perhaps, burning which bestowed the same fate on the corpse, like the offerings which one sent to the gods through the sacrificial fire, had its share in the origin of this belief. I shall not venture to assess this. But in any case, it is extremely probable that the concept of Agni as a psychopomp leading heavenwards entered as a new element the already extant mass of concepts concerning the fates of the soul at the time of death and of cremation:[209] it is, therefore, not surprising that the old and the new have not merged into a perfectly smooth whole.

It is not the cremated dead alone who are considered as living in heaven: the *Ṛgveda* speaks of those 'who, consumed by fire or not consumed by fire, feasting on offerings, in the midst of heaven'.[210] Therefore, it is but appropriate that the concept of heavenly life stands in a special, often explicit relation to the rite of cremation; the normal way for the dead to reach the heavenly world is the one led by Agni. Perhaps it is this relationship alone which, besides other factors—like the general preference of the Vedic theologians for Agni and for every rite connected with Agni[211]—, gave priority to cremation over the other rival types of funeral.

What is burnt by Agni or more precisely what is cooked and refined by Agni, appears to have been understood as the whole man, the body and the soul, which was likewise considered to be present. The *Ṛgveda* X, 16, 1 says: 'Burn him not, nor quite consume him, Agni: let not his body or skin be scattered. O Jātavedas, when you have cooked him well, then send him on his way to the fathers.' One will not be surprised at this idea in flux: after 'he', the deceased person with body and soul, has gone into the other world, 'he' is laid to rest in the earth in a later ceremony when the mortal remains are buried; the earth should not, oppress him as it is said; there shall be his house, his place of refuge, Yama shall prepare a place for him (p. 329).[212] What is more natural than this uneven shift and the fact that everywhere 'he', the self of the dead man is addressed regardless of the direction taken by the thought and rite?[213]

Things given with the Dead

The dead man does not go naked and alone to the other world. When clothes and ornaments are placed on the corpse, it is not to be understood as an act of piety; the idea is that the dead should wear them in the other world. The significance of this custom is also fully alive in the Veda. 'This cloth', it is said in the *Atharvaveda* (XVIII, 4, 31) to the dead man, 'is given to you by the god Savitar. Attired in it, go to Yama's kingdom...' The age-old custom of giving to the dead man of his main possessions has at first left its traces in the burning of the sacrificial utensils: precisely here, perhaps on account of the sanctity present in them which is dangerous for the survivors. Even the removal of the bow, the gold from the hand of the dead man[214] suggests that the dead were given once such possessions: only when the claims of the living became more imperative, a special rite was used to remove these things from the sphere of influence of the dead. It is not different in the case of the widow. That the Vedic rite excludes her burning is without doubt. But she climbs the funeral pyre and it needs a special ritual to bring her back to the world of the living: a clear remnant of real widow-burning, which was then revived, as is well-known, has never become really extinct despite the authority of the Veda.[215]

The burning of a goat or a cow along with the corpse does not really mean that the animal was given to the dead in possession. The covering of his limbs with the corresponding parts of the cow seems to suggest the idea that it meant, at least originally, a sort of substitution: in place of the dead man, an animal was thrust to the hostile powers in pursuit of the dead man in order to spare him. The *Ṛgveda* also interprets the rite thus—with special reference to the goat and the consuming power of fire.[216] Besides that, there are of course, other opinions elsewhere. The Maruts are to bestow coolness on the dead through the goat:[217]—I do not understand how this is meant. Further—

it is possible this is a genuine old feature—, one speaks of the paths trodden by the goats, upon which Pūṣan should lead the dead to the other world: perhaps steep mountain paths which are not accessible to any animal other than that of the divine ruler of paths and the psychopomp.[218]

If the rites discussed so far referred to the path of the dead into the other world and their fate there, then other rites have to do with the purification and the protection of the living: thus the wiping away of the foot-prints, the erection of a boundary stone, the water used in two ways—as a purifier and as a barrier, etc. The broad space these rites occupy, shows that a predominant viewpoint of the whole funeral ceremony is represented in them. Clarification of the details appears unnecessary; but it will be in order to refer cursorily to the mourning customs mentioned above (p. 328), namely the observances connected with the 'impurity' of the bereaved-chastity, sleeping on the bare floor, eating of food bought from or given by others.[219]

Protection of the Survivors; The Mourning Rites

These customs in themselves and also comparisons with similar mourning-rites of primitive races,[220] show clearly that there are at least originally acts here to ward off dangers coming from the dead. The law-book of Viṣṇu[221] says: 'As long as the impurity of the relatives lasts, the Preta (above p. 319) does not find a place to stay; thus, they return to them who give them offerings of dumpling and water.' Fully true, but naturally one has to return; the impurity remains as long as the return of the soul is feared, i.e., that condition of the relatives which makes continuous precautions necessary.[222] The nature of this precaution is especially clear with regard to eating. We may observe a few parallel customs of other people. The Indian rite must be related[223] to the Avestic rite, according to which the relatives of the dead are not allowed to cook anything during the first three days: Dastur Hoshangi says[224] that the Parsees do not cook even today under a roof where death has occurred, but receive their food from the neighbours; they are allowed to cook only when the kitchen is under a special roof. Exactly the same is said of the aborigines.[225] Amongst the Alfures in the Indian Ocean, the widower is not supposed to take for some time food prepared in the house where a death has occurred. Amongst the Samoans: '*While a dead body was in the house, no food was eaten under the same roof; the family had their meals outside, or in another house*.' Doubtless, it does not mean that one wanted to express sadness by not taking food. There is a danger in the food cooked by oneself or in the house where death has taken place. It can be infected by the death-bringing substance, bringing death, or by the soul-substance of the dead man, transferred to the one who eats it.[226] Sleeping on the floor may also rest upon similar ideas. Is it at bottom the idea that the soul may visit the survivors at night, that one escapes it by avoiding the accustomed resting-place? Or does it perhaps mean that the person who has now been the dead man could transfer traces of this contact on to his own resting-place and infect it thereby for the future? I would like to explain the abstinence from sex[227] by mentioning that, like the food prepared in the house of death, the semen of the person, who had been near the dead man was considered susceptible to impurity, and, therefore, likely to infect the wife or offspring.

In conclusion, our consideration of the funeral rite will have established that the Vedic Indians had long outgrown the fearful terribleness of the savage cult of the souls though they have especially preserved many vestiges of ancient forms of belief. The contents of the funeral *mantras* comprise pious faith in deities who protect the dead, and reverence to the dead and that, apart of course, a great deal of ritualistic trifles that cannot be ignored, and above all the eager concern for one's own well-being. If the language of that piety appears to lack something of that full glow of human feelings, of the sombre touching poetry of sorrow, we must then remember that only the ritual-texts with their impersonal formulas have survived. Had we possessed from the Vedic period the poetic descriptions which the Iliad accords to the funerals of Petrocles and Hector or had we a beautiful account of the *Mahābhārata* of the celebration of death for the fallen heroes in the great battle, we could have no doubt added to our description many a feature now lacking.

REFERENCES

1. According to the knowledge of the Vedic period this event is necessarily to take place before any other; man is by nature a 'mortal' (*marta, martya*). The view that death is traced back in every case to the accident of hostile attack has been since long done away with.

2. The same connection of macrocosmos and microcosmos—as has been observed long time back—, when according to *Ṛv*. X, 90, 13 the sun originates from the eye of the original man (*puruṣa*), and the Vāyu (god of wind) from his breath, etc. *Atharvaveda* VIII, 2, 3 may also be compared.

3. One cannot obviously expect to find the juxtaposition of ideas developed to absolute clarity so that one could, say, answer the question, how the surviving soul could see and hear, when its eyes and ears are sent to the sun and in all directions.

4. Thus speaks also verse X, 16, 3 cited above which lets the eye and the *Ātman* of the dead man be dispersed in the universe, and soon thereafter speaks of his whereabouts.

5. *Bṛhad Āraṇyaka Upaniṣad* IV, 3, 14. For parallels coming from outside of India see Frazer, *Journ. of the Anthropol. Institute of Great Britain and Ireland* XV, 70 note 1; *Golden Bough*[2] I', 257f.

6. *Kāṭhaka Upaniṣad*, IV, 12 f. Compare also the material on the soul as big as a span in Caland, *Wenschoffers* 17.

7. *Mahābhārata* III, 16763 ed. Calc.

8. Thus the word *ātman* (originally 'breath', then 'soul', 'one's own self') which got later a great significance in philosophical speculation; compare my 'Lehre der Upaniṣaden', 52 ff.

9. I do not think it necessary to remind one that we are speaking here in our language; the demarcation between the physical and the psychological was unknown in those ancient times.

10. Thus *Av*. VI, 104 1 where *asu* appears in connection with *prāṇa* and *apāṇa*; Then again in the *mantra* of the killer in Animal-sacrifice (*Ait. Br*. II, 6) where the eye of the animal is sent to the sun, the breath (*prāṇa*) to the wind, the *asu* to the air, the bones to the earth; thus *asu* is closely connected with *prāṇa*, but as it appears, thought of more as resting, while the other one is mobile (The *ātman* has in *Ṛv*. X, 16, 3 the place which *prāṇa*

has in *Av.* V, 9, 7 as against that, which *asu* has here. Further *Śatapatha Br.* VI, 6, 2, 6 where it is just said: 'Breath (*prāṇa*) is really *asu*'; compare also *ibid.*, II, 4, 2, 21. Compare Geiger, *Ostiran. Kultur*, 298 f. about the meaning of the corresponding *anhu* in the psychology of the *Avesta.*

11. *Ṛv.* VIII, 100, 5 'My *manas* has answered from heart' (if *ā* is the ablative in *hṛda*, compare my note on I, 17, 3). In many other hymns of the *Ṛgveda*, *manas* and *hṛda* or *hṛdaya* stand close to each other. Of the later Vedic texts, it is sufficient to refer to the *Atharvaveda* VI, 18, 3: 'In this heart lives, the little spirit (*manaskam*), the winged little thing' and to the verse in *Āśvalāyana G.* III, 6, 8 (to Agni): 'May he guide my *manas* in the heart'—compare Windisch, *Bericht der Sachs. Ges. d. Wiss.* 1891, p. 163 f.

12. 'Quick as the *manas*' is a popular expression for the highest speed. It is possible that one spoke of the roaming thought, but likewise, one might certainly have also thought of the movement of the *manas* from the unconscious body. We may also refer here to *Ṛv.* I, 163, 11 (regarding Horse-sacrifice): 'your (of the horse) thought (*cittam*) is like the flying wind'.

13. Like Bhṛgu who became unconscious and went 'into that world'; where he then saw various scenes from the other world (*Jaiminīya Br.* in Oertel, *Journ. Am. Or. Society* XV, 234).

14. What *Taitt. Saṃh.* VI, 6, 7, 2 says about the *gatamanas*, 'whose *manas* has gone', may be compared. When the observation of its mirror-image is indicated as medicine for it (compare *Hiraṇyakeśin G.* I, 11, 6; see also *Ath. Pariśiṣṭa* VIII, Caland, *Zauberritual* 32 note 7, Caland-Henry 364 f., v Negelein, *Traumschlüssel* 130 f.), it appears to be based on the belief, that in this image there is a part of one's soul. Therefore, it is also a premonition of death when one does not see one's image (*Taitt. Saṃh.* VI, 6, 7, 2, *Lāty.* III, 3, 6; compare *Āśv. Śr.* V, 19, 5; *Āpast.* XIII, 14, 3 f.; about the image, compare in general the literature in Zachariae, Ztschr. d. Vereins f. Volksk. 1905, 76 note 1; v. Negelein *Arch. f. Rel.* V, 1 ff). Like the superstition of the Germans and other people: one who has no shadow (Frazer, *Golden Bough*[2] I, 290)—is it taken, as when it is said in *Av.* XIII, 1, 56 f. in a curse: you shall not throw any shadow henceforth? About the shadow compare also T. Segerstedt, *Le monde oriental*, III, 1 ff. As in a dream the soul of the dreamer hovers around; it is also certain on the other hand—this may be just remarked here—also in India—that the dreaming of the dead man was traced back to the appearance of his soul (thus here, the hovering soul is the object of the dream and not the subject). I would like to recognise this idea in the custom that one wiped oneself off with the plant Apāmārga ('*Wiping of*') after returning from the *śrāddha* and said: 'Apāmārga, drive away the evil dream from us' (*Śat. Br.* XIII, 8, 4, 4). The belief appears also to be there that while yawning, something of the substance of the soul can escape from the wide-open mouth if it is not prevented with the words 'let there be in me power and wisdom' (*Taitt. Saṃh.* II, 5, 2, 4; from that *Hiraṇyakeśin G.* I, 16, 2; compare with it Frazer, *Golden Bough*[2] I, 251.

15. VIII, 1, 1. 15; 2, 26; V, 30, 1; VIII, 1, 7; 2, 3; 1, 9.3. From another source 'May we, Soma, remain firm in your commands, preserving the *manas* in our bodies, rich in our progeny' (*Vāj. S.* III, 56). At the funeral, prayer for survivors: 'May their *asu* not go to Yama' (*Av.* XVIII, 3, 62). On the other hand, for the dead: 'Let your *manas* go to those dear to you, hasten to your fathers' (2, 23). 'It (death) made the *asu* go to the fathers' (*ibid.*, 2, 27).

16. The difference in these two directions of the *asunīti* is very clear in the two verses of *Ṛv.* X, 15, 14; 16, 2 which are close to each other.

17. The story of the journey to the other world by Bhṛgu is quite unproductive.

18. It is said in *Ṛv.* about the fathers living in the other world: 'Those who have gone to their *asu*' (X, 15, 1 compare also X, 12, 1). It appears thus, that *asu* is shown here as preceding other beings which follow it and get united with it.

19. In the Upaniṣad of *Śat Br.* (XIV, 7, 2, 3), it is the *Ātman* which leaves the body in death. The Buddhists let the devil hover around the person just dead like a smoke-cloud, it tries to snatch its *viññaṇa* ('perception') (my 'Buddha'[6] p. 308). In *Rāmāyaṇa* (VII, cap. 55 to 57 ed. Bombay) the souls (*cetas*, *cetana*) of Vasiṣṭha and Nimi fly about in the form

of air (*vāyubhūta*) separated from the bodies on account of a curse. These later formulations for the being separating from the body in death can be just alluded to here.

20. I refer to note 21 below about the words to the dead: Unite yourself with your body'. (*Ṛv*. X, 14, 8; 16, 5).

21. Look up the story in the text about the appearance of *Uccaiśśravas*. Obviously, the body is only one element in the existence in the other world, (compare *Av*. XVIII, 2, 24: 'Let not something be lost here from your *manas*, from your *asu*, your limbs, your juice, your body') and not the best one; the expression of the *Ṛv*. (X, 14, 8; 16, 5) 'unite yourself with the body' shows that the real 'you' here is not the body.

22. See the passages in S. Lévi, *La doctrine du sacrifice dans les Brāhmaṇas* 94 and compare the important essay of Boyer, *Sur l'origine de la doctrine du Saṃsāra* (*Journ. as.* 1901, II).

23. The pressed Soma drips through the sieve made of goat's hair.

24. Yama, see p. 310.

25. I translate the word '*svadhā*' with the word 'spiritual food', the usual word for the food offered to the dead. I consider it to be identical with '*svadhā*' 'self-determination'; the free movement, the unbridled activity of the souls—somewhat comparable with the *acakrayā svadhayā* (*Ṛv*. IV, 26, 4) hastening through the air—depends upon the enjoyment of the spiritual food and it is embodied in it. The manes come to the Lord of creatures and they request him for their share in the world-existence. He speaks to them: 'Food shall come to you month after month; *svadhā* shall belong to you; quickness of thought should belong to you; the moon shall be your light' (*Śatapatha Br.* II, 4, 2, 2). Besides, the idea could be advanced that the word *svadhā* attained technical significance through its accord with the word *svāhā*, the sacrificial invocation to the gods.

26. Muir's appropriate comparison of the diction of verse 11 referred by us above to *Taitt. Br.* II, 4, 6, 6 (compare Zimmer p. 413) may be noted. The comparison of a later description of entering the world of heaven in *Kauś. Up.* I, 4 (my 'Lehre der Upaniṣaden' 143 f.) is also quite instructive.

27. Compare above p. 68, 137, on Vivasvant and Yama.

28. Compare above p. 178, note 502 on the Aṅgiras as the surrounding of Yama. When in the song of the dead *Ṛv*. X, 14, 15, beside Yama, the old deceased Ṛṣis are invoked as the 'makers of the path', does it not mean, that like Yama (X, 14, 1) they were also, together with him, the inaugurators of the path to the other world for human beings?

29. *pīlu* a tree (Careya arborea), and its fruit, which are mentioned as eaten by the doves. It is, therefore, not clear here, in what context *pīlu* is mentioned.

30. See Bergaigne *Rel. védique* I, 82 f. The mode of thinking referred to here is, as far as I think, quite understandable. Even without that, one associates it with the idea of union of Agni with the Sun, as it is also done by Bergaigne. But I have my doubts.

31. *Av*. III, 28, 5; VI, 120, 3.

32. *Av*. XVIII, 4, 32 ff. may be compared, where the idea is mentioned that seeds of grain and sesame strewn for the dead man should approach him in the other world as colourful milch-cows which remain quiet, while being milked (corn), with their calves (sesame).

33. From there, it is only one step to the conception of the Buddhists, that one can relieve or free the poor souls suffering from punishment of their sins, if an offering is made to a pious monk in their name or one gives them a heavenly reward for that. The Petavatthu consists mainly of stories which end with this point. At least, there is an allusion to such things in the Veda. Compare Deussen, *Allg. Gesch. d. Philosophie* I, 2, 294; my 'Lehre der Upaniṣaden', p. 32.

34. *Av*. IV, 34; *Kauś. Sūtra* 66, 6 ff.

35. At the time of the funeral. *Av*. IV, 34, 2. 4.

36. Such a thing is mildly suggested in Buddhism. See my '*Buddha*'[6], p. 378 f.

37. *Ṛv*. X, 154, 2.

38. *ibid.*, verse 3.

39. Thus Roth, *Journal Amer. Or. Soc.* III, 345.

40. Or, it is at least what is at first understood as regular. It can be little proved or re-

futed, that absolute destruction appeared to Vedic belief, besides heaven and hell, as especially unlucky. Compare my '*Lehre der Upaniṣaden*', 29, note 1.

41. See e.g. Zimmer, *Altindisches Leben* 418 f.; Scherman, *Romanische Forschungen* V, 569 f.; *Indische Visionsliteratur* 122 ff.

42. Compare above p. 297, note 535. One of them can be understood as the one with colourful spots and the other black. They also appear as messengers of Yama to fetch those who are to die. The dogs who guard the Cinvat-bridge in the Zoroastrian belief (Vend. 13, 9) may be compared.

43. I think it is quite risky to associate these dogs linguistically and historically with Cerberus (compare also Bloomfield, *Cerberus, the Dog of Hades*, 1905).

44. Literally: into the wrapping or enclosure (*vavra*). This word is often used for the rock-enclosure from which Indra freed the cows.

45. The same expression 'darkness that has no support' appears again in I, 182, 6 with reference to the bottomless depth of the ocean.

46. As a matter of fact, VII, 104 is no doubt a later hymn.

47. The same word as above (see note 44). Prison can be considered as endless; it remains prison, in as much as it is barred to the world of life.

48. The Ādityas are addressed.

49. The wolf of the nether world is thought of: without any reason. Wolf is often a symbol of powers that waylay and attack human beings. Thus the very bold suggestion made by their author (Scherman, *Rom. Forsch.* V. 570; *Ind. Visionsliteratur* 127), that the fire in IV, 5, 4 and VII, 59, 8 is the fire of the hell has to be rejected.

50. Probably, Soma is meant.

51. Compare I, 121, 13 (to Indra): 'Casting them forth beyond the ninety rivers you drove down into the pit the godless.'

52. Sieve of goat's hair which plays a main role in the preparation of the Soma and is the cause of many mystical fantasies.

53. I don't include IV, 5, 5 along with it where there is a mention of the 'abysmal station' meant for the sinners. I feel, the decisive phrases seem to explain something else. Compare my note on the verse.

54. Further description of such torments is found in the journey of Bhṛgus to the other world (*Śat. Br.* XI, 6, 1; *Jaim. Br.* I, 42 ff). I emphasise here one of its features: people wronged in this world do the same thing to those in the other world who were responsible for it.

55. One can interpret in this direction from the *Ṛgveda*, at X, 12, 8. It may be observed that this verse is close to the hymns to the Dead.

56. The royal assessors of Yama (*rājānaḥ sabhāsadaḥ*), of whom Av. III, 29, 1 speaks, need not be considered as the judges of the dead, even if the word *sabhāsada* would easily suit the interpretation (compare Jolly, *Recht u. Sitte* 132). With Hillebrandt (*V.M.* I, 511 f.), one may understand participants in a council. It is only said, that those raise the sixteenth part as a tribute from the reward of good works following the dead man as his possession into the other world. Ehni, *Die urspr. Gottheit des ved. Yama* 92, thinks otherwise. It may be added that *Śatapatha Br.* XI, 2, 7, 33 mentions really the concept of weighing good and bad deeds in the other world. This concept is very close to the concept of the last judgement; *ibid.* 1, 9, 3, 2 the two flames, at the sides of the way leading to gods or to fathers which burn the dead or let him go, depending upon his service. But I don't know how in *Ṛv.* X, 14, 11 a reference could be made to the Judge's sentence of Yama (Scherman, *Visionsliteratur* 159 f.).

57. But also for the living, independent of the funeral customs, the later Vedic period invented, if one may remark in passing here, a rite with lot of pomp, to secure for him the way to the heavenly world: the construction of the fire-altar (*Agnicayana*). An altar is built in the shape of a bird, which was seen as identical with the fire burning upon him. This bird-Agni should fly up to heaven, to the Sun, and along with it the sacrificer. Compare my paper in *NGGW.* 1917 9ff, on *Agnicayana*.

58. I refer to Schrader, *Reallex*, under 'Totenreiche'.

59. In Rhodes' Psyche.

60. *Taitt. Br.* I, 3, 10, 5.

61. It appears to me that *Atharvaveda.* XVIII, 4, 64 is to be understood thus.

62. *Śatapatha Br.* XII, 7, 3, 7; XIII, 8, 1, 5. Even according to the *Ṛgveda* (X, 15, 6; 17, 9) the direction of the fathers is the south, indeed, in accordance with the Indo-Iranian belief; compare above p. 275, note 100. This is correctly interpreted by Kern (*Der Buddhismus* I, 359) that the sun is on the southern-most point of its course on the shortest days in the period which is holy to the souls. Caland thinks otherwise in *Een Indogermaansch lustratiegebruik* 5 f.

63. This does not mean that this empire cannot include also regions where infernal punishments are carried out. The story of Bhṛgu's journey into the other world may be noted wherein—in contrast to the separation of the world of gods and the world of fathers just mentioned,—the world of Varuṇa with its joys is introduced as a special region of that empire (*Jaim. Br.* I, 44).

64. I refer to my essay on *pravat* in *Festschrift für E. Windisch* 116 ff.

65. Thus there flows water, the fact which is also noted by Scherman (*Ind. Visionsliteratur* 112 f.). The verse with which one puts the reed on the graveyard of the dead may be compared: 'Climb this reed as vehicle; go along the path on the reed; go away with the vehicle of the reed, go forward, go upward' (*Taitt. Ār.* VI, 7, 2). The later concepts of the river of the dead Vaitaraṇī are well-known.

66. I refer also to the concept of 'way leading to gods' and 'way leading to fathers' *devayāna* and *pitṛyāna* which is common to the Upaniṣads. (Compare my '*Lehre der Upaniṣaden*' 106 f. and p. 344, note 54.). It leads through the flame (of the cremation), the day, the brighter half of the month, etc.; the other one through the smoke, the night, the darker half of the month; then enters obviously the shift in the original idea, brought about by the doctrines of metempsychosis and salvation. Even in the *Ṛgveda*, death is asked to go its way (X, 18, 1), which is different from *devayāna:* thus it clearly refers to *pitṛyāna.* This is very clearly expressed in X, 2, 7.

67. A water-plant which appears often in the ritual as an expression for the idea that fire—in this case the fire of the pyre—should extinguish and coolness appear in its place.

68. Something like this also in *Atharvav.* IX, 5, 1. 3.

69. See e.g. *Taitt. Saṃh.* I, 3, 6, 1; VI, 3, 4, 2; compare also *Śatap. Br.* III, 6, 1, 13; V, 2, 1, 7. As Vāyu is the Lord of the air, Sun-god is the Lord of the sky, Yama is the Lord of the earth: *Pāraskara* I, 5, 10. We may also be reminded of the observances discussed above, (p. 226 f.) which appear to rest upon the connection of the earth with death and the dead, also of the Nārāśaṃsa-rite at the time of Soma-sacrifice (Caland-Henry 220. 350; IF. XXXI, 139; Can one also include *Āśvalāyana G.* I, 11, 4 with these?).

70. That (with the idea of Yama's world) the concept of light and salvation was not firmly associated, is shown also by verses like *Av.* II, 12, 7 where the poet, or more correctly the magician wishes his enemy 'Yama's seat'. In this context, one may also consider the verses mentioned in the text p. 326 f. in connection with the ritual of the burial, which speak of the earth's depths as a seat prepared by Yama for the dead, as his place of refuge; further the observation of a *Brāhmaṇa*-text, that the dead are active at the roots of the plants (p. 329).

71. There could be obviously other possibilities also. Thus the souls can reside in the 'earthly empire of the air' or in the villages (*Ṛv.* X, 15, 2). It can happen to them that they do not find the correct place in the other world (Compare my '*Lehre der Upaniṣaden*' 27). I also refer to pages 319 ff. to what is said about the existence of ghosts.

72. It is open to doubt as to how the view of moon as the seat of manes is related to the whole development. One comes across it in the Upaniṣads, but it could be dated back to remote antiquity. Compare my '*Lehre der Upaniṣaden*' 106 f. and arguments there in note 54 (p. 344 f.).

73. Caland has treated the sacrifice in detail in *Altindischer Ahnenkult.*

74. Between south and east: direction holy to the manes. Compare p. 315.

75. With mats or something similar.

76. Meat coming from the previous Animal-sacrifice stands in a special connection with the description of the celebration in Gobhila. It is generally dropped (Compare *Gobhila* IV, 4, 1, Caland, *ibid.* 114).

77. This is a characteristic of the sacrifice to the dead; in case of sacrifice to gods, the even number is valid (Compare *Śatap. Br.* XIII, 8, 1, 3; *Āśvalāyana G.* II, 5, 13, 14, etc.). Similarly, here the direction from the right to the left, there from the left to the right, and thus a constant contrastivity. Compare Caland, *Die altind. Toten- und Bestattungs-gebräuche* 172 f.; *Een indogermaansch lustratie-gebruik* 2 ff.

78. The rule of Kleidemos is well known: to dig a ditch to the west of the monument and pour water in it with the words: 'This ablution for those who need and deserve it'. Similarly then the anointment (*Athanaeus* IX, p. 410).

79. For the purification of oneself, which is made necessary by the action done to the dead (above p. 274, note 80).

80. Grandfather and great-grandfather. We don't have to point out especially, how here the Indo-European agnatic family is contrasted. When, on happy occasions, a sacrifice to the dead it celebrated for 'the happy-faced fathers', does it really mean, according to the original concept, the distant ancestors beyond the immediate 'tear-faced' three, as postulated by some? I doubt it. See material in Caland, *Über Totenverehrung* 36 f. As one can see, the ceremony discussed here is mainly for the ancestors of the sacrificer, there is also a general celebration for the dead, a celebration for all souls; compare above p. 237.

81. Compare the dedication of the three holy cakes in Parsee funeral ritual.

82. Certainly not originally 'to let the *pitaras* enjoy their share without disturbing looks' (Caland, *Über Totenverehrung* 20; *Altind. Ahnenkult* 180; as a matter of fact the Indian tradition is expressed in this sense), but to protect oneself from the dangers of proximity to the sinister. That is why the breath is held.

83. Instead of *sado*, *Vāj. S.* II, 32 gives *sato* which I think is the correct form. But the mistake must be quite old.

84. 'For cloth, he may give a fringe or a piece of cotton till he is fifty years of age, and then hair from his own body, with the saying: That is cloth for you, O fathers; do not take anything else from us, O fathers!' (*Āśvalāyana Śr.* II, 7, 6). I think, two originally different rites are combined here: the offering of clothing to clothe the soul and the typical common offering of hair to the dead—compare its treatment by G.A. Wilken, *Revue coloniale internationale* III, 225 ff., IV, 345 ff.; Samter, *Geburt, Hochzeit und Tod* 179 ff.; see also Wundt, *Völker psychologie* II, 2, p. 23; *Encycl. of Rel. and Eth.* IV, 431 f.: surrendering of the appropriate part of the body for the purpose of protecting the same as a whole. The idea of the dead who are clothed only with their hair must have played its part while bringing together the sacrifices of the clothes and the hair (e.g. Petavatthu I, 10, 2). That the gifting of hair is done only in old age, must be owing to the concept that life becomes more endangered; thus, the redemption by that offering becomes more necessary. 'He is then nearer to the fathers' says *Taittirīya Brāhmaṇa* (I, 3, 10, 7) with reference to this rite. Caland, *Altind. Ahenkult* 177 thinks otherwise.

85. Compare above p. 58 f., note 141. It may be noted besides, that the normal order, first Agni and then Soma, is invested here: obviously nothing other than the inversion carried out in so many externals of the sacrifice to the manes, as against the sacrifice to the gods (note 77 above). Compare also *Āśvalāyana Śr.* II, 6, 12, 13.

86. They are absent in the form of sacrifice to the dead (Piṇḍapitṛyajna) belonging to the Śrauta-ritual. Compare Caland. *Altind. Ahnenkult* 17, 154 ff.

87. The Indian practice, like that of the other peoples, appears to date back to the age-old belief that souls lived under the threshold; see Winternitz, *Altind. Hochzeitsrituell* 72; Samter, *Geburt, Hochzeit und Tod* 136 ff; Compare also Crooke, *Folklore* XIII, 238 ff.

88. See *Āpastamba Dh.* II, 8, 18, 16.

89. Caland, *Altind. Ahnenkult* 189. Such special features which are mentioned by me, to concretise Indian conceptions, cannot extend their validity beyond India.

90. Caland, *Altind. Ahnenkult* 180.

91. *Hiraṇyakeśin Gṛhya* II, 13, 2; *Kauśika Sūtra* 88, 28. This *mantra* is a parallel of the invitation-formula mentioned above (p. 317).

92. *Kauś. S.* 88, 27. I point out here also to a practice to call back one's own soul (*manas*), fallen into the company of souls of the deceased. (*Vāj. Saṃh.* III, 53 ff.; Kāty V. 9, 22).

93. *abhiramayatām*, *Śāṅkh. G.* IV, 2, 6.

94. A further difference is, that Viśve devās, i.e. veneration dedicated to 'all gods', appears alongside the normal sacrifice to the dead in the fairly recent ritual innovations of many schools. This is missing in the sacrifice to the individual dead. Compare Caland *Altind. Ahnenkult* 160 f., 181, where the theory of *devāḥ pitaraḥ* appears to me to be objectionable.

95. Material in Caland, *Totenverehrung* p. 22.27.34. I think the differentiation in question can be traced back to *Śāṅkh. G.* IV, 2, 7; 3, 5. 6; compare also *Pāraskara* III, 10. 21. 27 f. 49 f.; *Baudhāyana Gṛhya* III, 11 in Caland, *Altind. Ahnenkult* 217; *Bhāradvāja Gṛhya* III, 17.

96. The word stresses the reference to the process of dying which is still felt immediately, though blurred for those who had died earlier.

97. 'After a year Preta becomes Pitar': thus in *Baudhāyana Gṛhyasūtra, ibid.*

98. Kaegi, *Philol. Abh. für Schweizer-Sidler* 55, note 19 thinks otherwise.

99. One may compare the survey of G.A. Wilken in his essay on air-sacrifice in *Revue coloniale internationale* III, 256 ff.; see also *Encycl. of Rel. and Eth.* IV, 442 f.

100. Wilken *ibid.* 260. 261.

101. To mention a modern story, one may be reminded of the wicked hunter killed by a tiger in the forest, who haunts as a wicked spirit till a crow drags his remains to the Ganges, after which he goes to heaven as a redeemed one (*Garuḍa Purāṇa* in M. Williams, *Brāhminism and Hindūism*, 3rd. ed., 301).

102. As also indeed, that the heavenly world is not barred to the ones not burnt, although the cremation is the right means of transport to that world (see page 325).

103. Compare *Av.* XVIII, 3, 9=*Taitt. Ār.* VI, 4, 2 (to the dead:, 'Go where you like on the earth'. Compare *Ait. Br.* VII, 5, 3 with 'in the earthly air-region' mentioned here.

104. *Taitt. Saṃhitā* II, 6, 10, 2, Compare *Manu* IV, 168; XI, 207.

105. Texts as *Ath. Veda* V, 19, 3—I do not venture to include here the offenders of a Brahmana sitting in the midst of a stream of blood and eating hair; there it could mean easily the inhabitants of hell (or more easily) the ghosts dwelling on earth.

106. *Jaiminīya Upaniṣad Brāhmaṇa* III, 29 f.

107. *Śatapatha Br.* XIII, 8, 4, 12.

108. Compare above p. 32.

109. Mainly in the collection of stories of Petavatthu. One may think here also of the ghosts mentioned in the epics. Hopkins, *Epic Mythology* 29 ff. has given an excellent collection of these stories.

110. But there is no mention of the time-bound existence of a ghost, restricted, say, to the normal one year period. Like the existence of the god, man or animal, this creature represents its own stage in the scheme of metempsychosis.

111. *Pārājika* I, 10, 14; II, 6, 4.

112. Thus, the *Mahābhārata* also likes to compare the din of battle with the dreadful sound of ghosts.

113. *Petavatthu* IV, 3.

114. *ibid.*, II, 10.; IV, 1, 5. 8.

115. *ibid.*, II, 4.

116. *ibid.*, II, 8.

117. *Aṅguttara Nikāya* Vol. V p. 270.

118. *Petavatthu* I, 5. One may also compare *Kathāvatthu* VII, 6.

119. e.g., *Petavatthu* I, 10, 12; II, 7, 12.

120. p. 7f. ed. Cowell-Neil.

121. vol. IV, p. 2 f. ed. Fausböll.

122. *Abh. der Berl. Akad.* (Phil.-hist. Kl.) 1877. p. 16.

123. *Baudhāyana* II, 14, 9.10. Compare Johansson, *Solfågeln i Indien* 20 f.

124. See viz. Winternitz. *Der Sarpabali* 37.

125. See p. 329.

126. *Satapattajātaka*, *Jāt.* Vol. II, p. 388. The Buddhistic narrator expresses in his own way, that here is an occurrence, different from that of the usual metempsychosis. He does not let the dying mother be reborn as a jackal, but lets her become *opapāti sigālī*, i.e., one formed directly so and not being born *via* the mother's womb. See *Milindpañha* p. 272 for Buddhistic expressions on the bodies (sic) of the dead Yakṣas which appear as worms or as other kinds of animals.

127. More in my work '*Die Lehre der Upaniṣaden und die Anfänge des Buddhismus*' p. 27 ff. about the question raised at the end. Compare there particularly p. 27, note 2 on it, whether the common idea of 're-death' (*punarmṛtyu*) in the *Brāhmaṇas* dates back to the Ṛgvedic period. See also my note on *Ṛv.* X, 14, 14. Here one may further ask, whether the belief in rebirth of the father in the son (compare *Buddhas Geburt* 60 f. by Windisch; T. Segerstedt, *Le Monde Oriental* IV, 144 f.) is to be ascribed to remote antiquity in one form or the other. As far as I can see, this cannot be settled.

128. p. 329.

129. Compare particularly Barth, *Religions of India*[3] p. 23 note 2; Scherman, *Visionsliteratur* p. 29; Hillebrandt, *V.M.*, III, 420 ff.—there is a mention of moon as the seat (if not also as the embodiment) of departed souls; compare above p. 337, note 72. About shooting stars, see *Maitr. Saṃh.* I, 8, 6. *Ath. Pariśiṣṭa* LVIIIb 1, 3ff.; Haradatta in Bühler *SBE.* II[2], p. 96; Hopkins, *Ep. Myth.* 34.

130. *Mahābhārata* III, 1745 f. ed. Calc. Compare Hopkins, *ibid.* 53.

131. *Āpastamba* II, 9, 24, 14.

132. *Śatapatha Br.* VI, 5, 4, 8.

133. X, 107, 2; 154, 5. Does it concern the seven Ṛṣis in the sense of the Great Bear?

134. XVIII, 2, 47.

135. The main category of the relevant sacrifice is called *Śrāddha*, literally meaning 'that which rests on faith (*śraddhā*)'; what it means, as it is often with the word *śraddhā*, is the faith of the sacrificer in the Brahmanas (compare my essay in *ZDMG.* L. 448 ff.), in this particular case in those who were to be invited, fed and honoured in diverse ways by him, namely the Brahmanas or the recipients of 'the food offered in faith' (*saddhādeyyāni bhojanāni*), as the Pali-texts say. See Caland, *Altind. Ahnenkult*, particularly 152 ff. for more information on the relation of Śrāddha to the other types of the sacrifice to the dead.

136. See the sources in Caland, *Totenverehrung* p. 43 ff.

137. See Bergaigne I, 95f. for the *Ṛgveda.*

138. *Atharvav.* XVIII, 3, 15f.; *Ṛv.* X, 15, 8. It may be noted how in *Ṛv.* V, 31, 9 along Indra, Kutsa (compare above p. 84 f.), i.e., the soul of a human hero is invoked. Is perhaps also that Udalākāśyapa (?), to whom one sacrifices in the ploughman's festival, (*Pāraskara* II, 13, 2) an ancestor? Ritual characteristics of the sacrifice to the dead are, however, not mentioned in his case.

139. *Av.* IV, 15, 15; VII, 12, 1; XVIII, 2, 30; II, 12, 4. There is a special sacrifice to the dead to get a specific wish fulfilled. See e.g., *Āśvalāyana G.* IV, 7, 1; Caland, *Totenverehrung* p. 39.

140. *Ṛv.* VI, 75, 9.

141. *Taittirīya Āraṇyaka* V, 7, 8.

142. *Kauśika Sūtra* 88, 25.

143. *ibid.* 89, 6.

144. *Āśvalāyana G.* IV, 7, 15.

145. *Kauśika Sūtra* 84, 12.

146. *Atharvaveda* XIV, 2, 73. See my note to X, 40, 10 concerning the Ṛgvedic evidence about the interest of the 'Fathers' in the marriage of their progeny.

147. e.g., *Mahāvagga* (*Vinaya Piṭaka*), I, 4, 2; *Udāna* I, 10.

148. I am reminded of the supernatural knowledge of the Vetāla, etc., from the later

literature; Also the appearances of ghosts, like that of Daśaratha's ghost before Rāma may also be mentioned here. Further research is necessary to find out whether there were actually oracles of the dead. According to the conceptions of the great epic, the priestly magician can conjure up the dead in every case. This is shown by Putradarśanaparvan (*M.Bh.* XV, 766ff. ed. Calc.), where Vyāsa makes the ghosts of the fallen heroes come out of the waters of the Ganges.

149. *Taittirīya Brāhmaṇa* I, 3, 10, 7.

150. Non-Aryan enemies (above p. 81 ff.)

151. *Atharvaveda* XVIII, 2, 28; *Kauśika Sūtra* 87 30. Also, burying of some magical object in graveyards as a means to harm the enemy, (*Av.* V, 31, 8; X, 1, 18) can point out to the concept that the souls housing there—indeed, such places were considered also as the gathering place of other sinister demons—could do him harm. I see little traces of actual corpse-magic (comp. e.g., B. Monier Williams, *Brāhmanism and Hindūism*[3] 254) in older literature. It could be considered as related to it when corns strewn during the sacrifice to the dead were given to keep back the wife or servant who are inclined to run away (*Kauś. Sūtra* 89, 10). We may refer also to *Jātaka* Vol. I p. 456. It is quite understandable that a cult, like the Buddhistic cult devoted to the relics of their masters and other saints, also contained elements pertaining hereto.

152. Caland, *Altind. Ahnenkult* 32. This is the reason why the crime of the 'killer of the embryo' was considered as very serious; thereby, an exceptionally dangerous soul was activised.

153. Through such a Rakṣas, the soul causing harm is clearly seen, when it is narrated how a Rakṣas was born from the severed head of Namuci whom Indra had killed for breaking his oath of loyalty. The Rakṣas followed Indra and spoke to him, 'Where will you go? Where will you escape me?' (*Śatapatha Br.* V, 4, 1, 9; compare *Taitt. Br.* I, 7, 1; 7.8; *Maitr. S.* IV, 3, 4). Apparently, at bottom, the soul of the slain pursuing the evil-doer as an avenging spirit.

154. I refer mainly to Caland's excellent work '*Die altind. Toten und Bestattungsgebräuche*' (1896); in the following, cited in short as 'Caland'.

155. *Yājñavalkya* III, 1; *Manu* V, 68f. Compare *Pāraskara* III, 10, 5; Caland 93; Compare Dietrich, *Mutter Erde* 21f.; Charpentier, *Kleine Beiträge zur indoir. Mythologie* 2, note 1. It must be a more recent rule that the ascetics are also buried. (Cal. ibid.).

156. I, 3616 ed. Calc.

157. One may be reminded of the Avestic uzdāna, a stretcher to set out the corpses. Vend. 6, 50; Geiger, *Ostiran. Kultur* 267 note 1.

158. See on that Caland 164f. and my note on Ṛv. X, 18, 10ff.

159. The expression of *Pāraskara* (III, 10, 5) with reference to small children is characteristic (above note 155): 'They bury the body without burning it.' It is seen, that the treatment accorded to the bones after the burning of the corpse, was felt as similar to burying.

160. See p. 328f.

161. With this interpretation of *Ṛv.* X, 18, *Av.* XVIII, 2, 50-52 and similar verses also have, of course, been assessed.

162. I have tried to combine the most important features into a total picture; It cannot be my intention to mention numerous divergences of the sources and discuss them. For this and for the sources see Caland. Compare also my notes on *Ṛv.* X, 14ff.

163. Caland 8; Compare Dieterich, *Mutter Erde* 26f.

164. *Atharv.* XII, 5, 48; Caland 139.

165. Bloomfield, *American Journ. of Phil.* XI, 336 ff. deals with the wailing-women in the *Atharvaveda*; it is possible, women relatives also wailed (Caland, *Altind, Totengebräuche*, 140). The later literatures give lot of material on this; The following may be compared: *Cullavagga* XI, 1, 10; *Mahāparinibbānasutta, Dīgha Nikāya* II, 159, *Mahākapijātaka* (Jāt. vol. III, p. 374), Strīvilāpaparvan in *M. Bhārata* XI, *Rāmāyaṇa* II, 76, 20f. ed. Bombay, etc.

166. More exactly: fires, got from those fires by certain manipulations (*Śat. Br.* XII, 5, 2, 3; *Kauś S.* 80, 21; Caland 19).

167. *Ṛv.* X, 14, 7-12; compare my notes on X, 14 concerning the application of the ceremony at this place. The contents of these verses fit in correctly here in so far as Agni is not named as the guide who conducts the dead to the other side, thus, they are not concerned with the situation of the cremation itself (yet compare *Āśv. G.* IV, 4, 6), on the other hand, verse 7 appears to point to a real retreading of the way from the side of the corpse—of course with magic influence to let the soul progress on its way. The place mentioned in verse 9 is considered as the place of burning in *Kauś. S.* 80, 42, *Āśv. G.* IV, 2, 10, (*Śāṅkh. Śr.* IV, 14, 7 (see Caland 33f.); the reference to the place where the bones are buried (compare *Taitt. Ār.* VI, 6, 1) would have appeared to be closer, if the relevant *mantras* in *Ṛv.* had not been in another place (X, 18, 10f.).

168. One has discovered here the sentimentally tinged thought that dying is a return of the soul to its home. But do not the words really mean: go to the heavenly world and free yourself from all infirmities then return again to your body where your home is?

169. Compare above p. 312 f.

170. I am shedding the vague word *udumbalau*.

171. *Ṛv.* X, 18, 8. The meaning appears to be: you have reached a new marriage from the old marriage which is dissolved through death; you have become the wife of one who holds your hand and who makes you get up. It is possible, that it means here 'the brother-in-law who takes the place of the husband' which *Āśvalāyana* (*G.* IV, 2, 18) mentions in the rite referring to the above. The treatment of this *Ṛv.*-verse in Hillebrandt *ZDMG.* XL, 708 does not convince me; compare my note and literature there.

172. Later texts mention, correspondingly, other objects for the members of both the other castes; According to *Av.* XVIII, 2, 59 and *Kauś. S.* 80, 48f. it is a staff for the Brahmana and horn of the ox for the farmer. It is also prescribed that a piece of gold is to be taken from the hand of the dead which is then given to his eldest son (*Av.* XVIII, 4, 56, *Kauś. S.* 80, 46).

173. Caland (45f.) understands this verse differently; as against that, compare my note.

174. *Śatapatha Brāhmaṇa* XII, 5, 2, 14.

175. For such possessions of the dead are considered as affected by death.—Compare v. Negelein *JAOS.* XXXIV, 249 on treatment of the vessels of the dead.

176. The later Vedic texts think of other vessels; see Caland 51 with note 201.

177. In the diction of the *Ṛgveda*, this means some sort of a substance hailing from the cow; here, clearly the different parts of its body.

178. The fire is led from the three sacrificial fires surrounding him (p. 327) through the strewn dry grass.

179. If the apparent intention is, that it should run away (compare Caland 60), then the Ṛgvedic verse X, 16, 4 just quoted seems to show that it was originally intended to be burnt.

180. *Kauśika Sūtra* 81, 34-39 (compare Caland 64) prescribes a number of offerings to Yama, Aṅgiras and Sarasvatī; it can be doubted whether these sections of the *Ṛgveda* X, 14, 1-6. 13 ff.; 17, 7-9 are composed for this portion of the rite.

181. Caland 63.

182. Compare above p. 299 note 586.

183. Here rests the magic power in name (I think, independent of the barley's relation to Varuṇa; above p. 237), as it is shown by the relevant *mantra* (*Kauś. Sūtra* 81, 17 and otherwise often): 'You are barley (*yava*); keep away hatred (*yavaya*) from us, keep away ill-will.' Eitrem, *Opferritus und Voropfer* 169, note 1 interprets differently.

184. A well-known common feature in the treatment of sinister creatures which should not be allowed to know the door through which they could return.

185. In the more recent ritual (Caland 113f., where one can get more information) this happens only after the relics are buried. The location of the verses *Ṛv.* X, 16, 9 ff., which is of course no definite evidence, would lead to this order taken for granted here. The interpretation of Ṛv.-verses in particular entails lots of difficulties; compare my notes.

186. Caland 81 mentions further details. See p. 332 for the meaning of these customs.

187. *Śāṅkhāyana Sr.* IV, 15, 6.

188. Thus *Kauś. S.* 82, 25; other periods in other texts. Caland 99.

189. That means extinguish. The text is *Ṛv.* X, 16, 13f. Compare in addition Bloomfield, *Amer. Journal of Phil.* XI, 342ff.; above p. 258.

190. According to *Kāty.* XXV, 8, 1. 7 *inter alia* in a bag made of leaves; in an urn only when it is intended to celebrate the burial (this is discussed in the text).

191. See note 193.

192. *Gṛhya* IV, 5, 7-10. I am giving in full the verses of the *Ṛgveda* (X, 18, 10ff.) quoted there only with the initial lines.

193. *Kauś. Sūtra* 82, 32 speaks of burying at the root of a tree (compare Caland 107); for it the *mantra* of *Av.* XVIII, 2, 25; 'May not the tree hamper your movement. Not the great goddess Earth'. 'Tree' does not mean wooden coffin. Compare besides note 198 below.

194. Is the idea here, that misfortune can befall the dead to the extent of total destruction? It may also mean some other grave misfortune in the other world.

195. Here follows, in the more recent ritual, the doing away of the fire of the dead; see p. 328 with note 185 on p. 342. See Caland 115 for the ensuing divergences of the sources concerning the order of the various acts.

196. So to say, a second funeral: a very common ritual, compare above p. 319 f.

197. *Śatapatha* XIII, 8, 1, 2. Compare *Kāty.* XXI, 3, 1.

198. For that, when they are buried at the root of a tree (above note 193) the verse: 'Give him back, O master of the woods, who is resting with you, so that he can sit in Yama's house speaking of holy service.' *Av.* XVIII, 3, 70; *Kauś. S.* 83, 19.

199. *Kauśika Sūtra* 83, 22f. The following reference from Turner which I have taken from Frazer (*Journ. of the Anthrop. Institute of Gr. Britain and Ireland* XV, 96, note 1) may serve as a comparison: *In Somoa the relations spread out a sheet on the beach near where the man had been drowned, or on the battle-field where he had fallen, then they prayed, and the first thing that lit on the sheet (grasshopper! butterfly, or whatever it might be) was supposed to contain the soul of the deceased and was buried with all due ceremony.*

200. The original purpose must have been shaking away of the soul, compare Caland 171.

201. The *Kauśika Sūtra* 84, 9 lets instead an empty kettle be struck with a shoe. Old utensils often appear in the cult of the dead. The original purpose is naturally to scare away the evil souls and spirits.

202. Compare the ritual of the sacrifice of Tryambaka above p. 237. Further *Āśv. G.* IV, 6, 3; Eitrem, *Opferritus und Voropfer* 35. 43.

203. Before sunrise: funeral at night is common among several races; compare *inter alia Encly. of Rel. and Eth.* IV, 426.

204. *Śatapatha* XIII, 8, 1, 20 (compare *Av.* VI, 44, 3?).

205. The role could lead to something similar to the one played by the tree. See notes 193 and 198 above.

206. Quite like in the rite of building the altar of bricks, *Ind. Stud.* XIII, 245.

207. Also, other sacrificial gifts are mentioned; I do not wish to exhaust the details.

208. See above p. 276, note 107.

209. Compare also Wundt, *Völkerpsychologie* II, 2 p. 71f.

210. X, 15, 14. Compare Bergaigne I, 79.

211. In reality, a certain resemblance with the sacrificial rite clings to cremation—as Bergaigne I, 81 has emphasised. In free diction, the Ṛgvedic poet (X, 16, 5) could say that the dead man has 'surrendered himself' to Agni as sacrifice (*āhutaḥ*). (For more like examples, see Caland 175). But because of that, the act of cremation had in no way the technical construction of a sacrifice; it lacked all the poetical and liturgical embellishments that go together with the sacrifice. Therefore, one will agree that sacrifices were connected with it.

212. In the case of ancient India, the idea of the dead being present in the relics will have to be associated with that concrete vital force, which is difficult for us to grasp. This idea has the same association in modern India too, as illustrated by Mon. Williams, *Brāhmanism and Hindūism*[3] 301 with the help of a characteristic incident.

213. One will not, of course forget that again expressions occur, which show that the soul has a greater right than the body to represent the actual person. Compare above p. 335, note 21.

214. Above p. 327 with note 172 on p. 342.

215. It is quite clearly shown, e.g. by Tylor, *Anfänge der Kultur*, I, 459; compare also Bergaingne I, 78, note 1; Garbe, *Beitr. zur ind. Kulturgeschichte* 148 ff.—*Ath. Veda* XVIII, 3, 1 (similarly *Taitt. Ār*. VI, 1, 3) we read the *mantra*: 'This wife, choosing the world of the husband, O mortal, sleeps with you, the dead, fulfilling the old custom; may she be given progeny and possession.' Does not this clear emphasis on the fulfilment of the custom raise the suspicion that the old custom really desired nothing more, and that one was still aware of it? Compare Caland 45.

216. X, 16, 4. above p. 327. Compare Caland 176f.

217. *Āv*. XVIII, 2, 22.

218. ibid 53. Compare above p. 39. 118 with notes 351, 352 pp. 160 f.

219. Compare the section 'Cult observances', above p. 224ff.

220. See mainly Wilken, *Revue coloniale intern.* IV, 348ff.

221. XX, 32.

222. Thus also *Śāṅkhāyana Śr*. (IV, 16, 1): 'Delimiting-ceremony after the end of the observances'—the rite which definitively (or comparatively definitively) excludes the dead from the neighbourhood of the living.

223. As Kaegi ('Die Neunzahl bei den Ostariern') has already noted.

224. *Sacred Books of the East* V, 382, note 2.

225. Wilken *ibid.*, 352. Compare also Haberlandt, *Zeitschr. f. Völkerpsychol.* XVII, 379.

226. Similarly Frazer, *Journ. of the Anthrop. Institute of Gr. Britain and Ireland*, XV, 92f.

227. See parallels in Wilken *ibid.*, 352, note 41.

In Retrospect

At our journey's end, let us summarise the characteristic features of the phenomena considered by us.

A host of mighty gods holds a place of honour within the relatively narrow range of the religious life in India. This is revealed by the oldest sacrificial poetry in the light of its exclusively priestly style of thought and expression. Most of them, notably the mightiest among them, represent natural powers: thunder and storm, sun and moon, morning and evening, stars and fire, the friendly household companion of man. Besides them, there are also other types of deities, above all those presiding over specific types of action or definite areas of life, like the god 'Impeller', the god of paths and wayfarers, the priest-god, the Lord of prayer. But the original characteristics of many of these nature-gods have faded away and become blurred; developments over a long time—for the Veda is far away from the origin of these conceptions, in terms of time and its spiritual contents—have loosened, indeed dissolved, the connection with the nature-beings which were at their basis. The belief that it is the mighty natural powers upon wnom depend one's woes and fortunes, retreated increasingly into its shell: later, above all, the vital forces of human society determined the decisive hold over the individual; primarily, there have remained only man-like ruler-figures from among the old nature-deities: divine giants endowed with brute strength, others with unfathomable magic powers, or those entrusted with maintaining the ruling customs of Indian chieftains. On the one hand, these gods have very simple wants and preferences, yet on the other, they are capable of a peculiarly childish guile: they want to eat or to carouse, they have to be flattered by praising their greatness and their accomplishments; they love, however, to be entertained particularly by the priests in the subtle, glib, language of theological secret-mongering, with its concealed, dark and intricate allusions about the mystery of their nature and their deeds. Ethnic elements cling to these gods, on the whole only loosely and superficially: the Thunderer fades away and turns into the most powerful warrior-hero, which is to be expected of such a friend of man and inexhaustible bestower of mercies, a predominantly good and brave giant, but whence should he get the resplendent purity and majesty of lofty moral strength? The ethical powers desire nevertheless representation among the gods. They were represented—before the separate existence of the Indian people—by a group of gods of light, probably of alien origin; notable among them was a Moon-god, whose natural significance was later obscured by his rôle as the highest Lord and Patron of the Law. If thus, for example, there is a clear-felt difference between this God of the Law and the Thunderer, then it is because, they had been isolated from their natural moorings. Given the easy changeability, the lack of plasticity and the invariable phraseology of conventional flattery, it was but inevitable that the two gods became unmistakably identical with one another. Often, one is inclined to think that basically there was but one great deity, under whose umbrage the gods crept in, who were addressed one after the other on every occasion by the poets, with their differences and individual characteristics becoming increasingly obsolete in the process.

As for the stories of the deeds of these gods, we find, among stories of varying quality, historical reminiscences, serious as well as farcical productions of pure fantasy; but the most elegant pieces among the legends are the old natural myths like the battle of the Thunderer, the capture of the imprisoned red cows, probably the dawn, the journey of the morning and the evening stars with the sun-maiden. The meaning of such myths is almost wholly forgotten in the Vedic period. They have been transposed to superhuman, heroic actions. The picture has often become an incomprehensible hieroglyph. The stories are mostly limited to garish effects and to most elementary motives: tremendous deeds of strength, acquisition of splendid possessions, overpowering and outsmarting of fearful enemies, rescue from great plight, and occasionally, in the second place, sensual passions. There is, however, no deep involvement in spiritual processes, no intricate, logically arranged, artistic structuring of actions and fates. The innovative style, characteristic of primitive races, is apparent everywhere, with its baroque formlessness and arbitrariness of unrestrained fantasy. Where the old myths have continued in time, where they have absorbed more modern motives, it is not due to the deep sense of ethical ideas concealed in their garb, but among other things, mostly the pretentiousness of unconcealed oriental priestly greed: one may recall how the story of the acquisition of cows is twisted in favour of the victory of the priests who desired the cows, over the misers who wanted to deep the cows for themselves.

The sacrifice made to the Vedic gods is the sacrifice of the pastoral tribes, who do not lack the various sophistications of a culture by no means any more young. The urban cult-centres with their architectural art are missing, but the act of sacrifice which revolves around the sacred fire, the carpet of grass and the seat of god, is quite removed from the character of primitive simplicity. It is excessively burdened with ingenious priestly ceremonies and embellished by liturgic poetry, wherein the clumsy formlessness and the first clear signs of that excessively subtle artistry, so dominant in later Indian poetry, have formed a bond. Numerous priests, in their bustling loquacious fashion, are busy importunating the gods and humouring them. Once put in good mood, they will bestow on the sacrificer long life and prosperity, throw down his enemies. Everything is directed to the immediate desires and needs of earthly existence; the cult is the means to secure and to augment riches and estate for the rich and the nobles. Little more than mere beginnings are evident, which suggest that religious life could have developed into a great ethical force capable of educating the individual and the people.

Given the weak development of the individual life of clan and tribe, the cult-orders hardly became fully associated with any particular place or locality. Within the sphere of Vedic culture, whenever Aryan sacrificers and

Brahmanic priests perform great sacrifices, they address in almost same form the same gods who are free from local ties. We find the odd reference to local demons only where our sources from the field of the higher, exclusively priestly cult give us an insight into the deeper aspect of people's life. These local demons appear to be associated with water and mountain, forest and field; we hear of the lady of the woods who meets the wayfarers amidst solitude that is pierced by the noise of birds and mysterious voices; we find vestiges of worship offered to the tree-genii living in sacred trees and to the nymphs of rivers and ponds.

More creations of the myth and the cult are visible, given the limited scope of the oldest Veda, only in traces, that too only at a secondary level. These creations appear beside the gods and the sacrifices of the Ṛgvedic hymns, thus completing the picture of the ancient Vedic belief. The mighty gods are surrounded by the swarming crowd of primitive plebeians of the spirit-world, evil, misshapen and animal-shaped spectres, vampires and bringers of diseases. They nestle in houses, live on cross-roads or hover about. In addition, there are the souls of the dead, the 'fathers' of the family, who are fed by their progeny. There are also hostile souls, against whose wiles one must be on guard. There are again numerous substances which hover or move about, lie concealed here and there. Depending upon their bringing good or bad luck, one fills oneself with their healing power or avoids contact with them. Here the primitive cult holds sway: exorcisms and conjurations, propiatory and other kinds of magic. We have further, superstitious precautions at every step, like not looking-at, not looking-around, not touching, not eating, fear of taboos of all kinds. Such rites and observances accompany daily life and all events in the life of the family. Mastery over the technique governing them plays a more important rôle than the great sacrifices in the art of ensuring one's happiness and welfare. This is especially true for the poor people who cannot offer inebriants to Indra and the whole crowd of gods. Behind the comparatively recent belief in Indra and Varuṇa, the world of the Soma-sacrifice and the Ṛgvedic poetry—behind these regions flooded by the course of historical development, there opens the world of the eternally stable, hailing from remote, prehistoric times—basic forms of a religious way of life without a history, infinitely older than the Vedic creations and determined to survive them with seemingly inexhaustible tenacity. We recognize at every step those types dating back to the religious life of remote antiquity, not merely juxtaposed but deeply intertwined with the later belief and cult. The layer superimposed on them by later ages cannot conceal their form of construction. This form stands apart from all later creations in its ancient uniqueness. It will remain incomprehensible, if it is judged by later trends. Behind the near human Vedic gods, we think, we can perceive the crude formlessness of old animal-shaped deities or of the deities fluctuating between human and animal forms. We come across fetishistic incarnations of gods. From the figure of the Vedic sacrificial priest stand out features, which belong to the medicine-man, the rain-maker, of the savages; from the Vedic sacrificial fire, the image of the prehistoric magic fire; from the acceptance-ceremony of the Brahmana pupil, the girdling and the magic rebirth of the youth in the dedicatory puberty-rite of the savages. Thus a vista opens up, from the remote past of the Vedic belief into still further incalculable distances beyond the impress of the Indian, indeed the Indo-European, character. We have no more right today to despair of treading these distances, as though on unchartered territory, a territory not to be chartered.

Translator's Note

1. There are a few instances where incorrect numbering has been assigned by Oldenberg to quotations from the *Ṛgveda*. For example:

p. 62. *Ṛv*. VIII, 58, 2 should read VIII, 11, 2.

p. 139, note 48. VIII, 101, 15.16 should read VIII, 90, 15.16.

p. 269. VIII, 69, 11.12 should read VIII, 58, 11.12.

p. 387, note 54. II, 32, 11 should read II, 35, 11.

p. 415, note 197. I, 24, 9 should read I, 24, 10.

2. For quotations from the *Ṛgveda*, I have largely made use of Griffith's translation (R.T.H. Griffith: *The Hymns of the Rigveda*, Vols. I and II, The Chowkhamba Sanskrit Series, Varanasi, IVth Ed., 1963). Where Oldenberg's translation does not concur with Griffith's, I have preferred to translate Oldenberg faithfully. For example:

p. 275. *Ṛv*. V, 77, 2:
Griffith:
Worship at dawn and instigate the Aśvins:
nor is the worshipper at eve rejected.
Oldenberg:
Worship at dawn and instigate the Aśvins. In the evening worship does not reach gods; they do not like it.

3. Oldenberg's corrigenda have been appropriately incorporated in the text of the translation.

Index